CANADIAN STATE TRIALS
VOLUME I

LAW, POLITICS, AND SECURITY MEASURES,
1608–1837

Edited by F. Murray Greenwood
and Barry Wright

State trials reveal much about a nation's insecurities and shed light on important themes in political, constitutional, and legal history. In Canada, perceived and real threats to the state have ranged from dissent, disaffection, and the emergence of threatening ideologies to insurrection, riot, violent protest, and military invasion. The Canadian State Trials series will explore the role of the law in regulating such threats, from the period of early European settlement to 1971.

The first volume and the planned series as a whole present a great deal of new material by prominent Canadian historians and legal scholars. Although certain Canadian political trials and security crises have received scholarly attention in the past, there has never been a comprehensive and systematic examination of the country's surprisingly rich record in this area. The eighteen essays in Volume I examine this record for the period 1608–1837, covering proceedings in New France, the four Atlantic colonies, the Old Province of Quebec, and the two Canadas. They highlight security law during the American revolution, the wars against revolutionary/Napoleonic France, and the War of 1812; comparative treason law; and the trials of David McLane, Robert Gourlay, Francis Collins, and Joseph Howe, among others. The essays, which make extensive use of primary sources (the most illuminating of which appear in a documentary appendix), place the examination of the law and its administration during these events in socio-political and comparative context.

(Osgoode Society for Canadian Legal History)

F. MURRAY GREENWOOD is Associate Professor Emeritus of History at the University of British Columbia.

BARRY WRIGHT is Associate Professor of Law and Legal Studies at Carleton University.

PATRONS OF THE SOCIETY

Canadian State Trials

VOLUME I

Law, Politics, and Security Measures, 1608–1837

Edited by F. MURRAY GREENWOOD and BARRY WRIGHT

Published for The Osgoode Society for Canadian Legal History by

University of Toronto Press

Toronto Buffalo London

ISBN 0-8020-0913-1 (cloth)
ISBN 0-8020-7893-1 (paper)

Printed on acid-free paper

Canadian Cataloguing in Publication Data

Main entry under title:
Canadian state trials

Includes index.
Contents: v. 1. Law, politics and security measures, 1608–1837.
ISBN 0-8020-0913-1 (v. 1 : bound)
ISBN 0-8020-7893-1 (v. 1 : pbk.)

1. Political crimes and offenses – Canada – History.
I. Greenwood, F. Murray (Frank Murray), 1935–   .
II. Wright, Barry, 1957–   .   III. Osgoode Society for
Canadian Legal History.

KE226.P6C3 1996   345.71'009'03   C96-931135-4
KF221.P6C3 1996

This book has been published with the help of a grant from the Humanities and
Social Sciences Federation of Canada, using funds provided by the Social Sciences
and Humanities Research Council of Canada.

University of Toronto Press acknowledges the financial assistance to its
publishing program of the Canada Council and the Ontario Arts Council.

Contents

Foreword

THE OSGOODE SOCIETY
FOR CANADIAN LEGAL HISTORY

The purpose of The Osgoode Society for Canadian Legal History is to encourage research and writing in the history of Canadian law. The Society, which was incorporated in 1979 and is registered as a charity, was founded at the initiative of the Honourable R. Roy McMurtry, former attorney general for Ontario, and officials of the Law Society of Upper Canada. Its efforts to stimulate the study of legal history in Canada include a research-support program, a graduate student research-assistance program, and work in the fields of oral history and legal archives. The Society publishes volumes of interest to its members that contribute to legal-historical scholarship in Canada, including studies of the courts, the judiciary, and the legal profession, biographies, collections of documents, studies in criminology and penology, accounts of significant trials, and work in the social and economic history of the law.

Current directors of The Osgoode Society for Canadian Legal History are Jane Banfield, Tom Bastedo, John Brown, Brian Bucknall, Archie Campbell, Susan Elliott, J. Douglas Ewart, Martin Friedland, Charles Harnick, John Honsberger, Kenneth Jarvis, Allen Linden, Virginia MacLean, Wendy Matheson, Colin McKinnon, Roy McMurtry, Brendan O'Brien, Peter Oliver, Paul Reinhardt, James Spence, and Richard Tinsley.

The annual report and information about membership may be obtained by writing The Osgoode Society for Canadian Legal History, Osgoode Hall, 130 Queen Street West, Toronto, Ontario, Canada M5H 2N6.

Law, Politics, and Security Measures, 1608–1837, volume I of the Canadian State Trials series, launches a new and exciting venture in Canadian legal history. Under the editorship of two distinguished scholars, Professors Murray Greenwood and Barry Wright, the Canadian State Trials series as planned will include six volumes, to appear over the next decade, and will draw upon the work of many of this country's outstanding historians and legal scholars.

Volume I, dealing with the period 1608–1837, contains essays by prominent Canadian legal historians covering New France, the four Atlantic colonies, the Old Province of Quebec, and both Canadas. Among the highlights are security law during the American revolution, the wars against revolutionary/Napoleonic France, and the War of 1812; comparative treason law (Great Britain, Lower Canada, the United States); and the trials of Robert Gourlay, Francis Collins, and Joseph Howe. The essays stress socio-political context and are based on intensive use of primary sources, the most illuminating of which appear in a documentary appendix.

R. Roy McMurtry
President

Peter N. Oliver
Editor-in-Chief

Acknowledgments

This is a collective effort and we are grateful to our contributors for their support and much enlightened criticism, especially as we re-worked the introduction. We also thank them for exemplary patience and good-natured, useful responses to numerous editorial suggestions. Peter Oliver has been a staunch supporter of the project since its inception in 1988 and without his enthusiasm the project would likely have been stillborn. Peter's comments on essays, assistance in obtaining financial support, and encouragement are greatly appreciated. Marilyn MacFarlane, throughout, has played her usual roles of effective coordinator, wise administrative adviser, and foe to our occasional despondency.

One of our authors, Patricia Kennedy, has helped us immensely in locating documents held by the National Archives and assisting our editorial efforts. We are grateful to Wesley Pue and the Faculty of Law, University of British Columbia, for circulating drafts of the essays in collected working-papers form among the contributors. We also thank the Institute of Advanced Legal Studies, University of London, for providing facilities in 1993–4. Our research assistants – Julie Boudreau, Christopher Greenwood, Stewart Greenwood, Laura Landry, and Michel Roy – performed admirably, often at short notice.

Beverley Boissery (Greenwood) provided invaluable help as an unofficial 'assistant editor' and we are grateful for her diligence in taking on a diversity of tasks, especially research, word processing, stylistic editing, and preparation of the index. Meredith Kennedy provided moral and practical support. The copy editor, Curtis Fahey, made numerous helpful suggestions and has done superb work, professionally accomplishing a task made difficult by the anarchism of scholars.

Our three external reviewers, two selected for the publisher and one for the Humanities and Social Sciences Federation of Canada, made informed and constructive comments. Their advice is reflected in a number of the essays. We thank the Social Sciences and Humanities Research Council of Canada for a generous research grant in support of the editors' scholarship. This book has been published with the help of a grant from the Humanities and Social Sciences Federation of Canada, using funds provided by the Social Sciences and Humanities Research Council of Canada. Last, but not least, The Osgoode Society for Canadian Legal History has supported the project in a multitude of vital ways. We are grateful for its commitment to the important mandate of advancing the cause of legal history in Canada. Finally, excerpts from documents in the Colonial Office and War Office series are crown copyright and are reproduced with the permission of the controller of Her Majesty's Stationery Office.

Contributors

THOMAS GARDEN BARNES is a professor of history and law at the University of California, Berkeley.

D.G. BELL is professor of colonial law and institutions in the Faculty of Law, University of New Brunswick.

J. M. BUMSTED is a professor of history and director of the Institute for the Humanities at the University of Manitoba.

BARRY CAHILL is an archivist in the Government Archives Division at the Public Archives of Nova Scotia.

ERNEST A. CLARKE is a independent historian whose book *The Siege of Fort Cumberland 1776: An Episode in the American Revolution* has been recently published by McGill-Queen's University Press.

CHRISTOPHER ENGLISH is a professor of history at the Memorial University of Newfoundland.

JEAN-MARIE FECTEAU is a professor of history at the Université du Québec à Montréal and an affiliated researcher at the Centre internationale de criminologie comparée, Université de Montréal.

F. MURRAY GREENWOOD is an associate professor emeritus of history at the University of British Columbia.

DOUGLAS HAY is an associate professor of law at Osgoode Hall Law School and of history at York University.

PATRICIA KENNEDY is an archivist in the Manuscript Division at the National Archives.

EVELYN KOLISH is an archivist at the Archives nationales du Québec, Centre de Montréal.

JAMES LAMBERT is coordinator of the Historical Archives Programme at the Université Laval.

PETER N. MOOGK is associate professor of history at the University of British Columbia.

JIM PHILLIPS is associate professor and associate dean in the Faculty of Law, University of Toronto. He is also a member of the Department of History and the Centre of Criminology, University of Toronto.

PAUL ROMNEY teaches Canadian studies at the Nitze School of Advanced International Studies, Johns Hopkins University.

JEAN-PIERRE WALLOT is the national archivist of the National Archives.

BARRY WRIGHT is an associate professor in the Department of Law, Carleton University.

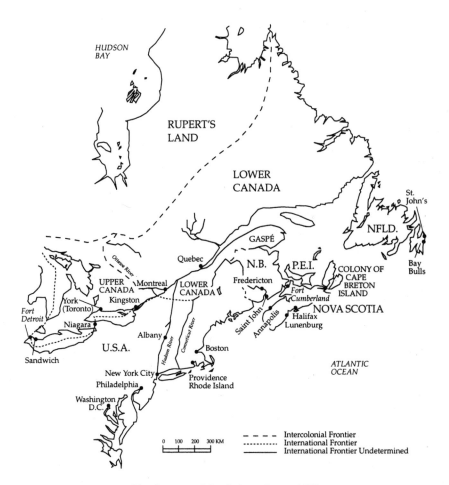

Northeastern North America, *c.* 1800

CANADIAN STATE TRIALS
VOLUME I

LAW, POLITICS, AND SECURITY MEASURES, 1608–1837

Introduction:
State Trials, the Rule of Law, and
Executive Powers in Early Canada

F. MURRAY GREENWOOD and
BARRY WRIGHT

STATE TRIALS AS A GENRE: THE ENGLISH COLLECTIONS[1]

After the multitude of fascinating seventeenth-century constitutional conflicts, grisly treason proceedings, and the return of stability in 1688–9, it was almost inevitable that someone would attempt to exploit public interest in past political or 'state' trials. The pioneer of the genre, historical and geographical writer Thomas Salmon, remarked that the absence of predecessors was almost impossible to explain, except for the fact, perhaps, that they had been deterred by the vast expense and trouble entailed. He remedied this 'strange' lacuna in 1719 by publishing four huge tomes of trials from King Henry IV to Queen Anne inclusive[2] and later in the year adding a fifth treating the *Ship Money* or *Hampden's* case (1637). In 1730 the renowned chambers counsel and editor of Sir Mathew Hale's *Pleas of the Crown*, Sollom Emlyn, brought out a second edition, adding material to Salmon's work and a sixth volume extending the series to the end of King George I's reign.

Emlyn's edition is distinctive in that the preface contains the most elaborate justification ever published in English of collected state trials, a preface admired greatly by his eighteenth-century successors and approximating the viewpoint of the editors of this work. He argued for such collections because they taught the law concerning the 'Life and Liberty of the Subject,' were at times a monument to learned eloquence, and were always an aid to historical understanding. The last involved forming proper opinions on the behaviour of judges in politically controversial cases: to revere those who acted impartially and to revile those who 'delivered Opinions in direct contradiction to the known fundamental laws of the nation' and those again who 'made no scruple to murder the Innocent, and ... acquit the Guilty, just as they received their directions from, or thought it would be best pleasing to those above them.' Emlyn also believed that state-trial collections would enable readers to understand the importance of maintaining the best in British laws, such as those provisions relating to the writ of habeas corpus[3] and the special guarantees afforded accused traitors (rights to counsel and various crown documents, the need for two witnesses, and so on). Such guarantees – which he thought should be expanded[4] – were absolutely essential where government was so deeply engaged, lest 'too great a latitude should be left to ... a Judge, who is the creature of the crown.' Readers would also, Emlyn believed, see the need for extensive reform of the criminal law. Most of the specifics he advocated, such as abolishing Latin in indictments and allowing accused felons defence counsel, have long since been achieved. Emlyn's arguments supporting reforms often strike a familiar chord; for example, he offered a 'modern' condemnation of capital punishment a generation before Cesare Beccaria.

Further eighteenth-century supplements and editions followed, culminating in the contribution of Francis Hargrave, a jurist of high reputation then and since. Aside from a perceptive preface, his ten volumes of 1775 simply reproduced the work of predecessors, a procedure recommended by him to the projectors and never concealed. An eleventh (1781) contained valuable new material – the result of much high-level searching: selected and annotated constitutional decisions either omitted from earlier editions or occurring after 1760, such as *Sommersett's* case (1772), which restricted the rights of slave-holders over their slaves in England.

Towards the end of the first decade of the nineteenth century, the eccentric reforming publisher William Cobbett decided to launch yet another edition of the *State Trials* to go along with his *Weekly Political Register, Parliamentary Debates,* and *Parliamentary History.* Cobbett's editorial assistant, John Wright, strongly recommended for editor Thomas Bayly Howell, a scholarly barrister of Lincoln's Inn, then forty years old.

Cobbett – a self-made man of farming origins – was reluctant in the extreme to employ Howell. The prospective editor was a lawyer, hence untrustworthy, and worse, had attended the elite Christ Church College, Oxford. 'I know,' Cobbett wrote Wright, that '*college* gentlemen ... always have ... the *insolence* to think themselves *our betters*,' despite 'our superior talents.' All authors – 'Damn them' – are so 'full of college conceit ... that I would sooner have dealings with an old lecherous woman that would be tearing open my cod-piece fifty times a day!' Howell, moreover, was greedy and a schemer, superficially clever no doubt, but a 'feeble' little fellow in body and mind, perhaps even 'an opium eater.'

Fortunately for posterity, sense prevailed and Howell was hired in December 1808. Yet Cobbett remained hostile and even as he agreed to the contract plotted his editor's early demise. Wright was to insist on a comprehensive outline of the series and information on sources: 'We shall find him [Howell] fail us, sooner or later, from one course or another; but if we can get out two or three volumes first, we shall ... be able to set him at defiance.' In the end, the owner was unable to satisfy his vitriolic envy. Wright probably assisted in minor ways for a while, but Cobbett took no further active interest in the project. Like the *Debates* and the *History*, the *State Trials* – contrary to the publisher's expectations – lost money. Facing insolvency in 1811, Cobbett sold these publications to his printer, T.C. Hansard, who removed Cobbett's name from the *Debates*, the *History*, and the *State Trials*, replacing it on the title page of the last with that of Howell.[5]

From 1809 to his death six years later, Howell was responsible for publishing twenty-one volumes of trials, a series that began in the late twelfth century with the treason proceedings against Thomas à Becket, archbishop of Canterbury (1163), and ending more than six centuries later with the prosecution of the Dean of St Asaph for seditious libel (1783–4). The first nineteen volumes and part of the next one reproduced the whole of Hargrave's edition, to which were added numerous new cases and notes. Including the material found in volumes twenty and twenty-one, Howell produced 'upwards of two hundred cases never before collected' – and some, such as Becket's and the *Case of Proclamations* (1611) denying royal legislative power, are of obvious importance to the historian.[6] His son and assistant, Thomas Jones, also of Lincoln's Inn, eventually took over editorial direction and from 1817 to 1826 was responsible for the publication of twelve equally full[7] and learned volumes carrying the story down to the trials of the Cato Street conspirators (1820) for plotting the murder of the cabinet.

The Howells have enjoyed high repute as editors and properly so. To have produced thirty-three thick volumes in eighteen years was a major achievement. Almost all cases of prime political importance were included, with every conceivable effort made to obtain accurate texts.[8] And readers were presented with thoughtful, if often provocative, commentary. It was in these elaborate footnotes that the Howells showed their political colours. State trials under the later Stuarts were presented through their advanced Whig eyes and those of Sir John Hawles, legal apologist and solicitor general for King William III, and Charles James Fox, in his role as party historian. Constructive or judge-made artificial treasons were intellectually demolished in the acid of the legal historian Alexander Luders and of anarchist philosopher William Godwin. Foot-of-the-page heroes included such near-contemporary dissidents as Fox, the supposed 'traitor' John Horne Tooke (1794), and John Philpot Curran, libertarian defence counsel for accused United Irish rebels (1798–1803). Leading the group was lawyer Thomas Erskine, eloquent protagonist of jury power in seditious libel cases, successful opponent of judicially constructed definitions of treason, and courageous defender of the English 'Jacobins' in the 1790s, virtually all of whom were acquitted or discharged.[9]

The Howells had successors, but, with one exception, none approached their standard of scholarship or willingness to embrace controversy. Twenty-four of their pre–1688 cases, all but three of them reporting treason trials, were summarized in 1826 by Samuel Phillipps of the Inner Temple, a scholar praised for his balanced judgment by such pre-eminent figures as Henry Hallam, Sir James Mackintosh, and Lord Cockburn. He provided readers with succinct political background; focused, clearly composed summaries; even-handed commentary; and plentiful references to legal authorities on such matters as allegiance, levying rebellious war, plotting the monarch's death, and the standards of proof required in treason proceedings. Not surprisingly, this ideological but moderate Whig tended to fault Tudor and Stuart judges (George Jeffreys in particular), but on the whole he found little to complain of in the constructive treasons 'from the period of the Revolution,' which were supposedly 'much less strained, than the [judicial] constructions put on most other branches of the criminal law.'[10] In 1850 the recorder of Macclesfield, William C. Townshend, put out a two-volume work of annotated abridgments entitled *Modern State Trials*, one purpose of which was to laud 'modern' judges, on whom no 'breath of suspicion ever seems to stain the purity of the judicial mirror.'[11] A four-volume study by H.L. Stephens, published at the turn of the century, was a scissors-and-paste abridgment of the Howells' great work.[12]

A few years earlier (1888–98) the eight-volume 'new' *State Trials* had appeared, covering cases from 1820 to 1858 and financed by the taxpayer. Safety was the watchword. Everything was vetted by a committee appointed by the lord chancellor and consisting of prominent members of the bar and bench, as well as such cautious academic luminaries as Sir James Fitzjames Stephen and Lord Acton. 'Messy' trials, such as that of Queen Caroline for adultery (1820), and those where only 'one-sided accounts by the defendants' could be found were omitted. No trial report could be published without the sanction of the lord chancellor and the lords commissioners of the Treasury. Opinionated notes in the style of the Howells were banned and a bureaucratic disclaimer denied responsibility for anything controversial which somehow managed to reach print.[13]

In 1882 English barrister G. Latham Brown published a two-volume collection of essays, *Narratives of State Trials in the Nineteenth Century* (1801–30). The narratives were impressively supported by Brown's relentless digging into printed correspondence, diaries and the like, and government records, including manuscripts. The author's approach to his task revealed assumptions radically different from those informing the near-contemporary new series. Judges were at times severely criticized. The trial of Queen Caroline was included, as were instructive examples of governmental corruption and abuse of power (for example, torture in Trinidad, unwarranted use of informers at home, and high-handed repression of dissent instead of measures remedying genuine grievances). Typical of Brown was his attempt to explore in depth Robert Emmet's attempted rising in Dublin (1803) by obtaining access to pertinent official records held by the government. More than three-quarters of a century after the events (1879) the home secretary, through his deputy, informed Brown that after consulting a variety of politicians and officials, 'he finds that there are strong reasons why, in the interest of the country, the request should not be complied with.' The author complained that this denial was a cover-up designed to protect the Irish government of the early nineteenth century, a government which informed public opinion was inclined to blame in part for the troubles.[14]

As was common in British thought, few definitions of a state trial or even hints of such were attempted. Closest to a formal one is found in the new series of 1888: 'State Trials' meant those 'relating to offences against the State, or trials illustrative of the Law relating to State Officers of high rank.' Readers will note that offences need not have been politically motivated and that the financial shortcomings of a cabinet minister or the sexual peccadilloes of a colonial governor came within the guidelines.[15] But this definition was utterly rigorous compared to Townshend's fuzzy, commercial inclination, which was to present those legal proceedings 'most likely to command the attention of all members of the community, and to be read by them with pleasure and profit.' This approach, he claimed, was justified by his illustrious eighteenth-century predecessors, Emlyn and Hargrave, who had published sensational trials for perjury and for witchcraft.

Predictably, the English collections did not always emphasize legal issues of national security, the most obvious types of state trials. Indeed, only in the Howells' work, Phillipps's summaries, and Brown's narratives did even three-quarters of the items clearly relate to such questions. The pioneering Salmon included trials for rape, heresy, sodomy, nonpolitical murder, forgery, and fraud, and Emlyn followed suit. Townshend gave the public *M'Naghten* (1843) on insanity, duelling cases, and the cunning abduction of a teenage heiress by political writer Edward Gibbon Wakefield, amid much other miscellany. The new series dealt in blasphemy, Bible printing, prize claims, appointment of coroners, and diplomatic privilege as well as rioting, sedition, and Chartist 'treason.'

It may also be remarked here that, despite publishing significant security material on, *inter alia*, the Whiskey Rebellion of 1794 in Pennsylvania, Lincoln's assassination, and dissent in the First World War, the seventeen-volume *American State Trials* collection was arguably misnamed. Considerably fewer than one-third of the items emphasized the safety of the state, the main thrust being to provide titillating tales, in legal dress, about larceny, arson, violent labour relations, train robberies, and slaves killing masters. Even passing muster was the 1873 trial of one Charles Hazeltine for exhibiting a classical nude statute ('Narcissus Listening to Echo') in puritan Massachusetts – a subject somewhat remote from the 'Boston Massacre' or the 'Boston Tea Party.'[16]

DEFINITION OF TERMS: CANADIAN STATE TRIALS AND RELATED PROCEEDINGS

The Canadian State Trials series is a more extensive, contextualized examination of a wider range of security proceedings than that offered by its predecessors. As many of the trials examined in this volume were never authoritatively reported, historical commentary is provided, supported by an array of reproduced primary documents, rather than verbatim transcripts of trials and editorial notes. In addition to trials for political offences, we examine other security measures and the political or military circumstances in which such proceedings took place. By doing so, the series allows for a rigorous but accessible examination of the uses of law in dealing with dissent and officially perceived security threats.

law & the exercise of power

Such an approach, generated partly out of necessity, has always been more familiar to historians than to lawyers and judges. Significantly, Cobbett's project had no pretense of 'legal science' and the Howells' notes and commentary openly reflected a libertarian/reform outlook. Samuel Johnson tells us that, in the eighteenth century, case reports were 'invented.' In the next century, as the legal profession increasingly embraced scientific models to justify and expand its trade, reports of trials acquired a more authoritative and objective image. Yet even then – and for long afterwards – legal history was marginalized in settings where the study of law was confined largely to specialized professional training, and it was hampered in settings where its methodology was limited largely to the professionally 'sanctified' sources. However, in recent years law has attracted more interdisciplinary interest. Legal historians no longer confine themselves to explaining patterns in case reports. Nor are they professionally bound to leave unquestioned the premises and formal claims of the rule of law which suggest that the development of law and its administration are free from immediate social influences.

The way is open to return to the tradition of the libertarian state-trials editors, where a critical eye may be cast at the contradictions between repressive or partisan practices and claims made about the impartiality of law. But this wider curiousity about law involves more than re-examination of those constitutional developments that led towards the better securing of the rule of law. It encourages sceptical consideration of the relations between law and authority. Security cases highlight an ongoing tension between the rule of law and the discretionary exercise of executive measures and reveal something about the role of law in the exercise of power.

The recent emergence of interdisciplinary legal history has also caused modern scholarly imperatives to bear more heavily on the study of law. While a trial report, where one exists, remains an important source, it sheds little light on the origins of the laws applied, administrative considerations, and how proceedings were experienced. Rigorous historical enquiry requires examination of the full range of law-related printed and manuscript sources in archives, where official concerns and strategies may be recovered and a limited picture of unofficial perceptions and popular responses may be discerned. The empirical limits are recognized; evidence from the surviving records represents only a partial and biased portrayal of the past and the historian intervenes as an interpreter of these records.

A broader, more sophisticated range of scholarly concerns makes the careful definition of the terms of reference for this collection all the more important. We examine trials for offences which allegedly threatened the safety of the state as well as other legal responses to officially apprehended security threats. There is no attempt to embrace the vast realm of interactions between law and politics. Partisanship in the ongoing administration of law, or politics in the more diffuse sense of the 'social-ordering' that arguably takes place as the result of the routine business of the courts, are important and complex issues lying beyond our scope.

A 'state trial' may be variously defined. At its most capacious it might be held to include any trial in which the political interests of government were specifically and obviously engaged. This would encompass innumerable kinds of trials relating to the interests of those who hold power – state security, of course, but also political corruption, federal/provincial disputes over jurisdiction, gender politics, native land claims, and so on. Somewhat less embracing are the definitions given by the *Oxford English Dictionary* and *Black's Law Dictionary*; these sources refer to 'offences against the state' (*OED*) and 'a trial for a political offence' (*Black's*), thus eliminating most civil and constitutional cases but retaining an immense scope in the area of criminal law, unless one adds that the trial is for an offence which allegedly threatens the security of the state. An exceedingly narrow definition of a state trial might be – as Lord Macaulay and Sir Thomas Erskine May seem at times to have suggested – one in which the accused was charged with high treason. Such an approach excludes a vast array of the uses of law for national-security matters.

The coherent selection process found in the Howells' edition of English state trials, which concentrates on state security cases – treason, sedition, riot, habeas corpus, and occasional politically inspired murder proceedings – is the most useful starting point. However, there is much of legal interest which lies outside or around actual trials, and it is in this respect that our collection ranges somewhat farther than the Howells'. As the suspension of habeas corpus suggests, attention must also be paid to uses of law and procedures which may not result in criminal proceedings. The exercise of the crown's prosecutorial prerogatives of ex officio informations and *nolle prosequi* stays caused security-related conflict around the administration of justice, as highlighted in Paul Romney's examination of the Collins case in this volume. Other executive measures figured prominently in the early Canadas, including summary deportations ordered and administered without recourse to the criminal courts. Thomas Barnes's study sets out another context – eighteenth-century Nova Scotia – in which such measures were implemented. The resort to courts-martial trithe focus.

als to deal with security threats is an ongoing theme from the British conquest (the essay by Douglas Hay examines the British military regime in Quebec) to the rebellions. The consideration of such proceedings as an alternative to regular trials is a central issue in the essay by Paul Romney and Barry Wright on the War of 1812 in Upper Canada. More generally, 'martial law' is studied in the piece by Jean-Marie Fecteau and Douglas Hay and also in the one by Fecteau, Murray Greenwood, and Jean-Pierre Wallot. Legislatures may act as courts and the uses of parliamentary-privilege proceedings for repressive security purposes, as well as counter-hegemonically in a manner that fuels security concerns, are analysed in an essay by Murray Greenwood and Barry Wright and in another piece by Evelyn Kolish and James Lambert. Contemplated, as opposed to actual, uses of the law to deal with perceived security threats also warrant attention, as suggested in the essays by David Bell, Jack Bumstead, and Christopher English. The specific content and enforcement of security legislation is treated at length in numerous other essays in this volume. Finally, the role of government officials in oppressive civil proceedings and officially sanctioned 'rough justice' are often revealing of the security intentions of governments and as a context for criminal trials, a point made in the essay by Ernest Clarke and Jim Phillips.

This volume examines such law-related dimensions of national security as well as providing the first comprehensive look at 'classic' state trials in early Canada. Later volumes will look at state trials during the rebellion period and after. As we move to the twentieth century, we will see that national-security legislation such as the War Measures Act, the Official Secrets Act, and the Immigration Act has extended executive powers at the expense, often, of access to the criminal courts. The issues of political espionage, access to information, and privacy rights fall outside the traditional concept of state trials.

A great deal of interest, therefore, lies beyond the confines of the trial of security offences in the criminal courts. The topics in this collection may be said to focus on incidents where government authorities perceive, or profess to perceive, fundamental threats to the state's internal or external security. Within this framework, a wide variety of legal forms and measures are analysed.

RECEPTION OF THE CRIMINAL LAWS OF ENGLAND

The proceedings examined in this volume focus largely on British-administered territories in what we now know as Canada. Peter Moogk's essay casts light on the security laws applied in New France, and the essays by Barnes, Cahill, Fecteau and Hay, and Clarke and Phillips deal with a period when British North America included the American colonies. Beyond the political dimensions of British conquest and retrenchment lie complicated constitutional matters related to the application of the imperial power's laws in early Canada. Since these matters concern most of the essays in this collection, they bear extended comment.

The reception date for a colony is the time down to which British statutes were in force. Thereafter, new British acts did not apply, unless they were explicitly imperial in reach, a colony was indicated, or a colonial legislature expressly adopted them.[17] The reception date is irrelevant to the common law, which was considered timeless in the eighteenth and nineteenth centuries. Thus, a court decision in England on sedition, rendered long after the reception date (since it supposedly 'discovered' rather than created a common-law principle), could be cited as authority in the colony. The reception dates were set in a variety of ways: provincial statutes in Newfoundland and Upper Canada, judicial decisions followed by enactment in Nova Scotia, imperial legislation in Quebec, executive fiat in New Brunswick, and usage in Prince Edward Island.

The issues around reception are complex. Lawyers are interested in fixing a 'true' reception date while historians are concerned with the circumstances and extent to which English laws were retained, modified, or rejected. Discussion here is necessarily confined to how reception relates to security laws and their administration.

The legal rules relating to reception can be stated succinctly although such statements conceal more than they reveal.[18] British subjects founding colonies by settling uninhabited territory took with them as a birthright English laws (not Scottish, Welsh, or Irish), statutory and common, civil and criminal, as of the date of settlement. The king or queen acting outside parliament could not legislate for the colony, except to establish a constitution. With regard to conquered colonial territory or that ceded by treaty (more often than not conquered/ceded colonies such as Quebec), most laws of the conquered and especially their civil laws remained in force until altered or supplanted by the conqueror. Exceptions in the British empire fell under the rubric of 'public law,' which included aspects of constitutional law, for example, the right to petition the crown and the powers of courts; admiralty rules; and an indeterminate portion of the criminal law. The 'conqueror' for our purposes was parliament, or, depending on the period, the monarch acting alone. The sovereign's legislative power in this area was denied by, among others, the attorney general and chief justice of Quebec (1766) and the lord chancellor (1766).[19] It was only in *Campbell v. Hall* (1774) that Lord Mansfield – in the first clear precedent – upheld the royal prerogative to legislate for conquered/ ceded colonies. Mansfield also held that the promise of a legislative assembly (in this case by the Royal Proclamation of 1763 in relation to Grenada) precluded any further royal legislation. This concept had earlier had some currency, causing doubts about the validity of laws in Quebec in the period 1764–74. Those doubts – and also the uncertainty about the very existence of the royal prerogative – led to the first parliamentary-based constitution for a colony in the Quebec Act of 1774.[20]

Precisely when the ordinary, non-political criminal laws of England were introduced to a conquered or ceded colony has never been finally decided. The most persuasive view – both in logic and authority – was that of British Advocate General James Marriott (1774) regarding Quebec:

But whatever the criminal law of England is in the great lines of treason, felony, &c. I conceive it must of course have taken place in the colony of Canada; and that no other system of criminal laws could exist there at any instant of time after the conquest: because this part of distributive and executive justice is so inherent in dominion, or, in other words, so attached to every crown, and is so much an immediate emanation of every government, that the very instant a people fall under the protection and dominion of any other state, the criminal, or what is called the crown law of that state, must ipso facto and immediately operate: it cannot be otherwise; for were it otherwise there would be no effective sovereignty on one side, and no dependence on the other. The dominant power can exercise and execute no laws but those which it knows, and in its own name, and with which its servants are conversant; and the subjects can obey none but such as arise out of the new relation in which they stand.

Marriott's position was adopted by several judges, including three chief justices of Lower Canada.[21]

Discussion of the reception issue often conveys the unfortunate impression that areas eventually governed by British law were juridically, even demographically, vacant. Reception is in fact bound up with the realities of conquest and the imposition of an outside legal order. Indigenous legal systems, often carefully moulded, were gradually and sometimes violently submerged. Pre-existing European systems such as the French were accommodated to a greater degree and elements continued to prevail.[22]

A line of authority from Lord Chief Justice Holt in *Smith v. Brown* (1707) through Blackstone (1765) to Joseph Chitty (1820) held that a colony had to have been entirely unpopulated to qualify as 'settled.' Thus, Virginia, the Carolinas, and Georgia were deemed to be conquered or ceded because of the prior existence there of indigenous people. This concept did not much affect the incoming European settlers to North America. Theoretically, aboriginal laws could prevail until the conqueror otherwise decided (and clear decisions were rare), except that, since these were 'infidel' countries, those laws against 'God' would be automatically replaced by 'natural equity.' The Royal Proclamation of 1763 recognized aboriginal rights, but it did so in a contingent manner because they were held in trust by the crown. In practice, through local legislation, usage, and judicial decision, modified versions of English law were applied without regard to native rights.[23] By the second half of the nineteenth century, an imperialistic ideology (which prevails still in current law texts) had become entrenched. It held that the presence of natives was entirely irrelevant and did not prevent such colonies from being 'settled.'

Lawyers seem to find dates of reception with ease and confidence, but often by distorting the historical record. Historians examining the question have uncovered complexity and confusion, not certainty. However, they have also used their questions as routes to historical insight. Even on a technical level each colony in British North America presents different problems to the researcher. Was Nova Scotia a conquered/ceded or settled colony and does that matter? Does it matter much in the case of Prince Edward Island or even Quebec, which certainly was one? Why did New Brunswick adopt 1660 and can that idiosyncratic decision be justified? Was Nova Scotia's date of reception 1758, when the representative legislature first met – as lawyers generally claim – or 1749, when large-scale Protestant settlement began and Halifax was founded? Or should Nova Scotia be considered a colony of reception at all? What statutes applied in Newfoundland prior to its date of reception in 1837? What criminal laws were in force in Quebec in the decade after 1763? Did the wide-ranging Treason Act of 1795 apply to Lower Canada and did Fox's liberalizing Libel Act of 1792 apply in Upper Canada?

Newfoundland

Prior to reception in the 1830s, as Christopher English explains in his essay, informality characterized the administration of criminal justice in Newfoundland. There were few juries outside St John's and few legally trained men of any kind, simple pleadings and rules of evidence, fines in preference to jail sentences, little use of the complex doctrine relating to benefit of clergy, private prosecutions (in contrast to the Canadas) without mutual-help prosecuting associations (in contrast to England), and so on.[24]

In 1833 the island's representative legislature began to operate, meaning that – for a short time as it proved – subsequent British criminal legislation was not in force.[25] Four years later the system was altered by local act.[26] Imperial statutes on crime until 20 June 1837 were to be enforced, because the 'Penal Code and Criminal Laws of *England* have lately undergone very considerable revisions and improvements; and it is highly desirable to extend the same to this Colony.' The statement probably referred to such changes as granting accused felons the right to make full defence by counsel (1836) and the virtual elimination of the almost ubiquitous capital punishment for felonies, except where the crimes had involved violence or sexual deviation (1837).[27]

Whether intended or not, the Newfoundland statute was 'ultra colonial' (contrasting with the procedures adopted by even the 'Loyalist' legislatures of New Brunswick and Upper Canada), in that it provided for the development of criminal law as dictated by the mother country: 'Statutes of the Imperial Parliament ... passed subsequently ... shall in *Twelve Months* after ... extend to ... this Colony.' However, in accordance with long, local tradition, criminal-law provisions were to be enforced only 'so far as the same can be applied' with benefit in the social circumstances of Newfoundland. Precisely which statutes were not applied, both before and after 1837, awaits scholarly research. The 1837 act was repealed in 1949 when the island joined Canada.[28]

Nova Scotia

The question of received law in early Nova Scotia is extraordinarily complex, but fortunately mostly with regard to civil-law statutes which are not a concern here.[29] The leading case on criminal-law reception is *R v. Young* (1756), at which Chief Justice Jonathan Belcher presided. He was assisted by two inferior court judges who seconded his opinions on all points of relevance.

The principal issue in the case was whether a Marian statute of 1553 was in force so as to make counterfeiting/circulating Spanish dollars (legal tender in the American colonies) high treason. Belcher held, first, that the date of settlement for his colony was that of the foundation of

Halifax and the granting of local legislative authority (with an elected assembly which did not meet until 1758) in 1749, and second, that the Marian statute applied. Both points had essentially been laid down by him in a civil case one year previously.

Belcher's approach followed British judicial authority with one possible exception. To the chief justice it did not matter whether Nova Scotia was a settled colony – which it eventually became[30] – or a conquered/ ceded one. In the first case, the Marian statute was not unsuitable and antedated the 1749 beginning of settlement. On the other hand, if Nova Scotia was a conquered or ceded colony, the laws, generally speaking, of the conquered people remained in force until altered or replaced by the king or parliament. But where there was a gap, that is, where the indigenous laws were silent, as they were in Nova Scotia, British acts were in force.

One might add to Belcher's opinion by noting that if, as we believe, Marriott was correct in 1774, all significant criminal laws of England came into force at the time of France's cession of Acadia under the Treaty of Utrecht in 1713. If Marriott was not correct, it does not matter. Governor Edward Cornwallis's commission (1749) – the conqueror's decision – authorized him to establish courts 'for the hearing & determining all causes as well Criminal as Civil according to Law and Equity.' That this meant the criminal law of *England* – as Belcher assumed – is certain: three sucessive governors in the 1750s had that law applied as closely as humanly possible.

To the chagrin of Belcher and contrary to authorities, past and future, the British law officers found the chief justice to have erred seriously: the concept that settlers of the colonies carried with them enacted British law was 'not true as a general Proposition.' Statutory reception would depend, in each instance, 'upon Circumstances, the Effect of their Charter, Usage and Acts of their Legislature.' Had this question later arisen in Nova Scotia, the argument from 'usage' might have conferred a positive presumption of reception of imperial criminal-law statutes. But such was not necessary.

Guided by Belcher and to eliminate uncertainty, the legislature, in 1758, enacted a number of criminal statutes. Mainly by adopting acts, this 'codification' covered *all* capital statutes – or that at least is how contemporary Nova Scotians interpreted it – with the death penalty retained for only fourteen crimes (rather than over two hundred, as in the mother country).[31] Misdemeanours such as perjury, receiving stolen goods, and petty larceny were also dealt with. Whether in this case British acts (for example, on 'cheating' or fraud) were impliedly repealed is not clear. Common-law crimes such as seditious or criminal libel, riot, and assault remained in force. Nova Scotia, it appears, became a colony of adoption rather than reception in 1758, as far as the criminal law was concerned. Imperial statutes on crime, enacted after the settlement date of 1749, did not apply unless the colony was referred to therein.[32]

Prince Edward Island

There is no published scholarship of substance or suggestive judicial decision on Prince Edward Island's reception of the criminal law. Île Saint-Jean was a colony ceded to England by the Treaty of Paris on 10 February 1763. Assuming that Marriott was accurate, Prince Edward Island received British acts on crime (and the common law) up to the Paris treaty. About eight months later the island was annexed to Nova Scotia by the Royal Proclamation.

This suggests that it came under the mother province's 'codification' of 1758 and that such dispensation would arguably continue after 1769, when P.E.I. was separated from Nova Scotia. Unlike New Brunswick, there was never an island statute dissociating itself from Nova Scotian law. If this reasoning is not correct, the date of criminal-law reception would be 1763 (à la Marriott), sanctioned retroactively by the 1769 separation. More likely the precise date is 4 August 1769, the date of the commission issued to Governor Walter Paterson, which contemplated his establishing courts to judge 'all causes, as well Criminal as Civil, according to [Our] Law and Equity.'[33] This was either the conqueror's introduction of criminal law or the updating of its application from 1758 or 1763 on the island.

New Brunswick

Legal scholars have advanced various times for New Brunswick's reception of statutory law: 1758, the year Nova Scotia's representative government commenced; 1784, when New Brunswick separated from its eastern parent; 1786, the year its new legislature began to operate; and the Stuart restoration of 1660![34] The last peculiar, reactionary date is arguably sanctioned by a judicial decision of 1830 and certainly by a Court of Appeal ruling in 1970 (still definitive).[35] How did this come about?

In the months preceding the first meeting of the full legislature, the governor-in-council (including all the senior judges) tacitly fixed on 1660, as did the pro-government assembly and the courts immediately thereafter. The most comprehensive justification is found in a set of 'General observations on the laws passed in the first Session' written in 1786 by Solicitor General and assemblyman Ward Chipman and endorsed by Governor Thomas Carleton. Chipman defended the date on two principal grounds, one technical and the other political. The technical ground argued that it was about 1660 that the imperial authorities began to notice the colonies: they 'were not of sufficient importance before this period to become an object of attention to the Parliament of Great Britain, and after it so many acts are found expressly noticing and binding the plantations that a presumption arose [that] they were not intended [to apply to the colonies] unless named.' This assertion, while generally accurate, was created out of 'wholecloth' and ignored one monumental precedent to the contrary – Elizabeth I's Act of Supremacy in 1559 – as well as at least two others from the same reign.[36] More important, it flew in the face of established authority, which held that usable statutes enacted by parliament *up to the time of settlement* – however defined – formed part of the colony's law. The political rationale is best given in Chipman's words: 'It appeared most *safe* and convenient in our present situation to reduce the number of laws ... and by admitting ... [only those] which were passed before the restoration as of force amongst us, the *stability* of the Province will be guarded from a *spirit of innovation*' (emphases added). Chipman's statement strongly supports the view of certain scholars that 1660 was chosen to enhance executive power (at the expense of the legislative branch) in the new Loyalist Eden. As Phillip Buckner wisely writes: the 'choice of this date precluded the application to the colony of subsequent laws limiting the monarchy and thus placed more authority in the hands of the crown in New Brunswick than the crown possessed in Britain.'[37]

But what post-1660 acts did Chipman and like-minded men wish to target? Precision is impossible but certain candidates spring to mind. We here do not exclude those statutory provisions that *may have* declared common law or those that *perhaps* or even *probably* did *not* apply to the colony,[38] since the Tories could not have been certain on these matters and may well have acted from an abundance of caution. Among our list of measures are King Charles II's reforming Habeas Corpus Act of 1679 and legislation extending toleration to Roman Catholics.[39] Others include the Bill of Rights, 1689, which among other things sanctioned the right to petition and free parliamentary debate, restricted the executive severely at voting time (ignored during the first provincial election of 1785), and virtually eliminated royal legislative power. We must also mention the Treason Act of 1695/6, a statute against corrupt elections of the same date, provision for secure judicial tenure (1701),[40] and laws against certain public servants sitting in the Commons.[41] Idiosyncratic even among Loyalists, New Brunswickers had thus rejected the Glorious Revolution of 1688–9.

Courts can and usually should aspire to clarity in defining law. But often that very decisiveness does a disservice to history, usually a messy process at best. In the case of New Brunswick reception, nothing was carved in stone. During the mid-1790s oppositionists in the House of Assembly, for example, thought it feasible to challenge this rejection of celebrated parts of their constitutional history (wishing to substitute 1749 or 1758), but Tories in the Council scotched such plans. Even more revealing of the unsettled state of the law on this 'much agitated' question is a draft letter to Nova Scotian Chief Justice Sampson Salter Blowers, written by none other than Ward Chipman in Saint John on 27 February 1800. Chipman noted that the 'general principle under which we have proceeded here is that no Act of Parliament made after the Restoration of K. Ch. 2 soon after which the Colonies first began to be noticed in the Statute books, shall be considered binding unless the Colonies are specially named therein.' But he also stated that 'some of our Judges' thought that all suitable acts 'passed down to the time when the first Assembly was called in Nova Scotia [1758], are in force here, or at least down to the time when Governors of that Province ... were first empowered to call assemblies [1749].' Alluding to three British court decisions, Chipman was inclined to think that the period when a colony was 'planted' was crucial and that such was to be determined by the 'calling of a legislative Assembly' since, until that time, 'the Colony must be without laws unless the laws of England ... are in force.' There had never been a judicial decision on this point and Blowers was asked for advice.[42] While Chipman's letter contains a hint that the 1660 date was soon reinforced,[43] his doubts nevertheless suggest that the New Brunswick Court of Appeal decision in 1970 is vulnerable to attack by constitutional historians and expert historical witnesses.

Quebec/Lower Canada

Just when the criminal laws of England were introduced into the newly conquered/ceded British colony of Quebec has never been clear.[44] Candidates include 8 September 1760, which is our choice, as an automatic effect of conquest (how else could the conqueror govern effectively?); and 7 October 1763, the date of the Royal Proclamation, which, read literally, either promised or enacted English laws, civil and criminal, for Quebec. Even the Quebec Act of 1774[45] can be supported on the contentious but possible grounds that international, and hence British, law maintained in force all legal rules, not only civil – which no one denied – but criminal as well (except those essential to sovereignty, such as treason law) until expressly changed by the conqueror. A subordinate argument is that the Proclamation, a public-relations document, did not enact anything for Quebec.

This arcane problem need not concern us, since from the establishment of civil government on 10 August 1764 the Quebec courts constantly applied English criminal law, to the entire exclusion of French rules and without being challenged on legal grounds. Moreover, the Quebec Act *'enacted'* that the procedural and substantive 'Criminal Law of *England* ... shall continue to be administered, and shall be observed as Law in ... Quebec.' This was either the legal introduction of English criminal law or a re-*enacting* of such. But even if the latter, it seems logical to assume that the 'Criminal Law of *England'* was meant as that existing at the later time of enactment (and not as of Septmber 1760 or October 1763). The time of passage, then, provides us with a date of reception.

The criminal laws of England introduced or re-enacted by the Quebec Act consisted of judicial decisions in the mother country declaring the supposedly 'eternal' principles of the common law, juristic writings by authorities such as Sir William Blackstone, and an untidy mass of parliamentary statutes dating back to the Middle Ages. It is with regard to these that questions of reception arose.

Certain pre-1774 criminal-law statutes enacted by parliament, so precisely tailored to conditions in England/Great Britain as not to be readily transportable across the sea, were not in force.[46] A rare example was King Charles II's liberalizing Habeas Corpus Act of 1679, which dealt with numerous officials and institutions foreign to Quebec/Lower Canada.[47] But it did not matter in the slightest that the vast majority of the pre-Quebec Act criminal-law statutes had been framed without the colonies in mind; they were 'received' statutes enforceable by the colonial courts. Thus, the notorious Black Act of 1723, which included as one of its multitude of new capital crimes the appearing disguised and armed in a forest where deer were present, became part of Quebec's criminal law, even though deer poaching with blackened faces was not the popular sport in the valley of the St Lawrence it had been at Windsor and elsewhere in

Britain for centuries.[48] The principle applied even to acts that expressly referred to the British Isles and had been enacted before England had possessed any overseas colonies whatever. And so, despite references in it to the 'realm,' King Edward III's Statute of Treasons, 1351/2, was in force.[49]

Parliamentary enactments on the criminal law passed after the Quebec Act did not apply to the colony unless it was named or the statute was made applicable to all dependencies or to a group of which Quebec/Lower Canada was one – an example being the imperial act of 1777 which suspended habeas corpus in British America during the American revolution.[50] There does not seem to have been any notion of 'necessary intendment' at that time, which explains the status of the Treason Act of 1795.[51] That statute contemplated persons (including those resident in the colonies) committing treasons 'within the realm or without,' but neither contained an application clause referring to the colonies nor directed the colonial courts to enforce its provisions. Whatever might be the modern view as to the statute's geographic reach, Canadian judges were clearly of the opinion that it formed no part of the law in either of the Canadas.[52] This is an important point to bear in mind when assessing the 'royalist' interpretations of the law of treason handed down by the judges of Lower Canada: they had no warrant to base them on the wide-ranging provisions of the 1795 act.

Upper Canada

Initially, Upper Canada's reception date was seen either as 1774, the year of the Quebec Act, or 1791, when the Constitutional Act divided the old Province of Quebec into two Canadas mainly along the Ottawa River.[53] The Loyalist community's desire for a separate province with the 'blessings of the British Constitution,' including English (rather than seigneurial) land tenure and civil law, were largely met by the 1791 act and measures following from it. The early constitution of Upper Canada not only reflected Loyalist and British reaction to the American revolution but growing concerns (after 1792) about the French revolution. These attitudes, elaborated in the field by Lieutenant Governor John Graves Simcoe and Chief Justice William Osgoode, had a impact on the structure of representative government (a powerful appointed legislative council) and on the administration of law (which, through the Judicature Act of 1794, was closely modelled on the English system but was also heavily centralized and executively controlled).[54] These measures strongly suggested that the reception date was that of the Constitutional Act. The reception of criminal law remained unclear, however, until legislation passed in 1800 settled the reception date as 17 September 1792 (when the new legislature first met).[55]

Such details are important in evaluating the constitutionality and legality of security measures in the province. For instance, as examined in Barry Wright's essay on Gourlay, the question arose whether received law included Fox's Libel Act, a liberating clarification of the scope of the jury's verdict in seditious libel trials. Fox's act, passed in Westminster on 31 January 1792, was proclaimed law on 15 June 1792, over three months before the provincial reception date. Robert Gourlay and his supporters thought that they could not benefit from the legislation in 1818, assuming that 1791 was the relevant reception date.[56] When the issue came up after questions were raised about judge Levius Peters Sherwood's instructions to the jury in the case of Francis Collins in 1828, the applicability of Fox's act was accepted by the crown.[57]

CONSTITUTIONAL RECEPTION

The structure of colonial government had important consequences for the administration of received laws and for the creation of new ones. Executive domination or influence was a particularly contentious element of that structure, the point at which conflict between the theory and practice of colonial constitutional arrangements most frequently occurred.

Despite claims that British North American constitutions were formed in conformity to the British constitution, reality was somewhat different. Quite apart from the existence of supervisory imperial review, colonial constitutions framed in or after the mid-eighteenth century reflected a response to perceived 'errors' in the constitutional arrangements of the Thirteen Colonies. Care was taken to ensure that the lid over troublesome American tendencies was firmly screwed on. Thus, New Brunswick's constitution was a model of executive domination, and that of Nova Scotia entailed the suppression of local government influences that had proved so problematic in New England. During the British parliamentary debates on the Constitutional bill in 1791, there was much rhetoric to the effect that the newly created provinces were to receive all of the benefits of the British constitution – they were to be its 'very image and transcript,' in Lieutenant Governor Simcoe's phrase. While Charles James Fox emphasized that the full 'blessings' of the British constitution would avoid a replay of the American difficulties, Edmund Burke, alarmed by events in France, stressed the constitution's counter-revolutionary qualities. The 1791 act indeed reflected such qualities, or at least it was given counter-revolutionary content in the field by administrators who drew heavily upon the Loyalist experience.

The effect of executive influences on the operation of provincial legislatures rapidly became the stuff of public and political disputes. Home rule, financial control of the executive, and the later battles for responsible government are the well-known examples of the issues that arose. Executive domination also had profound and contentious implications for the administration of law. These included the participation of judges – whose tenure depended on executive pleasure – in executive and legislative councils, the effective monopoly of criminal prosecutions by the attorney general, and the use of executively appointed magistrates and sheriffs both to provide local government and to manage strategically important legal matters such as the selection of jurors.

Much of the conflict between the formal claims of British constitutionalism and colonial constitutional realities found voice in historically neglected courtroom battles and in debates over the administration of the law. Those prosecuted in the courts and those who battled for legislative reforms to the law's administration used the language of the British constitution and the rule of law to highlight colonial disparities and denounce repressive government measures. This language was contentious, for although executive influences on the law had been reduced by the end of the seventeenth century through the introduction of security of judicial tenure, restraints on the crown's prerogatives in prosecutions, and jury trials with free verdicts, the British constitution remained an evolving and largely unwritten entity. Notions about the proper relationship between executive, legislature, and judiciary were still being worked out through the eighteenth century.

The legal conflicts that reflected and fuelled these constitutional debates were not confined to the trial of political offences. Nonetheless, prosecutions for treason and sedition and the suspension of habeas corpus were the main legal sanctions used to control activities officially perceived as threatening state security. The following section examines the state of eighteenth- and early-nineteenth-century law with respect to these major sanctions. Other techniques of repression, such as parliamentary privilege and a range of executive measures, illuminated the strengths and weaknesses of the main legal measures. These will be introduced in individual essays in the volume. The French security doctrine applied in New France is studied at length in the essay by Peter Moogk.

TREASON, SEDITION, AND HABEAS CORPUS

Treason Law

The basis of treason law in all British North American colonies was King Edward III's celebrated Statute of Treasons of 1351/2,[58] which limited the highest of crimes to seven cases proved by 'open deed.' The three most important were plotting the king's death, rebelling in arms, and adhering to enemies during a state of war. Treason occurred 'when a man doth compasse or imagine the death of our lord the king, of my lady his queene, or of their eldest sonne and heire ... or if a man doe levie warre against our lord the king in his realme, or be adherent to the kings enemies in his realme, giving to them aid and comfort in the realme or elsewhere ...' Edward's act, passed at the urging of the barons, was designed to restrict judicial interpretations resulting in the forfeiture of lands and life and in particular to do away with the notion of traitorously 'accroaching' on royal power, which could mean almost anything including interference with the courts and highway robbery. Over the centuries the terms of the act were expanded to favour the crown and repress serious political dissent. By the late eighteenth century 'constructive treasons,' as constitutional historian Henry Hallam remarked, were often 'repugnant to the general understanding of mankind' and even that of 'most lawyers.' These verbal sophisms were indeed widely condemned outside ministerial circles. Thomas Erskine's monumental and effective attack on constructive treasons in *Hardy's* case (1794) made him the darling of the London crowd, while even such a robust Tory as Samuel Johnson found them morally repulsive.

Compassing the death of the monarch meant wishing it, trying to bring it about, or conspiring for that purpose. It did not mean murder. The regicides of Charles I were found guilty of the incipient offence of compassing, of which the actual beheading was considered evidence. Like other treasons, compassing had to be proved by 'open deed' or 'overt act,' such as conspiratorial conversations. The word 'death' in Edward's statute seems clearly to have referred to physical death (not the political demise involved in losing territory), since the compassing head protected the queen consort and the eldest son as well as the reigning king.

From the late sixteenth century, judges magnified compassing well beyond the original intent. Decisions bringing plots to imprison or depose the king under this rubric reflected Machiavelli's dictum that 'between the prisons and graves of princes the distance is very small.' Inviting foreigners to invade the realm was classed as compassing, as was the actual levying of war by rebels, since the monarch's life was thereby imperilled. This last extension enabled the courts to hold that a mere conspiracy to rebel – which was *not* levying – nevertheless amounted to high treason under this head, which referred to simple intention. Whether compassing could occur in an overseas colony remained an open question until 1797 when Chief Justice William Osgoode decided that it could in the Lower Canadian case of *McLane*.

For almost a century after 1352, levying was interpreted as applying strictly to formal war – with organized armies – waged by magnates against the king. Some change occurred in the aftermath of Wat Tyler's 'peasants' revolt' of 1381, but only after Jack Cade's insurrection in 1450 did the courts clearly establish that popular risings aimed at overthrowing the government were to be classed as levying. This first important constructive treason was but a prelude to many far less justifiable. Between 1595 and 1710 it was laid down that riots were levyings if the insurgents held some *general* objective, such as to destroy all enclosures, dissenting chapels, or bawdy houses within reach or to force the monarch to alter ministers, policies, or law. If the insurgents' aim was local and particular – for example, to release specified prisoners from one jail – the offence amounted only to the misdemeanour of riot. By the late eighteenth century, then, there were two main types of levying: rebelling to usurp political power and rioting to pursue some generalized political aim falling short of revolution. We refer to the latter as 'treasonable rioting.' Although conspiring to levy war as rebellion was deemed by eighteenth-century jurists and judges to be compassing (it was not levying, which required *activity*), they denied such status to conspiracy to engage in mere treasonable rioting – since the monarch's life was not thereby usually threatened.[59] Such draconian elasticity – beloved of Pitt's anti-'Jacobin' law officers (as was the related concept of political death) – was incorporated in the Treason Act of 1795.

In 1765 Quebec legal officials decided that Canadien merchants who had provisioned the native rebel leader Pontiac were guilty of adhering to His Majesty's enemies.[60] No one, fortunately, was convicted on this untenable basis. Men in Pontiac's forces were subjects by British law, having become so no later (if formerly 'French') than the Treaty of Paris in 1763, and there was no solid evidence that France or Spain had orchestrated the rising. The legal authorities, then and later, stated the obvious: subjects in rebellion could not be enemies; assisting them was levying, not adhering. Enemies meant nations at war with Britain (whether declared or not) and raiders from countries at peace with the monarch.

Read literally, the adhering clause required actual help being given rather than intentions or attempts. The early jurists (Edward Coke, Matthew Hale, William Hawkins) and the Court of King's Bench in 1696[61] accepted this interpretation, illustrating it by pointing to such activity as selling arms, joining the enemy's forces, treacherously surrendering a defensible position, and communicating military intelligence. A major change occurred with *Gregg* (1707/8), an extra-judicial opinion of the twelve judges of England which enlarged the ambit of treason in a variety of ways.[62] One of these constructive treasons held that sending intelligence to the enemy was adhering even when that intelligence was intercepted by the British authorities. This proposition was adopted in a series of cases and by the later jurists (Michael Foster, William Blackstone, Edward Hyde East), but it remained questionable whether *any* attempt whatever to aid (for example, mere gathering of information) was sufficient. Foster himself postulated that the attempt must reach the penultimate stage; that is, the aid must at least be 'tendered.' Referring to *Gregg*, Foster wrote, 'The party in sending did all he could; the treason was complete on his part, though [because intercepted] it had not the effect he intended.' This restriction was ignored by Chief Justice Osgoode (despite his admiration for Foster as a treason jurist) in *McLane*.

High treason could be committed only by persons under the monarch's protection and hence owing a reciprocal duty of allegiance.[63] Because protection was absent, no allegiance was owed to a *de jure* king or queen while a *de facto* monarch – or by 1700 probably any kind of government – exercised power.[64] Similarly, invaders from a nation at peace with Great Britain (for example, the American invaders of Upper Canada in 1838) and wartime enemy spies (McLane) arguably did not commit treason.[65] Enemy invaders certainly did not do so. Until 1870 a person born in His or Her Majesty's dominions owed allegiance for life (as did children and grandchildren), however tenuous the later connection[66] and despite naturalization in a foreign country. According to British court decisions in the 1820s and 1830s, persons born in the older American colonies who remained there as permanent residents after 1783 were deemed not to come under this rule. Earlier, the question had been one of great doubt.[67] Foreigners who enjoyed protection – such as alien residents and travellers – owed a 'local allegiance' for the duration of their stay and could commit treason in British territory. An unprecedented and probably unworkable proposition in *Gregg* held that, if a departed foreigner had left behind 'family and effects' (as many did in Upper Canada after the outbreak of war in 1812), he or she continued to owe allegiance.[68] The Overholser and Hartwells cases of 1814 raise some of these complex issues and are explored at length in the essay by Paul Romney and Barry Wright.

Prior to the rebellions of 1837–8, colonial legislation – except when habeas corpus was suspended – affected the law of treason only occasionally and slightly. Nova Scotia (1758), for example, reproduced the essentials of King Edward III's act, while Lower Canada (1801) changed the punishment for women from being burned alive to hanging. More significantly, Upper Canada (1833) reduced the physical penalty to drawing, fatal hanging, and dissection from the traditional drawing, hanging, disembowelling when alive, beheading, and quartering. Property forfeiture and corruption of the blood (incapacity to inherit) were not affected.[69]

Two imperial statutes of vital procedural importance were King William III's Treason Act of 1696 and an amendment (1708) enacted under Anne.[70] They required two or more witnesses to an overt act or acts charged under one head of treason, enabled the prisoner to subpoena witnesses and make full defence through counsel (as accused felons could not until 1836), and guaranteed that the defendant receive copies of the indictment, along with annotated lists of crown witnesses and the jury panel, at least ten days before arraignment. These acts applied throughout British North America, except presumably New Brunswick. As mentioned earlier, the Treason Act of 1795, which legislated certain constructive treasons, including conspiracy to deprive the monarch of any overseas dominions, was not in force.

Sedition Law

Although the English law of sedition had its origins in the Court of Star Chamber, the most important form of the offence, seditious libel, was developed largely in the eighteenth century, particularly by three chief justices: John Holt, Lord Mansfield, and Lord Kenyon. The result was exceedingly favourable to the crown: a wide scope of prohibited behaviour, minimal burden of proof, and refusal to allow the jury to decide on the really critical question of the 'seditious' quality of the publication.

Sedition entailed criticism of the crown, government, or officials which was deemed to bring these authorities into 'disesteem.' As with other forms of sedition – conspiracy and words uttered orally – the libel had to manifest a seditious intention, defined by Kenyon in 1793 as 'calculated to put the people in a state of discontent,' the rationale being, as Holt had declared almost ninety years earlier, that if agitators 'should not be called to account for possessing the people with an ill opinion of government, no government can subsist.'[71] The object was to protect political authority – then, of course, deemed superior in importance to the citizenry or even the elite electorate – by preventing the spread of 'discontent,' 'disesteem,' or 'disaffection.' The spread of such things, indictments usually charged, increased the likelihood of public disturbance. But there was not the slightest hint in the cases that the accused must have directly incited violence or even caused an actual breach of the peace – such a requirement would await the twentieth century.[72] The bare freedom to criticize cabinet ministers, public servants, and government measures existed, but the tone had to eschew emotion, be deferential, and avoid attributing unworthy motives.[73] Even this bare freedom sometimes disappeared in British North America.

Although the seditious variety may be distinguished from other forms of criminal libel (defamatory, blasphemous, obscene, and, in the case of parliamentary privilege, contempt), this was not always clear. A defamatory libel was directed at an individual allegedly held up to hatred, contempt, or ridicule in writing.[74] A seditious libel was directed at the state, its intention allegedly being to undermine the authority of the government's policies or its representatives. Written defamations against individual officials could be either defamatory or seditious, although when criticism involved the exercise of their duties the tendency was towards the latter. Allegations in libel cases nonetheless tended to blur these distinctions in the attempt to portray the defendant's conduct in the worst light. As the eighteenth century progressed, the adjectives were often dropped altogether. Concerns about the jury made the precise wording of the indictment important; adding 'defamatory,' 'malicious,' or 'seditious' to libel was an invitation to the jury to reflect on intent, whereas an indictment of libel alone made it easier to restrict the jury to the fact of publication. In the English context the resulting distinction was usually reflected in the mode of prosecution: private ones tended to be defamatory; prosecutions taken by the law officers of the crown, particularly through the royal prerogative of ex officio informations, tended to be seditious. In the British North American context even this distinguishing element is muddied as the result of the attorneys general monopolizing all prosecutions of serious criminal offences. The vagueness of libel indictments and questions around the crown's prosecutorial powers are highlighted in Paul Romney's examination of the Collins case.

During King George III's first thirty years, conflicts between juries and judges in seditious libel cases became endemic.[75] Urged on by defence counsel such as Thomas Erskine and a host of pamphleteers, juries often combatted what they took to be oppressive laws or prosecutions by resisting instructions from the bench. Judges, notably Lord Mansfield, condemned this behaviour and attempted to restrict the jury to deciding upon the fact of publication (which included distribution) by the accused and whether any innuendoes were as the crown alleged. Although some reformers went so far as to argue that juries were entitled to judge law as well as facts, moderate opinion maintained that juries should at least be free to give general verdicts on guilt, which meant, as with most other criminal offences, that they must determine intent.

After Erskine had rendered one of his timeless arguments in *Dean of St Asaph* (1783–4), the jury declared that the accused parliamentary reformer was 'Guilty of publishing *only*.' A lengthy dispute ensued between Erskine and the trial judge as to meaning, and then the verdict was amended to read 'Guilty of publishing, but whether a libel or not the jury do not find.' On application for a new trial, Mansfield held that the second, limited verdict was undoubtedly proper. The lord chief justice also used the occasion to condemn the notion of ignorant juries usurping the judicial function by deciding matters of law – which he evidently thought general verdicts would entail: 'Jealousy of leaving the law to the Court, as in other cases, so in the case of libels is now in the present state of things, puerile rant ... [since] judges are totally independent of ... [cabinet] ministers ... and of the King himself.'[76] Such a claim by a former cabinet minister and a judge active in governing councils certainly deepened the conflict.

The *Dean of St Asaph* case intensified the struggle for and against reform, one that involved the meanings of criminal intent, jury nullification, judicial independence, freedom of the press, and other legal/political implications of the Glorious Revolution of 1688–9 and the 1701 Act of Settlement. The reformers finally triumphed, briefly, with the passage in 1792 of the Libel Act named after opposition leader Charles James Fox.[77] This legislation, after referring to 'Doubts,' ambiguously 'declared *and* enacted' that in any criminal libel case judges were entitled to instruct on law, but the jury could 'give a general Verdict of Guilty or Not Guilty ... and shall not be required ... to find the Defendant or Defendants Guilty merely ... of the Publication ... and of the Sense ascribed to the same.' The legislation arguably did not make new law but rather, in order to correct a judicial error, declared and reinforced the existing law. On this basis it applied throughout British North America as a clarification of the common law. Even if this were not the case, Fox's act applied through reception in Upper Canada, though not in Lower Canada. It was thought applicable in Nova Scotia, while analogous legislation was defeated in New Brunswick. The essay by Fecteau, Greenwood, and Wallot as well as those by Bumsted, Wright, and Cahill all deal with the applicability of the act.

Fox's act was a liberal but limited advance, and it was met by a generation-long reaction in parliament. In the decade following its passage, juries at times used their new power to ignore judicial opinion on the law by acquitting, for example, parliamentary reformers and persons making inflammatory statements when intoxicated or intemperate attacks on politicians (although not on the king or constitution). However, prosecutions increased dramatically and the conviction rate for sedition in the English provinces during the period 1793–1802 ran at about 70 per cent.[78] The legislation, of course, did not directly affect the elastic substantive law defining sedition and libel. Nor did it hinder the attorney general's resort to the crown's prerogative of ex officio information. This avoided the difficulties of indictment before a grand jury and enhanced jury-packing through requests for a special, crown-controlled, trial jury of 'gentlemen' in 'complicated' cases.[79]

The period that followed the first decade or so of Fox's Libel Act saw the emergence of new connections between political radicalism and labour movements – a joining of class and politics that would have a profound effect on dissent. A spate of prosecutions by Attorney General Sir Vicary Gibbs and the passage of the Six Acts in 1819 were responses to growing fears about the collective behaviour of political crowds.[80] By 1819–20 the public-order crisis had reached new levels and an anxious government searched for additional measures. Sedition law did not effectively address collective agitation and its doctrinal and procedural limits were increasingly apparent. Fox's Libel Act allowed wider questions to be decided by the jury, obliging magistrates and prosecutors to obtain more extensive evidence of matters such as intent and effect. The response was a shift in focus from sedition to breaches of the peace; elaboration of measures related to unlawful assembly for political meetings that were not riotous; and greater resort to readings of the Riot Act for meetings that were (it was a capital offence not to disperse within an hour).[81] The new measures were supported by reforms to the administration of English criminal law which made it possible to cast the 'net' much wider. Owing to the surveillance and law-enforcement capabilities of the newly established police, the laws of unlawful assembly and riot could be effectively utilized.

This shift in focus in the prosecution of minor political offences and in the administration of criminal law reflects a larger transformation recently addressed in the literature on 'state formation.'[82] Such changes did not have an impact in British North America until the 1830s, signalled by sweeping reforms to the criminal law and construction of the Kingston Penitentiary. Subsequent volumes will examine the watershed treason trials of 1838 and the shift from sedition to breaches of the peace in the 1840s.

As in the case of other misdemeanours, the penalties for sedition were fines and imprisonment, although the pillory was a common additional element at the discretion of the bench. Unlike accused felons (until 1836 in the United Kingdom and both Canadas), those charged with a misdemeanour were entitled to a full defence by counsel.

Habeas Corpus and Its Suspension

The writ of habeas corpus in criminal-law matters was used to test the 'legality' of imprisonment (when, for example, a person was charged with an offence unknown to law or which did not carry a penalty of jail, or when a person was jailed on mere *suspicion* of high treason or another crime). It helped to enforce the 'right' of misdemeanants, including those accused of sedition, to bail[83] and to ensure that accused felons and traitors, who were normally not bailable, had a 'speedy' trial, usually well before a year had elapsed from the time of imprisonment.

These features of habeas corpus existed at common law, but by the late seventeenth century undermining abuses had emerged, such as judges refusing to issue the writ in vacation, jailors secreting the prisoner in another jail or having the prisoner transported out of the jurisdiction, and immediate re-arrest. These were to a considerable degree effectively addressed in King Charles II's well-known Habeas Corpus Act of 1679.[84] As mentioned earlier, this statute was not in force in New Brunswick, with its 1660 reception date, or Quebec. And since the reason the statute did not apply in the latter lay in its being 'merely local, and confined to England,'[85] it may not have been in force in the other colonies either. Nevertheless, the royal instructions to Governor Cornwallis of Nova Scotia in 1749 and later instruments for Prince Edward Island (1769) and New Brunswick (1784) introduced the substance of some principles found in the 1679 act, such as the prohibition on re-arrest, but not all (for example, issuance in vacation).[86] These executive 'laws' were undoubtedly valid if the colony was a conquered/ceded one and probably *intra vires* in the case of a 'settled' dependency, as an exercise of the constitutive power affecting the courts and the liberties of the subject. The common-law right to the writ arguably existed throughout British North America, including Quebec after 1774 in criminal-law matters.[87] In 1784 the Quebec Legislative Council enacted an ordinance reproducing the essentials of Charles II's act. This ordinance became part of the law of both Lower and Upper Canada when the Province of Quebec was divided in 1791. New Brunswick passed a similar act in 1836.[88]

By virtue of the common law – but not the supporting statute of 1679 or the 1784 ordinance – the writ could be used to test the legality of detention in cases where no criminal charges had been laid. It was employed successfully in eighteenth-century England, for example, to enable persons held in madhouses to obtain medical reviews and to free a slave whose master intended to forcibly remove him or her from the realm (*Sommersett's* case, 1772). The procedure was used in Lower Canada to destroy slave-holding (1798–1800) and to free persons detained arbitrarily by the military (1791).[89] Habeas corpus was used to equal effect in Nova Scotia in the period 1797–1806, though unsuccessfully in New Brunswick (chiefly in 1800) – the lawfulness of slavery being the other pressing matter about which Chipman was seeking Blowers's advice.[90] Habeas corpus had failed, in practice, as a defence against imprisonment by King Charles I for reasons of state, rather than crime. But the Petition of Right, 1628, as retroactively sanctioned by the Glorious Revolution of 1688–9, made the writ available in such cases.

Despite being what Blackstone called 'another Magna Carta,' the habeas corpus procedure was regularly although briefly suspended in England/Great Britain – not explicitly but by denying bail and trial for persons accused or suspected of serious political offences. There were about a dozen such statutes from 1689 to 1794 inclusive. These suspensions occurred during times of perceived crisis when invasion and/or insurrection were apprehended – that is, at times when the writ was urgently needed to prevent abuse. The reasons were usually specified in the preambles. The 1794 act, for example, referred to the conspiracy 'for introducing the system of anarchy and confusion which has so fatally prevailed in France.'[91]

The suspension of 1777, which was annually renewed to the end of the American Revolutionary War, applied to all the British colonies in North America. In Nova Scotia and Quebec several dozen suspects were interned under the act.[92] In the latter colony some remained in jail for over three years. The bourgeois reformers' alliance – Canadien and English – which emerged in Quebec after the war to obtain representative government, an independent judiciary, and English commercial law also sought to 'entrench' the right to habeas corpus by enunciating it in an imperial statute and therein restricting its suspension to *actual* rebellion or invasion.[93]

The reformers failed – such a restriction is not entrenched in present law – with serious consequences for Lower Canada. During the war against revolutionary France,[94] 1793–1802, the writ was suspended (by local acts) during every year but the first and 1796. Again, dozens of political suspects were detained. The writ was suspended from 1803 to 1812 in the war against Napoleon (though it remained in force in the mother country), and this proved useful to the government under Governor Sir James Craig in 1810 when three leaders of the assembly majority (and three other oppositionists) known as the *parti canadien* were interned.[95] Ironically, the play of domestic politics following these detentions resulted in a situation where the writ was fully in force during the very 'hot' War of 1812, as it was in Upper Canada until March 1814.[96]

GENERAL THEMES AND ISSUES

The cases examined in this volume highlight the importance of the courts as pre-confederation political battlefields and the prominence of law in early Canadian constitutional debate and social conflict. Historians, long fixated by the struggles for 'responsible government,' and more recently by 'state formation,' have only started to explore the legal dimensions of early Canadian politics and political culture.[97] The essays in this volume provide further systematic forays into this important territory. Subsequent volumes on the rebellions in the Canadas and beyond will, we trust, illuminate still more the role of law and its administration in political conflicts and the reforms managed under lords Durham, Sydenham, and others.

Kenneth McNaught, who has applied some of the themes of political-culture historiography to an examination of security trials over a much larger sweep of time, suggested at an early point that we must not lose sight of the positive elements of Canadian political culture. The characteristics of 'Peace, Order, and good Government' and 'deference to authority' have arguably generated a more tolerant and pluralistic political culture than that enjoyed by many 'advanced' societies, including the United States. He was concerned that a selection of topics focusing on incidents of suppression ran the risk of underestimating the social and political benefits of Canadians' attachment to social order. McNaught's *a departure from trad. view*

views mirror those expressed in his well-known essay on political trials and the political tradition where he emphasized that Canadian courts, unlike American ones, have resisted becoming instruments of the political process. When forced to face security issues directly, the governing authority, including judges, has tended to display 'Burkean rigour' followed by 'remarkable lenience' once the crisis passed. The pattern reflects the 'basic British belief that both liberty and justice are impossible without order [and this] lies at the heart of the Canadian political tradition.'

Murray Greenwood has elsewhere written that the characteristics described by McNaught, although accurate and stimulating, are somewhat incomplete. His overview of security trials reveals additional patterns which suggest official anxiety about apprehended insurrection and consistent violations of procedural norms.[98] Appreciation of the positive legacies of Canadian political culture need not deter rigorous study of the more ominous manifestations of early Canadian politics. And while 'British justice' may have important resonance with some elements of early Canadian political culture, the common links need not overshadow the differences that existed.

There is certainly a formidable record of security proceedings in Canada. In interpreting this record the editors and authors have attempted to avoid applying modern standards of constitutional liberty to an earlier age. Resisting the dangers of presentist or teleological judgment – the temptation to view such proceedings through the filters of modern standards of legality and political pluralism – obliges us to hold the prevailing constitutional standards of the time as a central reference. The legal battles, like the struggle for responsible government in the legislative sphere, must be evaluated by those standards.

Although eighteenth- and early-nineteenth-century understandings of the constitution and the rule of law clearly differed from modern ones, the nature of those understandings remains contentious. Blaine Baker, in his examination of Upper Canadian political/legal controversies in the 1820s, has gone so far as to suggest that there was no concept of the rule of law in a political and legal culture which celebrated providential order, a peaceable kingdom ruled by virtuous men. Paul Romney's refutation of this position emphasizes the dangers of assuming a homogeneous culture and trivializing social conflict; doing so can blind the historian to the contemporary significance of legal and political debates. Romney finds extensive evidence of both popular and sophisticated understandings of the rule of law.[99] The plural understandings of the British constitution and the rule of law, introduced in the section of this essay dealing with

the Baker Romney Split

constitutional reception, were vital to the historical actors involved in the security proceedings and the larger political struggles that formed their context. Before we explore these issues further, it is necessary to clarify the reasons for their importance.

Interpretations of security cases generally tend to fall into two extreme positions. One holds that the defendants are isolated crackpots or extremists, and if the proceedings are indeed egregious they may be dismissed as marginal exceptions to the law's impartiality (or, as Baker suggests, acceptable within the prevailing standards of the time). The other extreme suggests that such cases illustrate the law's role as a repressive instrument conspiratorially manipulated for interested ends. The first position simply neglects the historical evidence – the sheer number of cases of this nature, the social conflict underlying many of them, and the prominent role of law in political conflicts. The other oversimplifies the nature of the legal process and the meanings of the proceedings for defendants and the broader public. It fails to provide an adequate account of the sometimes successful struggles that evidently frustrated and embarrassed governments. And although the official cliques that dominated colonial governments (later known by names such as the Château Clique and the Family Compact) appear to fit 'class instrumentalist' caricatures, careful study reveals internal factionalism and dependency on tentative alliances with other powerful groups. The regulation of politics through the law presents a truly complex picture. We can begin to arrive at more sophisticated interpretations of this picture by addressing what the above views largely neglect – namely, the claims and expectations surrounding the rule of law.

The prominence of the rule of law in the language of political conflicts in the pre-confederation period relates to its ideological power. As suggested earlier, security proceedings provide particularly clear illumination of the role of law in the exercise of power, highlighting an underlying tension between the formal claims about the rule of law and discretionary authority. While repressively inclined colonial governments were checked by imperial accountability from 'above,' popular expectations from 'below' proved to be the most demanding form of accountability. In high-profile security cases especially, popular expectations derived from formal claims of the British constitution, British justice, and the rule of law operated as a constraint on repression.

Part of the calculated advantage of resorting to law rather than unregulated state violence is the attempt to legitimate official perceptions and actions, to generate greater public support for them. Such legitimacy is lost if justice is transparently interested. As the late E.P. Thompson remarked: 'For what we have observed is something more than the law as a pliant medium to be twisted this way and that by whichever interests already possess effective power ... The essential precondition for the effectiveness of law, in its function as ideology, is that it shall display an independence from gross manipulation and shall seem to be just. It cannot seem to be so without upholding its own logic and criteria of equity; indeed, on occasion, by actually *being* just.'[100] The advantage of greater legitimacy gained by proceeding through the courts, then, carries a certain cost; the law can be stretched only so far and its manipulation cannot be apparent, precisely because of the constraints of popular expectations concerning its formal claims. Obvious distortion would jeopardize its effectiveness. This not only limits official repression; the exploitation of formal claims creates limited opportunities to contest repressive actions successfully. These elements of legitimacy and contestability were obviously diminished when the expedients of executive summary measures or military proceedings were resorted to.

What was the nature of these formal claims in British North America? As noted earlier, the reception of English criminal law and the purported benefits of the British constitution were accompanied by the complex baggage of British constitutional and legal understandings. Despite the different social conditions, the language of the British constitution and the rule of law permeated post-conquest political conflicts, with its use going well beyond the courtroom. It was activated by the manner in which executive influences affected both colonial government and the administration of the law. It was a language that had various meanings.

Colonial elites and opposition movements alike utilized the language of the British constitution and the rule of law to justify their attitudes and actions. This was hardly surprising since eighteenth-century English libertarian Whigs, Court Whigs, and Tories all differed in their interpretation of the constitution and, in particular, in their views of the political and legal implications of the revolution settlement. On the political front, the settlement made the crown more accountable to parliament; but cabinets depending on the confidence of a Commons majority, organized political parties, and even the notion of a 'loyal opposition' evolved gradually, only gaining widespread acceptance about the time of the Reform Act of 1832. On the less well-known legal front, the settlement sought to bury the executive abuses associated with the Court of Star Chamber by establishing security of judicial tenure, a genuine right to trial by jury, the requirement of reasonable bail, and the important procedural protections of the Treason Act of 1696. However, ideas about the rule of law, particularly institutional safeguards on its impartial administration and due process, remained contentious. Issues such as the inclusion of judges in government councils, the crown prerogatives on prosecutions, the freedom of the jury's verdict, and the right to defence counsel in felony cases were fought over for more than a century.

While colonial governments and opposition movements drew heavily on this British constitutional discourse, they were also affected by the American experience. Most obviously this was the case for governments that, influenced by the Loyalist refugees, reacted against the United States and sought to insulate subjects from its influences. It must also be recognized that in 1800 Nova Scotia, New Brunswick, and Upper Canada were inhabited largely by American immigrants who understood the mother country's constitution through the filters of American experience. The libertarian Whig view of the implications of the revolution settlement was vibrant in pre-revolutionary America. The *Zenger* case, for instance, was seen as vindicating the jury's freedom of verdict and setting a constitutional precedent on freedom of speech and the press.[101] *Zenger* may have been on the minds of the actors in the Nova Scotia cases of William Wilkie in 1820 and Joseph Howe in 1835 (the latter is examined in Barry Cahill's essay). The American legacy is harder to trace in the Canadas. By the nineteenth century Upper Canadian Reformers appeared anxious to avoid allegations of republicanism and situated themselves within progressive British and Irish Whig ideas.

Murray Greenwood's essay on Lower Canadian treason laws during the French revolution compares their interpretation and administration with the situation in England and, as well, in the United States, where the prosecution of alleged traitors was constitutionally restricted. The American Bill of Rights, extended to federal powers in 1791, curbed Congress, the state legislatures, and the courts. The 1798 Sedition Act was a desperate attempt by President John Adams to silence political opponents and proved a temporary anomaly; it was never tested in the courts and was repealed after the Federalists lost office in 1800.[102] The essay by Jean-Marie Fecteau, Murray Greenwood, and Jean-Pierre Wallot on Governor Craig's 'reign of terror' and its aftermath briefly compares the British and Lower Canadian powers to suspend habeas corpus with the constitutionally limited authority in the United States. We see from such examples that post-revolutionary America and British North America are a study in contrasts, one that reflects the implications of the executively dominated structure of colonial government under a constitution based on parliamentary sovereignty as opposed to fundamental law.

By contemporary British (notwithstanding William Pitt the younger) and even pre-revolutionary American standards, British North American governments interpreted and applied the law in a relentlessly repressive fashion. Reflecting the legacy of Loyalist and 'garrison mentality' anxieties, they were more inclined to view protest and organized opposition as 'disloyal factionism,' and through their colonial constitutions they wielded greater executive control over the administration of justice. It was hardly surprising, then, that the contentious claims surrounding the constitution and the rule of law were wheeled out in force. In Tory guise they figured prominently in the official considerations and justifications for measures to 'protect' the constitution. In Whig guise they were evidenced in the perceptions and strategies of defendants as well as protest and opposition leaders, and in the language of their appeals to supporters and the broader public as they battled for the liberties 'guaranteed' by the constitution. As seen in cases such as those of Robert Gourlay and Joseph Howe, compelling and well-grounded defences could be raised to challenge effectively the legality or constitutionality of repressive measures and to hold the government more popularly accountable.

The administration of law, as the security and politically motivated criminal cases examined in this volume reveal, richly nourished these competing positions. Constitutional/legal issues arose out of executive influence which ranged from the lowest to highest legal officials. The Executive Council's authority over the local administration of government extended to the appointment of sheriffs, whose powers in jury selection raised the potent issue of packing. Access to trial by jury was put into question by executive actions and executive-enabling security legislation which raised the spectre of the Star Chamber. The freedom of the jury's verdict was thrown into doubt through the frequent resort to seditious-libel prosecutions, which in turn touched off the issue of popular nullification of oppressive laws and prosecutions. The colonial organization of prosecutorial authority, where the crown possessed a *de facto* monopoly, clashed with a constitutional view which held that crown prerogatives should be exercised circumspectly and celebrated the private prosecution as a guarantee of liberties.

The matter of judicial independence was perhaps the most prominent of the constitutional/legal issues. In Britain, the revolution settlement established one formal guarantee of independence through security of tenure, but the other contentious issues surrounding the separation of powers were not resolved until the beginning of the nineteenth century. Colonial judges continued to hold office according to royal pleasure and were regularly included in Executive and Legislative councils until almost the end of the period examined in this volume.[103] The theme of judicial independence as it relates to judicial impartiality in times of perceived political crisis runs throughout Canadian state trials. One overarching question is to what degree, in such crises, judges have adopted a 'Baconian' stance by putting the interests of the executive power before the rule of law, the latter being a top priority of the 'Cokean' magistrate.[104] Readers of this volume will discover chief justices in both Canadas who acted as 'prime ministers' (a role that even the lord chancellor could not aspire to in Britain); judges sitting in the 'cabinets' of those and other colonies, contrary, it may be argued, to British norms (almost certainly so after 1806, the date of the last British precedent); and instances of chief justices helping to build the prosecution's case and providing extrajudicial opinions in security matters, far exceeding what the judges of England were prepared to do in like situations.

There are a number of other themes raised by Canadian cases beyond those directly related to the administration of justice. A prominent one examined here is security concerns about aliens, first the French and then Americans. These concerns reflected geo-political anxieties about France and the United States and the political worries of the social groups dominating governments. They were evident as well in later periods, particularly in the treatment of immigrant groups under the War Measures Act and in legislation related to the labour movement. Perhaps such tendencies have been facilitated by the related lack of a 'revolutionary moment' which would have defined citizenship, for the absence of such a tradition left legal entitlement to rights dependent on the malleable concept of British subject. The diverse and migrant populations of British North America, many with suspected loyalties, could be readily defined as alien and have their civil rights suspended. This opened the way to the wide use of executive measures such as summary deportation. Alternatively, when expedient, the doctrine of perpetual allegiance could be drawn upon to try foreign citizens for treason, as in the case of naturalized American citizens born as British subjects. The security-related manipulation of alien status was not limited to those of foreign citizenship, which was the approach taken by the severe Lower Canadian statute of 1794, or even to Britons from across the sea, as demonstrated in the application of Upper Canada's draconian act of 1804 to Robert Gourlay. Alienage often meant 'dangerous foreigners' (whether aliens by law or ethnicity) as perceived by colonial governments. Examples include the security measures that culminated in the Acadian deportation of 1755 (Barnes), the alarmist perceptions of Canadiens in Lower Canada from 1794 to 1814 (Fecteau, Greenwood, and Wallot), and the treatment of Americans in the upper province, particularly after the outbreak of the War of 1812 (Romney and Wright).[105] In later volumes we will examine this theme as it relates to the deportation of labour and immigrant-association organizers between the wars and the treatment of Japanese Canadians during the Second World War.

There are other interesting themes: for example, the intermixture of religion and the state in the security laws of New France, New Brunswick's early Stuart constitution, the perceived French-Irish threat in Newfoundland during the 'rule' of the fishing admirals, and the security fears provoked by the impeachment of the Lower Canadian chief justices. Comparisons between the British North American colonies illuminate subtle but important differences in their social composition and in their perceptions of internal and external threats.

The volume lends itself to more than the unique, for, as suggested earlier, the prevailing British practices of the time and other contemporary comparisons serve as useful reference points. Since it would not be feasible to provide comprehensive studies of security measures in Great Britain and the United States for the entire period studied in this volume, Murray Greenwood's essay on the treatment of treason in the 1790s, a period of intense security anxieties, acts as the primary comparative piece. The other essays refer to British and/or American practices throughout: the treason trials in Nova Scotia in 1777 and in Upper Canada during the War of 1812; the fairness or otherwise of jury selection and prosecutorial practices; the intelligence and integrity or otherwise of defence counsel; sedition cases in Nova Scotia, New Brunswick, and the Canadas; parliamentary privilege and security; controls on the press in Prince Edward Island (a particularly interesting case), Nova Scotia, and the Canadas; and habeas corpus suspensions in Nova Scotia and Quebec from 1777 to 1783, Lower Canada from the 1790s to the early 1800s, and Upper Canada in 1814.

The Canadian state trials project will attempt to address concerns that have traditionally been neglected in this area of scholarship, including the involvement of women and native peoples and the role of regions outside central Canada. Native peoples figured prominently in strategic alliances in the early period, and when European interests turned to repression they usually did so through violent force rather than the law. The exercise of repression became more refined over the course of the nineteenth century with the extension of regularized law enforcement and territorial courts. A number of essays in future volumes will focus on security uses of the law against aboriginal populations, most notably the Big Bear-Poundmaker-Riel trials of the 1880s. Security incidents involving women such as Corriveau, the 'Queen[s?] of Hungary,' who wreaked such rebellious havoc in Quebec during the early American revolution, and the participation of women in the Montreal Road Act riots of 1796 will be studied in the next volume as background to an essay on women caught up in the rebellions of 1837–8.

Interesting events and common themes abound in this first comprehensive examination of Canadian political trials and security proceedings. The combination of archival historical research and legal analysis will, we trust, contribute to greater insight into Canada's political and legal culture as well as into the experiences of its people with authority, from the old regime inhabitants of New France to the recent past. The historian William Dawson LeSueur aptly observed that the self-knowledge we gain from history could form a basis for reconciliation and mutual comprehension among the divergent people of this country. Perhaps we will find in our last volume that, in a era of fragmenting identities, internationalization, and new national formations, the repressive measures of the past have no place. Or perhaps they will be resurrected. Much of what the authors have examined will surprise. Much will not become part of solid, meaningful generalization until our last volume and a lengthy 'afterword' is written many years hence. Until then we are launched on an exploratory voyage of learning. As Emlyn wrote, more than two and a half centuries ago, let us profit and enjoy: 'Here will be matter ... of Instruction and Entertainment to all who are delighted with History.'

NOTES

1 Space limitations prevent extended comment on important collections relating to jurisdictions other than England, such as the American State Trials series and two admirable works written in the middle of the nineteenth century: Francis Wharton's learned collected/annotated reports (including several cases of sedition and of treason) from the administrations of George Washington and John Adams and Lord Cockburn's scholarly essays (with an exhaustive, stimulating introduction and fruitful comparisons to England) on sedition cases in Scotland from 1793 to 1849 (see Murray Greenwood's essay 'Judges and Treason Law in Lower Canada, England, and the United States

during the French Revolution, 1794–1800,' in this volume). Nor have we dealt with publications concerning trials arising out of single 'events,' such as the Jacobite rebellion of 1745, the Derbyshire workingman's march of 1817, and the Cato Street conspiracy of 1820. The editors thank Douglas Hay for showing them the importance of this topic and commenting perceptively on the more recent English and American collections. The basic history of the compilation of State Trials collections (hereafter St. Tr.) to 1781 may be found in the prefaces contained in Howell, vol. 1 (see n.6 below), at xix–liv.

2 *A Compleat Collection of State-Tryals, and Proceedings upon Impeachments for High Treason, and other Crimes and Misdemeanours, from the Reign of King Henry the Fourth, to the End of the Reign of Queen Anne*, 4 vols. (London: Timothy Goodwin *et al.* 1719).

3 See text below.

4 Emlyn thought that these guarantees could be expanded by, for example, immediately entitling the accused to a copy of the crown's witnesses list instead of waiting (as required by [1708] 7 Anne c. 21) for the death of the Pretender to bring this right into force. Emlyn was being very liberal here. Contrast his view with the opinions of treason jurist Sir Michael Foster (1762) and Lower Canadian Chief Justice William Osgoode (1797): 21 St. Tr. 721 at 730.

5 Cobbett to Wright, 11 Sept., 28 Oct., 21, 28, 29 Nov., 7, 9 Dec. 1808, 22 Feb. 1809; same to Howell, 9 Dec. 1808, William Cobbett Papers, B. L. Extracts from some of these are printed in E.I. Carlyle, *William Cobbett: A Study of His Life As Shown in His Writings* (London: Archibald Constable 1904), at 140–2, 168–73; particularly important in this volume are the letters of Cobbett to Wright written between 28 Oct. and 9 Dec. 1808. It appears that Howell was to be remunerated by sharing in the profits after a certain number of copies had been sold. Although that figure was not reached by 1811, Wright had advanced him some £1,400. What expenses Howell had is unclear, as is his remuneration after 1811. See G.D.H. Cole, *The Life of William Cobbett* (New York: Harcourt Brace n.d.), at 162.

6 On a more technical level, the trial of *Dr Hensey* ([1758], 19 St. Tr. 341) resulted in the first adjudicated precedent significantly expanding the treason of adhering to the king's enemies, and it contains references to important lost documents on the evolution of treason law. See F. Murray Greenwood, *Legacies of Fear: Law and Politics in Quebec in the Era of the French Revolution* (Toronto: Osgoode Society/University of Toronto Press 1993), at 32-4, 273n.82. All references to the first twenty-one volumes of the St. Tr. are to the second-edition reprint of them in 1816. The quotation in the text, from the title page thereof, did not claim that the new trials had never been previously printed (*Hensey* had been), only that they had not appeared in any collection of state trials.

7 Each page was divided into two columns (as was the case with Hargrave's edition). Volumes usually had between 1400 and 1500 columns, each of which could run to more than 500 words.

8 T.J. Howell even travelled to Edinburgh to examine the original records of the Scottish political trials of the 1790s and also to interview the participants in those proceedings: 23 St. Tr. 117. The report of the *McLane* treason trial in Lower Canada (1797) was derived from an eyewitness, shorthand account, by far the best and longest text of the five available. See 26 St. Tr. 721 and *Legacies*, at 300n.2.

9 8 St. Tr. 723; 9 St. Tr. 517, 793, 999; 11 St. Tr. 297; 15 St. Tr. 522; 21 St. Tr. 971, 988; 22 St. Tr. 448; 24 St. Tr. 210; 28 St, Tr. 1097.

10 *State Trials; or, A Collection of the Most Interesting Trials, Prior to the Revolution of 1688*, 2 vols. (London: W. Walker 1826), quotation at 1: at 312.

11 London: Longman, Brown, Green and Longmans. See particularly 1: at v–x.

12 *State Trials: Political and Social* (London: Duckworth 1899–1902), particularly 1: at vii–xiii.

13 *Reports of State Trials* (London: Queen's Printers), particularly 1: at v–vi.

14 Boston: Houghton, Mifflin. See particularly 1: at vii–xii.

15 See 1 St. Tr. (n.s.) 1263 for a case of government finance involving Lord Palmerston, the secretary of war (1822).

16 Published 1914–36. The subtitle gives a far better idea of the contents: 'A Collection of the Important and Interesting Criminal Trials which have taken place in the United States, from the beginning of our Government to 1920.'

17 Before 'formal reception' British legislation was deemed to apply unless colonial or imperial authorities decided it unsuitable for local conditions. Generally speaking, after reception, British legislation up to that date, along with the ever 'evolving' common law, made up the foundation of the provincial laws, amendable by colonial legislation but subject to imperial review (a process that was regularized after the War of 1812 under the Colonial Office) and superior legislation.

18 *Blankard v. Galdy* (1693) Salk 411; *Smith v. Brown* (1707) 2 Salk. 666; 'Memorandum' of 9 Aug. 1722, 2 P. Wms. 75; *Campbell v. Hall* (1774) 20 St. Tr. 239; *Sammut v. Strickland* (1938) AC 678; Sir William Blackstone, *Commentaries on the Laws of England* [1765–70], 4 vols., ed. George Sharswood (Philadelphia: J.P. Lippincott 1859), 1: at 108–9; Anthony Stokes, *A View of the Constitution of the British Colonies in North America and the West Indies* [1783] (London: Dawson 1969), at 9; Joseph Chitty, *A Treatise on the Law of the Prerogative of the Crown* (London: J. Butterworth 1820), at 29–30; J.E. Read, 'The Early Provincial Constitutions,' *Canadian Bar Review*, vol. 26 (1948), 621; E.G. Brown, *British Statutes in American Law, 1776–1836* (Ann Arbor: University of Michigan Press 1964); Kenneth

Roberts-Wray, *Commonwealth and Colonial Law* (New York: F.A. Praeger 1966), at 138–64; John D. Whyte and William R. Lederman, *Canadian Constitutional Law*, 2nd ed. (Toronto: Butterworths 1977), at 2–1 to 2–21; J.E. Cote, 'The Reception of English Law,' *Alberta Law Review*, vol. 15 (1977), 29; J.C. Bouck, 'Introducing English Statute Law into the Provinces: Time for a Change?' *Canadian Bar Review*, vol. 57 (1979), 74; Peter W. Hogg, *Constitutional Law of Canada*, 2nd ed. (Toronto: Carswell 1985), at 21–9.

19 Francis Maseres and William Hey, *Considerations on the Expediency of Procuring an Act of Parliament for the Settlement of the Province of Quebec* (London 1766), as reprinted in *Con Docs* 1: at 257–69; R.A. Humphreys and S.M. Scott, 'Lord Northington and the Laws of Canada,' *CHR*, vol. 14 (1933), 42.

20 14 Geo. III, c. 83.

21 For Marriott's report on Canadien laws in 1774, see *Con Docs* 1:445 at 453–4; *R. v. Maclane* [*sic*] (1797) 26 St. Tr. 721 at 823 (per Chief Justice Osgoode of Lower Canada); *Baldwin v. Gibson* (1813) Stuart's Reports 72 (per Chief Justice Sewell of Lower Canada); *Rudkin v. Smith* (1821) 2 Hag. Con. 371 at 382 (per Lord Stowell, judge of the Court of Admiralty); *Wilcox v. Wilcox* (1857) 8 LCR 34 at 51-3 (per Chief Justice Lafontaine of Lower Canada); *R v. Bordoff* (1938) 76 SC 74 at 81 (per Chief Justice Perrault of Quebec Superior Court).

22 Limited legal pluralism or a paternalistic tolerance of native systems gave way to hegemony of English law once European interests became firmly established, accompanied by local legislatures, courts, and policies of 'civilizing' assimilation. State repression of aboriginal peoples through legal means (as opposed to brute force) will be a prominent focus in future volumes. Pluralism continued in Quebec with the retention of civil law under the Quebec Act of 1774, but arguably the adoption of English criminal law, modified in its administration with the wider exercise of crown prerogatives on prosecutions, reflected security concerns.

23 See *Calvin's* case (1608) 7 Co. Rep. 1 and Blackstone, *Commentaries*, 1: at 108–9. For a useful primer on this subject see Brown, *British Statutes*, ch. 1.

24 See Christopher English's essay in this volume, 'The Official Mind and Popular Protest in a Revolutionary Era: The Case of Newfoundland, 1789–1819,' and his article 'The Development of the Newfoundland Legal System to 1815,' *Acadiensis*, vol. 20 (1990), 88 at 108–10.

25 This had been laid down in advance by the island's chief justice, Sir Francis Forbes: *Yonge v. Blaikie* (1822) 1 Nfld. LR 277 at 283.

26 1 Vict. c. 4.

27 Trials for Felony Act, 1836, 6 and 7 Wm. IV, c. 114; Offences Against the Person Act, 1837, 7 Wm. IV and 1 Vict. 1 c. 85; Burglary Act., ibid., c. 86. Two of the crimes of sexual deviance to remain capital were male buggery and carnal

knowledge of a young girl. From the 1730s, accused felons had often but not always been allowed *ex gratia* to employ counsel. The latter were not permitted to address the jury.

28 14 Geo. VI 1950 (Canada), Schedule (repealing Consolidated Statutes of Newfoundland, Third Series, c. 95). This act was an updated version of (1837) 1 Vict. c. 4.

29 This section is based primarily on three perceptive articles: Barry Cahill, '"How Far English Laws Are in Force Here": Nova Scotia's First Century of Reception Law Jurisprudence,' *University of New Brunswick Law Journal*, vol. 42 (1993), 113; Jim Phillips, '"Securing Obedience to Necessary Laws": The Criminal Law in Eighteenth-Century Nova Scotia,' *Nova Scotia Historical Review*, vol. 12 (1992), 87, but particularly at 92–106, 114–24; T.G. Barnes, '"As Near as May be Agreeable to the Laws of This Kingdom": Legal Birthright and Legal Baggage at Chebucto, 1749,' in *Law in a Colonial Society: The Nova Scotia Experience*, ed. J. Yogis (Toronto: Carswell 1984), 1.

30 *Uniacke v. Dickson* (1848) 2 NSR 287 (NSCh). In historical reality, of course, Nova Scotia was a ceded/conquered colony as of 1713, with the exceptions of Prince Edward and Cape Breton Islands and, possibly, the territory that was to become New Brunswick. The first two were ceded to Britain by France in the Treaty of Paris, 1763, as were her post-1713 pretensions to the last mentioned.

31 Penalties were radically re-arranged (for example forgery ceased to be capital), but the only major substantive change was to raise the dividing line between non-capital petty larceny and clergyable but capital grand larceny from one to twenty shillings. An offence that was clergyable was reduced to non-capital for a first conviction of it if the person convicted pleaded his or her 'benefit of clergy,' a relic of the middle ages abolished in 1827.

32 Belcher's position in the two cases of the 1750s was later supported by events in New Brunswick (1790s). Barry Cahill demonstrates in '"How Far English Laws Are in Force Here"' that *Uniacke v. Dickson* did *not* establish 1758 as the date of reception, despite the common opinion of law professors. However, 1758, which might be supported on the basis of the opinion of Chief Justice Forbes of Newfoundland in 1822, would make little difference because of the wide-ranging adoption.

33 Parliament of Canada, *Sessional Papers*, 1883, no. 70, at 2–6, particularly 4. We thank Jack Bumsted for valuable assistance on this murky question.

34 See David Bell's two notes [28 (1979) 195 and 29 (1980) 157 *University of New Brunswick Law Journal*] for lengthy analysis, quotations, and the historiography. Bell himself accepted 1660 in the sense that *stare decisis* now requires it.

35 See Bell's notes and Cahill, 'Nova Scotia's First Century of Reception Law Jurisprudence,' at 135–6.

36 1 Eliz. 1, c. 1, s. 16, which applied the statute to 'your Majesty's dominions or countries that now be or hereafter shall be.' See also Cahill's 'Nova Scotia's First Century of Reception Law Jurisprudence,' at 121, 136n.74.

37 Phillip Buckner, 'Chipman, Ward,' *DCB* 6: 135 at 138. David Bell had previously mapped out essentially the same position, a position later adopted by Barry Cahill.

38 Much, but not all, of the Bill of Rights, 1689 (1 Wm and Mary, Sess. 2, c. 2) declared common law, while the Habeas Corpus Act of 1679, for one, likely did not apply to any overseas colonies.

39 31 Chas II, c. 2; 19 Geo. III, c. 44. The second measure relieved some of the strictures of the 1688 Toleration Act.

40 7 and 8 Wm. III, c. 3, as extended by (1707/8) 7 Anne, c. 21.

41 See, for example, the Act of Settlement (1701), 12 and 13 Wm. III, c. 2 and its amendment in the Regency Act, 1707: 6 Anne, c. 41, ss. 24–30.

42 MG 23, D 1, Chipman Papers, vol. 6 (485–8), NA. Blowers's answer adds nothing to our understanding of New Brunswick reception and little to our understanding of Nova Scotia's except that in his view the question was unsettled and 1758 was not an unreasonable choice. See Blowers to Chipman, 2 April 1800, MG 23, vol. 1, 146–51. We thank Barry Cahill for bringing these important documents to our attention and Patricia Kennedy of the National Archives for laboriously transcribing Chipman's letter.

43 In his letter, cited in the previous note, Chipman mentioned that the question 'now stands for argument ... at nisi prius' with regard to a British statute of 1751 (24 Geo.II, c. 44) requiring a month's notice be given of an intended suit against a justice of the peace. While there is no known report of such a case (if indeed there was one), it is suggestive that in the 1801 session the assembly majority thought it necessary, or at least prudent, to enact a local version of the relevant statutory provisions: SNB 1801, c. 2. We thank David Bell for his valuable assistance on this point.

44 See, for example, Quebec Attorney General Francis Maseres to Richard Sutton, 14 Aug. 1768, in *The Maseres Letters 1766–1768*, ed. W. Stewart Wallace (Toronto: Oxford University Press 1919), at 101–18; British Attorney General Edward Thurlow's report on Quebec laws, 22 Jan. 1773, *Con Docs* 1: at 437–45; British Advocate General James Marriott's 1774 report on same, *Con Docs* 1: at 445–83; Cote, 'The Reception of English Law,' at 40–3; André Morel, 'La réception du droit criminel anglais au Québec (1760–1892),' *Revue juridique thémis*, vol. 13 (1978), 449 at 455–64.

45 14 Geo. III, c. 83 as reprinted in *Con Docs* 1: at 570–6.

46 *Ex parte Isaac Rousse* (1828), Stuart's Reports 321 (per Chief Justice Sewell of Lower Canada).

47 See text at nn.83–4 below.

48 9 Geo. I, c. 22; E.P. Thompson, *Whigs and Hunters: The Origin of the Black Act* (London: Allen Lane 1975).

49 See *The King v. David Maclane* [sic] (1797) 26 St. Tr. 721 at 811–24 (per Chief Justice William Osgoode of Lower Canada).

50 17 Geo. III, c. 9.

51 36 Geo. III, c. 7.

52 See *Maclane* [sic] and *Charge of Chief Justice Robinson to the Grand Jury of the Home District; April, 1833* (York, U.C.: Robert Stanton 1833).

53 31 Geo. III, c. 31. The province's first chief justice, William Osgoode, did not think it necessary to legislate explicitly the adoption of English criminal law, but confusion over the *corpus* of received English statutes and whether it included criminal legislation passed after 1774 led to 'An Act for the further introduction of the criminal law of England in this province, and for the more effectual punishment of certain offences' (40 Geo. III, c. 1).

54 See R.L. Fraser, '"All the Privileges Which Englishmen Possess": Order, Rights, and Constitutionalism in Upper Canada,' in *Provincial Justice: Upper Canadian Legal Portraits*, ed. R.L. Fraser (Toronto: Osgoode Society 1992), at xxi–xcii; F.H. Armstrong, *Handbook of Upper Canadian Chronology* (Toronto: Dundurn Press 1985).

55 The legislation also modified English secondary punishments. Banishment was largely substituted where transportation was specified.

56 'This act [Fox's Libel Act] was passed the year after the constitution was given to this Province. The right of juries, therefore, is here, still, only an arbitrary right. It might be well, therefore, to have it made absolute by provincial statute.' See *Address to the Jury, at the Kingston Assizes, in the Case of the R. v. Robert Gourlay, Kingston, August 20, 1818*, in app. 3, N, doc. 1, and Barry Wright, 'The Gourlay Affair: Seditious Libel and the Sedition Act in Upper Canada, 1818–19,' in this volume.

57 Following the conviction of Francis Collins (see Paul Romney's 'Upper Canada in the 1820s: Criminal Prosecution and the Case of Frances Collins,' in this volume) John Beverley Robinson stated that Fox's act did indeed apply in the province. See Robinson's testimony to the Select Committee on the Petition of Francis Collins, JHAUC, 1829, appendix, Report on Collins' Case; Sherwood to Lieutenant Governor Colborne, 26 March 1829, CO 42/388/134–41, NA. Robinson's view was confirmed by his successor as attorney general in assembly debates over libel-law reform in December 1831.

58 25 Ed. III, st. 5, c. 2. This section is based principally on the statutes mentioned in the text, dozens of cases in the Howells' *State Trials*, the writings of the treason jurists, and innumerable secondary works. The treason jurists (usually

referred to simply by surname) are here cited in full (with pages, chapter, or volume indicating the relevant portions): Sir Edward Coke, *The Third Part of the Institutes of the Laws of England* [1641] (London: W. Clarke and Sons 1809), at 1–19; Sir Mathew Hale, *Historia Placitorum Coronae/The History of the Pleas of the Crown* [*c.* 1670], vol. 1, ed. S. Emlyn (London: E. and R. Nutt and R. Gosling 1736); William Hawkins, *A Treatise of the Pleas of the Crown,* vol. 1 [1716] (London: Professional Books 1973), ch. 7; Sir Michael Foster, *A Report of Some Proceedings on the Commission for the Trial of Rebels in the Year 1746, in the County of Surrey; and of Other Crown Cases: To Which Are Added Discourses upon a Few Branches of the Law* [1762], ed. M. Dodson (London: E. and R. Brooke 1792), at 183–220; Blackstone, *Commentaries,* 4: at 74–93; Sir Edward Hyde East, *A Treatise of the Pleas of the Crown,* vol. 1 (London: J. Butterworth 1803), at 37–138. The quotation in the text is taken from Coke's translation from the law French (the Anglo-Norman language used in statutes until the late sixteenth century).

59 See particularly Hawkins and *Freind's* case (1696), 13 St. Tr. 1 at 61.

60 This paragraph is based on documents related to the cases of Jean-Marie Ducharme and François Cazeau in RG 4, B 16, vol. 34 ('Grand Jury, 1765'), NA. We thank Patricia Kennedy of the NA for alerting us to these interesting sources. Ducharme was indicted in April but (on a second bill) was discharged by the Grand Jury in August, as was Cazeau. See ibid. and Quebec *Gazette,* 25 April, 29 Aug. 1765. Whether Attorney General George Suckling and Chief Justice William Gregory ever realized their April mistake is not clear.

61 *Vaughan's* case (1696), 13 St. Tr. 485 at 531–8.

62 See Greenwood, *Legacies,* at 33, 273n.82.

63 *Calvin's* case (1608), Co. Rep. at 5a; Glanville L. Williams, 'The Correlation of Allegiance and Protection,' *Cambridge Law Journal,* vol. 10 (1948), 54.

64 *De Facto* Act, (1495) 11 Henry VII, c. 1; F. Murray Greenwood, 'The Chartrand Murder Trial: Rebellion and Repression in Lower Canada, 1837–1839,' *Criminal Justice History: An International Annual,* vol. 5 (1984), 129 at 144–5. Defences by accused regicides of King Charles I based on the De Facto Act had been rejected on the ground that the statute applied only to monarchical usurpers.

65 See, for example, John Beverley Robinson to Lieutenant Governor George Arthur, 6 Aug. 1838, John Beverley Robinson Papers, AO; Hale, *Pleas of the Crown,* at 94.

66 See particularly the case of *Aeneas Macdonald* (1747), 18 St. Tr. 857.

67 Paul Romney, 'Re-inventing Upper Canada: American Immigrants, Upper Canadian History, English Law, and the Alien Question,' in *Patterns of the Past: Interpreting Ontario's History,* ed. Roger Hall *et al.* (Toronto: Dundurn Press 1988), 78.

68 See Williams, 'The Correlation of Allegiance.'

69 SNS 1758, c. 13, s. 1; SLC 1801, c. 9, s. 1; SUC 1833, c. 3.

70 7 and 8 Wm. III, c. 3; 7 Anne, c. 21. On the jurors' and witnesses' lists, occupations and addresses had to be supplied. For a perceptive view of the significance and historical context of the 1696 act, see Alexander H. Shapiro, 'Political Theory and the Growth of Defensive Safeguards in Criminal Procedure: The Origins of the Treason Trials Act of 1696,' *Law and History Review*, vol. 11 (1993), 215.

71 *R. v. Lambert and Perry* (1793) 22 St. Tr. 953 at 1017 and *Tutchin's* case (1704) 14 St. Tr. 1095 at 1128. In general, see Greenwood, *Legacies*, at 117–19; Barry Wright, 'Sedition in Upper Canada: Contested Legality,' *Labour/Le Travail*, vol. 29 (1992), 7; William E. Conklin, 'The Origins of the Law of Sedition,' *Criminal Law Quarterly*, vol. 15 (1972–3), 277; P. Hamburger, 'The Development of the Law of Seditious Libel and Control of the Press,' *Stanford Law Review*, vol. 37 (1985), 661.

72 See particularly *Burdett's* case (1820) 1 St. Tr. (n.s.) 1 at 120, where Justice Best stated that the test was whether 'the people *may* be set in motion against the Government.'

73 See, for example, *Stockdale's* case (1789) 22 St. Tr. 237; *William Cobbett* (1804) 29 St. Tr. 1; *R. v. Lambert and Perry* (1810) 31 St. Tr. 335, particularly at 363–70.

74 The victim of defamatory statements had the option to choose between a civil suit (tort, delict) for damages or criminal proceedings only if the statements were in writing. All other non-seditious defamations had to be pursued in the civil courts.

75 See particularly Thomas Andrew Green, *Verdict According to Conscience: Perspectives on the English Criminal Trial Jury 1200–1800* (Chicago: University of Chicago Press 1985); Hamburger, 'The Development of the Law of Seditious Libel.'

76 27 St. Tr. 847, particularly at 950, 1033–40.

77 32 Geo. III, c. 60.

78 See particularly F.K. Prochaska, 'English State Trials in the 1790s: A Case Study,' *Journal of British Studies*, vol. 13 (1973), 63.

79 Clive Emsley, 'An Aspect of Pitt's "Terror": Prosecution for Sedition during the 1790s,' *Social History*, vol. 6 (1981), 155.

80 See Barry Wright's essay 'The Gourlay Affair' in this volume for further reference to these events.

81 M. Lobban, 'From Seditious Libel to Unlawful Assembly,' *Oxford Journal of Legal Studies*, vol. 10 (1990), 305.

82 See P. Corrigan and D. Sayer, *The Great Arch: English State Formation as Cultural Revolution* (Oxford: Basil Blackwell 1985); *Colonial Leviathan: State Formation in*

Mid-Nineteenth-Century Canada, ed. A. Greer and I. Radforth (Toronto: University of Toronto Press 1992).

83 Provided the sureties (or other security) offered were adequate, the misdemeanant had a *right* to be bailed by the committing magistrate, who was debarred by the Bill of Rights, 1689, from setting 'excessive' bail (except presumably in New Brunswick): 1 Wm. and Mary, st. 2, c. 2; Blackstone, *Commentaries*, 4: at 297; *R. v Judd* (1788) 2 TR 255.

84 31 Ch. II, c. 2. For a useful analysis of this act in its historical setting, see R.J. Sharpe, *The Law of Habeas Corpus*, 2nd ed. (Oxford: Clarendon Press 1989), at 1–20.

85 William Knox, *The Justice and Policy of the Late Act of Parliament for Making More Effectual Provision for the Government, of the Province of Quebec* (London: J. Wilkie 1774), at 62–5. See also Greenwood, *Legacies*, at 269-70n.46.

86 See Read, 'The Early Provincial Constitutions,' at 626–9, where extracts from the Nova Scotia instructions are printed.

87 See Greenwood, *Legacies*, at 25, 269–70nn.46-8, 52. For a contrary view with regard to Quebec after 1774, see Jean-Marie Fecteau and Douglas Hay, '"Government by Will and Pleasure Instead of Law": Military Justice and the Legal System in Quebec, 1755–83,' in this volume.

88 SOQ 1784, c. 2; SNB 1836, c. 3.

89 See Greenwood, *Legacies*, at 270, nn.53, 55–7, 271n.64.

90 The editors wish to thank Barry Cahill for this insight.

91 34 Geo. III, c. 54.

92 See two essays in this volume: Fecteau and Hay, '"Government by Will and Pleasure"'; and Ernest A. Clarke and Jim Phillips, 'Rebellion and Repression in Nova Scotia in the Era of the American Revolution.'

93 Greenwood, *Legacies*, at 42–3.

94 See Murray Greenwoods essay 'Judges and Treason Law' in this volume.

95 See Jean-Marie Fecteau, F. Murray Greenwood, and Jean-Pierre Wallot, 'Sir James Craig's "Reign of Terror" and Its Impact on Emergency Powers in Lower Canada, 1810–13,' in this volume.

96 SUC 1814, c. 6.

97 For good recent critical overviews of the historiography in this area, see R.L. Fraser, '"All the privileges,"' and B. McKillop and P. Romney,'Introduction' to S.F. Wise, *God's Peculiar Peoples: Essays on Political Culture in Nineteenth Century Canada* (Ottawa: Carleton University Press 1993), ix.

98 K. McNaught, 'Political Trials and the Canadian Political Tradition,' in *Courts and Trials: A Multidisciplinary Approach*, ed. M. Friedland (Toronto: University of Toronto Press 1975), 137 at 138; F. Murray Greenwood, 'L'insurrection appréhendée et l'administration de la justice au Canada,' *RHAF*, vol. 34

(1980–1), 57, and 'The Treason Trial and Execution of David McLane,' *Manitoba Law Journal*, vol. 20 (1991), 3.

99 B. Baker, '"So Elegant a Web": Providential Order and the Rule of Secular Law in Early Nineteenth Century Upper Canada,' *University of Toronto Law Journal*, vol. 38 (1988), 184; Paul Romney, 'Very Late Loyalist Fantasies: Nostalgic Tory "History" and the Rule of Law in Upper Canada,' in *Canadian Perspectives on Law and Society: Issues in Legal History*, ed. W. Wesley Pue and B. Wright (Ottawa: Carleton University Press 1988), 119.

100 Thompson, *Whigs and Hunters*, at 462–3. See also, in the Canadian context, Greg Marquis, 'Doing Justice to "British Justice": Law, Ideology and Canadian Historiography,' in *Canadian Perspectives*, ed. Pue and Wright, 43.

101 (1735) 17 St. Tr. 625 (New York Supreme Court). See also L.W. Levy, *Freedom of Speech and the Press in Early American History: A Legacy of Suppression* (New York: Harper 1963); J.P. Reid, *In a Defiant Stance: Conditions of Law in Massachussetts Bay, the Irish Comparison and the Coming of the American Revolution* (London: Pennsylvania University 1977). The editors thank David Bell and Barry Cahill for bringing the pre-revolutionary American legacy to their attention.

102 See J.M. Smith, *Freedom's Fetters: The Alien and Sedition Laws and American Civil Liberties* (Ithaca: Cornell 1956).

103 Until 1834, 1843, and 1848 in Upper and Lower Canada and Nova Scotia respectively.

104 For the derivation of these terms and their application to Quebec/Lower Canada from 1789 to 1811, see Greenwood, *Legacies*, passim but particularly chs. 1, 6–7, 10–12.

105 For the security context of the Acadian expulsion, see Thomas Barnes's essay in this volume, '"Twelve Apostles" or a Dozen Traitors? Acadian Collaborators during King George's War, 1744–7,' and Naomi E.S. Griffiths, *The Contexts of Acadian History, 1686-1784* (Montreal: McGill-Queen's University Press 1992), particularly at 125. For the deportation of Americans from Upper Canada, see Paul Romney and Barry Wright, 'State Trials and Security Proceedings in Upper Canada during the War of 1812,' also in this collection.

PART ONE

c. 1608–1783

1

The Crime of Lèse-Majesté in New France: Defence of the Secular and Religious Order

PETER N. MOOGK

In the jurisprudence of *ancien régime* France and its colonies, crimes against the state came under the description of *lèse-Majesté humaine et divine*. There was no division between defending the king's authority and imposing respect for the majesty of God. The monarch was 'by the grace of God, King of France and of Navarre' and bore the title 'His Most Christian Majesty.' Louis XIV had reduced the Roman Catholic Church in France, the state church, to dependency upon his government and he considered it his religious duty to impose conformity to the one true faith upon his subjects. He upheld the Roman Catholic faith and, in return, the Roman Catholic clergy blessed his reign and preached submission to the ruler that God had given to France. Church and state were mutually supporting institutions and both were protected by French criminal justice.

The Great Criminal Ordinance of August 1670 defined court procedure rather than crimes, but its preamble revealed the logic of French criminal justice. That justice, it said, 'not only ensures private individuals of the peaceable possession of their goods, as does civil law, but, moreover, it ensures public tranquility, and restrains by fear of punishments those who are not restrained by a consideration of their duty.'[1] It was axiomatic in *ancien régime* justice that the uneducated lower orders of society were motivated by fear and greed. Evoking fear was reckoned to be a cheap and effective way of containing the depraved multitude's brutish impulses; it was aroused by *punition exemplaire* [exemplary punishment]. Criminal punishments were public spectacles calculated to inspire the greatest fear among onlookers and, thus, to deter them from committing a similar offence. French governments compensated for the inefficiency of their policing agencies by imposing the harshest retribution upon the few malefactors who were caught and convicted. Before execution of the sentence, those who had offended against public morals performed *amende honorable* [ritual penance] while dressed in a white shift and holding a burning taper. Before the church door, the bareheaded offender knelt and, in a loud voice, begged for God's forgiveness for transgressing the king's justice, since both the divine and the secular orders had been violated. The malefactor then suffered physical punishment or death.

The definition of *lèse-Majesté* appears in various statutes rather than in the 1670 criminal ordinance. *Lèse-Majesté divine* (outrages against the majesty of God) comprised apostasy, heresy, atheism, magic, witchcraft, sacrilege, blasphemy, crimes against nature, and simony. Offences against the monarch and the state, *lèse-Majesté humaine*, had three levels. The first, high treason, included conspiracy to kill or overthrow the prince, his family, agents and governors, the concealment of such plans, incitement to armed rebellion, violation of a royal safe conduct, communication with the monarch's enemies, receiving payment from those enemies, and aiding their hostile designs. The next level, lesser treason (*lèse-Majesté au second chef*), covered private discussions of state affairs, unauthorized recruiting of soldiers, diversion of royal revenues and assets to personal use, refusal to vacate public charges upon dismissal, hindering execution of the king's orders, falsification of royal seals or signatures, private coining, alteration, or counterfeiting of money, and desertion from the king's armed forces. The third category of *lèse-Majesté humaine* comprised duelling, unsanctioned melting down of artillery pieces, levelling existing defences, and the erection of unauthorized fortifications. To these might be added *la rebellion à justice*: opposing or striking legal officials, such as court ushers, who were carrying out magistrates' orders and sentences. 'Le Roi est le principe et le terme de toutes les justices' was a maxim of royal absolutism and resistance to any level of justice was an affront to the crown. Most of the crimes against the state committed in New France belonged to the two lowest categories of *lèse-Majesté humaine* (see app. 3, A, doc. 1).

Colonial legislation added to the list of offences against the state. For example, in 1677 Governor General Buade de Frontenac decreed that no one could circulate collective petitions or hold 'any assemblies, [or] conventicles' without his expressed permission since unauthorized gatherings were usually a 'pretext for all the monopolies, cabals, and intrigues that evil-minded persons would wish to create.'[2] At Montreal in 1693 a surgeon was charged with passing around a petition and soliciting signatures, 'in contempt of the king's ordinances that forbid all popular assemblies and cabals.'[3] Personal petitions from individuals were tolerated, but the royal administration reserved for itself the right to represent collective interests.

Offences planned but not carried out were punishable, as were acts of disrespect whether by word or gesture. Even want of respect, say to a religious procession, was an offence. All were *cas royaux*, punishable by the high courts and beyond the jurisdiction of seigneurial justice. Speaking of high treason, the jurist Claude-Joseph de Ferrière wrote that 'the crime of *lèse-Majesté*, under the first heading, is concerned with public peace and the tranquility of all the prince's subjects. This crime is even more horrible when committed directly against the sacred person of the sovereign, who is the living image of God on earth, and who is entrusted by divine providence with the governance of those people under his rule. This is what gives the name of sacrilege to this crime.'[4] St Paul's dictum that 'there is no authority but by act of God ... consequently anyone who rebels against authority is resisting a divine institution' gave scriptural support to this view.[5] Thus were the worlds of divine and earthly majesty cojoined and both were worthy of protection by criminal justice.

THE FRAGILE SOCIAL ORDER

A central pillar of the *ancien régime* definition of sedition was the ideal of *bonne ordre* [good order] held by magistrates and public officials. This concept assumed that there was a sacred hierarchy of orders, occupations, and persons that the law must uphold. The monarch and the church were at the apex of that inviolable hierarchy. To tolerate the smallest challenge to it would sanction a progressive erosion that would sweep away all order and authority. Just as the Ten Commandments enjoined children to honour their parents, so servants were bound to submit to their employer. A servant's defiance of his master was classified as seditious because it threatened the social hierarchy. In Canada runaway domestics and apprentices were forcibly returned to their master with an injunction from the bench to behave more respectfully. Duchesne, author of *Code de la Police*, asserted that 'the unsettling of morals is a contagious evil, whose progress would lead to the destruction of the body politic.'[6] Without legal restraints, it was believed that the common people would quickly descend into anarchy. This belief in the fragility of civil society justified swift and harsh punishment of offenders.

The accession in 1594 of Henri de Bourbon, a former Protestant, to the throne of France after a civil war was opposed by many of his subjects. Law courts reacted vigorously to threats against royal authority, meting out severe penalties to intimidate conspirators. For example, Jean Chastel, who wounded the new king, Henry IV, in 1595, was sentenced to do public penance, to be chained in a public place, to have his right hand (which had held the knife) cut off, to be pulled apart by four horses, and finally to have his remains burned and the ashes cast into the wind. This end excited the fear and revulsion that *punition exemplaire* was intended to achieve.

On the principle that no one could escape the king's justice, even by suicide, dead bodies were tried and publicly punished. Suicide was an offence against God and the law. In 1687 Beauport's seneschal judged Pierre Lefebvre to be guilty of self-murder and ordered that his remains be twice dragged, face downward and attached to a hurdle, through the settlement before being suspended from a gallows, upside down, for 'four winters.' Furthermore, all of his property was confiscated and Lefebvre's widow was fined for concealing some goods, a punishment that left her destitute. A higher court, Quebec's *Conseil souverain* (Sovereign Council), however, found this penalty excessive; it returned the proceeds from the fine and confiscation to the widow and permitted her to bury her husband in a cemetery.[7] Title 22 of the 1670 criminal ordinance instructed court officials on how to try a corpse or the memory of a deceased person, when the accused was guilty of *lèse-Majesté* by duelling, suicide, 'or rebellion against justice with open force.' An appointed administrator, preferably a relative, would be required to answer on behalf of the dead offender. When a criminal was still alive but had escaped from confinement, the court's sentence was carried out on an effigy and the offender was considered to be legally dead. In this way, the king's justice was shown to be inescapable and ever-triumphant.

Betrayal of or hostility to one's God-given monarch was considered so heinous as to sweep aside all safeguards for the accused. Those convicted of high treason were automatically tortured to disclose their confederates, if any. Witnesses and testimony that would not be heard by a court for other crimes were admitted in cases of lèse-Majesté. There was no statute of limitation for high treason. Confiscation of property accompanied physical punishment and retribution extended to the conspirator's family: for example, the parents of François Ravaillac, Henri IV's assassin, were expelled from the kingdom and the murderer's siblings had to change their surname. A traitor's children could also be banished from the realm. This punishment of the malefactor's relatives, as well as the relaxed rules of evidence, show that high treason was the greatest crime one could commit. Those who threaten the monarch's life, wrote de C.J. de Ferrière, 'are called parricides, because they are reckoned to be dealing with their own father, for kings are, as it were, the common father of all their peoples.'[8]

CRIMES AGAINST THE STATE IN CANADA

'Parricide' was the term used by Canadiens to describe the execution of King Louis XVI in 1793. The killing of the French royal family was incomprehensible to France's former subjects in North America, who had an uncritical reverence for the Bourbon monarchs. The king's government in New France had imposed few burdens on them – unlike the French peasantry, they paid no direct taxes – and criminal punishments in the colony were light by current standards. The reason for government leniency was simply that the monarchy and the church were never seriously threatened in New France. The small number of educated immigrants and the rarity of Protestants meant that, even in the eighteenth century, there was no ideological challenge to Roman Catholic orthodoxy or to the king's divine mandate. The absence of serious challenges to the royal government permitted a restrained approach with transgressors.

This was not the case before 1663, when New France was administered by chartered trading companies. The companies exercised governmental and judicial powers on the king's behalf and, in one instance, the sword of justice was wielded with a vigorous hand. The first recorded state trial was that of several conspirators at Quebec in 1608. The ringleader was Jean Duval, a locksmith employed by the Du Gua de Monts trading company. Duval had already revealed his rebelliousness during a 1606 expedition to explore the North American coast south of Acadia. Jean de Biencourt de Poutrincourt commanded the expedition. Duval and four companions ignored their commander's order to return to the ship from Cape Cod, after Biencourt observed some suspicious activity among the local natives. The five feasted on freshly baked biscuits and fell asleep on the shore. All but Duval were killed or fatally wounded by the Amerindians. He escaped to the vessel with an arrow wound.

Despite this misconduct, Jean Duval was enrolled again to accompany Samuel de Champlain, Sieur de Monts' lieutenant, on another voyage to the Americas. Champlain was to establish a permanent post at Quebec, to control the river passage inland, because interlopers were buying furs from Canada's aboriginal peoples and violating the company's trade monopoly. The St Lawrence River led to greater sources of good-quality pelts. The expedition set out in 1608.

The only record of Duval's planned mutiny at Quebec and the subsequent trial is the published narrative of Champlain. In his journal Champlain wrote: 'Some days after my arrival at Quebec [on 3 July 1608], there was a locksmith who conspired against the king's service, and his plan was to put me to death, and having made himself master of our fort, to hand it over to the Basques or Spaniards who were then at Tadoussac.' Duval recruited three confederates and they 'resolved to seize me unarmed and to strangle me, or to give a false alarm at night and to shoot me as I came out ... All promised mutually to make no disclosure, on penalty that the first who should open his mouth should be stabbed to death.' They hoped that by selling the post at Quebec to foreign competitors, 'they would become very rich, and ... they did not wish to go back to France.' The four mutineers then set about to suborn other company employees to join their plot.

Antoine Natel was another locksmith who, despite being 'a comrade of Jean Duval ... did not desire the execution of the plot.' Natel divulged the conspiracy to Captain Testu, pilot of a pinnace [barque]. In the privacy of the forest, Testu passed on what he knew to Champlain, recommending clemency for the informant. Champlain agreed to be merciful and discreetly questioned Natel. The latter 'related to me the remaining details of their project [entreprise].'

Testu lured the conspirators on board his vessel to share some wine provided by Champlain, who had gathered a party of loyal men. The plotters were surprised, arrested, and placed in confinement that evening. All the other workers were promised a pardon 'on condition that they should tell the truth about everything that had happened.' 'On the following day,' wrote Champlain, 'I received all their depositions, one after the other, in presence of the pilot and sailors of the ship, and had them committed to writing.' Champlain was following French criminal procedure: the accused and witnesses summoned by a court attorney usually were questioned singly and in camera while a clerk recorded their testimony. The notes were read back to each testifier for confirmation and signature, if the subject could write. This was called récolement des témoins. 'The same day,' said Champlain, 'I had six pairs of handcuffs [menottes] made for the authors of the plot, one for our surgeon, named Bonnerme, one for another man named La Taille whom the conspirators had [falsely] accused' in the hope of shifting some of the blame from themselves.

Because Quebec still lacked a prison, the accused conspirators were kept on a ship that moved downriver to Tadoussac, possibly to prevent a rescue attempt by sympathizers. When the interrogation of witnesses was completed, the prisoners were to be brought back to Quebec 'to have them confronted with the witnesses. Then after hearing them we should order justice to be done according to the offence they had committed.' In criminal trials *confrontation* was the first opportunity for the accused to hear the charge and to challenge the testimony against them. Defendants had no right to legal counsel. Judges used this occasion to put supplementary questions to the prisoner.

When the plotters were faced with their accusers, 'all that had been stated in the depositions was reaffirmed, without any denial on the part of the prisoners, who confessed that they had acted wickedly, and deserved punishment, unless mercy should be shown them; and they cursed Jean Duval for being the first who had led them into this conspiracy as soon as they sailed from France. The said Duval was unable to say anything, except that he deserved death; and that everything contained in the depositions was true, begging for pity for himself and for the others who had sided with him in his wicked intentions.'

Although Samuel de Champlain had a delegated judicial authority, with the power of life and death, he was the intended victim of this conspiracy. Moreover, high crimes called for more than one judge. And so Champlain had educated and trustworthy men join him in judging and sentencing the mutineers. 'After [Captain François Gravé du Pont, known as] Pont-Gravé and I, along with the Captain of the ship, the surgeon, master, mate, and other seamen, had heard their depositions and cross-examinations, we decided that it would be sufficient to put to death Duval as the first mover in the conspiracy, and also to serve as an example to those who remained, to behave properly in future in doing their duty, and in order that the Spaniards and Basques who were numerous in the region, might not rejoice over the affair.' *Punition exemplaire* was deemed necessary to deter others. 'We decided that the three others should be condemned to be hanged, but meanwhile should be taken back to France and handed over to the Sieur de Monts, to receive fuller justice, according as he might decide, with all the papers and the sentence upon Jean Duval before him, by virtue of which sentence Duval was hanged and strangled at Quebec, and his head placed on the end of a pike and set up in the highest spot in our fort.'[9] The three other condemned men sailed for France with Captain Gravé du Pont and disappeared from history.

When the royal *Conseil souverain* was established at Quebec in 1663, it became the automatic court of appeal for all death sentences rendered in the other courts of New France. There were suspicions that the council would be too lenient in dealing with traitors. One person who felt this way was a naval captain, Nicolas Gargot. On its outward voyage from France, the royal supply ship *le Jardin d'Hollande* under Captain Jean Guillon stopped at Plaisance in Newfoundland, where a mutiny had just occurred. The mutineers had murdered the fort commandant, his brother, the post chaplain, 'and several other persons' as well as pillaging and demolishing buildings, including the royal storehouse after the liquor it contained had been stolen. The crew of Guillon's ship captured fifteen of the mutineers and took them to Quebec, where the warship *Aigle d'Or* under Captain Nicolas Gargot was already at anchor. In September 1663 Quebec's new Sovereign Council demanded that Guillon deliver the prisoners to the royal gaol for the council's judgment. Captain Gargot had more faith in naval justice.

Since the rebels were still on a vessel, Gargot summoned the two ships' officers to a council of war to judge them. The murderer of the chaplain was sentenced to have his thumb cut off and then to be hanged and burned by another prisoner acting as executioner. Landing the criminals would have placed them within the jurisdiction of the council and local governor, and so Gargot had a gallows erected on a raft in full view of the town and the sentence was carried out, to the governor's great annoyance.[10] There is no record of Gargot being disciplined for this defiant action nor an account of the other prisoners' fate.

Captain Gargot's suspicion about tendered-hearted civilian magistrates was not borne out by the early rulings of Quebec's *Conseil souverain*. When in 1671 Pierre Dupuy, living at St Louis opposite Montreal, said that 'the English had done well to kill their king,' Charles I, and denied God's existence, he was sentenced to perform *amende honorable*, after which he was chained to a post in a public place and branded on the cheek 'for having spoken ill of royalty ... and for making seditious statements.'[11] Even the memory of a Protestant king deserved respect. In later years the councillors were less severe. In 1695, when Quebec's Sovereign Council received a report that François Chauveau had said privately that he would not be surprised if the governor used soldiers to coerce the settlers and 'cut their throats,' no action was taken against Chauveau for this 'seditious remark.'[12] Colonists sometimes composed defamatory songs about their betters and in 1708 and 1723 the intendants threatened the originators and singers of such scurrilous ballads with fines and imprisonment. Governor General Buade de Frontenac observed that serious cases of sedition and treason 'hardly ever happen' in New France, although he was quick to accuse those who questioned his own actions of being treasonous.[13]

Secure in their positions, colonial officials and magistrates could afford to be gentle when dealing with popular unrest. Those who circulated collective petitions or who elected a spokesman were reprimanded and then released. Public protesters, provided they did not explicitly challenge royal authority, were also verbally chastised without punishment. Four protests were sparked by the high price of goods or a shortage of essential foodstuffs. Montreal district farmers expressed their anger over the high cost of salt in 1704 and in 1705. They did this without violence or threats and quickly dispersed. After the first protest, the governor general forbade such seditious gatherings. Following the second outburst, two of the principal agitators were arrested, tried, and, after receiving a reprimand, fined. In September 1714, three farmers from St Augustin and Lorette were charged with enlisting local country folk to protest 'the costliness of merchandise and to make known their misery.' Some of the protesters were armed with muskets and threatened to enter Quebec City to challenge the government if Intendant Michel Bégon did not deal with their complaint. They scattered when the town militia and garrison troops were called out to march against them. The *Conseil souverain* interrogated the three farmers and witnesses and, after eleven months, acquitted one and released the others on bond until more information could be obtained[14] (app. 3, A, doc. 2). A 1717 protest in Longueuil seigneury against compulsory labour on Montreal's defensive walls, across the river, earned ten protesters a two-month sojourn in prison. In 1757, during a wartime famine, Montreal women confronted the colony's governor, Pierre de Rigaud, Marquis de Vaudreuil, demanding bread from him and rejecting the offer of cheap horse meat from the king's butchery in place of beef. An observer reported that 'Monsieur de Vaudreuil dismissed the women and told them that the first time they should create a disturbance he would have them all cast into prison, and that he would have half of them hanged.' It was all bluster: the magistrate allowed the protesters to disperse and return home still 'holding seditious designs.'[15] Leniency was reasonable because the protesters acknowledged their dependence upon the government by demanding that it intervene; they did not threaten to take the law into their own hands. Women protesters benefited from the contemporary legal assumption that females were always under some man's authority. Thus, it was believed that women seldom acted of their own volition and were usually led into wrongdoing by a man.

By contrast with New France, those who joined food riots in Paris suffered public punishment and death. After a sharp rise in the price of bread in 1692, one Cavoy and his wife participated in the pillaging of bread sellers in Place Maubert. The couple was arrested and, because food thefts and unrest continued, the *Lieutenant-Général de Police*, G. Nicolas de La Reynie, decided to 'make a very great example' of the pair. Cavoy was to die on the gibbet and his wife was to be flogged and branded 'to restrain the licence of those who ... take, as this man has done, disorder and scandal to the ultimate limit.' La Reynie noted with satisfaction that a large crowd was present to witness the execution of the sentence: 'this example of justice ... cannot but produce a good effect.'[16]

As a rule, punishment was elevated in proportion to the danger posed to 'public tranquility' and to the government. The measured response was evident in the most dangerous protest that occurred in New France: the Louisbourg mutiny of 1744. In December, French and Swiss soldiers of the garrison protested the diversion of their pay as well as spoiled vegetables in their rations, a shortage of firewood, and denial of a share in the plunder from the British settlement at Canso. The men threatened officers, extorted goods from merchants at a 'just price,' and took control of the seaport. After a few days, the malcontents were appeased with some concessions and went back to their duties. When New Englanders landed in 1745 to besiege Louisbourg, the governor and *commissaire-ordonnateur* (the local equivalent of an intendant) promised the troops a full pardon for the mutiny. Despite the soldiers' loyal service during the siege, that promise was not honoured. The minister of the navy and colonies, Jean-Frédéric Phélipeaux de Maurépas, believed that news of discontent among the garrison troops had encouraged the New Englanders to attack Louisbourg and that the mutiny had contributed to the surrender of the fortress. He was determined to make an example of the rebels to restore discipline among the colonial regular troops. The loss of the reputedly impregnable fortress, which had cost the government so much to build, was a political scandal.

When the soldiers returned to France after Louisbourg's capitulation, the surviving leaders of the 1744 protest were identified and arrested. Thirteen mutineers were sentenced to death by courts martial. Most were hanged, one was beheaded, and two had their sentences commuted to life service in the galleys. A condemned Swiss soldier escaped execution, possibly with his officers' connivance. The two hanged at Rochefort were to be left dangling from the gallows for a full day 'in order to serve as an example for everyone.'[17] The crime, mutiny, and the severity of the punishment were exceptional in the colony's history. The trials in France answered the royal government's need to find scapegoats for a military catastrophe. Had there been no defeat and had the mutineers been tried in New France, the authorities would have been satisfied with the exemplary punishment of one or two soldiers. That was the characteristic pattern for state trials in the French colony and it would be the practice in the later British provinces of North America.

Although the history of state trials in New France began dramatically with the conviction of Jean Duval and his co-conspirators in 1608, most subsequent offences were mundane affairs. Resistance to lawful authority was usually of a lesser order of lèse-Majesté. Court ushers or huissiers delivering writs of seizure or summonses risked being reviled, threatened, assaulted, and having their documents torn to shreds by the recipient.[18] Defiance of court officials was termed la rebellion à justice. People charged with la rebellion à justice – hindering legal officials carrying out unpopular sentences – accounted for 5.8 per cent of those tried as criminals in New France during the 1700s.

Colonists also disliked public executions. For instance, in 1685, Montrealers uprooted a newly erected pillory post and threw it into the river to express their hostility to executions. Carpenters and carters were reluctant to assist in punishments; public executioners and their families were social outcasts. Releasing prisoners and aiding their escape was another expression of distaste; when the populace considered a sentence excessively harsh, a flight from prison was arranged. In 1709 a Montreal couple was heavily fined for helping two men under sentence of death to escape in women's clothing.[19] People in the Montreal region refused in 1732 to aid the road police or maréchaussée in pursuing a fugitive. Assisting army deserters, however, was a graver case of lèse-Majesté because military desertion was treason. The executioner's son, Pierre Rattier or Daunier, was convicted of plotting with soldiers confined in Quebec's prison to lead them out of New France, probably to the English colonies.[20] Ironically, his father had escaped the noose for his crimes by accepting the hangman's office and the son, who was a petty thief, became the public executioner in 1710.[21] Another condemned man became Louisbourg's executioner in 1741.

Cases against those who threatened the natural order by disobeying their superiors accounted for 3.1 per cent of the criminals tried during the eighteenth century. At Quebec in 1739, three crewmen of *Le Saint-Joseph* were punished for refusing their captain's orders to continue a voyage after their ship had struck a rock. They were sentenced to two hours of public exposure in the iron collar, bearing a sign identifying them as 'séditieux et désobéissants [seditious and disobedient].' On appeal, the sentence was commuted to a public flogging with rods.[22]

Counterfeiting money and payment vouchers was the most common form of *lèse-Majesté humaine* dealt with by courts, accounting for 6.4 per cent of all persons tried for crimes in Canada. Issuing money was a royal prerogative and, since it was a source of revenue, it was closely guarded even though milled coins were hard to duplicate. Paper currency was another matter. Forgery was assisted by colonial issues of card money from 1685 onward. Playing cards, and then cards with embossed stamps, had a value inscribed on them along with the endorsing signatures of two or more government officials. The cards were easily copied and were readily accepted by a largely illiterate population in the cash-starved colony. As was customary, the administration responded to the problem of catching counterfeiters (who most commonly were the underpaid soldiers) by increasing the punishment of the few it did apprehend; that was the measured response. For example, a surgeon was convicted in 1690 of fabricating 'eleven cards worth four livres apiece, by forging the writing and signature of Sieur De Verneuil, Naval Treasurer, with Sieur Duplessis' signature, and the seals of M. the Governor and M. the Intendant.' The forger was marched through Quebec and was flogged in various locations and, after making financial restitution to the recipients of his spurious notes, he was to perform hard labour for three years.[23] By the eighteenth century hanging and branding were used to deal with the growing number of counterfeiters, yet brutal punishments did not end this form of *lèse-Majesté humaine*.

THE DECLINE OF LÈSE-MAJESTÉ DIVINE

Blasphemy – the disrespectful use of divine names — was prosecuted in the 1600s, often as part of a litany of sins that included drunkenness and brawling. In 1681 a storehouse keeper was convicted of 'insults, blasphemies, and shocking and abominable oaths against God's holy name and dignity' while playing with dice at a friend's house.[24] The courts' zeal to prosecute blasphemers was founded on a belief that God's retribution would fall on any community that tolerated sin in its midst. The king's edict of July 1666 forbade his subjects 'to blaspheme, swear by or disdain the holy name of God, nor to proffer any words against the honour of the most holy Virgin, his mother, or the saints' because, by tolerating such sins, 'we would esteem ourselves unworthy of the title we bear of Most Christian King.'[25] Earthquakes, pestilence, and Iroquois attacks were accepted as divine punishment for moral failings.

In the more secure decades after the 1713 Peace of Utrecht, however, fear of collective celestial punishment waned and individual moral failings were tolerated. Worldliness was especially common among the well-educated, including magistrates. Sent out from an increasingly secular France because legal training was inadequate in the colony, eighteenth-century magistrates had little interest in lèse-Majesté divine. As a result, prosecutions for blasphemy and sacrilege diminished even as the population grew. Andre Lachance found fourteen prosecutions for blasphemy in the St Lawrence valley during the seventeenth century as opposed to just one in the next century.[26]

Prosecutions for witchcraft also declined, although the clergy and country folk remained convinced that one could acquire magical powers from the devil. In earlier times, the diabolic source of supernatural forces made magic heretical and a case of lèse-Majesté divine. In 1661 the Quebec Ursulines' mother superior wrote that New France was afflicted by 'sorcerers and magicians' who were blamed for 'a universal malady ... Such then are the two scourges with which it has pleased God to try this new Church.'[27] One of these sorcerers in the 1660s was Daniel Will, a Protestant miller, who was accused of bewitching a seigneur's maidservant for the purpose of carnal relations. The miller was hanged for blasphemy, profanation of holy objects, and providing liquor to Amerindians. Courts at this time cooperated in the detection of witches, seeking evidence of a satanic pact by tests such as probing the skin with pins to locate the devil's spot which marked Lucifer's servants.

Gradually, the respected parlement of Paris started to treat sorcerers as charlatans who deceived ignorant folk with imaginary powers. Since the courts and judgments at Paris served as a model for colonial justice, eighteenth-century magistrates in New France also adopted this sceptical attitude toward witchcraft. They were now less receptive to accusations from neighbours whose motives were a mixture of jealousy, superstition, and ignorance of the material causes for misfortunes. Strokes and sudden death were blamed on evil spells because there was no visible, external agency. In 1707 Jean Charpentier, a Boucherville coppersmith, complained that two farmers and a servant had told many that the craftsman 'was a sorcerer who had caused many of Captain de la Jemerais' cattle to die,' which prevented Charpentier from earning a living, 'being rebuffed by several people' on account of the story. The Montreal court investigated the charge, fined the accusers for malicious libel, and ordered them to make a public retraction.[28]

The only other prosecution for witchcraft in eighteenth-century New France proceeded because it also involved sacrilege, the profanation of holy objects. The abuse of sacred objects, not the claim to possess supernatural powers, was the crime, and it was still regarded as reprehensible. While attempting to identify a thief for a client, the prognosticator, a soldier called Havard de Beaufort, used a crucifix and prayer book in his ritual. In 1742 Montreal's court sentenced the self-styled wizard to make *amende honorable* and then to serve five years in the galleys. His client, whose home was the location of the ritual, was banished temporarily from Montreal. Quebec's *Conseil supérieur* (the renamed *Conseil souverain*), acting as an appelate court, reduced service in the galleys to three years and added a public flogging to the sorcerer's sentence; his customer merely received a reprimand and paid a small fine.[29] The final sentence was light because, though the king's edict of July 1682 made it a capital offence 'to add and join to superstition, impiety and sacrilege, under the pretext of performing so-called magical transactions,' it reduced penalties for fortune-tellers, magicians, and 'enchanters.'[30] By 1742 the councillors at Quebec were no longer outraged by impious or superstitious acts. The clergy and lower orders of the laity retained a belief in magic but the autocratic nature of French colonial government allowed officials to ignore popular delusions. If court officials at Salem, Massachusetts, had been as sceptical of public superstitions as judges in New France, that town would not have been the site of the notorious witchcraft trials of 1692! The evidence of judicial indifference to the violation of religious taboos is in the statistics. *Lèse-Majesté humaine* was the charge against 15 per cent of the 995 persons who appeared in Canada's criminal courts in 1712–59, whereas only 1.2 per cent of them were accused of *lèse-Majesté divine*.[31] The rest were charged with other criminal offences.

CONCLUSION

By the eighteenth century, *lèse-Majesté* usually meant an offence against secular authority; crimes against Roman Catholic orthodoxy and morality were a minor concern of the courts. Yet the two aspects of *lèse-Majesté*, secular and religious, remained linked even though crimes against the state received the most attention. Political allegiances were still determined by religion and loyal subjects followed their monarch's faith, which was protected from rival beliefs.

In New France, state trials rarely involved high treason; they were more concerned with petty treason and sedition against the 'good order' of a hierarchical society. The principal offences were interference with those carrying out sentences and court orders, acts of disobedience to one's lawful superiors, flagrant disrespect to superiors, counterfeiting money, prison escapes, military desertion, and flight to the British colonies, which was equated with desertion. Except when dealing with counterfeiters, the colony's magistrates tended to use their discretionary power to impose lighter punishment than the retribution inflicted on criminals in France. Since punishment was proportionate to the danger to society, the merciful hand of justice in Canada reflected the royal government's sense of security and the fidelity of the colonists.

NOTES

1 *Ordonnance de Louys XIV, Roy de France et de Navarre, Pour les matières Criminelles, Donnée à Saint Germain en Laye au Mois d'Aoust 1670* (Paris: les Associez 1671), at 2.

2 Ordinance of Governor Buade de Frontenac, 23 March 1677, *RAQ*, 1927-8, opposite xvi.

3 MG 8, C 5 (Archives judiciaires du District de Montréal), vol. 4 (1687-93), at 297-8, NA: Procès verbal ... contre le Sieur Martinet de Fonblanche, 10 Oct. 1693.

4 C.J. de Ferrière, *Dictionnaire de Droit et de Pratique, contenant l'explication des termes de droit, de coûtumes & de pratique*, 2 vols. (Toulouse: J. Dupleix 1779), 2: at 134 (pre-1734 editions are called *Introduction à la Pratique*). The same idea is more succinctly stated in Nicolas Guy du Rousseaud de La Combe, *Traite des Matières Criminelles* (Paris: Theodore Le Gras 1753), at 61: 'Le crime de lèse-Majesté humaine est une offense qui se commet contre les Rois & les Princes Souverains, qui sont les images vivantes de Dieu sur la terre, & que représentent dans le Gouvernement de leurs Etats, l'autorité que Dieu exerce dans le Gouvernement de l'Univers.'

5 *The New English Bible: New Testament* (Oxford, England: Oxford University Press/Penguin Books 1964), at 263 (Romans, XIII: 1-2).

6 Duchesne [Lieutenant-général de police at Vitry], *Code de la Police, ou Analyse*

des règlemens de police, 3rd ed. (Paris: Prault père 1761), at 40. The author's first name is unknown.

7 *Jugements et Déliberations du Conseil souverain de la Nouvelle-France* (1663–1716) [hereafter *JDCS*], 6 vols. (Quebec: A. Côté et Joseph Dussault 1885–91), 3: at 192–3.

8 De Ferrière, *Dictionnaire de Droit et de Pratique*, 2: at 134.

9 *The Works of Samuel de Champlain*, ed. H.P. Biggar, 6 vols. (Toronto: Champlain Society 1922–36), 2: at 25–34.

10 René Baudry, 'Du Perron, Thalour, *DCB* 1:296; *JDCS*, 1: at 6; Pierre-Georges Roy, *La Ville de Québec sous le régime français*, 2 vols. (Quebec: Redempti Paradis 1930), 1: at 301–2.

11 *JDCS*, 1: at 644–5.

12 NF 13, Dossiers du Conseil supérieur, vol. 1 (Police, 1695–1755), ff.1–4, ANQ (Quebec).

13 The character of this haughty and testy governor is well delineated in William John Eccles, *Frontenac: The Courtier Governor* (Toronto: McClelland and Stewart 1959).

14 *JDCS*, 6: at 834, 842–3, 997–9, and André Lachance, *La Justice criminelle du Roi au Canada au xviiie siècle* (Quebec: Les Presses de l'Université Laval 1978), at 22n.90. The argument that protests in New France conformed to George Rudé's model of pre-industrial riots is contained in Terence Crowley, 'Thunder Gusts: Popular Disturbances in Early French Canada,' Canadian Historical Association, *Historical Papers* (1979), at 11–31. Such protests were spontaneous, conservative reactions to an uncomfortable change in the status quo that offended the population's sense of justice. The movements were ephemeral and were focused on a specific grievance. Crowley writes that 'colonial officials ... unofficially recognized the legitimacy of demonstrations as long as they acted within certain bounds. Governors and intendants were overtly hostile ... but punishments were never harsh. This is explained by the non-destructiveness of the crowds, but also by the opinion among colonial officials that the people had no other way to express their plight.'

15 *Journal des Campagnes du Chevalier de Lévis*, (Montreal: C.O. Beauchemin et fils 1889), at 117–18, translated in *PACR*, 1943, at xxxii–xxxiii.

16 *Correspondance administrative sous le règne de Louis XIV*, ed. Georges Bernard Depping, 4 vols. (Paris: Imprimerie nationale 1850–5), 2: at 631, 635. Conversely, the danger of provoking a rebellion by public punishment stayed the hands of the authorities. In 1709, during a severe famine in a brutal winter, a Parisian *archer*'s wife stood before a portrait of Louis XIV and said 'si je savais qu'un coup de couteau dans ce portrait put pénétrer jusqu'à l'original, je le donnerai.' Despite this treasonous threat, the police magistrate decided not to

punish her, considering the Parisians' explosive temper at the time. See Jacques Saint-Germain, *La vie quotidienne en France a la fin du grand siècle, d'après les archives ... du lieutenant général de police Marc-René d'Argenson* (Paris: Hachette 1965), at 21–2.

17 Allan Greer, 'Mutiny at Louisbourg, December 1744,' *Histoire sociale – Social History*, no. 20 (1977), 305.

18 Juridiction royale de Montréal, Feuillets séparés, 5 nov. 1710, 9 sept. 1728, 24 sept. 1729, 28–30 juillet 1732, ANQ (Montreal); 8, B 1, 2: at 5, 3: at 261–2, 303–4.

19 Raymond Boyer, *Les Crimes et les Châtiments au Canada français du XVIIe au XXe siècle* (Montreal: Le Cercle du Livre de France 1966), at 194.

20 *JDCS*, 4: at 878.

21 André Lachance, *Le Bourreau au Canada sous le régime français* (Quebec: La Société historique de Québec 1966), at 63–6, 72–5.

22 Boyer, *Les Crimes et les Châtiments*, at 373; also noted in André Lachance, *Crimes et Criminelles en Nouvelle-France* (Montreal: Les Editions du Boréal Express 1984), at 68.

23 *JDCS*, 3: at 402–3.

24 *JDCS*, 2: at 613. In 1689 the Montreal baillif's court tried Jean Boudor and René Godefroy de Tonnancour for burlesquing a Roman Catholic burial service by covering Boudor's drunken and inert storekeeper with a black cloth, placing six candles in empty wine bottles around the body, and singing the *Libera me, Domine* while aspersing the 'corpse' with a bottle of wine and bucket of water. See MG 8, C 5, 4, 19 février, 19 juin 1689, NA.

25 *Edits, Ordonnances Royaux, Déclarations et Arrêts du Conseil d'État du Roi concernant le Canada* (Quebec: E.R. Frechette 1954), at 62–3.

26 André Lachance, *Crimes et Criminels en Nouvelle-France*, at 63.

27 Joyce Marshall, *Word from New France: The Selected Letters of Marie de l'Incarnation* (Toronto: Oxford University Press 1967), at 264–5.

28 Robert-Lionel Seguin, *La Sorcellerie au Québec du XVIIe au XIXe siècle* (Montreal: Lemeac 1971), at 111–14.

29 André Lachance, 'Havard de Beaufort, François-Charles,' *DCB* 3:278.

30 Duchesne, *Code de la Police*, at 71.

31 Lachance, *Crimes et Criminelles*, at 63, 65.

2

The 'Hoffman Rebellion' (1753) and Hoffman's Trial (1754): Constructive High Treason and Seditious Conspiracy in Nova Scotia under the Stratocracy*

BARRY CAHILL

... for this general decay of that settlement various reasons are given, some say its owing to the military form of government they are under but to say this in Nova-Scotia is treason.

– 'J.B.' [John Butler], 1756

'There has never been a trial for high treason in this province, as far as I can learn,' wrote Beamish Murdoch in 1833. 'The only instance of one in the present B.N.A. provinces, I have heard of, is that of McLean [sic], tried and executed in Lower Canada, about the close of the last century.'[1] Murdoch the lawyer-cum-legal historian, who – unlike Murdoch the narrative historian-cum-chronologist – had little or no interest in crimes against the state, thus ignored not only Nova Scotia's first, aborted treason trial in 1754[2] but also the two wartime treason trials resulting from the patriot siege of Fort Cumberland [Beauséjour] in 1776.[3] While the *grand dérangement* of the Acadians in 1755 is well known to students of Canadian colonial history as a quasi-legal

*The author wishes to thank Dr J.R. Phillips, associate dean, faculty of law, University of Toronto, for an incisive critique of the first draft of this paper; and a colleague, Patricia Kennedy of the National Archives of Canada, for numerous helpful suggestions.

response to an 'officially apprehended security threat,'[4] primitive state-security law as experienced by a group of continental European immigrants nearly contemporaneous with the Acadian deportees, the so-called 'foreign Protestants,' who arrived en masse in Nova Scotia a few years before the Acadians were expelled, is scarcely known at all. These mainly German- but also French-speaking immigrants, had they been eligible for naturalization within the statutory seven-year waiting period, would eagerly have taken the oath of allegiance, which the Acadians resolutely declined to do, because their status as resident aliens possessing all the legal rights and privileges (as well as liabilities) of natural-born subjects placed them in an invidious position. Though Nova Scotia during the first decade of Halifax hegemony (1749–58) was never officially under military rule or martial law, it was governed by a succession of army colonels, in whom were united not only the civil and military commands but also the executive, legislative, and supreme judicial branches of government. There was little delegation of authority, and no *de facto* separation of powers.

Into this authoritarian, if not totalitarian, milieu came both entrepreneurial, mercantile New Englanders – carrying with them their native traditions of unrestricted free enterprise and direct democracy in the form of township government – and the foreign Protestants, about 1500 of whom in the summer of 1753 were settled on the south shore of Nova Scotia, 92 kilometres west of Halifax, to found the coastal town of Lunenburg. The settlers' legitimate grievances, aggravated by suspicion that supplies intended for them by the British government had been intercepted and withheld by the Halifax 'bashaws,' was shrewdly exploited by an inside agitator with New England mercantile connections. The result was that the larger part of the militia which had been raised from among the immigrant population of the new town appeared in armed rebellion against the government in December 1753 – less than six months after the settlement had been founded, and barely six weeks after Colonel Charles Lawrence, president of the Council, had taken over as administrator of the province. In June 1753 Lawrence, the official responsible for directing the settlement of the 'foreign Protestants' at Lunenburg, had drawn upon the translation services of the man whom he would afterwards suspect of having plotted the insurrection. Whether Hoffman is to be identified with 'ye ringleader of these mutineers,' whom Lawrence accused of 'stirring up mutiny' among 'Some Germans of ye lower kind,' and whom he threatened to make an example of by returning him to Halifax in June 1753, is unknown.[5]

THE LUNENBURG CHRISTMAS PUTSCH: PRELUDE, PROGRESS, AND AFTERMATH

The eponymous inciter of the 'Hoffman Rebellion,' Johannes Wilhelm Hoffman[6] (fl. 1741–60) – the name had become anglicized as 'John William Hoffman' before his arrival in Nova Scotia – was reportedly born in the old German electorate of Hanover and immigrated to Philadelphia in 1741. What evidence there is, and it is entirely circumstantial, suggests that he was in London on business seeking a quick and economical passage back across the Atlantic when the Lords Commissioners for Trade and Plantations chartered the brigantine *Nancy* to transport (free of charge) a surfeit of mostly German-speaking Swiss immigrants to Halifax in June 1750. As neither the Board of Trade's agent nor the master of the vessel would have been able to communicate in French let alone in German, there was clearly a role for Hoffman to play as intermediary between shipboard officialdom and the non-English-speaking passengers. Whatever the timing and circumstances of Hoffman's arrival, it is certain that by December 1750 he had not only settled in Halifax but was also prominent enough to receive appointment as a justice of the peace.[7] Though this appointment was afterwards determined to be technically illegal – under the imperial Foreign Protestant Naturalization Act [(1740) 13 Geo. II, c. 7] the immigrant had to have resided continuously in the same colony for seven years – Governor Edward Cornwallis justified it on the grounds of necessity: a bilingual (or rather trilingual) German magistrate to arbitrate among such German-speaking immigrants as had already arrived would reduce the level of miscommunication and disaffection.[8] Hoffman had caught the governor's eye and been selected for such a prestigious and responsible office 'because he had some education, was competent in the English language, was in better circumstances than the rest, and had made himself popular among them.'[9] Further proof that Hoffman was a person of substance is his residence 'Within the Town [proper] of Halifax' rather than in the north suburbs, with the rest of the Germans, or in the south suburbs (or 'Within the Pickets'), where most of the Americans – mostly New Englanders – lived. Significant, too, is the fact that his household (consisting of himself and two servants) does not appear on the lists of those receiving government relief.[10]

It was inevitable that the legality of Hoffman's commission as a JP would be challenged by English-speaking settlers and soldiers when he attempted to exercise his authority beyond the confines of the immigrant community.[11] Despite the Council's support of Hoffman, neither the

Quarter Sessions nor the General Court were competent to address what was after all a political as well as a constitutional issue, and Governor Cornwallis thought it best to refer the matter to the Lords of Trade. Their lordships determined that the lack of naturalization meant that no foreign Protestant, however trustworthy, was eligible for appointment to government office. Having renewed Hoffman's appointment on his own authority in March 1752, therefore, Cornwallis took the precaution of issuing another commission of the peace a mere four months later, in order to exclude both Hoffman and the other – unnaturalized – foreign Protestant JP, Leonard Christopher Rudolf. So popular had been Hoffman's appointment that the new governor, Colonel Peregrine Thomas Hopson (Cornwallis left office on 3 August 1752), was immediately confronted with a memorial from the 'Whole body of [Rhineland] Germans and Swiss,' in which he was asked to 'again favour us with a capable Person (as we are very imperfect in the English Language) who under your Excellency's Direction, we might advise with, more easily determine our disputes, and direct and order things, and not in the future let us be titled Foreigners, as according to Act of Parliament we are on the same footing and Prerogatives as others ...'[12] Hopson acceded to the request, but not by commissioning another recent immigrant who might lie under the same suspicion and be vulnerable to the same accusation of alienness. Hoffman's replacement was Sebastian Zouberbuhler, a naturalized Swiss immigrant to the America colonies in the 1730s who had subsequently migrated from New England to Nova Scotia.[13]

Together with most of the new settlers, John William Hoffman moved on to Lunenburg in the summer of 1753, having profitably sold his remaining Halifax property to a Boston merchant, Andrew Faneuil Phillips, and intending to play no less prominent a role in the affairs of the new settlement than he had among the foreign Protestant immigrants at Halifax in 1750–2. His appointment as one of the eight militia captains conferred on him a position of authority and prestige, as well as some power and influence, and placed him on a more equal footing with his rival Zouberbuhler. He was directed by the expedition commander, Colonel Lawrence, to cooperate with Zouberbuhler – who, as well as being the only foreign Protestant JP, was senior to Hoffman in the list of militia captains – in translating for the settlers. The impact of Hoffman's services as a trilingual translator is concisely stated in W.P. Bell's standard work on the foreign Protestants: 'In connection with many of the episodes of the insurrection one might keep in mind that few, if any, of the Montbéliardians understood German, except what little they might have picked up from contacts in Nova Scotia with German immigrants, while a very few only of the Germans spoke any French ... One factor in J.W. Hoffman's influence with the people may have been his ability in all three.'[14]

The sequence of events during the Christmas rising at Lunenburg in 1753 is rehearsed in great detail by Bell and so is only sketched here. Eight days before Christmas, news reached Halifax that the Germans were in armed rebellion. Gossip about a spurious, perhaps non-existent letter – allegedly from a relation in London to one of the *montbéliardais*, Jean Petrequin – had planted the idle rumour that the settlers were not receiving all the supplies intended for them by the home government. The more disaffected among them thereupon took steps either to appropriate the letter or, failing that, to lay hands on its alleged recipient, who was suspected of having connived with the authorities at suppressing it. Petrequin was taken by the crowd and incarcerated in the militia blockhouse. Liberated on the instructions of the garrison commander, Petrequin was again taken by force and reimprisoned; he was harassed, interrogated, threatened, and ultimately tortured. Reading a proclamation under the Riot Act made no impression on the rioters, because they had many more men and firelocks than the garrison. Belying his true role as *éminence grise* masterminding the affair, Hoffman was careful not to appear publicly as one of 'the more active insurgents' but only as a go-between (and mediator of demands) between them and the *custos rotulorum* or chief magistrate, Patrick Sutherland.[15] After shots were fired at the hopelessly outnumbered rump of loyal militiamen – and returned by them – Sutherland had no alternative but to send secretly to Halifax for reinforcements. A tense few days ensued while Sutherland, resolutely refusing to hand over to the insurgents the magistrate to whom Petrequin had purportedly confided the letter, or otherwise to accede to their more unlawful demands, waited patiently for help to arrive. The insurgents held the militia blockhouse and its armoury and continued their unlawful detention of the hapless Petrequin, while forbearing to press their advantage through force of arms. Governor Lawrence quickly dispatched his second-in-command, Lieutenant-Colonel Robert Monckton, ordering him 'to see civil authority fully restored and the ringleaders of the rebellion apprehended for trial.'[16] With the aid of 200 regular troops from the Halifax garrison, Monckton quashed the rising without firing a shot and disarmed the militia holus-bolus. By Christmas Eve the week-long putsch was over.

The true nature and extent of Hoffman's behind-the-scenes involvement were neither known to, nor perhaps even suspected by, the local authorities until after the official inquiry was well under way. Hoffman, who initially had not lain under any degree of suspicion – he was not examined at all – was eventually denounced to the investigating magistrate, John Creighton, the senior militia captain. Lieutenant-Colonel Monckton sent a party of soldiers to arrest Hoffman, who was found at the house of Georg Hirschman, one of the suspected ringleaders. Under interrogation, Hoffman asserted that his accuser had been bribed to incriminate him. On being arrested by the soldiers, he appealed for the people's 'deputies'[17] to rescue him and indignantly protested his innocence. Circumstantial evidence weighed heavily against him, however, because 'Hoffman had been captain of the militia guard the night of the uprising.'[18]

PRE-TRIAL PROCESS

Accompanied by his two servants, three suspected militia officers, and at least one of the ringleaders, Hoffman was transported to Halifax under a guard of twelve soldiers. Ten days later, on 21 January 1754, Hoffman – only – was brought before the Council for a preliminary hearing. As the supreme judicial court of the province, the Council was also the tribunal by which he would be tried, should it (acting in an administrative capacity) resolve to order the king's attorney to indict him. The depositions that had been taken before the civil magistrates in Lunenburg were tabled, and Hoffman was accused of having been the 'Original Contriver and Promoter' of the insurrection. President Charles Lawrence, who entertained great expectations of succeeding to the then vacant lieutenant governorship, was anxious to impress the Lords of Trade by making an example of Hoffman, who 'had nothing material to say in his Defence.'[19] The secretary (also a member of Council) was directed to issue a mittimus (warrant) for committing Hoffman to the common jail, where he remained only temporarily. Lawrence, having decided that the accused was to be held incommunicado pending the spring session of the General Court three months hence, ordered Hoffman moved to the military prison at the 'Battery' on Georges Island in Halifax Harbour, a prohibited area from which civilians (other than state prisoners) were barred.[20] No distinction was made between committing an accused on remand and a convict serving a custodial sentence. As a result of Lawrence's determined efforts to prevent Hoffman from communicating with the outside world, several more or less incriminating letters written by the prisoner were intercepted by the deputy provost marshal (sheriff) and given in evidence at the trial.

As required by the English statutes of 1695/6 and 1708, the government was at pains to ensure that Hoffman's legal rights as a treason indictee were not violated. On 19 April, eleven days before the trial, clerk of the crown George Suckling paid an official visit to Georges Island, where he read to the accused six articles pertaining to the content of the indictment and to the arrangements for witnesses for both crown and defence. Hoffman gave his preliminary, over-long list of prospective defence witnesses to Suckling, who the following day made out the subpoenas.

R. v. HOFFMAN

Witnesses

Colonel Sutherland, chief magistrate at Lunenburg, was assigned the responsible task of 'selecting suitable witnesses to support the crown's case.'[21] In this process he was to be guided by a thirteen-point 'memorandum touching the Evidence necessary to support the Charge against the Prisoner,' which Lawrence had sent him early in February 1754. Among the eighteen or so prospective crown witnesses were Major Rudolf, the former JP;[22] Sebastian Zouberbuhler, Hoffman's nemesis and the only foreign Protestant JP – known to be a firm friend of government; and three of the alleged ringleaders: Almond, Hirschman, and Wüst (the only commissioned militia officer afterwards presented by the grand jury for trial).[23] As the *custos* could not be spared from his post, Sutherland was not given leave to attend, even though his evidence might have been essential to proving the crown's case. Witnesses were formally subpoenaed, but the exact number and identity of those crown witnesses who actually testified cannot be ascertained. At least one of them, moreover, was also scheduled to testify as a defence witness.

Four of the fifteen alleged ringleaders, including Johann Andreas Stahl, sergeant of the militia guard the night of the uprising, and Hirschman, in whose house Hoffman was apprehended, obviously had been conveyed from Lunenburg to Halifax for that purpose. They, too, were under arrest and in custody. The chief crown witness, one Jean Petrequin,[24] had also been incarcerated. Indeed the only material evidence supporting the treason charge against Hoffman was the discreditable testimony of a single witness – Petrequin – who had inculpated Hoffman during the course of his own rigorous re-examination by Monckton. 'Petrequin's testimony,' writes his biographer, 'was the only positive feature of the crown's case.'[25] Even Administrator Lawrence, supreme judge of the General

Court, would later have to admit that Petrequin had fatally injured his own credibility in the eyes of the jury, and as a result Hoffman was nearly acquitted on the charge as laid in the indictment.

Even if Petrequin had been a credible witness, however, his uncorroborated testimony would not have been sufficient to try – let alone convict – Hoffman of treason. Among the important reforms introduced by the Treason Trials Regulation Act of 1695/6[26] was the right to subpoena witnesses for the defence. Under an act of 1702 (1 An., st. 2, c. 9, s. 3), moreover, witnesses for the accused in a treason trial were on the same footing as witnesses for the crown. Indeed, Hoffman was shown such careful consideration in this regard that he may have attempted to take advantage. His preliminary list of thirty or so names included most if not all of the crown witnesses and did not spare even the chief magistrate himself, Sutherland, who was ordered by the secretary to ignore any such summons to testify on behalf of the accused. Hoffman also insisted on the appearance of all twelve of the deputies, some of whose identities he professed not to know. The grand jury seems afterwards to have consulted the document concerned in order to identify those ringleaders whom to present for trial, the principle of selection being that any prospective defence witness who was not also a crown witness incurred suspicion. The Council finally decided to limit the number of defence witnesses to six: 'That Six witnesses, Is Imagined, will be Sufficient for you [Hoffman], on your Trial And the bringing them up for you in the Governments Sloop, Is an Act of great Indulgence & Lenity in the Government, And which you are by no means Intitled to by Law.'[27]

Crown Attorney; Defence Counsel

King's attorney [attorney general] William Nesbitt and clerk of the crown George Suckling, two leading figures at the nascent provincial bar, prosecuted – the one as counsel, the other as solicitor. Nesbitt had replaced New Englander Otis Little as king's attorney the year before,[28] while Suckling, Nesbitt's former law partner, had succeeded Nesbitt as clerk of the General Court. Suckling, 'the English Attorney' – he had been admitted to the Court of Common Pleas at Westminster Hall – went on to become first attorney general of Quebec and subsequently chief justice of the Virgin Islands.[29] Nesbitt was afterwards to adduce *R. v. Hoffman* as one of the 'two remarkable trials'[30] he had prosecuted as king's attorney which justified his claim for remuneration from government.

It is not known whether Joseph Kent, the Massachusetts attorney who defended Hoffman, was retained by the accused or assigned by the court, as was provided for under the Treason Trials Regulation Act. Kent and Little, the disgraced former king's attorney, were not only Harvard classmates (1731) but also the principal professional rivals of Nesbitt and Suckling; it was England versus New England at the bar of New Scotland. Kent's flourishing law practice – he appears to have been the leading criminal defence counsel, as well as having an extensive civil practice in the Inferior Court of Common Pleas – was cut short by his premature death in November 1757 during the smallpox epidemic.

Grand Jury; Petit Jury

As the only representative body in the settlement before the summoning of the legislature in 1758, the Halifax grand jury maintained a system of checks and balances vis-à-vis the Council-cum-General Court, from the judgments of which there was no appeal in criminal cases. Rejecting the treason indictment, for example, was the means – the only legal means – whereby the grand jury could assert popular rights and exercise political influence, if not power, as a de facto pre-legislative constituent assembly.[31] To some extent, however, the Council had usurped even this inquisitional role by itself acting as a board of preliminary judicial inquiry for the purpose of ascribing criminal responsibility for the insurrection. The grand jury nevertheless had the right to dispose of the crown's treason indictment in whatever manner they saw fit.

The members of the grand jury for the year 1754 had been duly drawn and sworn up to the full legal maximum of twenty-three.[32] It is engaging to speculate as to possible partiality towards Hoffman on the part of the grand jury, nearly 40 per cent of whom are known to have come from New England and a majority of whom were merchants or traders; twelve had to concur if the indictment was to go forward. Neither the English nor the New England mercantile group was above suspicion; occupational cohesion and bourgeois class consciousness might have prompted them to close ranks around one of their own who was under attack by government – a government dominated by soldiers, not merchants. The foreman of the grand jury, Joshua Mauger, the leading merchant in the colony, was heavily involved in the economic and commercial life of Lunenburg, where Hoffman had set up as a retailer, perhaps in order to assist the Boston mercantile interests, whom he seems to have represented, in their efforts to remain competitive with Mauger. So too, to a lesser extent, was Malachy Salter.[33] John Webb, moreover, was a partner in the Halifax mercantile firm of Webb and Ewer, who were Hoffman's wholesalers.[34] Another grand juror, Henry Ferguson, baker and trader, was to act as one of Hoffman's sureties when he was released from prison on a bond.

The proclivities of the trial jury are less easy to determine. The political lines should not perhaps be drawn too finely, as jury personnel also split along ethnic-national, English-American lines: nine of the thirty-five members of the grand and the petit jury, including both foremen, had previously signed articles of impeachment for incompetence and partiality against the justices of the Inferior Court of Common Pleas, a majority of whom were from Massachusetts.[35]

High Treason and Seditious Conspiracy: The Two Indictments

The treason indictment, which had been drafted by clerk of the crown Suckling, was returned endorsed 'Ignoramus' by the grand jury, because the crown's evidence was insufficient in law; 'a charge of high treason could be sustained only by the concurrent evidence of two or more witnesses to overt treasonable acts, and to the principal such act in this case there was but one witness.'[36] (See app. 3, B, doc. 1.) It is amazing that the king's attorney had failed to bring to the Council's attention the fact that the two-witness rule, governing the sufficiency of crown evidence in a treason trial, precluded drafting a sustainable indictment for high treason in this instance. One can only assume that defence counsel, though not permitted to appear before the grand jury, was more attentive to procedural errors in the crown proceeding than either the king's attorney or the clerk of the crown who drew the indictment. The bill having been quashed, the accused ought to have been granted an absolute discharge; he was not. The government responded by ordering the king's attorney, who had been set to proceed against Hoffman for treason, to prepare a new indictment alleging 'High Crimes, Misdemeanours and Breach of the Peace' – in short, seditious conspiracy (see app. 3, B, doc. 2). The king's attorney did not distinguish explicitly between treason and sedition, because his chief concern was to circumvent the procedural requirement which had defeated the treason indictment.[37] If the government could not procure a trial on the capital felony charge, it would at least make the indictment fit the crime for which the accused was triable and potentially convictable. In conclusion, the difference between the two indictments was the difference between treason and sedition: on the first, the government could not obtain from the grand jury even the promise of a trial; on the second, the government was able to obtain from the petit jury a conditional, truncated verdict of guilty.

General Court Trial

Hoffman's trial began on 30 April 1754.[38] According to Lawrence, it lasted twenty-four hours, covering at least two, if not three, sitting days. The venue was the old courthouse on the northeast corner of Argyle and Buckingham streets, at the then northern extremity of the town of Halifax. Bell's statement that 'the court consisted of the Council sitting in its judicial capacity,'[39] though accurate, applies equally to the preliminary hearing which had taken place in January; thus the same individuals were deciding, not only whether or not to order that the chief suspect be charged, but also whether to try the accused on the sedition indictment as found by the grand jury. Hoffman was duly arraigned and pleaded not guilty. 'The Jury,' reported Lawrence to the Lords of Trade, 'brought him in Guilty of a part of the Charge only tho' the Evidence was very full against him for the whole charge, and I am apt to think they did not give sufficient Credit to one of the Witnesses [Petrequin] because he had before the Trial told different Storys about the matter, which I suppose proceeded from Mr Hoffmans having threatened him at different Times with the Effects of the Peoples Rage When he should return to Lunenburg.'[40]

The trial jury's special verdict ('Guilty of Misdemeanours') signified a compromise on the charge of seditious conspiracy, between 'high crimes' and 'breach of the peace.' It elaborated on the verdict as follows: 'for Advising to Add to Peterquins Declaration and for Misbehaviour to the Honble Col.° Monckton.' Not only had the lesser of the two indictments been accepted by the grand jury; the trial jury abridged it even further by finding the defendant guilty of only part of it. The accused having waived his right to speak to the verdict, the court sentenced him to pay a fine of £100 sterling and serve two years' imprisonment. Obviously, Hoffman was being punished for seditious conspiracy or slander, a high misdemeanour at common law, and not merely for contempt towards the grand inquisitor, Lieutenant-Colonel Monckton, during the interrogation preceding his arrest.[41] The convict was remanded to the common jail, to which doubtless he had been transferred from the military prison on Georges Island in readiness for the trial. Thereafter the state prisoner headed the list of criminals in jail.

About two weeks later, fifteen of the alleged ringleaders, including perhaps some of the twelve deputies, were presented by the grand jury; they were never tried. The administrator, President Lawrence, chose to exercise broad prosecutorial discretion unilaterally and arbitrarily in favour of executive clemency. Yet his motives were scarcely benign. Once he had the paramount leader in hand, Lawrence lost interest in the subordinates, except to the extent that their evidence could buttress the crown's case against Hoffman. In the end, Lawrence chose to proceed not even against those four alleged chief ringleaders – Hoffman's lieutenants – who were in Halifax as crown witnesses or suspects or both. The grand jury, taking the initiative, made the presentment but the government refused to commit the presentees for trial, while in the case of Hoffman the court refused to discharge the accused absolutely despite the indictment's having been thrown out by the grand jury. Hoffman had been ordered reindicted on substantially similar, though differently denominated, charges, while the alleged chief ringleaders – against whom there was more than enough evidence to justify a trial if not to ensure a jury conviction – were granted a conditional discharge. In his capacity as supreme judge of the General Court, moreover, Lawrence went so far as to use the verdict against Hoffman, 'who stood convicted as the Author of all the disturbances at Lunenburg,' as the pretext for discharging all fifteen of the alleged ringleaders.

On the award of this collective 'pardon,' judicial proceedings arising from the 'Hoffman Rebellion' ceased. Bell remarks on the 'anomaly' of the ringleaders' being pardoned without having been tried much less convicted, whereas Hoffman was paroled and banished after having served six additional months beyond his custodial sentence.[42] Hoffman, whom the supreme judge presumed guilty of treason, though the jury found him guilty only of sedition, ended up as the lone accused, tried, and convicted, as well as the scapegoat for crimes allegedly committed by the ringleaders – who, in Lawrence's prejudication of the case, 'had been greatly deceived & misled by Mr. Hoffman' and were therefore somehow less guilty by reason of their association with the convicted seditionist. High treason admitted of no accessories, of course, only principals – but Hoffman had not been tried, much less convicted of treason. The unequal treatment accorded the ringleaders subsequent to Hoffman's conviction makes clear that in Hoffman's trial a gross miscarriage of justice had occurred. While Lawrence's reluctance to summon the remaining eleven presentees from Lunenburg is perhaps understandable, given the special circumstances of the infant settlement and the season of the year, his refusal to commit for trial the four who were already under arrest in Halifax arraigns him for bias against Hoffman.

This entire postlude, however, must be weighed in the balance of politically tense and strained relations between president and Council qua supreme judicial court, and the self-assertive grand jury qua judicial board of inquiry. The former was administering to the latter a quid pro quo for having had the effrontery to quash the first indictment against Hoffman, thus forcing the crown not only to reindict but also to downgrade the charge from treason to sedition. The supreme judge of the General Court, after all, viewed *Hoffman* as an exercise in high politics which dovetailed with his personal strategy for capturing the vacant lieutenant governorship. If the grand jury could take it upon themselves to thwart the government's intention to prosecute for treason, on statutory grounds of evidence, then the supreme judge could reject the grand jury's presentment of the chief ringleaders on purely non-legal grounds and abuse the pardon process to boot. The only person eligible to be considered for a pardon was Hoffman, who instead not only was denied a pardon but also suffered the arbitrary readjustment of his parole eligibility and was illegally detained in prison after his sentence had expired. In view of Hoffman's inability to pay his fine, the proper legal course would have been a civil suit by the crown under the exchequer equity jurisdiction of the Supreme Court. Yet this would have contradicted Lawrence's firm stance on penal sanctions: Hoffman could be tolerated only in jail or out of the jurisdiction. Indeed, Hoffman was perennially *persona non grata*; even after Lawrence had ceased to be supreme judge of the defunct General Court, he continued to view the convicted seditionist as an undesirable alien or political prisoner too dangerous to be set at liberty within the province. In fine, however, Hoffman was neither.

Crime and Punishment

'I shall endeavour,' wrote Lawrence to the Lords of Trade shortly after Hoffman was taken into custody, 'if any thing can be proved upon him, to bring him to condign Punishment.' The supreme judge's zeal for retributive justice was to be somewhat tempered by the jury verdict of misdemeanours, the punishment for which at common law was imprisonment and fine at the discretion of the court. Presumably a discretionary fine of £100 sterling above and beyond the customary two-year custodial sentence was as harsh a sanction as Lawrence dared impose. When Hoffman, whose business had been ruined by his long incarceration, found that he could not pay the fine, his two-year sentence was indefinitely extended and he became in effect a debtor to the crown. His frequent petitions to be pardoned were rejected by the Council, Lieutenant Governor Lawrence (as he became in October 1754) treating him as an outlaw. The Lords of Trade, however, were willing to approve a remission of sentence after one year, on condition that after his release the convict should depart the province never to return. Their proposal eventually stirred Lawrence to purposeful action, though he contrived to keep Hoffman in jail until he could be banished. A deal was ultimately struck whereby the convict would be paroled on condition that he leave the province as soon as possible and not return on pain of reincarceration. Lawrence, taking no chances, insisted on a substantial – £200 – bond in order to guarantee Hoffman's compliance.[43] He was free by October 1756, three months after Lawrence had achieved *his* overriding ambition – the governorship – and was gone from the province by March 1757.

Though the accused had been tried and convicted of the offence now known to the Criminal Code as seditious conspiracy, Lawrence was criticized by his New England political opponents for having confiscated Hoffman's lands and goods, as if he had been convicted of treason under English law and had thus forfeited his property rights. The truth of the matter was that Hoffman conveyed, mortgaged, or relinquished his Halifax properties under execution in favour of a judgment creditor.

A MILITARIZED JUDICIARY

Though *R. v. Hoffman* was not a court martial, two-thirds of the six judges were current or former serving army officers. The bench, in order of precedence, consisted of President/Colonel Lawrence (administrator, army commander, and supreme judge); Treasurer Benjamin Green; William Steele (brewer and merchant); John Collier (judge of the Court of Vice-Admiralty and former chief justice of the county court); Secretary William Cotterell (formerly acting and deputy provost-marshal); and Lieutenant-Colonel Monckton (deputy army commander). Monckton's presence was salutary, because he had been, however unsuccessfully, counselling Lawrence against sterner measures of 'legal retribution.'[44] As one of the members (Collier) was a judge in his own right and another (Green) a former judge of the Court of Vice-Admiralty, it cannot be said that the General Court was altogether lacking in wider experience of non-criminal justice (as distinguished from formal legal education, which was conspicuous by its total absence). Of the two civilians (Green and Steele), the former was the sole New Englander on the board.

LEGAL ASPECTS OF THE 'HOFFMAN REBELLION'

The legal proceedings consequent on the 'Insurrection of December 1753' make clear that the Halifax authorities supposed they were confronted with armed rebellion. Perhaps 'reading the Riot Act' to an unlawful assembly, who understood little if any English, availed nothing because the die was already cast. The question remains whether there was anything more to Hoffman's role than conspiracy or incitement; whether the doctrine of constructive treason applied to Hoffman, or to the 'Principal Actors & Abettors' who were arrested by the government and presented by the grand jury, though not tried at all, or to the disloyal militia who fired the first shots. Chief magistrate Sutherland possessed neither the resources nor the authority to declare martial law; Monckton possessed both the resources and the necessary delegated authority, but he chose not to do so. He had been ordered by government to proceed as far as possible in his civil capacity, having as a member of Council ex officio jurisdiction as a JP throughout the province.

The eighteenth-century British state was amply possessed of ordinary common-law and statutory powers to suppress riot and rebellion. Such powers as were held by the imperium were also exercised analogically by colonial governments, despite reservations expressed many years later by Beamish Murdoch: 'It was at one time [17—] proposed,' wrote Murdoch,[45] 'to send prisoners from the colonies to England to be tried for treason, alleged to have been committed in the colonies, under the supposed authority of the statutes referred to in 4 B[lackstone] C[ommentaries] 303,[46] but those acts cannot apply to a colony like Nova Scotia, possessing regular criminal courts.' The origin and circumstances of this proposal are not clear, but it does suggest the possibility of uncertainty as to whether the English act regulating treason trials was *in force* in Nova Scotia before 1758 regardless of its having demonstrably been *enforced* further to a criminal proceeding.[47] Criminal procedure, however, was not entirely a matter of the reception of English adjectival law, whether judge-made or statute; it was in the first instance, if anything, a quasi-reception of colonial Virginian statute law, which furnished the prototype for Nova Scotia's judicial system. Criminal procedure had also been recently reregulated by the royal instructions to Governor Hopson in May 1752.[48] It is clear from the marginalia to 'Belcher's Laws' [1767], moreover, that the treason statute of 1695/6 was in force locally, which leads one to suspect that what was law in Nova Scotia before the legislature met was retrospectively confirmed as law afterwards. Nova Scotia's first legislated criminal code, An Act Relating to Treasons and Felonies,[49] provided that 'such acts of parliament as direct[ed] the proceedings and evidence against [and] trials of ... traitors, shall have their full force and effect, and be observed as the rule in all trials for treason in this province.'[50] That was an omnibus local statutory enactment of English criminal procedure, which had hitherto extended at common law – the particular statute concerned being pre-settlement; it was both necessary and applicable and was therefore in force. Just as the legality of all judicial proceedings was retrospectively confirmed by statute, moreover, so too – by implication – were the English laws which had been enforced as the mechanism for administering criminal justice.

Bell is correct to describe the Hoffman trial as having been conducted 'according to the usage of English criminal procedure.' The process could hardly have been otherwise, given that both the king's attorney and the clerk of the General Court were Englishmen, and the latter an attorney of the Court of Common Pleas at Westminster Hall. Bell misunderstands the relationship between the two indictments, however, supposing that they were concurrent, when in fact there was only a second indictment preferred after the grand jury had returned the first endorsed 'Ignoramus.'[51] The government's response to the grand jury's exposure of a fatal defect in the treason indictment – the crown's failure to adhere to the two-witness rule – was to reindict the accused in a manner better suited to the available evidence. Furthermore, the supreme judge of the court, almost as a matter of routine, played an active role in directing the preparation of the crown's case, but this was typical of the administration of criminal justice in eighteenth-century colonial societies – even under a partly separate judicial branch, which Nova Scotia acquired later in 1754, and an independent non-political judiciary of lawyers, which developed much more slowly. Such high-level, executive interference in the crown case reflected the fact that government – especially when its own political interests or prestige were involved, as in a show trial such as *Hoffman* – had little confidence in the prosecutorial effectiveness of the crown attorneys, who were often inferior lawyers.[52]

Would Jonathan Belcher have conducted the Hoffman trial any differently? Jim Phillips[53] has argued that this New England expatriate, Ango-Irish barrister appears to have arrived in Nova Scotia carrying among his 'legal baggage' many of the values of the English judiciary (despite twelve years' practice at the Irish bar) – most notably a belief that the assertion of state power through the criminal law was a vital pillar of received social and political institutions. Yet even Belcher, as the province's first professional chief justice, was going to have to cope, sooner rather than later, with independently minded grand juries who flexed their muscles and declined to accept direction from the upper bench. They remembered the palmy days when defying the court, as they had done over the Hoffman treason indictment,[54] was the most effective means of protesting government policy. The editor of Chief Justice Belcher's famous first charge to the grand jury (Michaelmas Term, 1754) takes the view that the 'recent incident at Lunenburg, although it occurred before Belcher's arrival, must have had some influence [on the tone and substance of Belcher's first charge] ... Hoffman was still in jail in Halifax in the fall of 1754, and the insurrection was still fresh in the minds of those concerned with order and good government in the Province. The Lunenburg incident, however, served to sharpen a more serious and pressing anxiety relating to civil order – the problem of the Acadian French.'[55]

THE POLITICAL CHARACTER OF HOFFMAN'S TRIAL

'A certain thread of tradition,' writes Bell,[56] 'seems to have persisted at Halifax that there had been some injustice in connection with the Hoffman case.' The purveyors of this tradition were the ex-convict's New England sympathizers, who also happened to be Governor Lawrence's most articulate, vituperative political opponents and who wished to exploit the state trial for short-term political gain. No such tradition persisted among the foreign Protestants at Lunenburg, because Hoffman disappeared from there without a trace, having been only a sojourner, not a settler proper. In Halifax, however, the situation was different. The sedition trial understandably aroused intense feeling among the New England expatriate community, because the defendant – like his rival Zouberbuhler – had business associates among them. As late as June 1757, nearly a year after the prisoner had been released, no less a figure than New Englander Joshua Winslow, commissary-general to the British army in Nova Scotia, was sending to A.F. Phillips, the Boston merchant who had purchased Hoffman's interest in a valuable Halifax property, a copy of the official record of the trial.[57] Three months earlier, former defence counsel Joseph Kent had sworn out an affidavit[58] in which he exaggeratedly accused then Governor Lawrence of having shown gross partiality against Hoffman by directing the king's attorney to prosecute personally, 'lest he should be found not Guilty.' Kent, though by no means a disinterested witness, cast his client more as a scapegoat and victim of Lawrence's personal vindictiveness than as the subject of a legitimate public prosecution.

After Kent came Robert Sanderson, a Boston *émigré* merchant who served as first speaker (1758–9) of the House of Assembly. Sanderson's 'enormously long' memorial, presented to the Lords of Trade three months after Lawrence's premature and unexpected death in October 1760, consisted of twenty-one grievances against the late governor, the first and most substantial of which concerned his alleged victimization of J.W. Hoffman.[59] Among the New England mercantile clique, Sanderson[60] epitomized Lawrence's most implacable opposition, which had become yet more extreme after the assembly was finally convoked and the governor's political enemies assumed a leading role in the management of its affairs. Having achieved their aim of representative government, the New England cabal revamped and broadened their agenda to include ridding themselves of the autocratic soldier-governor.

What Hoffman and the Massachusetts mercantile clique for whom he 'fronted' and who sprang to his defence may have wanted to introduce at Lunenburg was the town meeting form of local government, with Hoffman as moderator and the insurrectionist deputies as selectmen. Bell perhaps goes rather too far in describing this group as 'the extreme New England republican wing of the local opposition to Lawrence's government.'[61] He writes:

While one should doubtless beware of reading too much into Hoffman's activities at the time of the insurrection, he appears clearly to have had pretty close associations with some of the more radical New England element at Halifax; and it is perhaps not altogether unlikely that he had in mind some idea of bringing about a replacement of the officially appointed magistrates by leaders chosen by the settlers themselves, himself the chief one. Note, for example, the role played at that time by the elected 'people's deputies.'[62]

Is it possible that what Hoffman was preconcerting at Lunenburg in November–December 1753 was a microcosmic *coup d'état*, which resulted in a state of apprehended insurrection? All that is certain is 'that after Hoffman was removed from Lunenburg the settlement never again ... showed any tendency toward such mutinous activity as it had shown ... in December of 1753.'[63] Though the insurrection *tout court* must be considered to have been an ignominious failure, the political significance of the 'Hoffman Rebellion' lies in the fact that it was an escalation of what D.C. Harvey characterized as 'the struggle for the New England form of township government in Nova Scotia' – a struggle from which Governor Lawrence and Halifax rule emerged victorious.[64] Yet it was the trial (Bell's 'upshot'), not the rebellion, that was to have the more serious political implications and long-term effects.

'Hoffman's Trial,' as it early on became known in New England Planter demonology, furnished ammunition to use against the governor, allowing him to be depicted as a military dictator and tyrant. It was still being cited in polemical pamphlet literature on the eve of the American revolution as an example of oppression – twenty years after it had taken place. Writing in 1774 under an innocuous *nom de plume*, New Englander John Day, the non-partisan (and nonpareil) leader of the 'progressive conservatives' in the House of Assembly, instanced the Hoffman trial as a bad consequence of the confused, para-constitutional system which had prevailed during the decade of pre-representative government (1749–58), when the powers of the legislative and judicial branches were effectively combined and concentrated in the executive branch.[65] Though

the laws of *England* were referred to in Matters relating to Property or Trial for Offences, it [the Form of Government] was in Fact an undigested synthetic System of civil and military Laws and Regulations, which often betrayed Government into Measures that might be esteem'd arbitrary, without their intending it.[66] But *except in one Instance* [italics added], I could never find, that during this Period [1749–58], any Act of Oppression was really committed. The several Governors, *Cornwallis, Hopson,* and *Lawrence,* were Men of great Humanity and Disinterested-ness.[67]

Whatever the political reasons for the development among Nova Scotia's New Englanders of a mythology of 'Hoffman's Trial,' it is clear that the aspiring historian Dr Andrew Brown, who was collecting materials for his projected history of the province while several of the ringleaders of the insurrection were still alive, 'seems to have had no doubt of Hoffman's culpability, and attributed it to his resentment of Sebastian Zouberbuhler.'[68] The latter, who played no role at all among the foreign Protestant immigrants until after Hoffman's removal as JP, had, of course, a similar immigrant background. Zouberbuhler nevertheless demonstrated superior discretion as well as better political judgment and *savoir faire* in dealing with the powers that be in Halifax. Hoffman resisted central government authority and had a 'brief and stormy career in Nova Scotia,'[69] while Zouberbuhler collaborated and was rewarded with rapid promotion through the ranks of officialdom – crowning his considerable achievement with appointment to the Council in 1763. If history is the view that prevails, then the ultimate victors were Zouberbuhler and the Halifax oligarchs, whose ranks he eventually joined – not Hoffman and his fellow-travelling New England republicans. They were shortly to have as administrator of the government and then lieutenant governor of the province a chief executive more arbitrary and oppressive than the prematurely dead Colonel Lawrence could ever have been imagined to be – their high Tory compatriot, Chief Justice Belcher.

By then the Council had long since ceased to be a court of first instance, except in equity (until 1764). Nevertheless, the chief justice had by the force of destiny become head of government as well as of the Supreme Court, uniting in himself the chief judicial and executive authority. Such had been the *status quo ante* 1754, though at least in that period the 'supreme judge' had been the president of a tribunal rather than sole judge. 'The Humiliation of Jonathan Belcher,' as John Bartlet Brebner christened his disastrous, two-year lieutenant governorship in a memorable chapter in *The Neutral Yankees of Nova Scotia*, led in September 1763 to a generic amendment to the royal instructions to colonial governors which barred chief justices from ever assuming the government of the colony in the event of a vacancy. While it was constitutionally feasible for the administrator, as *primus inter pares* of a collective judiciary, to preside in the high court of justice *before* the introduction of representative government, it proved impossible for the chief justice, as ex officio president of the Council, to act as administrator *after* the introduction of representative government. Once the principle of the separation of powers had been put into operation, the clock could not be turned back to a time when the same powers were, for all practical purposes, undifferentiated.

NOTES

1 See F.M. Greenwood, 'The Treason Trial and Execution of David McLane,' *Manitoba Law Journal*, vol. 20 (1991), 3, the structure of which has been adapted as a model for this analysis of the sedition trial and imprisonment of John William Hoffman. For Murdoch's statement regarding treason trials, see his *An Epitome of the Laws of Nova-Scotia*, 4 vols. (Halifax: 1832–3), 4:126. Murdoch did not know of any instances of trials for sedition, of which there were at least four between 1754 and 1820. Ironically, less than two years after publication of the final volume of the *Epitome*, Murdoch was to be present at the sedition trial of the newspaper editor and job printer who had published it – Joseph Howe;

see the author's essay elsewhere in this volume. Though willing to serve as an amicus curiae, Murdoch forbore defending his then friend Howe against a charge of seditious libel.

2 *R. v. Hoffman* (Gen. Ct. 1754). The principal account of the Christmas rising is to be found in W.P. Bell, *The "Foreign Protestants" and the Settlement of Nova Scotia: The History of a Piece of Arrested British Colonial Policy in the Eighteenth Century* (Fredericton: Acadiensis Press; Sackville: Mount Allison University 1990 [repr. of 1961 ed.]), at 450: (s.63) 'The Insurrection of December 1753 and the Hoffman Trial.' See also Beamish Murdoch, *A History of Nova-Scotia, or Acadie,* 3 vols. (Halifax: James Barnes 1866), 2: at 227–30; Bell's account closely follows Murdoch's, which nevertheless he does not acknowledge.

3 See the essay by Ernest Clarke and Jim Phillips elsewhere in this volume. (I am grateful to Dr Phillips for allowing me to peruse his and Mr Clarke's chapter in manuscript.)

4 It is twice mentioned by Barry Wright in his ground-breaking article 'Sedition in Upper Canada: Contested Legality,' *Labour/Le Travail,* vol. 29 (1992), 7 at 18 and 21.

5 *Journal and Letters of Colonel Charles Lawrence : Being a Day by Day Account of the Founding of Lunenburg, by the Officer in Command of the Project, Transcribed from the Brown Manuscripts in the British Museum,* ed. D.C. Harvey (Halifax: Public Archives of Nova Scotia 1953), at 10, 24.

6 *Planters and Pioneers: Nova Scotia, 1749 to 1775,* rev. ed., comp. E.C. Wright (Hantsport, N.S.: Lancelot Press 1982), at 162, s.v.

7 Hoffman's pre-insurrection career is conveniently traceable in Bell, *"Foreign Protestants",* at 210, 210n., 306n., 307n., 357–9, 362–3n., 365n., 412, 422, 443n., 463. His complicated and obviously not very successful business activities can be reconstructed from the Halifax County Deeds, mfm., book 2, at 129 (#82), 169 (#175), 170 (#178), 224 (#97), and 254 (#151), PANS; and from the records of the county court/Inferior Court of Common Pleas, in which he was frequently impleaded for debt: RG 37 (HX), box A, vol. 1, PANS.

8 Cornwallis to Lords of Trade, 3 Nov. 1751: CO 217/13/36r, at 38r–39v, PRO.

9 Bell, *"Foreign Protestants,"* at 362–3n., summarizing a documentary source.

10 Bell's argument here is persuasive. See ibid., at 210–1.

11 See J.P. Martin, *The Story of Dartmouth* (Dartmouth N.S.: the author 1957), at 34–5.

12 Quoted in Bell, *"Foreign Protestants,"* at 365. 'The manner of this plea for Hoffman's reinstatement,' writes Bell (ibid., n.7), 'can suggest that he had a hand in the drafting of the memorial. The reference to the act of Parliament, too, might be more apt to come from the disgruntled ex-JP than from other immigrants.'

13 A.A. MacKenzie, 'Zouberbuhler, Sebastian,' *DCB* 4: 780. Bell, *"Foreign Protes-*

tants" (467–8), following the late-eighteenth-century Scottish historian Andrew Brown, attributes the genesis of the affair to the rivalry and resentment between Hoffman and Zouberbuhler, who was to resist successfully all attempts by the insurrectionists to dragoon, implicate, or scapegoat him.

14 Bell, "*Foreign Protestants,*" at 459n.9.

15 Sutherland was an army captain on half-pay who also held the posts of lieutenant-colonel of the militia and local army commander: C.B. Fergusson, 'Sutherland, Patrick,' *DCB* 3: 604.

16 Bell, "*Foreign Protestants,*" at 451.

17 There were twelve *Deputierten*, two for each of the six divisions of the town. 'The partition of the town into six 'divisions' not only served for identification of lots, but was used in the early days of the settlement as a principle of organization for musters of the settlers, and for other supervisory purposes': Bell, "*Foreign Protestants,*" at 427. It could also have been used for subversive purposes, for example, in order to organize an insurrection. Who better than Hoffman to have preconcerted it? – right under the nose of Major Rudolf, in whose division of the town he resided.

18 Ibid., at 460.

19 Council minutes; quoted in ibid.

20 This was the other 'and more isolated prison' to which Bell refers in ibid., at 466. It is clear that Lawrence's intention in removing Hoffman from the common jail to the military prison was to prevent his intimidating or suborning the chief crown witness, Petrequin. Bell suggests that the tactic worked: 'At the trial he [Petrequin] certainly stuck to his story about Hoffman' (ibid.).

21 Ibid., at 462.

22 On Major Rudolf's acting as an emissary from the insurrectionists to Colonel Sutherland, see ibid., at 456 (including n.13). It is possible that Rudolf's dissimulation was prompted by the fact that both Captain Hoffman and Caspar Schauffelberger, the alleged chief ringleader whose name was later to head the list of grand jury presentees, resided in Rudolf's division of the town.

23 Concerning Wendel Wüst, see T.M. Punch, 'The Wests of Halifax and Lunenburg,' in *Nova Scotia Historical Quarterly*, vol. 6 (1976), 69 at 70.

24 Petrequin was Hoffman's denouncer: R. Rompkey, 'Pettrequin (Petrequin), Jean,' *DCB* 3: 513.

25 Ibid. Bell, in contrast, states: 'It was, indeed, a weak feature of the Crown's case that it had no testimony except Petrequin's for Hoffman's reading of the purported letter at all': "*Foreign Protestants,*" at 463. The issue, of course, as will be seen, was not merely the factual one of the credibility of Petrequin's evidence but the legal one of the number of witnesses to the same overt treasonable act.

26 (1695/6) 7 and 8 Wm. III, c. 3. For a discussion of this act, see the introduction to this volume.

27 It must be borne in mind that as many as four of the prospective defence witnesses were already in Halifax, having been brought up with Hoffman in January 1754.

28 Nesbitt's oath (drafted by Suckling) placed less emphasis on the prosecutorial than on the solicitorial function of the office: 'fform [sic] of the Oath to be / taken by the Kings Att° / 25th April 1753 / Wm Nesbitt Esqr Sworn / Kings Att° in Open Court': RG 39, 'C' (HX), box 1, file 75(i)a, PANS.

29 The best account of Suckling's Nova Scotia career is J.B. Brebner, *New England's Outpost: Acadia before the Conquest of Canada* (Hamden, Conn.: Archon Books 1965 [repr.]), at 269–70.

30 The other was *R. v. Hovey et al.* (SCNS 1754), for murder; see J. Phillips, '"Securing Obedience to Necessary Laws": The Criminal Law in Eighteenth-Century Nova Scotia,' in *Nova Scotia Historical Review*, vol. 12, no. 2 (1992), 87.

31 Fully seven members of the grand jury originally drawn for the year 1754 were also to sit in the first assembly in 1758. (When the Supreme Court was established under Chief Justice Jonathan Belcher later in 1754, a new grand jury was summoned.)

32 One of the grand jurors, Malachy Salter (1715/16–81), was to be once tried and twice indicted for sedition during the American revolution: RG 1, vol. 342, docs. 77–80, 82–5, PANS. Unlike Hoffman – though for different reasons – Salter was not formally indicted on a charge of high treason.

33 Bell, *"Foreign Protestants,"* at 662, 668.

34 Ibid., at 433n., 467–8.

35 Among the signatories were prominent anglophile foreign Protestants, Zouberbuhler and Isaac Deschamps; also among them were two English attorneys, Daniel Wood and William Nesbitt. The latter, within three months, was to replace New Englander Otis Little as king's attorney: T.B. Akins, 'History of Halifax City,' in the Nova Scotia Historical Society, *Collections*, vol. 8 (1895), at 38–9.

36 Bell, *"Foreign Protestants,"* at 461n.25, which paraphrases Lawrence's dispatch to the Lords of Trade describing Hoffman's trial.

37 This conclusion is borne out by the penal sanction, which lay entirely within the court's discretion, and answers the difficulty which Bell had about finding any 'intimation of the court's basis for fixing the particular amounts of fine and imprisonment in the sentence on Hoffman': ibid., at 464n.32.

38 From Michaelmas Term 1754, the Council's judicial powers were residually exercised as a court of chancery and a court of error and civil appeal; there was

little to choose between the equitable jurisdiction, such as it was before the superior court reforms of 1764, and the appellate civil jurisdiction, which was shared with the new Supreme Court.

39 Bell, *"Foreign Protestants,"* at 460. The only other criminal court, the Quarter Sessions, had but summary or inferior jurisdiction and could not try felonies.

40 This is the only appearance of the allegation that Hoffman attempted to intimidate the chief crown witness.

41 'Colonel Monckton called him [Hoffman] Scoundrel & Villain; To which M.ʳ Hoffman replyed that he was no more a Scoundrel or Villain than himself.' Hoffman may have gone even farther: the second, effective indictment alleged him to have stated publicly that 'the Governor of Halifax [Lawrence] & the Governor of Lunenburg [Sutherland] were both rogues & both drank out of one Cup.'

42 'I fancy there was so little question that these men had been ringleaders in the insurrection that the irregularity could pass unnoticed': Bell, *"Foreign Protestants,"* at 464n.32. On pardons generally during the colonial period, see Jim Phillips, 'The Operation of the Royal Pardon in Nova Scotia, 1749–1815,' in *University of Toronto Law Journal*, vol. 42 (1992), 401.

43 The bond executed in favour of the provost-marshal is not extant; knowledge of its content depends on highly coloured statements made by Joseph Kent, Hoffman's attorney, as well as one of his two sureties.

44 I.K. Steele, 'Monckton, Robert,' *DCB* 4: 540. Monckton seems to have advocated a general amnesty and to have opposed legal proceedings of any kind being taken against the insurrectionists. But Lawrence nevertheless inferred from Monckton's own account that Hoffman would inevitably be convicted as an 'Instigator': Lawrence to Monckton, 30 Dec. 1753 [copy], RG 1, vol. 134, 34 at 40 (inland letter-book), PANS.

45 Murdoch, *Epitome*, 4: 178.

46 Chiefly the Treason Trials Regulation Act.

47 I owe this distinction to Jim Phillips ('"Securing Obedience,"' passim), who argues that all English criminal procedure was in force in Nova Scotia. See Phillips, 'Royal Pardon,' at 405n.43 ('English criminal law and procedure was fully introduced to Nova Scotia in 1749') and 411 ('In May 1749, with the founding of Halifax, the colony of Nova Scotia received the full panoply of contemporary English criminal law and procedure'). On the reception of the criminal law of England, see the introduction to this volume.

48 Both documents are conveniently reproduced in C.J. Townshend, *Historical Account of the Courts of Judicature in Nova Scotia* (Toronto: Carswell 1900), at 19ff.

49 (1758) 32 Geo. II, c. 13, s. 1 (N.S.).

50 *The Perpetual Acts of the General Assemblies of His Majesty's Province of Nova Scotia*, comp. J. Duport (Halifax: Robert Fletcher 1767), at 29.

51 Bell, *"Foreign Protestants,"* at 460–1. Procedure in sedition prosecutions was not statutorily prescribed, in contrast to treason prosecutions. Wright ("Sedition in Upper Canada," at 14) might well have been referring to *Hoffman* when he states, 'No such defence [truth] was available to the defendant charged with sedition.'

52 Nesbitt, for example, a clerk and notary by profession – he was Nova Scotia's first commissioned notary public – had been appointed king's attorney in April 1753.

53 Phillips, '"Securing Obedience,"' 106ff.

54 The grand jury would do so again two years later in R. v. *Young*, for statutory high treason: Phillips, '"Securing Obedience,"' at 98–9.

55 T.B. Vincent, 'Jonathan Belcher: Charge to the Grand Jury, Michaelmas Term, 1754,' in *Acadiensis*, vol. 7, no. 1 (1977), 103 at 104. Vincent was the first to identify Hoffman as 'the scapegoat of the affair.'

56 Bell, *"Foreign Protestants,"* at 464.

57 [Boston Public Library], *Canadian Manuscripts in the Boston Public Library. A Descriptive Catalog* (Boston, Mass.: G.K. Hall 1971), at 19 (s.205). Winslow may have replaced Hoffman as Phillips's Halifax agent.

58 See Brebner, *New England's Outpost*, at 255–7. Kent's affidavit comprised the fifth of five specific complaints against Governor Lawrence which were enclosed in a statement of grievances from the freeholders of Halifax, presented to the Lords of Trade in January 1758.

59 Bell, *"Foreign Protestants,"* at 362n.16a.

60 Concerning Sanderson, see Brebner, *New England's Outpost*, at 256–7 and *passim*.

61 Bell, *"Foreign Protestants,"* at 465.

62 Ibid., at 543n.34.

63 Ibid., at 468.

64 Harvey, on the other hand, did not undertake 'to discuss ... the New England influence on the struggle for representative government in Nova Scotia': D.C. Harvey, 'The Struggle for the New England Form of Township Government in Nova Scotia,' in the Canadian Historical Association *Annual Report*, 1933, 15 at 16.

65 'A Member of Assembly' [pseud.], *An Essay on the Present State of the Province of Nova-Scotia, With Some Strictures on the Measures Pursued by Government from Its First Settlement by the English in the Year, 1749* ([Halifax: Anthony Henry 1774]).

66 An asterisked footnote at this point in Day's account read, *'Hoffman's Trial.'*

Whether the note was intended to accompany what precedes or what follows is left a little ambiguous by the syntax and may affect exegesis of the passage.

67 Ibid., at 6–7. Bell (*"Foreign Protestants,"* at 464–5) cites this passage as further evidence 'for the fact that there did persist at Halifax talk to the effect that there had been something unfair about the Hoffman case.'

68 Ibid., at 466 (including n.35).

69 Ibid., at 210.

3

'Twelve Apostles' or a Dozen Traitors? Acadian Collaborators during King George's War, 1744–8*

THOMAS GARDEN BARNES

A decade ago, Antonine Maillet instructed a university audience at Berkeley, California, in how Québécois might be distinguished from Acadians: while closely resembling each other, the Québécois defends himself by claw and fang like the wolf, whereas the Acadian seeks protection in speed and cunning like the fox. There is merit in the analogy, quite beyond the inimitable witness of the poet-scholar who has given a consummately literary voice to *Acadie*. It has observational authenticity in the Acadians' fidelity to *survivance* as a primary cultural value as contrasted with the unforgetting and unforgiving *souvenance* which has long undergirded Québécois cultural, and latterly political, identity.[1] So strong has been the Acadians' sense of *survivance* that it has almost entirely suppressed other themes in the oral tradition as well as in Acadian literature, achieving apotheosis in Maillet's brilliant *Pélagie-la-Charette*, appropriately titled in its English translation *Return to the Homeland*. The oral tradition of Acadians everywhere erected the community's cultural cohesiveness on the unflagging resiliency of 'a generation of survivors. Survivors of life in the wilderness, survivors of exile, survivors of History,' as Maillet puts it.[2]

Survival emphasized forbearance not bitterness, aspiration rather than

* I am grateful to Barry Moody for the use of his notes on Paul Mascarane, which have provided me with much guidance to the documents that form the basis of this essay. All dates are Old Style, unless otherwise indicated.

reflection, and a certain present elation that banished past grief.[3] These qualities were raised on irenic, or at least unbellicose, sentiments that pre-dated the conquest of 1710–13 and enabled the Acadians afterwards to prosper and multiply as 'King George's neutral subjects.'[4] If such sentiments were unheroic, passive, neutralist, dependent on weapons of the spirit more than on musket and cannon, they enabled the fox to run and to dodge, and so survive. Should the fox step out of character to play the wolf he courted destruction. While the Annapolis Royal regime had but one 'division' – the 40th Foot – the Acadians had none.

Unlike the wolf, the fox is not a beast ennobled by courageous ferocity. So the Acadians have suffered twice over, at the hands of those who victimized them in the expulsion of 1755 and by historians who have taxed them with cravenness in not putting up even a show of resistance. One consequence has been a pronounced effort of late to find genuine heroes of resistance among the Acadians during the four unsuccessful invasions of Nova Scotia by their Canadian and French co-religionists in the years 1744–7. While the search has been extensive and keen, carried on by francophone scholars and vulgarizers on both sides of the Atlantic, the results have been scant. Despite extravagant predictions by the French commanders of all four failed military expeditions of King George's War (known in Europe as the War of the Austrian Succession) that the Acadians would rise up en masse given a sufficient show of force from Canada, only a dozen Acadians were prominent enough in their display of disaffection to invite demonstrably punitive action against them by the British authorities in Annapolis Royal. Those twelve, 'Les douze Apôtres de la cause Acadienne,' as a recent French popular historian, Robert Sauvageau, has termed them, were by his unsubstantiated reckoning singled out disproportionately for punishment, there having been 'a thousand Acadians who had compromised themselves with the French troops.'[5] Sauvageau's legion is quite hyperbolic, though there is evidence that more than merely the most obvious dozen Acadians were in some degree compromised by aid to the French. No matter how many 'Apostles' or traitors, however, there were only twelve tangible heroes.

THE ACADIANS ON THE EVE OF WAR

Few knew better than the Acadian 'ancients,' the elders of the four major Acadian communities along the Bay of Fundy – at the Annapolis River, Minas (comprising Grand Pré, River Canard, and Piziquid), Cobequid, and Chignecto – how little could or would be done by their people in support of French military activity in Nova Scotia. And none appreciated more than Major Paul Mascarene, president of the Council at Annapolis Royal and surrogate governor of Nova Scotia from 1739 to 1749, both the physical difficulties facing resistance and the communal restraints on those who wished to abandon the neutralism that had become statecraft with the Acadians. Mascarene admired the Acadians' sophisticated political temperament and preserved an almost unwavering confidence in their irenic good sense to avoid hostile acts in collaboration with French forces when war broke out between the two imperial powers. He was also the principal architect and latterly the astute and assiduous builder of a loosely structured polity which enabled less than a dozen British administrators, a handful of New England merchants, and a few score aging, often ill, always plaintive soldiers, at the ruinous fort at Annapolis Royal – who readily confessed that their power carried no farther than a cannon shot beyond the glacis – to oversee an Acadian population grown from 2000 to 10,000 in the three decades since the 1713 treaty.

To oversee, never quite to govern, for the Acadians exercised considerable autonomy in ruling themselves. Beyond the provision of judicature for the Acadians, almost wholly in civil litigation and that according to Acadian legal custom and only when the Acadians' internal machinery for dispute resolution could not cope sufficiently with problems, the routine relationship of the Acadians with the regime was largely economic and contractual and the extraordinary and political relationship virtually a matter of negotiation and treaty between the 'deputies' representing the communities and the Council.[6] So easy rested the yoke of British governance that the Acadians had few concrete grievances to direct against the regime. Beyond occasional friction over the choice and the activities of priests (Mascarene, born in the Languedoc of Huguenot parents and speaking an impeccable classical French, was adept at mollifying such) and a residual fear that the demand for an unconditional oath of allegiance might arise again (it had not since 1730), the prospect of any deeply divisive internal problems was slight. Moreover, the old men of the communities, enjoying the benign conditions of life which obtained by the mid-1740s, had more grounds for satisfaction than for complaint. Mascarene's policy was to that end, as he wrote Whitehall in 1740: 'Since I have had the honor to preside here, my study has been to make these French Inhabitants sensible of the difference there is between British and French Government, by administering impartial justice to them and in all other respects treating them with lenity and humanity, without yielding anything wherein His Majesty's honor or interest were concerned.'[7]

By 1744 the vast majority of Acadians (their fecundity contributing to the size of the majority) had come of age since the conquest of 1710 and had never known any other authority than the British one at Annapolis Royal. If an invasion, sufficiently strong to overcome the disadvantage of their relative impotency in the face of such power as the Annapolis Royal regime managed, was to persuade the Acadians to arise and throw off the British yoke, they would have to be motivated more by a remarkably deep, nostalgic, affection for roots, faith, and tongue than by any present dissatisfaction. Even then, a cold scepticism argued for reassurance that the French would be successful before the Acadians cast their lot with them. They were well aware of the old proverb, *Il ne faut pas chanter triomphe avant la victoire* (One must not hymn triumph before the victory).

THE FIRST THREE ATTACKS

The initial French attack after King George's War began with formal declarations of hostilities in March 1744 demonstrated French military weakness and dashed overly sanguine French expectations of Acadian revolt. The incendiary Spiritan missionary to the Micmacs, Abbé Jean-Louis Le Loutre, more warrior than confessor and no martyr, led some 250 Micmacs and Malecites against Annapolis Royal on 1 July. An attempt to mount siege turned into cattle stealing, and with the arrival at the fort of a small company of reinforcements from Boston, the shepherd took his lambs to Minas to await a major attempt coming from Louisbourg. Le Loutre's premature sortie cost the new expedition the element of surprise. The fact that apparently no Acadians were involved in Le Loutre's undertaking constituted an at least modest moral victory for the British.

The second attempt came after a hard march from Baie Verte via Minas to Annapolis, by a force of Canadien militiamen, Indians (this time wrangled by Abbé Pierre Maillard, Le Loutre having found it impossible to rally his lambs for a second try), and a few regulars, less than 300 in all, commanded by François Du Pont Duvivier. They arrived fatigued within a couple of miles of the fort, on 28 August, and Duvivier established his headquarters at Bellair, the commodious house and estate of Nicolas Gautier *dit* 'Bellair,' about two miles south of the fort. Duvivier moved his main force northward to within 1.25 miles of the fort to besiege it by a loose surround and noisy night patrols. The results were risible. Mascarene held fast, refused to surrender, and poured fire into the French positions, forcing Duvivier to move back nearer Bellair. After a handful of

Gorham's Rangers arrived from Boston on 26 September, Mascarene counter-attacked and the French withdrew to Minas.

Mascarene was too modest in failing to emphasize how far his own courage, leadership, and vigorous defence had contributed to beating off both attempts when he informed the Lords of Trade, 'To the Breaking the French measures; the timely Succours receiv'd from the Governor of Massachusetts [William Shirley], and our French Inhabitants refusing to take up arms against us, we owe our preservation ... if the Inhabitants had taken up arms they might have brought three or four thousand men against us.'[8] This handsome compliment, not at all disingenuous, was merely a statement of fact. It is not clear that any Acadians had borne arms against the British. Some, however, had been much less than dutiful subjects. Two Minas habitants, Armand Bigeau and Joseph Le Blanc *dit* 'Le Maigre,' had traded with Louisbourg and assisted the supplying of Duvivier's forces by sea. It is also clear from Duvivier's journal (of which Mascarene was ignorant) that both had not only helped transport Duvivier's force from Louisbourg to Baie Verte but had accompanied the expedition to Annapolis Royal and had served as scouts and couriers.[9] Upon being interrogated by the Council, Bigeau denied categorically that he had borne arms, and no evidence contradicted him. 'Le Maigre' denied having served the French actively during the siege by a bold, albeit unconvincing, confession and avoidance: Duvivier had made him return to Louisbourg and he feared 'ill consequences' if he disobeyed Duvivier.[10] The most serious offender appears to have been Nicolas Gautier *dit* 'Bellair,' proprietor of the estate of that name, major entrepreneur, shipowner, farmer, and merchant, who had welcomed Duvivier and placed his estate at his disposal as the 'French camp' overlooking Annapolis Royal.[11] Having lent his name and considerable influence to the French cause, giving it full and unalloyed support even after it had clearly failed, he stood in the gravest danger. Bigeau, 'Le Maigre,' and 'Bellair,' the most prominent of the *Douze Apôtres*, would in due course suffer the heaviest pains at the British regime's disposal.

As soon as Duvivier departed, the Acadian deputies from the Annapolis River came before the Council and vehemently denounced the coercion visited upon them by Duvivier and the threat from Le Loutre's Indian charges. Duvivier had been especially bullying, issuing written orders and requisitions upon the habitants at Minas and the river under threat of corporal punishment or death. Even a sceptic might credit 'Le Maigre's' fear of 'ill consequences' from Duvivier's order to him to go to Louisbourg 'sous peine a luy Refusant d'obeir au present ordre d'estre Livrez a la discretion des Sauvages pour y estre punie de mort.'[12] The Minas deputies asserted that they had persuaded Duvivier to continue his retreat to Chignecto. The missionaries to the Acadians convinced Mascarene that they had repudiated Le Loutre's threats to loose his Micmacs.

The third French attempt, a minor expedition of Canadiens and Indians led by Paul Marin de La Malgue, arrived in the vicinity of the fort in April 1745. They did nothing more menacing than prowling in the woods. If less of a threat to the British than Duvivier, Marin was a great deal more so to the Acadians, whom he roundly abused. Mascarene termed Marin's force 'banditti,' and Marin's subsequent career in New York and Pennsylvania during the Seven Years' War, when his name became a byword for fanaticism towards his own people and cruelty towards the enemy, indicates that the Acadians' fear of him was not exaggerated.[13] Certainly some of the allegations of collaboration brought against a number of the Acadian habitants can be put down simply to actions growing from Marin's menaces. But at least two of the Twelve Apostles, and the wife of the most prominent of them all, were caught assisting him. A sweep after Marin's retreat netted nine habitants, including 'Bellair's' wife, son Pierre Gautier, and Charles Raymond. There was sufficient evidence to hold the Gautiers, *mere et fils*, and Charles Raymond.[14] The rest appear to have been released.

RAMEZAY'S EXPEDITION

The fourth and final attempt, extending over the fall of 1746 into the winter of 1747, under Jean-Baptiste-Nicolas-Roch de Ramezay, was trite in strategic conception but brilliant in tactical execution. After briefly trying a surround without siege of Annapolis Royal in September 1746 while awaiting seaborne troops from France which never arrived, Ramezay and his troops from Quebec wintered over at Chignecto. That isthmus, connecting present-day New Brunswick to Nova Scotia, was effectively beyond the exercise of British power and it had a sizable new population of 'frontier' Acadians who had moved as far from British authority as they could and still remain in Old Acadia. More resonant to the historic appeal of roots, faith, and tongue than other habitants, they were susceptible to Ramezay's assiduous courtship of them. To the British, his was a persistent threat in the way none of the other three expeditions had been, for Ramezay did not merely hit and run. Governor William Shirley of Massachusetts, who in the face of the French threat posed by the war had become the protector if not guarantor of the Annapolis Royal regime and British dominion in Nova Scotia, overrode Mascarene's reluctance to undertake an offensive-defence by stationing troops at Minas. Five hundred fresh but raw Massachusetts troops, commanded by Colonel Arthur Noble, were quartered on the habitants at Grand Pré (Minas) to discourage intercourse with the French and provide an advanced picket against overland invasion. Without a blockhouse or even a palisade, dispersed among twenty-four Acadian households extending over one and one-half miles, the unblooded Yankees were an irresistable target. After a long forced and furtive march in deep snow, 300 of Ramezay's men under Nicolas-Antoine Coulon de Villiers fell upon the sleeping New Englanders in a roaring blizzard at 3 a.m. on 31 January 1747. Though the habitants had warned Noble of the danger and themselves abandoned their houses to avoid a fight, the Yankees convinced themselves that winter's rigours were sufficient safeguard, failing to credit how hardy Canadiens were in the most severe conditions. Surprise was complete. Five officers, including Noble, perished along with seventy other ranks. Though the survivors fought until mid-morning, they were forced to yield. Accorded the honours of war, they made a humiliating march to Annapolis Royal under parole guided by Acadian conductors to show them the way.[15] The 'Massacre at Grand Pré' was a signal French triumph of arms worked by boldness, leadership, tenacity, and bravery. But it was militarily inconsequential because Ramezay had too few troops, all of them much worn and fatigued, to attempt again to take Annapolis Royal. He withdrew to Chignecto, thence to Quebec.

Ramezay's expedition was the most serious French attempt of the war, not only by virtue of its bold execution and remarkable tactical success, but because it had elicited more support from the Acadians, enjoyed more of their collaboration, than the other enterprises. Ramezay cultivated Acadians along his line of march with the same care he had shown in recruiting the Chignecto frontiersmen, claiming to have enlisted twenty-five Acadians from Piziquid to Grand Pré ready to bear arms.[16] While there is no other evidence as to that number or whether in fact any habitants bore arms, it was certainly local intelligence that had pinpointed Noble's billets with stunning accuracy. Moreover, French fleet movements in Nova Scotia waters before the massacre enjoyed the help of Acadian pilots, among them the Apostles Nicolas Gautier dit 'Bellair,' his two sons Joseph and Pierre, and Pierre Guidry dit 'Grivois.' Mascarene in August 1746 noted (without naming them) that four pilots and four other habitants – eight more Apostles – had joined the 'enemy' at Minas before Ramezay attacked

Annapolis Royal.[17] These would have included Armand Bigeau and 'Le Maigre.' Of the lot, the most vigorous and dangerous was a forty-five-year-old *mauvais-garçon du village*, Joseph Broussard *dit* 'Beausoleil,' the Acadian hero of the 1750s and afterwards in Spanish Louisiana, where he lies yet in the heart of the Cajuns' Acadiana.[18]

COLLABORATION INVESTIGATED

Mascarene lost no time investigating the extent of collaboration and the damage done by it. Major Edward How, a long-time and capable member of the Council who had attended Noble as civilian commissary at Grand Pré, gathered much information. By late summer 1747, the Twelve Apostles had been identified as the major collaborators, some of them for delicts committed only during Ramezay's sortie, others for activities going back to Duvivier's time. Their crimes were compounded by their flight and refusal to be interrogated. All twelve were in effect, albeit not technically at law, outlawed by a proclamation originating with Governor Shirley of Massachusetts (who saw to its printing) and promulgated by the Council at Annapolis Royal, dated 28 October 1747. A reward of £50 sterling for the delivery of each of them within six months, and a pardon plus the reward to any Apostle who turned in another, was offered. All other habitants who had remained loyal were promised the king's protection and indemnity.[19] Shirley acted in the matter of the conditional pardon and indemnity at the explicit direction of Whitehall.[20] His role was neither remarkable nor sinister, given his increasing involvement in Nova Scotia. He filled a power vacuum left by the absence for two decades of a resident governor in Nova Scotia; Mascarene was merely president of the Council. Because of the heavy ship traffic between Boston and Britain, Shirley was in closer contact with Whitehall than Mascarene was. And in men and gear Massachusetts bore the brunt of the war effort.[21]

Much has been made of this proclamation, damned for its foreign provenance, the fewness of those it proscribed, and the lightness of the penalties it imposed. Sauvageau greets it with a sustained sneer: Mascarene was 'not able to fight back' more boldly for fear of provoking a rising among the Acadians, and his moderation only 'underlined [his] supreme craftiness.'[22]

In fact, the proclamation was right on target. It was aimed at the principal delinquents against whom there was substantial evidence of collaboration. It was directed at making the prominent Twelve amenable to justice. All twelve were actively pursued and heavy disabilities were laid upon them. Gautier's vessels, cattle, and realty had already been seized for his misdoing in Duvivier's time.[23] His wife and his son, Pierre, examined for complicity in Marin's attempt in May 1745, had been ten months in irons at the fort until they managed to escape in early 1746.[24] The entire family, including the other Apostle-son, Nicolas, hid at Chignecto or stayed at sea until in 1749 they settled finally on Île-Saint-Jean (Prince Edward Island), as did a number of other principal collaborators. The dwellings of Bigeau and 'Le Maigre' at Minas were fired, apparently after the cessation of hostilities, to the outrage of the commandant-general of New France.[25] The long collaboration of 'Bellair' and 'Le Maigre' had made notable contributions to French military efforts, as a recent historian has testified: 'What little progress Duvivier succeeded in making during the entire [1744] campaign, he owed almost exclusively to the efforts and the influence of the two richest Acadians of Nova Scotia, Joseph Leblanc and Joseph-Nicolas Gautier.'[26] Broussard retreated to modern-day New Brunswick, whence he had come, to emerge only when war began again in 1755.

Pursuit continued even after the cessation of hositilities in April 1748. Gorham's Rangers, dispatched to survey Chignecto for the erection of a fort there, were told to take 'Bellair' and his two sons, along with Bigeau and 'Le Maigre,' if they could be found.[27] Some of the Twelve were captured. Ten habitants of Minas were ordered to appear before the Council on 5 November 1748 to be crown witnesses against 'certain prisoners' (names unknown to us).[28]

Nothing happened. There were no trials, apparently no forensic examination of witnesses for the crown. Extant evidence establishes that most of the Twelve clearly acted in ways which, if the requisite criminal intent existed, constituted treason under the 1351/2 Treason Act. Since those in custody were triable, why did nothing further come of the matter? Was it weakness, cravenness, or Mascarenian 'craftiness'? In fact, none of these.

Mascarene never underestimated either the peril or the extent of Acadian collaboration with the French. The threat was real enough. After the first three testings – by Le Loutre, Duvivier, and Marin – Mascarene momentarily despaired of being able to prevent the fall of Annapolis Royal. Each defeat of the enemy seemed more fortuitous than effected; each further exposed the innate feebleness of the Annapolis Royal regime and its garrison; each constituted a new trial and another blow of the axe; and all collectively raised the spectre that the next attempt would be the last, not because it failed but because it succeeded. Mascarene feared that the Acadians' neutrality was evolving into a more actively pro-French stance as each incursion demonstrated that France could still extend its power into Nova Scotia from New France. By late 1745 his apprehension was so strong that he felt impelled to send on a hyperbolic report on the Acadians by Edward How and Erasmus Phillipps suggesting their deportation and replacement by Protestant settlers.[29] (See app. 3, C, doc. 1.) In fact, the report was less intent upon that rigorous course than directed at prying from Whitehall more men and materiel for defence. Moreover, Mascarene made clear in forwarding it to Whitehall, along with his own analysis countering the report and correcting its exaggerated assessment of the amount of collaboration, that deportation was too difficult and dangerous to be attempted.[30] (See app. 3, C, docs. 2, 3.) By spring 1746 Mascarene had suppressed his black thoughts. He convinced Shirley, hitherto the vociferous advocate of expulsion, that the Acadians were not so dangerous as to demand such a drastic solution. Shirley became the advocate of New English settlement *among* (not instead) of the Acadians, in order to keep them under surveillance and to dilute their capacity for trouble, a policy never seriously planned let alone implemented.[31] Curiously, Mascarene's faith in Acadian neutrality revived with the fourth attempt. Despite the heaviest collaboration yet, Ramezay failed. While his brilliant tactical achievement at Grand Pré had the potential of unravelling the regime's military power and moral authority among the Acadians, it had not done so. It confirmed that the mass of the Acadians would not rise. Without them a French strategic triumph was unachievable.

JURIDICAL LIMITATIONS

With the end of the war and Annapolis Royal saved, Mascarene was confident enough to write, rather disingenuously, to Whitehall in June 1748 that there had been only a 'few' Acadian collaborators.[32] He was more candid with the Duke of Bedford in September, referring to a 'faction' at Minas – the Twelve – who had openly appeared in the enemy's interest and had been 'exempted' from the declaration of protection for loyal Acadians. He admitted that time and 'good care' would be needed to wean such habitants from their natural inclination, growing from consanguinity and religion, towards the French interest.[33] But he had no doubt that he could do it. Official policy of the Annapolis Council in the nature of such 'good care' was made clear in a shake-up of Acadian under-officers – notary, deputies, and so on – to exclude any tainted by delinquency during the war. This was coupled with a harsh letter to the habitants at Minas taxing them with disobedience, divisiveness, hiding the Twelve, impeding government traffic, burning proclamations, harbouring rebels, obeying the orders of the 'banditti who are surely seeking your ruin as well as their own,' succoring deserters from the garrison, arming and clothing deserters and Indians, and the like.[34] Hardly a reign of terror; but then the idea was to win hearts and minds, not collect scalps.

Such tenderness would not have prevented taking twelve heads, *pour encourager les autres*. Mascarene was neither a weakling nor too clever by half. To give point to a policy of reconciliation and to cast it in bolder relief, Mascarene believed that sharp correction of the Twelve was appropriate. But, as a supreme realist well schooled over a third of a century in the limitations of his political and judicial powers, he attempted no more than he could expect to accomplish; he seized and destroyed property, imprisoned delinquents in irons, and so on. In the autumn of 1748, he wrote Whitehall:

The inhabitants mentioned to be brought here for having appeared openly in the enemy's interest have been under examination, but it is very difficult to bring to a regular tryal the breaches of duty and fidelity some of them have been guilty of by reason of the uncertainty we are in how far the power of the subsisting Council can extend in criminal cases, there being besides no officer to execute sentence in a civil way, and not even proper persons to keep any malefactor, this fort in proportion to the barracks and quarters being over crowded with officers and men.[35]

This should not have come as any surprise to their lordships. Three years before, Mascarene had begged for instructions and power to deal with the delinquents. Alluding to Madame Gautier, son Pierre, and Charles Raymond, the examinations of whom he enclosed, he wrote:

As there is here no person known in the law, and the Members who compose the Council for the Province are not qualified to advise me in this case, I don't know how to act with these or other of the French inhabitants in like circumstances, as it has always been a doubt here whether the Council could try, condemn, and execute in criminal cases. An instruction on that head has never been more wanted than at this time, when many delinquents may be found amongst these inhabitants who may deserve to be brought to a tryal.[36]

The Lords of Trade had ignored him then. They ignored him in 1748.

Procedural short cuts with the law of treason had become more remote in the aftermath of the Glorious Revolution of 1688 and during the Whig supremacy, and the Treason Trials Act of 1696 must perforce be as closely observed in New Scotland as in Old England.[37] Yet even had there been a learned judge of competent jurisdiction, ample provisions for the full panoply of due process, and clear instructions for implementing the law of treason – and a sheriff with a coil of hemp and a lock-up to hold the condemned – trial of the Twelve might have proved impossible. There were insufficient civilian British to serve as grand and petit jurors. Aside from the Acadians' unreliability in passing on such a sensitive matter, since they refused an unconditional oath of allegiance and were not bound to take the oath of supremacy, they were arguably not *probos et legales homines* as English law required for a jury. As well, treason law required two witnesses to treasonable acts in order to convict. Among the ten habitants summoned to give evidence for the crown it might have been difficult to find two who would agree to any one defendant's treason, perhaps to any treason at all. This, however, is speculation.

What is not is the inherent, long-demonstrated feebleness of the Annapolis Royal regime in the matter of doing justice. In civil matters it did well; in criminal ones it was constrained to no more than summary procedures in misdemeanor.[38] Treason resulting in death and forfeiture, as well as misprision of treason with imprisonment and loss of goods and loss of profits of land for life, would not allow for anything less than what the common law required in judicature and due process. Nova Scotia did not possess such until the Edward Cornwallis's new regime under new commission and full-strength articles arrived at Halifax in July 1749. Cornwallis demonstrated in an exemplary manner that he would use his juridical powers: Peter Carsal, convicted of murder, swung at the yard-arm of Cornwallis's floating government house a few weeks after the governor had anchored in Chebucto Bay.[39] Mascarene and the old regime had never possessed such authority or been able to exercise such legitimate power. It was, then, more a sign of strength than of weakness that Mascarene and his Council would not subvert the law in order to punish the guilty. Not even to hang a full dozen traitors.

JURIDICAL FAILURE AND 1755

For what was to become British North America, there was something anticlimactic about the story of Acadia's Twelve Apostles. It revealed the larger failing of the old British empire, which too readily relied upon inchoate or atrophied institutions insufficient to usher in and to nurture peace, order, and good government: myopia, indifference, ignorance, and indolence in Whitehall made effective direction of provincial government impossible while hampering the necessary exercise of authority and power by provincial governors in concert with colonial subjects. Representative institutions with the potential for responsible government and the promise of a popular franchise were requisite, and had been understood to be so in the older Atlantic seaboard colonies since the revolution of 1688, no matter how imperfectly implemented. Nova Scotia would begin the journey in 1758 with the summoning of the first legislature. Yet even before this there was the necessity of instituting the rule of law, not only because it was part of the birthright and the baggage of the British, but because the law, substantive and adjective, provided both instruction in civic virtue and the institutional memory of the polity. Nova Scotia began that journey only in 1749 in the new Athens (more properly, Athena, rising from the head of Zeus) on Chebucto Bay named for George Montagu Dunk, Earl of Halifax.

It proved a pity for the king's 'neutral subjects,' the hapless Acadians acquired by conquest in 1710, that what the second British regime instituted in 1749 at Halifax had not been begun by the first in 1713 at Annapolis Royal. The Acadians therefore received little instruction in civic virtue as the conqueror understood it. For more than a generation they had, with the at least tacit allowance of the British regime, lulled themselves into believing that the even tenor of their old ways would always be understood and respected by their new masters so long as they remained detached and distant from their former. But that proposition relied on maintainence of an institutional memory, which certainly would have been formed in jurisprudence and sustained by judicature had the regime at Annapolis Royal possessed authority to undertake it. Since it did not, when Mascarene handed over his charge to Cornwallis on 12 July 1749, the institutional memory of the first four decades of *vieille Acadie*- become-Nova Scotia ended abruptly. With it went the record of the Acadians' substantial though not entirely universal fidelity to their new allegiance during King George's War. In Shakespeare's words, 'the scraps of their good deeds past were devour'd as fast as they were made, forgot as soon as done.' Six years later Charles Lawrence and the rest of the Halifax Council, acting in the absence of memory and wholly focused on the present, expelled the Acadians. In ignorance of the past, Lawrence and his colleagues had not persevered in that steady practice of civility with the Acadians that had been Mascarene's great gift to empire. In 1755 Britain's honour-bright was left to hang 'Quite out of fashion, like a rusty mail / In monumental mockery.'

NOTES

1 *'Je me souviens'* of late has meant less 'I remember' than 'I don't forget' your mistreatment.

2 Antonine Maillet, *Pélagie-la-Charette* (Paris: Bernard Grasset 1979), at 291 (author's translation).

3 Thomas G. Barnes, 'Historiography of the Acadians' Grand Dérangement, 1755,' *Quebec Studies*, vol. 7 (1988), 74.

4 'By the end of the seventeenth century one can distinguish in Acadia many of the social customs, religious beliefs, political norms, economic practices, and artistic traditions that would blend in a unique fashion to form the distinctive Acadian identity.' Naomi E.S. Griffiths, *The Contexts of Acadian History 1686–1784* (Montreal: McGill-Queen's University Press 1992), at 33.

5 Robert Sauvageau, *Acadie: la Guerre de Cent Ans des Français d'Amérique aux Maritimes et en Louisiane, 1670–1769* (Paris: Berger Levrault 1987), at 203–4 (author's translation).

6 Thomas G. Barnes '"The Dayly Cry for Justice": The Juridical Failure of the Annapolis Royal Regime, 1713–1749,' *Essays in the History of Canadian Law*, vol. 3, *Nova Scotia*, ed. Philip Girard and Jim Phillips (Toronto: Osgoode Society/University of Toronto Press 1990), 10.

7 *Selections from the Public Documents of the Province of Nova Scotia*, ed. T.B. Akins (Halifax: Charles Annand 1869), at 109, Mascarene to secretary of state, 15 Nov. 1740.

8 Ibid., at 148–9, December 1744.

9 François Du Pont Duvivier, *Course à L'Accadie*, ed. Bernard Pothier (Moncton: Éditions d'Acadia 1982), at 78, 108–10, 120, 128–30, 139, 152. Duvivier called Bigeau a 'habitant de confiance' (ibid., at 78).

10 *Minutes of His Majesty's Council at Annapolis Royal, 1736–1749*, ed. C.B. Fergusson (Halifax: Public Archives of Nova Scotia 1967), at 59–62: interrogatories to and examinations of Bigeau and LeBlanc, 26 Jan. 1745; supporting documentation in their defence (and of others), including orders under pain from Duvivier: at 62–8.

11 Ibid., at 63, 94, 98.

12 Ibid., at 63.

13 W.J. Eccles, 'Marin de La Malgue (La Marque), Paul,' *DCB* 3: 431.

14 *Minutes of Council*, at 68–70.

15 RG 1, 13/39, Captain Benjamin Goldthwaite's report to Governor Shirley on the Grand Pré affair, PANS. Another version of the report is in RG1, 4A/102, 2 March 1747. Terms of capitulation of Grand Pré survivors: RG1, 13A/17a, 11 Feb. 1747 (NS).

16 CO 217/32/22–5, Ramezay to Acadian deputies from Beaubassin, 31 March and 24 April (NS) 1747, PRO; also, RG1, 13A/28d and 28e (copies), and RG1, 3/89, La Corne's account of Ramezay expedition, Montreal, 28 Sept. (NS) 1747.

17 Two of these were probably Paul Doucett alias Paul Laurent and Charles Pelerain alias Tuck, whose property along with that of 'Bellair' was proclaimed forfeit by the Council. See RG1, 21/[103], 21 Nov. 1746, 87–8.

18 He is buried at Broussard, on the outskirts of Lafayette, Louisiana; the author has been unable to find the exact site of the grave.

19 Beamish Murdoch, *A History of Nova-Scotia or Acadie*, 2 vols. (Halifax: James Barnes 1866), 2: at 117. The Twelve Apostles: Armand Bigeau (Bugeau, Bujold) of Minas; Joseph Broussard *dit* 'Beausoleil' of Shepody and Chignecto; Nicolas Gautier *dit* 'Bellair' of the Annapolis River; his sons, Joseph Gautier and Pierre Gautier of the same; Pierre Guidry *dit* 'Grivois,' possibly of Minas; Louis Hebert of Minas and the River; Joseph Le Blanc *dit* 'Le Maigre' of Minas; Charles Le Roy and Philippe Le Roy; Charles Raymond, possibly of the River; François Raymond of the River.

20 RG1, 13A/4, Duke of Newcastle to Shirley, Whitehall, 30 May 1747, for the king. See also RG1, 13A/33, and CO 217/31/67, Shirley to secretary of state, Boston, 20 Oct. 1747.

21 George A. Rawlyk, *Nova Scotia's Massachusetts: A Study of Massachusetts-Nova Scotia Relations, 1630–1784* (Montreal: McGill-Queen's University Press 1973), Chapters 9–11.

22 Sauvageau, *Acadie*, at 203–4 (author's translation).

23 Gautier's property was seized under a proclamation of Mascarene, issued by/ with the advice/counsel of the Council at Annapolis Royal, declaring forfeit all property of Nicolas Gautier (*inter alios*), real and personal, movable and immovable, as well as Gautier's schooner *Swallow*, for having 'perfidiously withdrawn their allegiance.' RG1, 21/[102–3], 87–9, 21 Nov. 1746.

24 CO 217/A27/257–8, Mascarene to Lords of Trade, 18 Dec. 1745.

25 CO 217/9/48, Marquis de La Galisonnière to Mascarene, Quebec, 15 Jan. (NS) 1749, and f.53, Mascarene to La Galisonnière, 25 April 1749.

26 Bernard Pothier's introduction to Duvivier's *Course à L'Accadie*, at 46 (author's translation).

27 RG1, 9/15[m], 233–5, Mascarene to Captain Charles Morris, 4 June 1748.

28 RG1, 21/[252], Mascarene to ten habitants of Minas. The letter is undated, but they were to appear before the Council on 5 November.

29 The low point was 8 Nov. 1745; 'Representation of the State' of the province, *Minutes*, 80–4, approved by Council.

30 CO 217/39/314, Mascarene to Newcastle, 9 Dec. 1745, enclosing Mascarene's representation on the state of the province, ff.316–17.

31 RG1, 13A/25, Shirley to Newcastle, Boston, 28 April 1747.

32 RG1, 17/45, Mascarene to secretary of state [Duke of Bedford], 15 June 1748.

33 RG1, 17/46, Mascarene to Duke of Bedford, 8 Sept. 1748.

34 RG1, 21/[220]: 166–70, Mascarene to deputies at Minas, 30 Aug. 1748; also, *Selections From the Public Documents*, at 162–4.

35 CO 217/32/102, Mascarene to Lords of Trade, 17 Oct. 1748.

36 CO 217/32/5, postscript to letter of Mascarene intended for Lords of Trade, 18 Dec. 1745, forwarded to Newcastle by R. Plumer, 23 April 1746 – a neat example of how little 'real time' intelligence Whitehall had of Nova Scotia affairs (and vice versa).

37 See Alexander H. Shapiro's valuable reminder of this point in his 'Political Theory and the Growth of Defensive Safeguards in Criminal Procedure: The Origins of the Treason Trials Act of 1696,' *Law and History Review*, vol. 11 (fall 1993), 217.

38 The author has discussed this matter at some length in '"The Dayly Cry for Justice"': the failure was more Whitehall's than Annapolis Royal's.

39 Carsal, a civilian sailor, received a proper show trial; he was indicted by a grand jury and convicted by a petit jury for murder, all done very correctly. See Thomas G. Barnes, '"As Near as May be Agreeable to the Laws of this Kingdom"': Legal Birthright and Legal Baggage at Chebucto, 1749,' *Law in a Colonial Society: The Nova Scotia Experience*, ed. Peter B. Waite, Sandra E. Oxner, and Thomas G. Barnes (Toronto: Carswell 1984), 20.

4

Civilians Tried in Military Courts: Quebec, 1759–64*

DOUGLAS HAY

When Governor François-Pierre de Rigaud de Vaudreuil surrendered in September 1760, the last courts of the French regime ceased to function. Following the cession of 1763, the new British government of Quebec was constituted in August 1764. One of its first acts was to approve an ordinance on 17 September establishing a new system of courts. The interregnum of 1760–4, often named 'the military regime,' was the period when all the inhabitants came under the rule of the army of the conqueror, but in the region of Quebec, which fell in September 1759, British military government lasted five years. The administration of criminal justice, like most aspects of government, lay in the hands of the officers of the occupying British army.[1] The experience of the army, the new French-speaking subjects of the crown, and the 'old subjects' – English-speaking civilian immigrants to Quebec – were all profoundly shaped by the absence of a structure of civilian courts. The expedient adopted by the English-speaking officers who effectively ruled Quebec was the one with which they were most familiar: military courts.

Those in Quebec, as everywhere the British army was stationed, were mainly concerned with the offences of soldiers. Of the almost 240 Quebec prosecutions that survive in the records of the War Office, at least 80 per cent were trials of soldiers for desertion, insubordination, conduct unbe-

*The support of the Social Sciences and Humanities Research Council of Canada, and the assistance of Samuel Marr and Daniel Condon, are gratefully acknowledged.

coming an officer, theft, rape, and other military and non-military offences. This was a jurisdiction conferred by the Articles of War, and it was a central part of military discipline and order. A few more prosecutions were of camp followers, women, or civilian employees of the army, who it was generally agreed fell under the Articles of War.[2] The variable punishments inflicted were characteristic of the eighteenth-century British army: from a pardoning to a hanging for desertion (serious because it constantly eroded the size of armies), and a wide range of other punishments for that and other offences. There was no fixed sentence for a given crime. Sentences of 1000 lashes with a cat-o'-nine-tails were common; there were even sentences of 2000 lashes in Quebec. Often the most severe flogging sentences were remitted in part. These trials and sentences of soldiers were similar to those found wherever the British army was stationed, throughout the empire.

But between forty and fifty of the charges heard before the General Courts Martial in Quebec, Montreal, and Trois-Rivières were cases in which benches of British army officers tried, convicted, and punished civilians accused of criminal offences.[3] In all, about twenty-one civilians with French names, another twenty-three with English names (some of them well known), and two women identified as 'a negro woman' and 'a negro slave' were tried by these military courts. The cases were almost all heard between 1761 and 1763: apparently, there were none in 1759 and 1760 and only two in 1764. The evidence strongly suggests that the army (or the civilians) only slowly came to the conclusion that courts martial were appropriate venues for trying even serious criminal cases. In 1761, the first year with a substantial number (about a dozen), the first cases, prosecutions of a Canadien's wife and of the two black women mentioned above for receiving and theft (by the slave), all resulted in acquittals, perhaps because the owner of the slave, La Corne Saint-Luc, did not offer any damning evidence.[4] But serious crime demanded remedies. A few days later a former French soldier robbed and stabbed to death a family of four, including two children, in the parish of Saint Francis and burned the house to try to conceal the evidence. Within a week he had been arrested, prosecuted before a court martial with the assistance of the *capitaines de milice* and five other Canadien witnesses, convicted, and sentenced to be hanged, with his body 'hung in irons on a Jibbet, in the same manner as practised in England, until his bones shall drop asunder, as a terror to all evil minded persons.' He was executed eleven days after he committed the crime.[5] A trial of a Canadien for killing another in a hunting accident resulted in an acquittal; one other man with a name that might be French was acquitted of theft and attempted murder after being accused by two women of the British army.[6]

There were a few other prosecutions that year of both old and new subjects, apparently civilians, for theft. Yet, in general, English names appeared rarely; indeed, those civilians with English names who were accused in 1761 were all former soldiers, with two possible exceptions. By 1762, however, the General Courts Martial were dealing with more contentious cases. That year there were a dozen prosecutions. Three were of English merchants, and in 1763, when over twenty prosecutions occurred, including some very controversial ones, the constitutional, legal, and political significance of military courts trying civilian offenders became a highly visible issue in Quebec, Montreal, and London. These cases probably helped to shape the meaning of government and of civil liberties in Quebec in the ensuing years, sharpening the disputes about law and military governance that arose in the period of the American revolution. In the final months of military government, January to August 1764, probably because of the controversy that had come to surround such cases, only two civilians appeared before a court martial.[7]

MILITARY COURTS AND PROCEDURE

For the military forces of the crown in the eighteenth century, the court martial, distinguished as either a Garrison Court Martial or a General Court Martial, was the fundamental instrument of order and discipline. Its punishments were harsh and its procedure significantly different from that of civilian courts.[8] Thirteen officers filled the roles of both judge and jury: they collectively heard the evidence, decided guilt on a majority vote (two-thirds in capital cases), and ordered the punishment. The prosecutor was another officer; the sentence, if one was passed, was confirmed by the local commanding officer. Without legal training and with only the outlines of a legal code in the Mutiny Acts and Articles of War, the members of the court inevitably relied on their own judgment of what seemed equitable and what the situation required. Charges were not cast in the extremely formal language required in the indictment used in a civil court; the technicalities that could result in acquittals in the ordinary criminal law were largely absent. Although flogging and execution were the common punishments for petty and serious offences, there were also some unusual military specialties, such as running the gauntlet. And punishments could be arbitrary in the most exact sense: where several or many men were convicted of a serious offence, particularly desertion, which carried the death penalty but which reduced military manpower, a few were sometimes selected for representative punishment, by lot.[9] All sentences were reviewed by the commanding officer, and many were reduced.

Enlisted men, particularly those charged with desertion, generally received harsh punishment quickly decided upon, after a brief outline of the evidence and an even shorter defence. Such cases, and charges of theft and drunkenness, constituted the majority of cases. In serious cases of non-military offences such as murder, trials of soldiers were longer and punishments probably less harsh than those in civilian cases in England. In the rarer instances of officers charged with 'conduct unbecoming,' many witnesses might be called, the evidence sifted in detail over a period of days, and the sentences (often public apologies) contrived to restore army etiquette. Because all proceedings of General Courts Martial were transcribed and sent to London to the judge advocate general (and, if necessary, the king), there was in theory a further level of protection for the defendant from the ignorance or malice of the members of the court. In most cases sentence would already have been carried out, but review of a case might result in better treatment of later defendants.[10]

The court martial, and military law in general, was the subject of occasional, sometimes violent public criticism from civilians in Britain. Most often it was aroused by the severity of military punishments, seen by the general public when the army was encamped near a town in the mother country or billeted on populations abroad. Moreover, Englishmen confidently believed their civilian criminal law, particulary its procedure, to be the fairest in the world, and the obvious differences between that law and the proceedings of courts martial troubled them. But the army was the army; few disagreed that deserters had to be deterred by the most severe punishments, and that, if officers had made the court martial into a court of honour, one of the places where the definition of 'an officer and a gentleman' was worked out, that was their business. Yet a court that suited the army had different connotations when it began to try civilians.

THE QUEBEC CASES

In Quebec, cases were tried before both General Courts Martial and Garrison Courts Martial, and civilians apparently appeared before the latter, too, for certain petty offences, although such cases are not considered here.[11] Arguably the reactions of the accused differed somewhat by national origin. For the Canadiens, any comparisons they drew were of course not to English criminal law but to that of the French regime. Apart from the significant fact that the military courts administered the law of the conqueror, and that much of the population seems in this period, as later, to have avoided the courts so far as possible, there were some striking similarities between English military justice and the criminal law of the *ancien régime*. French prosecutorial procedure emphasized separate examination of witnesses, the creation of a written dossier of evidence, trials in camera, few if any evidentiary rules, and active participation, with some distinctions, of both royal prosecutor and the judges in questioning and developing the case. In serious cases, where enough preliminary 'proofs' were held to exist, judicial torture could be applied. In all serious cases, too, appeal to higher levels was virtually automatic before sentence was carried out. Many of these characteristics (with the exception of judicial torture) were equally common in British army courts. Although the officers who tried cases did not have formal legal training, some of the chairmen and deputy judge advocates (the prosecutors) acquired a great deal of experience, in hundreds of cases.[12]

Military justice was charged with different emotional significance for some of the English-speaking 'old subjects' who found themselves accused before it. In the first place, as we have seen, there was a strong whiggish critique of military justice and military law in England, Scotland, and Ireland. Underlying it was the more general constitutional argument, since 1688, that British liberty should not be threatened by standing armies. One of the conventions of the constitution was that the administration of civilian justice should not be overawed by military force, and for that reason troops were almost always withdrawn from assize towns when the judges of assize, the circuit court that tried serious criminal and important civil cases, sat. Only serious disorder likely to threaten the administration of justice itself was considered to justify keeping soldiers nearby.

These political and constitutional positions were constantly sharpened, in Britain and in the colonies, by friction between soldiers and civilians wherever there were significant numbers of troops. Soldiers drank, they demanded loyalty toasts of suspected Jacobites in the period 1715 to 1760, they got into fights, and they often (both enlisted men and officers) scorned civilians. The fact that they were often billeted (as in Quebec) on local householders did not help matters. Taunts, alehouse brawls, and occasional riots were the consequence. And when large civil disorders in Britain, such as food riots, were put down by troops, any loss of life, or resulting murder trials, further exacerbated ill feeling between army and populace.

It therefore seems likely that many of the English-speaking 'old subjects,' who arrived in Quebec in the train of the army and later, were appalled to discover that they would have to seek justice in military courts. As such cases began to take place, from 1762, it also seems likely that characteristics of court-martial procedure that the French-speaking population found relatively familiar (written dossiers, no juries, combined prosecutorial and judicial roles, discretionary penalties, closed courtrooms) were perceived as oppressive by English defendants precisely because of the parallels with French justice. For French inquisitorial procedure, in the lexicon of Englishmen, was a synonym for oppression by the absolutist state. It was epitomized by the contrast between the *lettre de cachet*, which Englishmen believed allowed the French state to imprison anyone on the most frivolous of grounds, with their own writ of habeas corpus, which required the British state to prove it had grounds for detention. The fact that it was English officers who were administering unconstitutional justice in a former French colony was striking; the fact that those officers admired many aspects of the old regime was probably well known. And legal counsellors of the old regime were certainly consulted by them. To an English merchant inclined to a dark view of the matter, even the fact that many of the prosecutions were conducted by an officer named Cramahé, of French and Irish background, was not reassuring.[13]

THE CONSTITUTIONAL ISSUE IN LAW

Article 2 of section xx of the Articles of War apparently gave General Courts Martial in jurisdictions without civil courts the power 'to try all persons guilty of wilful murder, theft, robbery, rapes, coining ... and all other capital crimes or other offences and punish offenders according to the known laws of the land, or as the nature of their crimes shall deserve.'[14] The phrase 'all persons' was taken by the Quebec military to include civilians, and article 2 was explicitly cited in one of the earliest cases as the basis for the conviction.[15] But this was not the interpretation of the law in the Judge Advocate General's office at the Horse Guards. For the highest lawyers of the army fairly consistently took the position in the eighteenth century that not 'all persons,' but only army personnel, were subject to such courts.[16] This doctrine in effect made the trial of civilians by courts martial unlawful, but the situation in Quebec did not arouse concern for some years. Official copies of the proceedings of

General Courts Martial were forwarded regularly to London, apparently without arousing comment. Most of them, of course, related the cases of soldiers, but even the index pages of the office copies of the judge advocate general clearly distinguished the trials of civilians.[17] Perhaps they were read only by the clerks.

Dispute over the wide use of military law in Quebec apparently first arose over cases in other courts involving essentially civil matters.[18] Similar cases also came before the General Courts Martial. Some, like the proceedings taken against two servants (former soldiers) for running away from their master, Colonel Gabriel Christie, and the complaint of six canoemen against the Montreal merchant Edward Chinn that he had not paid their wages, fell in the category of what contemporaries called 'master and servant' cases. Christie lost at trial, for the contract was dissolved, but the 'sentence' was changed by the commanding officer and the men were forced to return to work for him, in spite of their complaints of great abuse at his hands.[19] Chinn, in his case against the voyageurs, successfully proved a custom to retain wages when furs had gone missing, and he also made successful use of the court against another canoeman for alleged theft of the furs he was carrying. Chinn was probably less pleased that not all the disputed furs were returned to him; the court ordered some to be given to the 'motherless children' of two soldiers.[20] There was also a successful prosecution of a publican for receiving stolen furs.[21]

This use of courts martial was a *de facto* recognition of the unsettled state of civilian justice in the colony and also of the importance of the fur trade. The employment cases perhaps seemed the most natural for the officers to consider, as master and servant cases in England could have penal consequences, at least for servants, and therefore straddled the distinction between criminal and civil cases. But in Quebec at least some such cases probably came before the military courts because English merchants insisted that they were not subject to French civil law, which was being concurrently administered by the *capitaines de milice*, and a military court of English officers was the only alternative.[22] And, of course, merchants successfully used courts martial to prosecute in criminal cases affecting them, such as a case of fraud,[23] a theft from a house by a servant boy,[24] and a hogshead of rum taken by a soldier from a wharf.[25]

Meanwhile, civil cases tried by the *capitaines* could be appealed to the governor, and by 1763 the military governor of Montreal, General Thomas Gage, was perplexed by the 'very ignorant lawyers of Montreal ... obstinate, Quibbling, Chicanning fellows,' who were exploiting 'a Labyrinth of the Law.' He appealed for advice from his superior in New York, but with the Proclamation of October 1763, the issue, it was thought, could be left for the subsequent establishment of civilian courts.[26] Moreover, the military jurisdiction of the province had already become highly contentious.

It was the famous and bloody case of Marie-Josephte Corriveau of Saint-Vallier, who murdered her husband with a hatchet and whose father was convicted of the crime before he implicated her, that forced the Judge Advocate General's Office in the summer of 1763 to realize that civilians were being tried and condemned by military courts in Quebec.[27] (See app. 3, D.) In the view of Charles Gould, the deputy judge advocate general, Corriveau's conviction, execution, and hanging in chains, her father's pardon – in short, all the proceedings – were irregular since there was no military jurisdiction. He was deeply embarrassed for not having noted earlier cases and for not being able to propose a solution that met both his assessment of military law and the acknowledged needs of the military governors of Quebec. General Gage, for one, thought the doctrine absurd and probably viewed Gould as another obstinate, quibbling lawyer. Lieutenant-Colonel Ralph Burton, who had succeeded Gage as military governor at Montreal and had continued with courts martial of civilians as late as June 1764, expressed the hope in July of that year that the 'good intentions' of officers would be taken into account in any litigation that might result against them.[28]

THE CONSTITUTIONAL ISSUE IN POLITICAL PRACTICE

The doctrine recognizing military jurisdiction over civilians in conquered territories without civilian courts came to be accepted in the early nineteenth century.[29] That it was not the law at the time of the conquest of Canada caused some anxiety and embarrassment, but no lawsuits, prosecutions, or other consequences appear to have troubled subsequently the officers who tried, convicted, and even executed civilians without legal mandate. Still, the use of such courts in Quebec arguably had more important results for the colony than the testy exchanges between military lawyers in London and military officers in Canada. In addition to the awkwardness of legally untrained officers dealing with civilian litigation, and the uncertain place of civil actions in the General Courts Martial, these courts exacerbated political passions in Quebec. We have already noted the predisposition of English civilians, particularly 'middling men,' to suspect military justice of despotism and to draw parallels with French criminal procedure. Courts martial became even more problematic in the eyes of 'old subjects' in Quebec when they tried civilians, English merchants, for insulting army officers. Such cases arose from the kinds of conflicts normal wherever armies lived with civilian populations, and particularly when there were other grounds for mutual suspicion and friction.

The first such cases, in 1762, brought the merchants William Grant, Edward Chinn, and Forrest Oakes before a General Court Martial in Montreal, charged with abusing, assaulting, and insulting Ensign Robert Nott.[30] In a coffee-house brawl partly caused by a very drunken Nott pressing drink on the reluctant Chinn, Grant was said to have knocked down Nott, prompting a quartermaster to draw his sword and threaten to cut off the limb of any man attacking an officer. Grant's version was that he was disarming the drunken quartermaster. In any case, Nott called the guard and had Chinn and Grant arrested (Chinn was dragged out a window by his hair) and confined, demanding apologies; when they were not given, a court martial was ordered. There, one of the defence witnesses was not allowed to testify since he had been named by Nott as an offender; much of the testimony revolved around whether, and when, Nott had formally informed Chinn of the charge against him. The court found for their fellow officer, and Chinn and Grant were sentenced to fines and to make formal public apologies to Nott before the Montreal garrison, in words specified by the court.[31] The issues of honour and status informed all the proceedings. Oakes, Nott said, had declared that he was a gentleman and could not be sent to the guardhouse, and he had challenged Nott to fight to prove whether he was a gentleman or 'a damned scoundrel.' Oakes 'further said two hundred pounds made a gentleman in the army, and that [he] ... was a gentleman for he was worth ten thousand pounds.' The court sentenced Oakes to fourteen days' imprisonment for 'scurrilous reflections cast by him on the army'; he, too, was sentenced to make a dictated public apology.[32]

The second important case bringing officers and merchants into conflict was the prosecution in December 1763 of Isaac Todd, Richard McNeall, George Knaggs, John Blake, and William Haywood for abusing and assaulting Captain John Campbell in the execution of his duty.[33] Among the witnesses for the prosecution was La Corne Saint-Luc, recently returned to Quebec and busily building his career by supporting the English military in all things. Campbell, the alleged victim, had married La Corne's daughter, probably earlier that year.[34] McNeall and Todd, very drunk after St Andrew's Day, had been arrested for having burst into the bedroom of Todd's landlady, who saved herself by jumping from the second-storey window. (Todd claimed that he had offered apologies the next morning but that she was bent on a malicious prosecution.) During the arrest some hearty insults were exchanged, and the other defendants had tried to rescue Todd and McNeall from the army guard led by Campbell, who seems to have been very drunk himself. They were led off, partially clothed, surrounded by soldiers with fixed bayonets. Again, part of the issue in the court martial was the legality of the arrest and the right to bail. Again, five defence witnesses were not heard by the court on the grounds that they were somehow involved with the defendants and hence were 'accessories.' The court sentenced the defendants to stiff fines and specified public apologies to Campbell; Burton reduced the fines but enforced the apologies.

The Judge Advocate General's Office in London was already exercised by the Corriveau case of the previous year when the transcript of the Todd case arrived early in 1764. Charles Gould clearly feared that the court martial that convicted Todd *et al.* was not only *ultra vires* because the defendants were civilians but guilty of a range of procedural irregularities. In a letter to Burton at Montreal, Gould analysed the shortcomings of the case 'to prevent inconvenience in future': the embarrassment of lawsuits in England against the military. The court had refused evidence of defence witnesses on dubious grounds and had not allowed the defendants proper opportunity to prepare their defences.[35] In short, to the general argument Gould mounted with respect to civilians – that courts martial strictly speaking had no jurisdiction over them, even in a country under military occupation – he now added the concern that irregularities because of military ignorance of the law, or because military standards of law were not acceptable to civilians, were a political problem. In the Corriveau case he had already stated the problem in explicit terms, undoubtedly referring to the contemporary Wilkite attack on authoritarian government in England and to recent controversies about impressment: 'Although there has been no Substantial injustice done in this case ... you are so well apprised, how many there are in this Kingdom, who view the Military Arm with a jealous Eye and are ever ready to take advantage of the least mistaken excess of Power.'[36] In the Todd case, he now admitted that substantial injustice *had* been done.

CONCLUSION

Military government, and particularly military justice, while necessary, was thus problematic in Quebec. As early as the 1760s its connotations of authoritarian government were heightened, in the eyes of the English-speaking merchants' community, by cases in which they were humiliated before courts of English army officers intent upon upholding the honour of officers and gentlemen. The result could only be to reinforce the determination of some of the merchants to refuse to recognize the legitimacy of the military jurisdiction or of the French civil courts. The Todd case so enraged the Montreal merchants that many of them refused to attend the customary levee of the governor, as representative of the crown, on New Year's Day 1764.[37] By that date Thomas Walker, a merchant from Boston, was a leading critic of military justice and army rule. A year later, having been made a magistrate and having curtailed soldiers' billeting privileges, he was beaten severely and had his ear cut off by masked men in his own house. This outrage and its aftermath convulsed the colony and made bad relations between soldiers and civilians much worse. The failure of the authorities to secure convictions of the soldiers whom Walker accused seemed, to some of the merchants, a continuation of the unconstitutional justice of the military regime. Governor James Murray wrote the Lords of Trade in March 1765:

The contempt which military men have ever entertained for mercantile peoples must have been greatly increased in this colony from the circumstances of it. The genteel people of the colony despise merchants and of course esteem the officers who shun them most. On the other hand our merchants are chiefly adventurers of mean education or if old traders such as have failed in other countries[;] all have their fortunes to make, and little solicitous about the means provided the end is obtained.

In Montreal, he added, relations between the military and merchants were particularly bad:

... as there had been frequent disputes between them and merchants which had been decided by courts martial, it may be supposed the civil establishment was by no means relished by the troops, as the new magistracy must be composed agreable to my instructions, of the very merchants they held so much in contempt ... it happened unluckily the merchants at Montreal[,] the most proper from their circumstances and understanding to be made Justices of the Peace, were those who had had the most disputes with the troops.[38]

Some of the merchants who had appeared as defendants before the courts martial of the 1760s continued to demand the constitutional rights of Englishmen in the following decades. One of them, Isaac Todd, helped lead the merchants' protests against the Quebec Act in the 1770s. He nonetheless remained loyal to Britain during the American revolution and went on to become a very wealthy merchant and father-figure of the fur trade before retiring to Bath.[39] William Grant, who had been convicted in the 1762 case of abusing Ensign Nott, also became wealthy. He, too, supported the government against the Americans, but by 1780 he was an opponent of Governor Frederick Haldimand, by 1784 he was calling for an assembly and habeas corpus, and within a few years he was one of the most outspoken critics of the 'French party' in Quebec, demanding English law and English justice.[40] Moreover, a few merchants in Quebec were tempted to join the American rebellion; others at least espoused its principles. The authoritarian cast of military government of Quebec intensified in the revolutionary years, and the conflict of army and civilian notions of freedom and justice became pronounced.[41] Those conflicts, between merchants and officers, officers and lawyers, had been rehearsed in the courts martial of the military regime of 1759–64. The legitimacy of the justice to be found in Quebec courts, particularly when the forms and precedents of English common law were ignored, was to be repeatedly called into question in succeeding decades.

NOTES

1 Civil cases 'among the inhabitants' were to be tried before local *capitaines de milice*, with appeals to the local British officer and then the governor: *Con Docs* 1: at 38–41. See also text at n.26.

2 The numbers are not exact because some accused are not clearly identified as civilians and may have been camp followers; there are also a few multiple charges.

3 The sources are the entry books and transcripts (some originals, some office copies) of General Courts Martial kept by the Judge Advocate General's Office, now deposited at the PRO, London, as WO 71/45–/6, /49, /68–/74, /132, /135–/8. Many but not all of these papers were used by Frederick Bernays Wiener, an American lawyer and reserve judge advocate, in his authoritative *Civilians Under Military Justice: The British Practice since 1689 Especially in North America* (Chicago: University of Chicago Press 1967). The records of the General Courts Martial used here, apparently all those surviving for Quebec, Montreal, and Trois-Rivières, are those beginning on the following dates: Quebec: 26 Sept., 16 Nov., 13 Dec. 1759; 30 March, 31 May, 11 June, 11, 13, and 17 July,

11 and 28 Aug., 26 Oct. 1760; 8 Feb., 9 and 23 March, 6 April, 1 and 11 June, 27 July, 17 Aug., 25 Sept., 19 Nov. 1761; 8 Feb., 11 May, 11 June 1762; 29 March, 15 April, 4 July, 27 Sept., 6 Oct. 1763; 11 June 1764. Trois-Rivières: 13 Nov. 1760. Montreal: 8 Dec. 1760; 19 Jan., 15 and 27 Feb., 14 and 26 March, 1 April, 3 June, 3 Aug., 25 Nov. 1761; 15 Feb., 26 March, 22 June, 31 July, 9 Sept., 12 Nov. 1762; 22 Jan., 2 and 13 June, 18 July, 16 Aug., 12 Dec. 1763; 4 April, 14 May, 26 and 28 June 1764.

4 Cases of Katherine David, Etien, Joset, 4 March 1761, Montreal, WO 71/135 and WO 71/68.

5 14 March 1761, Montreal, WO 71/135 and WO 71/68.

6 3 June 1761, Montreal, WO 71/68. 15 March 1761, Montreal, WO 71/135 and WO 71/68.

7 See below, 'The Constitutional Issue in Political Practice.'

8 For an overview see three articles by Arthur N. Gilbert: 'Military and Civilian Justice in Eighteenth-Century England: An Assessment,' *Journal of British Studies*, vol. 17, no. 2 (spring 1978), 41; 'The Regimental Courts Martial in the Eighteenth Century,' *Albion*, vol. 8, no. 1 (spring 1976), 55; 'Law and Honor among Eighteenth Century British Army Officers,' *The Historical Journal*, vol. 9 (March 1976), 75.

9 Wiener, *Civilians*, at 20. Two instances occurred in Quebec in 1759, under Murray: WO 71/68/29, WO 71/46/13.

10 See the comments of the deputy judge advocate general on the case of Todd *et al.*, below. Gilbert, 'Military and Civilian Justice,' argues that court-martial proceedings against officers were probably fairer than trials in the civilian courts, largely because no limit was set for the length of a court martial, but the comparison made is with felony trials, which few gentlemen ever endured. On misdemeanour charges, civilians in civilian courts enjoyed the protections (although also the expense) of an unhurried process. They also had right to full counsel and a jury of gentlemen. On the other hand, in the matter of felonies, the short and informal hearings of the General Court Martial in ordinary cases were similar to those of the average criminal case at the Old Bailey.

11 Wiener, *Civilians*, at 46, citing a printed edition: the cases at Montreal included liquor offences, petty fraud, false weights, disorderly houses, small thefts and assaults, and insults; the court also examined debtors.

12 See following note.

13 Hector Theophilus Cramahé, later lieutenant governor of the province, acted from 1759 to 1764 as deputy judge advocate (prosecutor) in most, if not all, the cases prosecuted in General Courts Martial held in Quebec City.

14 Quoted in Wiener, *Civilians*, at 23.

15 Joset, 4 March 1761. Murray, however, had doubts: A.L. Burt, *The Old Province of Quebec*, 2 vols. (Toronto: McClelland and Stewart 1968), 1: at 94–5.

16 Wiener, *Civilians*, ch. 1.

17 See WO 71/49, /70, /71, /74.

18 See the discussion below regarding appeals to the governor.

19 2 Aug. 1762, Montreal, WO 71/71. On master and servant cases in the empire, see P. Craven and D. Hay, 'The Criminalization of "Free" Labour: Master and Servant in Comparative Perspective,' *Slavery and Abolition*, vol. 15, no. 2 (August 1994), 71.

20 16 Dec. 1763, Montreal, WO 71/49; 17 and 20 Aug. 1763, Montreal, WO 71/73. He failed to get a conviction for theft against two men in another case, 22 Aug. 1763, Montreal, WO 71/73.

21 26 March 1762, WO 71/70.

22 Wiener, *Civilians*, at 39, 50.

23 17 March 1763, Montreal, WO 71/73.

24 8 Feb. 1762, Quebec, WO 71/136 and WO 71/70.

25 26 Oct. 1760, WO 71/68.

26 Wiener, *Civilians*, 50ff.

27 Luc Lacourcière, 'Corriveau, Marie-Josephte,' *DCB* 3: 142; WO 71/137. The case became a powerful image in Quebec popular culture. See the sources cited in Lacourcière, 'Corriveau, Marie-Josephte.'

28 28 June 1764, WO 71/138 and WO 71/74/213–16; Wiener, *Civilians*, 55ff and appendix I, D. Wiener's account suggests that Burton was making a general point; his remark, however, arose in reply to Gould's warnings in the Todd case: see below.

29 Wiener, *Civilians*, at 59–63.

30 15–20 Feb. 1762, Montreal, WO 71/136 and WO 71/70.

31 Gage reduced the fines.

32 Gage reduced the sentence to twenty-four hours' imprisonment, security for good behaviour, and no apology.

33 13 and 15 Dec. 1763, Montreal, WO 71/49.

34 Pierre Tousignant and Madeleine Dionne-Tousignant, 'La Corne, Luc de,' *DCB* 4: 425. Campbell was later accused by Thomas Walker of being one of his attackers: see below.

35 Charles Gould to Ralph Burton, Montreal, 14 April 1764, WO 71/49/261–3.

36 Charles Gould to Governor James Murray, 11 Aug. 1763, Wiener, *Civilians*, appendix I, D, 2, 251–2, reprinted in this volume's app. 3, D, doc. 1.

37 Burt, *Old Province*, 1: at 96–8.

38 The attack on Walker took place in December 1764, after the establishment of civil government and courts, and the affair profoundly affected relations for

years. In the abortive trial of some soldiers for the offence in 1766, a 'French protestant' JP was active. This was probably Pierre Du Calvet, recently appointed to the bench, who became a famous victim of military justice in the 1780s, when Walker was still in touch with him. See Governor Murray to the Lords of Trade, 2 March 1765, CO 42/3/559; Burt, *Old Province*, 1: 102ff; Lewis H. Thomas, 'Walker, Thomas,' *DCB* 4: 758; and Jean-Marie Fecteau and Douglas Hay, '"Government by Will and Pleasure Instead of Law": Military Justice and the Legal System in Quebec, 1775–83,' in this volume.

39 Myron Momryk, 'Todd, Isaac,' *DCB* 5: 818.
40 David Roberts, 'Grant, William,' *DCB* 5: 367.
41 See Fecteau and Hay, '"Government by Will and Pleasure."'

5

'Government by Will and Pleasure Instead of Law': Military Justice and the Legal System in Quebec, 1775–83*

JEAN-MARIE FECTEAU and
DOUGLAS HAY

This Swiss General ... carried his ideas of military authority, and Government by will and pleasure, instead of law, beyond even those other gentlemen of the same profession who were born subjects of the British Crown – Pierre Du Calvet, *The Case of Pierre Du Calvet* (London: 1784), at 229.

To explain the connections between state law and the power of the state it is crucial to understand political context. That context does much to determine the content with which the forms of law are filled and the degree to which invocations such as 'the rule of law' are persuasive. The security of civil liberties and the actual content of the notion of the rule of law are particularly illuminated by the glare of war.

Three major events defined the context in which Quebec's military and legal and civil authorities operated during the American Revolutionary War of 1775–83. First and foremost there was the conquest of 1760 and the cession of 1763, which established a legal system haunted by ambiguity and indeterminacy. The Royal Proclamation of 1763 was intended to end uncertainty, but the attempt to impose English law on a population of French-speaking Catholics accustomed to French law met resistance. The colonial authorities soon recognized that this fact had to be acknowl-

*Douglas Hay wishes to acknowledge the support of the SSHRC and the Canada Council.

edged, a recognition reinforced by the enthusiasm of the English officers in the colony for what they believed had been an effectively authoritarian form of government during the French regime. As early as 1767, Guy Carleton, the new governor, had doubts about the introduction of English law; by 1775 he was proposing the nearly complete re-establishment of French law, both civil and criminal.

The second determinant of our period, ten years after the Stamp Act, was the Quebec Act, promulgated in 1774. It was an attempt to reconcile the French Canadian elite's ambition to restore the old system with the needs of British colonial authority.[1] Hence the fundamental decision: to allow the restoration of French civil law but to retain English criminal law, which was held to be better and milder than the French and in any case a central pillar of state power. The result, however, was an unstable legal regime, one with significant discontinuities in the common law. Most of the rules dealing with criminal law and political and imperial authority were retained, but protection of the individual citizen's rights was weakened by the exclusion of trial by jury in civil causes and of habeas corpus in both civil and criminal cases.[2] The Quebec Act was rooted in the realpolitik of both the specific problems of Quebec and the urgent necessity of reinforcing imperial supremacy as the other American colonies sought to escape it.

The third major event was, of course, the war itself. The War of Independence looms as the defining event of the period. In the first place, it put enormous pressure on the political compromise which had produced the Quebec Act while also confirming an erosion of imperial power and directly threatening the fundamental principles of monarchical authority. The claims of democracy became the frame of reference of all contending parties. Secondly, the position of the Canadiens was critical, not so much because their support or repudiation of the cause of independence would determine the outcome of the struggle, but simply because they became the target of attempts by both sides to claim their allegiance. Quebec was a battleground for the competing views of authority, allegiance, and democracy that arose during the war. Pestered by the Thirteen Colonies to join them, but faced with the Quebec government's paranoid suspicions of their loyalty, the Canadien peasantry took a remarkably pragmatic stand: essentially, to wait and see. It was this context, alternately reassuring and deeply threatening to the civil authorities, this state of potential revolt in suspended animation, that shaped demands for the maintenance of order and claims for the protections of the law.

FROM CIVIL RULE TO MARTIAL LAW: THE BEGINNING OF THE AMERICAN REVOLUTIONARY WAR

The outbreak of the war and the early invasion of the province by the rebel forces in May 1775, followed by the fall of Montreal in November, was a brutal shock to the authorities in Quebec City and in London, the more so as the stance of friendly neutrality taken by the Canadien peasants towards the invaders was largely unforeseen. Why that should be the case is explained by the assumptions that had developed over the preceding decade.

Imperial Authority and the Law of Nations: The Canadien Case

Much has been written about England 'conceding' to Canadiens their original laws, a move described either as an act of political pragmatism at a time when the other colonies were in revolt or as a realistic attempt to resolve the legal contradictions issuing from the Royal Proclamation of 1763. But the political stakes involved were larger than such interpretations suggest. The terms of the proclamation implied that fitting Canada into the empire was to be a relatively straightforward matter of providing territorial protection for the fur trade and aboriginal peoples in the western part of what had been New France, and, in the colony's older settled parts, establishing a legal regime 'as near as may be agreeable' to the laws of England.[3] The aim was not to open a new territory to British colonization but rather to accomplish the gradual anglicization of a foreign people deeply attached to their homeland.

The Royal Proclamation: Allegiance and Fidelity

The policy embodied in the proclamation soon came to be seen in a different light. As the American colonies' protests against imperial policy grew, England found its relatively peaceful French-speaking colony more and more attractive. Even more reassuring was the fact that Quebec had never had representative government of a parliamentary form. The British parliamentary system had become widespread in the American colonies in the aftermath of the English revolutions of the seventeenth century; the crown therefore insisted on keeping colonial executive power subordinate to London policy as legislative assemblies attempted to acquire more and more powers. In the British Isles from the 1760s there were growing popular demands for more accountable parliamentary representation, for greater control of ministers of the state by the courts, and for government that was more attentive to the wants of the people, including the mob.[4] A North American colony with a quiescent population, unused to parliamentary representation and schooled in obedience to autocratic French government, became an increasingly prized possession. From the morrow of the conquest, the military officers who ruled Quebec showed an interest in reviving the modes of French government, some of them even suggesting the restoration of *haute, moyenne, et basse justice*. From James Murray to Frederick Haldimand, the governors were attracted by the image of a French governor wielding absolute power over deferential subjects. In Carleton's well-known words,

this System of Laws established subordination from the first to the lowest, which preserved the internal harmony until our arrival and secured obedience to the supreme seat of government from a very distant Province. All this arrangement, in one hour, we overturned by the ordinance of the 17th of September 1764 [which established English criminal law and courts modelled on the mother country], and laws, ill adapted to the genius of the Canadiens, to the situation of the province, and to the interests of Great Britain, unknown, and unpublished were introduced in their stead ... The most advisable method, in my opinion, for removing the present as well as for preventing future evils, is to repeal that ordinance ... and for the present have the Canadien laws almost entire.[5]

The attraction of authoritarian government was complemented by the old distrust, still significant, of plans for systematic settlement of the colonies: 'More attention is due to the native Canadien than the British emigrant, not only because that class is the most numerous; but because it is not the interest of Britain that many of her natives should settle there.'[6] The behaviour of the new subjects in Quebec also influenced British policy. The Royal Proclamation envisaged a smooth change in the legal framework which would allow gradual and peaceful integration of the Canadien population into the British empire. Yet as early as 1760, the military courts were forced to recognize the dominance of French law in the domestic and mercantile dealings of the vanquished people.

As soon as new courts on the English model were set up under the terms of the 1764 ordinance,[7] replacing the military courts of 1759–64, it became evident that the administration of justice, civil or criminal, was encumbered by the passive, yet steadfast, resistance of the Canadiens.[8] The colonial administration, the imperial government, and many historians have hastily concluded that this resistance constituted a mute, yet eloquent, testimony to the Canadien peasants' attachment to the French law. Such a conclusion, however, ignores the fact that the law of the old regime (like others) was not a coherent body of formal rules but a multifunctional normative magma of rulings which were often contradictory. For example, the French law, on the one hand, established a body of rules related to inheritance and the family, embodying norms of joint responsibility both in the community and in trade founded originally on ancestral arbitration and compromise. On the other hand, French law also sought to ensure the reproduction of a feudal authority relationship, through rules such as those governing the collection of seigneurial and ecclesiastical taxes. The eighteenth century saw a slowly widening gap between the rules that applied to life within the community, including the familial transmission of peasant landholdings, and the rules that reproduced feudal authority. But where France itself was dominated by 'feudist' lawyers whose sole purpose was to revive and extend feudal powers over the peasantry, in Canada developments followed an opposite course. The peasantry eventually could take advantage of a juridical haziness and their own bargaining position to sustain a refusal to pay feudal or ecclesiastical taxes. Their successful resistance to many of the claims of church and state under the French regime continued after the British conquest. Oddly, little has been written about this crucial phase of the law's 'suspended animation,' when passive resistance was mounted against the traditional French-speaking elites as well as against the new British masters. The seigneurs' forceful denunciations of the more democratic aspects of English law, including juries and private prosecution (criticisms with which the English military tended to agree),[9] and Governor Carleton's belief that anarchy had characterized much of the Canadiens' life since the conquest,[10] convinced London. The British authorities accepted the restoration of French law after ten years of civil administration of the colony, not only to satisfy the petitions of the Canadien elite and as a response to the prejudices of the British military governors, but also to ensure respect for the institutions of the state.

At this juncture, dominated by the fears, ambitions, and hopes of the British government and the Canadien elites, the Quebec Act was adopted. It rested on a gamble: that the return of French civil law would ensure stability and secure the allegiance of the Canadiens to their new king, and that the social and political settlement which the act embodied would re-establish the nobility as the 'effective' dominating class while avoiding the cost and faction of a legislative assembly. As customary practices and institutions returned, enfolded within them would be the peasants' ancestral deference to their masters since time immemorial. This notion of deference in *ancien régime* Canada was an assumption of the British officer class, indeed their Arcadian myth of the Canadiens. Reiterated again and again in the official correspondence, it underlay the authorities' attitude to legality and force in the maintenance of order.

The American war, the invasion itself, activated a deeply paranoid attitude towards the Canadien peasantry. In the eyes of the British in Quebec, this transplanted French peasantry, ignorant and gullible, subordinated to the arbitrary domination of seigneur and absolute monarch for centuries, quiescent until it exploded in its traditional uprisings, could, in the short term, be subdued and brought into subjection only through the powerful return of its old masters. Only time would allow the transformation of ignorance into entrepreneurship, subjection into citizenship.

That this analysis of pre-conquest society had little basis in fact partly explains the reaction of the Canadiens to the American invasion. For, to the amazement of their new masters (and probably of some of their former masters also), the Canadien peasant did not wait to be emancipated by slow acculturation to British civil society. Their reaction to the American uprising profoundly shocked and unsettled the colonial and imperial authorities. As early as February 1775 Carleton understood that the restoration of French civil law by the Quebec Act had not reawakened the hierarchical deference he imagined was part of it, and to explain this fact he resorted to the idea of sedition, the poison of disloyal opinion:

Considering all the new ideas they have been acquiring for these ten years past, can it be thought they will be pleased at being suddenly and without preparation embodied into a militia and marched off from their families, lands and habitations to remote provinces, and all the horrors of war, which they have already experienced; it would give an appearance of truth to the language of our sons of sedition, at this very moment busily employed instilling into their minds that the Act was passed merely to serve the present purposes of government, and in the full intention of ruling over them with all the despotism of their ancient masters.[11]

Some months later, when Benedict Arnold attacked Saint-Jean, the governor found even more evidence. On 7 June he wrote Lord Dartmouth, secretary of state for the colonies: 'The consternation in the towns and country was great and universal, every individual seemed to feel our present impotent situation ... All subordination overset, and the minds of the people poisoned by the same hypocrisy and lies practised with so much success in the other provinces, and which their emissaries and friends here have spread abroad with great art and diligence.'[12]

The more than conciliatory attitude of the Canadien peasantry towards the American rebels infuriated and disillusioned the governors of the colony. William Hey, the chief justice, echoed the governor in a letter to the lord chancellor in London:

Your lordship will remember how much has been said by us all of their loyalty, obedience & gratitude, of their habitual submission to government, & their decent civil and respectful demeanor to those who had the conduct of it, but time and accident have evinced that they were obedient only because they were afraid to be otherwise and with that fear lost (by withdrawing the troops) is gone all the good disposition that we have so often and steadily avowed in their names and promised for them in ages to come. Yet I am sometimes willing to think that fear, joined with extreme ignorance and a credulity hardly to be supposed of a people,[13] have been overmatched by the subtlety and assiduity of some colony agents who were very busy here last winter, and that they are not at bottom an ungenerous or disobedient people ... English officers to command them in time of war, and English laws to govern them in time of peace, is the general wish; the former they know to be impossible (at least at present) and by the latter if I understand them right, they mean no laws and no government whatsoever ... Gen. Carleton had taken an ill measure of the influence of the seigneurs and clergy over the lower order of people whose principle of conduct founded in fear and the sharpness of authority over them now no longer exercised, is unrestrained, and breaks out in every shape of contempt or detestation of those whom they used to behold with terror and who gave them I believe too many occasions to express it.[14]

The Case of the Old Subjects

To these anxieties about the new subjects of the king were added those caused by the old subjects, the English, Scots, and American traders who set up shop in the colony after the conquest. Historians of the Quebec Act who have praised the realism and even the generosity of the English authorities towards the Canadiens have tended to evaluate the reaction of the merchants solely in terms of their self-interest or their desire for political hegemony. The merchants, part of an army of occupation, could hardly have expected to be warmly received by the Canadiens, especially since their first reaction was to attempt to exclude all Catholics from juries. The claim that British freedoms should benefit only old subjects suggested to the Canadiens an ambition to oppress; the Quebec Act thus could be promoted as the Canadiens' charter of protection against the foreign profiteers. Both the old Canadien elite and the new British governors used that argument. Both groups were composed largely of officers and gentlemen, and whether French or English they shared a common contempt for the incoming traders and merchants, their social inferiors. It seems clear that the behaviour of the merchants, by alienating the Canadiens in the early years, prevented the explosive alliance between merchants' interests and the claims of the people which had caused England to lose control over the Thirteen Colonies.

What is less noticed is that the imperial authorities were also alienating the most liberal fringe of the Quebec mercantile bourgeoisie. In the Walker affair of 1764, there was a palpable undertone of hostility between the merchants and the military, the latter being closely connected to the colonial authorities.[15] The Quebec Act not only slighted the merchants' narrowly mercantile interests in matters juridical (restoring French law, ending civil juries) but also deprived them of fundamental rights claimed by all British subjects since the seventeenth-century revolutions.

That was the argument of the British merchants, and their view was not without merit. The re-establishment of French law affected the whole body of regulations relating to property and civil rights.[16] In the parliamentary inquiries and debates that preceded the Quebec Act, it was clearly stated that the right to a jury trial in matters civil and the right to habeas corpus were abolished.[17] The merchants' case, represented by Francis Maseres, emphasized their dismay at the loss of English private law as well as the most important constitutional protection for civil liberties, namely

for those parts (of the English law) which relate to actions for the reparation of injuries received, such as actions of false imprisonment, and of slander, and of assault, and whatever relates to the liberty of the person. And most of all for the writ of habeas corpus, in cases of imprisonment which we take to be, in the strongest and most proper sense of the words, one of the benefits of the laws of England, of which His Majesty has promised us the enjoyment by his proclamation above-mentioned and which we apprehend to be a part of the English system of jurisprudence, to which our new Canadien fellow-subjects will not object.[18]

The British government temporized, not restoring habeas corpus in the

Quebec Act but recommending its future enactment in its confidential instructions to the governor.[19]

The merchants' protest at the betrayal of their interests was couched in the highest of constitutional rhetoric:

We are deprived of the Franchises granted by your Majesty's Royal Predecessors and by us inherited from our Forefathers; That we have lost protection of the English laws so universally admired for their wisdom and lenity and which we have ever held in the highest veneration and in their stead the Laws of Canada are to be introduced to which we are utter strangers disgraceful to us as Britons and in their consequences ruinous to our properties as we thereby lose the invaluable privilege of trial by juries; That in matters of a criminal nature the habeas corpus act is dissolved and we are subjected to arbitrary fines and imprisonment at the will of the Governor and Council who may at pleasure render the certainty of the criminal laws of no effect by the great power that is granted to them of making alterations in the same.[20]

From this moment on, the merchants were regarded as another danger to public order, liable to rally to the side of the American rebels; some of course were, and did, but the official correspondence reports sedition everywhere. Two days before applying martial law, Carleton denounced the merchants' conduct: 'To defame their king and treat him with insolence and disrespect, upon occasions to speak with the utmost contempt of the government, to forward sedition and applaud rebellion seem to be what too many of his British American subjects in those parts think their undoubted right.'[21] And he thought that restoration of all the old French law might be the best solution: 'For my part, since my return to this province, I have seen good cause to repent my having ever recommended the Habeas Corpus Act and English criminal laws; these Laws, now used as arms against the State, require more public virtue, and greater fidelity to their Prince, than is generally to be met with amongst the set of people here, that take the lead upon all occasions; to render the colony of that advantage to Great Britain, it certainly is capable of, would require the reintroducing the French Criminal Law, and all the powers of its Government.'[22]

An unforeseen consequence of the Quebec Act was that the merchants, forsaken by parliament, beleaguered in a colony whose rulers despised them, did not simply make contacts with representatives of Congress. They also attempted to create ties with prominent French-speaking Canadiens who might share their views. The result was that the act of 1774 led to an enlarging of democratic claims as the merchants became willing to seek and accept the support of the 'enlightened' parts of the Canadien population. In the petition against the Quebec Act that was presented to the House of Commons, the distinction is already drawn. Referring to the petition signed by those who were in favour of the act, the merchants stated that: 'The said petition was never imparted to the inhabitants in general (that is) the freeholders, merchants and traders, who are equally alarmed with us at the Canadien laws being to take place, but was in a secret manner carried about and signed by a few of the seigneurs, chevaliers, advocates, and others in their confidence, at the suggestions, and under the influence of their priests.'[23]

Trapped between old subjects in open revolt and Canadiens who showed little enthusiasm for the crown, the colonial government was very much aware that an alliance, even if only tactical, between the mercantile lobby and a section of the French-speaking bourgeoisie massively seconded by the peasantry could bring about the demise of the British empire in America. Its aim, then, was to use all available means, whether legal or arbitrary, to prevent this possible union of interests. Its efforts were enhanced by the war and the powers granted the executive by the Quebec Act. As much as invasion, those ruling Quebec came to fear democratic and republican propaganda which, in their view, held in thrall not only the despised merchants but also a good proportion of the new subjects. This is the context in which demands for order and loyalty met demands for legality and justice.

THE FIRST TROUBLES AND MARTIAL LAW

The Proclamation of June 1775 in Canada

The Quebec Act was to come into force on 1 May 1775, and in the weeks leading up to this date Carleton acted quickly in setting up a juridical structure that would meet the colony's needs until the definitive creation of the civil and criminal courts. On April 27th he named Adam Mabane, Thomas Dunn, John Fraser, and John Marteilhe to the Court of Common Pleas and installed Hertel de Rouville and Jean-Claude Panet as keepers of the peace in Quebec and Montreal. Already, rumours were rampant throughout the province that secret meetings were being held and that contacts had been established with the emissaries sent by the rebels.[24] On May 1st the bust of King George III in Montreal was found smeared with paint and hung with a necklace of potatoes; on a wooden cross were the words 'Voilà le pape du Canada ou le sot anglais.' A 50-guinea reward brought no information. The following day, a Canadien nobleman recently named to the Legislative Council, Picoté de Bellestre, declared that the culprit should be hanged; the son of an American merchant just arrived in the country, Salisbury Franks, expressed astonishment at the remark. A fracas ensued. Tensions between the French noblemen and English officers, on the one hand, and the American and British merchants, on the other, characterized the colony even at this stage; the war would exacerbate them. The immediate outcome also prefigured later events. The younger Franks was immediately jailed and all bail denied by the zealous new Canadien JP, Hertel de Rouville. The governor, Carleton, regretting the excessive enthusiasm of the Montreal justices, succeeded in convincing them that Franks should be freed. Their eagerness to help the executive, their sensitivity to any hint of sedition, and their ignorance of or contempt for the forms and spirit of English law (the warrant of committal was highly irregular) were characteristic of many of those on the bench in this period.[25] Abuse of the law became a major grievance of their opponents and proof to them of the tyranny imposed by the Quebec Act.

On 17–18 May Benedict Arnold raided the town of Saint Jean, underlining the weakness of the British troops and the lack of enthusiasm of the Canadien militia. As a first resort, Carleton called forth his allies under the Quebec Act: Monsignor Jean-Olivier Briand issued a pastoral letter on 22 May denouncing the American rebellion and urging the Canadiens to remain faithful to their king.[26] Perhaps because it achieved little, Carleton decided, two weeks later, to proclaim martial law. His famous letter of June 7th to Darthmouth, from which we have already quoted, reveals his state of mind two days before the proclamation. The Quebec Act had not enlisted the support of the mass of the peasantry. Worse, the seigneurs seemed to have less influence with their peasants than did the American rebels' agents, and the latter were also able to enlist the more or less open collaboration of some of the most prominent Quebec and Montreal merchants. In these circumstances, resorting to martial law, even though there was no open rebellion in the colony and the civil and criminal courts were sitting regularly, was a necessary course of action. As the proclamation stated:

To the end therefore that so treasonable an invasion may be soon defeated, that all such traitors with their said abettors may be speedily brought to justice, and the public peace and tranquility of this province again restored, which the ordinary course of the civil law is at present unable to affect, I have thought fit to issue this proclamation, hereby declaring that, until the aforesaid good purpose can be attained, I shall, in virtue of the powers and authority to me given by His Majesty, execute Martial Law, and cause the same to be executed throughout this province and to that end I shall order the militia within the same to be forthwith raised.[27]

Rather surprisingly, Carleton waited three weeks before informing Dartmouth of his decision; he then justified the proclamation by noting the lack of any other possible alternative: 'Circumstanced as we are, no other measure is likely to secure the province.'[28] The political and legal context of his decision reveals much about how the authorities of the period regarded the justifications for military rule and the supercession of normal law.

Martial Law, Common Law, and the Colonial Context

Apart from the fears of the government and the conspiratorial manoeuvres of some of the British merchants, the colony was relatively quiet when Carleton proclaimed martial law. The rebels had withdrawn their troops from the colony at the end of May. On June 1st, the Congress, in Philadelphia, had voted a resolution stating that it had no intention of invading Canada.[29] A week later, Ethan Allen published his letter to the Canadiens, in which he called for their neutrality. Carleton's proclamation appears even more premature in view of the fact that in Boston General Thomas Gage, with the city virtually besieged and the courts of justice systematically boycotted, waited until *June 12th* before proclaiming martial law.[30] Its imposition in Quebec, therefore, could not be justified by immediate urgency, by an existing state of war or rebellion in the colony, or by the closure of the regular courts. Moreover, English legal doctrine at the time tended to deny the right of the military to arrest or try civilians. In the 1670s Sir Matthew Hale, the lord chief justice, had enunciated the classic dictum: 'Martial law, which is rather indulged in than allowed, and that only in cases of necessity, in time of open war, is not permitted in time of peace, when the ordinary courts of justice are open.'[31] Following the Mutiny Act of 1689, the term 'martial law' became more and more associated with the body of law applied to the soldiers of the regular army, and the Bill of Rights of the same year declared void 'the pretended power of laws, by regal authority, without consent of Parliament.' From this period, martial law seems to have been progressively abandoned as part of the repressive means used by the British state; in parallel terms, sensitivity to its unconstitutional associations grew. The

Riot Act of 1714 expressed the concern that military intervention to suppress civilian riot be controlled by the civilian legal authorities. Again, in 1780, during the Gordon Riots, Chief Justice Lord Mansfield, although keen to justify the intervention of the military by the simple operation of the common law, dismissed the idea that this intervention was justified by the exercise of the 'King's extraordinary prerogative to proclaim martial law (whatever that may be).'[32] This systematic denigration of martial law in England culminated in the case of *Grant v. Gould*, in 1792, when Lord Loughborough, the English chief justice of Common Pleas, equated martial with military law and declared that since its only existence in England was under the terms of the Mutiny Act, it applied exclusively to the military.[33] The development of a legal doctrine giving prerogative powers to decree martial law in the British Isles during insurrections developed substantially only at the end of the century, in connection with the Irish resistance and the growth of Jacobin revolutionary political organization.[34]

In America, the crisis of the Revolutionary War resulted in earlier deviations from the official doctrine. At the end of the Seven Years' War, the army in Quebec found itself forced to govern conquered territories while awaiting the formal declaration of peace. Military law thus came to be applied to civilians by right of conquest, as it was in several other colonies, until the regimes established by the Royal Proclamation of 1763.[35] Perhaps for the first time, martial law was not looked upon as the brutal exercise of the power of the military in a state of war when normal resort to the regular laws is not available, but, rather, as an alternative form of administration of justice which, in a critical situation, may allow the military efficiently and swiftly to control the civilian population.[36] Once this 'precedent' was established, the military leaders in the American colonies, with Gage the first among them, did not hesitate to call repeatedly upon the army to repress civil disorder. Thus, the proclamation of martial law in Quebec was, for the military, a natural extension of a repressive tool that gave them wide latitude and allowed them to act freely against agitators, *in parallel* with the ordinary administration of justice:

The King did not issue his proclamation, branding the dissident colonists traitors and declaring that they were at war against him, until August 1775 ... Throughout the period of rising unrest, except when suspended by Parliament itself, the ordinary civilian organs of colonial government were open and in competent exercise of their powers. Once the threshold of revolution was crossed, military force had to be recognized as appropriate and lawful; but it was the British resort to such force, and to elements of martial rule before that threshold was crossed, that inflamed the passions of the masses of colonists and steeled their minds to revolution ... Once again, the use of military troops against disorderly civilians had served as a catalyst to precipitate revolution.[37]

On the eve of the Revolutionary War, America thus became, before Ireland, the experimental ground for a new distribution of repressive powers between civil and military authority. Martial law began to justify the prompt use of military force as the needs of the moment seemed to dictate.

The Application of Martial Law in Canada

Carleton's proclamation of 9 June 1775 is an illustration of the development. Recall that it had a double purpose: to proclaim martial law and to raise the militia.[38] The failure to effect the latter demonstrated that the Canadien nobility had little influence over the peasantry. But martial law seemed to the merchants a complete justification of their fears that the Quebec Act would encourage or allow arbitrary government by military rule, *lettres de cachet* unchallenged by habeas corpus. Maseres, now a cursitor baron of the Exchequer in London, presented their arguments in print and in person. He published a letter in September 1775 which offered a critical analysis of the proclamations by Gage and by Carleton in June 1775 of martial law, this strange beast that was 'neither common law, nor statute law, nor civil law.'[39] Relying on the 1628 Petition of Right, he argued that martial law could be applied only when civil courts were unable to sit and, then, exclusively against the military and their personnel; it was, in short, 'a summary kind of criminal law adapted to the government of an army.'[40] The conclusion followed: 'as to the proclamation establishing Martial Law in the province of Quebec, I can hardly conceive it to be legal in the state in which the province was reported to be when it was published, that is, on the 9th of June last: for according to all the accounts we have had from thence, that province was then, and I hope is still, in a state of perfect tranquility.'[41] If the state of the province could not justify Carleton, there remained the hypothesis that it was a measure he believed would give him powers to raise a militia, thus restoring to him a prerogative his French counterpart had before the conquest. But this, continued Maseres's account, was a mistaken conclusion. The constitutional authorities, he argued, showed that 'the establishment of martial law in the province, even if the situation of the province had been such as to make such a measure legal, would not have authorized him in the least degree to press the Canadiens into service on this occasion.'[42]

The debate on the validity of martial law in Quebec undoubtedly reflects the opposition of the merchants to all military power, and it is very similar to the reaction of the Americans faced with the tactics of General Gage in Boston. This indignation over the arbitrary uses of military force and the law was one of the springs of the revolution. The irony is that in Quebec all the indications are that the proclamation of martial law was intended not so much to deal with internal opposition as to mobilize the population to face the external enemy.

From 9 June to 5 December 1775, when Carleton retreated inside the walls of Quebec, besieged by Montgomery, only two men were arrested and imprisoned by the army. One was Pierre Charlan, arrested 1 August, who was carrying a letter from John Brown, a delegate of Congress, to Thomas Walker. The latter was arrested, in a siege on his house at Assomption, only on October 5. There were no more such arrests, in spite of many American raids, scattered resistance to the raising of the militia, and great activity on behalf of the Americans by some English and American merchants, notably Walker, James Price, and James Livingstone.[43]

All the other detainees in 1775 whose names we can find in the archives seem to have been identified as Canadiens who were made prisoners during a scuffle with the rebels.[44] Of course, Carleton knew only too well that, with barely 1000 regular troops and a population fully aware of the weakness of the British army, he could not risk abusive measures. He restrained seigneurs who showed too much enthusiasm in their efforts to recruit militiamen, and he gladly pardoned Canadiens unwilling to enlist who showed the least sign of repentance.[45] From June to September 1775, shows of force and arbitrary use of the law were useless, if not dangerous, against a peasantry that successfully practised passive resistance. From October, such measures became impossible as the rebels advanced and Carleton was obliged to fall back to Quebec City.

The Reopening of the Civil Courts and the End of Martial Law

At the end of June 1776 the American force withdrew from the province. With reinforcements coming in from England and the Americans retreating to their bases, Carleton continued his policy of moderation. The troops newly arrived from England were billeted so as not to create too many problems for the habitants. He did compel the peasants to participate in some road repairs and to protect army convoys. A few peasants opposed to these measures were arrested in the summer of 1776; that was the extent of the repressive measures.[46]

At the end of the summer, the re-opening of the civil courts came up for discussion.[47] On August 8th, the secretary for the colonies, Lord George Germain, wrote to Chief Justice Hey: 'His Majesty's province of Quebec being cleaned of the rebels, it is become highly necessary that the Courts of Justice should be forthwith opened and public business carried on there in the usual forms.'[48] The regular application of the law was clearly regarded as an essential means to restore order, as Germain explained to Carleton: 'there still remains another part of your duty to be undertaken which will require all your abilities and the strictest application, the restoring peace and the establishing good order and legal government in Canada ... The rewarding those who preserved their loyalty, and the punishing those who have forsaken their allegiance will tend to the future safety of your province by convincing the inhabitants that the laws can be executed for the protection of the innocent and the punishment of delinquents ... No time should be lost in beginning so important a work.'[49]

This legalistic vision of the pedagogical benefits of English justice must have amused Carleton. He had already set out to ensure, in his own way, the restoration of order. In the second week of May he had appointed three commissioners to visit parishes in the Quebec and Trois-Rivières districts, with power to dismiss and replace the militia captains who had accepted commissions in the ranks of the rebels; they were also to enquire about the conduct of the peasantry while the country was occupied.[50] These commissioners were strongly supported by the seigneurs, and even more strongly by the church hierarchy, and their activities exemplified Carleton's paternalistic approach: their inquiries had virtually no penal consequences, repentance on the part of the guilty being deemed sufficient.

Carleton, without consulting the Legislative Council, had seen fit to organize two civil courts, in Montreal and in Quebec, and to replace the keepers of the peace who had been installed prior to the invasion. He briefly notified Germain of these decisions, in a letter that Germain received only after sending out his own of 22 August: 'As neither the season or circumstances of the Province, at this time, admit of calling together the Legislative Council, and establishing the Courts of Justice by ordinance, I issued a commission for that purpose in the districts of Montreal and Quebec, and in the same manner have established a court of Appeals.'[51] From this moment, even if no formal text proclaims it, we may conclude that martial law was no longer in force in the province.[52] In the end, its only use had been as a supplementary power to a government that tempered arbitrary legal measures with a genuine paternalism. Martial law was a creature born of the 'system of the generals.'[53] In Quebec its character was precisely that given it a century later by Lord Chief Justice Cockburn: 'Martial law, when applied to the civilian, is no law at all, but a shadowy, uncertain, precarious something, depending entirely on the conscience, or rather on the despotic and arbitrary will of those who administer it.'[54] With martial law set aside, other means had to be found to circumvent the normal administration of law. One unresolved question dominated much of the ensuing struggle: whether the English remedy of habeas corpus was part of the law of the province.

HABEAS CORPUS IN ENGLISH AND COLONIAL LAW AND POLITICS

The writ of *habeas corpus ad subjiciendum* and the Habeas Corpus Act of 1679 loomed large in the rhetoric of Englishmen, both at home and in the American colonies. By the seventeenth century the ancient writ had been transformed from an instrument by which the crown compelled appearance before its courts to its quite different modern role as the principal protection from arbitrary imprisonment. As Chief Justice Sir John Vaughan of Common Pleas expressed it in 1670, 'The Writ of *habeas corpus* is now the most usual remedy by which a man is restored again to his liberty, if he have been against law deprived of it.'[55] There had been evident deficiencies of the writ at common law. It was sometimes unavailable in the vacations between law terms, was no help to those transferred to other jails or out of England, and could too easily be flouted by re-arrests or evasions that required the victim of injustice to make repeated applications to the court. Hence the famous act of 1679, which extended its reach in criminal cases.[56] The combined effect of this 'most celebrated writ in the English law'[57] and the 1679 act was that, once probable grounds were shown that a person was committed to prison and charged with a crime without cause, unless it was for treason or felony plainly expressed in the warrant, the common law judges or the lord chancellor would award habeas corpus; the writ had to be returned in a limited time, depending on the distance, and at most within twenty days; on the return, if the offence was bailable, the prisoner was allowed bail; all those accused of treason or felony could demand to be indicted or bailed at the next sitting of the relevant court.[58] But two significant shortcomings (from the perspective of a state prisoner) remained. Neither the act nor the writ applied to prisoners committed by either of the houses of parliament.

And in 1689 parliament had begun the practice, which was to become common, of suspending the act when the security of government seemed threatened. Moreover, English governments clearly believed that rebellious subject populations could not be granted its benefits: in 1758 Lord Hardwicke pointed out that its extension to Ireland had always been refused. 'It has been often attempted and has as often, in the best of times, been rejected on account of the state of Ireland, which made it not safe for the King's Protestant subjects there.'[59] It was an argument that would be used with respect to Quebec.

British colonists in America liked to believe that they had taken with them all the constitutional elements of English liberty, especially liberty from oppressive government. The two most important were trial by jury and habeas corpus. Trial by jury was introduced for criminal cases in Quebec in 1764; it was not available for civil cases until 1785, although the argument that it had necessarily been introduced by the conquest was made. About habeas corpus there was even less clarity, and that lack of clarity made the arguments between a nascent democratic movement and an intransigent executive particularly sharp. When the government imprisoned its critics, and courts closely identified with the executive refused to grant habeas corpus, the argument became virulent.

Whether the writ and the act were in force was a matter of distinct inquiry in each British colony, with sometimes conflicting explanations, depending on differing theories of reception, different charters, different colonial legislation. But by the mid-eighteenth century, the writ was in operation in all of the thirteen colonies that were to rebel in 1776, and the advantages conferred by the act were found in Virginia, North Carolina, South Carolina, and Georgia; sometimes courts in other colonies also behaved as if it was law.[60] But what of Quebec? With respect to the act, the issue seemed clear, but only at first; the question of the writ was even more obscure.

Habeas Corpus and the Special Problem of Quebec

The Policy of the British Government

Carleton and Hey, the governor and chief justice, recommended to the Board of Trade in 1769 that the act be introduced into Quebec to complement the English criminal law already in force. In recommending the creation of crown attorneys, they urged that all warrants of commitment should exactly specify the crime, on the oath of a credible witness, 'so that the Habeas Corpus Act may take it's proper Effect, and the Party, if entitled, be admitted to Bail.'[61] Carleton had changed his opinion by the time the Quebec Act was passed,[62] and Alexander Wedderburn, England's solicitor general, reported in 1772 that although the common-law writ was part of the received criminal law of Quebec, greater proofs would be needed of the Canadiens' 'fidelity and attachment' before the boon of the act could be granted.[63] The effect of the advice the British government received from Quebec and from its own law officers led to the deletion of any mention of habeas corpus in the act. In 1774 the American Congress, seeking to gain the support of Quebec, deplored the omission of 'that great bulwark and palladium of English liberty.'[64]

The British government did make weak, and secret, obeisance to that belief of Englishmen. Carleton's instructions recommended that the governor and council consider and follow the example 'which the *Common Law* of this Kingdom hath set in the Provision made for a *Writ* of Habeas Corpus' to ensure 'security to personal liberty' in Quebec, 'a fundamental principle of justice in all free governments,'[65] a recommendation that would be repeated in Haldimand's instructions of 1778.[66] It seems unlikely that a crown lawyer would understand this to be an instruction to enact a version of the act of 1679; at the most, Quebec might be granted the more limited benefit of the common-law writ, expunged in 1774 by the grant of French law with respect to 'property and civil rights' in the Quebec Act. This was certainly the opinion of the former attorney general, Francis Maseres, who believed that there hence was no remedy for false imprisonment by government. During the debates on the Quebec Act, he was asked, 'Among those civil rights under the laws of England which this bill is to abolish, do you not understand the laws of habeas corpus to be a part? – I understand they are. If not, there should be a proviso that the laws of habeas corpus continue.'[67] The instruction thus appears to have been based on the assumption that the writ, itself part of the common law, was not yet part of the laws of Quebec.[68]

Carleton never acted on that instruction to introduce the remedies of the writ. Haldimand, Carleton's successor, was anxious to have the issue clarified before going to Quebec in 1778, but he clearly wanted to believe that there was no right of habeas corpus in Quebec, at least during war. In 1780, defending his decision not to communicate to the council his instruction (identical to Carleton's) to introduce habeas corpus, he argued that during war and rebellion such a remedy was 'highly dangerous.'[69]

There was nonetheless confusion over whether habeas corpus obtained in Quebec, arising in part from genuine uncertainty about the legal niceties, in part from deliberate ambiguity, and in part from changes in policy, in Quebec and London, as the American rebellion developed. The implication that we suggest can be drawn from Carleton's instructions, namely that neither act nor writ obtained in Quebec after the Quebec Act, was contradicted by some apparently authoritative sources. The secretary of state for the colonies responded to protests from Quebec in early 1775 with the words, 'They are entitled to [habeas corpus] by the laws of England,'[70] and the undersecretary of state, in a published defence of the Quebec Act, stated that the right to habeas corpus stood on the same footing as in the other American colonies.[71] Yet these statements were designed to placate the highly critical parliamentary opposition in England; in Quebec in 1778 the attorney general, like Maseres and Hey, apparently believed that habeas corpus was not part of the law of the province.[72] And this seems to have been the prevailing view in the colony, on the part of both the government and its merchant opponents: that without specific legislation (such as Carleton's secret instructions of 1775 recommended) no right of habeas corpus existed at all — neither the writ nor the act.[73] But it is ultimately up to the judges to decide what the law is. Clarification might have followed the appointment of Peter Livius as chief justice, because Livius held the belief, or came to hold it, that the writ, as part of the *criminal* law of England, was in force in the colony. The colonial government provided him very shortly with a test case. But the outcome was extraordinary and left the law unclear.

The Livius Affair

Livius arrived in Quebec in November 1775, holding an appointment as a judge of the courts of Commons Pleas and Vice-Admiralty; in August 1776 he became chief justice of the Court of King's Bench and the only legally trained member of the Court of Appeal, new courts set up following the Quebec Act. He had arrived after Carleton's declaration of martial law and just before the Americans laid siege to Quebec at the end of 1775. His short tenure as chief justice was engulfed by the war.[74]

In the aftermath of the invasion Governor Carleton and those about him deeply suspected the Canadiens and the British merchants of continuing treason, and on 24 September 1777 the lieutenant governor, Hector Cramahé, locked up Louison Giroux, a tanner, and his wife in the military prison on grounds of spreading false news and being suspected of disaffection. Ten days later Livius wrote Cramahé that he had discovered not only that the Giroux had been locked up in a military prison, itself an impermissible act, but that the supposed warrant from Cramahé was defective in not charging a specific offence; their accusers had not been bound to prosecute, and no offer of bail had been made to them. He also believed that the accused had not been examined before committal. In the military prison they were 'out of the way of trial and deliverance if innocent, and of conviction and punishment if guilty.' Livius expressed his astonishment as well as his dismay that he had not been asked for advice if Cramahé (who was a magistrate as well as lieutenant governor) had acted in ignorance.

Livius was reciting the requirements of some of the basic procedural requirements of the English criminal law on committals,[75] and he initially urged Cramahé to release the Giroux so that a new and proper warrant could be used to commit or bail them, to be followed by a proper prosecution and imprisonment should that be the case. Livius's indignation mounted as Cramahé and his men refused to agree. It soon became evident that Livius felt at stake his prestige as chief justice and that he appeared to believe that something like a military despotism was in place in Quebec, destroying respect for the law and for government; as guardian of both the law and civil liberties, he declared that he had to act. The ensuing quarrel between Cramahé, the officer son of a French Protestant soldier who had settled in Dublin, and the judge, son of a German merchant father and English mother settled in Lisbon, was in part one of social status. It made clear the relative powers of military governors and chief justices as well as the contempt that military men could have for troublesome lawyers. Cramahé's scorn was probably heightened by the fact that, for four years after the conquest, he had been the chief prosecuting officer in hundreds of courts martial in Quebec, including trials of civilians.[76]

But the Giroux were not released on the writ, and the place of habeas corpus was not clarified. The inconclusive nature of the case arose in part from uncertainties about the law,[77] uncertainties that were exacerbated by the fact that Livius was forced to try to act alone on issues which, in England, would have been raised by private counsel or by the attorney general. Nor could he command the immense prestige, and the support of an organized political opposition, which occasionally allowed high court judges in England to wage contests with the executive. Although rare, contests such as that conducted by Charles Pratt, later Lord Camden, in the Wilkite cases in the 1760s continued to establish civil liberties and the importance of habeas corpus, as they had in the seventeenth century.[78] Livius could not hope to win such a battle in Quebec.[79] His language to

Cramahé suggests that he thought he could do so: he denounced him for 'illegally, wantonly, and unnecessarily' hiding prisoners of state through *'lettres de cachet.'*[80] The phrase, shorthand for Englishmen's traditional scorn of the absolutism of the French monarchy, was perhaps also a reference to Cramahé's origins. Cramahé rejected the judge's charges with contempt, and, as Livius's subsequent fate shows, knew that he could do so. Although Carleton supported Livius in the Giroux case, when the chief justice pressed Carleton the following spring to reveal his secret instructions to enact habeas corpus and trial by jury for civil cases, and tried to force the issue through the Council, he incurred his enmity. Within months the governor summarily dismissed him, not long before Haldimand, the newly appointed governor, arrived to take up office.[81]

The Giroux case thus did not establish the status of habeas corpus in Quebec: the writ never issued. Livius clearly believed that it was part of the law of the province.[82] Cramahé clearly stated his belief that it was not, and cited Carleton's instructions as proof. But the episode reveals a great deal about the relative importance of legal probity and reasons of state for the government of the province. Cramahé frankly argued that 'the ordinary course of law' could not meet the threat of sedition and that the times would justify going beyond the 'strict letter' of the law, at least in the eyes of 'every friend to government.'[83]

'Under the Inquisition of the Tyrant Haldimand'[84]

Shortly before Haldimand embarked for Quebec in early 1778, he begged the secretary of state for the colonies to clarify the matter of habeas corpus, since Livius (still chief justice, although his dismissal by Carleton took place within weeks of Haldimand's inquiry) had made the issue inescapable by his contention that it had been introduced with the criminal law of England.[85] He does not appear ever to have received an answer; his instructions simply repeated the ambiguous advice given Carleton years before.[86] It seems likely that, as a German Swiss, he was also ignorant of the niceties of English constitutional law with respect to arrest and imprisonment.[87] Certainly he thought that arresting men of questionable loyalty was essential. Within a year of his arrival in Quebec he began a series of arbitrary imprisonments that went far beyond anything even contemplated by Carleton or Cramahé, and in doing so he brought into being an opposition, a binational democratic alliance, that demanded for all residents of Quebec the constitutional protections of Englishmen.

After Livius's dismissal, the office of chief justice was held in commission for eight years by three men close to the governor; only one of them was a lawyer.[88] They constituted the court that offered recourse to those unjustly imprisoned, if any court in Quebec could do so, by issuing a writ of habeas corpus. But again the context was that of war. Shortly after his arrival as governor, Haldimand published a 1777 act of the British parliament authorizing arrest and detention without bail of anyone suspected or accused of high treason in America.[89] (See app. 3, F.) And arrests followed quickly. Of the twenty-five[90] interned during the war on suspicion of furthering republican sedition, four in particular raised the issue of imprisonment without trial in constitutionally important ways: Fleury Mesplet, Valentin Jautard, Charles Hay, and Pierre Du Calvet.[91]

Mesplet, a printer, and Jautard, a lawyer, were locked up from June 1779 to September 1782 (see app. 3, E, doc. 1). They represented a new force in Quebec politics: enlightenment journalism with a subtext of republicanism. They had received permission from the governor to publish, provided they showed respect for the church and the government. Their *Gazette littéraire* of Montreal, begun in 1777,[92] was not overtly seditious, and Jautard was careful to include attacks on Voltarian ideas as well as extracts from the *philosophes*. But the very fact that such debates were being conducted by laymen offended the church. The government probably had similar reactions to the anonymous articles: even before the war, it was said that nothing could be printed in the official *Gazette* without the approval of the lieutenant governor.[93] The editors were objects of suspicion in any case. Mesplet, who had immigrated to Philadelphia from France, had first arrived in Montreal with the invading American forces as their propagandist. Jautard, who had moved to Quebec from France in 1768, had welcomed the invading Americans with a public address in 1775. When Jautard tried to begin an academy, the bishop complained to the governor. Then in 1779 Jautard used his infant newspaper to attack René-Ovide Hertel de Rouville and Edward Southouse, lay judges of the Court of Common Pleas whom Jautard believed to be incompetent, partial, and hostile to his own advocacy in that court. Haldimand acted against the 'seditious cabal.' Jautard and Mesplet were arrested and imprisoned by executive order, although the governor doubted that there was sufficient proof to sustain a conviction.[94] But he had little respect, as an embattled soldier surrounded by poisonous sedition, for 'the suggestions of lawyers,' including the new instructions sent to him in the late summer of 1779.[95] They were to the effect that the government of Quebec should reform the judicial system, in part by appointing the chief justice to the Court of Common Pleas.[96] By the time the instructions arrived, of course, Livius had been dismissed and the cause of legal reform had clearly failed.

Du Calvet was prosecuted in connection with the same article about Hertel de Rouville in the Gazette littéraire of 26 May 1779, because it was his case that Jautard, as advocate, was arguing unsuccessfully, and his open letter to the judge that Jautard, as editor, published. Du Calvet accused the judges of acting as counsel against him, of partiality and lack of decorum, of applauding libellous statements against him, of overtly favouring counsel opposed to him and of excluding Jautard, his lawyer, for fear of his knowledge and expertise.[97] In September, Monk, the attorney general, exhibited a King's Bench information against Du Calvet for this seditious libel on the judges of Common Pleas. Such a charge, at the instance of the highest government lawyer, could result in heavy sentences of fines and imprisonment, but the process also allowed the defendant to delay his plea to the next sitting of the court. In March 1780 Du Calvet pleaded not guilty and was able to delay the trial again until its next sitting at Quebec on 7 September, on the grounds that his lawyer was ill. On that day a special jury (all English-speaking old subjects from Montreal) acquitted him.[98]

The government was unwilling to leave such a presumptuous and dangerous critic at liberty. In Quebec on legal business later that month, Du Calvet visited the governor and told him of his intention to sail to England in a months' time.[99] Two days later, less than three weeks after his acquittal, he was arrested on his way back to Montreal by two military officers.[100]

This time there was no formal charge. Du Calvet was held, on slim evidence, on grounds of having corresponded with the rebel Americans and of attempting to persuade Canadiens to join them. He undoubtedly had been an object of suspicion to the government for some time, a government convinced that the province was 'surrounded by enemies without' and 'infected with spies and secret enemies from within.'[101] He had been investigated after the American invasion, because their army had requisitioned supplies from him (for which he sought payment years later) and he was suspected of collaboration.[102] The grounds of his arrest were suspicions only, but Haldimand thought it best to intern him and, justifying his actions two years later, in the face of Du Calvet's campaign for freedom, he assured London that releasing him (and others, including Hay, whose case is mentioned below) would inflame the disaffected in Quebec.[103] It is clear, however, that Du Calvet endured prison without charge from September 1780 to May 1783 for much less substantial reasons. Haldimand in fact had been prepared to release him on bond two months after his arrest, but he changed his mind when Du Calvet wrote a letter of bitter recrimination to the governor.[104]

Du Calvet was disagreeable to those in power and on the bench, and in the small society of Montreal and Quebec personal and political disagreements were closely entwined. Because he was a Protestant, Du Calvet had been one of the few French-speaking JPs in the province from 1766 to 1775. He was apparently a good one[105] when most of the bench were not; their oppressions (which he claimed to have helped uncover) led to wholesale dismissal of the provincial justices. He had not been reappointed, and he was convinced that his troubles, including his arrest in 1780 and his long imprisonment, were strongly influenced by the enmity of Captain John Fraser[106] and Hertel de Rouville of Common Pleas, and hence of Dr Adam Mabane, their influential friend, who was, like Fraser, a member of the Legislative Council and also (after 1777) close to the governor and one of the three commissioners who assumed the role of chief justice.

Du Calvet's quarrels with Fraser may have preceded but certainly increased after a decision in Common Pleas in 1770 that the merchant believed to be most unfair. Within months the contemptuous English officer and indignant French merchant had a public affray; soldiers began harrassing Du Calvet and attacking his property; and in 1771 he openly blamed Fraser's servants for a night-time attack on his house with stones and gunfire. (He later blamed the attacks on his house for his wife's miscarriage and death in 1774.) After the appointment of Hertel de Rouville to the commission of the peace in 1775 (when Du Calvet was dropped from it) and then to the bench of Common Pleas in Montreal, things grew worse. There were bitter exchanges in Common Pleas, where Du Calvet felt that his lawyer was threatened and ignored and his opponents' causes favoured by both Fraser and Hertel de Rouville; his lawyer felt that he could no longer represent him without danger to his career. The merchant's frustration was enormous: large sums in litigation were involved; the judges of Common Pleas were clearly of limited competence besides being his enemies; the chief justice could hear civil cases only on appeal, by the existing local law.[107] When Livius was dismissed in 1779 not even that protection remained. Du Calvet's great indignation at what he felt was an unfair arbitration award at the end of years of litigation in one dispute finally prompted the libel for which he was acquitted in 1780. But he was convinced that his subsequent imprisonment was due to the social enmity of soldiers like Fraser and Haldimand, the opportunism and ignorance of incompetent judges like Hertel de Rouville and Mabane, and the deeply conservative suspicions and hostility to liberty that characterized the government of the colony.[108]

Meanwhile, others had been arrested, including the Scots cooper and merchant Charles Hay (held from April 1780 to May 1783), whose brother was an officer with the American rebel army. Du Calvet and Hay, Jautard and Mesplet, and some others passed their imprisonment in a large room at the residence of the Récollets. From there they organized a remarkable campaign for civil liberties and their own freedom. For these four, and others in the colony, were the germ of a new phenomenon in Quebec: a binational mercantile and intellectual party of opposition, one whose republican leanings informed a critique of military government. To the rulers of Quebec their social standing was inconsiderable, their politics anathema. In the context of the American rebellion against the crown, a military governor and a bench of lay judges were not interested in the niceties, or even the broad principles, of English legal doctrines on the liberty of the subject. So those imprisoned set out to instruct their jailers in the rule of law.

The Search for a Legal Remedy

They appealed both to executive clemency and to the courts. Jautard the lawyer made repeated appeals to Haldimand, all unanswered. His demands for a judicial examination of his confinement, a testing of the vagueness of the charge, were totally ignored.[109] By 1782 he wrote the governor's secretary with angry irony:

I dare not think that only in this tiny corner of the British Empire are the rights of the individual of no concern ... I keep silent lest I commit an offence. I know that I am allowed to think, but I do not know if I should say what I think.

Thus I do not despair of gaining my freedom, but neither am I hopeful. Hence I demand what can be refused me neither in law nor equity. Tell me why I have been arrested and held so that I may know if the offence merits the penalty.[110] (See app. 3, E, doc. 5.)

But the misery of his imprisonment, described in his many letters to the governor and his secretary, broke him. When he was eventually freed through the intercession of a few prominent Canadiens, after almost four years of imprisonment, his thanks to Haldimand were carefully couched in the most obsequious language.[111]

Two of the other prisoners did not so capitulate. Charles Hay's wife, Mary, applied almost immediately for a writ of habeas corpus to free her husband, imprisoned in April 1780, in part on the grounds that he had been refused a copy of his committal warrant and hence the charge under which he was being held was unknown. This was a conclusive ground for obtaining the writ in England.[112] Her petition was rejected (the governor reporting to London that this had 'very much strengthened the hands of government'), and a few months later the lawyer assigned to her by the court, Robert Russell, declined to act for her, fearing harm to his career.[113] Mary was not deterred. At the May 1781 sitting of the court she re-petitioned, giving the commissioners of King's Bench a lesson in constitutional law as she did so.[114] (See app. 3, E, doc. 4.)

Her petition dissected their reasons for refusal the year before. They had confused the right under the writ with the right under the statute, refusing the latter when she had asked for the benefit of both; they had required her to identify the charge, whereas her grounds for proceeding were that she had been refused a copy of the warrant, indisputable grounds for the writ in England; they had stated that the writ had not been introduced by the Quebec Act, whereas that statute confirmed English modes of prosecution and trial, which necessarily (she argued) included the writ. They had also cited the 1777 act authorizing detention without bail of those suspected of treason in America, a statute she argued applied only to the Thirteen Colonies. Her petition repeatedly cited technical law (for example, that the 1777 statute could be cited in the return but not as a reason for refusing the writ; that it dealt with high treason, not treasonable practices), and general principles of the common law (for instance, that temporary penal statutes should be construed with the greatest strictness; that a witness in court had to be sworn.)

What the not-very-learned commissioners of King's Bench made of this is not known; in her conclusion, Mary 'humbly' entreated them 'to consider how ill qualified she is for discussing points of law' and prayed that they would again grant her husband the assistance of counsel, counsel undeterred by fear of retaliation. The court refused to grant the writ. Over a year later, having finally received a copy of his warrant of committal ('on suspicion of treasonable practices') from Haldimand's secretary, Charles Hay petitioned the judges from prison.[115] After oral argument by Russell (again appointed to represent him) that this was a bailable charge, the judges dismissed this third request for habeas corpus.[116]

Meanwhile, Du Calvet protested the loss of his property and the fact and conditions of his imprisonment in sardonic, impassioned letters not only to the governor and Cramahé but also to London. He sent Edmund Burke, then paymaster of the forces, strongly worded petitions to Lord Shelburne and Charles James Fox, the principal secretaries of state. He protested his innocence and loyalty and demanded the protection of the constitution. Declaring that the 'foreigner' Haldimand was the real rebel against the constitution, he advised the British government to secure the loyalty of the inhabitants of Quebec by introducing habeas corpus.[117] Du Calvet also sent his brother-in-law, Jussome, to England in the winter of 1781–2 to present his case to the imperial government. Jussome returned in May in the belief that Chief Justice Livius (whom he probably met) was about to sail for Quebec to enforce English criminal law.[118] When the news reached Quebec later that summer that Livius was not to return (probably foreseeing that he would lose the battle with Haldimand over the issue of arbitrary imprisonment as he had with Carleton), Jussome first petitioned Haldimand (who did not reply) on behalf of Du Calvet and then sailed again to England 1782 to ask for relief from the British government.[119]

Du Calvet apparently believed by that autumn that Haldimand was prepared to allow him to be released and that therefore an appeal to King's Bench (at the time of Hay's third attempt) for a writ of habeas corpus might succeed. It did not.[120] Finally, in May 1783, the war over, Du Calvet and Hay and others were released by orders of the British government.[121]

An Appeal to State Justice

Immediately upon his release in 1783, Du Calvet prepared to take his case to England, and by September he was in London making preparations to sue Haldimand in the English courts. Charles Hay apparently began taking similar steps about the same time.[122] It is clear that their ensuing campaign for the support of English and Canadien public opinion was strongly supported by Livius and Francis Maseres, respectively the former chief justice and attorney general of Quebec, both now living in London. Livius had begun a lawsuit of his own against Carleton, the former governor, in 1782, for his losses in being dismissed.[123] Maseres, of Huguenot extraction like Du Calvet, was also critical of the regime established by the Quebec Act, in part because of its disregard for legality. He probably helped plan Du Calvet's legal strategy; certainly he was passionately committed to his cause and wrote Burke to intercede, apparently without effect.[124]

Du Calvet believed that he had to persuade the British government to recall Haldimand to London because he could be sued only there.[125] A year of petitioning the government did not seem to bring that any closer. In the spring and summer of 1784, to apply pressure, to prepare public opinion for the case, and to educate his compatriots in the rights of British subjects, he published two lengthy pamphlets, 600 pages in all. In them his personal tribulations became the symbol of the suffering of the province of Quebec under 'principles that prevail at Algiers and Tunis, or according to the mere will and pleasure of the Governour, with a declared contempt of all the restraints or rules of Law.'[126] In the English version he presented his imprisonment as a constitutional issue before the bar of British opinion. In the French, much of it a 'Lettre aux Canadiens,' 'tant anciens que nouveaux sujets,'[127] he also demanded restoration of habeas corpus and trial by jury in civil matters, and, significantly, the creation of an elected assembly with the power of the purse, to control the executive. Other proposals included elections to the Executive Council, greater religious freedom (including greater independence from government for the Catholic Church), judicial reforms, higher education, and public schools. In short, he contested almost all the assumptions on which Quebec had been governed since 1774, and indeed from the distant past, and laid out a program that inspired liberal and democratic reformers in Quebec, French and English, for the next half-century.

The *Times* of London, in its first year of publication, tended to support the protests from Quebec, reporting the impending lawsuits against Haldimand for his 'arbitrary and oppressive' regime and raising the danger that Quebec might be lost, like the Thirteen Colonies, if her citizens were not conciliated. Yet it also noted that the king had decorated[128] rather than censured Haldimand, who now moved in the highest circles of English society.[129] Certainly Du Calvet would not have been optimistic about the outcome of his appeals to the government if he had been able to read Haldimand's correspondence, as Haldimand was able to read his.

For that was the situation by February 1785. Advised by Maseres, Du Calvet had sued Haldimand in the Court of Common Pleas for £30,000 for false imprisonment; the general had to put in bail of £5000. Du Calvet had also mounted a collateral attack in Chancery to fight Haldimand's delaying tactics in the case. The general, meanwhile, asked to be defended by the attorney general and solicitor general of England. He was also receiving detailed reports from Du Calvet's secretary Roubaud, a former government secret agent, who was spying on Haldimand's behalf, pumping Maseres for the plaintiff's strategy, and sending reports to his employer Haldimand of the increasingly despairing state of mind of his other employer, Du Calvet.[130] Whether Haldimand's dishonourable spying would have defeated Du Calvet in court we cannot say.[131] He is reported to have been prepared ultimately to challenge the general to a duel if necessary.

That moment epitomizes in some ways their entire struggle. Haldimand scorned lawyers but was prepared to win at all costs in the courts, the choice of weapon of his merchant opponent. Du Calvet was prepared, if he lost there, to follow the general onto his own turf, the field of honour. Just as their quarrel invoked both honour and law, they were protagonists of two notions of constitutionality. For Haldimand, the German Swiss who was knighted by King George, it was fealty to his monarch, the code of an aristocratic order, and the identification of the king's enemies with his own. (After all, Haldimand had kept Du Calvet in prison in December 1780 for a slight on his honour).[132] For Du Calvet, the French Protestant, it was embodied in the forms and institutions of English law, habeas corpus, trial by jury, and the promise of justice before the courts. In the constitutional monarchy of eighteenth-century England, dominated by an aristocratic oligarchy, both could find support for their definitions of constitutionality.

Du Calvet did not live to see the results of his 'appeal to state justice,' nor to challenge the general to personal combat. Returning to England from a trip to Canada in 1786, he was shipwrecked and drowned. It was for Charles Hay to seek and find a little justice in the English Court of King's Bench, having been so often denied it in the Quebec court of the same name. His action for trespass and false imprisonment 'in a loathsome cell' for three years and sixteen days, begun in February 1785 (when Haldimand's bail was set at £3000), came before Francis Buller of Common Pleas and a special jury in June 1787.[133] Thomas Erskine, the most famous barrister in England, defended General Haldimand on the grounds that his conduct was meritorious, that he had full authority in his commission, and that it was 'not to be imagined, that every officer was sufficiently a lawyer to know what may be the point of law in every part of his conduct.' Hay's counsel, Edward Bearcroft, argued that Haldimand's conduct, 'by no means to be considered as intentionally wrong,' was nonetheless not justified in law. Buller instructed the jury that the commitment of Hay was irregular and probably unjustifiable. The jury found for Hay, awarding him damages of £200 and hence costs.

Perhaps that is why a year later the British government granted Haldimand £2500 for 'law expenses' while governor of Quebec.[134]

CONCLUSION

In the period of the American revolution, civil liberties in Quebec were largely in abeyance, at least in the courts. Under Carleton, in the period to June 1776, few opponents of government were detained, reflecting first his confidence that the Canadiens would reciprocate the trust shown them and then the importance of conciliation, or simply impotence, in face of the American invasion. Carleton initially also showed some sensitivity to the constitutional niceties surrounding arrest, detention, and criminal charges. Franks, the young man arrested by a French magistrate on a defective warrant in 1775 for insufficient loyalty, was freed. And the governor at first supported Livius, in spite of his self-importance, probably because the chief justice's emphasis on the exact forms of English justice was recognized by all educated gentlemen to be a foundation of British liberty.

But British liberty was different in the colonies, especially in new Catholic colonies, and emphatically different in time of war. The Habeas Corpus Act had never been extended to Ireland; it became clear after the Quebec Act that most agreed that neither it nor the common law writ extended to Quebec. Livius, pressing for its recognition in time of war, was dismissed in 1778 for trying to force Carleton to act on his secret instructions to introduce habeas corpus. In the aftermath of the American invasion, probably Carleton, certainly his deputy Cramahé, were disinclined to listen to lawyers' advice that could weaken the defence of the colony. Carleton openly doubted that the Canadiens were advanced enough in civilization to enjoy the more libertarian aspects of English law without danger to the crown. Cramahé took the view that legal niceties had to be ignored in time of war.

That was emphatically Haldimand's opinion also, and he justified his many arrests and detentions as crucial to the security of Quebec. The long imprisonments without trial of Du Calvet, Hay, and many others were acts that could not be questioned in the courts because of the compliance of King's Bench in Quebec. Its acting justices were at one with the government; the notion that the law might take a different view of constitutional rights than did the soldiers heading the executive never arose. By the time of the war, too, claims for such rights had acquired a taint of faction, and then treason, in the eyes of those soldiers and the magistracy.

The crisis of the war was the culmination of the friction between civilian old subjects – the English, Scots, and American traders who followed the army – and the officer class that had begun immediately after the conquest. During the 'military regime' of 1760 to 1764, the period when no civil courts sat, army officers had conducted justice for civilians under military forms, and their jurisdiction had sometimes been contentious. In English constitutional terms, the use of courts martial to try civilians was indeed remarkable, and the confusion of military and judicial roles ominous.

The suggestion of incipient military despotism was confirmed in the minds of some civilian old subjects by the Quebec Act's abrogation of what they believed to be established English legal rights in Quebec, including habeas corpus and juries in civil litigation. Their fears were heightened by the imposition of martial law and the absolute refusal of the courts to recognize even the common-law claim to habeas corpus. For those sympathetic to republican and revolutionary ideas, the subjugation of civil rights in Quebec was analogous to the English parliament's unjust and tyrannical imposition of penal laws on the American colonies.

It is in this context that the resistance of Du Calvet, Jautard, Mesplet, Hay, and others in Quebec has great historical significance. In recent decades historians have explored the notions of civic humanism that informed much political writing on civil liberties in the Atlantic world of the seventeenth and eighteenth centuries.[135] It generated a critique of executive power as always prey to corruption and a corresponding celebration of the probity and wisdom of independent landed gentlemen. This set of attitudes probably influenced some of the old subjects in Quebec, directly or indirectly, in their critique of the power of the governors and their supporters. More recently, some historians have returned to an older emphasis, a law-centred account of English political thought and action. For in England, and throughout the empire, many Englishmen (and Scots and Irish) took with them the convictions that due process, scrupulous regard for the detail and spirit of legal forms, legislatures open to the pressure of a wider political public and debate, and courts protected from executive coercion were at the core of English, and British, political identity and freedom.[136]

What Englishmen claimed, new British subjects learned to take as ideals also. The claims of Du Calvet were cast explicitly in this language: he took entirely seriously the claims of British justice, and his outrage and despair were fuelled by that belief and his hope that his wrongs would be righted. And in campaigning first for his freedom and then for redress, he and his friends began to create a French-speaking expertise in English constitutional law in Quebec, a generation before Bédard. But at this earlier juncture, there was another important ingredient in claims for liberty in Quebec. Mesplet and Jautard, and English-speaking republicans like Walker and others in the colony, also celebrated democratic ideals, in the widest sense, ideals that horrified those who headed both church and state. The short-lived *Gazette littéraire* published arguments for non-sectarian education, religious freedom, and liberty of the press; its editors attacked the courts as biased, reprinted Voltaire, and praised the American rebels. This was a political program that went beyond advanced Whig notions of English liberty. It anticipated Jacobinism. And it did so a decade before Painite ideas in England convinced its governors that aristocracy and monarchy themselves were at risk. In England the repression of the 1790s marked their response. In Quebec, that response had already been well rehearsed under 'L'inquisition du tyran Haldimand.'

NOTES

1 Philip Lawson, *The Imperial Challenge: Quebec and Britain in the Age of the American Revolution* (Montreal: McGill-Queen's University Press 1989).
2 Those exclusions turned in part on the unclear distinctions in English usage, and perhaps law, between 'civil law' and 'civil rights.' The former was usually a distinction drawn to mark a contrast with criminal, ecclesiastical, or military law, or all three. In that sense, it meant the English law governing private relations between subjects. 'Civil rights' often meant those legal claims enforceable as a consequence of state law alone, that is, ones not arising from natural law. It seems likely that both connotations are strong in the language of the Quebec Act, which stipulates that 'in matters of controversy, relative to Property and Civil Rights, resort shall be to the Laws of Canada, as the rule for the decision of the same; and all causes that shall hereafter be instituted in any of the Courts of Justice, to be appointed within and for the said province, by His Majesty, His Heirs and Successors shall, with respect to such Property and Rights, be determined agreeably to the said Laws and Customs of Canada' (14 Geo. III (1774) c. 83, s. 8). At the same time, some of the more modern connotations of 'civil rights' as civil liberties, particularly against state oppression through the criminal law, were current: see the quotation at n.67.
3 Proclamation of 7 Oct. 1763, in *Con Docs* 1: at 165.
4 Recent treatments include H.T. Dickinson, *Liberty and Property: Political Ideology in Eighteenth-Century Britain* (London: Weidenfeld and Nicolson 1977);

John Brewer, 'The Wilkites and the Law,' in John Brewer and John Styles, *An Ungovernable People: Englishmen and the Law in the 17th and 18th Centuries* (London: Hutchinson 1980); Nicholas Rogers, *Whigs and Cities: Popular Politics in the Age of Walpole and Pitt* (Oxford: Clarendon Press 1989).

5 Carleton to Shelburne, 24 Dec. 1767, *Con Docs* 1: at 289–90.

6 Report of Solicitor General Alexander Wedderburn, 1772, Ibid. at 430. In the debate on the Quebec Act, Wedderburn remarked, 'The situation of the British settler is not the principal object of my attention. I do not wish to see Canada draw from this country any considerable number of her inhabitants. I think there ought to be no temptation held out to the subjects of England to quit their native soil, to increase colonies at the expense of this country ... With regard to the English who have settled there, their number is very few. They are attached to the country either in point of commercial interest, or they are attached to it from the situations they hold under government. It is one object of this measure (Quebec Act) that these persons should not settle in Canada.' Henry Cavendish, *Debates of the House of Commons on the Quebec Bill* (London: Ridgeway 1839), at 51–8.

7 According to the spirit of the Royal Proclamation, the 1764 ordinance created tribunals for the administration of *English* law.

8 See, among others, André Morel, 'La réaction des Canadiens-Français devant l'administration de la justice de 1764 à 1774,' *Revue du Barreau*, vol. 20 (1960), 53, and Douglas Hay, 'The Meaning of the Criminal Law in Quebec, 1764–1774,' in *Crime and Criminal Justice in Europe and Canada*, ed. L.A. Knafla (Waterloo, Ont.: Wilfrid Laurier University Press 1981), 77.

9 Report of Attorney General Thurlow, 22 Jan. 1773, *Con Docs* 1: at 443; Haldimand to Germain, 25 Oct. 1780, CO 42/23/276, NA; Hay, 'Meaning of the Criminal Law.' This and further references to the CO series in the NA are to the microfilmed copies of the originals held by the PRO.

10 'As to the Habitants or peasantry, ever since the Civil Authority has been introduced into the Province, the Government of it has hung so loose, and retained so little Power, they have in a manner emancipated themselves and it will require time and discreet management likewise to recall them to their ancient habits of obedience and discipline' (Carleton to Gage, 4 Feb. 1775, *Con Docs* 1: at 661); 'These people have been governed with too loose a rein for many years and had imbibed too much of the american spirit of licentiousness and independence administered by a numerous and turbulent faction here, to be suddenly restored to a proper and desirable subordination' (Carleton to Germain, 9 May 1777, ibid., at 677).

11 Carleton to Gage, 7 Feb. 1775; Ibid., at 661.

12 Carleton to Dartmouth, 7 June 1775, Ibid., at 665.

13 In the same letter, Hey gives interesting evidence of popular beliefs in the aftermath of conquest and the conflicting demands on the habitants' allegiance. The Canadien peasants feared enlistment and forced exile, even being sold to the Spanish: 'A mixture of ignorance, fear, credulity, perverseness and prejudice never yet I believe took possession of the human mind or made it more difficult what to do with them.' See Murray Greenwood, Jean-Marie Fecteau, and Jean-Pierre Wallot, 'Sir James Craig's "Reign of Terror" and Its Impact on Emergency Powers in Lower Canada, 1810–13,' in this volume.

14 Hey to the lord chancellor [Henry Bathurst, Lord Apsely, later Lord Bathurst], 28 Aug. 1775, *Con Docs* 1: at 669–70.

15 All this was an echo of the opposition, in the mother country, between Wilkites and 'Old Corruption' (see n.4). On the Walker affair, see Douglas Hay, 'Civilians Tried in Military Courts: Quebec, 1759–64,' in this volume.

16 See n.1.

17 See text at nn. 67, 68.

18 Case of the British Merchants Trading in Quebec, 1774, *Con Docs* 1: at 517.

19 See below, 'Habeas Corpus and the Special Problem of Quebec.'

20 Petition to the King, 12 Nov. 1774, *Con Docs* 1: at 589.

21 Carleton to Dartmouth, 7 June 1775, ibid., at 665.

22 Ibid., at 665–6.

23 Petition to the House of Commons, 12 Nov. 1774, ibid., at 593.

24 On April 3rd Carleton was advised by an anonymous correspondent that 'the pig-headed subjects of supposed liberty constantly distribute all kinds of libels and try to intimidate the poor Canadiens'; CO 42, 34/126. See Gustave Lanctôt, *Le Canada et la Révolution américaine* (Montreal: Beauchemin 1965), at 49–53.

25 'The judges, through excess of zeal, laid hold of the words that had given offence to the canadian gentlemen ... to commit the young man to gaol, and refused at first to bail.' Carleton to Dartmouth, 15 May 1775, CO 42/23/276; for the warrant, see Pierre Du Calvet, *The Case of Peter Du Calvet, Esq., of Montreal in the Province of Quebeck. Containing ... An Account of the Long and Severe Imprisonment He Suffered in the Said Province by the Order of General Haldimand ...* (London: 1784), at 69.

26 'Your oaths, your religion, impose upon you an obligation, from which you cannot be exempted, to defend, with all your might, your country and your King. Therefore, dear Canadiens, close your ears, do not listen to these seditious persons who are trying to make you unhappy and to smother in your hearts the feelings of submission to your legitimate superiors which education and religion have etched thereon.' Pastoral letter issued by Mgr. Briand, 22 May 1775, in Lanctôt, *Le Canada et la Révolution*, at 223.

27 Proclamation of 9 June 1775, *PACR*, 1918, at 18. Briand assisted further, on June 13th, with a circular letter enthusiastically greeting the levy of the militia, without a single word about martial law: 'With the re-establishment of the militia in this province, General Carleton adds today another favour to his previous good deeds.' Lanctôt, *Le Canada et la Révolution*, at 293.

28 The governor offered a very pessimistic picture of the situation: 'The truth is, that those who retain their fidelity to the Crown, are astonished at [the rebels'] ... numbers and activity, and greatly intimidated at seeing no force or power able to protect them.' Carleton to Dartmouth, 26 June 1775, CO 42/34/155.

29 'As this Congress has nothing more in view than the defence of these colonies, resolved that no expedition or excursion ought to be undertaken or made by any Colony, or body of Colony, against or into Canada,' quoted in S.D. Clark, *Movements of Political Protest in Canada, 1640–1840* (Toronto: University of Toronto Press 1959), at 82.

30 F.B. Wiener, *Civilians under Military Justice. The British Practice since 1689 Especially in North America* (Chicago: University of Chicago Press 1967), at 83. As justification for his decision, Gage cited the fact that the civil courts had ceased sitting.

31 Quoted by G.M. Dennison, 'Martial Law: The Development of the Theory of Emergency Powers, 1776–1861,' *American Journal of Legal History*, vol. 18 (1974), 52.

32 Quoted in Dennison, 'Martial Law,' at 53–4.

33 Ibid., at 54–5. William Blackstone described this as the peacetime doctrine: *Commentaries on the Laws of England*, (London: 1765–9), 4 vols. 1: at 413–14, 4: at 436. *Grant v. Gould*: 2 H. Blackstone 69; 126 English Reports 434.

34 D.E. Engdahl, 'Soldiers, Riots and Revolutions: The Law and History of Military Troops in Civil Disorders,' *Iowa Law Review*, vol. 57, no. 1 (October 1971), 1; John Phillip Reid, *In a Defiant Stance: The Conditions of Law in Massachusetts Bay, the Irish Comparison, and the Coming of the American Revolution* (Penn State University Press 1977); R.B. McDowell, *Ireland in the Age of Imperialism and Revolution, 1760–1801* (London: Oxford University Press 1979), ch. 18.

35 See Hay, 'Civilians Tried in Military Courts'; Wiener, *Civilians under Military Justice*, at 34–63.

36 General Gage had suggested in 1765 that civilians facing criminal accusations in the western territories be judged by military tribunals: Engdahl, 'Soldiers,' at 24.

37 Ibid., at 28.

38 The two purposes were linked by a recent British statute providing that in cases of war or open rebellion the militia be submitted to the authority of the military law and governed by the Articles of War: 30 Geo. II (1757) c. 25, s. 45.

39 Francis Maseres, *Additional Papers Concerning the Province of Quebec* (London: 1776), at 174.

40 Ibid., at 182: 'It is clear beyond a doubt, that commissions to execute martial law ... are illegal in time of war, as well as in time of peace, unless the war be at home in the heart of the Kingdom, and the success and the power of the enemy so great, that the courts of justice cannot sit to administer justice upon the offending soldiers and mariners according to the known laws and statutes of the realm'; see also ibid., at 179–80.

41 Ibid., at 191.

42 Ibid., at 195–6. In his instructions to Carleton, as quoted by Maseres, the king gives the governor 'full power and authority ... to execute martial law in time of invasion, war, or other times, when by law it may be executed' (ibid., at 200–1). In fact, this clause does not appear in any of the instructions: see *PACR*, 1904, app. E, and *Con Docs* 1: at 301–24, 422, 594–636.

43 The Americans later delivered Walker, on November 11. For all this period, see Lanctôt, *Le Canada et la Révolution*, at 67–122; Carleton to Dartmouth, 14 Aug. 1775, CO 42/34.

44 Such an event happened on 26 September at Longue-Pointe, where Ethan Allen was captured together with twenty Americans and eleven Canadiens. Carleton shipped the Americans to England and kept the Canadiens in the local jails. Apparently, they were freed at the same time as Walker: Lanctôt, *Le Canada et la Révolution*, at 95.

45 He did it notably for the militiamen of Terrebonne and those of Saint-Denis.

46 Lanctôt, *Le Canada et la Révolution*, at 86.

47 When the Quebec Act came into force on 1 May 1775, the old courts were officially closed and were never really replaced by keepers of the peace. They must therefore be considered as never created instead of closed.

48 Germain to Hey, 8 Aug. 1776, CO 42/35/77.

49 Germain to Carleton, ibid., at 84–5.

50 A similar commission was set up, on June 26th, for the district of Montreal: Hilda Neatby, *Quebec, The Revolutionary Age, 1760–1781* (Toronto: McLelland and Stewart 1966), at 156–8. It must be noted that nowhere do we find that Carleton notified Germain of this initiative.

51 Carleton to Germain, 10 Aug. 1776, ibid., at 112. On this episode, see A.L. Burt, *The Old Province of Quebec*, 2 vols. (Toronto: McLelland and Stewart 1933; repr. 1968), 1: at 226–8.

52 'The resumption of civil government occurred in the summer of 1776, although, as far as is known, the proclamation of martial law was not revoked.' Burt, *Old Province*, 1: at 227.

53 The expression was coined by François Baby, one of the commissioners

named in 1776 with the mandate to re-establish order in the Canadien parishes.

54 *R. v. Nelson and Brand* (1867), cited by W.S. Holdsworth, 'Martial Law Historically Considered,' *Law Quarterly Review*, vol. 18 (1902), at 127–8.

55 *Bushell's Case*, 124 English Reports 1007; quoted in William F. Duker, *A Constitutional History of Habeas Corpus* (London and Westport, Conn.: Greenwood Press 1980), at 54. This paragraph follows Duker, chs. 1 and 2, except where noted.

56 31 Charles II c. 2. The statute 16 Charles I c. 10 had made the writ obtainable in both Common Pleas and King's Bench.

57 Blackstone, *Commentaries*, 3: at 129.

58 By the Bill of Rights, 1 Wm and Mary st. 2 c. 2, excessive bail was not to be required. The improvements embodied in the act of 1679 applied only to those accused of crime; in the eighteenth century soldiers and sailors claiming to be unlawfully pressed, and wives, children, relations, or domestics 'confined for insanity or other prudential reasons,' were limited to what they could obtain by the writ alone.

59 P.C. Yorke, *The Life and Correspondence of Philip Yorke, Earle of Hardwicke, Lord High Chancellor of Great Britain*, 3 vols. (London: Cambridge University Press 1913), 3: at 11.

60 Duker, *Constitutional History*, at 115 and ch. 2, passim.

61 Report of Guy Carleton and William Hey, 15 Sept. 1769, printed in *Reports on the Laws of Quebec, 1767–1770*, ed. W.P.M. Kennedy and Gustave Lanctôt (Ottawa: King's Printer 1931), at 68–72.

62 See text at n.22.

63 *Con Docs* 1: at 431.

64 Quoted in Duker, *Constitutional History*, at 115. See also F. Murray Greenwood, *Legacies of Fear: Law and Politics in Quebec in the Era of the French Revolution* (Toronto: Osgoode Society/University of Toronto Press 1993), at 24–7.

65 *Con Docs* 1: at 600, (authors' emphasis).

66 Ibid., 1: at 697.

67 *Debates of the House of Commons on the Quebec Bill* (London: Ridgway 1839), 2 June 1774, 133–7. Chief Justice Hey's answer was more tentative: 'If the habeas corpus is not allowed, is not arbitrary imprisonment in the power of the governor, without legal relief?' 'I should apprehend there are abundance of restraints upon the governor, which will intimidate him; and that the courts of justice would relieve against such. It would not be so instantaneous, perhaps, as the case may require ... They would not give instant relief; but I apprehend the party would be delivered at the commission of the oyer and gaol delivery. If out of term time, not.' Hey was referring to the normal course of gaol deliv-

ery, several times a year, when trials were held and accused persons tried or released. The difference made by habeas corpus was that it allowed 'instant relief,' even out of term (when the courts were not sitting). Hey's questioner continued, 'Suppose the imprisonment private, what remedy then?' 'No remedy' (a reference to the fact that the writ of habeas corpus was available in such cases). Ibid., 3 June, at 153. Hey's optimistic assessment of the Quebec courts' willingness to grant relief were not borne out. See below, 'Under the Inquisition of the Tyrant Haldimand.'

68 A version of the instructions to be found in the Dartmouth Papers states: 'Security to personal Liberty to be provided for; And the Writ of Habeas Corpus, as a part of the Criminal Law, to be adopted to its full Extent' (M 385:485, quoted in *Con Docs* 1: at 600n.1). The last words might be cited in support of the assumption, made by some authors, that the instruction recommended enactment of the act. But both policy considerations and the text of the instructions do not appear to justify this interpretation. For a contrary view, see Greenwood, *Legacies of Fear*, n.90 at 25, 269–70nn.46–8, 52. This view is also reflected in the introduction to this volume at nn.85, 90.

69 Haldimand to Germain, 25 Oct. 80, CO 42/23/276. On the 1778 query, see text below at n.85.

70 *Parliamentary History*, xviii: at 662.

71 William Knox, *The Justice and Policy of the Late Act of Parliament for Making More Effectual Provision for the Government of the Province of Quebec* (London: J. Wilkie 1774), at 63.

72 Haldimand to Germain, 14 April 1778, CO42/23/276; whether the Quebec or English attorney general is meant is not clear, but the context suggests Monk of Quebec.

73 An opinion by the law officers was usually considered strongly authoritative, but see text below at n.85 on the reluctance of the British government to provide such an opinion. On the general impression in Quebec, see Neatby, *Quebec*, at 68.

74 See L.F.S. Upton, 'Livius, Peter,' *DCB* 4: 484, the most recent biography. The following account of the conflict with Cramahé, unless otherwise noted, is based on CO 42/37/178–202v.

75 Any justice could find the relevant information in his books of practice: among other points, that a commitment (now more commonly called a committal) should be to the common gaol unless otherwise authorized by statute; that it should contain the cause, or charge. Richard Burn, *Justice of the Peace* (12 ed., 1772), 'Commitment'; William Hawkins, *A Treatise of the Pleas of the Crown*, 2 vols. (1716), 2: ch.16.

76 See n.13 of Hay, 'Civilians Tried in Military Courts.'

77 In addition to the question of whether habeas corpus was in force, there was the issue of whether Cramahé had in fact committed the Giroux not in his role as JP but as lieutenant governor, since the authorities recognized the right of a Privy councillor in England to commit persons for offences against the state (Hawkins, *Treatise*, 2: at 117); Livius argued that Cramahé had no such right while the governor was still in the province (fol. 191), an argument Cramahé rejected.

78 Douglas Hay, 'Scandalizing the Court: A History of the First Hundred Years,' *Osgoode Hall Law Journal*, vol. 25 no.3 (fall 1987), at 451–4.

79 Two details of his struggle with Cramahé illustrate his dilemma. He threatened to issue a writ to bring the parties before him with the cause of their commitments, an apparent reference to habeas corpus (fol. 182v); Cramahé retorted that he was informed that no judge could issue the writ ex officio but only by a party standing in need (fol. 200). Livius's problem was that the Giroux clearly did not have counsel willing to make such a case. Secondly, Livius said that had Cramahé been any other JP he would have directed an information against him (fol. 183v); Cramahé retorted that he was informed that judges could only order criminal informations to be filed by private persons coming before the court (fol. 201v). He was wrong: ordinary criminal informations were so filed, but in England ex officio informations as well as ordinary criminal informations could be filed against erring magistrates. An attachment for contempt was also possible. Livius's problem here was that only attorneys general could file informations ex officio, or generally filed attachments for contempt, and apparently he could not rely on Monk, the attorney general, to side with him against the lieutenant governor. We do not know who was providing legal advice to Cramahé in these exchanges, but Monk apparently thought habeas corpus not in force: Haldimand to Germain, 14 April 1778, CO 42/10–11. For an instance of an ex officio information later filed by Monk, see the case of Du Calvet below.

80 Fols. 189v, 192.

81 See Neatby, *Quebec*, and *DCB* for the importance of other disagreements between Livius and Carleton.

82 Livius to Germain, 9 May 1778, cited in Neatby, *Quebec*, at 68. In 1782, contemplating his return to Quebec, Livius announced or at least implied his intention of granting habeas corpus and the necessity of Haldimand accepting it if there was not to be an explosion. Livius to Germain, 13 March 1782, CO 42/42/109.

83 Fols. 200v, 201v.

84 'A L'inquisition du tyran Haldimand' was Du Calvet's heading on his letters

of protest to the English government: for example, Du Calvet to Lord Shelburne and Charles James Fox, secretaries of state, 30 June 1782, CO 42/44/23.

85 Haldimand to Germain, 14 April 1778, CO 42/38/10–11.

86 *Con Docs* 2: at 600, 697; Neatby, *Quebec*, at 83.

87 For Maseres's opinion some years later, see Roubaud to Haldimand, 23 March 1785, Haldimand MSS, vol. 206: at 117, NA.

88 The three were Adam Mabane, Thomas Dunn, and Jenkin Williams. Livius went to London and was reinstated after inquiry, but he never returned to Quebec. William Smith came to Quebec with Carleton (now Lord Dorchester) on the latter's return in 1786; Smith became chief justice that October. In England habeas corpus could issue from the Court of Common Pleas, but it did so rarely.

89 17 George III c. 9, continued annually to 1783; Haldimand was sent the statute by the secretary of state in January 1778: Haldimand MSS, B–205: at 5–6.

90 Murray Greenwood, *Legacies of Fear*, at 25; see also Pierre Du Calvet, *Appel à la Justice de l'Etat* (London: 1784), at 151–2, which claims 'hundreds' but names nineteen.

91 Aff four figures are profiled in *DCB* 4: Mesplet and Jautard, by Claude Galarneau (532, 390); Hay, by Guy Dinel (336); Du Calvet, by Pierre Tousignant and Madeleine Dionne-Tousignant (227). The following account is based on these biographies, except where noted.

92 Du Calvet, *Case*, at 75. The full title was *Gazette littéraire pour la ville et district de Montréal*.

93 Du Calvet, *Case*, at 60–1.

94 Haldimand to Germain, 7 June 1779, 13 Sept. 1779, CO 42/39/93–4, 229. Hertel de Rouville had been one of the enthusiastic oppressors of Salisbury Franks in May 1775. See text at n.25.

95 Haldimand to Germain 24 Oct. 1779, CO 42/39/386.

96 *Con Docs* 1: at 706.

97 QBC 28/17/4/7–8, ex officio information exhibited 6 Sept. 1779, ANQ: Du Calvet to Hertel de Rouville and Edward Southouse, 26 May 1779, printed in the *Gazette littéraire* of that date. A few words in the letter are missing from the copy in the information.

98 QBC 28/17/4/7–8.

99 It seems likely that Du Calvet told Haldimand that he intended to take his appeal in *Watson and Rashleigh v. Du Calvet* to the Privy Council, on the grounds that Haldimand and his council would not give him justice. If so, his meeting with Haldimand was less amicable than he later represented it. Du Calvet, *Case*, at 82–4.

100 The Tousignants' account in *DCB* 4: at 229 is erroneous in saying that the arrest was sixteen months after his trial: it misdates the trial to May 1779.

101 Haldimand to Germain, 25 Oct. 1780, CO 42/23/185: Haldimand defends the imprisonment of Hay and Cazeau in this letter but does not mention that of Du Calvet, a much more prominent merchant.

102 The evidence is summarized in the Tousignants' biography in *DCB* 4: at 229–30.

103 Haldimand to Shelburne, 16 July 1782, Haldimand MSS, vol. B–55 at 152. See also Haldimand to Shelburne 15 Aug. 1782, CO 42/43/109.

104 Du Calvet, *Case*, at 44, 109–24.

105 This was his opinion but apparently also that of Maseres: see the latter's testimony in 1774, *Debates*, at 128.

106 Du Calvet, *Case*, at 46. Du Calvet apparently had been active in 1766 investigating the Walker affair, for which Fraser and Luc De La Corne, among others, stood trial. See Lewis H. Thomas, 'Walker, Thomas,' *DCB* 4: 758 and n.38 of Hay's 'Civilians Tried in Military Courts.'

107 New instructions to Haldimand in July 1779 were to remedy this situation by appointing the chief justice to the Court of Common Pleas; see text at n.96.

108 For the foregoing, see Du Calvet, *Case*, at 35–79, 156–85.

109 Jean-Paul De Lagrave and Jacques G. Ruelland, *Premier journaliste de langue française au Canada: Valentin Jautard, 1736–1787* (Quebec: Griffon d'Argent 1989), at 310, 314, Jautard to Haldimand, September 1780, 7 Aug. 1782.

110 Ibid., at 315, Jautard to Robert Matthews, 19 Sept. 1782 (authors' translation).

111 Ibid., at 309–19.

112 Petition of Mary Hay to Commissioners of King's Bench, 15 May 1780, QBC 28/17/10/5.

113 QBC 28/17/10/3; copy Russell to Mary Hay, 23 Sept. 1780; Haldimand to Germain, 25 Oct. 1780, CO 42/40/185.

114 Quebec T–0006–14, ANQ.

115 Quebec T–0006–14, memorial 11 Nov. 1782, ANQ.

116 Ibid.

117 Du Calvet to 'My lord,' 10 Aug. 1781, CO 42/42/170; Edmund Burke to 'Dear Sir,' 22 Jan 1783 forwarding letter from Maseres, CO 42/44/21; Du Calvet to Lord Shelburne and Charles James Fox, 30 June 1782, ibid., fols.23ff.; Du Calvet to Burke, 30 June 1782, ibid., fol.27; Du Calvet to Burke, 1 Sept. 1782, ibid., fol.29; Du Calvet to the secretaries of state, 1 Oct. 1782, ibid., fols. 31ff.; Du Calvet to the secretaries of state, 1 Sept. 1782, enclosing letters of 30 June, 18 July, 19 Aug. 1782, ibid., fols. 33ff.

118 This was Livius's intention: memorandum of 13 March 1782, CO 42/42/109; however, his wording does not make it entirely clear whether he would pro-

vide a remedy for those imprisoned by delivering the jails or by granting habeas corpus.

119 Du Calvet, *Case*; also, Livius to Earl of Shelburne, 7 April 1782, CO 42/42/135–6.

120 See text at n.116; Du Calvet, *Case*, at 238–9; 21 Nov. 1782, QBC 28/17/10/8.

121 Cazeau and Pillon are also mentioned. See Townshend to Haldimand, CO 42, 44/46. Also see Haldimand MSS, B–205:9, in which Haldimand later claims that he set the prisoners free at the end of hostilities without waiting for orders from England.

122 Hay was in dispute with Russell in December 1783.

123 Livius to the Earl of Shelburne, 7 April 1782, CO 42/42/135–6.

124 Roubaud to Haldimand, 23 and 26 March 1785, Haldimand MSS, B–206, fols. 113–126. On Du Calvet's death in 1786 Maseres took responsibility for his orphaned son: see the Tousignants' biography of Du Calvet in *DCB* 4: at 232.

125 Du Calvet, *Case*, at 265–7.

126 Ibid., at 108.

127 *Appel à la justice*, at 65–262.

128 He was installed as Knight of the Bath on 19 May 1788; see *Times*, 15 April 1788.

129 *Times*, 4, 22 Jan. 1785; 1 Feb. 1785; 14, 20 Oct. 1785. Also: Stuart R.J. Sutherland, Pierre Tousignant, and Madeleine Dionne-Tousignant, 'Haldimand, Sir Frederick,' *DCB* 5: 887.

130 Haldimand MSS, vol. B–205: 400–11; Haldimand to Sydney, 1 Feb. 1785, Haldimand MSS, vol. B–58, fols. 43–4; Auguste Vachon, 'Roubaud, Pierre-Joseph-Antoine,' *DCB* 4: 685; Roubaud to Haldimand, 23 and 26 March 1785, Haldimand MSS, vol. B–206, fols. 113–26.

131 Maseres thought not, according to Roubaud: see preceding note.

132 See text at n.104.

133 *Hay v. Haldimand*, King's Bench deposition of Charles Hay, 10 Feb. 1785, Haldimand MSS, vol. B–205: 333–42; *Times*, 9 June 1787. James Cuthbert, later dismissed from the Executive Council by Haldimand, also sued him in King's Bench in February 1785.

134 *Times*, 26 June 1788.

135 Notable in this regard is the work of J.G.A. Pocock.

136 For example, see David Lieberman, *The Province of Legislation Determined: Legal Theory in Eighteenth-Century Britain* (Cambridge University Press 1989); Brewer, 'The Wilkites and the Law'; Hay, 'Scandalizing the Court.'

6

Rebellion and Repression in Nova Scotia in the Era of the American Revolution*

ERNEST A. CLARKE and JIM PHILLIPS

The last days of 1776 were not happy ones for Lord George Germain, His Majesty's secretary of state for America. On Christmas Eve he received word that the revolt of the Thirteen Colonies had spread to a fourteenth when a small band of Patriots laid siege to Fort Cumberland in northern Nova Scotia.[1] As it turned out, this was not the beginning of a general insurrection, and the siege was quickly lifted. A confident secretary of state expected to 'hear by the next ship' of 'exemplary punishment' meted out to 'the instigators of the insurrection,'[2] but in this he was wrong. Official response to the rebellion was characterized more by leniency than by vengeance, and in particular the heavy hand of the law of treason was stayed. Only two patriots were tried for high treason, and while both were found guilty neither was executed.

This essay provides an account of the treason proceedings resulting from the Cumberland rebellion, but while that is its focus it is by no means the only issue covered. The Nova Scotia government dealt with disloyalty in Cumberland and elsewhere in the colony through a variety of measures, administrative and curial, which involved both carrots and sticks, encouragements to loyalty and punishments for past offences. The use of formal law was a relatively minor aspect of the official response to the rebellion, which included hostage taking, property confiscation, and

*The authors thank Darlene Moore, Rebecca Veinott, Anne Kinsman, and Kemi Odujirin for their assistance with the research for this essay. Barry Cahill, Murray Greenwood, Peter Oliver, and Barry Wright provided helpful comments on previous drafts.

compensation through private civil litigation for those who remained loyal. An account of official reaction to the rebellion would be incomplete if the treason trials were not placed in this broader context.

NOVA SCOTIA AND THE AMERICAN REVOLUTION

At the outbreak of the American revolution Nova Scotia society was marked by two principal characteristics.[3] First, although it was 'a society of remarkable ethnic complexity' in this period,[4] comprising Micmac and Maliseet native peoples, non-English-speaking Europeans – Acadians, Swiss, Germans, and Huguenots – anglophones from North America and Britain, as well as free and enslaved blacks, a substantial majority, perhaps three-quarters of the more than twenty thousand people in 1776, were relatively recent immigrants from colonies to the south.[5] These 'planter' settlers made pre-revolutionary Nova Scotia essentially a New England colony in population and social structure if not in forms of government. The planters spread English-speaking settlement thinly throughout the colony in many farming and fishing communities. They brought with them dissenting religious traditions and a taste for the New England township form of local government, both of which resulted in substantial tensions between these scattered communities and the Halifax administration.

This cleavage between the official establishment in Halifax and the many 'outsettlements' represents the second significant characteristic of the colony in the mid-1770s. The division in part reflected the unusual history of the colony. Although Britain established an administrative centre at Annapolis Royal after acquiring Acadia from France in the 1713 Treaty of Utrecht, large-scale English settlement did not follow immediately. No effective attempt was made to govern the French-speaking population, and control over the part of Acadia north of the Bay of Fundy was not achieved until nearly half a century later, after the capture of Fort Beausejour in 1755 and the fall of New France a few years later. The history of Nova Scotia as an English colony really dates from the founding of Halifax in 1749. The new capital was founded for strategic reasons, as a counterweight to the French fortress of Louisbourg, and in British eyes Halifax's role as a major naval station remained the reason for the colony's existence throughout the eighteenth century. Halifax's ruling class and its merchant elite looked eastward across the Atlantic or southwards to Boston and cared very little for the travails of the growing number of settlers elsewhere.

Despite the close ties between Nova Scotia and New England, the reaction of the former to the growing imperial crisis in the mid-1770s was relatively muted.[6] Sympathizers with the patriot cause were few, isolated, and unable to galvanize the general population to a more radical stance. As relations between New England and the mother country deteriorated in 1774 there were meetings in the outsettlements of Nova Scotia to express support for colonial rights, and even an attempt to hold one in Halifax to protest the importation of East India Company tea. But the former attracted little support and the latter was cancelled by the authorities and its organizers dismissed from their government offices.[7] The House of Assembly did protest attempts to increase Halifax influence by reducing its quorum and the 'tyranny' of naval impressment, and there is evidence of some arson and sabotage.[8] In addition, a sustained campaign unseated the unpopular Governor Francis Legge in 1775, but this was essentially a dispute within the Halifax elite, not a battle between political ideologies.[9] When Nova Scotians made public statements about their political beliefs in this period, one in which the colony's defences were weak and an uprising would have encountered little resistance, they expressed loyal sentiments.[10]

Only on one issue was there sufficient discontent to unite a substantial number of Nova Scotia's diverse communities in opposition to government. In the fall of 1775 the assembly passed two bills relating to the militia. One provided for the selection of militiamen in local communities and for a fifth of those chosen to be stationed in Halifax. The other levied a tax to cover the expenses of the new militia.[11] These bills were prompted by the largely defenceless state of the colony and by government fears of an American invasion, fears given credence by the increasing scale of privateer attacks on coastal communities as well as by preparations for the assault on Quebec. But for many Nova Scotians these measures were severely flawed in two principal ways. First, they made it clear that government considered the defence of Halifax more important than that of the outsettlements. Secondly, they would squeeze money, labour, and defensive capacity out of many impoverished settlements already hard put to defend themselves. Legge's militia policy was a disaster, producing 'a universal ferment throughout the whole people'[12] which was expressed in petitions of protest from many, though not all, communities, including the oft-quoted petition from the inhabitants of Yarmouth asking to be allowed to remain neutral.[13]

Protests against the militia acts were most vociferous in Cumberland and Sunbury counties and in the Cobequid district of Halifax County, the result of the particularities of their social structure and histories. Since these districts provided the vast majority of the defendants in subsequent legal proceedings, a little more should be said about them and about their responses to the revolution.

The Cobequid district proved to be the least rebellious of the three.[14] A prosperous farming area situated on the north shore of the Minas Basin, it was comprised of three townships with a total population of perhaps 1000 people in 1775. Half of these lived in Londonderry, a community made up largely of Ulster Protestant dissenters. Truro was peopled by co-religionists from Scots-Irish settlements in New Hampshire, and Onslow's original inhabitants came largely from Massachusetts. Dissenting religion, Ulster or American frontier backgrounds, and in some cases fondness for the 'Charter Governments' they had known to the south made these communities distrustful of the Halifax oligarchy and potentially sympathetic to the revolution.[15] This tradition of political dissent was exploited in 1775–6 by a coterie of patriot sympathizers among prominent locals, men such as Thomas Faulkner, John Fulton, Matthew Archibald, John and William Cutting, and assembly members Samuel Archibald (Truro), Joshua Lamb (Onslow), and John Morrison (Londonderry). There was plenty of anger over the militia acts, principally in Onslow, but the patriot leaders could not persuade more than a small minority of residents to join them, in part because the district's influential religious leaders, Presbyterian ministers David Smith of Londonderry and Daniel Cock of Truro, were unsympathetic to republicanism. The clique of local patriots was reduced to individual rather than community action. A few of the more committed of Onslow wrote to Massachusetts for assistance and some two dozen from the townships eventually joined the insurrection in Cumberland.

The most dramatic incident in the Cobequid district was the remarkable forbearance of Onslow residents towards two parties of American privateers who appeared suddenly in their midst in September 1776. One party had travelled overland from Canso after their ship the *General Gates* ran aground in Petit de Grat harbour with a British naval vessel in hot pursuit.[16] The other party, which belonged to the privateer *Washington*, had fled from Halifax after breaking out of jail there.[17] At Onslow these fugitives joined forces and, in full view of many of the inhabitants and with the assistance of some, outfitted a local vessel and made good their escape to New England. This event infuriated Halifax and led later to the abortive prosecution of seven of those responsible.[18]

Patriots had rather more success in Sunbury County (now part of New Brunswick), far from the seat of government and relatively close geographically, socially, and politically to the communities of northern Massachusetts.[19] English settlement in this frontier district extended from Portland Point at the mouth of the Saint John River (the present city of Saint John) to Maugerville, some ninety kilometres up river. Farther up the valley was Aukpaque, capital of the Maliseet nation, and from there Acadian settlers were scattered as far north as Meductic. Maugerville, with 300 or so people the most substantial settlement, had been founded in the early 1760s by Massachusetts veterans, notably Francis Peabody and Israel Perley. While Halifax approved its establishment and gave formal title to land grants, it had little other contact with the settlement. The classic New England institutions of Congregational church and town meeting were the instruments by which the community governed itself; even after the county was formally established in 1765 and assembly elections held, those chosen rarely bothered to take their seats.

Revolutionary New England found fertile ground in this remote area, particularly at Maugerville and Aukpaque. Encouraged by the recently arrived Congregational minister Seth Noble, local pro-American residents of Maugerville such as Israel Perley, Elisha Nevers, Jonathan Burpee, and, particularly, committee of safety chairman Jacob Barker had taken control of the community by mid-1776. In May of that year residents passed a series of resolutions in which they declared themselves willing 'to submit ... to the government of the Massachusetts Bay.'[20] This document was carried up and down the river and, while 'Canoes full' of Maliseets stood threateningly by, chairman Barker obtained some 125 signatures.[21] Barker became the *de facto* head of local government, rewarding supporters and plundering and imprisoning Loyalists.

While the hub of patriot activity in Nova Scotia through most of 1776 was the Saint John River valley, as events unfolded it was Cumberland that would provide the most dramatic challenge to British rule.[22] This district comprised the Chignecto Isthmus, which connects modern-day Nova Scotia and New Brunswick, and the land immediately to the northwest, around Shepody Bay and the Petitcodiac and Memramcook rivers, now in New Brunswick. Following the Acadian expulsion the area was settled primarily by people from Rhode Island who founded the townships of Cumberland, Amherst, and Sackville. By the mid-1770s Cumberland County was peopled by these planters, Acadians living at Jolicure, Bloody Bridge, and in the Memramcook valley, and a community of Yorkshire immigrants whose presence dated only from the early 1770s. To the north at Cocagne was a large native settlement of Micmacs. The European population of the district at this time was about 800–900 people. In its strategic location on the Tantramar marsh at the head of the Bay of Fundy, Cumberland was largely a farming community although it also relied on the economic activity – jobs and contracts – generated by the presence of Fort Cumberland (formerly Fort Beausejour).

In 1775 a group of energetic patriot leaders, drawn almost entirely from the planter fragment, worked politically to bring the county, and indeed all of Nova Scotia, into the revolution. The best known is Jonathan Eddy, originally from Massachusetts, a retired army officer who had settled in Cumberland after the Seven Years' War and become a successful farmer with ample landholdings and a minor official at Fort Lawrence. He represented Cumberland Township in the assembly until 1775. Another leader was John Allan of Bloody Bridge (now Upper Point de Bute, New Brunswick); raised among the planters of Cumberland, he had spent part of his youth in Boston. Eddy and Allan were the principals, but there were other leaders – Samuel Rogers, Josiah Throop, Zebulon Roe, William How, Parker Clarke, and Elijah Ayer.[23] These men and others laboured in 1775 to persuade the population to rebellion. They were able to draw on unique local grievances,[24] and as a result the protest over the militia acts was most vehement in Cumberland. Its petition stated bluntly that its signers 'cannot comply' with the acts, for if they did their families 'must inevitably perish.' The petition also demanded dissolution of the assembly and the election of a new one.[25]

Neither in Cumberland, however, nor in any other region of the colony did the protest over the militia acts or anti-Halifax feeling or any other local grievance impel the populace in general to join the continental cause. MHAs Archibald and Rogers had declared in the assembly that 'the People would rise in Arms to oppose the Execution of the [militia] Acts,'[26] but they were proved wrong. Most districts remained at least tentatively loyal and in Cumberland and Cobequid support for the patriot cause ebbed as a result of the suspension of the militia acts, the recall of Governor Legge, and a variety of other government initiatives including a declaration of martial law, propaganda campaigns, and a successful tour of many outlying districts by the new lieutenant governor, Marriot Arbuthnot.[27]

There was, nonetheless, one dramatic incident of insurrection in 1776, the Eddy rebellion at Cumberland which attracted dissidents from other districts. When the fort there was re-garrisoned in the summer of 1776 with the Royal Fencible Americans, a provincial regiment commanded by Colonel Joseph Goreham, local patriot leaders were forced underground.[28] The attention of Jonathan Eddy and other patriots was directed almost entirely to attempts to persuade the Americans to invade. In fact, although Congress endorsed Eddy's proposals, only token support was forthcoming via Massachusetts in the form of arms and supplies and permission to recruit in that state. The result was an 'invasion' in October led by 'Colonel' Eddy. He had twenty-one men when he left Machias and seventy-two when he reached the Chignecto Isthmus on 29 October, having collected disappointingly few recruits at Passamaquoddy and among the Maliseet and the European settlers of the Saint John valley. Many former New Englanders, about two dozen Acadians, and only four Micmacs joined Eddy to form a small but heterogeneous military force of a little over 200. Defending the fort was about the same number of provincial troops and local Loyalists.

A month-long siege of Fort Cumberland ensued, during which the communities on the isthmus were ruled by Eddy's 'committee-of-safety' and the patriots subjected their loyal Yorkshire neighbours to a variety of indignities.[29] They also captured a large provision ship belonging to the fort, destroyed the garrison hospital and other buildings, and took sixty-one prisoners. The patriots killed or wounded at least nine Fencibles. Eddy's attempts to take the fort failed and the rebellion collapsed when reinforcements arrived from Halifax, broke the siege, and routed the patriot army at the 'battle' of Camphill.[30] Eddy and fifty-eight of his men fled immediately to the south and others followed.

Though the insurrection at Cumberland had been crushed, the threat of an American invasion increased. Even as the siege was lifted that other leading patriot, John Allan, was lobbying in the United States and the result was that in January 1777 Congress resolved to raise a 3000-man army in Massachusetts to invade Nova Scotia that winter 'or early in the spring.'[31] An elated Allan returned to Machias and when the plans for invasion fell behind schedule he led a small military force of Americans and Nova Scotia refugees across the border to Sunbury County in May 1777. This advance party occupied the lower valley of the Saint John River where at the Maliseet village of Aukpaque Allan located his headquarters and prepared to welcome the main American assault. When news of Allan's incursion reached Halifax, the loyal militia mobilized promptly and was shipped to Portland Point at the mouth of the river. The patriots were defeated in a skirmish at nearby Manawagonish Cove on 1 July 1777 and the remnants of John Allan's force were driven from the valley.[32] The Nova Scotia naval commander followed up this success with raids along the Maine coast, beginning at Machias in late August. As a result, American invasion plans were quietly 'laid aside.'[33]

The transformation of an almost defenceless colony at the time of the Cumberland rebellion to an aggressor in the American revolution reached a climax in the spring of 1779 when an expedition from Halifax established an outpost at the mouth of the Penobscot River in Maine. This guaranteed the security of the colony less than three years after the siege of Fort Cumberland. It was during the same period that legal proceedings were taken against those Nova Scotians who had rebelled at Cumberland.

THE SHORT-TERM RESPONSE TO ARMED REBELLION IN CUMBERLAND

Pacification of the County

Lord George Germain may have hoped that the rebels who besieged Fort Cumberland would be punished severely, but an immediate barrier to a sweeping policy of revenge was presented by Goreham, who elected to clean up the district through a mixture of aggressive pursuit and an offer of amnesty. The latter was issued the day after the siege was broken, and in it Goreham promised that he would do all in his power to obtain pardons for anybody who surrendered within four days, four principals excepted.[34] He could not do more, for he had no power to pardon the crime of high treason; arguably, he should have done less since his action had not been authorized. Halifax officials accepted his amnesty policy although we do not know whether they approved of it. Offering an amnesty certainly represented a change of heart for Goreham,[35] but the 'critical situation' in Cumberland after a month of civil strife motivated him to prevent excessive revenge by Loyalists and desperate rearguard actions by the dispersed remnants of Eddy's army. House burnings had occurred under the committee of safety's rule, the garrison troops had added fire to the sword in the Camphill rout, and revenge arson was a feature of the immediate aftermath of the siege. The cycle had to be broken. Goreham's 'conditional pardon' specifically referred to the need to prevent 'the horror and devastations, the loss of lives and destruction of houses and property.'[36]

Hard realities in the field guided Goreham; Halifax had to devise a policy to suit the larger context. Two principal goals animated policy making in the capital during the last weeks of 1776 and the early months of 1777. The first was the need to reimpose order at Cumberland and throughout the colony, which was achieved by a variety of measures put into effect in January 1777. These included the disarming of combatants who surrendered at the fort, the dismissal from government employment of two men not directly involved in the armed rebellion but who had been at best highly equivocal, limited financial sanctions against others, and enforcement of the laws against seditious utterances and correspondence.[37] A massive program of administering the oath of allegiance was instituted at Cumberland and special envoys were dispatched in April to Cobequid and Sunbury for the same purpose. This is not to say that civil government was quickly or fully restored as a result of these measures. Neither in 1777 nor 1778, for example, was it deemed advisable to allow the Supreme Court judges to include Cumberland on their annual circuits.[38] Continued acts of lawlessness led at least one resident in 1782 to seek out 'a more Peacable part of the Country,'[39] and as late as 1783 it was still considered that 'operations of the civil authority are very feeble there.' But pacification, if not reconciliation, was quickly achieved.[40]

The Treason Proceedings of 1777

The second goal of post-rebellion policy was the identification, apprehension, and punishment of those involved. The record of government activities and decision making on this issue is not nearly as full as one would like it to be, but a general picture can be outlined. Apprehension was greatly assisted by the amnesty offer, for in the days following the lifting of the siege over 100 took advantage of it.[41] Many nonetheless refused the offer, preferring to flee to Maine.[42] While a number of these men returned later, including two of the principals, many others stayed in the United States and afterwards received land grants from Congress.[43]

As he received the submission of his former besiegers Goreham also collected information and names from local Loyalists, who inundated him with accusations.[44] They likely provided details of Zebulon Roe's behaviour sufficient to convince Goreham to exclude him from the amnesty offer.[45] Despite all of this activity, only about seventeen individuals were captured. Five were taken on the day of the Camphill rout – James Avery, Parker Clarke, Benoni Danks, Thomas Faulkner, and Richard Uniacke – and conveyed to Halifax.[46] Three other patriots, who were implicated in the seizure of the *Molly* at Pictou by one of Eddy's patrols, were taken on December 5th when that vessel was chased ashore at Baie Verte by the naval sloop *Hunter*. These three – William Ball, Richard Simpson, and Charles Swan – were transported across Northumberland Strait to the colony of St John's (Prince Edward) Island and confined at Charlottetown.[47]

At least nine others were captured during the winter of 1776-7, although there is little information on when and where. By April these nine – Nathaniel Earle, Hugh Logan, Robert McGowan, Henry Miller, Alpheus Morse, Charles Oulton, Robert Sharp, John Simpson, and John Stewart – were incarcerated in the Halifax jail.[48] Some had been picked up in early December by naval vessels operating in Cumberland Basin and Shepody Bay. Sharp and Stewart had fled with Eddy but then returned to their homes at Cumberland, where they were captured later that winter.[49]

Investigations on the ground in Cumberland were supplemented by interrogations at Halifax of those taken prisoner and conveyed there. Although there is no record of any such decision, it seems to have been quickly and clearly understood that Halifax, not Cumberland, was to be where the majority of prisoners would be interrogated and any trials would occur. As a practical matter the authorities did not want to send the judges to Cumberland in its unsettled condition, but there was also general and local legal justification for the decision. Treason trials in England were generally held in the Court of King's Bench, and it was the Supreme Court at Halifax that exercised that jurisdiction in Nova Scotia, although its judges also operated under special commissions of oyer and terminer and as assize judges on circuit. Moreover, it had long been the practice to hold some criminal trials in Halifax even when the offence had taken place in another county.[50]

The authorities had a sheaf of local and imperial laws to deal with offenders.[51] The crime of high treason was received into Nova Scotia in 1749 at the latest and re-enacted locally in the first section of the Treasons and Felonies Act of 1758. This section was comprised of extracts from a variety of English acts and defined high treason as, inter alia, to 'compass or imagine the death of the King,' or to 'levy war against him or adhere to his enemies, or give them aid or comfort.' It also stated that 'all treasons declared by acts of Parliament of England or of Great Britain shall be deemed and adjudged to be treason within this ... Province.' This provision formed part of a general local re-enactment of the major English criminal statutes undertaken by the first colonial assembly; it did nothing to alter English law, although there had earlier been doubts about which aspects of English treason laws relating to counterfeiting had been received into the colony.[52] Those who had taken part in the Cumberland rebellion were clearly guilty of treason so defined, for they had unmistakably waged war against the crown, and the indictments presented in the Supreme Court in April 1777 charged that the accused did 'Wage and Levy a Public and Cruel War against ... the King.'[53] English law also recognized lesser political offences at this time, including sedition and 'high misdemeanours.' The latter covered a broad range of activities; for our purposes, relevant examples include such acts/omissions as refusing to take the state oaths and refusing to assist in the defence of the realm when ordered to.[54]

The government therefore had a more than sufficient legal armoury to begin prosecutions, and as early as mid-January 1777 it probably had enough information on offenders. It also had two crown witnesses – Avery and Uniacke – among those captured.[55] Avery had been Eddy's 'commissariat officer,' and Uniacke was clearly implicated in the forcible detention of a loyal settler.[56] Yet, even with the added weaponry of accomplice witnesses, the government delayed prosecutions until April and the only persons presented to the grand jury in Hilary Term (January) were seven Cobequid men accused of 'comforting, aiding and assisting ... Rebel Privateers.' All of them – Samuel Archibald, Thomas Archibald, Charles Dickson, Adams Johnston, John Savage, Joseph Scott, and Matthew Taylor – were presented 'from Information on Oath of James Avery.' While their actions would certainly have supported an accusation of treason, the authorities chose not to apply the law in all its rigour and they were charged only with 'misdemeanour.' Moreover, those charges came to nothing. Some were dropped in January; others were put off at the prosecution's request – likely because Avery, the principal prosecution witness, had by then escaped – and later dropped.[57] Thus, the government's first efforts at prosecutions for disloyal acts proved abortive; it is more than likely, although there is no conclusive evidence of this, that the accuseds bought their freedom by agreeing to take the oath of allegiance.[58] Dickson's change of heart was genuine and he made striking progress as a born-again Loyalist, procuring a government appointment that same year and becoming an inferior court justice in 1778. The policy of leniency in return for loyalty had begun.[59]

The Easter Term (April-May) of the Supreme Court brought substantial activity in cases arising directly from the Cumberland rebellion. In stages throughout the month of April, at least thirty-five, and probably forty-two, men were named on indictments for high treason.[60] The list included major figures such as Eddy, How, Roe, Rogers, and the Acadian captain Isaiah Boudreau, but not the native leader Ambroise St Aubin.[61] Also indicted were the only prisoners tried, Parker Clarke and Thomas Faulkner. Clarke, who was tried first on 18 April, had been a member of the committee of safety in Cumberland and during the period of republican rule he made himself notorious as the principal in what can only be described as an extortion racket. He and others, all armed, called on Loyalists to collect old and previously settled accounts for medical services. When one of his victims, Thomas Robinson, protested that he had already paid his bill, Clarke's companion at the time, Zebulon Roe, 'demanded in a threatening manner' and said that if Robinson did not pay 'he would oblige [him] ... to go prisoner.' Robinson paid. Clarke's prosecution was conducted by both Attorney General William Nesbitt and Solicitor General Richard Gibbons, who called three witnesses to attest to these activities, to the fact that Clarke had made many derogatory comments about government and loyal Yorkshiremen, and to the circumstances of his apprehension.[62] According to the evidence, Clarke 'had gun and bayonet fixed at the time the forte was invested' and 'Col. Roe, Major How and Clark were in company once before in arms.'

During the one-day trial leading criminal lawyer Daniel Wood defended Clarke, but he does not appear to have examined the prosecution witnesses or to have called any on behalf of the defence. The jury had no difficulty in finding Clarke guilty of high treason, a verdict presumably based principally on his being in arms against the crown.

The following day Faulkner came up for trial. He was from Cobequid district and his strongly pro-American sympathies had come to the fore during the crisis over the militia acts. He had been sufficiently prominent to be arrested and charged with 'treasonable practices' before the Supreme Court at Halifax in 1776, although the grand jury refused to indict him.[63] Shortly afterwards Faulkner became the 'captain' of the twenty-five men from Cobequid district who joined Eddy's force. On 29 October, after the Camphill rout, he fled east with James Avery to Fort Lawrence, where the two of them were captured and disarmed. When taken he had apparently 'trembled much' and 'seemed much terrified,' and he hardly cut a defiant picture in the months spent in jail awaiting trial. At one point, describing himself as 'a prisoner now in Irons,' he petitioned the court for his release, arguing that he had been apprehended while doing nothing more illegal than travelling from Cobequid to New England, a journey he had undertaken 'on account of the hardships he suffered in Gaol during the last Summer.' He called 'God to witness' that 'he never took up arms against any of his Majesty's subjects, that he was not anyway concerned in joining ... the ... parties which attacked ... His Majesty's Garrison at Cumberland.' In fact he 'was Eight miles distance from the Rebels at the Time of their last Skirmish ... and had not been in the County of Cumberland Forty Eight Hours when he was taken a Prisoner.' He claimed that he could produce 'Evidence now in Town to prove' this story, and he argued that he had been apprehended only because of general suspicions. Not surprisingly, the judges did not believe that he was a victim of such outrageous coincidence, and he stayed put to await trial.[64]

At his trial Faulkner was, like Clarke, prosecuted by Nesbitt and Gibbons but, unlike Clarke, he apparently chose to defend himself. The prosecution established the circumstances of his capture – that he and Avery had been in arms, that they had initially run from the soldiers, and that in flight Faulkner had thrown away his ammunition. There was also testimony from William Milburn, a Yorkshireman, that while Milburn had been held prisoner he saw Faulkner at Eddy's headquarters on Camphill 'with Avery and two other Cobequid men.' As with Clarke, it seems to have been a simple matter to establish that Faulkner had been in arms against the crown, and that brought a verdict of guilty of high treason. Faulkner did offer a defence almost as unlikely as his earlier claim to be merely travelling through Cumberland County, but it obviously did not impress the court.[65]

Both Clarke and Faulkner had their sentencing put off until the following term, and in the interim Clarke submitted a petition for a pardon from the death sentence that would inevitably follow a conviction on a charge of high treason.[66] The Halifax authorities could only reprieve them, since pardons for murder and treason had to be granted in London.[67] A few weeks after conviction, on 11 May 1777, both men escaped as part of a mass jailbreak that included four others charged with treason.[68] They were never retaken. Faulkner fled across the border and served out the war in the American military, and after a brief delay Clarke also ended up in New England.[69]

Imperial Intervention and the Saint John River Campaign

Two convictions followed by jailbreaks were not much of a haul for the government, yet that was all the authorities achieved. No more rebels went to court on treason charges in 1777 or at any time thereafter. This is easy to explain for the period from July 1777 onwards, since that was when news arrived of a British statute ordering that 'no judge or justice of the peace shall bail or try any ... person' detained on suspicion of committing high treason in America.[70] This statute's principal purpose was the suspension of habeas corpus to permit detention without trial, one of at least a dozen such suspensions between 1688 and 1800,[71] but in Nova Scotia it served as a barrier to trial of those already detained. Originally passed for twelve months only, it was renewed four times before finally expiring at the end of 1782.[72] (See app. 3, F.)

The British statute was a godsend for patriots captured in the summer and fall of 1777 following John Allan's brief occupation of the Saint John valley. That second incursion into Nova Scotia marked a triumph for the Loyalists in two respects. First, the attack was not supported by a local rebellion as had been the case in the siege of Fort Cumberland. This change reflected the mood of the populace in the wake of Eddy's fiasco and was a tribute to special envoys (especially Councillor Arthur Goold) sent out in the spring to administer the oaths. Secondly, the relief expedition was mounted promptly from Windsor and Cumberland as well as from the capital, and it was joined this time by a militia no longer reticent to travel outside home districts, even to remote Sunbury County. Much had 'the complexion of the times changed,' exclaimed Arbuthnot at this upsurge in loyalty.[73] Considering the militia protests of only a year and a half before, the lieutenant governor was not exaggerating.[74]

Although the loyal militia mounted a spirited attack to rout the patriots at Manawagonish Cove on 1 July 1777, as in the Eddy affair few prisoners were taken and the leadership escaped altogether.[75] Allan retreated upriver after Manawagonish, with loyal troops in close pursuit. Unable to escape from the valley except by an arduous overland trek to Maine, he split his force into two parties. One fled via the Oromocto River while the second party, including Allan, retreated first to Aukpaque, soon abandoned to the advancing government force, then much farther upriver to Meductic, from where they escaped to Maine. It was in the course of pursuing Allan to Meductic that a patrol captured three of the refugees on 7 July at an isolated Acadian home several kilometres north of Aukpaque. As the soldiers approached along the river bank three men dashed from the house, 'without clothes except britches and their blankets which they were drawing after them.' One managed to escape into the woods but Samuel Crath of Cumberland was stabbed with a bayonet while trying to climb a fence and James Crawford, also of Cumberland, surrendered in the dooryard. Found hiding under a bed was John Fulton of Truro, whom the soldiers dragged out of the house just before burning it to the ground. The three prisoners were taken downriver to Aukpaque to face Major Gilfred Studholme, military commander of the expedition and the officer who had led the attack at Manawagonish Cove. Having also led the charge on Camphill that ended the siege of Fort Cumberland, he recognized these veterans of Eddy's army and the evidence of their continued rebellion (firearms, powder, and ball had also been found in the

Acadian home) did not please. As Fulton recalled, the major cursed him 'with a Dozen or two damns ... telling me I would be hanged.'[76]

Fulton and his two colleagues were protected from Studholme's dire prediction, if not his rage, by the British statute. It also spared four other patriots captured that summer and fall. These four – Robert Wilson of Campobello Island in the Passamaquoddy district, William Crow and William Elvill, probably also of Passamaquoddy, and Donald MacDonald of Pictou – were taken in unknown circumstances. The statute halted proceedings against these seven and also clearly prevented the prosecution of another patriot, Charles Oulton, who was recaptured in the same period. Having broken out of the Halifax jail in May, Oulton joined John Allan at Aukpaque before returning to visit his family at Cumberland where he was taken by Goreham.[77] Fulton, Crath, and Crawford were in the Halifax jail by the end of July 1777, and there they languished until presented to the Supreme Court at Halifax early in 1778, charged with high treason.

A grand jury found true bills against Crath, Crawford, and Fulton, but rejected those against the other four. All seven suffered the same fate, however, being incarcerated under the British statute. Halifax had not by then heard whether the act had been renewed, but Deschamps expected it to be.[78] Fulton, and perhaps others, escaped from jail in mid-March 1778, and he made his way back to Cobequid.[79] The statute also blocked proceedings against at least one other patriot after this date, Lewis Delesdernier, who had been indicted for high treason for his part in the siege. He was captured near Machias by a provincial naval vessel on 7 August 1778 and imprisoned in the Halifax jail.[80]

Official Leniency and Colonial Loyalty

It is not at all clear that any other men would have been prosecuted after the trials of Clarke and Faulkner even had Britain not intervened. While there are indications that the authorities were interested in further prosecutions in mid-1777[81] and at the end of the year,[82] nobody else was tried in Easter Term despite the presence of ten men in the Halifax jail before the breakout of May 11th and five thereafter. There were a variety of reasons for this reluctance to prosecute in the first half of the year, some the result of circumstances, others reflecting the deliberate thrusts of government policy.

The first, rather prosaic, reason is that the authorities did not have many available to be prosecuted. All the principals and many lesser lights had absconded or taken advantage of amnesty offers. Secondly, to have prosecuted those in custody merely because they had been captured just before the amnesty or had tried to escape to Maine but failed would have seemed heavy-handed in the circumstances. Government was deprived of the opportunity to pick and choose those to be prosecuted according to levels of guilt. Many rebels could not be prosecuted simply because they had escaped capture on 29 November and walked into Fort Cumberland to take an oath of allegiance a day later under Goreham's offer of amnesty. Clarke made the point implicitly in his petition for pardon when he stated that he had surrendered 'in order ... to acquire and obtain His Majesty's mercy' under proclamations to that effect.[83] Clarke was gilding the lily here, of course, for, although he does seem to have surrendered rather than been captured, the post-siege amnesty was proclaimed a day later.[84] But the force of the general argument was probably not lost on policy makers in the early months of 1777 as they contemplated how many and whom to bring to trial.

A third, and related, reason is that events conspired to deprive the colony of legal leadership at a crucial time, for Nova Scotia lacked any professionally trained judges in 1777. The line between political and judicial functions was often blurred in the North American colonial world of the late eighteenth and early nineteenth centuries. Many judges sat on governing councils, taking active roles in formulating policies of all kinds, including those relating to political prosecutions. Jonathan Belcher, the colony's first chief justice, was a man very much in this tradition of colonial 'political' judges, even serving for a time as chief executive of the colony.[85] His replacement, Bryan Finucane, was appointed in December 1776, but he did not arrive in Nova Scotia until April 1778 and thus for two years there was no lawyer to take charge of the courts.[86] During this period, Charles Morris, appointed to the Supreme Court as an assistant judge in 1764, was acting chief justice; soldier, surveyor, land speculator, and councillor before and after his elevation to the bench, but never formally trained in the law, Morris presided over the trials of Clarke and Faulkner. He was joined on the bench by Isaac Deschamps, another lay judge.[87] Almost as important as Morris's lack of legal training, perhaps, was the fact that he had been a principal supporter of the despised Legge and so in 1777 was a figure with little moral, legal, or political weight. In the absence of a dominating chief justice, legal leadership might have been assumed by the government law officers. But remarkably, Attorney General Nesbitt also had no legal training, and he was by then in his seventies.[88] Solicitor General Gibbons was a relatively accomplished lawyer but he had only been appointed to his post in January 1777, and he, too, had been a Legge protégé.[89]

Hesitancy, prevarication, and unwillingness to take responsibility seem to have been the hallmarks of government policy on prosecutions during the early months of 1777. In part this was the result of what Arbuthnot recognized as 'the enfeebled state of our First Lawyers' which made 'the presence of ... [a new] Chief Justice entirely necessary.'[90] Nobody seems to have been willing or able to take charge. In mid-April, for example, Nesbitt reported to the Council that he had collected 'more than 200 names' of people who had taken part in the rebellion, many of whom had come in under Goreham's amnesty. Since that time, however, 'several ... had ... been guilty of diverse misdemeanours and atrocious behaviour,' and he wanted the Council's advice as to whether 'all persons committing any offence since the proclamation should be tried simply for such offences' or whether there should be 'prosecution in general for rebellion.' It is not at all clear what these offences were, but they likely involved disloyal statements and/or revenge arson. In any event, the rather unhelpful guidance of the Council, of which acting Chief Justice Morris was the senior member, was that 'all such persons should be prosecuted for such misdemeanours and atrocious behaviour at the discretion of the Attorney-General.'[91] Although the government seems to have changed its mind on this two weeks later,[92] the fact remains that Nesbitt received little assistance from his superiors.

A fourth reason, the most important, was that prosecutorial decisions were not made in a political vacuum. The relative lightness of the government's touch reflected concerns about the political wisdom of extensive treason trials. Government policy on the use of the courts was, in the final analysis, driven by two beliefs that informed general policy making after the Eddy rebellion. The first was that, the rebellion and other lesser incidents aside, the colony was fundamentally loyal. What struck the authorities as significant in 1777 was the evident unwillingness of so many inhabitants to support the rebellion; indeed, hundreds worked hard to suppress both it and the later invasion of the Saint John valley.[93] This first belief led in turn to a second – that the best post-rebellion policy would be one of general leniency, leniency designed to encourage and reward loyalty. This policy reflected the confidence of government in the loyalty of the population.

Conciliation was also the natural preference of the lieutenant governor; it was the hallmark of Arbuthnot's governing style, whether he was harmonizing Nova Scotia's political factions after Legge's departure, touring the outsettlements to promote the new administration, or simply preventing his two chiefs of the army and navy from shooting at each other in a duel. To be sure, Arbuthnot could feel personally affronted by an instance of disloyalty, as he did on hearing that Cobequid residents had sheltered privateers after his tour of their district. Yet, after flying into a blustering rage (another part of his personality) at the news, his countermeasures were designed always to leave the door open to reconciliation. This chief executive was naturally optimistic and seemed to understand the peculiar task of nurturing loyalty in Nova Scotia – 'I think I can root out the weeds and leave a great number of loyal subjects.'[94]

Forgiveness did not mark every aspect of the official response to rebellion. That response was a mixture of rigorous measures and leniency, and the mixture was differently constituted at different times. The rigorous measures, however, were largely military responses to invasion threats. While the immediate aftermath of the Cumberland rebellion included an intense investigatory process and threats of treason proceedings, by the time cases were prepared and men might have been brought to court the news from the outsettlements was highly favourable. Treason trials were not required as a signal of royal power in the circumstances. Indeed there was always the danger that a spate of trials would have been counter-productive, giving credence to outsettlement distrust of the Halifax oligarchy. Here we see the influence of the reverse side of Nova Scotians' ambivalent politics. If loyalty was the fundamental precept that underpinned Nova Scotians' attitudes in 1776–7, and it was, it was nonetheless always loyalty infused with a suspicion of oligarchic government. Government could provoke serious opposition, as it did with its militia acts, but serious support for the rebellion was not a feature of local politics.

Leniency in the encouragement of loyalty was thus the preferred policy of government, with much stress placed on bringing wayward citizens back into the fold. Goreham's amnesty began the policy. Under his proclamation it was possible even for prominent patriots to surrender at the fort, take the oath of allegiance, and thereby remain at large. One notable example was Eliphalet Read, whose farm had been Eddy's military headquarters and was one of the first properties destroyed on the day the siege was lifted. Read chose not to flee with Eddy and was allowed to live quietly at Cumberland.[95] Lenity continued thereafter. As late as mid-April 1777, with prosecutions well under way, men could still avoid the courts and prison cells by taking the oaths of allegiance and abjuration.[96]

Alpheus Morse, imprisoned in Halifax in April, was freed, soon became a JP, and was remembered in the community as a Loyalist.[97] Others were accepted back into the fold even later, including John Bent of Cumberland, who had prayed 'with ardency' in 1776 for Washington to attack Nova Scotia and was a member of the committee of safety.[98] More cases could be cited, with political rehabilitation going on still in the early 1780s.[99] While there was some reluctance to extend amnesty to those who had decamped,[100] we must assume that all those imprisoned but not otherwise accounted for took advantage of it.[101] The zenith of the amnesty policy was the Act of Oblivion of 1783,[102] but its roots clearly go back to 1776–7. The same approach was taken when news arrived in mid-April 1777 of congressional approval of Allan's invasion. The authorities, while quickly applying defensive measures,[103] also offered amnesty in return for allegiance in the three potential trouble spots of Cumberland,[104] Cobequid (where it was less than successful[105]), and Sunbury (where it was completely vindicated).[106]

This explanation of events begs an obvious question – why, if policy was driven by leniency and a desire to cement provincial loyalty, were any proceedings taken at all? Perhaps, with so much effort having been put into suppression of the rebellion and investigation of the principals, it might have seemed like weakness not to have taken any action. In this respect the government was using the legal process in a classic eighteenth-century display of discretionary power and mercy.[107] Moreover, the vast majority of those indicted had absconded, including the principal military leaders of the rebellion. In the circumstances there was therefore no prospect of having to prosecute all these men, and official disapproval of the obviously guilty could be voiced via the indictment process without running the risks of mass prosecutions. It is also worth observing that the Clarke and Faulkner trials did not proceed until news was received of the American plans for invading the colony. This may have been coincidence, but the decision to go ahead with the trials might equally have been a signal of government resolve at a time of danger.

Finally, if examples were needed in mid-April of the state's power and willingness to punish its enemies, Clarke and Faulkner were far and away the best candidates. The former, with his unsavoury reputation and his penchant for committing ordinary criminal acts under the guise of rebellion, was also no doubt a popular defendant among loyal Cumberlanders. Faulkner, as leader of the Cobequid men and one formerly accused of treason, was also a prime choice for prosecution. Indeed, to some extent both these men had been singled out as early as January 1777 when Avery and Uniacke were allowed to strike bargains with the authorities. While all five men captured on 29 November and sent to Halifax by Goreham were said to have had 'particular complaints exhibited against them,'[108] the fact remains that these two were the most notable catches. Although Clarke and Faulkner were convicted, there does not appear to have been any intention that they be hanged for the crime. In this respect, they also would have benefited from prosecutorial decisions which reflected both confidence in the overriding loyalty of the population and concern that executions might give credence to republican charges of British tyranny.

This account of post-rebellion policy sheds new light on what has been a mystery of Nova Scotia's early history – the ability of Richard John Uniacke to participate in the rebellion and yet emerge later as a major figure among the colony's legal and political elite, becoming solicitor general in 1781 and attorney general in 1797.[109] He had arrived in Hopewell Township from Philadelphia with his business partner and future father-in-law, Moses Delesdernier, in 1774. He joined Eddy's force in 1776 and was captured on 29 November, the final day of the siege.[110] The next four and a half months were spent in captivity, mostly in the Halifax jail. He was probably released in April 1777.[111] It has been variously argued that he was not involved in the rebellion[112] and that he was but proved able to use family influence to escape his just deserts.[113] Both explanations miss the context. Uniacke's greatest error was to be captured before the amnesty. There was nothing sinister or remarkable about the failure to prosecute him, nor did that failure indicate a lack of involvement in the rebellion. As with many others, the authorities abandoned proceedings in return for his allegiance. Similarly, there is nothing extraordinary about Uniacke's rapid transformation from patriot to Loyalist. The aftermath of the Cumberland rebellion provided many such examples of political about-faces.

THE AFTERMATH OF THE REBELLION

While government chose largely to stay its hand as far as treason trials were concerned, the consequences of the Cumberland rebellion were not limited to criminal court proceedings. Other official measures were adopted or contemplated – principally the use of families as hostages and efforts to seize and/or confiscate property. In addition, the authorities permitted the civil courts to be used for private retribution, as the loyal sued their former enemies for damages suffered during the rebellion.

Rebel Families as Hostages

When so many of Eddy's followers chose to flee to the United States they abandoned 'Family and Estates to the Mercy of an Enraged Enemy.'[114] Not only were their families despised and shunned,[115] many were destitute and unable to work farms which had been put to the torch at the end of the siege, the fences destroyed and livestock plundered or dispersed.[116] What to do with the families of absconded patriots – some two hundred women and children, many of whom were homeless and dependent on charity – was a critical question in Cumberland.[117] Spiteful Yorkshiremen demanded that Goreham 'take all the Families into the Fort as Hostages.' Goreham resisted until orders from Halifax compelled him to take some of them in.[118] At least five families were later taken to Halifax and held under house arrest, and in 1779, after two attempts at exchange schemes were vetoed by government, those who wished to leave the province were finally allowed to do so.[119]

It is difficult to describe the treatment of the families of the Cumberlanders as anything other than hostage taking. There is no evidence that they were being held as some sort of wider negotiating policy, and simple vindictiveness would surely not have lasted so long, particularly since the retention of the families cost the government money. As far as we can discern, therefore, the only point to holding them was to make those who had absconded think twice about what might happen to their families if they were again to threaten Nova Scotia. Release came only when it was clear that no further invasions would be forthcoming.

Confiscation of Property

Another retributive government policy was the confiscation of the property of absconders. Three legal methods of attaching the property of rebels were available to Nova Scotia authorities in the late 1770s. First, persons convicted of capital felonies, including treason, could lose their estates to the crown through the feudal incident of escheat.[120] However, only Clarke and Faulkner had actually been convicted, and if the property of those who had not had the foresight to dispose of it before rebelling was to be seized this had to be achieved through a second procedure, that of outlawry.[121] Outlawry was a sentence prescribed, following certain well-established procedures, for those who did not appear in court to answer a charge when required; in such circumstances 'the law interprets the party's absence as sufficient evidence of his guilt ... without requiring any further proof.' A judgment of outlawry was effectively the same as a conviction for our purposes, its principal consequence being that it brought about 'forfeiture of his whole estate, real and personal.'

At first glance it would seem that the events of 1776–7 provided a bevy of prime candidates for property confiscation, either through escheat following conviction (Clarke and Faulkner) or outlawry (the absconders). Moreover, confiscation of property had many advantages. It punished without appearing too repressive, it provided funds for the war effort, and it would doubtless have been popular with Cumberland's Loyalists. Yet there appear to have been very few, if any, confiscations. Not only are there no records which suggest that Clarke and Faulkner lost their property via escheat, there is positive proof that both men still owned land and personal property in 1780 and 1784 respectively. The former had his lands attached and then sold when he was successfully sued in a private action by Christopher Harper in 1779–80.[122] The latter lost large tracts of land in the mid- to late 1780s as part of the process by which many old land grants were forfeited to provide for the influx of American Loyalists. Between 1783 and 1790 the Nova Scotia Court of Escheats and Forfeitures granted over one hundred largely uncontested applications for forfeiture. All of these, including those against the estates of Faulkner and Benoni Danks, were made on the grounds that the original grantees were in contravention of the conditions of settlement and improvement. The rebels were treated no differently than any other persons, and for our purposes the point is not that Faulkner lost his lands then but that he still had them to lose despite his conviction for treason almost a decade earlier.[123]

The situation is somewhat more complicated regarding those who were indicted and absconded and who were thus liable to outlawry. In fact the evidence is contradictory. There are indications that such confiscation was contemplated in 1777. The first two stages of the outlawry process – indictment and the issuing of an arrest warrant – were completed for a substantial number of men. But there is no evidence of the authorities proceeding to the third stage – the issuing of a writ of *exigi facias*. In some instances there was no point to outlawry proceedings, for cautious and knowledgeable men had disposed of their property before committing treason.[124] Not many escaped this way, however, and the government's intentions to proceed are revealed by a court order of April 1777 for the seizure of the estates of many absconders.[125] Yet in only one instance is there definite evidence that this was acted on.[126] It is possible that other families of absconders also lost possession of their lands. John Allan stated in mid-1777 that 'Several Famelys' had been 'turnd out of their Homes' and that in a number of cases personal property had been seized and sold.[127] When in 1779 'certain persons' who had taken part in the rebellion petitioned to be allowed to take the oath of allegiance and return, they asked to be 'settled on uncultivated lands,' an unnecessary request if they had retained lands.[128] But this request is as consistent with temporary seizure or private sale as it is with confiscation, and in other instances families of rebels continued to occupy lands.[129]

Not only are there few indications of a general policy of outlawry and confiscation, most absconders kept title to their property through the late 1770s and beyond. A number of them still had lands and personal effects to be taken and sold by writs of execution when they were, like Clarke, sued by Loyalists in civil actions. Men in this category included Elijah Ayer, Simeon Chester, Atwood Fales, Robert Foster, Ebenezer Gardner, William How, John MacGowan, Nathaniel Reynolds, Zebulon Roe, and John Starr. Others lost lands in the late 1770s and early 1780s when they were seized for non-payment of taxes.[130] Again, as with the cases of Clarke and Faulkner, the point is that they still had property three to four years after absconding. One can also cite the case of Josiah Throop, whose family, by his own admission, were the victims of plunder and arson but had nonetheless 'built a house' to replace one lost and been 'allowed to possess and occupy his lands' after his flight.[131] The local Act of Oblivion of 1783 forbade future prosecutions for treason or any consequent civil proceedings and pardoned past deeds, and therefore there could be no confiscations afterwards. But it appears that there were very few before then; even the leader of the Eddy rebellion kept his property.[132]

This is not to suggest that those who deserted Nova Scotia in 1776–7 did not suffer economically. A few clearly did lose at least control of their lands via official action. Many had their buildings burned down in revenge arsons, and almost all of them lost livestock and other goods through private plunder in the days and weeks following the lifting of the siege. The authorities took action also in other ways. In January 1777 the Council ordered the seizure of the effects and cattle of those who had been in arms, and there is evidence that some of this was done even if it is difficult to discern any legal justification for it.[133] In addition, a number of absconders, including William Eddy, Elijah Ayer, and William Maxwell, were successfully sued by government for the recovery of money paid to them before November 1776 for goods to be supplied to the garrison at Fort Cumberland but not provided.[134] Using the courts to collect debts, however, is not confiscation, and again demonstrates that absconders had property unmolested by official seizure policy.

Seizures of property were thus limited to at most a small number of individuals and then largely to personal effects, not substantial landholdings. One might lay the failure to carry through with the outlawry proceedings at the door of the British statute. Although there is no evidence of discussions on this point, it is possible that the law officers assumed that outlawries as well as treason trials were precluded because the former required the state to be willing and able to bring absconders to trial. Certainly there was not time, in the very few weeks between the arrest warrant which marked the second stage of the outlawry proceedings and the arrival of news of the statute, to complete the third stage. But this does not explain why Clarke and Faulkner kept their lands. Nor does it explain why the property rights of so many other absconding patriots remained intact following the enactment locally of a third method of seizing the property of absconders. In 1779 the assembly passed a statute which gave the crown power to seize all property of persons who had 'joined with His Majesty's rebellious Subjects of the other Colonies' and who 'would have forfeited to His Majesty all their Goods and Chattels, Lands and Tenements' had they actually been convicted of treason.[135] This act stayed in force for the duration of the rebellion,[136] and commissioners to enforce it were appointed in August 1779.[137]

The 1779 act does provide some indirect evidence that the local law officers believed they could not employ the law of outlawry to confiscate property. Why else would a measure be passed which duplicated that law, indeed which did not go so far as outlawry did for it talked only of temporary seizures of real estate rather than confiscation? Yet this statute appears to have been more honoured in the breach than the observance. No proceedings of the commissioners have survived, and we suspect there were none, for there is no other evidence of its operation. A large number of those who should have been its targets kept their property even if they lost it through civil litigation or forfeited it years later. The only indications that it was used were likely misleading special pleading by patriots.[138] And so we are again left with the impression of a government whose bark was very much worse than its bite. It needed to threaten so as not to appear powerless, and for that reason it enacted the local seizure statute. Other than that, it did little. In taking this lenient approach the authorities incurred the wrath of some Loyalists. Irascible Cumberland clergyman John Eagleson, for one, bemoaned the 'indulgence and lenity of Government towards the delinquents,'[139] and no doubt others did so. But policy in this area was in fact quite consistent with the government's overall approach to the rebellion.

Civil Litigation and the Reconstruction of Cumberland County

The most damaging blows to the patriot community, both to those who fled and to those who quickly repented of their role in 1776, came from legal action initiated by private citizens, not by government. In a series of lawsuits launched between 1778 and circa 1782, principally *Eagleson v. Oulton et al* and *Harper v. Ayer et al*, Cumberland's Loyalists sued former patriots for damages sustained in 1776.[140] Their motives were obvious and are exemplified by Eagleson's comments that, since he had 'sustained heavy losses by the rebels' and saw 'no hopes' for 'restitution from Governm't,' he 'thought it a duty I owed myself to Endeavour to Recover ... some part of my Property out of the Estates of the Absconding Rebels & from some of the Inhabitants present, who I knew were most forward & Active in the Insurrection.'[141] There were more than a dozen lawsuits begun by at least seven individuals, and the defendants, perhaps as many as fifty men, were drawn from among those patriots who had absconded and those who had taken advantage of the amnesty offer. The plaintiffs were largely successful in winning judgments, and they were substantially if not entirely able to make good on these judgments by seizing and in some cases eventually selling the real property of former patriots.

Those ex-patriots fought back in a variety of ways. At some point, probably in early 1779, they tried to head off the litigation by invoking Goreham's amnesty. They were even able to persuade Goreham himself to intercede on their behalf with the Halifax authorities. According to Eagleson, this intervention occurred 'shortly after I had entered my suit,' and he found it scandalous that Goreham had dared to support the defendants, to 'in a dark and Underhand manner ... Use all his Influence & Interest ... to have my suit laid aside.'[142] Government, however, rejected the patriots' argument unequivocally: 'The petitioners may be entitled by your declaration and by several proclamations to their Liberty and the repossession of their property and to pardon for offences they committed against the Crown,' Goreham was told, but not to 'an exemption for the injuries they may have done to private people.' To intervene would be to exercise 'an authority arbitrary and illegal' for 'the course of Law cannot be stopped and the injured have a right to seek remedy.'[143]

The government's refusal is instructive. In part it may have derived from the stated motive, an unwillingness to interfere with the civil courts. But the explanation is surely not that simple. There is a fine line between 'offences against the crown' and 'injuries done to private people,' a line so fine that it often becomes invisible. Presumably the authorities would not have countenanced private criminal prosecutions or damage suits based on the death or wounding of men who had fought on the government's side, and it could equally well be argued that amnesty for acts of rebellion should have included amnesty for property destruction or damage caused in the course of rebellion. If it was considered necessary to reimburse those who had lost property during the rebellion, some form of official compensation scheme could have been arranged, similar to the Loyalist Claims Commission put into place after 1783. Instead, by not stopping these private suits, government was effectively permitting Loyalist claims to be charged directly to individual rebels – including rebels who had returned to their allegiance.

When the authorities learned of this use of the civil courts they may well have positively approved of the process, for two reasons. First, the litigation represented an effective form of punishment of patriots, making them pay for their actions. Yet it was not official repression; the 'law' was not 'government,' and thus charges of heavy-handedness could be avoided. Eagleson's suit, and those that followed, may therefore demonstrate the limits of leniency, the existence of a desire to see the former patriots punished in some way. Secondly, Loyalists were compensated without cost to government. Moreover, and this is speculative, the litigation was probably beneficial to Loyalist psyches. It not only put them in control of a retributive mechanism, it may also have assuaged dissatisfaction with the treason proceedings.

Yet the litigation had adverse consequences also. It played a role in substantially retarding the very process of reconstruction and reconciliation that government was attempting otherwise to achieve. It certainly engendered other defensive responses from the ex-patriot community once the appeal to the amnesty had been rejected. One such response was defensive counter-litigation, patriots suing each other to make lands safe from executions obtained by Loyalists by making those lands answerable to ones already awarded. In fact this strategy was entirely unsuccessful, the Supreme Court in Halifax holding that the litigation was collusive.

The patriot community also took more direct action, as exemplified by an anonymous letter written in the late summer of 1780 to Thomas Watson, deputy provost-marshal of Cumberland County and the officer responsible for carrying out court orders for the seizure of property following the lawsuits. It was said to come from 'R. Revenge' of 'Scrutiny River' and singled out justice of the peace Christopher Harper for his 'diabolical proceedings.'[144] Watson was warned to 'desist from executing any instrument of what name or nature so ever against any person or persons in your county who have been under arms against the Fort'; if not he would 'neither have house nor barn many days after.' Halifax's response was to offer a £100 reward for 'the discovery of the author or authors of said letter.' According to Eagleson, 'several anonymous seditious letters' were sent to 'the Sheriff and other executive Officers of justice' which threatened 'to burn and destroy their property, and mal-treat their persons, should they presume to execute any writ or verdict of the Courts.'

Patriot complaints about the suits and about other, unspecified, activities by Loyalists were also pursued through more legitimate channels and eventually received the sympathy of the assembly. In June 1782 that body demanded a judicial inquiry into the 'oppressive measures' which 'have been exercised towards the Inhabitants of Cumberland'; it asked also for the immediate suspension of all executions.[145] The judicial inquiry did take place, justices Brenton and Deschamps visiting the county in the summer of 1782 and reporting in September. They first noted that 'many inhabitants who took an active part with the rebels' had since been 'harassed by law prosecutions ... for damages sustained in the general devastation.' In some instances they apparently 'adjusted' matters 'consistent with the principles of law and justice,' and they also ordered the cessation of executions consequent on lawsuits.

The judges' report discussed other grievances also. A major problem was that Harper, in his capacity as a JP, had 'in a variety of instances been guilty of violent and oppressive measures against a number of inhabitants,' who had suffered 'injuries and oppressions' because of his 'abuse of Authority.' In consequence Harper had 'made himself exceedingly obnoxious to most of the principal settlers in the ... county,' and the judges recommended his dismissal 'from the Commission of the Peace and every judicial power that he holds under government' as 'one means of quieting the minds of the inhabitants.' Other problems were noted also, particularly the 'improper use of military power.'

The most serious problem in the county, however, was that caused by the civil litigation, even where it had been prosecuted with propriety. In a tone distinctly sympathetic to the former patriots, the judges noted that many of them 'had had their whole property seized and taken from them,' leaving their families 'destitute of every support,' and that even those who had to date escaped lived 'under the Terror' of the 'same persecution' and the 'continual dread of being reduced to a Wretched Indigence.' They recommended that this 'evil' could be remedied by the appointment of commissioners to calculate all losses and 'apportion the whole equitably upon such of the inhabitants or their estates as were any ways concerned in supporting or aiding the rebels.' In this way, compensation 'would fall on a number, and not be laid on a few.'

Although the judges' report asserted that the idea of apportionment of losses had the support of both factions in Cumberland,[146] it was not adopted in 1782 and the tense atmosphere did not improve. Indeed it worsened in 1783 with the infusion of American Loyalists, and Harper was finally removed from the commission of the peace over an incident involving an assault by one newly arrived individual on seventy-year-old Moses Deslesdernier.[147] More important, measures were taken to deal with the fundamental cause of the unrest, the civil litigation for rebellion losses. A statute of 1783 recorded the assembly's conviction that persons who had successfully launched suits for losses 'sustained ... by reason of the depredations of the enemy' had actually received judgments 'for a much greater amount than the losses really sustained,' and that 'the manner in which the said judgments have been carried into execution is grievous and oppressive' because 'the estates of a few individuals [had] ... been wholly seized to satisfy the same.'[148] The statute provided for the apportionment of liability recommended by the judges the previous year. The task would be carried out by commissioners whose work would be overseen by the Supreme Court. The final section of the act suspended the operation of all current suits and executions.

The 1783 statute was a start, but it hardly provided a solution. The commission was not established until late in 1784[149] and it seems to have done very little, perhaps because at the same time the British government was putting into operation its scheme for compensating Loyalists who had lost lands in the newly independent American states. It may well have been the existence of this imperial compensation scheme that was partly responsible for the dilatory and half-hearted approach to putting the local one into operation.[150] More immediately, factional bitterness and complaints about the actions of Loyalist JPs in the county continued, and in 1784 the judges were sent back for another investigation.[151] Arson also continued to haunt the county in the mid-1780s; indeed it spread to New Brunswick, where in 1788 Christopher Harper's new house, which happened to be committee of safety man Elijah Ayer's old house, was burned to the ground.[152]

The siege of Fort Cumberland is the only instance of rebellion in Canadian history in which privately initiated litigation played an important role in the state repression that followed. This repressive measure was taken with the explicit compliance of government and government intervention was required to control its excesses. Effects of the litigation were sometimes as severe as the causes; for example, suits seeking redress for arson resulted in more arson while attempts by judges to disentangle improprieties created grounds for their own attempted impeachment.[153] The privatization of repression after the Cumberland rebellion is illustrative of the strain placed on legal systems when political conflict adjourns to the civil courts. Legal proceedings extended the bitterness and deferred reconciliation but also revealed an essential aspect of government policy in a colony in which the American revolution failed. While leniency distinguished that policy, government maintained the intent that unsuccessful revolutionaries should pay for damages they had caused.

CONCLUSION: REPRESSION AND LENIENCY, LOYALTY AND NEUTRALITY

Official responses to the Cumberland rebellion are not easy to assess. As a result of the peculiar circumstances of the period and of the twists and turns of government policies, little of note occurred in the realm of treason and related legal proceedings. Moderation, not retribution, marked the legal process. Yet government leniency in the courts was counterbalanced by other methods of punishing the rebellious – holding their families hostages and, largely indirectly, enforcing the payment of reparations. It is therefore necessary to see the treason proceedings, the most obvious method of dealing with rebels, as but one of several strands in the government's policy of quieting dissent. Reluctance to invoke the law to the ultimate also marked Nova Scotia government reactions to a dozen or so other instances of actual or alleged disloyalty during this period. None of these involved armed rebellion; they ranged from the Reverend John Seccombe preaching a sermon which the Council thought tended 'to promote Sedition and rebellion amongst the people,' to merchant Malachy Salter's corresponding and trading with associates in Boston as he had done before 1775, to Maugerville assemblyman Israel Perley providing information about government activities to John Allan in 1777. But neither in these nor in other cases was government heavy-handed. Seccombe was admonished and asked to recant any republican principles, Salter was briefly imprisoned but the charge against him was dropped on Arbuthnot's orders, and Perley suffered little more than removal from the commission of the peace and was sufficiently rehabilitated in the mid-1780s to obtain a substantial grant of land in New Brunswick and become deputy surveyor general of the colony.[154]

The Nova Scotia story is different in a number of ways from other Canadian examples of the official response to rebellion or political crime. Historians of these phenomena in Canada have tended to emphasize two, apparently but not necessarily inconsistent, themes.[155] First, severe political crises have brought rigorous enforcement while the threat to the social and political order was perceived as very real, and leniency once that threat passed. Secondly, political authorities have consistently tended to overstate the danger to the state and have just as consistently been willing to subvert due process in attempts to ward off that danger, with the result that legitimate but dissenting political activity has been punished in defence of the existing order. The foregoing account of Nova Scotia in the American revolutionary era seems to fit the first of these two themes well. The authorities dealt vigorously with the Cumberland rebellion in late 1776, but, with the danger past the following and succeeding years, their conduct was not marked by retribution. Nova Scotia does not seem to fit the second theme at all well. Here was not dissent depicted as treason, but rather the reverse. The policy of leniency towards the Cumberlanders, albeit perhaps a policy dictated to some extent by circumstances, was nonetheless one that treated true treason, armed rebellion against the crown, as excusable dissent. How different this was to the later reactions of both the Upper and Lower Canadian authorities to the 1837 rebellions, which featured many abuses of process and a bevy of executions.[156]

If this essay provides a contribution to the historiography of political crime in Canada, it also, we believe, suggests a need for some rethinking of the paradigms that have dominated the traditional historiography of the popular response to the American revolution in Nova Scotia. Explanations of why Nova Scotia did not become the 'fourteenth colony' have stressed a long-standing desire for neutrality among the inhabitants of the region and a religious revivalism caused by social and political dislocation which led in its turn to a preference for religion over political involvement.[157] Recent work by one of the authors of this chapter argues that historians should pay more attention to the degree of loyalty that the population in general exhibited in 1775–6. Noting its prevalence in the rebellious colonies as late as 1774,[158] this account argues that loyalty continued to be the norm in Nova Scotia throughout the revolution. This was not surprising. The thousands of New England planters who removed to Nova Scotia in the early 1760s avoided the period of radical political change that preceded the military events of 1775–6, a period that John Adams termed 'the real American Revolution.'[159] Thus the planter majority along with other Nova Scotians need to be viewed in their capacity as Loyalists. In formulating its legal response to disloyalty, the Nova Scotia government viewed its constituents in largely this way. The heavy hand of legal repression was stayed precisely because it was not required.

NOTES

1 No less than three letters from Nova Scotia's top colonial appointees confirming the attack at Cumberland reached London on 24 Dec. 1776: Arbuthnot to Germain, November 1776; Collier to same, 21 Nov. 1776; and Massey to same, 22 Nov. 1776, CO 217/52/232–50, PANS.

2 Germain to Massey, 14 Jan. 1777, CO 217/53/1–3. The secretary of state wrote similarly to Collier and Arbuthnot on the same date: ibid., 4–9.

3 This section on the early history of Nova Scotia is drawn principally from J.B. Brebner, *The Neutral Yankees of Nova Scotia: A Marginal Colony During the Revolutionary Years* (New York: Columbia University Press 1937); J.M. Beck, *The Politics of Nova Scotia: Volume One* (Tantallon, N.S.: Four East Publications 1985); D.C. Harvey, 'The Struggle for the New England Form of Township Government in Nova Scotia,' Canadian Historical Association *Report* (1933), 15.

4 Bernard Bailyn, *Voyagers to the West: A Passage in the Peopling of America on the Eve of the Revolution* (New York: Knopf 1986), at 373.

5 The literature on pre-revolutionary immigration is very large. See E.C. Wright, *Planters and Pioneers: Nova Scotia, 1749–1755* (Hantsport, N.S.: Lancelot Press 1982); W.O. Sawtelle, 'Acadia: The Pre-Loyalist Migration and the Philadelphia Plantation,' *Pennsylvania Magazine of History and Biography*, vol. 51 (1927), 244; J. Stephenson, 'The Connecticut Settlement of Nova Scotia Prior to the Revolution,' *National Genealogical Society Quarterly*, vol. 42 (1954), 53; C.B. Fergusson, 'Pre-Revolutionary Settlements in Nova Scotia,' *Collections of the Nova Scotia Historical Society*, vol. 37 (1970), 5. See also many of the essays in *They Planted Well: New England Planters in Maritime Canada* (Fredericton: Acadiensis Press 1988) and *Making Adjustments: Change and Continuity in Planter Nova Scotia* (Fredericton: Acadiensis Press 1991), both edited by Margaret Conrad.

6 This brief summary of general Nova Scotia responses to the American revolution is drawn from Ernest Clarke, *The Siege of Fort Cumberland, 1776: An Episode in the American Revolution* (Montreal: McGill-Queen's University Press 1995); Brebner, *Neutral Yankees* and 'Nova Scotia's Remedy for the American Revolution,' *CHR*, vol. 15 (1934), 171, W.B. Kerr, 'Nova Scotia in the Critical Years, 1775–1776,' *Dalhousie Review*, vol. 12 (1932), 96, 'The American Invasion

of Nova Scotia, 1776-1777,' *Canadian Defence Quarterly*, vol. 13 (1935–6), 433, 'The Merchants of Nova Scotia and the American Revolution,' *CHR*, vol. 13 (1932), 20, and 'The Stamp Act in Nova Scotia,' *New England Quarterly*, vol. 6 (1933), 552; George Rawlyk, *Nova Scotia's Massachusetts: A Study of Massachusetts-Nova Scotia Relations, 1630-1784* (Montreal: McGill-Queen's University Press 1973), chs. 12 and 13.

7 See the following at PANS: Council Minutes [hereafter Minutes], 16 and 19 Sept. 1774, RG1 vol. 189: 234–7; Bulkeley to Smith, 16 Sept. 1774, RG 1, vol. 136: 177; Legge to Dartmouth, 20 Sept. 1774, CO 217/51/3–4; Monk to Dartmouth, 16 Nov. 1774, ibid., 67–9.

8 Minutes, 16 and 29 June 1775, RG 1, vol. 189, 309 and 314–17; Address of Assembly to Legge, October 1775, *Journal and Votes of the House of Assembly* [hereafter *Assembly Journals*]; Legge to Dartmouth, 31 July 1775, CO 217/51/275.

9 No more recent account of Legge's reforming efforts and the opposition to them has surpassed that of Brebner in *Neutral Yankees*, at 212–54. For Legge see also J.M. Bumsted, 'Legge, Francis' *DCB* 4: 449.

10 Legge to Dartmouth, 27 Nov. 1775, CO 217/52/18–19. For other examples see Clarke, *The Siege of Fort Cumberland*, at 9.

11 SNS, 1775, c. 1 and 7.

12 Arbuthnot to Sandwich, 14 Jan. 1776, in *The Private Papers of John, Earl of Sandwich, 1771–1782*, ed. G.R. Barnes and J.H. Owen, 4 vols.(London: Naval Records Society 1932), 1: at 116–17.

13 Inhabitants of Yarmouth to Legge, 8 Dec. 1775, CO 217/52/36–7. For the other petitions see Inhabitants of Cumberland to Legge, 23 Dec. 1775, ibid., 78–78v; Inhabitants of Truro to Legge, Inhabitants of Onslow to Legge, and Inhabitants of Hopewell, Hillsborough and Memramcook to Legge [all December 1775], Dartmouth Papers, 2922–4, 2927–8, and 3802–3, PANS.

14 For the early history of the district and its role in the revolutionary period see M.E. Wright, 'Of a Licentious and Rebellious Disposition: The Cobequid Townships and the American Revolution,' *Collections of the Royal Nova Scotia Historical Society*, vol. 42 (1986), 27; Carol Campbell, 'A Scots-Irish Plantation in Nova Scotia: Truro, 1760–1775,' in *Making Adjustments*; A.W.H. Eaton, 'The Settling of Colchester County by New England Puritans and Ulster Scotsmen,' *Transactions of the Royal Society of Canada* (1912), 221; Clarke, *The Siege of Fort Cumberland*, at 66–8.

15 Quotation from Michael Francklin cited in Wright, 'Cobequid Townships,' at 28.

16 'Petition for a Commission for William Carleton to Command the Massachusetts Privateer Schooner *General Gates*,' 8 Aug. 1776, in *Naval Documents of*

the American Revolution, ed. W.B. Clark, 9 vols. (Washington: United States Government Printer 1964–86), 6: 112. A first-hand account of her capture is in the *Hope* log, 27 Sept. 1776, Adm 52/1794, PRO. See also *Diary of Simeon Perkins*, 4 vols. (Toronto: Champlain Society 1948–67), 3: at 133–4, and *Independent Chronicle* (Boston), 24 Oct. 1776.

17 For details of the *Washington* and her captain, Sion Martindale, see the *Freeman's Journal* (Portsmouth, N.H.), 27 July 1776.

18 This incident is described in the depositions of John Cole, 31 Oct. 1776, of Mary Morrison and others, 16 Nov. 1776, and of Peleg Card, 7 Nov. 1776, RG 1, vol. 342, nos. 73, 74, and 76; and Interrogation of Charles Dickson, 23 Nov. 1776, ibid., no. 75. The Halifax reaction is in Arbuthnot to Smith, 19 Nov. and 4 Dec. 1776, and Bulkeley to Cobequid Magistrates, 19 Nov. 1776, RG 1, vol. 136, 241–4. For the prosecutions see text accompanying nn.57–9.

19 For Sunbury County in this period, see D.M. Young, 'Planter Settlements in the St. John Valley,' in *They Planted Well*; W.O. Raymond, *The River St. John* (Saint John: *Daily Telegraph* 1905); Clarke, *The Siege of Fort Cumberland*, at 40–3; J.M. Bumsted, 'Noble, Seth,' and S.E. Patterson, 'Perley, Israel,' *DCB* 5: 627 and 665.

20 This document is reproduced in F. Kidder, *Military Operations in Eastern Maine and Nova Scotia During the Revolution* (Albany, N.Y.: Joel Munsell 1867), at 62–5.

21 Claim of Charles Jadis, 24 Oct. 1776, AO (Audit Papers) 13, NA. Even Jadis, a passionate Loyalist, felt compelled to sign.

22 For Cumberland in this period see Clarke, *The Siege of Fort Cumberland*, 'Cumberland Planters and the Aftermath of the Attack on Fort Cumberland,' in *They Planted Well*, and 'The Cumberland Glebe Dispute and the Background to the American Revolution in Nova Scotia, 1771–1774,' *University of New Brunswick Law Journal*, vol. 42 (1993), 95; E.C. Wright, 'Cumberland Township: A Focal Point of Settlement on the Bay of Fundy,' *CHR*, vol. 27 (1946), 27; J. Snowdon, 'Footprints in the Marsh Mud: Politics and Land Settlement in the Township of Sackville, 1760–1800,' MA thesis, University of New Brunswick, 1974; George Rawlyk, 'Eddy, Jonathan,' *DCB* 5: 295.

23 Rogers was the member for Sackville until ejected from the assembly in 1776. Throop was a former MHA, a well-educated, successful businessman, and a surveyor by trade who also taught school and was clerk of the Inferior Court of Common Pleas. Clarke was a physician from Fort Lawrence and also a farmer. How lived at Fort Lawrence and was county coroner and treasurer of the Congregational Society.

24 Three in particular stand out. First, the Methodist and Loyalist Yorkshire settlers had taken lands that New Englanders believed should have been given to

them by land speculator and Lieutenant Governor Michael Francklin. Secondly, the Cumberland economy, never strong and always to some degree reliant on the economic activity of the fort, was plunged into recession when the garrison was withdrawn in 1768, a recession sufficiently severe to induce some to return to New England. Thirdly, the community had been badly fractured in the early 1770s by a dispute in which the New Englanders' Congregationalist church had lost its glebe lands to the resident Church of England clergyman, John Eagleson.

25 Inhabitants of Cumberland to Legge, 23 Dec. 1775, CO 217/52/78–78v. The Cumberland petition was signed by 246 people including many of the county's Yorkshire residents, a group that neither then nor later was prepared to countenance disloyalty.

26 Gibbons's Observations on the state of Nova Scotia, 1775, in Dartmouth Papers, 2932.

27 For Arbuthnot see D.F. Chard, 'Mar[r]iot Arbuthnot,' DCB 4: 29, and Ernest Clarke, 'The Error of Marriot Arbuthnot,' Nova Scotia Historical Review, vol. 8 (1988), 95.

28 MHAs Allan and Rogers were expelled from the assembly, as was Joshua Lamb of Onslow. While six of the seven constituencies whose members were expelled returned Loyalists, Sackville, the centre of patriot activity in Cumberland, returned Robert Foster, chairman of the committee of safety. In addition to these expulsions, Eddy and others found themselves with a price on their heads: see Rawlyk, 'Eddy, Jonathan,' at 296.

29 These included the taking prisoner and shipping to New England of the Reverend John Eagleson, the Loyalist Anglican clergyman, and the plundering of the houses and farms of other Loyalists. For Eagleson's travails see Clarke, 'Cumberland Planters,' at 53–4, and Ernest Clarke, Jim Phillips, and Stephen Waddams, 'The Trials and Trial of John Eagleson,' unpublished ms., 1995. For one example of losses by plunder, that of Charles Dixon, see the list of goods taken from his Sackville home in MC 251, MS 1: 64, PANB.

30 For the period of republican rule and the siege see Clarke, The Siege of Fort Cumberland, and 'Journal of Joseph Goreham,' Report of the Public Archives of Canada (1894), 355 (hereafter Goreham's Journal).

31 Elbridge Gerry to John Adams, 8 Jan. 1777, in Papers of John Adams: Series III – General Correspondence and Other Papers of the Adams Statesmen, ed. R.J. Taylor et al., 7 vols. (Cambridge, Mass.: Harvard University Press 1977–89), 6: at 66; Journals of the Continental Congress, 34 vols. Washington, 1904–37), 7: at 20, 34.

32 For details see Ernest Clarke, 'The Occupation of the St. John Valley,' unpublished ms. 1992.

33 State of Massachusetts to Congress, 13 Aug. 1777, in Documentary History of the

State of Maine, ed. J.P. Baxter *et al.,* 25 vols. (Portland: LeFavor-Tower 1869–1916), 15: at 11–12.

34 Goreham's Proclamation, 30 Nov. 1776, CO 217/53/52A. The four excluded were Eddy, Rogers, Allan, and William How.

35 During the siege he had warned Cumberlanders not to join the rebels, for they would thereby 'subject themselves to an immediate military execution': Proclamation, 7 Nov. 1776, CO 217/53/46. When Goreham later demanded that his besiegers surrender, they not unreasonably adverted to this proclamation and told him that they 'had no encouragement to retract' and would 'rather die like men than be hanged like dogs': Inhabitants of Cumberland to Goreham, 11 Nov. 1776, CO 217/53/50A.

36 In fact rebellion-related arsons did continue until as late as 1788. In all at least forty-nine such fires were set from 1776 on, which left at least three hundred people homeless: see Clarke, 'Cumberland Planters,' at 44.

37 Minutes, 6 Jan. 1777, RG 1, vol. 189: 421–2, and Bulkeley to Massey, 6 Jan. 1777, RG 1, vol. 136: 245. The two dismissed were Samuel Wethered and Moses Delesdernier. Delesdernier 'by the whole course of his conduct gave full proofs of his disaffection to government.' Wethered had apparently used the occasion of a dispute between himself and Loyalist Christopher Harper 'to speak in the most abusive and contemptuous manner of the government.' He had also kept a tavern near Fort Cumberland and during the siege had regularly entertained Eddy's troops; General Massey called the Wethereds 'the family of the worst rebels in this Province' and Samuel, according to John Eagleson, was a man of 'Desperate Fortunes.' Two months later Wethered died of a wound received during the siege: Clarke, 'Cumberland Planters,' at 47. Goreham asserted that Delesdernier 'stood tryall and was acquitted' for his alleged wrongdoing (Goreham to Haldimand, 5 Oct. 1778, Haldimand Papers, B 149: 19, NA) but we have no evidence of any 'tryall.'

38 The circuit had previously been cancelled in the spring of 1776 but it did take place in September of that year. It was not renewed until 1782, and even then it was not deemed advisable to send the judges to Cumberland without a militia escort: see Minutes, 30 April 1776, 14 April 1777, and 15 April 1778, RG 1, vol. 189: 405, 425, and 439; Bulkeley to Morris, 26 Aug. 1777, and to Tonge, 23 Aug. and 2 Sept. 1782, RG 1, vol. 136: 254 and 304–5; Diary of Isaac Deschamps, Dalhousie University Archives.

39 Robert Smith to his uncle and aunt, 13 May 1782, cited in A. Calabresi, 'Letters Home: The Experience of an Emigrant in Eighteenth Century Nova Scotia,' PhD thesis, Yale University 1986, letter 15, Appendix I. Robert's father, Yorkshireman Nathaniel Smith, moved to Cornwallis.

40 Fox to Carleton, 3 Oct. 1783, British Headquarters Papers, 392–3, PANS.

41 Arbuthnot to Germain, 31 Dec. 1776, CO 217/53/12.

42 A week and a half later Goreham issued a further proclamation against these men, excoriating those who 'have most daringly and in violation of the sacred laws of society stood out many days beyond the limited time against every humane method to bring them to reason,' and stating unequivocally that the period of grace had ended and that 'of this date I will receive no submission of ... persons but as prisoners to be dealt with as the laws, civil or military, may deem fit': Goreham's Proclamation, 10 Dec. 1776, CO 217/53/56–56v.

43 It is difficult to establish precisely how many active service refugees the Cumberland rebellion produced, but we put the figure at 70–80. The activities of some of them can be followed in Kidder, *Military Operations*, passim. See also C.M. Layton, 'Canadian Refugee Lands in Ohio,' *CHR*, vol. 24 (1943), 377–80, and Eddy's list of refugees reproduced in *Maine Historical Magazine*, vol. 9 (1894–5), at 64. Two principals who returned to Nova Scotia were committee men Elijah Ayer, Sr and Samuel Rogers.

44 See the two depositions taken before JP Edward Barron at Fort Cumberland early in December 1776, in J.T. Bulmer, 'Trials for Treason in 1776–1777,' *Collections of the Nova Scotia Historical Society*, vol. 1 (1876), at 111–16. These alone implicated eighteen individuals including most members of the committee of safety. See also Goreham's Journal, 365–6.

45 Goreham's Proclamation, 3 Dec. 1776, CO 217/53/54.

46 Danks was a retired British army officer who had settled in Cumberland after the Seven Years' War. Ironically, his earlier service had included the campaign in which Britain acquired Fort Cumberland from the French: *Captain John Knox: An Historical Journal of the Campaigns in North America for the Years 1757, 1758, 1759 and 1760*, ed. A.G. Doughty, 3 vols. (Toronto: Champlain Society 1914), 1: 196–203. He had been wounded in the 1776 siege and died at Windsor from his injuries late in December of that year. The other four were marched in irons from Windsor to Halifax: see Clarke, 'Cumberland Planters,' at 51, 58–9.

47 See P.E.I. State Papers, CO 229/1, NA; Log of the *Hunter*, Adm 52/1799, PRO; Goreham's Journal, 363. For a description of the *Molly* incident see Clarke, *The Siege of Fort Cumberland*, at 197–8.

48 'Return of Prisoners,' 18 April 1777, in Benchbook of Isaac Deschamps, RG 39, Supreme Court Records, Halifax County, series C [hereafter RG 39– C], box A, no. 3 [hereafter Deschamps Benchbook], PANS. The preceding entry in the benchbook, of the same date, is 'John Fillmore of Cumberland took the Oaths.' It is almost certain that Fillmore was one of Eddy's soldiers and that he was also captured and taken to Halifax jail where he avoided appearing on the return of prisoners by taking the oath of allegiance before the judge. John's

two brothers – Asa and Spiller Fillmore – were patriot soldiers and Charles Oulton, one of the prisoners in the return, was his brother-in-law.

49 For the naval clean-up see Clarke, *The Siege of Fort Cumberland*, at 207. Sharp and Stewart appear in Eddy's return of those who fled: Kidder, *Military Operations*, at 76–7.

50 English treason procedure is discussed in J.R. Phifer, 'Law, Politics and Violence: The Treason Trials Act of 1696,' *Albion*, vol. 12 (1980), 235, and L.M. Hill, 'The Two-Witness Rule in English Treason Trials: Some Comments on the Emergence of Procedural Law,' *American Journal of Legal History*, vol. 12 (1968), 95.

51 Accounts of the law of treason can be found in W.G. Simon, 'The Evolution of Treason,' *Tulane Law Review*, vol. 35 (1961), 669; J.F. Stephen, *A History of the Criminal Law of England*, 3 vols. (London: Macmillan 1883), 2: at 241–97; William Blackstone, *Commentaries on the Laws of England*, [1765–9], 4 vols. (Chicago: University of Chicago Press 1979), 4 ('Of Public Wrongs').

52 SNS 1758, c. 13. For the prior difficulties over the reception of English treason statutes, and for the reception of English criminal law generally, see Jim Phillips, '"Securing Obedience to Necessary Laws": The Criminal Law in Eighteenth Century Nova Scotia,' *Nova Scotia Historical Review*, vol. 12 (1992), 87.

53 Indictment of Clarke and Faulkner, in Bulmer, 'Trials for Treason,' at 113.

54 See the list of examples in Blackstone, *Commentaries Book IV*, ch. 9

55 Presentment of Archibald *et al.*, 31 Jan. 1777, RG 1, vol. 342, no. 58, and Indictment of Clarke and Faulkner, April 1777, in Bulmer, 'Trials for Treason,' at 112–13.

56 Depositions of William Black and William Milburn in Bulmer, 'Trials for Treason,' at 113–16.

57 For these cases see RG 39, series J [hereafter RG 39–J], vol. 1: 276 and 292; Presentment of Samuel Archibald *et al.*, 31 Jan. 1777, and Indictment of Charles Dickson, RG 1, vol. 342, nos. 58 and 72.

58 This was certainly the case in the other jurisdiction where patriots were held. 'Having prayed for the Benefit of His Majesty's Mercy and requested to take the Oaths of Allegiance, and the same being tendered to them,' Swan, Ball, and Simpson (see above, text accompanying n.47) were discharged by the council board of the colony of St John's Island on 19 Feb. 1777. Charles Swan, whose exploits were enumerated for the board, had been seen in arms: Council Minutes, 19 Feb. 1777, CO 229/1.

59 Dickson was appointed registrar of deeds for Cobequid in 1777. Samuel Archibald was MHA for Truro. Thomas Archibald, Adams Johnson, Matthew Taylor, and John Savage were from Truro and Joseph Scott lived at Onslow. The Archibalds, Johnson, and Taylor had on at least one occasion refused to

take the oaths. Samuel and Thomas Archibald were in Machias in November 1779 and Thomas died in the West Indies in 1780. Adams Johnson received an American land grant for his patriot service. See S.B. Elliott, *The Legislative Assembly of Nova Scotia 1758–1983: A Biographical Directory* (Halifax: Queen's Printer 1984); Wright, *Planters and Pioneers*; and C.N. Smith, 'Revolutionary War Refugees from Canada and Nova Scotia,' *National Genealogical Society Quarterly*, vol. 59 (1971), at 270.

60 RG 39–J, vol. 1: 283, 286, 294, and 296–7; Deschamps Benchbook; RG 39–C, vol. 17, no. 30; Bulmer, 'Trials for Treason.' The different figures given are the result of the fact that the surviving indictments do not name seven of those captured. However, given that so many absconders were named, it is most unlikely that these men were not also included. Certainly it is fair to say that a total of forty-two were either indicted or imprisoned, or both. In addition to the seven noted in this paragraph, those indicted or arrested included nine members of the committee of safety in Cumberland County – Elijah Ayer, Sr, John Bent, Michel Bourg, Simeon Chester, Robert Foster, Amasa Killam, William Maxwell, Alpheus Morse, and Nathaniel Reynolds, Sr. There were also eighteen other members of the Cumberland planter community – Simon Austin, Elijah Ayer, Jr, Anthony Burke, John Casey, Ibrook Eddy, Atwood Fales, Ebenezer Gardiner, Edward Hampson, Robert MacGowan, Charles Oulton, Nathaniel Reynolds, Jr, Robert Sharp, James Sharpe, John Simpson, John Starr, John Stewart, James Story, and Jabez West – and the Acadian, Isaiah Boudreau, and the Swiss, Lewis Delesdernier. From Cobequid there was Matthew Taylor, one of the six indicted in January and reindicted in April, presumably for being in the Cobequid contingent that joined Eddy, and Henry Miller, Hugh Logan, and John Morrison. Abiel Peck hailed from Hopewell and Nathaniel Earle from Pictou district, Halifax County.

61 All ethnic groups in Eddy's varied band except the natives were targets of treason proceedings. The Maliseet and Micmac were regarded as separate nations for this purpose.

62 The only account of the trials is a relatively brief summary of the evidence contained in Deschamps Benchbook. A bare account of proceedings is at RG 39–J, vol. 1: 288, 290–1, and other documents are reproduced in Bulmer, 'Trials for Treason.'

63 There is little evidence either about what Faulkner had done or about what transpired in the court proceedings. It is clear that he was arrested and conveyed to Halifax, for on 15 July 1776 he petitioned the Supreme Court for a trial or bail. Nesbitt opposed bail and requested a continuance, on the ground that the crown's chief witness was out of the colony. The court agreed, and Faulkner stayed in jail until he was brought before the grand jury on October

14th on an indictment for 'treasonable practices.' That body threw out the bill, and Faulkner was discharged just in time to lead the Cobequid contingent in the siege of Fort Cumberland: RG 39–J, vol. 1: 259, 262.

64 Petition of Thomas Faulkner, n.d. [pre-April 1777], RG 1, vol. 342, no. 59.

65 He claimed that John Bent, another Cumberlander indicted in April 1777, owed him some money for a horse and that he, Faulkner, had gone to Fort Lawrence to demand payment. He was unable to find Bent and on the evening of the 29th, still in pursuit of his debtor, happened to arrive at Parker Clarke's house. While he was there news came that the rebel army had been dispersed, and Faulkner managed to locate and pursue Bent who was on the retreat. He overtook Bent, who apparently asked Faulkner to take his gun and powder horn and to carry them for him, which of course the obliging Faulkner agreed to do; this accounted for his carrying arms when apprehended. Prosecuting counsel intervened when this story was recited and noted that Faulkner had not offered it when apprehended.

66 The petition is reproduced in Bulmer, 'Trials for Treason,' at 117–18.

67 For the pardon process see Jim Phillips, 'The Operation of the Royal Pardon in Nova Scotia, 1749–1815,' University of Toronto Law Journal, vol. 42 (1992), 401.

68 Minutes, 12 May 1777, RG 1, vol. 189: 426. News of the escape reached fellow revolutionary John Allan at Machias at the end of May: Kidder, Military Operations, at 91. See also the report of the escape in Boston's Independent Chronicle and Universal Advertiser, 19 June 1777. Ironically, Clarke at least may have been released from jail by another method in time. On 22 April 1777 the Massachusetts Council wrote to naval commander-in-chief Sir George Collier proposing to exchange one Dr Madden for him, and it even sent a cartel ship to Halifax with Madden on board: see Mass. Council to George Collier, 22 April 1777, vol. 166: 358, Massachusetts Archives (hereafter MA); and Captain Glover to Jeremiah Powell, 30 May 1777, vol. 197: 103, MA.

69 A 'family tradition' holds that Faulkner killed a pursuing soldier on his way to Cobequid district, from where he escaped by boat to the United States: Letter to the Morning Chronicle (Halifax), 10 Jan. 1922. Both men received land grants in the United States: for Thomas Faulkner, 230 acres in Maine and 750 in Ohio; and for Parker Clarke even larger tracts – 500 acres in Maine and 1000 in Ohio. Faulkner died at Attleboro, Massachusetts, age sixty, on 7 July 1803 (gravestone). Clarke lived another twenty years and died at Machias, Maine, age seventy-five, on 25 March 1823. See Mass. Resolves, 4 July 1785, at 662–3; Smith, 'Revolutionary War Refugees,' at 266–73; and G. Sanborn, 'Genealogies on Families Settling both in New England and Nova Scotia,' unpublished ms., 1961, in MG 1, vol. 1691c, PANS.

70 17 Geo III, c. 9 (1777). Despite the fact that it was passed in February, news of it

did not reach Nova Scotia until July: Arbuthnot to Germain, 4 Aug. 1777, CO 217/53/166.

71 See Murray Greenwood 'Judges and Treason Law in Lower Canada, England, and the United States During the French Revolution, 1794–1800,' in this volume.

72 18 Geo III, c. 1; 19 Geo III, c. 1; 20 Geo III, c. 5; 21 Geo III, c. 2.

73 Arbuthnot to Sandwich, 13 Sept. 1777, Barnes and Owen, *The Private Papers of John, Earl of Sandwich*, 1: at 296–8.

74 See Clarke, *The Siege of Fort Cumberland*, at 3–16.

75 In fact Allan had with him a good number of Nova Scotia's principal rebels. There were three members of the Cumberland committee of safety – Ebenezer Gardener, William How, and William Maxwell – and three of Eddy's captains from the siege – Jabez West, Isaiah Boudreau, and Lewis Delesdernier. Tempting fate, the notorious Parker Clarke, a convicted traitor and escapee from the Halifax jail, lingered with Allan at Sunbury rather than flee directly to New England (as Faulkner had the good sense to do). Also at Sunbury were Charles Oulton and Robert Sharp, who had broken out of jail with Clarke and Faulkner.

76 Fulton to Allan, 1 April 1778, vol. 218: 55–6, MA. Fulton's account notes that he was subjected to the unusual humiliation of being tied up with his own garters! For the capture of these three see also depositions of John George Pyke and Ensign John MacDonald, RG 1, vol. 342, nos. 67 and 68, and Allan's Journal and Allan to Mass. Co., 10 July 1777, in Kidder, *Military Operations*, at 115, 202.

77 By the time Oulton was recaptured the act had arrived. He was detained under its provisions for about six months and then released on bail: Bulkeley to Barron, 17 Oct. 1777 and 25 Feb. 1778, RG 1, vol. 136: 257 and 260.

78 For these cases see RG 39–J, vol. 1, 314–17; RG 1, vol. 342, nos. 66 and 67, and Deschamps Benchbook.

79 Fulton to Allan, 1 April 1778, vol. 218: 55–6, MA.

80 Delesdernier's capture is described in Allan to Mass. Co., 9 Aug. 1778, in Kidder, *Military Operations*, at 248. His imprisonment is described in Gallatin to Badelot, 29 Aug. 1780, in H. Adams, *The Life of Albert Gallatin* (New York: Smith 1943), at 30–1.

81 In June a statute was passed by the assembly which permitted those captured in outlying counties on suspicion of treason to be brought to and jailed in Halifax if the county jail was 'insufficient.' It also allowed for such persons to be tried by the Supreme Court at Halifax before a jury, 'any Law, Usage or Custom to the contrary Notwithstanding,' for the duration of the rebellion: SNS, 1777, c. 7. This latter provision may have reflected some doubt about the legal-

ity of the trials of Faulkner and Clarke, although there is no evidence of that. The purpose of the act is unclear, in fact, for it merely confirmed procedural options already available to the authorities, but for our purposes its significance lies in the fact that it does afford some indication of interest in further prosecutions.

82 As the British statute was about to expire the council debated what should be done about those in the Halifax jail awaiting trial 'for promoting rebellion and such treasonable practices.' It decided to keep them incarcerated until the next meeting of the court while seeking the advice of the law officers: Minutes, 30 Dec. 1777, RG 1, vol. 189: 436, and Bulkeley to Nesbitt, 16 Dec. 1777, and to Gibbons, 26 Dec. 1777, RG 1, vol. 136: 258.

83 Petition of Parker Clarke, April 1777, in Bulmer, 'Trials for Treason,' at 117–18.

84 For the circumstances of his apprehension see the testimony of William Black, Deschamps Benchbook.

85 For Belcher see Susan Buggey, 'Belcher, Jonathan,' DCB 4: 50; C.J. Townshend, 'Jonathan Belcher, First Chief Justice of Nova Scotia,' Collections of the Nova Scotia Historical Society, vol. 18 (1914), 25.

86 For Finucane's appointment see Germain to Arbuthnot, 6 March 1777, RG 1, vol. 32, no. 39. Finucane's career is described in J.B. Cahill, 'Fide et Fortitudine Vivo: The Career of Chief Justice Bryan Finucane,' Collections of the Royal Nova Scotia Historical Society, vol. 42 (1986), 153.

87 For Morris and Deschamps see Phyllis Blakeley, 'Morris, Charles,' DCB 4: 559, and Gertrude Tratt, 'Deschamps, Isaac,' DCB 5: 250.

88 Nesbitt was one of the original Halifax settlers in 1749 and had been attorney general since 1753. For his career see J. Doull, 'The First Five Attorney-Generals of Nova Scotia,' Collections of the Nova Scotia Historical Society, vol. 26 (1945), 33, and Lois Kernaghan, 'Nesbitt, William,' DCB 4: 581. In November 1776 Arbuthnot had expressed concern that Nesbitt's health was so bad that he would not survive the winter: Arbuthnot to Germain, Nov. 1776, CO 217/52/239.

89 For Gibbons, who had served a legal apprenticeship under a former Supreme Court judge, see Warrant of Appointment, 23 Jan. 1777, RG 1, vol. 347, no. 38, and J.B. Cahill, 'Richard Gibbons' "Review" of the Administration of Justice in Nova Scotia, 1774,' University of New Brunswick Law Journal, vol. 37 (1988), 34.

90 Arbuthnot to Germain, 31 Jan. 1777, CO 217/53/22.

91 Minutes, 14 April 1777, RG 1, vol. 189: 424.

92 See Bulkeley to Goreham, 26 April 1777, RG 1, vol. 136: 249: 'The Offers made by your Proclamation to those who had been in arms on a surrender will be held good and valid,' but the amnesty covered only 'offences against the King' and not 'private offences.' Thus 'all persons who have surrendered being

guilty of any crimes, such as misdemeanours or Misprision of Treason, after their surrender, will be liable for prosecution for the whole of their offences, that is for Rebellion.'

93 Clarke, 'Cumberland Planters,' at 45–7; Bulkeley to Tonge, 22 Jan. 1777, RG 1, vol. 136: 245.

94 Arbuthnot to Germain, 12 June 1777, CO 217/53/101v.

95 Read acquired the use of another property at Cumberland; see his lease agreement with Dorothy Wethered (widow of Samuel) dated 31 May 1777 in RG 48, Halifax County Probate Records, Wethered Estate, PANS.

96 See the case of John Fillmore, discussed above at n.48.

97 Typical is the family history recounted in a local newspaper in the late nineteenth century, which includes the statement that Morse's 'loyalty was unimpeached': *Chignecto Post*, 17 March 1881. See also Clarke, 'Cumberland Planters,' at 60. For Morse's appointment to the commission of the peace see *Nova Scotia Gazette*, 24 Dec. 1793.

98 Ayer, Bent, *et al.* to Washington, n.d. [March 1776], in *American Archives: Consisting of a Collection of Authentick Records ...*, comp. P. Force, 9 vols. (Washington: Government Printer 1844), 4th series, vol. 5: 524. Bent was indicted and then took the oaths in June 1777: RG 39–C, vol. 17, no. 30.

99 Robert Sharp's mother presented a memorial on his behalf in 1782, supported by loyal Cumberland JPs. She was told that Sharp could 'return into the province and remain on his taking the oaths to government': Bulkeley to Barron, 20 June 1782, RG 1, vol. 136: 297.

100 Bulkeley to Studholme, 10 June 1779, RG 1, vol. 136: 274, refusing permission for 'certain persons ... who had been in arms' to 'return to their allegiance' and 'be received.' The authorities' opinion was that 'no such people could with propriety or safety be received.'

101 See the case of Hugh Quinton, Eddy's commander of the Saint John River detachment, who just a year after the siege was a loyal militia captain in Sunbury County and 'turned out sundry times and fought the rebel parties': 'Studholme's Report on Operations on the Saint John River,' *Collections of the New Brunswick Historical Society*, vol. 1 (1894), at 114. His militia commission is in RG 1, vol. 168: 524. See also generally Bulkeley to Barron, 20 June 1782, RG 1, vol. 136: 296. While we know very little about the process, it does seem that most or all of those in prison in Halifax were released sometime in 1777, and some may have been shipped to the other colonies, to Rhode Island or New York, along with prisoners captured in war: see Minutes, 16 Sept. and 6 Nov. 1777, RG 1, vol. 189: 430, 436.

102 SNS 1783, c. 3. This measure assisted Elijah Ayer, Jr, and Jonathan Eddy, Jr, who had been indicted for treason in 1777 and who later privateered in the

Bay of Fundy, to escape prosecution when taken in Cumberland in August 1783: James Brenton's Benchbook, 54, Acadia University Archives.

103 Minutes, 14 April 1777, RG 1, vol. 189: 423–4, and Arbuthnot to Massey, 24 April 1777, RG 1, vol. 136: 248.

104 See the instructions to Cumberland magistrates to require all those who had not yet taken the oath of allegiance to do so forthwith: Minutes, 14 April 1777, RG 1, vol. 189: 423.

105 Two Halifax county magistrates, John Cunningham and John George Pyke, were sent to the townships to administer the oath of allegiance. Although the district proved to be no more rebellious in 1777 than it had been in 1776, 148 refused to sign in May 1777 and in June the assembly refused to allow the townships' members to take their seats. Under considerable government pressure, which included a resolution to prosecute, many more did eventually take the oaths, although in October 1777 there were still holdouts: Minutes, 14 April and 5 May 1777, RG 1, vol. 189: 424–5; *Assembly Journals*, 1777, 46–7; Council resolution, July 1777, RG 1, vol. 342, no. 47; Arbuthnot to Germain, 12 June 1777, CO 217/53/101–101v; Deschamps Benchbook, entry for 27 Oct. 1777. The tenor of political attitudes in Truro at least can be gathered from the fact that a later petition requesting reinstatement of its representative also demanded remission of a land tax levied and collected when the township was unrepresented: Petition of the Inhabitants of Truro, n.d. [1778], RG 1, vol. 222, no. 87.

106 Almost all of those who had declared for Massachusetts in 1776 signed the oath of allegiance, and only three Sunbury residents, all of whom had previously fled the valley, joined John Allan. They were the Reverend Seth Noble (now Private Noble), Dr Phineas Nevers, and William Tumball: see 'Muster Roll for the non-commissioned officers and soldiers of Capts Dyer and West's Companys that marched to St. Johns in Nova Scotia in May 1777,' vol. 35: f64, MA.

107 See generally Douglas Hay, 'Property, Authority and the Criminal Law,' in Hay *et al.*, *Albion's Fatal Tree: Crime and Society in Eighteenth Century England* (London: Allen Lane 1975).

108 'Goreham's Journal,' at 362.

109 Uniacke's career is detailed in Brian Cuthbertson, *The Old Attorney-General: A Biography of Richard John Uniacke* (Halifax: Nimbus 1980), and 'Uniacke, 'Richard John,' *DCB* 6: 789.

110 See Deposition of William Milburn, 10 Dec. 1776, in Bulmer, 'Trials for Treason,' at 115–16, which implicates Uniacke but makes him out to be nothing more than a peripheral figure, a 'foot soldier.'

111 It is difficult to trace his movements during the critical period or to establish

precisely why he was released. His name disappears from the record of treason proceedings after he gave evidence before the grand jury in the Clarke and Faulkner cases: Indictment of Clarke and Faulkner, in Bulmer, 'Trials for Treason,' at 112–13. Both Bulmer and P. Hamilton, 'History of the County of Cumberland,' typescript 1880, 81, PANS, state that on 22 April 1777 the solicitor general 'moved that the provost-marshall assign over the bail bonds in the King vs Avery and Uniacke, the defendants not having entered their appearance, and the motion was allowed and entered accordingly.' From this one can probably conclude that Uniacke was released on turning King's evidence and that he was not in Halifax shortly thereafter even though he was around later before abandoning his pregnant teenaged wife and returning to Ireland.

112 His most recent biographer asserts that Uniacke 'did not play even a minor role in the Cumberland rebellion': Cuthbertson, The Old Attorney-General, at 10.

113 Hamilton, 'History of Cumberland,' at 81. See also Cahill's comment that Uniacke was able to 'bluff his way out of a treason trial,' in 'Chief Justice Finucane,' at 157.

114 Petition of Elijah Ayer, 6 Dec. 1782, in Documentary History of Maine, vol. 20: at 136–7. Only Jonathan Eddy had the foresight to move his family to New England before the siege.

115 They were frequently the subject of verbal and physical abuse. John Allan's wife, Mary, was one of those left behind and he complained that she and other women were called 'Damn'd Rebel Bitches and whores' and were often 'kicked when met in the street.' Allan explained why his wife was shunned – 'forsaken by those who I Expected would have helped her, for fear of being Ruined themselves': Allan to Mass. Co., 24 June 1776 and 22 Sept. 1777, in Kidder, Military Operations, at 196–7, 228–31.

116 For accounts of arson, destruction, and plunder by Loyalists see, inter alia, Memorial of John Allan to Congress, 26 March 1800, RG 1, vol. 364, no. 94; John Allan to Mass. Co., 25 Feb. 1777, in Documentary History of Maine, vol. 14: at 181; Memorial of Josiah Throop to Governor and Legislature of New York, 10 Jan. 1780, in Public Papers of George Clinton, First Governor of New York, comp. H. Hastings, 8 vols. (Albany: Nynkoop 1899–1904), 5: at 453–4; Letter from the Commissioners Appointed Pursuant to the Act Entitled an Act for the Relief of the Refuges from the British Provinces of Canada and Nova Scotia, Enclosing Certain Documents Relative to the Claims of Elijah Ayer, Deceased, and Elijah, Jr. (Washington 1802), at 6–7, 12, 19–20.

117 This estimate is based on a sample of only 17 absconded patriots whose dependants totalled 96 women and children. The number of children in each

family ranged from 0 to 10 and the average number of women and children
was 5.3 per household. Applying this average only to those 59 patriots who
fled directly after the siege (46 Cumberlanders and 13 Acadians) results in
more than 200 women and children. See 'A List of the Familys in the County
of Cumberland to Be Brought of[f] in the Flag,' vol. 183: 175, MA, and 'A List
of the Inhabitants of Cumberland Countie in Nova Scotia Who Left that Place
on account of the Enemy and Arrived at Saint Johns River and afterwards at
Machias,' in Kidder, *Military Operations*, at 76–7.

118 It is not possible to compute exactly how many were taken into the fort and
how many remained in the community. The families of Simeon Chester and
Parker Clarke, for example, were two that did stay on their husbands' lands,
aided by John Bent, Mrs Chester's brother, after he had taken the oaths in
June 1777.

119 For this see Minutes, 16 Sept. and 6 Nov. 1777, and 24 April 1779, RG 1, vol.
189: 431–3, 450; Bulkeley to Barron, 17 Oct. and 20 Dec. 1777, and to Goreham, 26 April and 30 May 1779, RG 1, vol. 136: 257, 259, 271–2; Fulton to
Allan, 1 April 1778, vol. 218: 55–56, MA; Clarke, 'Cumberland Planters,' at 45
and 50.

120 See Beamish Murdoch, *Epitome of the Laws of Nova Scotia*, 4 vols. (Halifax:
Howe 1832–3), 4: at 94.

121 This section is based on H.E. Richards, 'Is Outlawry Obsolete?' *Law Quarterly
Review*, vol. 18 (1902), 297, quotations at 299–300; R.B. Pugh, 'Early Registers
of English Outlaws,' *American Journal of Legal History*, vol. 27 (1983), 315; M.D.
Howe, 'The Process of Outlawry in New York: A Study of the Selective
Reception of English Law,' *Cornell Law Quarterly*, vol. 23 (1937), 559; Black-
stone, *Commentaries, Book IV*, at 314–15; J.H. Baker, *An Introduction to English
Legal History* (3rd ed., London: Butterworths 1990), at 77. Outlawry, like all
English criminal procedure, was in force in Nova Scotia: see generally Phil-
lips, 'The Criminal Law in Eighteenth Century Nova Scotia.'

122 This process is described below, in the section on civil litigation in Cumberland County.

123 Records of the Court of Escheats and Forfeitures, RG 1, vol. 377. For the process of freeing up land for the influx of Loyalists, see Margaret Ells, 'Clearing
the Decks for the Loyalists,' *Canadian Historical Association Report*, 1933: 43,
and 'Settling the Loyalists in Nova Scotia,' *Canadian Historical Association
Report*, 1935, 105; Magaret Gilroy, *Loyalists and Land Settlement in Nova Scotia*
(Halifax 1937); N. Mackinnon, *This Unfriendly Soil: The Loyalist Experience in
Nova Scotia, 1783–1791* (Montreal: McGill-Queen's University Press 1986), at
13–14.

124 John Allan, for one, 'put [his property] into a friend's hands to secure [it]

from confiscation,' and others presumably did also: Memorial of John Allan to Congress, 26 March 1800, RG 1, vol. 364, no. 94.

125 RG 39–J, vol. 1: 283. The law permitted the temporary seizure of property, as a prelude to forfeiture, when outlawry proceedings were in process.

126 The June 1777 report of Deputy Provost Marshall William Martin, who had been ordered to seize the farm of John Morrison of Cobequid, noted that it was being leased to another man, and the government was content for the latter to stay provided no rent was paid to Morrison or his family: RG 39–C, vol. 17, no. 48. See also King vs John Morrison, 24 April 1777, RG 39 – J, vol. 1: 296, and Petition of Martha Morrison, n.d. [1777], RG 1, vol. 342, no 49.

127 Allan to Mass. Co., 18 and 24 June 1777, in *Documentary History of Maine*, vol. 14: 435, and vol. 15: 196.

128 Bulkeley to Studholme, 10 June 1779, RG 1, vol. 136: 274.

129 Evidence of this comes from a later Chancery Court inquiry: see Depositions of Alpheus Morse, Ephraim Church, and Rhoda Terrace, 24 June and 3 July 1789, Chancery Court Records, RG 36, vol. 13, no. 82, PANS.

130 *Nova Scotia Gazette*, 6 July, 3 and 10 Aug. 1779; Registry of Deeds, Cumberland County, RG 47, reel 555, vol. C, nos. 78, 146, 237, 246, 247, 277, 296, 297, and 303, PANS.

131 Memorial of Josiah Throop to Governor and Legislature of New York, 10 Jan. 1780, in *Papers of George Clinton*, vol. 5: 454.

132 SNS, 1783, c. 3. On 22 March 1786 Jonathan Eddy, Jr, of Machias, acting on a power of attorney granted him by his father, sold to Peter Etter of Halifax, for £150, lands in Cumberland County, N.S., and Westmorland County, N.B., belonging to his father: Power of Attorney, 10 Oct. 1783, and Deed of Sale, 22 March 1786, both in RG 47, reel 555, vol. C: 336, 338, PANS. Of course it is possible that Eddy's lands were taken in 1776–7 and returned to him after 1783, but there is no evidence of this.

133 Minutes, 6 Jan. 1777, RG 1, vol. 189: 421. Much of the evidence comes from the later Chancery Court inquiry: see Depositions of Jesse Bent and Rhoda Terrace, 25 June and 3 July 1789, RG 36, vol. 13, no. 82. Military officers also confiscated cattle in 1777 from residents of Maugerville who continued to support the American side: Massey to Germain, 10 June 1777, CO 217/124.

134 RG 39–C, vol. 17 (1777).

135 SNS, 1779, c. 7. The act did not pass without controversy. The first draft was drawn up by the council in June 1779, and the assembly proposed amendments to it, although we have not been able to discover the substance of their disagreement. The bill was enacted following a conference between the two legislative chambers: *Assembly Journals*, 1779, 96–8.

136 The act was amended in 1780 following advice from London. The original
     1779 version contained a clause designed to prevent fraudulent conveyances;
     it provided that all conveyances 'made by ... Deserters within three months'
     before their departure 'shall be adjudged to be fraudulent, and shall have no
     force or effect for the Conveyance of ... Lands,' even if registered. London
     objected to this clause, stating that in some cases 'it may surely happen that
     purchases may be fairly made upon valuable consideration by men not
     knowing nor suspecting the principles of the parties of whom they purchase.'
     Believing, however, that the act as a whole was 'a very reasonable and
     becoming regulation,' London did not disallow it but chose to recommend 'a
     mitigation of this clause.' The assembly concurred. For all this see Board of
     Trade to Hughes, 15 Dec. 1779, CO 218/7/505–7; SNS, 1780, c. 10; *Assembly
     Journals*, 1780, 112; Hughes to Board of Trade, 9 May 1780, CO 217/28/56.
137 Minutes, 3 Aug. 1779, RG 1, vol. 189: 457; Commission of Appointment, 6
     Aug. 1779, RG 1, vol. 168: 555–7.
138 Robert Foster and Elijah Ayer, Jr, both complained in petitions to American
     authorities that, in Foster's words, they had been 'strip'd of what property
     they had in [Nova Scotia].' Yet they were not specific as to how this had been
     done, and whatever may have happened to Foster, the Ayer, family lost its
     lands as a result of Christopher Harper's lawsuit against Elijah Ayer, Sr. His
     son's statement was made as he was submitting a claim for compensation to
     the American government, and no doubt he preferred to let the American
     authorities believe that the property had been confiscated by the British
     rather than lost in the civil courts. See Foster to the Senate and House of Rep-
     resentatives of Massachusetts, 15 April 1782, in *Documentary History of Maine*,
     vol. 18: at 468; Ayer, *Letter from the Commissioners*, at 6. The process of Ameri-
     can settlement of refugee claims is briefly described in Layton, 'Canadian
     Refugee Lands.' Ayer was successful, as were Clarke, Faulkner, Eddy, and
     many others.
139 Eagleson to Society for the Propagation of the Gospel, 7 May 1781, MG 17,
     vol. 2: 257, PANS.
140 This section provides a necessarily brief summary of a long and complicated
     process, and is based on Ernest Clarke and Jim Phillips, '"The Course of Law
     Cannot Be Stopped": The Aftermath of the Cumberland Rebellion in the Civil
     Courts of Nova Scotia, 1778–1808,' unpublished ms, 1995, which deals with
     the post-rebellion litigation in much greater detail.
141 Eagleson to Chipman, 8 April 1788, Chipman Papers, F1, packet 6, no. 34,
     New Brunswick Museum, and to Society for the Propagation of the Gospel,
     30 July 1779, MG 17, vol. 2: 670.
142 Eagleson to Society for the Propagation of the Gospel, 30 July 1779, MG 17,

vol. 2: 670 and 671. He felt that he 'must observe' that Goreham was *'born & Educated* in *New England.'* He must also have said more than this locally, for in June 1779 Goreham sued Eagleson for 'scandal and defamation,' asking for £5000 in damages. The case does not seem to have proceeded past the initial filing stage: *Goreham v. Eagleson,* RG 39–C, vol. 20; RG 39–J, vol. 99: 10.

143 Bulkeley to Goreham, 8 June 1779, RG 1, vol. 136: 272–3.

144 RG 1, vol. 170: 307–8; Minutes, 22 Sept. 1780, RG 1, vol. 189: 471–2; Eagleson to Society for the Propagation of the Gospel, 7 May 1781, MG 17, vol. 22: 258.

145 *Assembly Journals,* 1782, 171. The resolution also required that all prosecutions of absconders be halted and that they be invited to return to their allegiance to the crown. This brought the interesting response from the lieutenant governor that he was 'perfectly disposed to give them satisfaction in respect of the Fugitives from this province, as far as he is impowered, and can legally do it': ibid., at 176.

146 Report of the Supreme Court Judges, 8 Sept. 1782, RG 1, vol. 221, no. 61.

147 For this incident see the documents in RG 1, vol. 223, nos. 7 and 8, and Minutes, 22 Aug. 1783, RG 1, vol. 189, 498. An account of it appears in McKinnon, *This Unfriendly Soil,* at 100–1. Harper later became a JP in New Brunswick: see Ayer, *Letter from the Commissioners,* at 28.

148 SNS, 1783, c. 2.

149 Minutes, 8 Dec. 1784, RG 1, vol. 190: 47.

150 In June 1783 the Loyalist Claims Commission was established, and the work of assessing claims and making compensatory payments and land grants went on in London and in the British North American colonies until 1790. For the commission see *The Royal Commission on the Losses and Services of American Loyalists,* ed. H.E. Egerton (London: Oxford University Press 1915), and Wallace Brown, *The King's Friends: The Composition and Motives of the American Loyalist Claimants* (Providence, R.I.: Brown University Press 1965). The reports of the commissioners are reproduced in *Second Report of the Bureau of Archives for the Province of Ontario* (Toronto: King's Printer 1905). One of those successful in making a claim was Christopher Harper: see Ernest Clarke, 'Christopher Harper: Loyalist,' *Loyalist Gazette,* vol. 24 (1986), at 16.

151 Minutes, 12 Jan. 1784, RG 1, vol. 190: 5.

152 Clarke, 'Cumberland Planters,' at 57.

153 For this and related issues, see Clarke and Phillips, '"The Course of Law Cannot Be Stopped,"' at 49–59.

154 For these and other 'cases,' see Ernest Clarke and Jim Phillips, 'Ambivalent Loyalties: Politics, Trade and Religion in Nova Scotia in the American Revolutionary Period,' unpublished ms. One of these cases is also discussed in Barry Cahill, 'The Sedition Trial of Timothy Houghton: Repression in a

Marginal New England Planter Township during the Revolutionary years,'
Acadiensis, vol. 24 (1994), 35.

155 For a review of the literature see J.B. Wright, 'The Ideological Dimensions of
Law in Upper Canada: The Treason Proceedings of 1838,' *Criminal Justice History*, vol. 10 (1989), at 131–2. See also Kenneth McNaught, 'Political Trials and
the Canadian Political Tradition,' in *Courts and Trials: A Multidisciplinary
Approach*, ed. M.L. Friedland (Toronto: University of Toronto Press 1975).

156 See especially Wright, 'The Ideological Dimensions of Law,' and F.M. Greenwood, 'The General Court-Martial of 1838–1839 in Lower Canada: An Abuse
of Justice,' in *Canadian Perspectives on Law and Society: Issues in Legal History*,
ed. W. Wesley Pue and Barry Wright (Ottawa: Carleton University Press
1988).

157 Brebner, *Neutral Yankees*; M.W. Armstrong, 'Neutrality and Religion in Revolutionary Nova Scotia,' *New England Quarterly*, vol. 19 (1946), 50; George
Rawlyk and Gordon Stewart, *A People Highly Favoured of God: The Nova Scotia
Yankees and the American Revolution* (Toronto: Macmillan 1972). For reviews of
this literature, see George Rawlyk, 'The American Revolution and Nova
Scotia Reconsidered,' *Dalhousie Review*, vol. 43 (1963), 379, and 'J.B. Brebner
and Some Recent Trends in Eighteenth Century Maritime Historiography,' in
They Planted Well.

158 See especially Mary Beth Norton, *The British-Americans: The Loyalist Exiles in
England 1774–1789* (Boston: Little, Brown 1972).

159 Adams to Niles, 13 Feb. 1818, in C.F. Adams, *The Works of John Adams*, 10 vols.
(Boston: Little, Brown 1856), 10: at 282–3.

PART TWO

c. 1783–1814

7

Sedition among the Loyalists: The Case of Saint John, 1784–6

D.G. BELL

It is commonplace to say that Canada was conceived in negation: in a rejection of the secular republicanism introduced to a wondering world by the revolution in the Thirteen Colonies and then carried to its atheistic apogee a decade later in France. While, indeed, it would scarcely be possible to overestimate the influence of the revolution in France in crystallizing British America's anti-democratic ethos in the 1790s, it was the earlier, American conflict that gave rise to what late-Victorian historians would fashion into English Canada's founding myth. That myth was built around the northward flight, in 1783, of upwards of 30,000 American Loyalists into what remained of Britain's mainland colonies. Defeated and exiled in the eighteenth century, it was said, the Loyalists and their rejection of republicanism and democracy were vindicated in the nineteenth century as the United States proved vicious and unstable, while the virtuous British colonies to the north resolved the Blackstonean sovereignty paradox that had wrecked the first British empire and became the brightest jewels of the empire-commonwealth.[1] As with most mythologies, that which depicts Loyalists as the anti-republican, anti-democratic founders of English Canada has a measure of truth. Their advent more than doubled the non-French-speaking population of British America, triggered the division of two old colonies and the creation of three new ones with their attendant official hierarchies, and provided critical local content for a strain of anti-Americanism that would be invoked often in the nineteenth century.

Yet, when moving from mythology to fact, it is always well to be cautious in generalizing about the Loyalists. Their outlook varied greatly according to background in the old colonies, wartime experience, and place of resettlement. Upper Canada's primitive new townships were a world away from the polished and highly differentiated societies at Shelburne and Saint John. Conversely, the War of 1812 added to Upper Canada's Loyalist history whole chapters that were of infinite service to mythmakers, whereas in the Maritimes the war had no such effect and the ideological need for it was less pressing.[2] Yet despite these and other differences, a survey of the principal Loyalist communities at the very beginning of the exile experience discloses similarities which, together, were described aptly by one startled observer as 'amazing discontents.'[3] In the mid-1780s such distempers beset Loyalists in Sorel, Kingston, Cornwall, Prince Edward Island, Shelburne, Annapolis-Digby, and at Saint John harbour.[4] In every case they arose chiefly from a conjunction of two factors: delay in getting onto surveyed farms, coupled with suspicion that Loyalist leaders were engrossing a disproportionate share of land at the expense of the rank-and-file, with a view to entrenching themselves as a local elite. In two notable cases – Shelburne and Saint John – this discontent and suspicion led to major riots, and Digby and Cornwall were only a hair-breadth from organized violence. Each of the major and some of the minor civilian Loyalist communities were, then, characterized at their inception by a contest to establish a local hierarchy. In the course of this struggle, embattled elites did not hesitate to delegitimize their critics by labelling them as seditious. In this ineffably ironic, almost Kafkaesque epilogue to the revolution, exiled Loyalists came to be branded by other Loyalists as disloyal.

The particular story of nine sedition prosecutions and related acts of official repression at early Saint John would repay attention even if those troubles lacked such arresting parallels in other Loyalist communities of resettlement. Here the contest for power lasted longest and assumed the most extreme rhetorical and legal dimensions. While not the largest of the Loyalist settlements, Saint John was the most important in that it became the political focus for a whole colony in a sense that Shelburne or Cornwall or Kingston did not. Research on Saint John's founding is enriched incomparably by the presence of rival newspapers and the survival of important collections of private correspondence. Moreover, the ultimate phase of Saint John's troubles was preceded by the 1785 provincial general election campaign which, conducted on a nearly universal manhood suffrage, served both to heighten the rhetoric of debate and to provide some idea of the relative strength of the competing factions. As part of its struggle to intimidate electoral opponents, New Brunswick's governing elite initiated a multifaceted campaign of repression punctuated by trials for seditious libel.

Over several months beginning in May 1783 the harbour at the mouth of the Saint John River was the debarkation point for over 10,000 Loyalist evacuees from British-occupied New York City. By origin, most were from the middle colonies and Connecticut, though a significant minority was British. About half of the arrivals were civilian refugees; the others were disbanding 'provincial' soldiers of the various Loyalist regiments, with their families, and some disbanded British regulars. They landed in an almost entirely unsettled (though not ungranted) area of Nova Scotia. Because little preparation had been made for their advent, most were forced to spend the winter of 1783–4 at Saint John rather than moving upriver to their promised farmland. It was from this winter of delay and despair that, in a sense, all later troubles sprang. Discontent was manifested not so much against Governor John Parr and his administration at Halifax as against the Loyalist leaders he chose to deal with at Saint John. For the most part these were either the leading men designated by British military at New York to have charge of the various civilian migration groups or ex-officers of the disbanded regiments. The Nova Scotia government simply commissioned several of this number as justices of the peace and let it be known that it would deal with the settlement through their agency. Against these 'agents and directors' it was popularly alleged that, in distributing town lots at the river's mouth, they had awarded themselves and their friends a disproportionate number of the situations useful for commerce. True to their American political heritage, those who opposed the town's unelected leaders convened publicly to select representatives, establish 'committees of correspondence,' and issue 'remonstrances.' The town's first newspaper, the *Gazette*, begun in December 1783, made itself the organ of this disaffected group. Thus, only a few months into exile, some Saint Johners showed the world that, while they might not be republicans, they were not political naïfs.[5]

The principal source of information on the opposition faction is the Saint John *Gazette* between 1783 and 1786. Virtually every surviving issue contains anonymous letters, poetry, and more versatile literary creations denouncing with striking vehemence the settlement's unelected leadership. Even in the agitated context of the time, however, one such production, published on 4 March 1784, was sensational. Addressing his remarks to the many disbanded provincials in the settlement, 'A Soldier' concluded his letter with a veiled but unmistakable allusion to the possibility of collective violence:

I would not wish you to think I mean to cause discontent or excite discord among you. I mean to warn you of your impending inevitable ruin should government withdraw her bounty, leaving you inhabitants of the barren rocks or tenants to a fortunate few that either by bribery or fraud possess all the habitable lands expressly contrary to the King's order. No feeling men whose hearts are warm with loyalty could wish to rob you of your just rights, and those miserly wretches (void of principle and compassion) must feel the force of a justly enraged soldiery ... should they succeed in their mercenary attempts.

In a community that had experienced one minor outbreak of mob violence already and was declared with some frequency to be 'in a state of Anarchy' in which the 'common people' were becoming 'insolent & rude' and betraying 'stron[g] Symptoms of Discontent,'[6] Saint John's weary magistrates were quick to seize on these references to 'discontent,' 'discord,' and 'a justly enraged soldiery' as the pretext for administering an exemplary check to their critics. Within a day of the paper's publication the magistrates used their power to trace the author of the piece and the chain of communication that had brought it to the newspaper. They selected for prosecution the two printers themselves and the man responsible for leaving the letter at their publishing shop, who not by coincidence was the brother-in-law of Elias Hardy, the foremost figure in the town's dissident faction. The actual author of the piece, though exposed, was not charged; it was the leaders of the opposition faction who were to be targeted, not their pawns. So it was that William Lewis and John Ryan (the printers) and William Huggeford were arrested, brought before a grand jury, and indicted by it on 10 March 1784 for publishing 'among the subjects of our said lord the King a certain seditious and scandalous libel.'[7]

The outcome of these prosecutions is unknown. Trial before the county sessions of the peace would have put in play the awkward possibility that a jury of twelve would acquit the proprietors of what was still the town's only press. It may be, then, that the absence of records on the fate of the prosecutions means simply that the accused were put on recognizance and trials never proceeded with. In this way the managers of the town – the very men who in their capacity as JPs would have presided over any trial at sessions – could suppose that they had put their critics on the defensive without risking the possibility of a humiliating reversal from the jury.

Three months later, in the summer of 1784, for reasons that had little to do with unrest at the mouth of the Saint John River, the British government divided all Nova Scotia into three parts. The Saint John valley became the backbone of a new province called New Brunswick, and Colonel Thomas Carleton, brother of the last British commander-in-chief at New York, arrived in Saint John on 21 November 1784 as governor. Carleton himself was an Englishman whose colonial experience was purely military, but the central officers of administration who followed him to New Brunswick were all Loyalists and practically unconnected with the detested agents and directors who had managed Saint John to this point. Carleton soon fixed the new colony's intended capital in the remote hamlet of Fredericton, but Saint John remained the seat of government and judiciary until late in 1786, by which time the tumults noted below must have made the decision to relocate the capital seem wise indeed.

Almost everyone assumed that once Loyalists themselves were in charge of an almost purely Loyalist colony, all of the earlier troubles would vanish. The newly arrived governing elite approached its task with self-flattering heroism: Solicitor General Ward Chipman likened the planting of Saint John to the founding of Carthage and Rome, Admiralty judge Jonathan Sewall called the town the Loyalists' 'New Jerusalem,' Surrogate General Edward Winslow vowed that the colony would enjoy the most 'Gentlemanlike' government 'on earth,' and, on half a dozen occasions, various writers declared that New Brunswick would soon be the flourishing 'envy' of the American states.[8] Moreover, thousands of Loyalists formerly stranded unhappily at Saint John were now scattered inland on their promised farm lots and a second Saint John newspaper, the *Royal Gazette*, had been established, this one supportive of Carleton's regime. Under such favourable auspices the governor moved with confidence in the fall of 1785 to call New Brunswick's first general election. As formal land grants had for the most part not been issued yet, it was impossible to decree a voting qualification based on property holding. Accordingly, with a daring they would soon regret, governor and council awarded the franchise to all adult white males of three months' residence.

In the key Saint John constituency, which was to choose six of twenty-six members in the House of Assembly, the government ticket was headed by Attorney General Jonathan Bliss and Solicitor General Chipman. To the 'utter astonishment of every body' in the governing circle, the election in the town where all of them still resided turned into an intense and sophisticated anti-government campaign. Banners, badges, placards, and handbills were as much in evidence as if the election had been in pre-revolutionary New York, although the parallel invoked by some Saint Johners themselves was that of John Wilkes and 'shameful and corrupt practices à la mode de Westminster.'[9] The early days of the election were punctuated by a major riot of opposition supporters at Mallard's coffeehouse, the headquarters for the government candidates. The disturbance was suppressed only through intervention and arrests by British troops, a constitutional blunder reflecting the depth of Carleton's surprise and panic, and an act that itself became a popular grievance.[10]

Here, in the midst as it were of the protracted 1785 election campaign at Saint John, it is useful to examine the rhetoric employed by the two sides. Almost everything known of it comes from the two weekly newspapers, which overflowed with earnest, bitter, witty, and learned productions from writers styling themselves 'Horatio,' 'Claudius,' 'Britannius,' 'A Loyalist,' 'Mrs Mira,' 'Aesop,' 'A Native American Loyalist,' 'A Plain Dealer,' 'Urbanitatis,' and the like. Although elaborate literary rituals may seem extraordinary in a community of only four or five thousand, on the edge of the wilderness, in which true anonymity must have been impossible, they are a further sign of how much the politics of Saint John owed to the rhetorical techniques Americans had honed in the decade of debate preceding the outbreak of rebellion.

Even some of the issues dividing Saint Johners were connected directly to political tensions in the old colonies, particularly New York. The two opposition leaders at Saint John, for example – Elias Hardy and Tertullus Dickinson – had led a major protest by rank-and-file Loyalists in British-occupied New York City.[11] Similarly, the proprietors of the Gazette and the Royal Gazette had been rival printers there.[12] When Saint Johners were exhorted not to vote for Jonathan Bliss and Ward Chipman because they were lawyers and government placemen, they were reminded of an issue that had become a staple of eighteenth-century colonial politics, and varying precedents from pre-revolutionary New York, Pennsylvania, and Nova Scotia were duly canvassed.[13] Similarly, when opposition agitators urged voters not to support Bliss and Chipman because they were from Massachusetts, and exiles from that colony were already too powerful in New Brunswick, where the great majority of people came from New York, Connecticut, and New Jersey, they invoked a long-standing colonial prejudice against natives of the Bay colony.[14] By continuing to discuss the delayed and unequal distribution of land, opposition campaigners focused on a subject that resonated deeply with many American colonists – former New Yorkers in particular – who were acutely aware of the vast, neo-feudal manors in the Hudson valley, with their thousands of tenants. When, therefore, opposition polemicists alleged that deliberate delays in the settlement process were part of a plan to reduce the rank and file to the status of 'slaves' (that is, tenants), they invoked 'a central concept in eighteenth-century political discourse' and played on one of pre-revolutionary New York's most sensitive public issues.[15]

In the rhetoric of government supporters, two interrelated themes emerged to portend the regime's subsequent legal offensive against its detractors. One was what may be called the 'patriotic' issue. In their election handbill the government candidates styled themselves the 'disinterested patriotic candidates,' implying thereby that their opposers were seeking to gain public office for private advantage. Other publications characterized Attorney General Bliss and his fellow candidates as 'divested of any interested motive,' 'without any selfish views, or considerations of private interest,' and the like.[16] Conversely, opposition candidates were maligned repeatedly with the favourite eighteenth-century epithet of 'factious' and its synonyms. They were 'plotters,' a 'party,' a 'cabal,' 'interested,' 'artful,' 'scheming,' 'designing,' and 'ambitious'; their success came from deluding the ignorant and unthinking. Such rhetoric led almost irresistibly to the insinuation that those who opposed Carleton's regime were seditious and disloyal.[17] One might have thought such epithets taboo in a community composed almost exclusively of Loyalists, but the course of the 1785 election campaign at Saint John so alarmed the governing circle that even this constraint was shattered. Thus, one anonymous writer complained that the opposition's rhetoric made him 'shudder,' for it was reminiscent of the propaganda responsible for the 'late American usurpation.' Another warned that defeat for the attorney general's slate in the Saint John election would prove to the world that 'the seeds of sedition and rebellion are already sown.' A third charged that Elias Hardy and other opposition leaders were of a 'Republican craft.' Their principles, it was said, 'correspond exactly with those of the rebels'; they brought with them 'all that *restless turbulence* and *levelling* disposition, that characterized the enemies of loyalty.'[18]

Such language was already in the air when Governor Carleton's supposition that the first New Brunswick election would be a quiet affair began manifestly to go wrong. Because voting at Saint John was conducted over a number of days it was soon evident that the opposition's slate was well ahead. Then occurred, as noted above, the Mallard House riot, its suppression by military intervention, and the arrest of several second-rank opposition figures for their part in the disorder. Carleton's circle had misjudged the temper of the town entirely, and government forces both at the polls and in the streets were desperately on the defensive. What was to be done?

The first thought was to overwhelm the opposition by resorting to the constitutionally dubious expedient of extending the right to vote to the 160 officers and men of the 54th Foot, who had lately been so useful as police. The sheriff himself was agreeable, and his deputy actually admitted the vote of one sergeant.[19] When the six opposition candidates heard this news they sent protests to both sheriff and governor-in-council which raised the delicate question of just what election – and other – laws governed a new colony where the legislature had yet to sit. Nova Scotia had never succeeded in enacting an election statute, and so there was no question of accepting passively the voting laws of that notoriously republican colony.[20] Instead, the council had fixed by ordinance the principles on which the election would be conducted, but it had done so only in the briefest terms. None of the English statutes specifying who could vote or become a candidate or regulating the conduct of the sheriff had been invoked. In the wake of the riot, when it became urgent to think of extending the franchise to the garrison in order to save the election for the government, these lacunae in the voting ordinance suddenly became the focus for agitated consideration.

In effect, government forces determined to have it both ways. On the one hand, the two law officers (themselves election candidates) advised the sheriff that the English electoral regime – with its careful curbs on participation by those holding office under the crown – did not extend to the province: 'You will remember Sir,' opposition candidates later reminded the sheriff, 'that the Statute Law of England relative to Elections was repeatedly urged by us and as often rejected as not Extending hither and with it of course the Bill of Rights, which is an English Statute and the Basis of Parliamentary Freedom.'[21] On the other hand, when the sheriff thought it in the government's interest to grant a scrutiny of the votes cast, the lack of any legal warrant for such a proceeding proved no impediment to his professing to take as precedent 'the Late Election at Westminster,' although in fact he followed it only to the extent convenient. In the end, however, the garrison was not allowed to vote. It is tempting to think that this was because – as the English radical William Cobbett, one of the soldiers stationed at Saint John, later claimed – the privates of the 54th Foot were actually in sympathy with the opposition.[22] Quite apart from this possibility, one suspects that Carleton was deterred from allowing military votes because such a manoeuvre would have become a constitutional grievance of such magnitude that even far-off London could not have overlooked it. If the Saint John election were to be salvaged for Carleton's regime it would be in some other way.

The means fixed on – a scrutiny of voter eligibility conducted by the bitterly partisan sheriff – rejected nearly 200 opposition votes on grounds of non-residence, producing thereby a narrow win of six seats for the government.[23] Opposition candidates protested the sheriff's conduct to the House of Assembly when it convened, early in 1786, but its pro-government majority vindicated him. By this time, however – in the wake of the Mallard House election riot and its attendant arrests, the intervention of troops, and the stolen election – the opposition's front-rank leaders had lost control over their disillusioned Saint John supporters, who now became so extravagant in their conduct as to give the government pretext for a stern and concerted campaign of suppression.

That campaign had a number of aspects, all exemplary, and all involving the notion of sedition. In one minor though vivid episode, a second-rank opposition figure, who had protested the legislature's vindication of the sheriff by remarking in a coffeehouse that 'the House of Assembly ought to be tore limb, from limb' or that 'he wondered the People did not tare them limb from limb,' was denounced to the assembly and ordered arrested for 'publickly speaking and uttering certain opprobrious Words in Contempt and Breach of the priviledges of this house and tending to excite Sedition.' Brought to the bar of the house on 26 January 1786, the offending speaker was ordered committed until he should 'ask pardon of this House, on his knees.'[24]

Within a month of the 'kneeling man' ritual the authorities were enabled to turn their attention to the opposition press when Lewis and Ryan unguardedly published a long and vehement anti-government letter from a writer styled 'Americanus.' The bulk of the composition was a lurid rehearsal of the emotive theory that the Loyalist leadership had delayed distribution of farm land deliberately so as to reduce the mass of exiles to such desperation that they would be willing to become tenants ('slaves') to the great. As with the 'Soldier' letter of two years earlier, it was the writer's desperate exhortation to action that sealed the printers' fate: 'We are distressed in looking forward. We scarcely dare view tomorrow. Our Provisions almost gone. Our lands not brought into cultivation. Our Loyalty suspected ... Tear the mask from their Faces, and exhibit their naked Enormities to the whole World. Let us not disgrace Loyalty with Cowardice. My distressed Countrymen, let us oppose every the least Violation of our Privileges ... Submit not to petit Tyrants ... In Fine,

let the world know ... the Rights you are jealous of, manifesting yourselves to be the Descendants of Britons.[25]

Publication of these inflammatory urgings – reflecting the agitated dis-
illusion caused by the assembly's complicity in the theft of the Saint John
election – led predictably to the arrest of Lewis and Ryan for 'printing
and publishing a scandalous and seditious libel.' Just two weeks later,
and even before they came to trial, the printers announced the dissolution
of their partnership, and the *Gazette* ceased publication. 'The Printers
have laid aside their paper,' the governor chortled, 'and the Citizens disown these incendiaries.'[26] Thereby Carleton's regime succeeded in silencing the principal vehicle of opposition expression.

At the very time Attorney General Bliss was bringing his case against
the opposition press, the assembly was moving to intimidate and silence
the entire New Brunswick population. The means chosen was one of the
most overtly repressive statutes in the whole Canadian experience
between the American revolution and the War Measures Act: a law
against political petitioning. Petitioning was a ritual of political expression which carried considerable freight in English constitutional history.
The same had been true in the old colonies, where petitioning gave a
voice to those who were excluded otherwise from the political process.[27]
And so, when the newly convened legislature – alarmed that petitions
against its vindication of the sheriff's conduct in the Saint John election
were attracting hundreds of signatures – resurrected from the reign of
King Charles II a statute against petitioning, it sent a uniquely repressive
signal to its detractors while also setting at defiance the Glorious Revolution's Bill of Rights. The professed purpose of New Brunswick's 'Act
against Tumults and Disorders, upon pretence of preparing or presenting
Public Petitions, or other Addresses, to the Governor, or General Assembly' was to 'prevent tumultuous and other disorderly soliciting ... of
Hands, by private persons, to Petitions, Complaints, Remonstrances, and
Declarations ... to the Governor ... for alteration of matters established by
Law, [or] redress of pretended grievances in Church or State ... being
made use of to serve the ends of factious and seditious persons, to the
violation of the Public peace.' The effect of the legislation was to outlaw
petitions 'for alteration of matters established by Law in Church or State'
with more than twenty signatures unless they had the prior consent of
three justices of the peace or a grand jury. Violators would receive three
months' imprisonment and a £100 fine.[28] (See app. 3, G.)

Introduced into the council, the Tumults Bill was passed by the House
of Assembly on 1 March 1786 and given Carleton's assent the day follow-

ing. It was a direct response to the petition campaign which had been under way for a month and which was attracting support in rural counties as well as Saint John. Only one of these petitions survives, but it alone contains upwards of 300 signatures, all from Saint John. Just days after the Tumults Bill became law, four of the petition's leading sponsors called on the provincial secretary to present it. Jonathan Odell declined that honour but said that they might call the next day to offer it to the governor personally, at the same time warning them formally that the law against petitioning had come into effect. Accordingly, when the presenters waited on Carleton on 7 March to hand in the document, both sides were engaged in a self-conscious ritual of confrontation. The four – Claudius Charles, William Thompson, Joseph Montgomery, and John Carnes – were arrested quickly, examined before Saint John's mayor, and charged with publishing a seditious libel.[29]

Among many remarkable political compositions surviving from the tempestuous early history of Saint John, the petition of March 1786 is uniquely compelling. None of the leading opposition figures signed it, and it conspicuously lacks their rhetorical polish. It is, however, this very quality of artlessness that makes it such an arrestingly eloquent expression of grievance, despair, and desperation. Something of its special character is captured in its sonorous opening sentence:

We His Majestys dutiful and Affectionate Subjects, Electors of the City & County of St. John, after having suffered every Evil which could be inflicted upon loyal Subjects by the cruel Hand of Usurpation, for an Adherence to the Person of Our King and His Government, and a most oppressive Tyranny since our Arrival in this Place, patiently have borne those Hardships from a due Regard to the British Constitution, under the firm Persuasion of being relieved from our Bondage upon Your Excellency's arrival, cannot now sit silent under the complicated Grievances we suffer and the fearful Apprehensions of what this infant Settlement must undergo, if such dangerous measures are persisted in, which threaten no less than a speedy Dissolution of the same or a Revolution, to us no less dreadful: particularly the most daring, violent and alarming Invasion of our Liberties striking directly at the Vitals of our most excellent Constitution.[30]

These sensational allegations – with references to 'a most oppressive Tyranny,' 'Bondage,' 'complicated Grievances,' and the possibility of mass return to the United States or a 'Revolution' – were alone enough to invite prosecution. But there was more. After a lengthy catalogue of election-related grievances and a request that Carleton call a new vote, the petitioners concluded with a threat which no government could ignore. They asserted that laws made by an assembly 'so unconstitutionally composed' could have no binding force. It cannot be wondered, therefore, that the four presenters were arrested on a warrant alleging that they had published 'a certain inflammatory, seditious and scandalous libel purporting to be a petition to the Governor ... tending to excite sedition and rebellion against our Government, which said libel also denieth the authority of the Laws ... and the legality of the Assembly now sitting.'[31] Through such averments Carleton's regime contrived to equate criticism of a colonial government with opposition to the king, and it proceeded on that basis to prosecute Loyalists for disloyalty. Indeed, in the excited imagination of the regime's attorney general, circulation of this 'most seditious' document was 'little short of an overt act of High Treason.'[32]

Printers William Lewis and John Ryan and the four petition presenters all came to trial at Supreme Court sittings in May 1786, the occasion on which the Mallard House rioters also had their trial. None of those charged with sedition was indicted through means of the county grand jury. An administration in which both law officers were from Massachusetts had ample reason to fear the reluctance of an American grand jury to indict for seditious libel.[33] Instead Attorney General Bliss adopted the safer course, usual in sedition prosecutions in England, of proceeding ex officio to lodge informations with the Supreme Court. Once charges were procured in this manner, the actual trial presented relatively little political risk. At trial of a seditious libel the petit jury decided only the factual question of whether the prisoners had 'published' the words in question and whether any innuendoes were as the crown alleged. It was the judge – and in New Brunswick all judges were members of the privy and legislative councils, and Chief Justice George Ludlow was styled the regime's 'prime Minister'[34] – who decided whether the publication in question was seditious.[35] Prosecuted and tried under such an arrangement, and in the context of the prevailing campaign of suppression, it is not surprising that the two printers and the four presenters were convicted and fined.

These six convictions for seditious libel, together with the trials of the election rioters, were the denouement of the official campaign against political dissent in early Saint John. The election of six opposition assemblymen had been forestalled, the opposition press had been silenced, public petitioning had been suppressed. Even prior to the trials Attorney General Bliss thought that the opposition had 'discovered some Symptoms of Fear & Dejection, & some of them of Penitence & Reformation.'

Within a week of their close, Governor Carleton reported complaisantly to London that his policy of ruling New Brunswick with a 'strait hand' had met with 'every success.' The province had been brought into 'perfect order and obedience.' His factious opposition had, he noted discreetly, 'failed' to win election to the assembly. Following this failure they had 'procured by every Artifice libellous petitions and published inflammatory pieces in a Newspaper.' He continued: 'A prosecution has been carried on in the Supreme Court against the promoters of these disorders. The Rioters, Printers, and those who presented the Petition have been severally convicted and punished and ... faction is at an end here.'[36]

To the outward eye, Carleton was correct. In December 1786 the rector of Saint John preached a special sermon before the town's most influential dissidents on the *Pleasure and Advantage of Brotherly Unity*.[37] Although the sermon had reference ostensibly to the fluctuating fortunes of ancient Israel, no doubt he preached and was understood in a double sense. The 'late calamities, owing to civil dissention' were Saint John's; so also, apparently, was the 'love and harmony' that now prevailed in the town. In the short term, at least, political dissension was at an end. Carleton could assure his superiors truthfully that the 'most perfect tranquillity' now prevailed over every part of the province.[38]

And what of the future? While the political faction that emerged in early Saint John, first in opposition to the agents and directors and then to Carleton's high Tory administration, was still discernably at work as late as 1793,[39] there is no apparent link in personnel between the politics of the settlement era and the opposition faction that was to dominate New Brunswick politics beginning in the mid 1790s under the brilliant Scotch emigré James Glenie. By then, many who had opposed Carleton's regime through the tumultuous election of 1785 and its crushing aftermath had long since slipped back to the land of rebellion, such as the printer William Lewis; by 1792 Saint John's population had fallen to a mere 2000. Others, like Elias Hardy, made their peace with the dominant order. In this way New Brunswick's initially pronounced tendency towards what historians of the American revolution call 'Whig loyalism'[40] was attenuated greatly.

But though there may be no overt link between events in early Saint John and New Brunswick's constitutional controversies of the 1790s associated with the clash between Carleton and Glenie, there is an evident structural parallel. In both cases what might have been a routine political squabble was transformed into a full-dress crisis of grand proportion because the colony's governing clique chose to make it so. In each case

Carleton's administration might have chosen to respond to political challenge by political art but instead it opted for unflinching confrontation. In each case its ultimate weapon was delegitimization of its opposition through the charge of disloyalty. From this perspective the crises of the 1780s and the 1790s are effects of the same cause – the attempt of New Brunswick's governing elite to achieve psychological redemption through creation of a model Loyalist colony. Any deviation from that model was resisted to the uttermost.

Finally, it is instructive to reflect on the tactic used by Carleton's regime as its political trump card in the 1780s (as again in the 1790s) – the 'loyalty cry.' When it felt its 'Gentlemanlike' vision of New Brunswick in political jeopardy through the rise of an opposition, the governing circle instinctively equated support for themselves with loyalty to king and constitution, and opposition to themselves with disloyalty and republicanism. In this sense, the sedition trials and related acts of official repression at Loyalist Saint John are the earliest notable setting for a tactic that would become a familiar one in nineteenth-century Canadian politics. It was a similar loyalty cry that was invoked during Lieutenant Governor Sir James Craig's 'reign of terror' in Lower Canada in 1810–11 and that smashed the Upper Canadian Reformers at the election of 1836, triggering the rebellion of the following year. It was the same tactic that induced New Brunswickers to reverse their opposition to intercolonial union in 1866, thereby making possible confederation. It was a loyalty cry that frightened Canadians away from free trade with the United States at the federal election of 1911. In different settings, in different generations, politicians would find the loyalty cry useful in crushing their opponents because, for most of their history, British North Americans could not take continued independence from the United States for granted. Consciously or subconsciously, 'loyalty' was almost always in question.

Yet it will be noted that on this prototypical occasion, in early Saint John, the loyalty cry failed to work, at least in immediate terms. Despite the government's attempt to stampede the electorate by branding political dissenters as rebels, it was the opposition that, prior to the scrutiny, won a large majority at the Saint John polls on an almost universal manhood suffrage. In resisting the cry, the Loyalists themselves evinced a confidence in their attachment to the British constitution which their children and grandchildren would evidently lack. Ironically, however, the refusal of most Saint Johners to heed a counterfeit loyalty cry only triggered more overtly coercive measures from government. Carleton's regime demonstrated that it would go to almost any lengths to render eighteenth-century New Brunswickers passive and obedient: the transition from Whig Loyalist to New Brunswicker had begun.

NOTES

1 Carl Berger, *The Writing of Canadian History: Aspects of English-Canadian Historical Writing, 1900–1970* (Toronto: University of Toronto Press 1976), ch. 2; Murray Barkley, 'The Loyalist Tradition in New Brunswick: The Growth and Evolution of an Historical Myth, 1825–1914,' *Acadiensis*, vol. 4, no. 2 (1975), 3.
2 David Mills, *The Idea of Loyalty in Upper Canada, 1784–1850* (Kingston: McGill-Queen's Press 1988), ch. 2.
3 William Tyng to Brook Watson, 25 May 1783, WO 60, vol. 33/1, PRO.
4 This striking parallel in the founding of the various Loyalist communities seems to have received comment only in Wallace Brown and Hereward Senior, *Victorious in Defeat: The Loyalists in Canada* (Toronto: Methuen 1984), ch. 7, apart from my own work. For Sorel and Kingston, see Larry Turner, *Voyage of a Different Kind: The Associated Loyalists of Kingston and Adolphustown* (Belleville: Mica Publishing 1984), ch. 6, 9; for Cornwall, see Elinor Senior, *From Royal Township to Industrial City: Cornwall, 1784–1984* (Belleville: Mica Publishing 1983), ch. 3; for Annapolis-Digby, see Neil MacKinnon, *This Unfriendly Soil: The Loyalist Experience in Nova Scotia, 1783–1791* (Kingston: McGill-Queen's University Press 1986), at 45–6; for Shelburne, see Marion Robertson, *King's Bounty: A History of Early Shelburne...* (Halifax: Nova Scotia Museum 1983), at 52–7, 126–8, and MacKinnon, *Unfriendly Soil*, at 79–81; for Prince Edward Island, see J.M. Bumsted, *Land, Settlement and Politics on Eighteenth-Century Prince Edward Island* (Kingston: McGill-Queen's University Press 1987), ch. 7.
5 I call the settlement Saint John by way of convenience; it was not given that name formally until incorporation as a 'city' in 1785. This account of the settlement's founding is adapted from D.G. Bell, *Early Loyalist Saint John* (Fredericton: New Ireland Press 1983), ch. 2, 3.
6 John Cochran to John Wentworth, 14 Dec. 1783, Wentworth Papers, PANS; Edward Winslow to B. Watson, 10 Jan. 1784, CO 217/56, PRO; Joseph Aplin to William Smith, 6 March 1784; CO 217/56.
7 'Soldier''s letter appeared in an issue of the Saint John *Gazette* which no longer survives. Everything known of the seditious-libel prosecutions comes from Edward Jack's 'The Liberty of the Press in Parrtown in 1784,' printed in the [Saint John] *Daily Sun* for 5 Nov. 1894 in the context of late-nineteenth-century attacks on press freedom in New Brunswick: see D.G. Bell, 'Judicial Crisis in

Post-Confederation New Brunswick,' in *Glimpses of Canadian Legal History*, ed. Dale Gibson and W. Wesley Pue (Winnipeg: University of Manitoba 1991), 189 at 197–9. Jack, who had access to the examinations of the principals and the grand-jury presentments from the files of the clerk of the peace for Sunbury County, is silent on the fate of the prosecutions, from which I infer that he saw no evidence that they went forward. The materials seen by Jack and any judicial record connected with the affair are themselves not known to be extant.

8 For extensive citations, see D.G. Bell, 'Paths to the Law in the Maritimes, 1810–1825: The Bliss Brothers and their Circle,' *Nova Scotia Historical Review*, vol. 8, no. 2 (1988), 6 at 8–9.

9 Jonathan Sewall to Jonathan Sewell (*sic*), 5 Dec. 1785, Sewell Papers, MG 23, GII, 10, NA.

10 On use of the military for policing as a grievance, see Petition of the Electors of Saint John, 3 March 1786, RS 42, *R. v. Charles et al.* (1786), PANB; John P. Reid, *In Defiance of the Law: The Standing-Army Controversy, the Two Constitutions, and the Coming of the American Revolution* (Chapel Hill: University of North Carolina Press 1981); and Bernard Bailyn, *Ideological Origins of the American Revolution* (Boston: Harvard University Press 1967), at 61–5, 112–17.

11 *Documents of the American Revolution, 1770–1783*, vol. 21, ed. K.G. Davies (Shannon: Irish University Press 1981), at 98; Marion Gilroy, *Loyalists and Land Settlement in Nova Scotia* (Halifax: Public Archives of Nova Scotia 1937), at 147–53; William O. Raymond, *The London Lawyer: A Biographical Sketch of Elias Hardy...* (Saint John: New Brunswick Historical Society 1894), at 3-5 [CIHM #12376]; W. Stewart MacNutt, *New Brunswick: A History, 1784-1867* (Toronto: Macmillan 1963), at 37.

12 Timothy M. Barnes, 'Loyalist Newspapers of the American Revolution, 1763-1783: A Bibliography,' American Antiquarian Society *Proceedings*, vol. 83 (1973), 217 at 230, 237–8.

13 *Royal Gazette*, 22, 29 Nov. 1785, 6 Dec. 1785. For New York, see Patricia U. Bonomi, *A Factious People: Politics and Society in Colonial New York* (New York: Columbia University Press 1971), at 241–5; for Nova Scotia, see Joseph W. Lawrence, *Judges of New Brunswick and Their Times* (Saint John: Acadiensis 1907), at 177.

14 John Parr to Lord Sydney, 26 July 1784, CO 217/50; St John *Gazette*, 13 May 1784; *Royal Gazette*, 8 Nov. 1785, 6 Dec. 1785; Mary Beth Norton, *The British Americans: The Loyalist Exiles in England, 1774–1789* (Boston: Little, Brown 1972), at 67–8.

15 Petition of the Electors of Saint John; 'Americanus' seditious libel: RS 42, *R. v. Lewis and Ryan* (1786), PANB; *Gazette*, 29 Jan. 1784, 13 May 1784; 'Gentleman of Halifax,' *Vindication of Governor Parr and His Council, against the Complaints of*

Certain Persons... (London: John Stockdale 1784), at 24, 31 [CIHM #37513]; Bailyn, *Ideological Origins*, at 232; Rowland Berthoff and J.M. Murrin, 'Feudalism, Communalism, and the Yeoman Freeholder: The American Revolution Considered as a Social Accident,' in *Essays on the American Revolution*, ed. Stephen G. Kurtz and J.H. Hutson (Chapel Hill: University of North Carolina Press 1973), at 256; Robert C. Calhoun, *The Loyalists in Revolutionary America, 1760–1781* (New York: Harcourt Brace Jovanovich 1973), ch. 37.

16 The only extant copy of the handbill is in W.O. Raymond scrapbook, vol. 5, at the Saint John Regional Library; *Royal Gazette*, 1 Nov. 1785.

17 On the link in Loyalist thought between ideas of faction and disloyalty see J. Potter [MacKinnon], *The Liberty We Seek: Loyalist Ideology in Colonial New York and Massachusetts* (Cambridge, Mass.: Harvard University Press 1983), ch. 2-4.

18 *Royal Gazette*, 1 Nov., 15 Nov. 1785, 24 Jan. 1786.

19 Tertullus Dickinson *et al.* to Thomas Carleton, 21 Nov. 1785, RS 60, vol, 1 PANB.

20 John Garner, *Franchise and Politics in British North America, 1755–1867* (Toronto: University of Toronto Press 1969), at 14–19.

21 Tertullus Dickinson *et al.* to W.S. Oliver, 22 Dec. 1785, RS 60, vol. 1. One detects here the earliest hint of what would become explicit the following year: that New Brunswick's governing circle had selected as the colony's reception point for English statute law the implausibly – though perhaps defensibly – early date of 1660, thereby omitting from the province's constitution, at least symbolically, the Glorious Revolution: D.G. Bell, 'A Note on the Reception of English Statutes in New Brunswick,' *University of New Brunswick Law Journal*, vol. 28 (1979), 195. In the context of election legislation in particular, the issue is perhaps more complicated; but nothing save Tory fear and perversity can have deterred the governor-in-council from adopting by reference English 'pure election' safeguards in its electoral ordinances of 1785.

22 [London] *Political Register*, 13 Dec. 1817.

23 Particulars of voting and scrutiny are given in Bell, *Early Loyalist Saint John*, at 107–10.

24 Arrest warrant: Ganong Papers, Box 36, 1, NBM. This form of humiliation had colonial precedent: Leonard W. Levy, *Emergence of a Free Press* (New York: Oxford University Press 1985), at 19.

25 'Americanus' seditious libel: *R. v. Lewis and Ryan*. The number of the *Gazette* for 22 Feb. 1786, in which the 'Americanus' letter appeared, is not extant. The only version of the piece to survive is that copied into the Supreme Court record, which is here excerpted without the attorney general's interpolated averments. Authorship of the piece was never uncovered.

26 Thomas Carleton to Lord Sydney, 14 May 1786, CO 188/3.

27 John P. Reid, *Constitutional History of the American Revolution: The Authority of Rights* (Madison: University of Wisconsin Press 1986), at 21–3.

28 SNB 1786, c. 58; it disappeared only with New Brunswick's general statute revision in 1854. Its Restoration original was 13 Car. II c. 5, which was not repealed until 1986.

29 Since the Tumults law had been passed for the very purpose of suppressing this petition and since the presenters had been explicitly warned under the legislation, it is surprising that the four were charged not with its violation but with seditious libel. The only obvious reason to prefer seditious libel was the advantage it gave the crown in limiting the role of the trial jury, as noted below.

30 Petition of the Electors of Saint John, 3 March 1786: *R. v. Charles et al.*

31 Arrest warrant, 8 March 1786; Lawrence Collection, MG 23, D1, NA.

32 Jonathan Bliss to Sampson S. Blowers, 17 March 1786; Bliss Papers, vol. 1603, PANS.

33 Levy, *Emergence of a Free Press*, ch. 3.

34 See n.32.

35 Levy, *Emergence of a Free Press*, at 11–12; Thomas A. Green, *Verdict According to Conscience: Perspectives on the English Criminal Jury, 1200–1800* (Chicago: University of Chicago Press 1985), ch. 8.

36 Thomas Carleton to Lord Sydney, 14 May 1786; CO 188/3, PRO.

37 George Bisset, *The Pleasure and Advantage of Brotherly Unity* (Saint John: 1787), at 5. The address was a Saint John's day sermon to the Masons of the 54th foot, but Saint John's civilian lodge – which was dominated by first- and second-rank opposition leaders – would also have attended: see William F. Bunting, *History of St. John's Lodge, F. & A.M. of Saint John* (Saint John: J. and A. McMillan 1895), ch. 1 [CIHM #00329].

38 Thomas Carleton to Evan Nepean, 1 June 1786, CO 188/3. It is striking how little resort was had to seditious libel prosecutions after 1786. The nine cases noted here are probably more than half of all such trials in the entire history of the province. I have found other cases only in 1801 (2), 1805, 1821, 1828, and 1830. The sedition panic of the 1790s in other jurisdictions seems not to have found judicial reflection in New Brunswick.

39 Ward Chipman to Jonathan Odell, 23 Feb. 1793, quoted in Lawrence, *Judges of New Brunswick*, at 186–7.

40 On Whig loyalism see, for example, Calhoon, *Loyalists in Revolutionary America*, at 563.

8

Judges and Treason Law in Lower Canada, England, and the United States during the French Revolution, 1794–1800

F. MURRAY GREENWOOD

In the famous treason trial of Thomas Hardy at the Old Bailey in 1794, defence counsel Thomas Erskine had the attorney general argue that advocacy of universal manhood suffrage, 'by pamphlet and speeches,' was a plot to bring about revolution. Such advocacy by reform societies could result in drastic social levelling and even erode the foundations of aristocracy, a development that in turn 'might lead to the fall of the monarchy, and, in the end, to the death of the king,' which is what those francophile democrats had intended all along. Hence they were guilty of 'compassing' the king's death, which was high treason.[1] Counsel concluded by likening the attorney general's argument to 'the play with which we amuse our children. "This is the cow with the crumpledy horn, which gored the dog, that worried the cat, that ate the rat," etc. ending in the "house which Jack built."'[2]

This passage, which must have amused the jury, was perhaps the most dramatic in Erskine's more than two-hour, multifaceted attack on 'constructive treasons,' meaning judicial extensions of King Edward III's restrictive Statute of Treasons of 1351/2 by artificial reasoning. Any extensions at all by judges had been expressly prohibited in the statute itself, but this prohibition had had little effect on the courts through the ages.[3] The subject became a matter of great political controversy from time to time: in the period surrounding the Glorious Revolution of 1688–9 and again in the 1790s, for instance.

This essay compares judicial behaviour relating to treason trials in

Lower Canada, England, and the United States during the war between the British empire and revolutionary France. 'Behaviour' includes, indeed mainly consists of, judges construing the substantive law. Within this general theme, emphasis will fall on the treatment of constructive treason, an approach that is intended to illuminate the history of treason law and the administration of justice in each jurisdiction during a period of perceived security crisis. Besides pointing up particular institutional differences, the comparison will allow an assessment of the degree to which each bench was 'Baconian,' favouring the executive power despite the law, or 'Cokean,' upholding the law despite governmental desires.[4] The essay also provides a tentative explanation of differing judicial behaviour in terms of differing legal traditions.

FEAR OF THE FRENCH REVOLUTION

The three jurisdictions, palpably different though they were in handling treason judicially, had one common feature: the trials took place in and were influenced by an atmosphere of alarm permeating the governing elites, a phenomenon common in the entire western hemisphere.

Lower Canada

One of the most obvious features of Lower Canadian public life from 1793 until 1812 was the 'garrison mentality' of the colony's small English elite, which consisted of officials, merchants, seigneurs, army officers, and professionals. This mentality was at its height in the years 1794–7, when revolutionary France threatened all of west/central Europe and even North America, and subsided only after 1812, when France was preoccupied with Napoleon's campaign in Russia. Newfoundland was attacked in August 1796 by Admiral Joseph de Richery's fleet, which escaped the British blockade at Brest and was widely thought in Lower Canada to be headed for Quebec City. In these years several spies working for the French ambassador at Philadelphia gathered military and political information on Lower Canada as well as the United States. And the colony experienced widespread rioting (erroneously thought by the English to be the work of French agents) among workers and farmers against militia conscription (1794) and forced labour on the roads (1796–7).

The concept of the garrison mentality has various shadings which I have described elsewhere in detail.[5] In its pure form it was based on exaggerated assessments of danger. The French were likely to attack the colony, and if they did the conquered Canadiens, former subjects of the pitiless enemy, would rise *en masse*, except for the seigneurs and Roman Catholic clergy, in armed and bloody rebellion. Severed English heads on Canadien 'Jacobin' pikes or similar, if less precise, images formed part of the common refrain in these years. One resident, in late 1793, summed up the feelings of many: he was 'sure the moment a Descent was made by the Republicans of France that the French [Canadien] Inhabitants would Cut the throats of all that they thought to be in the British interest.'[6] Merchant-magistrate William Lindsay of Montreal wrote in December 1796 that only the recent dispatch of British troops to the rioting city had frustrated the 'Junto in this neighbourhood,' which had been and perhaps still was 'planning the destruction of the English within the walls.'[7]

This frame of mind was generated by numerous factors – among them the small number of regular troops in the Canadas; the absence of professional police; a sense, by no means confined to loyalists, of the fragility of the social order; and the common eighteenth-century belief in the efficacy of a few conspirators manipulating the ignorant masses, examples of such supposed situations being the American colonies in 1776 and France in 1789. But of the greatest importance was the simple fact that the English were outnumbered about fifteen to one by people still culturally French and often, among the 'lower orders,' anglophobic.[8] The large majority of the 160,000 or so Canadiens in 1793 were farmers (or members of farming families) who had hunting guns and lived along the two expected routes of invasion, the St Lawrence and Richelieu rivers. The fears expressed by the English were almost all genuine, but of course their perception of Canadien disloyalty could be and was used for other purposes: careerism, justification for various anglicizing policies, defence of the executive in its contest with the assembly, and so on.

Great Britain

For the British Isles in the 1790s, the equivalent of the garrison mentality was called then – and the label has survived in historical writing – 'Alarmism.' Influenced greatly by Edmund Burke, the ultimate Alarmist, it projected all-out revolution led by supposedly francophile popular societies calling for annual parliaments and universal male suffrage, a revolution that would be supported by aid, and perhaps invasion, from France. Future research will, it is hoped, compare and contrast Alarmism with the garrison mentality. In Lower Canada, the English elite was 'surrounded' by a culturally French people. Great Britain's elite was not. However, it confronted angry, interconnected reform societies, with at times massive support, mainly from the 'lower orders,' and faced a real possibility of invasion. Lower Canada's elite did not have to contend with such dangers.

Proof of Alarmism appears in virtually all the specialist texts on the impact of the French revolution on England.[9] The Leeds *Mercury* recalled, with definite exaggeration but more truth, a generation after that 'the French Revolution made the whole country Tory.' Advanced Whig though he was, Erskine publicly conceded that the fears were widespread, profound, and genuine.[10] As for Scotland, Lord Cockburn, the renowned legal historian, had been a boy when he first met the Attila-like judge Lord Braxfield and other extremists. He later wrote: 'Everything rung and was connected with the Revolution in France; which, for above twenty years, was, or was made, all in all. Everything, not this thing or that thing, but literally everything, was soaked in this one event.'[11] One could say exactly that for Lower Canada in the years 1793–1811.

The government of Prime Minister William Pitt has sometimes been accused, as it was in its own time, of manufacturing the crisis for such political reasons as gaining public support for entry into the war, killing parliamentary reform, and detaching the Duke of Portland's conservative Whigs from Charles James Fox.[12] Yet this theory is belied by the Alarmist tone of letters written by such important cabinet ministers as Secretaries of State Henry Dundas and Lord Grenville and Lord Chancellor Loughborough as well as by the later recollections of Attorney General John Scott, who decided that the leaders of the reform societies should be prosecuted for high treason as a necessary public-relations exercise rather than on the more easily winnable charge of seditious conspiracy.[13] Nor should we underestimate the impact of exaggerated reports of spies, often self-serving, and of others. The lord advocate of Scotland, Robert Dundas, to cite one, informed his brother Henry in August 1793 that he was about to prosecute radical reformer Thomas Muir for sedition as 'an emissary [undercover agent] from France or the disaffected in Ireland.'[14] And the government acted fearfully: building barracks in industrial towns (1792),[15] altering security laws in drastic ways (1793–5), preparing the volunteer corps for police work,[16] and investing huge amounts of money and energy on informers and the prosecution of political offences throughout England as well as in Edinburgh and Ireland.[17] The last two mentioned activities continued long after the beginning of the war in February 1793, the overwhelming defeat of Charles Grey's motion for modest parliamentary reform in May of that year, and the successful assimilation of the Portland Whigs into Pitt's administration in July 1794. As for Pitt personally, one of his 1793 letters reveals serious concern for internal security, as does his high attendance rate and prosecutorial activism during the crucial early examinations of the state prisoners in 1794.[18] A year or so later he was heard to remark: 'My head would be off in six months were I to resign.'[19] In 1798 Pitt wrote Dundas suggesting that they seriously consider prosecuting former opposition leader Fox – whose radical followers had recently seceded from parliament *en bloc* – as a subversive.[20] While somewhat sparse, the evidence is sufficient to indicate genuine apprehension, although not necessarily panic. As his biographer concludes, the prime minister, by the spring of 1794 at the latest, was at least a moderate Alarmist.[21] He and his colleagues of course *used* Alarmism for a variety of political purposes in consolidation of their power, but, as in Lower Canada, they did not manufacture the fear for these purposes.

United States

As with Lower Canada and Britain in the 1790s, some contemporaries suggested – and their claims have been echoed by later historians – that Federalist expressions of fear were strictly opportunistic, uttered to vilify their democratically inclined opponents, the Jeffersonian Republicans.[22] That the aristocratic, pro-British majority party of the period commonly exploited its perception of the security danger for precisely that end is beyond doubt. In the election year of 1800, to give one of hundreds of possible illustrations, 'Marcellus' argued in the New York *Spectator* that the aim of Jefferson 'and of course the Jacobins at large' was the overthrow of the constitution.[23] But it is highly unlikely that, an occasional individual aside, the 'fear' was *created* for partisan purposes.

The general situation argues for such a conclusion. As a leading student of the political psychology then prevalent has written, 'the first generation of American administrators knew partisanship only as a prelude to revolution' rather than as a norm of electoral politics.[24] A great many prominent Republicans, such as James Monroe, ambassador to France in the middle years of the decade, and Benjamin Bache, fiery editor of Philadelphia's polemic *Aurora* and a grandson of Ben Franklin who earned the nickname 'Lightning Rod, Junior,' made no secret of their admiration of French republicanism and of French foreign policy. Ministers sent by Paris to the United States, particularly citizens Edmond Genêt (1793–4) and Philippe-Auguste Adet (1796–7), openly favoured the Republican party and engaged in strategic intrigues contrary to the interests of the American governments. Adet, for example, sent a spy, General Victor Collot, to the Ohio-Mississippi river valleys in 1796 to collect political and military information so that France would be prepared to detach the trans-Appalachian region from the United States.[25] In the years 1798–1800 the two countries fought each other in an undeclared naval war over the shipping rights of neutrals.

Governmental action did not square with an orchestrated charade. Officials took the Collot plot seriously, expending considerable funds as well as energy on counter-intelligence and later minatorily inducing the general to leave the country. The war years saw the enactment of truly Draconian legislation against aliens and the hysterical enforcement of the Sedition Act of 1798. Equally telling is evidence from letters written by Federalists to Federalists which were not intended for publication. If references to Republicans as 'Jacobins' or 'Democrats' – both analogous to 'communist' or 'red' in the late 1940s and 1950s – regularly appeared in public speeches and conservative newspapers, so too did they regularly appear in private correspondence.[26] Other examples follow.

A careful study of President George Washington's correspondence has revealed his conviction (from 1793 to 1798 at least) that dangerous plots were afoot, inspired by the anarchistic French and involving the newly mushrooming democratic societies and Republican politicians. The 'Whiskey Rebellion' against excise taxes, which broke out in western Pennsylvania during the summer of 1794, was one major result, he thought, of these machinations to destroy the union.[27] Other well-known Federalists whose alarmist views found expression in private letters include Secretary of State Timothy Pickering; Alexander Hamilton; Senator James Lloyd, father of the Sedition Act; and President John Adams's wife and mentor Abigail, who usually reflected her husband's political viewpoint.[28] She wrote to a female friend in 1798 that 'French emissaries are in every corner of the union ... spreading Sedition' and hoping to force Adams to resign in favour of 'the Man of the People [Jefferson].' If the Republican newspapers were 'not suppressed, we shall come to civil war.'[29]

From 1795 to 1800 the Federalist clergy of many denominations continually sermonized and published on the theme of a 'French-Republican-democratic societies' plot. In the last years of the century these sermons and articles became more specific, adopting the demented (but historically understandable) conspiracy interpretation of the French revolution so popular in elite circles of Great Britain and Lower Canada.[30] According to this horror story – deriving principally from Edinburgh chemistry professor John Robison and emigré priest Abbé Augustin Barruel – it was a mad Bavarian intellectual, Adam Weishaupt, working with a small group of henchmen and through the secret German illuminati and French Masonic lodges, who had made the revolution. And had in fact made all of it, from undermining religious belief and respect for governmental authority in western Europe through the elections to the Estates General, the march of the women on Versailles, and King Louis XVI's execution to the Jacobin war and the Directory. Weishaupt's tentacles had been quietly effective everywhere in the conquered parts of the continent and were at work in such places as the British Isles, Lower Canada, and the United States.[31] Among many Federalist believers of this theory were George Washington and Abigail Adams (both in private letters); outspoken journalist William Cobbett; Timothy Dwight, the president of Yale College; and in all probability Supreme Court Justice James Iredell.[32]

Fear of a local version of the French revolution, then, informed the elites of Lower Canada, Great Britain, and the United States, and this fear propelled the bench of each jurisdiction in an authoritarian direction. But differences in handling security trials were marked and had a great deal to do with legal traditions.

THE TRIALS: GREAT BRITAIN (LONDON, 1794)

Space forbids treatment of the political background, the activities of the reform societies, the rabid loyalist associations or government spies, the general issue of freedom to dissent, or even the factual evidence presented in court. Such matters are capably handled in the secondary literature.[33] This essay concentrates instead on judicial behaviour in the prosecution of thirteen so-called 'Jacobins': six from the middle-class Society for Constitutional Information (SCI) and seven members of the London Corresponding Society (LCS), which had economically redistributionist as well as radical constitutional aims.

In early October 1794 the thirteen state prisoners were brought before the grand jury of Middlesex and a special commission of judges led by Chief Justice Sir James Eyre of the Court of Common Pleas, who presided at these proceedings and in the first two trials: those of master shoemaker Thomas Hardy, the highly intelligent, dedicated secretary of the LCS; and the sharp-tongued philologist, political theorist, cleric, and gentleman of means John Horne Tooke, a leader of the SCI. Eyre was assisted by

Alarmist Sir Archibald Macdonald, lord chief baron of the Exchequer Court; Sir Beaumont Hotham of the Exchequer; Sir Francis Buller of the Common Pleas, a former protégé of the ultra-royalist Lord Mansfield; Sir Nash Grose of the Court of King's Bench; and Sir Soulden Lawrence, also of that court.[34] All but the last assisted in *Hardy* and Lawrence replaced Buller in *Tooke*. Thus, fully half the twelve common-law judges of England sat on these cases, making them a good test of Cokean or Baconian tendencies in the English judiciary.[35]

Twelve of the thirteen state prisoners were indicted for high treason, but only three – Hardy, Tooke, and political lecturer/orator John Thelwall, an LCS activist – were actually tried. All were acquitted. This essay deals almost exclusively with the first two trials because of space limitations and the absence of any accessible report of Thelwall's trial.[36] Hardy and Tooke were prosecuted by ultra Tories, Attorney General Sir John Scott (later Lord Chancellor Eldon) and Sir John Mitford, who was to become lord chief baron and then lord chief justice of the Common Pleas. The great Erskine, himself later lord chancellor, and talented advocate Vicary Gibbs, afterwards chief justice of the Common Pleas, acted for the accused. Each side was assisted by a battery of prominent barristers and of course by solicitors. Counsel certainly put their energies into these trials. Scott opened *Hardy* in nine hours, Erskine in seven. It took Eyre a day and a half to summarize and assess the testimony (often lengthy) of fifty or so witnesses and mounds of written exhibits. The Old Bailey was jammed with spectators every one of the nine trial days. All of England, it seemed, waited anxiously for news.[37]

Preliminary Proceedings: Privy Council Examinations

In May and June the seized papers, state prisoners, and informers were examined by the cabinet sitting as a privy council of magistrates, assisted by the law officers and some non-cabinet councillors, including three judges. These were Sir James Eyre, destined to preside at the two main trials; Macdonald, who would sit with Eyre before himself presiding in *Thelwall*; and Sir Richard Pepper Arden, master of the rolls, who took no part in the court proceedings. This participation was fully in accord with traditional practice. Chief Justice Lee had attended examinations of accused Jacobite rebels prior to presiding at several of their trials in 1746. Lord Loughborough, then chief justice of the Common Pleas, who was present when the anti-papist rioters of 1780 were interrogated, sat on the bench which tried Lord George Gordon.[38]

Describing the attempts to scare those examinees who were not 'gentle-men'[39] and assessing the weight of evidence lie beyond the scope of this essay. Its purpose is rather to explain the role judges played in the pro-cess so that role can later be compared with judicial behaviour in Lower Canada. Writing in the 1840s, Lord Campbell construed the judges' responsiblity as strictly limited: when the state prisoners of 1794 'were apprehended and examined before the Privy Council, the judges were called in to listen to the evidence and join in the commitment.'[40] This assessment, while technically inaccurate, correctly conveys the idea of self-restraint, a point corroborated by primary sources. Attorney General Scott, for example, was later to recall that the judges' function, important though it may have been, was essentially passive: having been 'present at the many and long Examinations of the parties apprehended, the reading of the papers seized, and the Examination of the Witnesses, being called upon for their Opinions, [they] stated that in their Judgement the parties were guilty of High Treason.'[41] As Scott and the text below make clear, the judges felt entirely free to change their minds at trial after hearing fur-ther evidence and counsels' arguments.

Unfortunately, the privy council register held by the Public Record Office in London conceals much of interest.[42] With one notable exception mentioned below, the register does not indicate who did the questioning. Nor does it allow us to penetrate the discussions. On 19 May 1794, for example, it tersely records that Tooke and five others should be charged with treason rather than 'treasonable practices,' the undefined initial charge: 'Their Lordships having maturely considered the Evidence ... were unanimously of Opinion, that Warrants should be issued for com-mitting ... [Tooke et al.] to the Tower for High Treason.' Eyre, Macdonald, and Arden joined in this opinion – a critical early decision.

The register does help in some respects. Although the three judges attended the first meeting of 19 May, they did not sign the warrants which were issued that day. This certainly suggests some attempt, by oth-ers or by the judges themselves, to distance them from a prosecutorial function. The source also indicates that the judges were far from regular attenders. Of the twelve 'treason' sessions from 12 to 19 May inclusive, Eyre turned up for six, Macdonald for five, and Arden the same. None sat on Hardy's third examination or on those of Thelwall or Tooke. Of the twenty-three other individuals who participated in these proceedings, twelve attended more regularly than Eyre. The most regular participants were Secretary Dundas (12), Lord Aukland (not of the cabinet, 12) and Lord Chancellor Loughborough (11). Despite constant calls on their time,

Pitt came to nine sessions and Foreign Secretary Lord Grenville to eight. The judges were clearly not consumed by prosecutorial desires.

The author has located accounts of examinations conducted with six of the state prisoners: John Richter, Tooke, Jeremiah Joyce, John Augustus Bonney, Hardy, and Thelwall.[43] Taken together, they indicate clearly that Secretary Dundas normally took the lead in questioning (often in a bullying manner) and this is corroborated by the register's record of Tooke's appearance – the notable exception referred to above.[44] Other active questioners were a sometimes petulant, minatory, excitable Pitt, who called one prisoner a liar and threatened another with the gallows; Alexander Wedderburn, Lord Loughborough; and the law officers. The judges are never referred to.[45] Unfortunately, only Hardy's *Memoir* deals with sessions attended by both the prisoner and Eyre/Macdonald, but his silence on the issue of judicial involvement is significant. Though Hardy listed twelve examiners by name or office who had sat upon his various interrogations, he omitted mention of any judge except the lord chancellor. Their questioning, if any, made little impression on the accused.[46]

The limited role of the judges in the pre-indictment proceedings is further indicated by Lord Castlereagh's 1806 speech in the Commons defending the controversial appointment of Lord Chief Justice Ellenborough to the cabinet.[47] Chief Justice Eyre, Castlereagh claimed, 'was summoned to the privy council ... to hear evidence against the prisoners, to decide whether it was sufficient to warrant a committal, and for what crime.' If Eyre had gone beyond these tasks and 'consulted in Cabinet on the political expediency of bringing those persons to trial, if he had engaged in all the councils of government ... it would be monstrous to contend ... he would with propriety have been sent to sit in judgment upon the parties accused.' Castlereagh's statement, consistent with the deeply imbedded ideal of an impartial judiciary, went uncontradicted in parliament and was made when several men privy to what had transpired were still alive.[48] The pre-indictment role of the English judges, then – always excepting the lord chancellor – was conceived of as magisterial, not prosecutorial. They did *not*, in particular, help to *construct* the crown's litigation strategy.

Grand Jury Proceedings

Less than four months before the grand jury proceedings, Charles James Fox had warned the Commons that any parliamentary assertions of treasonable plots would be unfair to the state prisoners.[49] Nevertheless, the

chief justice opened his address to the grand jury by quoting the preamble to the Habeas Corpus Suspension Act of 1794, with its reference to a
conspiracy of traitors aimed at introducing Britain to anarchy.[50] This
august declaration pointed to a crime of 'deep malignity which loudly
calls upon the justice of the nation to interpose.' Later in his charge Eyre
twice reminded his audience of the statute, once stating that the allegation, even though emanating from 'the highest authority,' was 'extrajudicial' and as such 'not a ground upon which you ought to proceed'
without courtroom proof.

The chief justice made certain other points common among Alarmists.
Reform associations, for example, 'but too easily degenerate ... even to the
enormous ... crime of high treason.' Eyre, did, however, instruct that the
burden lay on the crown to prove that ostensible aims were but veils and
the societies stalking horses for the ultimate evil. The projected 'convention' would doubtless engross much of the jurors' attention. In the
present time, 'with the example of a neighbouring country before our
eyes,' the law looked jealously on such mass meetings. They were always
dangerous and always 'criminal' in some sense. Adoption of the language and procedural usages of the French revolutionaries would tend to
show the treasonable nature of the proposed organization.

The evidence, the chief justice asserted, might lead to one of three conclusions about the convention, each with its own legal ramifications.
First, the jurors could find that there was no intention by the projectors of
the convention to use force or the threat thereof to bring about manhood
suffrage and annual parliaments. Such a plan amounted to some kind of
an offence but not treason. Secondly, the convention might have been
designed as a means to the violent overthrow of the 'whole government
of the country, to pull down ... the British monarchy, that glorious fabric
... cemented with the best blood of our ancestors.' This type of plot had
not been included as a distinct head in King Edward III's statute nor
mentioned as an overt act of compassing by Mathew Hale and Michael
Foster, probably because the case was so obvious. To hammer home this
conclusion, Eyre went far (entirely without necessity) towards sanction-
ing the idea that 'death' included political death: 'The constitution of our
government is so framed, that the imperial crown of the realm is the common centre of the whole; that all traitorous attempts upon any part of it
are instantly communicated to that centre; and ... they are punishable as
traitorous attempts against the king's person.' Taken literally, this would
mean that a conspiracy to resist physical efforts to collect customs duties
at a number of ports was treason. Indeed, had Eyre persisted in this rea-

soning, he might well have affected the trial jury's perception of the third position, namely a plot to collect formidable power at the convention and use it to 'overawe the legislative body, and extort a parliamentary reform from it.' The actual deployment of force (as in *Gordon*) would be treason, even with no intent to usurp overall control of the state. But, Eyre went on, he was not warranted by authority to assert 'as clear law, that the *mere conspiracy* to raise such a force, and the entering into consultations respecting it, will alone, and without actually raising the force, constitute the crime of high treason.' This was 'a new and doubtful case' which should go to trial for resolution. The grand jury should indict accordingly. It did so, accusing twelve state prisoners of compassing, in that they had conspired to levy war (which included treasonable rioting) as well as 'to subvert and alter the legislature rule and government ... happily established ... and to depose our ... lord the king.'[51]

To the knowledge of the author, no scholar has analysed the legal authorities bearing on the third position and such an analysis must be done to evaluate Eyre's behaviour both in the grand jury proceedings and at trial. Judicial decisions relating to the destruction of enclosures, bawdy houses, and dissenting Protestant meeting houses, and juristic commentary thereon, made clear that rioting for a political purpose of a general nature (as opposed to attempting rebellion) constituted the treason of levying war. But when no rioting took place (as in 1794), what was the legal characterization of plotting to bring it about? Such plots could not be levying since that required the actual application of force. Armed *rebellion*, however, was not only treason as levying but proof of compassing the king's death as well. It therefore followed that *conspiracy to rebel in arms* was also proof of compassing, a crime of mere intention. But did this rule include *conspiracy to riot treasonably*, an object that was hostilely aimed at the royal office or majesty but not at the royal person and that therefore would not normally endanger the monarch's life? The weight of authority argued for a negative answer.

Referring to insurrections to redress public grievances where the insurgents had no 'direct Design' against the king's person (that is, treasonable rioting), the jurist William Hawkins had stated in 1716 that it was 'certain ... a bare Conspiracy to levy such a War can not amount to Treason ... [although] a [bare] Conspiracy to levy War against the King's person may be alledged [sic] as an Overt Act of compassing his Death.' The same clear distinction had been drawn by Chief Justice Holt in *Freind's* case (1696): 'There may be a war levied without any design upon the king's person ... which if actually levied, is high treason; but a bare designing to levy

[such] war, without more, will not be treason. As for example; if persons do assemble themselves, and act with force in opposition to ... [statutory] law ... and hope thereby to get it repealed; this is levying a war and treason, though [merely] purposing and designing it is not so.'[52] The treason specialist Michael Foster and William Blackstone, both writing in the 1760s, made the identical point.[53] Up to and including Blackstone, not a single published author had wrestled directly with the legal ramifications of rioting to intimidate parliament.

In *Lord George Gordon's* case (1781), which had arisen out of massive anti-popery riots in London designed to coerce parliament into repealing the Toleration Act of 1778, the accused was charged with levying but *not*, significantly, with compassing King George III's death. At the trial, which resulted in an acquittal, Lord Mansfield held that using a mob to intimidate parliament (by *inter alia* having it surround both houses) was the high treason of levying war even though the rioting targeted the king's regal office rather than, as full-scale rebellion would have done, his person. This characterization, be it noted, was given despite the need for the king's assent to any repealing bill. *Gordon's* case, at least by implication, suggests that *conspiracy* to riot in order to overawe parliament into enacting new statutory law, not being directed at the king's person, did not amount to compassing or of course any other treason.[54] This implication was drawn from the case by jurist Sir Edward Hyde East in 1803. In *Hardy*, Erskine appealed to Justice Buller, who had also sat in the 1781 trial, to confirm that it had 'never ... entered into the conception of any man living, that such an indictment [for compassing] could have been maintained ... against' Gordon.[55]

The most devastating attack on the address – 'Cursory Strictures on the Charge delivered by Lord Chief Justice Eyre to the Grand Jury, October 2, 1794' – was published by the London *Morning Chronicle* and the *Courier and London Evening Gazette* four and three days before *Hardy's* trial, which began on the 25th.[56] (See app. 3, H, doc. 1.) This all-out offensive against judge-made extensions of Edward's III's act has most often been attributed to the anarchist philosopher William Godwin and lauded for its cogency of argument. It has also been credited with enlightening the public on the dangers of constructive treason, as well as raising the morale of the accused and their defence counsel.[57] After reading 'Strictures' Tooke chortled to a fellow state prisoner in the Tower: 'By G_d, Joyce, this lays Eyre completely on his back.'[58] If the Pitt-worshipping *Times*'s spluttering, detailed invective in response is indicative, the articles had widespread, immediate impact on public opinion.[59]

'Strictures' slammed into the address at every possible point. It condemned as 'atrocious' Eyre's use of the 'Jacobin' brush and noted that respectable pacific 'conventions' of delegates (including a recent one in Scotland on municipal government) were far from unknown in British history. While admitting that a reform society could degenerate into a nest of traitors, the writer added that the same was true of 'a card club' or the cabinet. Most energy was devoted to attacking the chief justice's sponsorship of constructive treasons, contrary to Edward's statute, which reserved the discovery of new ones to parliament. In particular, Eyre had created out of whole cloth a new and vague treason called 'conspiracy to subvert the monarchy.'

The author of 'Strictures' had properly sensed something awry, but he did miss the technical point. If those constructive treasons that had been enunciated by courts and jurists as forms of compassing (plots to depose, imprison, or physically constrain the king or to encourage foreign invasion) were acceptable – a point 'Strictures' admitted – then surely so was a conspiracy to subvert the monarchy by force. Although worded a bit differently, such a charge amounted to conspiring to raise rebellion or to depose the monarch, both of which had long been considered as overt acts of compassing.[60] Really at stake was Eyre's tacit assumption – made explicit in the trials – that any of these plots if proved became a *presumption of law necessarily entailing intent to kill the king*. This debatable proposition is discussed below.[61]

The author was on far stronger ground in attacking Eyre's invitation to indict on the basis of a possible conspiracy to 'overawe' parliament, which was 'a new and doubtful case.' The chief justice, he claimed with reason, had here 'quit the character of a criminal judge' to assume that of an 'experimental anatomist ... willing to dissect' the accused and imperil their lives so that 'we [judges] shall then know how we ought to conceive of similar cases.' 'Strictures' concluded strongly: basic political freedoms were in dire jeopardy and, if Eyre's interpretations should ever prevail, the British people would 'certainly have reason to envy the milder tyrannies of Turkey and Ispahan [Spain?].'

Before the Trial Juries

The handling of the trials themselves by Eyre and his colleagues and the former's charges (with the one exception noted below) have been consistently praised by specialist scholars, most of them highly experienced legal historians, from at least the middle years of the last century. We

read of the chief justice 'displaying ... some of the highest judicial qualities, patience, impartiality, and the power of sifting relevant from irrelevant matter'; presiding with 'conspicuous patience, impartiality and
fairness'; and proving himself an 'excellent Judge ... formed on the best
examples of our legal history.'[62] There are many other like assessments.[63]

While glimpses of the expected political bias towards the crown are certainly given in the trial reports,[64] and proof possibly pointing to guilt was
never omitted in the charges, any careful reader comes across dozens of
examples where rulings and opinions – some very important – favoured
the accused. During his exhaustive summing up of the factual cases presented in *Hardy*,[65] Eyre cautioned the jury several times to be careful
before accepting as truth the testimony of Dundas's spies, who had
attempted from the witness box to link the defendants to intended revolutionary violence.[66] He also made clear that the Scottish insurrectionary
plot which had resulted in the conviction of Robert Watt and David
Downie, the former being executed as a traitor the previous month, had
not been tied to the accused and that the testimony to Hardy's 'peaceable'
disposition had been given 'by a cloud of respectable witnesses.' They
should be believed as to former times, although not necessarily as to the
recent past.[67] The crown's burden was put in unequivocal terms which
required proof so 'clear and convincing ... as shall leave no doubt in your
minds.'[68] Attorney General Scott, annoyed by Eyre's impartial charge,
complained in later life that 'the Judge, who summed up the Evidence,
after hearing both Sides, had more doubt whether the Case of high Treason was made out, than he had when he attended the Privy Counsel.'[69]

In *Tooke*, Eyre granted, reluctantly it is true, the accused's highly
unusual request to sit with counsel – a major concession as it turned out –
and ruled admissible, after lengthy arguments, writings by the defendant
that proved his past support of monarchy and aristocracy.[70] Tooke was
permitted every latitude in conducting much of the defence, a fact that
was later found inexplicable by the conservative writers of Eyre's otherwise fulsome obituaries, published by the *European Magazine* and the *Gentleman's Magazine* in 1799: 'It appeared to us that he did not resist the bold
irregularities of Horne Tooke as [judge] Sir Michael Foster would have
resisted them.'[71] Tooke certainly took advantage of Eyre's tolerance and
often with caustic wit.[72] He not only elicited positive testimony stressing
his scholarly bent and his fundamental acceptance of the principles of the
balanced constitution (with a radically reformed Commons), but he often
made the prosecution look ridiculous by, for example, doggedly discom-
fiting an erstwhile parliamentary reformer, none other than Prime Minis-

ter Pitt, a witness for the defence![73] In his charge, Eyre expressed the view, one that Tooke had tried to hammer home, that the SCI was a 'mere club' in no way comparable to the potentially dangerous LCS, which represented the 'lower orders.' He also emphasized the ostensible unlikelihood of such a scholarly, quiet, sickly character as the accused having done the things alleged, and with the violent motives alleged: 'Mr. Horne Tooke, with his principles, his habits, and his infirmities, would, in truth, [seem to] be the last man in England that could be justly suspected of being engaged in a conspiracy of this kind.'[74] Eyre did go on to show in some detail that this impression was not necessarily the correct one, but his caveats did not affect the jury, who returned a verdict of not guilty after less than eight minutes of deliberation. The accused – who had earlier privately expressed scornful hatred for the chief justice[75] – returned 'my most sincere thanks to your lordship, and to the bench' for their conduct towards him throughout the trial. In his thank-you speech to the jury, Tooke spoke of Eyre's 'sagacity and integrity' which had 'assisted him to clear many things up to you.'[76]

Eyre on Overt Acts

Counsel's intensity focused on the impact to be attributed to a conspiracy to depose, supposing it to be proved to the satisfaction of the jury. Obviously fearing that they might find such a conspiracy, Erskine and Gibbs cited authorities at length in an attempt to show that plots to depose or physically constrain the king, even when clearly established by proof, amounted to no more than presumptions of fact, admittedly strong but only *prima facie* and hence not *binding* the jurors to infer compassing. They must be convinced of such by all the evidence.[77] Because there was no proof of any plan to assassinate George III, although not for want of effort by the prosecution to discover it,[78] Scott and Mitford laboured long to convince the jury that such overt acts when proved had always constituted irrefutable presumptions of law, and they emphasized instances where plotters had been executed as traitors under the compassing head despite having no intent to harm (as opposed to control) the monarch.[79] Chief Justice Eyre briefly upheld the crown's position:

The overt-act charged in this indictment, is ... that the prisoner [and others] ... have conspired to depose the king, and to subvert the monarchy ... It is indeed a known presumption of law, acknowledged by the best writers ... and particularly by every one of those writers who have been referred by the counsel on both sides

[Coke, Hale, Foster, Blackstone] ... The conspiracy to depose ... is evidence of compassing ... the death of the king, conclusive in its nature, so conclusive that it is become a presumption of law, which is in truth nothing more than a necessary and violent presumption of fact, admitting of no contradiction. Who can doubt that the natural person of the king is immediately attacked and attempted by him who attempts to depose him.[80]

In *Tooke* Eyre confidently elaborated his position. The jurists had characterized conspiracies to depose as legally 'decisive'; Holt's judgment in *Freind* was a precedent directly on point; Chief Justice Francis Pemberton in *Russell* could be distinguished in law since the overt act there involved 'was of a different nature ... more capable of explanation' (a dubious proposition); his brother judges were unanimous in support; and the law as he had stated it had been so 'understood for centuries.'[81]

These assertions by Eyre were criticized by Samuel Phillipps and Lord Cockburn in the nineteenth century, just as they have been by Alan Wharam in his recent monograph *The Treason Trials, 1794*.[82] Was the chief justice wrong?

The early jurists – Edward Coke, Matthew Hale, and Henry Hawkins – characterized conspiracies to depose, imprison, or forcefully restrain the king as overt acts sufficient 'to prove' compassing. The verb thus employed was ambiguous, in that it might mean 'prove conclusively' or merely 'prove in most circumstances.' Erskine's clever argument that Coke had not added the words 'AS A PROPOSITION OF LAW' and Hale had not asserted that a relevant, proved overt act *'is high Treason'* weakens claims of the first meaning but does not establish the second.[83] Sir Michael Foster appears to have accepted the presumption as final: 'the overt act *is* the charge, to which the prisoner must apply his defence,' and again, if any one alleged overt act be 'proved ... the verdict *must* be for the Crown' (emphases added). Sir William Blackstone wrote that to conspire to imprison the monarch and 'move towards it by assembling company, is an overt act of compassing the king's death ... and *is a strong presumption* of something worse intended ... by such as have so far thrown off their bounden duty to their sovereign.' Using a notion deriving from Machiavelli and found in Foster, Blackstone explained his view by citing the 'old observation, that there is generally but a short interval between the prisons and graves of princes.'[84] As this example suggests, the treason jurists agreed that overt acts of compassing included not only plots aimed directly at taking the king's life but also conspiracies which, as Hawkins put it, 'shew such a Design as cannot be executed without the apparent

Peril thereof,' or, in Hale's phrasing, aim at 'something that in all probability must induce it.'

There were at least three judicial precedents on this point. The first
arose out of the trials of the Earl of Essex – found guilty of high treason in
1600, executed the following year – and his confederates. According to
Sir Edward Coke, who prosecuted as attorney general, these men, then
out of royal favour because of the Earl's Irish policy, had intended using
the force they had assembled 'to goe to the court where the queen was,
and to have taken her into their power, and to have removed divers of
her counsell.'[85] The trial report indicates that no physical harm to Elizabeth was planned.[86] The two chief justices and the lord chief baron nevertheless advised the lords that attempting to 'compel the king [sic] to
govern otherwise than according to his own royal authority and direction
... is manifest rebellion' and that 'in every Rebellion *the law intendeth* ...
the compassing the death ... of the king' since no rebel would 'suffer that
king to live ... who might [later] punish ... his treason.'[87] Upon the
arraignment of confederates Sir Christopher Blunt, Sir John Davis, and
others, Lord Chief Justice John Popham asserted that 'wherever the subject rebelleth ... the laws of this land maketh this construction of his
actions, that he intendeth to deprive the king both of crown and life.'[88] Sir
John Mitford made the *Essex* case a major point of the crown's closing
address to the jury.[89]

The trial of William Lord Russell in 1683 provided a second precedent.
Russell had joined with other hawkishly Protestant Whigs in a conspiracy to foster insurrections in London, Bristol, Cheshire, and Newcastle
and seek armed support from Scotland, with the design of overthrowing
King Charles II. The accused had not been involved in or even known of
the most secret affair called the 'Rye-House Plot' in which plans were
made to waylay, then assassinate, Charles together with his 'papist'
brother and successor James.[90] At trial, it came out that Russell had conspired not only to raise rebellion but also to seize the king's guards. Lord
Chief Justice Pemberton, ignoring the solicitor general's argument that
presumptions of law had arisen, instructed the jurors in quite another
sense. Unlike earlier cases involving the Rye-House plotters, he said, they
had no evidence before them of any direct conspiracy to kill. Whatever
the presumptive strength of the facts, 'this whole matter ... is left to you'
to decide whether to 'believe the prisoner ... conspired the death of the
king.' When Russell was brought up for judgment before Sir George
Treby, recorder of London (later chief justice of the Common Pleas), the
latter concurred on this point with the presiding chief justice. Vicary

Gibbs cited the Pemberton/Treby opinions as unanswerable against any hard and fast legal presumption.[91]

The third precedent arose in the trial of Sir John Freind (1696). Although he had not been party to the contemporary plot to assassinate King William III, he certainly conspired to replace the latter with James II and for that purpose had solicited a French invasion and prepared men to be levied to assist in the Jacobite restoration. There was evidence presented that Freind and his immediate circle intended William to escape unharmed to Holland. Despite this and notwithstanding Erskine's attempts to prove the contrary, Lord Chief Justice Sir John Holt had spoken to the jury in terms indicative of a presumption of law. Referring to the law in general, he said that a conspiracy to depose, imprison, or physically restrain the king, to be effected by levying war, 'is high treason' in that such a plot constitutes 'an overt act proving the compassing the death of the king.' While the word 'proving' can bear two interpretations, 'is' cannot and 'proving' therefore likely meant 'proving conclusively.'[92] In 1795 Attorney General Scott, speaking in the Commons, paraphrased a supposed passage from Holt's charge, as given by Chief Justice Treby, which was even clearer in favour of the crown.[93]

The Statute of Treasons lists seven varieties of the crime, among them those occasions 'when a man doth compasse or imagine the death of our lord the king,' and later requires that the accused 'thereof be provably attainted of open deed by people of their condition.' It does *not* say that an overt act established by proof conclusively establishes guilt and hence does not authorize judges to tamper with the general rule that it is the province of the jurors to draw inferences of fact. In argument Erskine referred briefly to a recent case he had pleaded in which the House of Lords held it improper for the '*effect of evidence*' to be withdrawn from the jury and '*transferred to the judges, and converted into matter of law.*'[94] However widely the principle was then applied, it was certainly relevant to this species of high treason, particularly since the historical record included cases of conspiracies to depose or constrain where conspirators intended no physical harm. Eyre and his colleagues, in the guise of ruling upon evidentiary law, no doubt in good faith, had created or recreated a substantive or constructive treason not found in Edward III's act. Plotting the death of the king had now definitively gained an offspring: 'plotting a scenario in which the monarch's life was put at serious risk.'[95] The Statute of Treasons had been enacted to prevent precisely that kind of thing, one portion of it reading: 'That if any other Case, supposed Treason, which is not above specified, doth happen before any Justices, the Justices shall tarry ... till the Cause be shewed and declared before the King and his Parliament, whether it ought to be judged Treason or other Felony.'[96]

Thus it seems that Eyre's royalist interpretation was wrong and one cannot but wonder how thoroughly the bench probed this question, potentially one of life and death. But considering the authorities, the error was somewhat excusable. Within a decade of the 'Jacobin' trials Sir Edward Hyde East paraphrased Eyre's charge in *Tooke* on this point, without any comment suggestive that the question was open to the slightest doubt.[97] The chief justice's interpretation was expressly followed with approval by Lord Chief Justice Ellenborough in 1817.[98]

Given the weakness of the crown's factual case, the legal characterization of plots to 'overawe' parliament into enacting legislation was probably of far greater practical importance. Eyre had successfully recommended that the grand jury indict in this 'new and doubtful case' so that the question could be resolved at trial. The law officers naturally tried to give the bench some plausible pegs on which to hang a constructive treason and of course the accused. Scott argued that the use of force to compel the king to assent to a bill (whether or not the two houses were overawed) was to usurp power at the 'highest and most essential act of the sovereignty of this country' and was 'unquestionably an overt act in deposing him, and in compassing his death.'[99] Scott did not confront the authorities and had not adduced proof of an intention to have a mob surround the king's residence or threaten him on the way to give or refuse royal assent to the 'reform bill.' Sir John Mitford misrepresented what Erskine had said in *Gordon*[100] to arrive at the wide-ranging position that any 'conspiracy against the constitution of the state is a conspiracy against the life of the prince; the life of the prince being so interwoven with the constitution of the state, that an attempt to destroy the one is justly held to be a rebellious conspiracy against the other.'[101] This concept, which would have reintroduced the elastic 'accroaching' of the fourteenth century, also assumed that 'death' in the Statute of Treasons included 'political' as well as natural death, though the protection afforded by the compassing head extended beyond the sovereign to the queen and their eldest son.[102] Despite Eyre's inclination to a similar view, he and his colleagues said nothing at all on what has been called here the third position, namely the characterization of plots to 'overawe' parliament as treason. The law had been left where it had been after *Gordon*: that conspiracies to riot treasonably, including plots to overawe parliament, did not amount to high treason. More cogent for Hardy, the jury was left with the stark choice of finding only between a legal pursuit of parliamentary reform and a plan to depose George III by use of force. They opted for the former.

Reflections and Denouement

There can be little doubt that a large majority, if not all, of the twelve judges of England who held office between 1794 and 1799[103] shared the Alarmism prevalent in the Pitt government. The nervous tone of Eyre's address to the grand jury involved fully six of them. And in *Thelwall* Lord Chief Baron Macdonald expatiated on the dangers that had resulted from contact between the reform societies and French revolutionaries: 'Every man alive ... must be convinced of the hazard ... French principles ... [having brought] their king to the scaffold.'[104] Two years earlier William Henry Ashurst of the King's Bench had given a similar direction to the Middlesex grand jury: now was the 'time for every sober man who is at all interested in the ... safety of his country ... to endeavour to crush such pernicious doctrines' and the organizations that spread them.[105] Judge Giles Rooke of the Common Pleas contended in a 1795 seditious-conspiracy trial that a speech on the corruption of the House of Commons and the need for radical parliamentary reform, when made before a large crowd at a time of great popular excitement, threatened the very fabric of society and was therefore seditious.[106] Along with Lord Mansfield, Justice Francis Buller had denied the jury's right to give general verdicts in seditious libel cases (1783–4) and in *De la Motte* (1781) he had adopted a highly elastic construction of adhering.[107] In the 1790s Buller, like John Heath of the Common Pleas and Lord Chief Justice Kenyon of the King's Bench, had a reputation for being an extreme Tory who commonly favoured the crown in criminal trials and punished the convicted with severity.[108]

But most of these men cannot be characterized as strongly Baconian in security cases. During the trials of Hardy and Tooke, Eyre and his colleagues were generally fair to the accused. In a later treason case (1796) the bench, again presided over by Eyre and consisting of John Heath, Macdonald, and Sir Alexander Thompson of the Exchequer Court, virtually directed an acquittal, which verdict was duly rendered.[109] Judge Rooke did not expand the law of sedition as then understood,[110] and Heath took the lead in raising a technical defence in the seditious-conspiracy trial of Manchester radical merchant Thomas Walker (1794).[111] In a 1798 trial presiding judge Buller indicated his strong belief in the character testimony given by prominent opposition Whigs in favour of accused traitor Arthur

O'Connor, a militant leader of the United Irish. O'Connor was found not guilty.[112] Only Lord Kenyon was close to being a thoroughgoing Baconian. He continually distorted Fox's Libel Act in seditious libel cases, provided the king with a covert extrajudicial opinion on Roman Catholic emancipation in Ireland, and on at least one occasion sent the attorney general copies of opposition newspapers he thought seditious.[113]

With the major exception of the grand jury proceedings and the less serious one of judicial characterization of conspiracies to depose the king, the bench in *Hardy* and *Tooke* admirably controlled what must have been a strong ideological bias towards the crown. This record becomes the more striking when contrasted with the Scottish sedition trials held before the High Court of Justiciary from August to March 1793–4.[114] There, the judges pronounced advocacy of radical constitutional change to be anarchic and in itself seditious, if not treason, as was participation in the British convention of parliamentary reformers which had met in Edinburgh in November 1793. All this was justified because the 'British Constitution is the best that ever was since the creation of the world, and it is not possible to make it better.' The bench imposed some vicious sentences of fourteen years' transportation, contrary to law or arguably so; packed the fifteen-man juries with members of the Scottish Loyal Association; and in calling for convictions encouraged the jurors to vote their prejudices against lovers of the French, those 'monsters of human nature.' The presiding lord justice clerk (functioning head of the court), Lord Braxfield, set an example extreme even among his colleagues. This expert on feudal law favoured transportation for life, mused publicly *before* one trial about giving the accused 'a hundred lashes together with Botany Bay,' and became notorious for reassuring hesitant prosecutors thus: 'Bring me prisoners and I'll find you law.'[115] No wonder Charles James Fox exclaimed in the Commons: 'God help the people who have such judges.'[116]

After the acquittals of Tooke and then Thelwall (December 1794) the government dropped its cases against the remaining state prisoners and several dozen suspects in the provinces must have felt triumphant relief. Hardy went so far as to claim that on the eve of his verdict the government 'had prepared eight hundred [treason] warrants, three hundred of which were actually signed,' in anticipation of a guilty finding.[117] The offensive against the reform societies for traitorously attempting to subvert the constitution was over. In the succeeding years of the war thirteen men were tried for more specific treasons in England. One was executed; twelve were acquitted.

So, the juries in *Hardy*, *Tooke*, and *Thelwall*, Erskine, Gibbs, the *Morning Chronicle*, the *Courier*, and the author of 'Strictures' had decapitated the serpent of 'constructive treasons' at a critical moment – when human lives were at stake. But they did not have the last word on the law. Pitt's Alarmist majority in parliament did. Using as a pretext a minor attack on the king during his progress to open parliament late in October 1795[118] and adopting the thesis of Edmund Burke's disciple, MP William Windham, that Hardy was 'an acquitted felon' – that is, that the societies remained nests of traitors despite the trial results – the parliamentary majority enacted a new treason law by an overwhelming vote in the Commons of 226–45.[119]

The Treason Act of 1795 made several constructive treasons into indisputable law: among them, conspiracies to depose, imprison, or physically restrain the king, plots to procure foreigners to invade the realm, plots to overawe either house of parliament, and conspiracies to deprive the monarch of any colonial territory. These things could be proved by overt acts of course but also through words, oral or written, uttered by the accused.[120] While apparently a dead letter in the war against revolutionary France,[121] the legislation was put to fatal use, in conjunction with charges under Edward III's act, in 1803 and after.[122]

THE TRIALS: LOWER CANADA (1797)

Analysis of the judicial application of treason law in Lower Canada concentrates on two events: Montreal Chief Justice James Monk's address to the grand jury at the March assizes in 1797 (see app. 3, H, doc. 3), and the famous trial of David McLane in June-July of that year.[123] McLane was an American citizen who had worked as a spy for France. He had attempted to recruit a 'fifth column' in the colony to attack the Quebec City garrison in coordination with a French naval invasion.

Both legal proceedings had as a brooding backdrop the Road Act riots, which broke out all over the colony in the period from late August 1796 to January 1797. Besides widespread refusal to do forced labour, they featured the newly elected overseers being 'imprisoned,' beatings of constables and one magistrate, a plot to starve Montreal concocted by habitant farmers on the south shore of the St Lawrence, and much talk of bloodshed. The English elite mistakenly attributed the rioting, a near-insurrection in their view, to the doings of undercover agents working for Citizen Adet. Fear reached a high point among the senior English officials responsible for maintaining law and order. In early 1797 Montreal merchant-magistrate John Richardson, head of provincial counter-intelligence, advised the government that Richery would return with up to 30,000(!) troops. 'No man,' he wrote, 'can doubt of a contemplated invasion, to be aided by exciting a Revolt.' Martial law should be declared to protect persons of property from 'all the horrors of assassination.'[124] At the outset, Attorney General Jonathan Sewell warned a subordinate that any serious 'opposition to the laws of a Country, if not timely checked may end in perfect Anarchy and the Destruction of the government.'[125] Shortly after, provincial Chief Justice William Osgoode harped on the 'Ignorance and Disaffection of the whole [Canadien] Race,' concluding that 'open Resistance to all Civil subordination is prevented merely by the Troops that are quartered among us.'[126]

Chief Justice Monk on Levying War

Monk asserted that any violent, generalized resistance to law enforcement, an obvious allusion to the recent rioting, amounted to levying war: the guilt of high treason 'attaches upon all those who rise in tumultuous assemblies and openly by force, oppose the execution of the Laws.'[127] Was this an accurate reading of Edward III's Statute of Treasons?

In *Dammaree* (1710), the leading eighteenth-century precedent on constructive levying, the court held that the crowd's actions in tearing down Presbyterian meeting houses amounted to an attempt to render the Toleration Act ineffectual and for that reason among others constituted high treason.[128] Earlier, in *Freind*, Chief Justice John Holt had given, in *obiter*, a terse, related example: 'if persons do assemble themselves, and act with force to ... [some] law, which they think inconvenient and hope thereby to get it repealed.'[129] Neither case dealt explicitly with a situation where resistance was directed against government officials attempting to enforce a statute, much less one in which the resisters had a clear personal interest in resisting.

There were, in short, no reported cases on this point. In 1803 the jurist Sir Edward Hyde East cited obscure manuscript judgments showing that, during the Seven Years' War, some Yorkshire and Northumberland militia rioters had been convicted of treason and sentenced to death. Of this group, some were in fact executed.[130] These judgments had been briefly alluded to by Lord Mansfield in *Gordon* (1781) but were not discussed there. Nor was the point treated by Sir Michael Foster, Blackstone, or 'A Barrister at Law' in his 1793 pamphlet on treason.[131]

Thus, in terms of authority, the question was open. And the general test laid down by Foster, if anything, inclined against Monk's position. The jurist summarized constructive levyings as insurrections 'for the reformation of real or imaginary evils of a public nature and *in which the insurgents have no Special Interest* [emphasis added].' Virtually all of the Road Act rioters might have claimed a 'Special Interest' in that their resistance was designed to avoid having to work on the roads. Monk was therefore construing the law in a genuinely grey area. While he certainly opted for the 'royalist' solution, this was not necessarily wrong in law, although possibly so. Both Chief Justice William Osgoode (1794) and American President John Adams (1800) harboured serious doubts that forceful resistance to a single statute, where opponents had a personal interest, could be equated with levying war.[132] On the other hand, the Federalist judges of the United States (1795, 1799–1800) and East (1803) would have agreed with Monk on this point.[133]

Monk also explained to the grand jury that it did not matter at all whether a participant in the resistance was aware of the treasonable design. This doctrine, intended to eliminate in advance arguments based on the supposed illegality of the Road Act, ignorance, or sudden impetuousness, accepted the precedent in *Purchase* (1710), another meeting-house case.[134] This held that 'if a man knowingly join with others in breaking the peace, and ... if in that breach ... they were rebels, he is so too, whether he knew them to be so or not.' In rebellions 'few are let into the real design, but yet all that join in it are guilty of the rebellion.' The isolated decision in *Purchase*, with three dissents, did not commend itself to Hawkins or Foster[135] and ran directly counter to the fundamental notion of high treason as conscious betrayal, reflected by the almost universal use in indictments of the adverb 'traitorously' and/or the characterization 'false traitor(s).' The Federalist judges in the United States did not adopt *Purchase*, although given every opportunity to do so. Nor did Lower Canadian Chief Justice Jonathan Sewell in 1812. Obstruction of law enforcement, he told the Quebec grand jury, changed from a misdemeanour into treason only if the accused could be shown to have acted 'with intent against the King.'[136]

Monk's court indicted four persons, allegedly involved in Citizen Adet's attempts at subversion, for adhering and compassing. Three of them were tried and acquitted in September 1797. Although no record of the trial appears to have survived,[137] we can nevertheless conclude from the indictments that Monk and his colleagues assumed that fomenting insurrection in a distant colony endangered the life of King George III. This point would be raised and decided in the trial of David McLane.

Since the author has recently published extensively on that trial and McLane's grisly execution (see app. 3, H, docs. 7, 8, 9), the present account offers only a brief summary of findings relating to the conduct and holdings of the judges.[138]

The Prosecution of David McLane

Two crucial crown witnesses, to whom the impetuous McLane had revealed his plans, were Montreal tavernkeeper Elmer Cushing and William Barnard, a shopkeeper of the same city. They testified on the understanding (ultimately realized) that each would receive a township of land. This bargain, concluded in November 1796, was sanctioned by Governor Sir Robert Prescott, Civil Secretary Herman Ryland, Attorney General Sewell, and Chief Justice Osgoode, Prescott's 'prime minister' in 1796–7.[139] Sewell later wrote that, on the orders of the governor, 'Mr. Ryland ... accompanied me and we had a long conference with the Chief Justice ... [with the] result ... that we were all of opinion that the expected information appeared of sufficient importance to justify an absolute promise of the Township of Shipton to Mr. Cushing.'[140] (See app. 3, H, doc. 4.) The government through Ryland later made it clear to Cushing that unless his testimony was very helpful he could expect no land.[141] (See app. 3, H, doc. 5.) At trial, defence counsel asked Barnard if he had received 'any promise or reward from the government.' Witness 'braved' a perjury charge by answering 'None.' Osgoode, who presided, interjected that the 'question has been allowed; but I think it was an improper one.' Cushing made a similar, safe denial. Counsel did not attempt to pursue the point. Sewell, who led for the crown, said nothing.[142]

This was not the only contribution Osgoode made to the crown's litigation strategy. It was he who successfully advised Prescott to, first, prosecute McLane for high treason rather than treat him as a spy subject to death or as a prisoner of war; second, to do so immediately; third, to conduct the prosecution by a special commission confined to treasons in the Quebec District, thus avoiding, for the time being, the trial of the three accused Canadien traitors jailed in Montreal, which the prudent Prescott did not then want to risk; and, finally, to hold the proceedings before a political court consisting of all executive councillors (except Anglican Bishop Jacob Mountain), whether judges or not.[143] Osgoode also 'took' Cushing's important deposition and together with Prescott permitted a potential witness to turn king's evidence.[144] The chief justice, considered a proper recipient of opinions on the danger of invasion/insurrection,[145] chaired the council's special security committee, where shortly before the trial he learned of a supposed plot to liberate McLane.[146] Quite clearly Osgoode greatly exceeded Eyre's magisterial role and in fact acted as a prosecutor, indeed the co-chief prosecutor with Sewell.

There were other, minor ways in which the chief justice assisted the crown: referring to the legislature's 1797 act suspending habeas corpus as telling proof of danger, and remaining silent when Sewell, without proof, rang the changes on the government's well-publicized but shaky thesis that McLane's conspiracy had involved massacring the English and Canadien elite.[147] Two elements of Osgoode's handling of the case, however, were particularly important: choice of counsel and the interpretation of substantive treason law.

The court appointed two lawyers in their early twenties to defend McLane: George Pyke and George Germaine Francklin. Pyke was a protégé of Nova Scotia's Tory solicitor general, Richard John Uniacke, and (if not then, very soon) of Chief Justice Monk. Francklin had been admitted to the bar the previous January after finishing his five years of articles with Sewell. He was, in July 1797, living in the attorney general's house as a virtual member of the family. And he was Cushing's representative in his negotiations for the promised township! As might be expected, counsel were largely ineffective – whether through inexperience, intimidation at the outset of their careers, or something more sinister is not clear. They allowed an all-English jury of wealthy merchants or their economic dependents to be struck, called no defence witnesses, and did not dissuade their client from his disastrous, patently false claim that he had come to Lower Canada to escape his creditors. Nor did they present the accused's obvious first line of defence: that as an alien working in a military capacity for the enemy, he had had the status of hostile enemy alien in the colony and hence owed no allegiance to George III. Sir Mathew Hale and Lord Chief Justice Holt in the well-known case of *Vaughan* (1696) could have been cited as authorities. One wonders what might have happened had McLane's defence been entrusted to one or more intelligent and courageous lawyers – and they existed.[148]

No juristic commentary or judicial decision dealt with the question whether plots or attempts to foment rebellion or otherwise assist the enemy in an overseas colony constituted compassing. Yet Chief Justice Osgoode, for one, had no doubts. It was, he told the grand jury, an 'inference of law[!], that he who adheres to the king's enemies, engages in and supports a warfare, by which the king's personal safety is endangered, and therefore such traitor compasses his death.' This supposed presumption of law applied everywhere in the empire, it having 'no limitation of place.' In their only competent move, defence counsel attacked the idea as absurd: the plot's locale and the monarch were thousands of miles apart. Francklin argued that 'it must strike you as monstrous to suppose, that the subversion of the government of this province would endanger his majesty's natural life.' After all, the American 'revolution, which severed thirteen colonies from the British empire did not in the least affect his sacred person.' In charging the trial jury Osgoode reiterated his holding but suggested that, if they nevertheless found the doctrine too artificial, they could convict on the basis of the adhering count alone. (See app. 3, H, doc. 6.) What the jurors actually thought about this instruction (they returned a simple verdict of guilty) is unknown, but it is possibly relevant that Sewell had argued the Mitford-Scott thesis strongly. He claimed that a long line of unimpeachable authority, not disclosed, demonstrated that the 'political or civil death of the sovereign is clearly within the purview of the statute [of Treasons].' Osgoode did not comment on this contention.[149]

The Statute of Treasons prohibited anyone from being 'adherent to the kings enemies ... giving to them aid and comfort.' As mentioned in the introduction to this volume, a literal construction of the clause suggests that *actual* assistance must have been given, such as selling arms, joining the enemy's armed forces, treacherously surrendering a fortified position, or *successfully* transmitting useful military intelligence. The early jurists – Coke, Hale, Hawkins – assumed no less, as did Lord Chief Justice Holt in *Vaughan*.[150]

The law of treason was radically altered in this as in many other areas by an extrajudicial opinion of the judges of England rendered in 1707/8. A manuscript discovered in the British Library recording the questions and answers indicates clearly the dangers to impartiality involved in the process: absence of defence counsel and publicity, tendency to give the answers desired by political masters, and, above all, the lack of reasoned justifications given (except the occasional brief reference to a case or statute). The opinion asserted many things unfavourable to potential accused: that *enemy aliens*, for example, owed allegiance if resident in the realm. The question and answer of interest here read: 'Whether the writing and sending Intelligence to the Enemy be not an Overt Act ... of adhering to her Majestie's Enemies tho such intelligence be Intercepted before it comes to the enemy. R. – Agreed by all that it is.'[151] This opinion was accepted by Foster and Blackstone, and it was adopted in *Hensey's* case (1758) and other cases later in the eighteenth century. But neither the case law, including the opinion, nor juristic commentary compelled judges to conclude that *any* attempt whatever to aid the enemy (for example, to *gather* intelligence, with or without the enemy knowing about it) amounted to adhering. An intermediate position, stated by Foster, stressed that tendering aid (money, supplies, arms, intelligence) must have reached a penultimate stage: 'the party in sending [such things] did all he could; the treason was complete *on his part, though it had not the effect he intended*' (emphasis added). Such a holding might have cleared the incompetent McLane of adhering and perhaps of a guilty verdict and is probably arguable in the United States today.[152]

In the three jurisdictions of the 'North American triangle' it was the Lower Canadian chief justices Monk and Osgoode who pushed constructive treasons to their limits. The American courts, while hardly liberal, were at the other end of this tripartite 'spectrum.'

THE TRIALS: UNITED STATES

The trials examined in this section arose out of two disturbances involving taxation in Pennsylvania. The first was the 'Whiskey Rebellion' of 1794 against the 1791 imposition of a stiff excise (25 per cent). In the 'west' whiskey was often both a medium of exchange and the only practical means of bringing grain to market. In the four western counties of the state, excise officers were terrorized and a small body of regular troops forced to surrender to the 'rebels.' Talk of attacking Pittsburgh, or even Philadelphia, the national capital, alarmed government. Disaffection began to infect Maryland, the Carolinas, and Georgia. President Washington effectively called upon the states to supply about 13,000 militia, and the rebellion soon sputtered out. The leaders escaped justice; in the end, 1795, only two secondary activists, a Philip Vigol and a John Mitchell, were convicted of treason. The president pardoned the former as insane and the latter as a simpleton.

The second disturbance broke out in the spring of 1799 among the usually frugal German- and Dutch-speaking farmers and other residents of the northeastern counties. It involved violent opposition to the so-called house tax (1798) on land, slaves, and dwellings. The most sensational incident involved a ragtag army sporting tricolour cockades and led by auctioneer John Fries which liberated two prisoners detained at Bethlehem for resistance to the tax. The rescue was effected by threat, not action, and the 'insurrection' soon melted away. In 1799–1800 Fries and two associates were tried (Fries twice) and convicted of treason. They were pardoned by President Adams.[153]

That the senior federal judges shared in the alarmist outlook of the Federalists seems beyond doubt. Their extremist, almost hysterical enforcement of the Sedition Act of 1798 (treated below) supports this claim, as does their authoritarian, although often not unprofessional, interpretation of treason law. Far from isolating themselves from politics, the judges revealed in their correspondence a constant concern with it and in a definite partisan manner.[154] The only letters the author has been able to study are those to and from Supreme Court Justice James Iredell. Those received certainly revealed a sense of the fragility of the social order,[155] although Iredell himself was more confident. In addresses or charges, Iredell stressed the security danger. At Charleston, on 7 May 1798, he expanded on this theme at length, generalizing for the grand jury's benefit that the 'present situation of our country is alarming to a very great degree.'[156] In his charge to the trial jury in *Fries* (1799) Iredell – a moderate conservative intellectual and constitutional expert – expressed a belief in the conspiracy theory of history, one that featured the ubiquitous, but secretive 'they' who 'go about their design by more insidious means; art will be used, and pains taken to promote a dislike to a certain law; their evil prejudice is encouraged until it becomes general among the people, and they become as ripe for insurrection as in the present case.'[157] Attorney General, later Chief Justice, Sewell would have agreed entirely.

Article 3, section 3 of the American constitution reads in part as follows: 'Treason against the United States, shall consist *only* in levying War against them, or in adhering to their Enemies, giving them Aid and Comfort' (emphasis added). The use of the word only, the failure to include 'compassing the death of the President,' and the very fact that this definition of a crime was constitutionalized indicate that the fathers intended to limit judge-made or constructive treasons. And the desire to forestall political or judicial abuse was further made clear by the evidentiary clause: 'No Person shall be convicted of Treason unless on the Testimony of two Witnesses to the same overt Act, or on Confession in open Court.'[158] This liberalized the British rule holding that the testimony of two witnesses was sufficient even when each applied to distinctly different overt acts, provided they referred to the same kind of treason (for example, adhering rather than adhering *and* compassing). It also foreclosed the arguable proposition discussed by Foster that confession out of court, witnessed by two persons, was enough for conviction. In Federalist Paper number 43 Madison wrote: 'But as new-fangled and artificial treasons, have been the great engines, by which violent factions ... have usually wrecked [sic] their alternate malignity on each other, the Convention have with great judgment opposed a barrier to this peculiar danger, by inserting a constitutional definition of the crime.' As had Pennsylvania delegate James Wilson at the Philadelphia conclave itself, Madison here articulated assumptions common among partisans of the proposed new constitution. Alexander Hamilton alluded to something similar in number 84, while the state campaigns for ratification were full of such sentiments.[159]

Article 3(3) of the constitution of course prevented Congress from adding to the substantive law. Any positive Federalist thoughts there were about emulating parliament's 1795 act must have been fleeting. When Congress in 1798 plugged perceived gaps, by dealing with conspiracies to rebel or engage in treasonable rioting, it did so by making the crimes misdemeanours, punishable by fines up to $5000 and jail terms between six months and five years.[160] An attempt the same year in the Senate to make adherence to the French, widely defined, treason and subject to the death penalty – although the United States and France were not officially at war – proved short-lived, whether for tactical reasons or because of constitutional doubts or both (the most likely interpretation) is not clear. This was apparently the only legislative attempt ever made in peacetime to articulate the meaning of treason.[161] But it is the possible impact of constitutionalization on judicial activities and decisions that most concerns us here.

As in the case of Congress – and of the president – judges could hardly, in any obvious way, undermine the accused traitor's protections guaranteed by the constitution. And they did not. Without hesitation or obfuscation they determined, for example, that conspiracy to levy even rebellious war was not treason, a logical deduction in view of the absence of any compassing head.[162] A full assessment of their stance on the treason provision requires consideration of what the Federalist judges of the 1790s held to be the law, perceptions they expressed about the value of the restrictive constitutional clauses, and those prosecutorial doctrines they might have advanced but did not.

In relation to both 'risings,' the Federalist judges upheld the constructive concept of treasonable rioting, applying it to cases of violent resistance to statutory enforcement. This latter application was disputable but arguably professional, since the framers of the constitution did not explicitly rule out constructive levying.[163] In *Fries* the judges properly rejected defence counsel's argument that in *Gordon* Lord Mansfield had specified only one type of statute – Militia Acts – violent resistance to which could entail charges of high treason. Mansfield had included this example as but one of a number of holdings illustrative but not exhaustive of treasonable rioting, and he had noted that 'many other instances might be put.'[164]

Another authoritarian aspect of the judgments that can be defended was the judges' action in directing the conviction of Fries. There was no evidence, as recorded by Francis Wharton's *State Trials*, that the accused and his associates had attempted to liberate *all* accessible prisoners or threatened to force the release of all who had resisted or would resist the House Tax Act.[165] Indeed, after the two targets of release had been freed, the 'rebel' army dispersed. This would seem to be an obvious case of a 'particular' rather than a 'general' object held by rioters, a point made, if badly, by defence counsel.[166] Foster (later East as well) and the *Porteous* case (1736) strongly suggest that a focus on a limited number of prisoners amounted to a riot, not treason.[167] Unfortunately for the accused, Justice Richard Peters of the United States Supreme Court and a judge in Fries's first trial had induced him to confess that 'his motive in going to Bethlehem to rescue the prisoners was not from personal attachment, or regard to any of the persons who had been arrested, but proceeded from a general aversion to the law.'[168] This admission certainly muddied the waters, but it did not necessarily imply treason.

The Federalist judges, despite political temptations, in fact insisted on the proposition that to be treasonable the rioting had to have a general, not a private, object. As expressed by Willard Hurst, one of the leading authorities on American treason law: 'Even Federalist-minded judges laid down the law with significant and reiterated emphasis on the need for finding that the force was exerted for a general and public purpose and not merely to stop the collection of particular levies, or collection from particular persons, or by a particular exciseman.'[169] This emphasis was expressly applied by Justice Henry Livingston in *Hoxie* (1808) to direct a verdict of not guilty where smugglers to Canada had used violence against troops seeking to enforce the embargo on trade with Britain and its colonies.[170]

A secondary point: in *Vigol* (1795) Judge William Patterson held that a defence of duress required proof of 'an immediate and actual danger, threatening the very life of the party.' This certainly did not help the actual or potential accused. But the holding was consistent with the leading British judicial precedent and the strong consensus among treason jurists, with the important exception of Blackstone who, anticipating the future, wrote of 'a fear of death *or other bodily harm.*'[171]

The constitutional provisions were frequently lauded as barriers against abuse by legislative, executive, and judicial authorities. In *Fries*

Judge Peters told the jury that the 'doctrine of *constructive treason* has produced much real mischief in another country' but the absence of any compassing head in Article 3 had foreclosed most of this problem for the United States. In the second trial of the accused, Mr Justice Samuel Chase, hardly a liberal, allowed that 'too much praise cannot be given to this [limited] constitutional definition of treason, and the requiring such full proof for conviction.'[172] Judge Iredell's addresses to the grand juries at Boston (1792) and Philadelphia (1796, 1799) and his charge in *Fries* have as a recurrent theme the great care the wise framers had taken to forestall 'an unprincipled government in tempestuous times' by insisting on a vigorous standard of proof and to undermine 'judicial tyranny' by precisely defining the crime so that 'plausible subterfuges' to extend its ambit were impossible.[173] (See app. 3. H, doc. 2.) The Federalist judges, then, acknowledged the dangers of treason prosecutions, unless strictly controlled, a point of view not expressed by the English bench in 1781 or 1794 or by the Lower Canada chief justices in 1797. Indeed, Osgoode expressed the opinion in *McLane* that the accused were overly and dangerously protected by the special guarantees enjoyed under (1708) 7 Anne, c. 21.[174]

Equally important, three legal interpretations from England favouring the prosecution might easily have been adopted but were not. The doctrine in *Purchase* was not referred to and indeed the repeated stress laid on the need to establish the accused's traitorous intention would seem to have firmly shut the door on it.[175] A second instance occurred in the Whiskey Rebellion case of *Mitchell* (1795) where the evidence *could* be seen as indicating that the defendant had been part of the preceding conspiracy but not the levying. Defence counsel argued that the English doctrine making conspirators traitors if war was levied *by others* was grossly unfair in that it did not allow for genuine repentance and later opposition to those whose actions could not be controlled. Both the district attorney and the attorney general of the United States contended that the English rule ('in treason all are principals') was sound and authoritative. Despite this invitation, however, Justice Patterson did not mention the principle at all, instructing the jury to convict on another basis.[176] In *Fries* Judge Chase enunciated what appeared to be the English rule ('In treason, all the *participes criminus* are principals; there are no accessories to this crime'), but he did not apply it to persons who had engaged *only* in the conspiracy. His wording in fact arguably implied that they were not caught by it: 'If a number of persons combine or conspire [to levy war] ... any act of violence done by any one of them, in pursuance of such combination ... is, in consideration of law, the act of all *who are present when such act of violence is committed.*'[177]

Even more remarkable, considering the post-1688 writings of Hawkins, Foster, and Blackstone and especially Lord Mansfield's far-reaching summary of constructive levying in *Gordon* (which included riots directed against Protestant meeting houses, brothels, landlords, food prices, and manufacturing employers), the Federalist judges did not hold treasonable rioting to be high treason except in the cases of attempted intimidation of government or violent resistance to the enforcement of a federal statute. In particular, they appear, at least by implication, to have excluded rioting aimed at private parties, such as landlords, adherents of religious sects, creditors, slave-owners, employers, and so on. In doing so these judges gave much more force to the words 'levying War *against them* [the United States]' than English commentators and judges had attributed to the comparable words in the Statute of Treasons: 'if a man doe levie warre *against our lord the king.*' The clearest expression is found in Judge Iredell's charge to the jury in *Fries*. It was only when rioters 'aim at the destruction of the government, that the nature of the offence attains the aspect of, and essentially becomes, *treason.*'[178] This thrust in the 1790s treason decisions was conspicuously and decidedly taken up and made more explicit in the leading case of *United States v. Hanway* (1851), which dealt with resistance to the fugitive slave law. Mr Justice Grier, citing as examples, *inter alia*, riots against slave-owners or mortgagees, wrote that the 'conspiracy and the insurrection connected with it must be to effect something of a public nature, to overthrow the government, or to nullify some law of the United States.'[179] This kind of distinction between targeting 'government' directly and aiming only or mainly at classes of fellow subjects was not even hinted at in the English courts until 1817 or at all in those of British North America.[180]

The tendency to Cokean interpretations of treason lies in striking contrast to the judiciary's ferocious application of the Sedition Act of 1798.[181] This statute, aimed at 'Jacobin' (Republican) editors by a Federalist Congress, was on its face a model of legislative moderation. Unlike the comparable statutory provisions in Lower Canada (1794–5), it applied only to *written* libels on the federal government, did not make the meaning of sedition any more elastic than it was conceived to be by the courts at Westminster, severely limited punishments, and adopted the principle of Fox's Libel Act of 1792, which may *not* have been merely declaratory of existing law.[182] The American sedition statute also softened the common law on two potentially crucial points. The act required the prosecution to prove 'malice' and allowed the defence to establish truth as a defence.

In short, the statute was highly protective of the accused, even of dissent.[183] But since sedition, unlike treason, was given no specific protection by the constitution, the Federalist judges did not hesitate to rewrite the act. The words 'malicious ... intent' were simply ignored, with 'seditious tendency' substituted in their place. Such tendency was presumed until the defendant could prove otherwise – a reversal of the central principle of criminal-trial procedure. The accused arguing truth had to establish every single impugned statement 'to the marrow,' as Justice Chase put it. Since the courts refused to distinguish between facts and opinions and since no *opinion* could be proved accurate 'to the marrow,' this test was strictly window dressing. Indeed, in one trial, Chase ruled that the defendant's attempt to prove the truth of his publication demonstrated defiance of government and therefore malice!

Judges' partiality extended to gross procedural irregularities: partisan rhetoric issuing from the bench and summarily dismissing counsels' attempts to argue the act's unconstitutionality, to cite two examples.[184] Chase was especially at fault in this regard; he boasted before one trial in Richmond that he would teach Virginians the difference between liberty and licence of the press, and he berated a Delaware grand jury for not heeding his command to indict a Wilmington printer. One historian quoted Chase saying to the federal marshall before the Richmond proceedings: 'Have you any of those creatures called democrats on the [jury] panel? Look it over, sir, and if there are any of that description, strike them off.'[185]

This procedural behaviour again contrasted with the judges' handling of treason cases. With the exception of Chase in the second trial of *Fries*, where his written prejudgment of the law led defence counsel to retire (a somewhat less serious abuse than might appear), there were no procedural irregularities in the Whiskey Rebellion or house tax cases as reported in Wharton's *State Trials*. In fact, three examples of exemplary fairness to the accused are recorded: in *U.S. v. Stewart* and *v. Wright* (1795), where the trials were postponed to canvass the characters of prosecution witnesses; in the selecting of the jury in *Fries*, second trial[186]; and, above all, in *Fries* (1799), where a motion for a new trial was granted by Iredell and Peters on the grounds that one of the jurors had been prejudiced against the accused.[187] The former wrote his wife: 'Evidence ... was produced so irrefutable of one of the persons having made strong, prejudiced declarations against Fries, previous to his trial, that contrary to my wishes, bias, and inclination, I was at length compelled to vote for his having a new trial, and Judge Peters, with some hesitation, acquiesced.'[188]

The executive, as well as Congress and the judiciary, were bound by the limitations imposed upon treason prosecutions. This was made evident by President Adams in pardoning Fries and his associates. While humanitarian motives and prudent statesmanship were at play, the impact of the constitutional definition and the restrictive gloss upon it were fundamental. 'My judgment was clear,' he wrote many years later, 'that their crime did not amount to treason.'[189] Why is not so obvious but the primary sources indicate one of (or a combination of) four possibilities. Alexander Hamilton, in his political attack on Adams in 1800, claimed that the president had rashly embraced defence counsel's argument that resistance to the enforcement of any single statute but a Militia Act (which was inherently linked to sovereignty) did not constitute high treason.[190] The other possibilities are suggested in a memorandum of queries the president sent to his heads of department shortly before the pardons.[191] One question was certainly suggestive and may well be relevant to the law in the United States of today[192]: 'Was it a design of general resistance to all law, or any particular law?' Adams also wished to know whether the rising was sufficiently general to qualify and in particular whether there was 'evidence of a secret correspondence or combination with other anti-federalists ... in other States in the Union, or in other parts of this State.' A third question ('Was this any thing more than a riot?') suggested the significance of a lack of a clearly thought-out, preconcerted plot. In an 1815 letter Adams contended, 'They had been guilty of a high-handed riot ... attended with circumstances hot, rash, violent, and dangerous, but all these did not amount to treason.'[193] This last approach was adopted in *United States v. Hanway*, but the extent of its direct influence, if any, is unclear.[194] Each of the four substantive grounds reinforces the point that Chief Justice Monk was not necessarily correct in characterizing the Lower Canadian Road Act riots as treasonable. Again, the impact of the American constitution is clear. Adams had taken a quasi-judicial stand eliminating *constructive* levying except when *aimed directly* at intimidating government.

CONCLUSION

Although the French revolution lent an authoritarian cast to judicial behaviour in Great Britain, Lower Canada, and the United States, significant differences in approach are obvious: Lower Canada was at one end of this triple comparison, the authoritarian one; the United States was at the other; and Great Britain was somewhere in between. What explains these differences? The following hypotheses should be considered.

The author has elsewhere written that the colonial status of the Lower Canadian judges, although important, does not provide a complete explanation of their Baconianism, which was unrelievedly prevalent in security matters during the period 1794–1811. The judges' Baconian approach was rooted in a profound historical experience – the emergence of the garrison mentality. In contexts where that kind of experience was lacking, judicial behaviour was much different. Examples of the impartial behaviour of colonial judges dealing with security issues encompass the old province of Quebec, Upper Canada, and India.[195] Recent scholarship has provided one additional and striking example, relating to seditious libel in the penal colony of New South Wales in the 1820s.[196]

Whereas fear of the French revolution and political partisanship were countered in the United States and Great Britain by significant elements in their legal traditions, this was not so in Lower Canada. Moreover, the judges held office at the crown's pleasure and were therefore naturally inclined to internalize thoroughly the central imperialist value that dependencies should be kept dependent. Moreover, the legal ideals of the mother country relating to an impartial judiciary were not exported across the ocean. Both Osgoode and Jonathan Sewell after him received not the slightest criticism from the Colonial Office for their prosecutorial approach to security cases. Indeed, both were generously rewarded.[197] Judges remained on executive councils, with Chief Justice Sewell often acting as 'prime minister' into the late 1820s – more than two decades after the last, controversial appointment of a judge to the British cabinet. The giving of extrajudicial opinions continued into the late 1830s, almost eighty years after the last known opinion of the judges of England prepared for the executive and at a time when no reputable jurist in the mother country would have supported the practice. Again, the imperial authorities were indifferent. The absolute lack of sensitivity from the centre towards the rule of law in Lower Canada was best illustrated by London's acquiescence in the appointment in 1805 of judge Thomas Dunn and in 1819 of Chief Justice Monk as political heads of the province (administrators). The concept of a politically independent judiciary in the colonies was simply not of importance to imperial politicians in the 1790s and for decades after. Hence, the influence of the garrison mentality on the Lower Canadian bench was not checked by any significant force of legal tradition. The result was Baconianism.

In the case of the United States, the constitution put a brake on judicial despotism, a constitution the Federalists were attempting to protect from the Republican onslaught and so tended to glorify. The brake lay not merely in the restrictions therein enacted but in the fact that the dangers of abuse in treason cases, clearly articulated by several of the framers, had been accepted as real by such influential Federalists as John Adams, Alexander Hamilton, and justices Iredells Peters, and perhaps even Chase. The contrast in the treatment of treason and sedition, the prosecution of which was not explicitly restricted by the constitution, seems too blatant to be coincidental. Of course, subordinate factors – clearer targeting of opponents (editors, not farmers or workingmen), the offences not being capital,[198] and a conviction on the bench, as in Lower Canada, that freedom of the press meant only freedom from *prior* restraint[199] – undoubtedly played a role.

In Great Britain the brake on fear and partisanship came not only from a relatively free press, far freer than that of Lower Canada, but also from two important elements in the legal culture, both antedating but having been strongly reinforced by the Glorious Revolution.

The concept of a politically independent judiciary was not a matter of hypocrisy but a genuine ideal and had been a strong one since the revolution, which had been provoked in part by the grossly partial judges, such as Jeffreys, appointed by the later Stuarts. Laudatory statements that independence was a central principle of the constitution emanated from, among others, constitutional law experts such as Blackstone (1765) and Jean-Louis De Lolme (1771–2), popularizer William Paley (1785), Lord Chief Justices Holt (1693) and Mansfield (1784), King George III (1760), and parliament. In a statute enacted at the outset of the new king's reign (1760), parliament referred approvingly to His Majesty's declaration in the speech from the throne that he looked 'upon the independence and uprightness of judges, as essential to the impartial administration of justice, as one of the best securities to the rights and liberties of your loving subjects, and as most conductive to the honour of ... [the] crown.'[200]

Parliament by 1794 had acted upon the principle several times. The Act of Settlement in 1701 made mandatory the post-1688 practice of commissioning the common-law judges during good behaviour rather than royal pleasure.[201] Following in the train of several earlier acts, the 1760 statute just quoted from guaranteed judicial salaries by removing them from executive control and enacted that judges would no longer vacate their offices upon the monarch's demise. From the time of King James I, the judges of England, for technical reasons, had been disqualified from sitting in the House of Commons – in great contrast to Lower Canada.[202]

Additional disqualifications were enacted in 1734 and 1792 barring the Scottish judges and stipendiary magistrates of Middlesex respectively.[203] That the ideal had potency is also apparent in other ways. An attempt by a member of the cabinet to tamper with King's Bench judge Joseph Yates during the period of the general warrants cases (1763–8) was rebuffed and the government later was criticized in the Commons for this appalling breach of judicial independence.[204] In the last known instance of the common-law judges advising the executive extrajudicially on a point of law (1760), Lord Mansfield made it clear that they found the practice distasteful, distinctly implied they had no duty to respond to such requests, and explicitly reserved the right to change their minds should the matter arise in the courts.[205] Finally, in the very year Lord Chief Justice Mansfield retired from the cabinet, 1765, Sir William Blackstone pronounced that nothing 'is more to be avoided, in a free constitution, than uniting the provinces of a judge and a minister of state.'[206] No further such nominations occurred until 1806, when the appointment of Lord Chief Justice Ellenborough – the last precedent – raised a storm of protest damaging to the government.[207]

The second element of importance in Britain's legal tradition was the presumption of innocence. The ideal that many guilty people should go free to prevent an innocent person being condemned can be traced back at least to John Fortescue in the fifteenth century and had become part of conventional wisdom by the latter half of the eighteenth century. In the interval, it had received an enormous boost in the wake of the Glorious Revolution. Political philosophy had then shifted from a position favouring the crown to one in which the individual took pride of place. The same pamphleteers, or some of them, who made this case also argued for a return to the basic thrust behind Edward III's act: no judge-made treasons. Their main reform was King William III's liberating act on procedure in treason trials. But they also argued at length in favour of the presumption of innocence, which the act was designed to protect, and, a deduction from it, that 'treason' should not be manufactured by judges.[208]

Hostility to constructive treasons continued to find expression among the learned in the eighteenth century: for instance, in the works of jurists Sollom Emlyn, editor of the second edition of the *State Trials*, which appeared in 1730, and Blackstone.[209] Even that convinced Tory Samuel Johnson agreed: 'He said he was glad Lord George Gordon had escaped [1781] rather than a precedent should be established for hanging a man for *constructive treason*; which ... would be a dangerous engine of arbitrary power.'[210] During the *Hardy* trial, hawkish Attorney General Scott expressly disavowed judicial extensions of Edward III's act, while of course advocating the very opposite.[211] Scott's biographer claimed in 1844 that Tories of 'the higher and better-informed classes' divided into two groups: those who wanted a conviction and those who, while condemning the reform societies, 'were yet disquieted by an apprehension lest the law of treason should be dangerously extended by construction.'[212] The *Annual Register* for 1794, referring to the acquittal and defence counsel's role therein, stated that 'the public' was loud in its praise for the 'forcible and effective manner in which they silenced every attempt to establish the fatal doctrine of constructive treason.'[213] This silencing was reversed by the politicians in the panic of 1795, although even the politicians did not remove the special procedural guarantees for accused traitors. And the official line took heed of the feelings against constructive treasons. Scott characterized the act merely as a clarifying one; it 'did not go beyond the statute of 25th Edward 3rd,' and clarification of doubtful cases had been expressly left to parliament by that statute.[214]

The negative responses of 1794 probably owed a great deal to 'Cursory Strictures.' T.J. Howell wrote in 1818 that the tract 'drew much attention and excited much interest at the time.'[215] Thelwall and Godwin himself, likely the author, thought that the pamphlet had had a major impact on public opinion and had thereby, unspecifically but in an important way, aided the state prisoners.[216] William Hazlitt believed it responsible for the jury verdict in *Hardy*.[217] This could well be the truth, particularly as mediated through Erskine. A decent case can also be made that 'Strictures' influenced the bench.

Is it only coincidence that Eyre's charge differed markedly in important respects from his address to the grand jury and that much omitted in the former had been ridiculed by 'Strictures'? The chief justice made no mention of reform societies being particularly prone to foster treason, nor did he describe conventions as necessarily illegal in one degree or another. The dangerous contagion of revolutionary France, which he might have harped upon, made one appearance in passing, but in relation to the largely irrelevant Scottish convention.[218] It is true that Eyre made explicit his assumption that conspiracy to depose always amounted to compassing, but 'Strictures' had argued this issue badly from a technical (but not a political) point of view and the authorities were, if anything, on Eyre's side. More important, the chief justice made no reference or allusion to any constructive treason of conspiring to ovewawe parliament.[219] It seems highly probable that 'Strictures' and the impact it had had affected the charge, particularly in burying, for a short while, this 'new and doubtful case.'

The Glorious Revolutionary legal tradition in Great Britain, the impact of the revolutionary constitution in the United States, and the absence of brakes on the garrison mentality in Lower Canada conditioned the administration of 'treason' justice in the three jurisdictions. Revolutions had a manifest liberalizing impact on the judges of two countries – but not on our own.

NOTES

1 On compassing, see this volume's introduction and the text below.

2 *R. v. Hardy* (1794), 24 St. Tr. 199 at 906.

3 25 Ed. III, st. 5, c. 2. For constructive treason, see the volume's introduction and text below. Erskine addressed the jury for seven hours in all.

4 For the derivation of 'Baconian' and 'Cokean' and their meaning in Lower Canada, 1793–1811, see the author's *Legacies of Fear: Law and Politics in the Era of the French Revolution* (Toronto: Osgoode Society/University of Toronto Press 1993), passim but particularly at 27–8, 257–8.

5 Ibid., passim but particularly ch. 5, 'The Garrison Mentality.'

6 Quoted in Mason Wade, 'Quebec and the French Revolution of 1789: The Missions of Henri Mezière,' *CHR*, vol. 31 (1950), 345 at 364.

7 Lindsay to Attorney General Jonathan Sewell, 1 Dec. 1796, Sewell Papers, MG 23, G II 10, vol. 3, NA.

8 Writing to the secretary of state in October 1796, Governor Prescott advised that, if a French attacking force managed to land in the colony, the situation would be critical since 'His Majesty's English subjects here compared to the former [the Canadiens] are not in a greater proportion as Seventy to Two Thousand [a gloomy exaggeration of population ratios]': Prescott to Portland, 28 Oct. 1796, MG 11, CO 42/108, NA.

9 See, for example, George Stead Veitch, *The Genesis of Parliamentary Reform* [1913] (London: Constable 1964), at 211, 240, 259–51, 326, 337, 341–2; Philip Anthony Brown, *The French Revolution in English History* (London: George Allen and Unwin 1918), passim but particularly 131–3; Cyril Matheson, *The Life of Henry Dundas: First Viscount Melville 1742–1811* (London: Constable 1933), ch. 9–15 passim; J.R. Western, 'The Volunteer Movement as an Anti-Revolutionary Force, 1793–1801,' *EHR*, vol. 71 (1956), 603; Austin Mitchell, 'The Association Movement of 1792–3,' *Historical Journal*. vol. 4 (1961), 56; Carl B. Cone, *The English Jacobins: Reformers in Late Eighteenth Century England* (New

York: Charles Scribner's Sons 1968), at 198–202; F.K. Prochaska, 'English State Trials in the 1790s: A Case Study,' *Journal of British Studies*, vol. 13 (1973), 63; Clive Emsley, *British Society and the French Wars 1793–1815* (London: Macmillan 1979), at 25; Albert Goodwin, *The Friends of Liberty: The English Democratic Movement in the Age of the French Revolution* (London: Hutchinson 1979), ch. 7–12 passim, particularly 246, 259, 266, 331; Robert R. Dozier, *For King, Constitution, and Country: The English Loyalists and the French Revolution* (Lexington, Ky.: University of Kentucky Press [c. 1983]); John Ehrmann, *The Younger Pitt*, vol. 2 (London: Constable 1983), ch. 11.

10 *Mercury*, 10 Oct. 1835, quoted in Mitchell, 'Association Movement,' at 77; Hardy at 892.

11 Quoted in Brown, *French Revolution in English History*, at 168–9.

12 See for examples discussed, ibid., 131–3; Veitch, *Parliamentary Reform*, at 211, 240. For a modern example see Betty Kemp's review of Ehrmann, *Younger Pitt*, vol. 2, in *EHR*, vol. 100 (1985), at 629–32.

13 Veitch, *Parliamentary Reform*, at 250–1, 337; Brown, *French Revolution in English History*, at 132; Matheson, *Life of Henry Dundas*, at 154–72, 191–2; Mitchell, 'Association Movement,' at 57–60, 75–6; Goodwin, *Friends of Liberty*, at 264, 288, 387; *Lord Eldon's Anecdote Book*, ed. Anthony L.J. Lincoln and Robert Lindley McEwen (London: Stevens and Sons 1960), at 55–8.

14 Quoted in Brown, *French Revolution in English History*, at 288.

15 Ibid., at 26.

16 Western, 'Volunteer Movement,' at 607–10.

17 See, for example, Clive Emsley, 'An Aspect of Pitt's "Terror": Prosecutions for Sedition during the 1790s,' *Social History*, vol. 6 (1981), 155.

18 See Matheson, *Life of Henry Dundas*, at 171–2, and text below under 'The Trials: Great Britain.'

19 Quoted in Veitch, *Parliamentary Reform*, at 326.

20 Ibid, at 327.

21 Ehrmann, *Younger Pitt*, 2: at 398–400.

22 See, for example, Elizabeth Lawson, *The Reign of Witches: The Struggles against the Alien and Sedition Laws* (New York: Civil Rights Congress 1952), at 19.

23 James Morton Smith, *Freedom's Fetters: The Alien and Sedition Laws and American Civil Liberties* (Ithaca, N.Y.: Cornell University Press 1956), at 341. *Freedom's Fetters* (passim) and Marshall Smelser, 'The Jacobin Phrenzy: Federalism and the Menace of Liberty, Equality and Fraternity,' *Review of Politics*, vol. 13 (1951), 457, are the most useful studies on this point which I have found. For general background, see Alexander De Conde, *Entangling Alliance: Politics and Diplomacy under George Washington* (Durham, N.C.: Duke University Press 1958), supplemented for Adams's presidency by Frederick Jackson Turner,

'The Policy of France towards the Mississippi Valley in the Period of Washington and Adams,' *AHR*, vol. 10 (1904–5), 249; John C. Miller, *The Federalist Era, 1789–1801* (New York: Harper and Row 1963).

24 Marshall Smelser, 'George Washington and the Alien and Sedition Acts,' *AHR*, vol. 59 (1953–4), 322 at 324n.7.

25 George W. Kyte, 'A Spy on the Western Waters: The Military Intelligence Mission of General Collot,' *Mississippi Valley Historical Review*, vol. 24 (1947), 427; *William and Mary Quarterly*, 'Notes and Documents: General Collot's Plan for a Reconnaissance of the Ohio and Mississippi Valleys, 1796,' 3rd series, vol. 10 (1952), 512; Smith, *Freedom's Fetters*, at 51, 164–9; Miller, *Federalist Era*, at 192. See also Greenwood, *Legacies*, ch. 4.

26 See, for example, *Life and Correspondence of James Iredell* [1857], 2 vols, ed. Griffith J. McRee (New York: Peter Smith 1949), 2: at 480, 503; n.29 below.

27 Smelser, 'Washington and the Alien and Sedition Acts,' passim.

28 Smith, *Freedom's Fetters*, at 15–16, 96n.6, 110, 182–3, 283, 416.

29 Quoted in ibid., at 191. Mrs Adams used a phrase in this letter suggesting the president agreed with her: '*We have renewed information* ... [of the French] System' of subversion (emphasis added). John Adams of course received numerous panicky messages in his correspondence with Federalists. One wrote (7 Nov. 1799) that the Republicans were 'Jacobins, Democrats, [and] enemies to God and Man': ibid., at 315.

30 See *Legacies*, at 114–15, 171–2.

31 Robison, *Proofs of a Conspiracy against all Religions and Governments of Europe* [1797], 2nd ed. (London: T. Cadell Jr and W. Davies 1797); Barruel, *Mémoires pour servir à l'histoire du jacobinisme*, 5 vols. (Hamburg: P. Fauche 1798–1800).

32 Smelser, 'Jacobin Phrenzy,' at 470; Lawson, Reign of Witches, at 21–2; Eugene Perry Link, *Democratic-Republican Societies, 1790–1800* (New York: Octagon Books 1965), at 198–9. For Iredell's charge to the jury in *Fries* (1799), see *State Trials of the United States during the Administrations of Washington and Adams* [1849], ed. Francis Wharton (New York: Burt Franklin 1970), at 591–2.

33 See the works cited in notes 9, 17 above and Alan Wharam, *The Treason Trials, 1794* (Leicester: Leicester University Press 1992).

34 Edward Foss, *The Judges of England*, vol. 8 (London: John Murray 1864), at 253–4, 301. For Macdonald, see text below.

35 Four judges each of the Common Pleas, Exchequer, and King's Bench were called collectively the twelve judges of England, the twelve common law judges, or the common law judges (of England).

36 See n.104.

37 Sir William Holdsworth, *A History of English Law*, vol. 13 (London: Methuen/

Sweet and Maxwell 1952), at 162; Brown, *French Revolution in England History*, at 127.

38 *Cobbett's Parliamentary Debutes* [hereafter *Parl. Deb.*], vol. 6 (3 March 1806).

39 See Veitch, *Parliamentary Reform*, at 309–12; Brown, *French Revolution in English History*, at 120–2.

40 *Lives of the Lord Chancellors and Keepers of the Great Seal* [1845–7], vol. 8 (Jersey City: Fred D. Linn 1885), at 418–19. Campbell criticized the practice as having been improper, but *as of 1794* any sense of impropriety must have been a minor one in the bar and among judges. It was undoubtedly changed into a consensus following the Ellenborough cabinet appointment discussed below.

41 *Lord Eldon's Anecdote Book*, at 55–8.

42 PC 2/140: 34–131, meetings of 12, 13, 14 (2x), 15, 16 (2x), 17 (2x), 18, 19 (2x) May 1794. The draft minutes for the register (PC 1/22A36[a]) and those Treasury Solicitor's papers examined (for example, TS 11/957/3502) did not prove of any benefit.

43 John Richter's 'Narrative of his Arrest and Examination before the Privy Council, 1794,' Additional Manuscripts, Place Papers, 27816, BL, as summarized in Veitch, *Parliamentary Reform*, at 311; 'Horne Tooke's Diary,' *Notes and Queries*, vol. 11, 8th series (1897), at 21 (16 May); *An Account of Mr. Joyce's Arrest for 'Treasonable Practices'; His Examination before His Majesty's Privy Council ...*, 2nd ed. (London: J. Ridgway and others 1795), at 4–7 and 7–9 (Bonney's examination); Thomas Hardy, *Memoir of Thomas Hardy* (London: James Ridgway 1832), at 32–3; Cecil Thelwall (John's widow), *The Life of John Thelwall* (London: John Macrone 1837), at x, 165–74.

44 PC 2/140: 93 (16 May 1794), PRO.

45 This is particularly striking with regard not only to Hardy, as the text explains, but also to Tooke, whose diary shows almost an obsession with the proceedings of the Privy Council in the treason cases. See entries for 16, 23, 24, 26, 28 May 1794; 6, 7, 8,9, 22, 27 June 1794; 4 July 1794. Pitt and Dundas emerge as the villains in these entries.

46 Both had attended Hardy's first examination (12 May) and Eyre had also attended his second (13 May).

47 *Parl. Deb.*, vol. 6 (3 March 1806). While Castlereagh seems to have accepted the practice, all shades of parliamentary opinion (for instance, Fox and Eldon) were strongly represented in attacking it. See Greenwood, *Legacies*, at 31, 167.

48 These individuals included, in parliament, lords Eldon, Redesdale (formerly Sir John Mitford), Melville (formerly Henry Dundas), and Grenville; and, outside it, Lord Chief Baron Macdonald, Spencer Perceval (counsel consulted by Scott in 1794 on the Society for Constitutional Information), Thomas Hardy, Horne Tooke, John Thelwall, and Thomas Holcroft, an untried state prisoner.

The parliamentary opposition (for example, Eldon) stressed the difficulties of having judges in cabinet during another round of state trials, and it therefore would have had an obvious interest in stressing any undue prosecutorial behaviour on the part of the late Chief Justice Eyre. But it did not. The former state prisoners had no reason to remain silent on this issue in 1806 although they apparently did, if *Parl. Deb.* and the *Annual Register* are trustworthy guides.

49 Goodwin, *Friends of Liberty*, at 337–8.

50 24 St. Tr. 199 at 200–10.

51 For the indictments see ibid., at 224–38.

52 13 St. Tr. 1 at 61.

53 For full references to the treason jurists, see this book's introduction, n.58. See also Sir William Blackstone, *Commentaries on the Laws of England* [1765–70], 4 vols. (Philadelphia: J.P. Lippincott 1859), 1: at 108–9.

54 21 St. Tr. 485, particularly at 644–7.

55 At 907.

56 The *Chronicle* printed additions on the 24th. The author's account relies on the copy printed in 24 St. Tr. 199 at 210–32.

57 *Chronicle*, 28 Oct. 1794; Thelwall, *John Thelwall*, at 213–14; C.K. Paul, *William Godwin: His Friends and Contemporaries*, vol. 1 (London: Henry S. King 1876), at 128–35; Veitch, *Parliamentary Reform*, at 313; Brown, *French Revolution in English History*, at 126–7; Goodwin, *Friends of Liberty*, at 341–2. In an editorial note (210) Thomas Jones Howell suggested 'on sufficient [but undisclosed] authority' that the author was Felix Vaughan, a member of the LCS, who would assist the defence lawyers in the trials and was counsel for one of the untried prisoners, Jeremiah Joyce. But see n.216 below. Wharam is alone (or almost so) among scholars in his unqualified criticism of 'Strictures,' writing that 'it was a travesty of what the Lord Chief Justice had said and does not ... merit any of the esteem which it has received over the years': *Treason Trials, 1794*, at 133, 291–2nn. 21–2. Despite 'Godwin's hyperbolic style and his missing the point on one issue (see text below), Wharam's criticism is itself exaggerated.

58 Quoted in Thelwall, *John Thelwall*, at 214.

59 25 Oct. 1794. Both Godwin and Thelwall were certain that 'Strictures' had had a great, to them positive, impact among 'impartial men.' See references in the preceding notes.

60 See for example *R. v. Russell* (1683) 9 St. Tr. 527; *R v. Freind* (1696) 13 St. Tr. 1.

61 For the tacit assumption, see *Hardy* at 203, first paragraph and first full paragraph where Eyre uses the verb 'to be.'

62 *Directory of National Biography* article on Eyre by 'J.M.R.'; David Walker, *The Oxford Companion to Law* (Oxford: Clarendon Press 1980), at 453; For a rare

exception to the consensus, see Wharam, *Treason Trials, 1794*, at 188–91, 196, 275–6, 296n.7.

63 Examples include Campbell, *Lord Chancellors*, 8: at 111; Henry Thomas, Lord Cockburn, *An Examination of the Trials for Sedition which have hitherto Occurred in Scotland* [c. 1853], 2 vols. (Edinburgh: David Douglas 1888), 1: at 259–68, 285–6, 2: at 100; Foss, *Judges of England*, 8: at 282–5; William Massey, *A History of England during the Reign of George the Third*, 2nd ed., vol. 3 (London: Longmans, Green 1865), at 385; editorial note appended (1897) to 'Tooke's Diary' at 163; Holdsworth, *A History of English Law*, 13: at 162; Goodwin, *Friends of Liberty*, at 352.

64 See, for example *Hardy* at 861–5, 1382. See also Massey, *History*, 3: at 377–8; Goodwin, *Friends of Liberty*, at 354.

65 Cols. 1293–1383.

66 Cols. 1306, 1318, 1322, 1380.

67 Cols. 1346–7, 1381–2.

68 Col. 1362.

69 *Lord Eldon's Anecdote Book*, at 57.

70 Cols. 6–15, 344–61.

71 *European Magazine*, July 1799, at 7–9; largely reproduced identically by the *Gentleman's Magazine*, August 1799, at 709–11.

72 To emphasize the idiosyncratic injustice of his having been refused a graduate degree by Cambridge, he asked the bishop of Gloucester (his witness): 'Is not the degree of master of arts such a one as would be given to any creature that could answer a rational question?': Wharam, *Treason Trials, 1794*, at 216–17.

73 Ibid., ch. 16.

74 Cols. 731, 741–3; Goodwin, *Friends of Liberty*, at 356.

75 Wharam, *Treason Trials, 1794*, at 194.

76 Cols. 743–4.

77 *Hardy* at 895–911, 1116–20.

78 See particularly the saga of Jane Partridge, who had claimed that, while in a coach from her native Nottingham (which the accused had never visited) to London some two years before, 'I [Hardy] said to her ... I would no more mind cutting off the King's head than I would shaving myself.' The prosecution went to great pains to organize a viewing of the suspect in the Tower. When called to testify twice Partridge twice fainted and never took the witness stand. Whether she was simply mistaken or willing to commit perjury for the crown, and how the law officers were involved, are unknown. See Hardy, *Memoir*, at 43–7; Wharam, *Treason Trials, 1794*, at 134–5.

79 *Hardy* at 246–68, 1180–204. As Phillipps noted, Scott in one short passage (col. 255) could be interpreted as conceding the contrary position, but it was obviously not his intent: *State Trials*, 2: at 80.

80 *Hardy* at 1361.

81 *Tooke* at 725. Considering that Russell was involved in plotting rebellion (hence deposition) and also *plotting* to attack the guards (rather than actually doing it without clear planning), Eyre's attempt to explain away Pemberton's instructions seems weak: 'It was there properly stated to be evidence upon which the jury might exercise a judgment, and in which by possibility, they might say that the man who attacked the king's guards might not mean to compass the king's death; but it might be in some affray, or some way or other, which might take off the force of that evidence.'

82 *State Trials*, 2: at 78–80; *Trials for Sedition in Scotland*, 1: 229–31; *Treason Trials, 1794*, at 188, 293–4n.5. Neither Cockburn nor Wharam advance arguments of their own but rely on those of Erskine, Gibbs, and Phillipps. Wharam seems clearly wrong in stating that Eyre's conclusion contradicted the position taken by the law officers. For Phillipps, see the first section of this book's introduction. His 'argument' was based wholly on what he claimed as the weight of authority to the time of writing (c. 1826).

83 *Hardy* at 897, 900 (emphasis in original).

84 *Commentaries*, 4: at 79 (emphasis added).

85 Sir Edward Coke, *The Third Part of the Institutes of the Laws of England* [1641] (London: W. Clarke and Sons 1809), at 11–12; Phillipps, *State Trials*, 1: at 41–2.

86 *R. v. Essex and Southampton* (1600) 1 St. Tr. 1333 at 1347–50.

87 Ibid., at 1355 (emphasis added).

88 *R. v. Blunt et al.* (1600) 1 St. Tr. 1410 at 1410–11. See also the remarks of queen's counsel.

89 *Hardy* at 1187–9.

90 Thomas Babington Macaulay, *The History of England from the Accession of James II* [1848–55], 4 vols. (New York: Harper and Bros. 1856), 1: at 199–201.

91 9 St. Tr. 577, particularly at 625–36, 666–8; *Hardy* at 116–20.

92 Macaulay, *History of England*, 4: at 515–42; 13 St. Tr. 1, particularly at 14, 33–4, 54–5, 59, 61–2.

93 *Parliamentary History* (hereafter *Parl. Hist.*), vol. 32, cols. 484–5 (30 Nov. 1795). Neither Scott nor Mitford nor Eyre made reference to this supposed instruction in *Hardy*. It does not appear in Howell's report.

94 *Hardy* at 895. No details were given by Erskine.

95 Scott argued this explicitly (col. 254).

96 As quoted by Hawkins at 43.

97 *Pleas of the Crown*, 1: at 60.

98 *R. v. Watson* (1817) 32 St. Tr. 1 at 579.

99 *Hardy* at 267–8.

100 *Gordon* at 589; *Hardy* at 907, 1182.

101 Ibid. at 1183, 1193, 1199.

102 The great constitutional historian Henry Hallam thought Mitford's idea of political death was the most expansive of all constructive treasons in history: *The Constitutional History of England from the Accession of Henry VII to the Death of George III* [1827] (London: Alex. Murray and Son 1871), at 711n.1.

103 The year 1799, rather than 1802, has been chosen as the terminal date here since one of the judges functioning in the crucial year of 1794 died and another resigned in 1799. A third died in 1800.

104 Charles Cestre, *John Thelwall: A Pioneer of Democracy and Social Reform in England during the French Revolution* (London: Swan Sonnenschein 1906), found an obscure printed account of the trial (15–16, 90n.3) and quoted a few passages from Macdonald's charge (99–102). This account had not been found by the Howells (see this volume's introduction) and was not used either by Goodwin (*Friends of Liberty*, at 358), who seems not to have known of it, or Wharam (*Treason Trials, 1794*, at 227–8), who did.

105 *Times*, 20 Nov. 1792.

106 *R. v. Yorke* (1795) 25 St. Tr. 1003 at 1149–54.

107 *Dean of St Asaph* (1783–4) 27 St. Tr. 847 at 943–55; in *De la Motte* (21 St. Tr. 687 at 808) Buller, in *obiter*, instructed the jury that any preliminary attempt to adhere (for example, gathering intelligence) constituted treason. See text below at nn.151–2. Justice Heath had sat with Buller.

108 Foss, *Judges of England*, 8: at 254–5, 302; Frida Knight, *The Strange Case of Thomas Walker* (London: Lawrence and Wishart 1957), at 140, 158–9. For Kenyon, see text below. The author has been unable to find any relevant evidence with regard to Richard Perryn of the Exchequer Court.

109 *R. v. Crossfield* (1796) 26 St. Tr. 1 at 190–222.

110 See the introduction to this volume.

111 *R. v. Walker* (1794) 23 St. Tr. 1055 at 1148–51. Defence counsel Thomas Erskine asked that the case go to the jury rather than be decided on a technicality. This was done and Walker was acquitted.

112 *R. v. O'Coigley, O'Connor and others* (1798) 27 St. Tr. 1 at 42–53, 133–4. Goodwin (*Friends of Liberty*, at 448) wrote that 'the testimony offered by Fox, Sheridan, Whitbread ... [among others] as to O'Connor's immaculate political principles and unblemished character, though later revealed as completely false, was allowed by the presiding judge to weigh unduly in his favour.' O'Connor had attempted to secure a full-scale invasion of England and/or Ireland by France: ibid., at 436–49, passim.

113 A.G. Mitford to Kenyon, 5 Feb. 1801, in Horace Twiss, *The Public and Private Life of Lord Chancellor Eldon*, 3 vols. (London: Cary and Hart 1844), 1: at 358;

John Campbell, *Lives of the Chief Justices of England*, vol. 4 (Boston: Estes and Laurait 1873), at 54–67, 94–5; Greenwood, *Legacies*, at 256–7.

114 This section is based principally on Cockburn, *Trials for Sedition in Scotland.* See also Brown, *French Revolution in English History*, at 95–9; Goodwin, *Friends of Liberty*, ch. 8; Wharam, *Treason Trials, 1794*, ch. 5, 6.

115 This statement is quoted and confirmed as accurate in Cockburn, *Trials for Sedition in Scotland*, 1: at 87.

116 Quoted in Goodwin, *Friends of Liberty*, at 290.

117 *Memoir*, at 42.

118 As the royal coach proceeded to the House of Lords, it was met with large crowds crying out 'No Pitt, No War, Bread, Bread, Peace, Peace' and one of its windows was broken by a stone or ball from (apparently) an air gun. See Goodwin, *Friends of Liberty*, at 386n.152. This 'outrage' was referred to in the preamble to the Treason Act of 1795.

119 See Goodwin, *Friends of Liberty*, at 366–7; *Parl. Hist.*, vol. 32 (debates in cols. 244–527).

120 36 Geo. III, c. 7.

121 Emsley, 'Pitt's "Terror,"' at 156–7.

122 See, for example, *R. v. Despard* (1803) 28 St. Tr. 345 at 349, 485–6; *R v. Watson* (1817), 32 St. Tr. 1 at 578–82; *R v. Ludlam* (1817), *The Trials of Jeremiah Brandeth etc.* 2 vols., ed. William Brodie Gurney (London: Butterworth and Son 1817), 2: 75 at 295–6. Despard and Ludlam were executed. Watson was acquitted.

123 *R. v. Maclane* (sic), 26 St. Tr. 721.

124 Richardson to J. Sewell, 23 Jan., 6 Feb. 1797, Sewell Papers, vol. 3.

125 Sewell to Foucher, 3 Oct. 1796, ibid., vol. 9.

126 Osgoode to [?], 13 Oct. 1796, CO 42/22; same to King, 14 Nov. 1796, ibid. For the fears expressed by other judges, see Greenwood, *Legacies*, at 148.

127 Montreal *Gazette*, 20 March 1797. For levying war, see this volume's introduction.

128 15 St. Tr. 521, particularly 608–9.

129 13 St. Tr. 1 at 61.

130 See the terse reports in the *Gentleman's Magazine* for April (191) and May (239) of 1758. It seems improbable that Monk knew of these judgments.

131 21 St. Tr. 485 at 644; *A Treatise upon the Law and Proceedings in Cases of High Treason* (London).

132 See text below and Osgoode to John King, 14 Nov. 1794, CO 42/22.

133 See text below. East asserted that it was treason 'to obstruct the execution of some general law [as opposed, for example to a private turnpike or enclosure act] by armed force.' See also Greenwood, *Legacies*, at 135–7. East's authorities

were the manuscript judgments mentioned in the text; he gave no explanation from principle.

134 15 St. Tr. 521, particularly at 699–702.

135 Greenwood, *Legacies*, at 138. Foster wrote that 'his [Purchase's] case, in point of law and of real guilt too, came far short of *Demaree's*.'

136 Quebec *Gazette*, 24 Sept. 1812.

137 See Greenwood, *Legacies*, at 83–85, 131–2. For adhering, see the introduction to the present volume.

138 See Greenwood, *Legacies*, ch. 7 and 250–1 and F. Murray Greenwood, 'The Treason Trial and Execution of David McLane,' *Manitoba Law Review*, vol. 20 (1991), 3.

139 For evidence of this relationship, see particularly Prescott to Portland, 18 March 1797, Prescott Papers, MG 23, G II 17, vol. 13, NA; Osgoode to [?], n.d. [1798], CO 42/22. Prescott praised Osgoode 'for his readiness on all occasions to give the whole weight of his Abilities and knowledge towards enabling me to carry on His Majesty's Government in this Province.' Even lord chancellors in Great Britain could not aspire to this role: Greenwood, *Legacies*, at 272n.80.

140 Sewell to Samuel Gale, 9 July 1797, RG 4, A 1, S series, vol. 68, NA. See also Stephen to Jonathan Sewell, 14 Nov. 1796, ibid., vol. 65; Greenwood, *Legacies*, at 141–4.

141 G. Francklin to Ryland, 17 April 1797, Prescott Papers, vol. 9; Ryland to Francklin, 18 May 1797, ibid.

142 *McLane* at 765, 769.

143 Ryland to Monk, 13 April 1797, Prescott Papers, vol. 9; Prescott to Portland, 27 May 1797, CO 42/109; *McLane* at 721.

144 23 Nov. 1796, CO 42/108; Richardson to J. Sewell, 23 March 1797, Sewell Papers, vol. 3. This witness did not in fact testify against McLane but in all probability was called by the crown in the Montreal treason case held in September.

145 See particularly Greenwood, *Legacies*, at 109–10.

146 Ibid., at 155–6.

147 *McLane* at 722, 754, 790; Greenwood, *Legacies*, at 127–31, 146–7.

148 The primary and secondary sources and historical judgments on which this paragraph is based may be found in Greenwood, *Legacies*, ch. 7, particularly 155, 168, 304n.35, 306nn.52–5; Jacques Boucher, 'Pyke, George,' *DCB* 8: 726. After moving out of his house, Francklin thanked Sewell for allowing him to experience 'the most perfect and disinterested Friendship, and a Tenderness of Conduct, that I could only expect from a near Relation': Francklin to Sewell, 15 Aug. 1798, Sewell Papers, vol. 3.

149 *McLane* at 729, 750–1, 785, 787, 794.

150 13 St. Tr. 485 at 531–3.

151 Unsigned document entitled 'In this vacation vist Decem. 1707' in Solicitor
General (1756–62)/Attorney General (1762–3, 1765–6) Charles Yorke's 'Legal
Precedents 1602–1752,' Hardwicke Papers, BL. This contemporary record of
the questions and answers is probably the only one known today, although
four others circulated in the eighteenth and early nineteenth centuries. See
Hensey (1758), 19 St. Tr. 341; *Joyce's* case (1946) AC 347 at 367, 375. After much
detective work by both of us, the author and his wife, Beverley Boissery,
located this document among Yorke's uncalendared and unorganized papers
in a volume which also, for example, contained gardening information.

152 J. Willard Hurst, *The Law of Treason in the United States: Collected Essays* (Westport, Conn.: Greenwood Publishing 1971), passim.

153 For brief résumés of the facts about these two disturbances, see Miller, *Federalist Era*, at 155–60, 247–8; Bradley Chapin, *The American Law of Treason: Revolutionary and Early National Origins* (Seattle: University of Washington Press
1964), at 85–97.

154 McRee, *Iredell*, 2: at 480–3, 495, 513, 537, 539–40. Judge Iredell corresponded
privately with the district attorney of Philadelphia: ibid., at 537.

155 Ibid., at 429–30, 483, 503, 539, 544–5, 548–50, 572, 577–8.

156 Ibid., at 523–7.

157 Wharton, *State Trials*, at 591–2.

158 Article 3, section 3 also allowed Congress to set the penalty. This was implemented in 1790 when capital punishment was prescribed. Congress was
barred from imposing corruption of the blood.

159 *The Federalist Papers by Alexander Hamilton, James Madison and John Jay*, ed.
Garry Wills (New York: Bantam Books 1982), at 319. See also Chapin, *American Law of Treason*, at 83–4; Hurst, *Law of Treason*, at 136–40, 152–4, 169–71.
Hurst remarked (at 138) that in many of the states 'advocates of the Constitution cited the treason clause as a valued part of the document, and the opposition maintained silence.'

160 This was s. 1 of the Sedition Act of 1798 (*Statutes of the United States*, 1798, 5th
Congress, Sess. 2, c. 74). The restrictive nature of the constitution is illustrated
by the fact that prior to 1787 five states had made conspiracy to levy war treason: Chapin, *American Law of Treason*, at 40.

161 Such a provision was in Federalist Senator James Lloyd's initial draft of the
sedition bill but was dropped in committee: Smith, *Freedom's Fetters*, at 107–
11. The provision made it treason to adhere to the government *or to people* of
France designated as enemies of the United States. Some Republican newspaper attacks on it cited the constitution. See Smith, *Freedom's Fetters*, at 106–9.
The British treason jurists' gloss on the adhering clause in the Statute of Trea-

sons included as 'enemies' nations engaging in undeclared war against His or Her Majesty.

162 Justice Patterson in *Mitchell* (1795), Wharton, *State Trials*, at 183; justices Iredell and Chase in *Fries* (1799–1800), ibid., at 589, 635. Per Chase: 'The Court are of opinion that a ... conspiracy to levy war against the United States is not treason ... some actual force or violence must be used, in pursuance of such design to levy war.' Chase's reading was endorsed in subsequent cases. See, for example, *United States v. Hanway* 26 Fed. Cas. (no. 15,299) 105 at 127–8 (per Justice Grier).

163 Chapin, *American Law of Treason*, ch. 6; Hurst, *Law of Treason*, at 140.

164 (1781) 21 St. Tr. 485 at 644.

165 Wharton, *State Trials*, at 496–537.

166 Ibid., at 571–2.

167 17 St. Tr. 993; *Porteus* (1737) 17 St. Tr. 993.

168 Wharton, *State Trials*, at 534.

169 See *Law of Treason*, at 196, 224n.34 where authorities are listed. See particularly Justice Patterson in *Mitchell* (1795), and Wharton, *State Trials*, at 182.

170 26 Fed. Cas. (no. 15,407) 397 at 398–9.

171 *R. v. M'Growther* (1746), Foster's *Crown Cases* 13; Blackstone, *Commentaries*, 4: 30; Wharton, *State Trials*, at 176.

172 Ibid., at 586, 633.

173 12 Oct. 1792, McRee, *Iredell*, 2: at 367–8; 12 April 1796, ibid., at 468–9 (quotations are taken from this address); 11 April 1799, ibid., at 568–9 and Wharton, *State Trials*, at 480; ibid., at 590, 594. Iredell also held (ibid., at 590) that American judges were not bound to follow arbitrary precedents drawn from 'the bad times of English history.'

174 *McLane* at 730. One of the statute's main new guarantees was the provision of a list, with addresses and occupations, of intended crown witnesses at least ten days before arraignment.

175 Justice Patterson in *Vigol* and *Mitchell*, Wharton, *State Trials*, at 175, 183; justices Peters, Iredell, and Chase in *Fries*, ibid., at 586, 594, 635.

176 Wharton, *State Trials*, at 177, 179, 182–3.

177 Ibid., at 636 (second emphasis added). In the *United States v. Burr* (1807) Chief Justice Marshall considered this question an open one and unnecessary to decide: Chapin, *American Law of Treason*, ch. 7.

178 Wharton, *State Trial*, at 589.

179 See n.162. Hurst, *Law of Treason*, at 199–200 gives numerous examples from the late nineteenth century where, on the basis of the English authorities, 'private' rioting might have been dealt with as treasonable but was not.

180 *R. v. Ludlam* (1817) as reported in Gurney, *Trials of Jeremiah Brandeth [and oth-*

ers], 1: 75 at 297–8 (per Justice Abbott). Abbott's comment was not quite explicit and Phillipps's favourable reference to it was downright ambiguous (*State Trials*, 1: at 311–25). Significantly, the widespread 'Captain Swing' riots of 1830 (breaking threshing machines, burning ricks) in southern England were not treated as treasonable. Nor were the serious anti-employer Chartist outbreaks of 1842. All this, it seems, took place by way of practice, without legislation, clear precedents, or clear juristic writings.

181 *Statutes of the United States*, 1798, Fifth Congress, Sess. 2, c. 74. The author's source for enforcement, unless otherwise specified, is Smith, *Freedom's Fetters*.

182 See Greenwood, *Legacies*, at 116–20 and Jean-Marie Fecteau, F. Murray Greenwood, and Jean-Pierre Wallot, 'Sir James Craig's "Reign of Terror" and Its Impact on Emergency Powers in Lower Canada, 1810–13,' in this volume. The common-law penalty for misdemeanours was imprisonment and/or fine, the extent of both being at the entire discretion of the court. Lower Canada prescribed transportation for a second offence. The American maximum was two years in jail and a $2000 fine.

183 A determined Republican opposition and an occasionally divided Federalist majority help account for the moderate provisions.

184 For the complicated questions of the act's *vires*, see Justice Iredell's address to the grand jury at Philadelphia, 11 April 1799, McRee, *Iredell*, at 551–70; Smith, *Freedom's Fetters*, ch. 8.

185 Lawson, *The Reign of Witches*, at 49.

186 Ibid., at 620, 637.

187 Ibid., at 604–9.

188 16 May 1799, McRee *Iredell*, at 575.

189 Adams to James Lloyd, 31 March 1815, *The Works of John Adams*, vol. 10, ed. Charles Francis Adams (Boston: Little, Brown 1856), at 154.

190 Quoted in Wharton, *State Trials*, at 644. See also ibid., at 647.

191 Adams, *Works of John Adams*, vol. 9 (1854), at 57–9.

192 See Hurst, *Law of Treason* at 197–8, but contrast this analysis with Chapin, *American Law of Treason*, at 111. Justice Grier in *Hanway* (see n.162) did retain violent opposition to a single statute as a *possible* case of treason (128).

193 See n.189.

194 See n.162. Excluded from the category of treason was a mere 'sudden "conclamatio" or running together.'

195 Greenwood, *Legacies*, ch. 7, 11 and pp. 27–34, 256–60.

196 David Neal, *The Rule of Law in a Penal Colony: Law and Power in Early New South Wales* (Cambridge: Cambridge University Press 1991), at 110.

197 S.R. Mealing, 'Osgoode, William,' *DCB* 6: 557 at 559; F. Murray Greenwood and James H. Lambert, 'Sewell, Jonathan,' *DCB* 7: 782 at 784.

198 See, for example, Justice Iredell's reasons for granting Fries a new trial, in Wharton *State Trials*, at 608.

199 See Justice Iredell's address to the grand jury, Philadelphia, 11 April 1799, ibid., at 458–9; Fecteau, Greenwood, and Wallot, 'Craig's "Reign of Terror."'

200 1 Geo. III, c. 23, preamble. References to the other authorities cited may be found in Greenwood, *Legacies*, at 271n.59.

201 12 and 13 Wm. III, c. 2, s. 3.

202 Judges were eligible to sit in the assembly until 1811. One of them, Pierre-Amable De Bonne, who sat from 1794 to 1810, acted as the government's house leader and as an electoral campaign organizer. The Colonial Office remained indifferent until 1809. See Greenwood, *Legacies* at 29–30, 218, 229–32.

203 7 Geo. II, c. 16, s. 4; 32 Geo. III, c. 53, s. 13.

204 *Parl. Hist.*, vol. 16 (6 Dec. 1770); Foss, *Judges of England*, 8: at 412.

205 Mansfield to Lord Keeper, 3 March 1760, 2 Eden (case reports) 371–3.

206 *Commentaries*, 1: at 269. The Mansfield appointment was attacked on principle and with vitriol by Lord Shelburne some ten years later: *Parl. Hist.*, vol. 18 (7 Feb. 1775).

207 *Parl. Deb.*, vol. 6 (3 March 1806); *Annual Register* for 1806, at 27–33.

208 Alexander Shapiro, 'Political Theory and the Growth of Defensive Safeguards in Criminal Procedure: The Origins of the Treason Trials Act of 1696,' *Law and History Review*, vol. 11 (1993), 208.

209 Emlyn's preface in T.B. Howell's *State Trials*, vol. 1 at xxvi; *Commentaries*, 4: at 85. For Emlyn, see this volume's introduction.

210 *Boswell's Life of Johnson* [1791] 2 vols., ed. Humphrey Milford (Oxford: Oxford University Press 1922), 2: at 397.

211 *Hardy* at 251–2. Scott claimed that, if judges decided a case by enunciating a new proposition and parliament did not react, the proposition was not a constructive treason! (cols. 254–5).

212 Twiss, *Life of Lord Chancellor Eldon*, 1: at 268.

213 *Annual Register*, 1794 at 278–9. See also, for example *Courier and London Evening Gazette*, 6 Nov. 1794.

214 *Parl. Hist.*, vol. 32 (30 Nov. 1795, cols. 482–4).

215 24 St. Tr. 199 at 210.

216 Thelwall, *Life of Thelwall*, at 213–14; Paul, *William Godwin: His Friends and Contemporaries*, at 135, where Mary Shelley, Godwin's daughter, remembers that it was her father's 'honest boast, and his most grateful recollection, that he had contributed to the glorious result [the acquittals] by his letter to Chief-Justice Eyre.' This strongly suggests that Godwin authored or at least co-authored 'Cursory Strictures.'

217 Wharam, *Treason Trials, 1794*, at 274. At the time of the trials, Hazlitt was only in his mid-teens. He was, however, a prodigy who had published an essay on law in 1792.

218 *Hardy* at 373. There were many occasions on which Eyre might have inserted some pointed francophobia: ibid., at 1325, 1327, 1363, 1366.

219 Eyre made no mention, either, of parliamentary assertions about 'Jacobin' plots. 'Strictures' had not, however, commented on this point.

9

The Official Mind and Popular Protest in a Revolutionary Era: The Case of Newfoundland, 1789–1819

CHRISTOPHER ENGLISH

In the revolutionary age spanning the years of unrest and war between the outbreak of the French revolution in 1789 and the final defeat of Emperor Napoleon Bonaparte in 1815, Newfoundland was not immune from dissent, street demonstrations, and official fears of insurrection. Such phenomena occurred in England and Ireland, in western Europe, in the United States, and in the British North American colonies. The liberal use of prosecutions for seditious libel in the mother country embraced even John Reeves, a respected historian, member of the Royal Society, framer of the judicature acts of Newfoundland in 1791–2, and the island's first chief justice.

As a result of the wars, the local population, whose numbers had been greatly increased by a unique wave of wartime immigration, was caught in the grip of a crippling economic depression. In this, too, Newfoundland was typical of the wider North Atlantic community. What appears to have differed was the official response to real or apprehended popular protest.

For reasons examined below, sedition was not charged locally. Fox's Libel Act of 1792, which did much to temper the arbitrary application of a blunt weapon, is not mentioned in official correspondence. The same is true of the Treason Act of 1795. While no sustained scholarly examination has been made of the surviving unreported cases of the supreme, [governor's] surrogate, or sessions (magistrates') courts in the period before the first reported cases (1817–28), it is unlikely that these British statutes were invoked. From what we know to this point, common and statute law on seditious libel and conspiracy went unnoticed. Neither the first newspaper, the *Royal Gazette*, which appeared, with the governor's permission, in 1806, nor the three others that had joined it by 1820 were charged or threatened with prosecution. That the law on seditious libel was not invoked does not mean, of course, that it was unavailable. We will return to this distinction.

It also appears, on the basis of research to date, that popular disturbances did not give rise to charges of seditious conspiracy or, with one exception in Harbour Grace in May 1819, a reading of the Riot Act. There were certainly occasions for such measures during three hard winters from 1816 to 1818 around Conception Bay. In a few instances, prosecutions for disturbing the peace occurred, but these were largely confined to 1814 when they were employed by a zealous chief justice, Caesar Colclough, government administrator in the absence of the seasonally resident governor. No consideration of the more serious step of suspending habeas corpus appears in the official correspondence. The few lawyers and amateur part-time special pleaders evidently found no need to invoke habeas corpus because the authorities usually brought an accused before a magistrate for summary justice or a bail hearing on the morning following arrest.

When habeas corpus was applied for, it accompanied a writ of certiorari and was employed by the Supreme Court to seize jurisdiction over the proceedings or verdict of a surrogate or sessions court. It was a rare procedure before a reforming chief justice, Francis Forbes (1816–22), endorsed it in *Clift v. Holdsworth* (1819), a judgment that outraged Governor Hamilton and, subsequently, elicited a contrary opinion by the law officers of the crown in London. Nevertheless, the procedure stood and the appellate jurisdiction of the Supreme Court over all causes pursued in subordinate ones was asserted. Forbes was unsympathetic to the plea that statute, when it denied jurisdiction to a superior court, was to prevail. The basis for his decision was the right of free-born Englishmen, settled in Newfoundland, to have access to the benefits of English common law, one of which was the need to have a final court of appeal wherein the applicable law would be finally decided. A sign of the rarity of the procedure in the early days of judicature is that it seems to have been first employed in *R. v. Kent* (1817), a case that was unreported a dozen years later when the first volume of Supreme Court reports was edited, perhaps because the same issue was raised by the better known case of 1819.[1]

During an age of revolution and war in contemporary England (and elsewhere in the empire), official practice in Newfoundland may seem anomalous when assessed against the relatively wide use of the common law on sedition, Fox's Act, the Riot Act, and the suspension of habeas corpus. But the fact that these measures were not employed does not mean that they had not been received as good law into Newfoundland. What was lacking was the means to administer such laws.

For what is the last but one of the foundations of the common law which by definition English settlers carried with them to the plantations, lands, or, in the case of Newfoundland, a migratory fishery that over time became a settled one?[2] English law, and there was never a question of any other, operated in Newfoundland from the earliest days of renewed European contact at the end of the fifteenth century. The royal charters granted to private individuals (Sir Humphrey Gilbert in 1583, Sir George Calvert, Lord Baltimore, in 1623, and Sir David Kirke in 1637) and to joint stock companies (the London and Bristol Company, represented by Sir John Guy, in 1610, and the Western Company of Adventurers in 1634, 1660, and 1676) all provided for the importation and application of English law. When these initiatives failed, through a combination of under-capitalization, ill-prepared and inadequately supplied settlers, isolation, and an unforgiving climate, then civilian 'fishing admirals' who pursued the annual migratory fishery on the Grand Banks and along the island's coasts administered their own form of law. Over time, however, fishermen and seamen stayed behind at the end of the fishing season. Neither private fishing interests nor the Royal Navy had the resources or the inclination to pursue illegal settlers or to winkle them out from isolated coves along an uncharted and difficult coastline. In addition, an English presence that required neither supervision nor administration was a useful foil to the territorial and fishing claims of the Spanish, Portuguese, and especially the French in the eighteenth century.[3] The governing statute of 1699 sought to reserve Newfoundland as a migratory fishery and nursery for seamen, but de facto settlement and international politics demanded an official response. In the result the governing statute was considered to be limited to the fishery, permitting an ad hoc response to local developments via the royal prerogative.

A state-appointed seasonal governor, usually a serving naval officer, succeeded the civilian 'fishing admiral' as the supreme authority on station in 1729. In that year courts of session, exercising a criminal jurisdiction in the seasonal absence of the naval governor and his surrogates from the end of the fishing season in mid-October until his return the following July, were set up in eleven centres on the Avalon peninsula and northeast coast. According to the attorney general, their commissions instructed them to follow the laws of England. Cognizant of King William's Act of 1699, they should act 'as near as the circumstances of the case would admit.' A superior criminal jurisdiction of Oyer and Terminer and General Gaol Delivery was an annual feature of the judicial calendar in St John's, the capital, from 1750. A Vice-Admiralty jurisdiction (1710) was regularly exercised by the governor from at least 1729 and was permanently established with resident William Keen's appointment in 1736. L.A. Anspach in 1827 noted that during the war with Spain in 1741 the court prevented 'the expense and risk of sending the prizes to England for trial and condemnation.' Later in the century it also sat at Placentia, the former capital of French settlement which was transferred to England in 1713. It invoked a jurisdiction in prize (contraband and captured goods in wartime) and instance (salvage, wreck, collision, bottomry, and so on) and in causes concerning the revenue of the North American colonies. A court of civil jurisdiction was established by imperial statute in 1791. It was intended to break the logjam of writs for debt and to address both the fallout from local bankruptcies following the American Revolutionary War and a judicial challenge to the jurisdiction over debts that the magistrates had exercised for years. They had done so illegally, it was declared in 1787 (R. v. Hutchings), in light of King William's Act. Largely as a result of Chief Justice Reeves's sojourn of 1791, during which he heard cases in St John's and on circuit to outlying harbours in a summer's residency, civil jurisdiction was expanded the following year to a

supreme court of judicature ... with full power and authority to hold plea of all crimes and misdemeanours committed within the island of Newfoundland, and on the islands and seas to which ships or vessels repair from the island of Newfoundland, for carrying on the fishery, and on the banks of Newfoundland, in the same manner as plea is holden of crimes and 'misdemeanours committed in ... England, and also ... of suits and complaints of a civil nature ... according to the laws of England, as far as the same can be applied to suits and complaints arising in the islands and places aforesaid.

There were courts, and there was English law. But how much of the latter was to 'be applied'? The verb was carefully chosen and it offers a key to the always tangled question of precisely what English law was operative in Newfoundland.[4]

All Englishmen carried the common law with them as their birthright. The royal prerogative had been exercised, via their commissions and instructions, by seasonally resident governors since 1729. Their right to do so was unchallenged in an era preceding the sovereign's grant of power to local inhabitants to establish a legislature (1832). At this point, as well, imperial statutes ceased to apply *ex proprio vigore* unless they specifically made reference to the island or its dependencies. The contentious issue was how much of the earlier English parliament's domestic legislation was operative in Newfoundland. The answer lay in the imperial statute of judicature of 1792: Newfoundland courts would exercise the jurisdiction of English courts and apply English law to the extent that it was appropriate to local needs.[5]

Just what elements of English criminal law would be applied in Newfoundland were unclear and would be left to judicial decision and, after 1832, the will of the legislature. In 1837 the legislature, by (1837) 1 Vict., c. 4, adopted English criminal law and all future amendments thereto after the passage of twelve months. It did so without controversy, despite bitter sectarianism which had contributed to legislative gridlock on a range of issues: a revenue bill, roads, the Education Act of 1836, and supply. Only ten of thirty-two bills passed by the Legislative Assembly were forwarded by the Legislative Council to London for confirmation. The act of 1837 was perpetuated in successive judicature acts down to 1949 when it was finally repealed as part of Newfoundland's coming under the provisions of the Canadian Criminal Code. The act may seem curious in retrospect, a gauge of the depth of loyalty to an English heritage and an English model. It could not be locally adopted before the establishment of a local legislature. But no previous request had gone to England for an imperial statute which would accomplish this. It is noteworthy that the act makes specific reference to the fact that 'the Penal Code and Criminal Laws of England have lately undergone very considerable revisions and improvements.' From a Newfoundland perspective, an end to the most egregious provisions of the Black Act, other elements of the 'Bloody Code,' and benefit of clergy (repealed in 1827) brought English criminal law closer to local practice. Newfoundlanders had applied English law 'as far as the situation and circumstances of the said colony will permit.' They were far from accepting or applying that law in its entirety.[6]

'AS FAR AS THE SITUATION ... OF THE SAID COLONY WILL
PERMIT'

We have noted the different, if not unique, circumstances of an island (to which Labrador had been returned in 1809) in transition from fishing schooner to colony which was without representative government until 1832. The courts were in place, capped by a supreme tribunal in 1791. However, the scope of the latter's appellate jurisdiction would be judicially contentious for a generation. Chief justices after John Reeves disregarded official instructions that they be permanently resident on the island. The first chief justice since Reeves to be legally trained was Caesar Colclough in 1813, and there may have been two qualified lawyers, as distinct from special pleaders, at war's end in 1815. One of them, James Simms, who continued to carry on commercial activities, was deputy clerk of arraigns, assuming carriage of criminal prosecutions before the Court of Oyer and Terminer in 1816 and in 1822, years in which chief justices Forbes and Tucker, newly appointed, were not yet in residence. We are a long way from reconstructing the practices of the Supreme Court of the period but it appears that Thomas Coote simultaneously held the posts of chief [stipendiary] magistrate in St John's, supreme surrogate judge, and clerk of arraigns of the Supreme Court for several years before his retirement in 1819. Simms had carriage of crown cases before Oyer and Terminer because Coote sat on that court in both 1816 and 1822. In the governor's eyes, this arrangement was no substitute for a crown prosecutor and at least from 1819 he pressed London for an attorney general. An English lawyer named Westcott proved unsatisfactory after his appointment in 1821 and was succeeded by John William Molloy, who vacated the office for the Supreme Court bench in 1825. Simms acted as attorney general until confirmed in 1827 and served until 1846.[7]

The first reported cases are notable for the absence of criminal actions, and in all likelihood these continued to be handled almost entirely by magistrates and by the governor's surrogates until 1824 when their office was abolished. In addition, alternative mechanisms existed for the settlement of personal disputes which had been accompanied by violence, physical (battery) or verbal (assault) although in local practice the term *assault* covered both: fisticuffs, mediation, exhortation, private discipline (masters over servants), charivari, compounding (private reimbursement), or arbitration. All were quick, effective, locally sanctioned, inexpensive, and less formal avenues than actions pursued through the courts.

Statistics on the number and type of actions pursued before the Supreme Court in St John's and on its three circuits (after 1825) indicated that in the years 1826–8 civil causes outnumbered criminal in a ratio of ten to one (1,550 to 144). And these were *common law* cases: the figures did not include proceedings in equity and probate or the large number of actions brought by indigent petitioners who agreed on the facts and submitted themselves to a summary ruling by a judge in chambers. As noted above, most criminal cases were litigated by private parties in magistrate's court. No handy statistical summary of those actions is available.[8]

At the stage of criminal prosecution antecedent to bringing an accused to court it is apparent that the policing authority of the state was almost entirely undeveloped. The citizenry provided a source of special constables but for most of the time they would be concerned with their private pursuits. In St John's, tavern owners comprised a constabulary by virtue of holding a licence. Governor Sir Thomas Duckworth changed this arrangement in 1812 by using higher licence fees to hire twelve stipendiary constables. No evidence has come to light to indicate that justices of the peace assumed any role in the investigation of complaints. They imposed the terms of recognizance and bail or committed an accused pending trial, and they presided at trial. The relative inability of the state to police and prosecute may help to explain the almost entire absence of court cases arising from the intimidation and violence that attended the activities of the poor and vagrant who roamed the settlements of Conception Bay in the hard winters of 1816–18. Many had been displaced by the post-war collapse of the fishery and were new to the neighbourhood. Hard to identify and faced by a constabulary of private citizens, the vagrants could disappear anonymously into the woods or the squatters' camps which were their temporary seasonal refuge. In an age when the apprehension of criminals relied heavily on informants, a community that closed ranks presented the authorities with a wall of silence. And beyond the settled communities of the Avalon peninsula and the northeast coast lay a vast, largely unsettled, and entirely unpoliced frontier of hundreds of coves which might offer a new beginning or a way station to the mainland of British North America or the New England states.[9]

A haphazard policing power and the absence of a state prosecutor may have meant that criminal prosecutions were pursued by private parties at their own expense, in keeping with the undeveloped nature of government and of societal institutions. All may be said to have been grounded in the uncertain constitutional status of Newfoundland. A population of 60,000 by war's end in 1815 comprised a settled society which might justify local governance, colonial status, and, eventually, representative government. But for the first fifteen years of the period under examination there were few government institutions in place outside the courts and their ancillary personnel: sheriff, clerk [registrar], and grand jury. The last passed on bills of indictment and made presentments to the governor on administrative matters. There were few facilities for more than brief incarceration. Attempts to tax fishermen in order to build jails had run into stiff opposition locally and from the West Country merchants ever since 1729. The usual penalty was a fine or forfeiture. Jails were scarce, and the cost of housing a prisoner was a charge on the successful plaintiff. Clearly, a fine was to be preferred, especially after 1788 when it had to be split with the crown.

Societal institutions were largely the result of private initiatives and only recently established. The first newspaper appeared in 1806, preceded by several philanthropic societies (1803), two private schools (1804), a postal service (1805), a mercantile society (1806), various benevolent and fraternal organizations, a public reading room (1810), a volunteer fire brigade and the beginnings of a hospital (1811), and a constabulary in St John's (1812). Evidently, English ministries and parliament continued to resist funding governance, with the exception of the courts. The island appeared in the parliamentary estimates only from 1787. In 1791 the £1,182 budgeted was slightly less than that provided for the Island of St John (Prince Edward Island), slightly more than half the allocation for Cape Breton, and less than a fifth of that for mainland Nova Scotia. Instructions to Governor Holloway, still only seasonally resident in 1806, echoed the continuity of imperial policy stretching back through the statutes of the eighteenth century to that of 1699: 'You are to make the most attentive inquiries, – whether any measures could now be taken for the further encouragement and promoting the return of every such seaman and fisherman to the part of our European dominions to which he belongs.' In sum, settlement patterns, an absence of state prosecutorial or policing function, underfunding, and an ambiguous constitutional status largely denied local authorities the means to monitor or move against real or apprehended seditious speech and conspiracy.[10] The likelihood that such manifestations of disloyalty might occur or threaten imperial authority is a question to which we now turn.

NEWFOUNDLAND IN BRITISH DEFENCE STRATEGY

Sedition and disloyalty, with a consequent threat to social unity and state security, are typically identified by the official mind in areas which the enemy most closely threatens and in which his propaganda might be most appealing. This was as true of the southeast coast of England or of John Bull's back door in Ireland as it was of France's northeastern departments during the Revolutionary and Napoleonic Wars. But Newfoundland was far from the front lines of war during the eighteenth century, and it remained so until well into the twentieth. With British naval power supreme in the Atlantic by 1763, and unassailable after Trafalgar in 1805, Britain did not need to provide either a strong garrison or a strong naval presence in Newfoundland. British defence strategy was to overawe and blockade the French navy in its home ports (Bonaparte's strongest naval squadron never made it out from its home port of Brest for Trafalgar) to prevent its access to the North Atlantic and to the Mediterranean. Thereby England's imperial interests, territorial and commercial, were safeguarded. This strategy sufficed to deny France the role of rival or challenger overseas. Wedded to a policy of supporting and subsidizing continental allies which forced France to divert her energies to Europe, it brought victory and, by 1815, supremacy. A watching brief on Newfoundland could be kept by convoys, escorted by the navy from the Caribbean and from home metropolitan waters, which made their rendezvous off St John's. The Gulf of St Lawrence and Britain's mainland colonies were guarded from Halifax. The entry of the United States into the war in 1812 momentarily raised the spectre of a renewal of the successful Franco-American alliance of 1778, but by then France was tied down in eastern and central Europe and on the Iberian peninsula. The Americans were not strong enough to threaten Britain's naval predominance on the Halifax–St John's station. Privateers had some initial success off the south coast in 1812 but they were countered by reinforcements to the local squadron which captured ten American vessels for every loss. For a short time, the defences at St John's, and those at Placentia which had been dismantled in 1811, were renewed. Given Britain's naval domination, however, the practical and less expensive policy was to permit the fall of Newfoundland to the enemy, for it could always be recaptured in the next campaigning season. But after Trafalgar the threat from France in this respect was removed and the Americans were not strong enough to try.[11]

Newfoundland was a case study in the success of Britain's imperial strategy. At the outbreak of war with France in 1793, England had one fifty-gun ship on station, accompanied by four smaller craft. From the English Channel a fleet of seventy-five ships of the line kept Newfoundland and the North American and Caribbean colonies secure. Of 345 British naval losses between 1803 and 1815, only three occurred off Newfoundland. All three ships were wrecked, in a notoriously hostile maritime environment, as distinguished from being captured, between 1812 and 1815. Britain's naval domination of the North Atlantic was evident.

By the end of 1796 France had been shut out from the region; from then until 1811, not a single enemy cruiser appeared off Newfoundland's coast. The threat from the United States in 1812 was short-lived as well. Two hundred American prisoners were exchanged for the captured *Alert* in 1812, and five hundred more were housed in a prison hulk in St John's harbour at war's end.

As a result of its successful war strategy, Britain was spared the task and expense of garrisoning large contingents of regular troops or maintaining a militia. Private attempts to raise and equip fencibles soon petered out. The third and most successful of these initiatives was the creation of the Royal Newfoundland Volunteers, which in 1793 replaced troops dispatched to take and garrison St Pierre. Given bi-weekly rations but not the bounty (pay) to which they felt entitled, they rapidly faded from the scene. Even their successors, the Royal Newfoundland Regiment of fencibles from 1795, equipped and paid as regular troops, were a luxury that imperial policy did not need and that local pride and loyalty could not sustain. A garrison, with or without local fencibles and volunteers to back it up, was not a military necessity.[12] On the one occasion when a French squadron slipped through the British net to maraud in the North Atlantic, it gained only short-term success and finally had no option but to return home, once again to run the British blockade of French ports.

ADMIRAL RICHERY IN 1796: A MOMENTARY CHALLENGE

The activities of ten ships under the command of Admiral Joseph de Richery in 'ravaging the coast' south of St John's and at Chateau Bay, Labrador, in the late fall of 1796 have been hailed in the nationalist literature as the final attempt by the French to conquer Newfoundland. In truth, his mission appears to have been more modest: possibly to destroy St John's, to recapture St Pierre, and generally to make a nuisance of himself in a region where the Royal Navy was unchallenged. In September 1795 Richery had slipped out of Toulon with nine warships and three frigates and gained three weeks' sailing advantage on Rear Admiral Robert Mau, who had been shadowing him. Two days after Mau gave chase Richery captured thirty ships out of a Levant convoy of sixty-three off Cape St Vincent and put into Cadiz. In light of the impending Franco-Spanish alliance of 19 August 1796, Mau withdrew his surveillance on 29 July. Five days later Richery sailed, reaching the Grand Banks on 28 August and patrolling off St John's for two days in early September. Of the four or five ships that Governor Vice-Admiral Sir James Wallace had on station, only one (of thirty-two guns) was available in St John's. The garrison and volunteers, after the declaration of martial law, totalled fewer than 700 men. By contrast, Richery's ten ships ranged from thirty-six to eighty-four guns, with 2000 troops aboard. The town was mobilized, a chain was stretched across the harbour, and news was sent to Halifax. The next step lay with the French admiral. He considered landing to the north of the town at Torbay, but he lacked a local pilot. At Bay Bulls, about thirty kilometres south of St John's, he may even have begun an overland march. In the end he destroyed the settlement and its fishing vessels, took the inhabitants prisoner, dispatched two or three ships to Labrador to raze fishing premises, and sailed to recapture St Pierre. There he put his prisoners on board a captured vessel for Halifax. By 11 December he was back in Brest, too late to participate in the French expedition to Ireland.

Two fishing masters, Charles McCarthy and John Morridge, were captured at Bay Bulls and interviewed by an English-speaking French officer. They later claimed that they had passed on misleading information about the strength of the St John's garrison, stressing Governor Wallace's determination to fight to the death. In the nationalist folklore, the town and Newfoundland were thereby saved for England. But what would the French have gained by taking St John's? They could neither defend it for long nor reinforce it. McCarthy reported that the seventy-four-gun *Jupiter* was leaky, requiring the pumps to be manned every two hours, and that 'no discipline seemed to be preserved on board.' Wallace remained confident for the long run. By 29 September, in writing London of Richery's success at St Pierre, the governor welcomed the release of the prisoners as a sign that the French intended to depart: they had not landed elsewhere, and 'we are in no apprehension of them coming here.' Wallace sailed for home on 31 October, leaving St John's 'well supplied with every necessary, and under no apprehension from the enemy.'

Under a British naval umbrella and without a local newspaper before 1806, St John's was doubly insulated. 'From 1796 to 1811,' Gerald Graham writes, 'Newfoundland remained untouched by the war.' Except for occasional consignments of French prisoners there appears to have been no pool for the development of local sympathy for France. There is no indication of any in the correspondence of the governors or of Roman Catholic Bishop James Louis O'Donel. The citizenry responded loyally and, according to Wallace, the 'volunteers behaved very well.' Thomas Paine's *Age of Reason and the Rights of Man* was known in St John's, noted Anspach, but it is less certain that it had 'poisoned the public mind.'[13] Occasional manifestations of opposition to the military authorities did not emanate from pro-French sentiment, and they were not given life by Richery's foray of 1796. Rather, it was local discontent with press gangs and the natural, even justified, grousing of seamen and soldiers against the conditions of their service that would raise the spectre of disaffection in the official mind. Outbreaks were taken seriously, but they inspired no popular wave of discontent and were accepted at the time as isolated incidents. However, sedition in the military is mutiny. It was that threat, real or apprehended, that occupied the official mind in 1797 and in 1800.

THE LATONA, 1797

'The greatest mutiny in the history of the Royal Navy,' which began at Spithead, near Portsmouth, and spread to the Nore in Kent in April and May 1797, had repercussions in Newfoundland.[14] The crew of the *Latona*, which was obviously disaffected, had sailed from Spithead to the Nore without permitting her captain to board. Nevertheless, the mutineers undertook to go to sea if the French appeared. Supplemented by pressed men who can only have made the situation more volatile, the *Latona* sailed uneventfully in convoy to St John's. Trouble did not occur until she was set to depart Newfoundland on the morning of 3 September. When the foretopmen were ordered aloft, the first step in taking the ship to sea, they refused. Captain Sotheron had the ringleader seized, officers and marines drew their arms, the crew was prevented from rescuing its leader, and he was flogged. Only he appears to have been punished, despite the continuing discontent. According to Governor Vice-Admiral William Waldegrave, 'the language of the seamen when in their hammocks was terrible. The Marines were threatened with being thrown overboard and bloody work was promised as soon as the ship would again be in blue water. The conduct of these wretches on shore has been no less wicked and daring; they have certainly endeavoured to sow sedition within the garrison, besides committing many outrages on diverse occasions.'

Perhaps the public flogging sufficed. No other crews in the convoy rose up. And when news came via a newly arrived vessel that the mutinies at home had been suppressed but that the seamen's demands for reform had been met, it was left only for Waldegrave to temper a public lecture on loyalty and discipline with a call for unity and a common front against the enemy. To this end, a public example was made of Sergeant James Dailey of the Royal Newfoundland Regiment who had declared to some seamen of the *Latona* that five or six hundred soldiers were ready to follow their example were they to take the lead.

This was serious stuff. Upon inquiry it was agreed that Dailey had been drunk at the time. Claiming no recollection of what he may have said, Dailey offered a public recantation, staged by Waldegrave, before being sent to Halifax for court martial. Whether or not disaffection, which the governor called sedition, was rampant, the official mind was prepared to assume that it was. Public protestations of loyalty were solicited from other service units but nothing has come to light to confirm active disloyalty, as distinguished from grousing, among the servicemen, much less among the civilian population. Waldegrave reported no further on the matter when he sent his next dispatch to London two months later. In retrospect, however, Dailey's drunken mutterings appeared prophetic when his regiment seemed to be a hotbed of United Irish sympathy and, by definition, sedition in 1800.

THE MUTINY OF 25 APRIL 1800

The transition from a migratory seasonal fishery to one carried on by permanent residents comprised several factors, all of which perpetuated, even increased, the insecurity of life in Newfoundland. But war was good for trade; it strengthened demand for salted and pickled cod, and it increased Newfoundland's access both to the English market and to markets controlled by Britain in the empire and Europe. Wages reached unprecedented heights in 1815.

Wartime prosperity had attracted thousands of immigrants, most from the southeastern provinces of Munster and Leinster where the merchant and fishing ships stopped to pick up agricultural supplies and young men for the fishery. The wave of migrants was unprecedented and never to be duplicated: 670 in 1807, the vast majority Irish, was a modest prelude to the rush of immigrants in the last few years of the Napoleonic Wars, 7000 arriving in 1815. In the five years down to 1816 the Roman Catholic population of St John's doubled to 21,000 to comprise half the town's residents.[15] How many of these were transients intending to make their way to greener pastures on the North American mainland is uncertain; many probably intended to try their luck locally to see what developed. The immigrants, most of whom were young men without resources – 'dieters,' in local parlance – sought subsistence during the off-season against work and clearing off their debt in the following fishing season. With them came factional rivalries and loyalties.

Who among them were fishermen declining to return home at the end of the fishing season, and who were deserters from the Royal Navy or the merchant marine, were questions that worried the authorities. Gubernatorial decrees enforcing the statutes against deserters were publicized, as were the offers of reward ('straggling money') for their apprehension. In a seaport town, predominantly male and liberally blessed with taverns (thirty-three in 1797 and thirty-five in 1807), opportunities for verbal and physical violence were legion. These were increased by the exigencies of war: reduced imports and higher food prices, foreign privateering, and war prize. Bishop O'Donel lamented in 1794 that 'all our first fleet to the foreign markets has been taken near the Western Islands; this destructive war has ruined this part of the New World.' Boredom, penury, cheap rum, poor housing (much of it illegal until 1811 as infringing on the shore facilities reserved by law to the use of the fishery), and random swoops by press gangs might ignite violent and inchoate protest. Seamen as 'bondsmen of the sea' had always been vulnerable to being pressed, and the statutes exempting fishermen were often ignored, especially during a war in which the Royal Navy's demand for seamen seemed insatiable.

In 1792 riots occurred in Trepassey on the southern Avalon peninsula and in St John's. The following year Lieutenant Lawry of the Royal Navy was killed in St John's while heading a press gang. The perpetrators were hanged, drawn, and quartered. In 1794 the captain of a merchant ship about to sail for Portugal gained the governor's permission to press eight or ten men from the St John's waterfront. The next afternoon, when one of his officers accompanied two of the men ashore to retrieve their clothes and some money owed them, he was murdered by a mob which set the pressed men free.[16]

Relations between successive Roman Catholic bishops (O'Donel, Patrick Lambert, and Thomas Scallen) and the English governors, commercial elite, and military commanders were cordial. Both sides pursued a policy of cooperation and accommodation in the interests of social peace. And while the bishops found their flock obedient on the whole, both elites kept a weather eye out for sympathizers of the Society of United Irishmen. The swearing of secret oaths of loyalty to that and other revolutionary organizations was illegal in England and the law was enforced in Newfoundland. The memory of the failed French attempt to invade Ireland in 1796 and the spectre of the rising of the United Irishmen under Wolfe Tone in 1798 made the local authorities, both lay and ecclesiastical, vigilant, especially in St John's. Fears of pro-Irish disaffection in town and within the Royal Newfoundland Regiment had informed official responses to the *Latona* episode in 1797. They did so again on 23 April 1800 when approximately fifty soldiers were party to a plot to desert. Twenty or so acted precipitately under the mistaken impression that the plot had been discovered. Twelve were captured. After court martial five were hanged and seven sent to Halifax for execution on 7 July. (Even the numbers are uncertain, David Webber recording that three were executed and eight had their death sentences commuted to life imprisonment.) There had been previous official doubts about the loyalty of the regiment; the Duke of Kent reported from Halifax to London in December 1799 that fully two-thirds were United Irishmen and that the whole regiment should be transferred. This step was accomplished as a consequence of the April events and the regiment was almost entirely replaced by British regulars.[17]

The affair still raises more questions than it answers. How many men were disaffected and/or party to the plot? How many deserted? Were they acting in liaison with local United Irish sympathizers? How far did the plot spread outside St John's, and what did the conspirators seek to accomplish? There is no consensus in the literature, and Cyril Byrne's authoritative preliminary account of 1984 does not appear to have been followed up. The regiment itself was undermanned and had not received the provisions, rations, or official support it had been promised. In his previous command Brigadier-General John Skerret had distinguished himself against the United Irishmen at home and had carried that reputation to St John's. Civilians were also aggrieved and apprehensive. The magistrates had recently enforced a ban on hogs running free in St John's. This gave rise to such a protest that rewards totalling 300 guineas were offered for information on the parties posting bills which threatened the person and property of the magistrates. Evidently, local feeling ran high on the issue.

Uncertainty about the war may have been another factor, for the last ship in harbour in 1799 had brought news of the destruction of the United Irish cause in Ireland, of Bonaparte's return to France from Egypt, and of successes by the combined French and Spanish fleets. Even the weather and the time of the year may have been factors. It was unseasonably mild, the warships were absent, and provisions and diversions after a long winter were in short supply. What is certain is that the danger did not persist. Governor Pole reported to London in October that on a visit to Placentia he found 'no appearance of ill humour.' In November he reported the 'present tranquil disposition of the inhabitants of this island.' To what extent that was due to the suppression of the mutiny, the cowing of local United Irish opinion, or the transfer of the Royal New-foundland Regiment (though a large section of the successor 66th was Roman Catholic) is not recorded. By autumn, of course, the rigours of the previous winter were a memory, the fishing season was just completed, and, presumably, the hogs were still running free in St John's. With the Peace of Amiens of 1801 about to offer a respite from war, the Act of Union between England and Ireland imposed, the Royal Navy in control of the North Atlantic, and the imperial government finally willing to sanction some, if largely locally generated, improvements to the security and quality of life in St John's, internal developments and consolidation were to dominate the local scene for a decade before the great waves of Irish immigration after 1811 presented new challenges.

ST JOHN'S FACTION FIGHTS

'Yellow-belly Corner,' D.W. Prowse notes, marked the spot where those wounded in street fights between rival immigrant gangs from Munster and Leinster washed themselves in a small brook running into St John's harbour. The factions had deep roots in rural eighteenth-century Ireland where their activities were distinguished by secrecy, oath taking, recruit-ment on the basis of friendship, kinship and community, ritual, escalating warnings to those they singled out, night-time intimidation and violence, and public displays of solidarity. The startling increase in the incidence of Irish immigration to Newfoundland, especially to the Avalon peninsula and Conception Bay, served to transfer these traditions and loyalties to Newfoundland. As at home, rival gangs in St John's appear to have had their local turf, their taverns, and their hangers-on. In the late war years the prosperity of the fishery meant that labourers had unaccustomed wealth, and as the long winter wound down they had time on their hands to get up to what Prowse good-naturedly dismisses as 'diversion and divilment.' However, Caesar Colclough, chief justice and administrator of the island, lately transferred from the same post in Prince Edward Island, saw in their activities a threat to law and order. In a celebrated dis-patch to Governor Sir Richard Keats on 21 March 1814, he told a long, detailed, and scaremongering story of incipient violence and riot. He was the hero of his own story, as he intervened forcefully to track down the perpetrators of social disruption and bring them to justice. The height-ened drama of the account was consistent with his recurring complaints about the misfortunes of health, finances, family, and career which marked his three unhappy years in St John's. Although the story was alarmist, he was himself an Irishman who prided himself on his reading of the national character. He was convinced of the existence of widespread gang violence which was difficult to eradicate.

Briefly summarized, his view was that high wages in the fishery had given rise to a desire for 'combination' by the workers. To this the employers offered a double negative: resistance and a wage cut. The chief justice foresaw the end of wartime prosperity and a period of serious readjustment ahead. Several nights of gangs marching to and fro and of crowds milling about the streets climaxed, perhaps significantly, on St Patrick's Day night when the chief justice weighed into crowds of 'some thousands' (of a winter population of perhaps 10,000), protesting, exhorting, arresting, and, by his own account, dispersing them. He reported no grievances or demands on the part of the men he encountered, being preoccupied with the crowds, the prevalence of oath taking, and the potential for trouble. Having mobilized the leading citizens, the magistracy, the constables, and the Roman Catholic bishop, Colclough commissioned a printer to post extracts from the Riot Act. Then he proceeded to head up a frantic and directionless search for unnamed ringleaders of rival bands bent on violence. He dismissed as naive cooler heads among his advisers, recognizing that not all shared his zeal. In an admission that is striking for our purposes, he noted that 'there is no design to attempt anything against the Government of this Country.' Of the few arrested, he later reported that the 'jurors have honourably and fairly performed their duty [but] the witnesses for the Crown, even the Constables, were unwilling ones.' Three of those arrested in the crowd received a week in jail and a three years' peace bond. One guilty of participation in 'two riots' was 'to be publicly whipped tomorrow from Sawyer's Corner to the Court House for the first, and confined six months for the last.' But because the guilty man was the sole support of wife and sisters, his remaining time would be forgiven when the fishing season recommenced if he would take ship for an outharbour. It was unlikely that three or four others whom he had in mind would be brought to court since not a single informant had come forward. There the affair rested. For the rest of his career in Newfoundland, Colclough refrained from leading in the streets by example, warning only that 'we must discover and put down the administering of oaths.'[18]

The episode may not have been unique, for faction fights and confrontations continued for some years in St John's, notably in 1819. That same year at Harbour Grace, the island's second town, the magistrate read the Riot Act and called upon St John's for reinforcements. Mustering the 'respectable inhabitants,' swearing in special constables, setting in place 'patroles and other measures of precaution,' and the arrival of a war ship sufficed to quieten lively spirits and reassure the official mind.[19]

It was not surprising that in the period 1793–1815, years of pervasive Irish immigration and undreamt-of wages, single men would seek diversion and sociability with their compatriots and release from a long hard winter by taking to the streets with the first signs of spring. Those experienced in Newfoundland ways took the faction fights in their stride, of a piece with mummering and the attendant settling of personal scores which in later years was to lead to the prohibition of mummering, yet another import from an English past. The risk perceived by cooler heads when faced by Colclough's forward policy was that a danger might be created where none was before. They may even have feared the loss of a socially sanctioned source for the release of individual tension and high spirits. The *Royal Gazette* from 1806 could not provide such an outlet, being both dull and deferential to authority. Only with the grant of representative government in 1832 was there an institutional mechanism which met the local propensity for lively debate, theatrics, occasional bombast, and a highly individual and personal form of politics. Succeeding generations of Newfoundlanders have proved enthusiastic players.

CRIPPLING POST-WAR WINTERS AND SOCIAL UNREST

Peace with France in 1815 and an end to hostilities with the United States brought a rapid and unwelcome readjustment to the Newfoundland economy. Markets, which months before had seemed insatiable, dried up. Unprecedented wage levels and heady talk of worker combinations gave way to unemployment, business insolvencies, and social distress. French fishermen, largely excluded from Newfoundland waters for a generation, returned to the French Shore. The Americans also came back, especially to the south coast, and in 1818 a convention implementing the Treaty of Ghent (1814) confirmed their right to fish from Ramea west and north to the tip of the northern peninsula, along the coast of Labrador, and into the Gulf of St Lawrence. Adding to the misery were a series of long, bitterly cold winters, the failure of a seal hunt which now supplemented the traditional reliance on cod, and fires which destroyed public buildings and jerry-built urban premises. Churches in Harbour Grace (1816) and Carbonear (1817) were destroyed. Half of St John's disappeared in successive fires on 7 and 21 November 1817. In September 1818, 20 houses went up in flames; in the following year, 120. Commentators muttered darkly of arson and decried the working classes' unwillingness to volunteer as firemen. They were guilty of looting; the only question was whether it was spontaneous or premeditated. And in the late winters of 1816–18 around the settlements of Conception Bay, a rabble of homeless Irish strangers intimidated the inhabitants into sharing their remaining potatoes, salt beef, and root crops. These were the 'winters of the rals' (rascals) when fire, frost, and famine stalked the land. (See app. 3, I.)

There were several reasons why this volatile mix did not lead to social confrontation, sedition, riot, or collective violence. First, contemporaries early recognized the nature and extent of the suffering. They organized relief and petitioned London for assistance. Captain David Buchan, administrator in the absence of governor and chief justice, took the lead in St John's and put his own crew of the *Pike* on short rations in order to share. Governor Francis Pickmore arrived in the spring of 1816 with £10,000 and the following spring Earl Bathurst provided another £3000, with £333 for funeral expenses. A meeting called by the high sheriff on the instructions of the surrogate and the magistrates at the courthouse in St John's on 10 January 1818 raised £300 'for the purpose of taking into consideration the distressed state of the town and the best method of relieving it.' An imperial statute in 1820 laid down regulations for rebuilding the town in a more permanent and secure form. Money and supplies were shipped by public subscription from Halifax and Boston.[20] And, whether out of fear, self-interest, or generosity, many private individuals shared staples with strangers. When confrontation and violence occurred around Conception Bay it was often when the poor or the vagrant who had been once to the well returned for more! In short, all shared in a general appreciation of the seriousness of the crisis and were determined, for whatever reason, to mitigate its worst effects. The word *starvation* was often used, but it was used advisedly.

Sometimes philanthropy had a sterner edge. The 'merchants and principal inhabitants' of Harbour Grace were summoned to the courthouse on 2 January 1817 'to take into consideration the best method of providing for or sending out of this country, the number of poor creatures now in a starving condition in this town.' Twenty-six male 'distressed objects of pity' were listed for deportation. They and their dependants were wished a 'safe passage ... and a happy sight of your native country.' Those failing to catch the boat to St John's would be flogged and jailed on a diet of bread and water for the remainder of the winter. In October the same solid citizens called for further deportations. In the aftermath of the fires of 1817, a meeting of the respectable inhabitants of St John's chaired by the chief magistrate, Thomas Coote, petitioned the governor to supplement the nightwatch kept by the citizens with a military guard of fifteen soldiers. He refused, but remained open to a renewed request should an emergency arise.

A measured response was consistent with the general view that the crisis was exceptional. War and peace, international politics, wartime immigration, and the weather had all somehow conspired. No one was immune. The propertied and relatively wealthy lost their livelihood as suddenly and irredeemably as did fisherman and 'dieter.' In the month following the closing of the seasonal accounts in October 1815, 700 writs were issued and 40 firms declared insolvency. Cases heard by Chief Justice Francis Forbes after his arrival in the fall of 1817 attest to the large sums of money involved: *Patrick Coleman v. John Kennedy* (11 August), for a debt of £643 remaining on a contract of £1200; *James Bristowe and John Bristowe v. Trustees Butler and Jodrey Estates* (20 August), for £723 owing on a bottomry bond; *John Cookesly and Wife v. Francis Buckley* (25 August), for a debt of £2108; *John Square v. Matthew and Co* (30 August), for a debt of £3716. Nearly all merchants in the fish trade, having exhausted their credit with English suppliers and being owed fish or funds by the local fishermen, are said by Prowse to have gone bankrupt.

Self-interest likely loomed large in the donations and exertions of some who brought relief. From Renews and Bay Bulls on the southern Avalon peninsula and from around Conception Bay came news of starving crewmen and bands of strangers. The West Country merchants who appeared before a parliamentary committee reporting on the crisis were unsympathetic, calling for mass deportations, bounties for the fishery, and exceptional aid. But the few witnesses from the front line whose letters were received or who testified stressed the all-encompassing nature of the crisis. Beyond the natural rapacity of shiftless vagrants which provided the *leitmotif* of the English merchants' view, James Henry Attwood, a delegate of the merchants of St John's, argued the wider context of the crisis. The French had returned and were expelling English fishermen from the French Shore. The Americans had undercut the market. Spanish duties were high. The island was a settled colony in all but name, but its governance reflected King William's Act of 1699, 'now ill adapted for the regulation of a community so extensive as that which at present exists ... in Newfoundland.' He testified that 'thousands ... of hardy industrious men were daily walking the streets, without money ... provisions ... lodgings ... [or] employment ... depending on casual charity ... and ... lodging on the snow-covered ... merchants' wharfs.'[21]

To what extent a determined stand by the authorities served to contain the possibility of widespread violence is unclear. Was the swearing-in of 121 special constables in 10 communities around Conception Bay in the 13 months after 30 July 1816 a sign of strength or weakness? Constables were in short supply, even when the new ones were summoned, according to some complainants. Affidavits were sworn by those who had lost supplies, but few prosecutions resulted. Perhaps the obvious penury of the perpetrators weighed with the aggrieved. And there was no denying that, once eaten, that which had been carried away could not be recovered. Often the 'rals' disappeared into the woods. Only when they were known could they be identified. When it came to barrels of potatoes, restitution was preferred to revenge. In addition, the cost to the plaintiff of jailing the guilty ruled out that remedy. Often the intervention of a respected figure, priest or neighbour, served to cool hot tempers. It would have to be contemporaneous if the goods were to be recovered and restitution effected, an unlikely confluence of events.[22] Isolation, the lack of police, the large number of strangers, and the end of a long and bitter winter appear at this distance to have been determining factors. With spring came berths on the sealing fleets, followed by the summer fishery. For those with the leisure for politics, optimism was spurred by Britain's implicit recognition of the permanence of settlement, the right from 1811 to private property, the decision in 1818 to have the governor join the chief justice in year-round residence, the appointment of a governor's executive council in 1823, and the recognition that changes were imminent within the empire. The propaganda war for recognition, colonial status, and representative institutions continued, but from 1815 Newfoundland, like other white imperial dependencies, was pushing at an open door.[23]

Throughout Newfoundland's uncertain past, local pride and a sense of identity had grown from the simple fact of survival. In 1815, legally and practically, imperial attitudes still reflected statutory priorities reiterated from 1699: a migratory fishery that would exclude European rivals, increase England's mercantile wealth and imperial status, and serve as a nursery for seamen for the Royal Navy, all as cheaply as possible. But at the end of two and a half centuries of wars against European rivals for naval and imperial influence, Great Britain stood pre-eminent. The empire was now a useful adjunct, not of an inward-looking and exclusionary mercantilism, but of industrialization and free trade. That prospect opened the door to new priorities, world power, and an imperial policy that encouraged rationalization, participation by the colonies in their own governance, and a degree of partnership which would serve England's interests and her new world role.

In an age of self-determination and world politics, Newfoundland would assume a new form of dependency. No longer a 'great English ship moored near the Banks' to provide fish and seamen,[24] she would now serve England's interests by trying to stand on her own. Although granted the rights and responsibilities of a colony and then a dominion, she would face the challenges they presented without the resources, population, institutions, or experience of her contemporaries.

The conclusion is a sober one and clearly subject to revision as the legal history of the jurisdiction is developed. But to this point it appears that, during an age of revolution when so many on either side of the Atlantic were swept up in challenge and change, Newfoundland remained apart. Change had been, and would continue to be, slow and sometimes painful. Continuity distinguished the Newfoundland experience down to 1815. Settlement had been discouraged since 1699, but it was governance that was withheld. The ad hoc provision of the basic institutions and machinery of a legal system through the exercise of the royal prerogative after 1729 was dictated by the statutory priorities of 1699. In law, this was still true a century later. Newfoundland's dependence on Britain and the insulating protection of the Royal Navy left little occasion for sedition. While English law was applicable in Newfoundland, the statutory legitimacy of her courts for the long run was affirmed only in 1809. Title to land was sanctioned from 1811.[25] A large enough population with a sense of permanence necessary to build a settled society was apparent by 1815. Sedition and riot as tools against the state can only be employed when a state is in place. In the absence of a full-time governor, a civil service, a garrison of more than a few troops, and representative institutions, only the rudiments of a state had been achieved. For the immediate future the priorities of most Newfoundlanders, if indeed they were beginning to see themselves as such, would continue to be survival, communal methods of dispute resolution, and accommodation to the harsh realities of an uncertain life in an unforgiving environment.

NOTES

1 R. v. John Reeve [sic] (1796) 26 State Trials, at 591, as cited in Sir James Fitzjames Stephen, A History of Criminal Law of England, 3 vols. (London: 1883), 2: at 368. The jury decided that 'the pamphlet which has been proved to have been writ-

ten by John Reeve. Esq., is a very improper publication, but being of the opinion that his motives were not such as laid in the information, find him not
guilty.' John Reeves, *History of the Government of the Island of Newfoundland*
(London: J. Sewell 1793). Peter Neary, 'Reeves, John,' *DCB* 6: 636. *Clift v. Holdsworth* (1819), in *Select Cases of Newfoundland, 1817–1828*, ed. R.A. Tucker (Toronto: Carswell 1979), 189. All Newfoundland cases are in the Supreme Court
unless otherwise indicated. Supreme Court Minutes, 1811–1855, GN 5/2/A/1,
31 (1819–21), Colonial Secretary Lord Bathurst to Governor Hamilton, 12 Sept.
1820, PANL. (1817) *R. v. Patrick Kent* [unreported], ibid., Letter Books of the
Colonial Secretary (Nfld), at 28, 164 (November/December 1817).

2 Leon Radzinowicz, *A History of English Criminal Law and its Administration from
1750*, 4 vols. (London: Stevens 1948) 1: at 25, proposes habeas corpus, Magna
Carta (1215), the Petition of Right (1628), the Bill of Rights (1689), and the jury
system as foundations of the common law. Keith Matthews, *Collection and
Commentary on the Constitutional Laws of Seventeenth Century Newfoundland* (St
John's: Maritime History Group 1975). Seaman was the contemporary term for
sailor. On the continuity of the Newfoundland nationalist school of historiography, which sees English West Country fishing interests and their allies or
puppets in government as the insuperable bar to local governance, see Keith
Matthews, 'Historical Fence-Building: A Critique of Newfoundland Historiography,' *Newfoundland Quarterly*, [*NQ*], vol. 74 (1978), 21, and Christopher
English, 'From Fishing Schooner to Colony: The Legal Development of Newfoundland, 1791–1832,' in *Law, Society and the State: Essays in Modern Legal History*, ed. Susan Binnie and Louis Knafla (Toronto: University of Toronto Press
1995), 141. The indispensable study of official policy and the seasonal migratory fishery is Keith Matthews, 'A History of the West of England–Newfoundland Fishery' (D.Phil. thesis, Oxford University, 1968).

3 Matthews, *Collection* and 'Newfoundland Fishery.' *Newfoundland Discovered:
English Attempts at Colonisation, 1610–1630*, ed. Gillian T. Cell (London: Hak-
luyt Society 1982). F.F. Thompson, *The French Shore Problem in Newfoundland:
An Imperial Study* (Toronto: University of Toronto Press 1961), provides
excerpts from the relevant acts. The 'French Shore' was defined in the Treaty
of Utrecht (1713) as running north and west from Cape Bonavista to Point
Riche on the western shore of the northern peninsula; from the Treaty of Versailles (1783) to 1904, it was seen as running from Cape St John to Cape Ray
and embracing the northwest and west coasts of the island.

4 (1699) 10/11 William III, c. 25 [King William's Act]. All statutes are imperial
unless indicated otherwise. Ralph Greenlee Lounsbury, *The British Fishery at
Newfoundland, 1634–1763* (Hamden: Archon 1969), at 272–309. Frederic F.
Thompson, 'Osborn, Henry,' *DCB* 4: 594. Lewis Amadeus Anspach, *A History*

of Newfoundland (London: Sherwood, Gilbert and Piper 1827), at 144. Keith Matthews, 'Hutchings, Richard,' DCB 5: 443. (1791) 31 Geo. III, c. 29, (1792) 32 Geo. III, c. 27, s. 1. Opinions of Eminent Lawyers on Various Points of English Jurisprudence, ed. George Chalmers (Burlington: C. Goodrich 1858), at 541–3. The statutes between 1699 and 1792 are parsed in Christopher English, 'The Development of the Newfoundland Legal System to 1815,' Acadiensis, vol. 20 (1990), no.1, 89.

5 On reception, see the introduction to this volume. To the sources cited there in n.18 add: Christopher P. Curran, 'Introduction: The Judicature Act: A History of the Early Acts,' in Newfoundland Law Reform Commission (NLRC), Legislative History of the Judicature Act, 1791–1988 (St John's: NLRC 1989); E.M. Archibald, Digest of the Laws of Newfoundland (St John's: Henry Winton 1847), at 37–8, 45; Chalmers, Opinions, at 511; (1809) 49 Geo. III, c. 27; Buyers Furniture v. Barney's Sales and Transport (1983) 43 Nfld and PEIR (CA) 158; Christopher English, 'Newfoundland's Early Laws and Legal Institutions: From Fishing Admirals to the Supreme Court of Judicature in 1791–92,' in Canada's Legal Inheritances, ed. DeLloyd Guth and W. Wesley Pue (Winnipeg: University of Manitoba Press 1995), 59.

6 Gertrude E. Gunn, The Political History of Newfoundland, 1832–1864 (Toronto: University of Toronto Press 1966), at 39. (1837) 1 Vict., c. 4 (Nfld) s. 1.

7 J.M. Bumsted, 'Colclough, Caesar,' DCB 6: 161. David Davis, 'Simms, James,' DCB 9: 720. Diane Janes, 'Dawe, William,' Encyclopedia of Newfoundland and Labrador, 5 vols., ed. J.R. Smallwood (Newfoundland Book Publishers 1981), 1: 600. Rupert W. Bartlett, 'The Legal Profession in Newfoundland,' The Book of Newfoundland, 6 vols., ed. J.R. Smallwood (Newfoundland Book Publishers 1967), 3: 519. Patrick O'Flaherty, 'Forbes, Sir Francis,' DCB 7: 301. C.H. Currey, Sir Francis Forbes (Sydney: Angus and Robertson 1968). Leslie Harris and P.G. Cornell, 'Tucker, Richard,' DCB 9: 794. Tucker succeeded Forbes in 1822. (1809) 49 Geo. III, c. 27 returned Labrador to Newfoundland. GN 5/6/A/1, Court of Oyer and Terminer, 1816, 1822, PANL.

8 GN 2/1/A, 31 (1819–21), Governor Hamilton to Lord Bathurst, 19 Nov. 1819, 65–6, 26 July 1821, 508–11, PANL. The governor noted that 'in all cases in which the Crown, the officers of Government or the Magistracy are concerned there is no person capable of conducting causes on their part, or advising thereon, the causes are generally lost, there being no advantage that these Petty Attorneys are not ready to take and magnify to the utmost, nor is it possible in some cases to bring a culprit guilty of the most atrocious crime to the punishment which the law directs, mainly owing to the want of a proper Prosecutor.' He also asked for an advocate to act for the government in the court of Vice-Admiralty. Unlike the situation in contemporary England, no activities

by (private) prosecuting associations or thief takers (bounty hunters) have come to light in Newfoundland.

9 William H. Whiteley, *Duckworth's Newfoundland: The Island in the Early Nineteenth Century* (St John's: Harry Cuff 1985), at 18.

10 Keith Matthews, 'Brooking, Thomas Holdsworth,' *DCB* 9: 84 at 85. Patrick O'Flaherty, 'Government in Newfoundland before 1832: The Context of Reform,' *NQ*, vol. 84, no. 2. (1988), 26. Helen Taft Manning, *British Colonial Government after the American Revolution, 1782–1820* (New Haven, Conn.: Yale University Press 1933), at 194. By 1810 the parliamentary grant was £4551 of which £1500 paid the salaries of governor and chief justice. Whiteley, *Duckworth's Newfoundland*, at 15. (1788) 28 Geo. III, c. 35. Gerald Graham, 'Fisheries and Sea Power,' in *Historical Essays on the Atlantic Provinces*, ed. G.A. Rawlyk (Ottawa: Carleton Library 1967), 7 at 12.

11 Gerald Graham, 'Fisheries' and *Sea Power and British North America, 1783–1820* (Cambridge: Harvard University Press 1941), passim; 'Newfoundland and British Strategy from Cabot to Napoleon,' *Newfoundland: Economic, Diplomatic and Strategic Studies*, ed. R.A. Mackay (Toronto: Royal Institute of International Affairs 1946), 245. Graham's continuing influence is evident in Paul M. Kennedy, *The Rise and Fall of British Naval Mastery* (London: Allen Lane 1976). Olaf Janzen, 'Napoleonic Wars,' *Encyclopedia*, 4:5, and 'The Royal Navy and the Defence of Newfoundland during the American Revolution,' *Acadiensis* vol. 16 (1984), 28. William Laird Clowes, *The Royal Navy* (New York: AMS Press 1966), 5: at vi.

12 Clowes, *Royal Navy*, 4: at 197–8, 548–55. G.W.L. Nicholson, 'Skinner, Thomas,' *DCB* 5: 762, and *The Fighting Newfoundlander. A History of the Royal Newfoundland Regiment* (St John's: Government of Newfoundland 1964), at 16–32. Stuart R.J. Sutherland, 'Skinner, Robert Pringle,' *DCB* 5: 762, and 'Pringle, Robert,' ibid., 647. David Webber, *Skinner's Fencibles: The Royal Newfoundland Regiment, 1795–1802* (St John's: 1964), and *The St. John's Volunteer Rangers: 1805–1814* (St John's, n.d.).

13 D.W. Prowse, *A History of Newfoundland from the English, Colonial and Foreign Records* (London: Macmillan 1895), at 367–73. Paul O'Neill, *A Seaport Legacy: The Story of St. John's, Newfoundland* (Erin: Press Porcepic 1976), at 97–8. The story is best told in Clowes, *Royal Navy*, 4: at 277–91, and in CO 194/39 (1796–7), Wallace to the Duke of Portland, 9, 29 Sept. 1796, 2 Feb. 1797, PANL. Cyril J. Byrne, *Gentlemen–Bishops and Faction Fighters* (St John's: Jesperson 1984), passim. Anspach, *History*, at 228.

14 Captain A. Fisk, 'Mutiny in Newfoundland, August 1797' *Canadian Defence Quarterly*, vol. 16 (1984), 58. CO 194\39, Waldegrave to Portland, 14 Aug. 1797, 86–216. Patrick O'Flaherty, 'Waldegrave, William,' *DCB* 6: 795. Webber, *Fencibles*, at 21–39.

15 Grant Head, *Eighteenth Century Newfoundland* (Ottawa: Carleton Library 1976), at 198, 206, 237. Paul O'Neill, *The Oldest City: The Story of St. John's, Newfoundland* (Erin: Press Porcepic 1975), at 51. Raymond J. Lahey, 'Scallan, Thomas,' *DCB* 6: 690 at 691.

16 For the governors' decrees against desertion, see MG 24, A 45, Series A, decree of [Governor Sir] Maurice Pole, 16 Aug. 1800 (at 3333), and decree of [Governor] James Gambier, 31 Aug. 1803 (at 3388), NA. See also Webber, *Fencibles*, at 61–2, decree of Governor Waldegrave, 16 Oct. 1799. On taverns, see Prowse, *Newfoundland*, at 375, 381, 394. He notes that, in 1813, 426,000 gallons of rum were imported, supplemented by the spirits captured from French and American prizes. Byrne, *Gentlemen–Bishops*, 125 at 127, O'Donel to Troy, 28 Nov. 1794. J.R. Hutchinson, *The Press Gang* (London: Eveleigh Nash 1913), at 7, 20, 30–3, 51, 95. Nicholson, *Fighting Newfoundlander*, at 27.

17 Byrne, *Gentlemen–Bishops*, passim. O'Donel's account of the mutiny is in ibid., O'Donel to [Archbishop] Plessis [of Quebec] 14 May 1800, at 171–3. Terrence Murphy, 'The Emergence of Maritime Catholicism, 1781–1830,' *Acadiensis*, vol. 12 (1984), 29. CO 194\42 (1799–1800), Portland to Governor Maurice Pole, 2 July 1800, Pole to Portland, 14 Aug. 1800 (enclosing letter from Jonathan Ogden to Waldegrave, 2 July 1800), at 155–69, and Pole to Portland, 25 Oct. 1800, at 213–16. Ogden's account of the mutiny is reproduced in Prowse, *Newfoundland*, at 418–19, and Webber, *Fencibles*, at 65–7. The most comprehensive secondary account, unfootnoted, is Byrne, 'Ireland and Newfoundland: The United Irish Rising of 1800 and the Fencibles' Mutiny in St. John's, 1799 [sic],' ms. (St. John's: Newfoundland Historical Society 1977). See also, Lahey, *James Louis O'Donel in Newfoundland, 1784–1807* (St John's: Newfoundland Historical Society 1984), at 25–8. G.W.L. Nicholson, 'Skerrett, John,' *DCB* 5: 761. M.P. Morris, 'A Crisis in Newfoundland History,' *The Irish Monthly* (1878), 101.

18 Prowse, *Newfoundland*, at 390–3, 401–2. Paul E.W. Roberts, 'Caravats and Shanavests: Whiteboyism and Faction Fighting in East Munster, 1802–1811,' in *Irish Peasants: Violence and Political Unrest, 1780–1940*, ed. Samuel Clark and James S. Donnelly (Madison: University of Wisconsin Press 1983), 64. Bumsted, 'Colclough,' at 163. CO 194/55, Colclough to Governor Keats, 21 March 1814, 233–41. Despite dismissing the danger discerned by Colclough, Prowse notes that in 1813 a 'very large commission of the Peace was issued' to twenty-one justices of the peace in specific communities and seven for the island as a whole.

19 GN/2/1/A, 30, Magistrate of Harbour Grace to Colonial Secretary, 20, 21, 28 May 1819, 118–21.

20 *Royal Gazette*, 29 Aug., 3 Sept. 1816, 10 Jan. 1817. Anspach, *History*, at 265–76. Prowse, *History*, at 403–10. Frederic F. Thompson, 'Pickmore, Francis,' *DCB* 5: 671. (1820) 1 Geo. IV, c. 51.

21 *Royal Gazette*, 10 Jan. 1817. Prowse, *History*, at 404, cited Chief Surrogate Coote to Keats, December 1815, on the number of writs issued since October. GN 5/2/A/1, Supreme Court (15 July–17 Dec. 1817), 40–2, 85, 88–94, 95, 110. GN 2/A/1, Petition from Harbour Grace to Governor Pickmore, 30 Oct. 1817, at 93. Ibid., Petition from St John's to the Governor, 6 Jan. 1818, at 257–8. Great Britain, House of Commons, *Select Committee on Newfoundland Trade*, 26 June 1817, testimony of James Henry Attwood, at 23. The committee reported in less than a page and appended the witnesses' testimony. It proved more sympathetic to the popular suffering than the West Country businessmen. There was a 'pressing urgency' to recognize 'the sufferings experienced by the great majority of a very exhausted population, amounting ... to the certainty of absolute Famine; and which has already involved ... the violation of private property and the destruction of civilized order. Unless ... immediate relief ... be granted ... the horrors of the ensuing winter will ... be ... increased.' At risk was the viability of the fishery and its nursery for seamen. On the economy of the period under study, see Shannon Ryan, 'Fishery to Colony: A Newfoundland Watershed, 1793–1815,' *Acadiensis*, vol. 12 (1990), 34.

22 GN 2/1/A, 31 (1818–21), 'Special Constables Sworn in Conception Bay, 30 July 1816 to 30 July 1817.' Excerpts from some of the affidavits sworn during the troubles are appended.

23 On imperial policy, see Phillip Buckner, 'The Colonial Office and British North America, 1801–50,' *DCB* 8: xiii. For a less sanguine view of British policy at war's end, see Graham, *Sea Power*, at 269–70.

24 Great Britain, House of Commons, *Reports from the Committee on the State of the Trade to Newfoundland* (1793), vol. 10: 413, testimony of William Knox.

25 The governor was permitted to grant title to property by (1811) 51 Geo. III, c. 45. It took the form of thirty-year leases.

10

Sir James Craig's 'Reign of Terror' and Its Impact on Emergency Powers in Lower Canada, 1810–13*

JEAN-MARIE FECTEAU,
F. MURRAY GREENWOOD, and
JEAN-PIERRE WALLOT

Legal history, like other history, is rooted in context. Its course is determined by the interplay of underlying forces, whether social, economic, political, ideological, military, or other, and in immediate events. Because Craig's 'reign of terror' has been the subject of much advanced research, it is peculiarly suited to an analysis that focuses on context, and such an analysis in its case again illustrates how complex historical explanation can be. The 'reign of terror' (1810–11) also invites exploration of issues raised by the suspension of the right to apply for the writ of habeas corpus, the means of contesting arbitrary imprisonment in political cases. This exploration is particularly illuminating when a comparative approach with the United States and Great Britain is adopted, as it is here. The subject, too, allows for a revealing examination of the 'Baconian' judiciary in early Lower Canada, a judiciary that invariably favoured the executive power in security cases. Although obvious in general outline, the significant impact of the 'reign of terror' on emergency powers, including martial law, during the War of 1812 has been neglected in the historiography.

Laws, of course, define the rights and rules by which individuals and

*Fecteau is responsible for the sections of the essay dealing with disturbances at La Malbaie, the Lachine riot (with Wallot), and martial law (with Greenwood). Greenwood supplied the immediate context to the Craig crisis and its legal aftermath, including the fate of the Better Preservation Act. Wallot provided the general context to the 'reign of terror.'

groups socially interact in an ordered fashion, whether in private or public matters. The state, which embodies the sovereignty of a nation and in which is vested the power to maintain 'Peace, Order and good Government,' and those who control it, create, amend, and apply the laws so as to ensure social stability in conformity with their perceived legitimate interests, often identified with those of the whole society. In its operations, the state or rather the interests controlling it define and rank needs, allocate resources to them, redistribute wealth, and try to maintain stability.[1]

In Lower Canada the situation was complex. The military government spent much more money than the civil government and occasionally invested in civil projects, although such might have been undertaken ostensibly for military reasons. The civil government itself was divided. On one side there was a governor who disposed of all executive powers and was advised by an Executive Council as well as by a Legislative Council, with members of both councils named by the British government. On the other side there was a House of Assembly, elected by the vast majority of heads of families (mostly owners of land or renters). In the British parliamentary system, cabinet, practically speaking, had to be supported over time by a majority of the elected members of the House of Commons. In the colony, however, the Executive Council was accountable to no one except the governor, and the latter only to the imperial government. Moreover, the Constitutional Act of 1791 did not specify how the two houses of the colonial parliament or they and the executive were supposed to interact. The working of the parliamentary machinery had to be learned by trial and error, mostly through conflict. Thus, in practice, the diverse interests in the colony could pick among various streams to promote their needs: the military government or the civil government or one of its components – between 1799 and 1807 the heads of the military and civil governments were different persons – while each branch of the legislature rested its legitimacy on different grounds, more or less derived from the cryptic text of the Constitutional Act and from British precedents.

The implementation and evolution of the political apparatus took place in the midst of important socio-economic upheavals, with a demographic surge through natural growth and immigration that finally sputtered, the explosion of exports-imports, financial changes, and more generally the accelerating pace of market forces in society as well as the rise of new social groups and the stagnation of others.[2] Moreover, Great Britain in 1791 had split the province of Quebec into Lower and Upper Canada in order, among other reasons, to divide its two ethnic groups, the English being concentrated to the west and the Canadiens to the east. Yet the most dynamic, richest, and powerful British North Americans (the 'English') lived in Lower Canada amidst a strong majority of conquered French Canadians or Canadiens, dreaming of a united, homogeneous, familiarly 'British' colony, blessed with the language, laws, and customs of the mother country and acting as the conduit of trade between Great Britain and its breakaway colonies to the south. They controlled virtually all the important patronage, contracts, and places through ascendancy in both councils and their links to the governor. The Canadiens, however, turned to their strong base in the assembly to try to carve a larger share of power for themselves and impose their own vision of a loyal Canadien colony inside the British empire.

The explosion under Craig was not so much a matter of law as of power. Laws and precedents were indeed used by both sides to justify their measures and countermeasures – and the revealing nature of the government's main legal offensives is dealt with below. But in the end, the governor, trying to crush a perceived plot and the enemies supposed to have hatched it, aimed at imprinting a new dynamic into the development of Lower Canada. Sir James Craig hoped to transform Lower Canada into an essentially British, subservient colony, with Canadien inhabitants destined for eventual assimilation, a fate that would supposedly benefit everyone, including them.

But why in 1810? Historians have specified constitutional struggles (the beginning of the inevitable quest for popular government, or 'responsible government,' and for financial control), more or less occurring in all colonies but especially acute in Lower Canada because of its longer history (except for Nova Scotia) and its population mix.[3] Others have focused on the clash of two mentalities, two cultural programs, which themselves nourished class struggles just at the time of the restructuring of the economy and of more aggressive competition from the United States.[4] With variations, others have picked up the same dichotomy but added to it a triggering element: an agricultural crisis abruptly breaking out in 1802, and the ensnaring of the impoverished masses by an opportunistic, conservative bourgeoisie of the *ancien régime*, feudal and economically impotent but using the House of Assembly as its springboard and nationalism as its mobilizing ideology to promote its own rise in society.[5] There is also the well-known picture of an ethnic struggle between 'British' and 'French' colonists, each attempting to build, on the same territory, its own ethnically differentiated society and both competing for overall domina-

tion. Such a conflict could lead only to violent confrontation and a decisive, predictable response by the mother country in 1840.[6] Some Marxists
have described a class struggle imbedded in a national conflict, or the rise
of a democratic, bourgeois, antifeudal and anticolonial movement, or
essentially a class conflict due to the rise of capitalism.[7] One can also add
to those factors the daily frictions resulting from different languages, cul-
tures, religions, customs, and laws.

Without denying these mostly internal sources of strife, Pierre Tousignant has suggested that the evolution of Lower Canada and its political
struggles cannot be grasped without reference to the British aristocratic
model of parliamentary government, which was the basis for the 1791 act,
and to its interpretation in Great Britain as well as by the ruling English
elite in the colony. This 'feudal' weight of metropolitan polity was the
more oppressive as the Canadiens' interpretation was based on theoretical
British principles but shaped or mediated by the much more democratic
North American practice.[8] And beyond the opposing interests, the class
struggles, the opportunistic use of government and laws to favour certain
sectors of society, and the attitudes of the English elite was the 'garrison
mentality' described by Murray Greenwood. The minority in Lower
Canada was fearful of the majority of Canadien subjects, their traditional
enemies and potential allies of France, which had been at war with Great
Britain since 1793 (except for the Peace of Amiens in 1802–3). Worse, the
English feared the influence on the Canadiens of the democratic principles
bred by the American and French revolutions. The rallying of the masses
to the parliamentary 'game' by 1800 through their attachment to the *parti
canadien* seemed as suspect if not more so than the anarchic popular riots
of the 1790s which had been led by mainly ad hoc local elites. The 'dema-
gogues' or 'traitors' of the *parti canadien*, moreover, threatened the dominance of the English ruling groups by espousing a constitutional
parliamentary system in order to raise a Canadien nation in a British
colony. This combination of perceived democracy and nationalism nourished the worst fears in government circles.[9] Thus, apart from the 'objective' causes or mix of them, different views of the world and conflicting
ideologies should not be passed over even when they were expressed in
the same constitutional language. Finally, one cannot deny the role of
opportunism and self-interest on both sides; each used all the means at its
disposal to, in one case, maintain British supremacy (and the class of
placemen benefiting from it), and, in the other, to strengthen the *nation
canadienne* and prevent British immigration and colonization.[10]

Perhaps, instead of pointing to a single cause or to a set of concomitant occurrences, historians may want to combine these different strands into a living texture, as a composer would join the scores of different musical instruments into a complex symphony. Life, after all, is more than the sum of its parts.[11] It is a dynamic combination of subprocesses that constitute, in the end, the society being 'instituted.'[12]

What triggered the explosion of 1810 was the *parti canadien's* emerging program of demands. These demands included: assembly control of government subsidies (financial appropriation); the selection of some of the governor's main advisers from the *parti canadien's* own ranks because it had a solid majority in the assembly (embryonic ministerial responsibility); the ensuring of Canadien supremacy in the assembly through measures of exclusion (directed at, for instance, judges); and the recognition of such principles as the independence of the assembly from both councils and the governor and the supremacy of the elected house.[13] Nearly all these were part of the program of Canadien reformers between 1784 and 1791,[14] and then of the *parti canadien* in the 1790s, but they had emerged as concrete demands by 1810. The whole strategy was to link the colonial constitution with that of the mother country and thus acquire for the colonial assembly the same extensive powers (subject to imperial authority) as those of the House of Commons in Britain. The response both from Britain and from the English party was blunt. Lower Canada was a colony and the *parti canadien's* constitutional principles amounted to democratic subversion 'from the voluntary suffrage of the rabble, already contaminated by the disturbers of society ... Even the English House of Commons, would be little better than a democratical club were it not for the boroughs [rotten/pocket] and the influence of the crown, and the influence of illustrious houses. What then may ... [be expected] in Canada from a population virtually french, without any one of these restraints?'[15]

The debates over financial control, sparked by the spectacular rise of revenues, echoed the underlying socio-ethnic conflicts between the English party and the *parti canadien*, and, indirectly, between the two communities they claimed to represent. No wonder that, according to Governor Craig in 1810, the house intended to impose its complete ascendancy over the colony by controlling the public finances and thereby dictate governmental policies.[16] No wonder also that the English party, particularly in the context of the *parti canadien's* efforts to equate the House of Assembly with the interests of the people and the councils and governor with the overly privileged rich, fought any measure that would have increased the assembly's power. What was at stake, ultimately, was power, as Sir James Kempt, after Craig, would realize in 1828–30.[17] But, however strong were the placemen and English merchants, they could not coerce the House of Assembly into voting the laws and taxes they thought were needed to encourage immigration, develop the economy, and build a strong 'British' Lower Canada. Naturally, other less grand issues also surfaced, as the executive systematically favoured the British colonists in the granting of land, contracts, positions, and pensions. Although constituting at least 90 per cent of the population during the period 1792–1811, Canadiens never received more than 25 per cent of the total sum of salaries, about one-sixth of the pensions, and less than 1 per cent of the contracts. Principles, objectives, and private interests all interfered to create a field of clashes.

The debates and conflicts can be schematized in the form of interactive layers of frictions which left few choices for resolving a complex cleavage. The table below[18] outlines the sharpness and diversity (in part) of these numerous conflicts. First, at the constitutional level, a struggle common to all colonies was developing between the traditional imperial sovereignty, embodied in the executive and legislative councils as well as in the governor, and the embryo of local sovereignty, rooted in the elective assembly which, moreover, had a democratic composition because of the liberal franchise. This dichotomy, compounded by the imprecise rules of the constitutional 'game' (not clearly defined in the Constitutional Act), extended into a second, social confrontation: the 'haves' versus the 'have nots.' The 'haves' came from the bureaucratic aristocracy and rich merchants, 'people' in the Blackstonian sense and in conformity with the British constitutional model invoked by members of the English party, whose power derived from and was asserted through the instruments of metropolitan or imperial sovereignty, essentially the governor and the councils. Opposing them were the 'real people,' the popular masses, whose leaders dominated the House of Assembly, the instrument for asserting local sovereignty. There is no doubt that both groups sincerely thought they were implementing British parliamentary principles, but their contextual references were divergent. An aristocratic notion of parliamentary government in which the 'majority,' even in the 'popular' house, emanated from the large landowners and the crown was answered by calls for the vesting of power in the people as a whole, as in a democracy. Finally, the aristocratic 'people' who looked to the mother country and defended an aristocratic form of government were mostly British in origin, while the 'people,' the heads of ordinary families admitted to vote, were essentially Canadien. In a colony without this particular ethnic structuring, many members of the English bourgeoisie would have tried to reinforce the power of the assembly and thereby assert more of their own importance in the hierarchy. In Lower Canada, any strengthening of the powers of the assembly meant also the reinforcement of the *parti canadien*'s aim of fostering a self-centred Canadien nation in the colony. That could not be. Finally, the two blocs had conceived and promoted economic programs that encompassed sometimes widely divergent interests: a strategy of transcontinental development pursued by the English party and the executive (the union of both Canadas, the establishment of large British banks, abolition of seigneurial tenure, radical changes to the civil laws, later the projected construction of canals towards the Great Lakes to channel all the western trade through the St Lawrence valley); and, on the other hand, the *parti canadien*'s economic strategy of regional development, the ideal of a capitalism tailored to the needs and interests of Lower Canada and its overwhelmingly French-speaking population (an American-like development of local banks, tenure reform to allow the ordinary colonist to become a landowner without disbursing capital, and later the building of canals inside the province or joining Montreal to New York). Religious, linguistic, and other cultural conflicts could be added to this brew.

A Schematized View of the Structure of Conflicts

Level of conflicts	Basis of these conflicts
1 Constitutional	Metropolitan sovereignty vs local control
	Councils and governor vs the House of Assembly
2 Social	Aristocratic compact vs people
3 Ethnic	English vs Canadiens
4 Economic	Continental trade and large agriculture and property vs regional development

From this simplified sketch, it is easy to grasp the depth of the conflicts, the reasons for their long duration, and the inability of all concerned to find a viable compromise. The complexity of the situation also explains the exasperation of the parties, after years of sometimes cautious, sometimes impetuous manoeuvres. Craig, in the end, thought that he could solve the crisis by resorting to the only method he knew: while awaiting important constitutional changes (which, as it turned out, would not be realized at this time), he would cow the popular branch through a calculated use of force. In this he acted honestly out of a commitment to the

British social and political order and his desire to create a similar, albeit modified, order in the colony; and out of his total opposition to Canadien nationalism and the democratic principles which he thought he recognized in his political adversaries. One must also include his irascible nature and authoritarian style as explanation for his behaviour. While the executive councillors, many of regime's newspapers, and the governor himself could have known (had the garrison mentality not operated so strongly) that there was no plot against the British government, no links with France, they in fact and quite naturally generated alarming rumours and pointed to an 'apprehended insurrection' because they were fighting for the survival of a British North America that they could recognize as British, not a 'French republic' masquerading under the guise of a British parliamentary system. Of course, the garrison mentality, sincere though it was, could be exploited out of self-interest, as it had been in myriad ways since its emergence in 1792–3 – for example, to access patronage, repel constitutional change, or press for anglicization.

Without this wider context, the English party's strategies and outcries would be nothing more than tantrums of the well-off barking at beggars, while Craig's actions could be dismissed as the result of one governor's eccentricities. Such interpretations, of course, fail to explain why political clashes persisted beyond the War of 1812 and until the crushing of one side in the rebellions of 1837–8, despite the changes in governors, unless one holds that, by definition, the latter were all maniacs. At the same time, ignoring the larger context makes it impossible to decipher Great Britain's role, which was decisive all along but especially in forcing the union of the Canadas in 1840. It also encourages the untenable view that the social vision defeated in 1837–8 was necessarily less rational, logical, and economically sound simply because the imperial power did not support it.

The complexities of the crisis of 1810–11 should be evident. There are at least three overarching ideas to explain it. The Laurentian thesis, mostly associated with Donald Creighton and Fernand Ouellet, posits a battle over the economic destiny of the colony: commerce versus agriculture, and the underused, magnificent trade route of the St Lawrence versus some kind of feudal Arcadia. In this view, cultural conflicts over constitutional issues and such matters as seigneurial tenure grew out of economic division. English expressions of fear were manufactured and most elements of the Canadien way of life were not threatened. None of us agrees with this thesis.

Jean-Pierre Wallot has written of a virtually inevitable explosion, dating to the conquest, involving two radically different ethnic groups that shared the same political territory. Also, with Gilles Paquet, he has developed the notion of a whole series of reinforcing conflicts. For instance, in this interpretation, commerce versus agriculture takes its place as but a single element of conflict interacting with others. Murray Greenwood, for his part, sees the garrison mentality as a major explanation of constitutional, political, and ethnic battles – for example, he shows why (as Wallot does from a different perspective) by the early nineteenth century almost all aspects of Canadien culture were very much under assault. As mentioned earlier, while the English elite was mainly sincere in its expressions of fear, alarmism could be and was used to foster self-interested purposes.[19] Though the crisis was about power more than law, the way in which the latter was administered is illuminating. In this essay, legal perspective is supplied by considering suspensions of habeas corpus in Great Britain, Lower Canada, and the United States.

SUSPENSIONS OF HABEAS CORPUS: ENGLAND/GREAT BRITAIN

The vital role the court writ of habeas corpus played in moderating arbitrary imprisonment by allowing the legality of detentions to be tested, affording protection to the right to bail in cases of misdemeanour, and ensuring a reasonably speedy trial for accused felons/traitors is treated in the introduction to this volume. Despite its having been widely regarded, in Blackstones words, as 'another Magna Carta,' access to the writ had been suspended by parliamentary statute in cases of apprehended invasion and/or insurrection about a dozen times from the Glorious Revolution of 1688–9 to 1794 inclusive.[20]

In a 1689 debate, some MPs expressed the hope that the suspending bill under consideration would 'not ... be drawn into example' by future generations.[21] Those who lived into the 1720s must have been sadly disillusioned by the ease with which personal liberty could be eroded more and more as each perceived crisis led to suspension. The crown was given increased flexibility in terms of issuing warrants, the length of possible incarceration, the crimes for which unappealable political charges could be laid, and the protection afforded members of the Commons and of the House of Lords. The ever more authoritarian direction is most dramatically captured in the changing titles of the first three suspending statutes. The act of 1688–9 empowered the king 'to apprehend and detain such persons as he shall find *just cause to suspect*' are conspiring against the government. Its 1696 successor referred to 'such persons as he shall find *cause to suspect.'* The statute of King George I (1714) applied simply to 'such persons as his Majesty *shall suspect'* of conspiracy.[22]

Preambles to the suspending acts normally announced justifications in extreme terms, designed to scare and thus forestall most questioning. In 1696 the statute referred to the 'most horrid, barbarous and detestable conspiracy ... by papists ... for assassinating his Majestys royal person in order to the encouraging an intended invasion from FRANCE.'[23] As mentioned in the introduction, the 1794 act conjured up a threatening plot (not really there) 'for introducing the system of anarchy and confusion which has so fatally prevailed in France.' Parliamentary supporters of the suspending bills often argued that at times the constitution could be preserved only by temporarily abandoning fundamental portions of it. Pitt made this point in the 1794 debate.[24] But not everyone accepted such justifications. The Foxite Whigs fought valiantly against this manifestation of Pitts 'reign of terror,' dividing the Commons fourteen times and threatening to secede from parliament before losing the vote 146 to 28.[25] One of the English 'Jacobin' state prisoners at the time of passage, philologist-political theorist John Horne Tooke, wrote a passage in his diary which in the years following must have been echoed in one respect or another by thousands of internees in Great Britain, the United States, British North America, and Canada: 'Sunday, June 8, 1794. In last night's *Courier* is the Act of Parlt "To empower his Majesty (*i.e.,* the Minister) to secure & detain (*i.e.,* to rob, ruin & murder ...) such persons as his Majesty (*i.e.,* the Minister) shall suspect (*i.e.,* pretend to suspect) are conspiring against his person & Government" (*i.e.,* who are displeased with the ministers measures, or to whom the minister is for any reason, or misinformation, or mistake or caprice, hostile).'[26]

The 1794 act, as several previous ones had, authorized privy councillors to intern persons charged with high treason, imprisoned on suspicion thereof, or charged with something called 'treasonable practices.' This catch-all phrase was obviously convenient to government, since no one knew what it meant and hence no one could mount a telling argument that an internee had not been guilty of the supposed crime. It certainly had not been defined by statute and Lower Canadian Chief Justice Jonathan Sewell stated in 1810 that 'the precise import of the phrase "treasonable practices" has never been settled by any legal decision.'[27] Not surprisingly, the English 'Jacobin' state prisoners of 1794 were initially held under this charge, a point of law that annoyed the precise linguist in Horne Tooke. According to the Privy Council register, the accused asked, at his examination, for proof that 'there had been any

Information upon Oath against him for Practices full of Treason, for that he understood Treasonable practices to mean.'[28] This was as sharp a definition as any to that time.

SUSPENSIONS OF HABEAS CORPUS: QUEBEC/LOWER CANADA

The writ of habeas corpus was suspended in Quebec and the power of internment gravely abused during the American Revolutionary War.[29] Afterwards, Canadien and English constitutional/legal reformers tried to have the writ 'entrenched' so that it would be sacrosanct, except during *actual* invasion or rebellion. They did succeed in having Council pass an ordinance (1784) extending in substance the important benefits of King Charles II's procedural act of 1679 to persons incarcerated in the colony on criminal charges. But they failed in their three attempts (1784, 1786, 1791) to have the imperial parliament enact entrenchment. Thus, in Lower Canada, there were no constitutional barriers to suspensions by the legislature. From 1794 to 1812 inclusive, the only entire calendar year that habeas corpus applied in cases of suspected subversives was 1796.

The first statutory interference with this second Magna Carta came in the 1794 Alien Act, drafted by Attorney General (later chief justice of the Montreal District) James Monk and passed at a time when the distorting garrison mentality of the tiny English elite was at one of its recurrent high points. In particular, invasion by revolutionary France or by France and the United States, the first at war with Britain and the second threatening it over British retention of fortified posts in western American territory, was more than possible. If either invasion occurred, it seemed certain to nervous government officials, merchants, and others that the Canadiens would rise in massive armed rebellion.[30]

The Alien Act, which was mainly concerned with registering and regulating foreigners (including their summary deportation), also suspended habeas corpus for persons 'who are or shall be charged with or suspected of the crime of high treason.' Where prisoners had been charged with a seditious offence, the writ was partially suspended. Bail could no longer be granted these misdemeanants by a single magistrate, but only by the governor, chief justice, a puisne judge of the Court of King's Bench, or two or more justices of Oyer and Terminer. Unlike a magistrate operating under the common law, these officials could refuse bail even when the sureties offered were sufficient. Such a suspension, partial as it was, had never occurred in Great Britain and would have been unconstitutional in the United States.

Monk's act also contained a section making much more expansive an already elastic definition of seditious offences found in the common law. In contemporary England (but not Scotland) criticism, moderate in tone, of government policies, the competence of crown ministers, the constitution, or social relations was not seditious. In Lower Canada virtually any complaint about any of these things was, arguably, now criminal. Nor did Monk extend to accused the benefits found in Fox's Libel Act of 1792 dealing with jury verdicts, as was later done in the United States in the Sedition Act of 1798. As was so often the case in Canadian history, when security legislation was enacted, it went beyond comparable provisions in the mother country, whether statutory or common law, in a royalist direction.

In the late spring, summer, and autumn of 1794, the internment provisions were used by Monk to conduct a virtual witch-hunt of dissidents. More people per capita were probably then interned than during the October crisis of 1970–1. Dozens more fled across the American border to avoid the tentacles of the attorney general. By 1795 the crisis had abated. Under orders from Governor Dorchester, government supporters in the assembly, when renewing the Alien Act, allowed the sections on habeas corpus and sedition to lapse.

The legislature again suspended habeas corpus in 1797 by the statute known as the Better Preservation Act.[31] (See app. 3, J, docs. 2, 3.) Again, there was pervasive fear of French invasion and Canadien insurrection. Attorney General Jonathan Sewell was the draftsman and he went well beyond his British model, the 1794 suspending act (see app. 3, J, doc. 1). In addition to high treason or suspicion of it, internment could take place upon charges merely of misprision (or concealment) of treason and, if the act was read literally, upon mere suspicion of the undefined treasonable practices rather than on charges thereof as required by the equivalent British provision. This was how Sewell himself interpreted the local act in 1801 when six suspected subversives (all Americans, who were thought, on weak evidence, to be working for Vermont adventurer Ira Allen and, through him, France) were jailed for about two months.

One intriguing feature of the drafting was Sewell's clever obfuscation of the government's aim to empower itself to intern members of the assembly should it become necessary – particularly the 'Jacobin' or 'democratical' leaders of the *parti canadien*, Joseph Papineau and Speaker Jean-Antoine Panet. The British statute required that no MP or peer could be imprisoned, during the sitting of parliament, 'until the matter of which he stands suspected be first communicated to the house of which he is a member, *and the consent of the said house obtained for his commitment or detaining.'*[32] Sewell deliberately abandoned his model on this point, including only a vague proviso in one section 'that nothing in this Act shall extend or be construed to extend or be construed to invalidate or restrain the lawful rights and privileges of either Branch of the Provincial Parliament in this Province.' But parliamentary privilege did *not* apply to charges of any serious crime (including treason, misprision, treasonable practices), although it *may* have applied where incarceration was based on suspicion, not charges.

The Better Preservation Act was annually renewed until the brief Peace of Amiens in 1802–3. It was revived in 1803 with the continuation of the Napoleonic Wars and renewed every year until 1812, in contrast to the United Kingdon which fought throughout the conflict without the suspension of habeas corpus. Evidence indicates that in certain years government officials could have made a case for possible invasion (1797, 1801, 1803, 1807–8, 1810) but not imminent invasion, let alone actual invasion. And without French invasion, even the English elite did not think that there would be any serious insurrection. In Britain, too, there had been times (for example, 1795) when the writ was in suspension even though invasion and/or insurrection were highly unlikely. Both jurisdictions operated under the doctrine of parliamentary sovereignty, Britain, of course, generally but its colony also in particular areas, of which this was one. Suspensions were conditioned by political factors, not fundamental law. This contrasts greatly with the United States.

SUSPENSIONS OF HABEAS CORPUS: THE UNITED STATES

Article 1, section 9, paragraph 2 of the American constitution reads as follows: 'The Privilege of the Writ of Habeas Corpus shall not be suspended, unless when in Cases of Rebellion or Invasion the public Safety may require it.' Despite its restrictive thrust, several of the framers thought the paragraph illiberal and it passed, after much discussion, by the relatively close margin of seven states to three. Thomas Jefferson, writing James Madison in 1788, went so far as to suggest that suspensions during rebellion should be prohibited.[33]

The provision was recurrently found, in the later history of the United States, to contain two major ambiguities: first, whether the president alone or only congress could suspend; second, as to the precise circumstances when suspension would be legally justified. The first is of no concern here. The second raises the question whether *actual* invasion or rebellion was a condition precedent to suspension, even though the word actual was not used. Or could such Draconian action be taken when either of those situations was proveably imminent? We confine our remarks to the 1790s and the first decade of the new century.

The 'imminent' school included Supreme Court Justice James Iredell (1793), but he also suggested that even in such cases the burden of demonstrating necessity 'to save the public from destruction' lay upon those proposing suspension.[34] Among proponents of the 'actual' school was the Republican leader in the House of Representatives, Albert Gallatin (1798).[35] The House debates in 1807 on a Senate bill to suspend, in the wake of Aaron Burr's abortive attempt to detach trans-Appalachia from the union, are illuminating (see app. 3, J, doc. 4). Every one of the eight members (of ten who spoke) expressing a constitutional opinion agreed that at a minimum there must be actual invasion or insurrection.[36] These included two who favoured the bill. Indeed, six of the eight constitutionalists claimed that the test was not merely actual rebellion or invasion but one of those *plus* demonstrably acute public danger. As put by a Mr Elliott: 'Have we a right to suspend it in any and every case of invasion and rebellion? So far from it, that we are under a Constitutional interdiction to act, unless the existing invasion or rebellion, in our sober judgment, threatens the first principles of the national compact, and the Constitution itself.' The Senate bill was defeated 113 to 19.

In the period under discussion, Britain and Lower Canada could suspend the writ whenever their legislatures thought fit. Congress could do so only when, one, the danger was *manifestly great and manifestly imminent*, two, there was actual invasion or rebellion, *or* three, such existed *and* the public safely was manifestly threatened. Certainly, the contemporary American constitution would not have permitted what happened in Lower Canada in 1810–11.

THE CRISIS OF 1810–11

Prelude

In the wake of the *Chesapeake* crisis in 1807 over maritime rights which brought Britain and the United States to the brink of war, Whitehall decided that Lower Canada must be governed by an outstanding field officer who would also command the regular troops throughout British North America. Lieutenant-General Sir James Henry Craig, one of the captors of Dutch South Africa (1795), who had been appointed in 1805 to command an expeditionary force in the European theatre (this plan was aborted), landed at Quebec in October 1807. He arrived at a time when relations between the English party and the opposition *parti canadien*, which had controlled the assembly since 1797, had reached one of their lowest points. The Gaols Act dispute of 1805–6, which involved imposing import duties on trade merchandise rather than land taxes and featured assembly orders to arrest three political opponents of the majority (see the essay by Murray Greenwood and Barry Wright in this volume), had embittered the English party. Its members, too, had been alarmed both by the foundation of the partisan French-language newspaper *Le Canadien* late in 1806 and its aggressive early battling against the equally partisan Quebec *Mercury*, and by the *parti canadien*'s increasingly frequent and forceful articulation of constitutional radicalism. By 1810 that radicalism would encompass the assembly's claims to the privileges of the House of Commons, including those relating to the expulsion of members and control of public finance and the right to censure individuals in the local 'ministry.'

Sir James was aristocratic, paternalistic, and, above all, autocratic. Yet, despite these extreme Tory character traits, he at first believed that the francophone population, including the *parti canadien*, was loyal. It was only during the vitriolic general election of May 1808 that he began to internalize the assumptions underlying the garrison mentality that inspired not only his executive advisers but the English elite generally. By early August Craig had convinced himself that Bonaparte's desire for worldwide conquest would, sooner rather than later, result in a French attack, perhaps via Spanish Florida and the Mississippi. The mass of the people, anglophobic and as French as they had been the day after the British conquest, would rise in bloody, supportive rebellion. The *parti canadien* leaders, almost certainly, and the Roman Catholic hierarchy very probably, were working for Napoleon through his ambassador to Washington. And, in Craig's thinking, the Americans, with some token help from France, might invade. That, too, would spark insurrection. The 'general opinion among the english part of the Inhabitants,' the governor informed the colonial secretary, 'is, that they [the Canadien "lower orders"] would even join an American Force, if that force were commanded by a french officer.'[37]

The Outbreak

Passions clashed momentously in the legislative session of 1810 and the ensuing election. Led by lawyer Pierre-Stanislas Bédard, the *parti canadien* attempted to establish its agent (lobbyist) in London, generously 'offered' to appropriate all government revenues, and, by simple resolution of the house, expelled its main political enemy, Judge Pierre-Amable De Bonne. Governor Craig thought this last move a precursor to excluding all placemen and to a 'vote that no Englishman could be eligible' for a seat in the assembly. As he had a year before, Craig prematurely dissolved the legislature, in February, setting the scene for the third agonizing election in three years. He wrote that the opposition leaders 'have hitherto been making [only] gradual advances to their Object, but as was the Case in Charles the First's Reign, the time of the Explosion is now come.' True. Craig, a man moved above all by a sense of duty, would do his part for the empire.

The electoral campaign reached new depths of hatred. Craig, the *parti canadien* charged, was about to impose conscription. The placemen, all of them public thieves, parasites living off the people's toil, had forced dissolution to prevent the assembly gaining any supervision over the civil list. The long-standing theme of *sans culottes* flowed from the lips and pens of government supporters. Bédard was another Robespierre or perhaps a Wat Tyler trying to provoke a peasant jacquerie. The Canadien revolutionaries held secret meetings at each other's houses, 'Camillus' wrote to the Quebec *Mercury* on 19 March, and at a mass gathering in the Quebec City market had burned pro-government literature 'amidst shouts of "Vive la Nation."' There could be no doubt that 'this faction have in view to [re-en]act now the same enormities which were committed' during the French revolution.

Rumours abounded. Most of the tales involved financial aid from France. The historian Robert Christie, then residing in the colony, later recalled stories that the 'french minister in America [General Louis-Marie Turreau] had supplied large sums in gold, to promote the views of the seditious in Canada,' while the scholarly artist George Heriot convinced himself that 'French Money, as well as influence have for some time past found their way into this province.' There was even a fantasy tale that priests at the Seminaire de Saint-Sulpice – emigrés who detested the 'usurping' Bonaparte – were sending intelligence and funds to General Turreau. In this hysterical atmosphere the party newspaper *Le Canadien* published an electoral song suggesting the people exterminate the 'scum' (*canaille*), that is, officialdom, whom the governor hoped to reward from taxes on land.

Craig struck, putting the military on alert status. The next priority was to gather evidence of high treason or treasonable practices. On 16 March two English tavernkeepers were sent to the printing office of *Le Canadien* to become subscribers. Their depositions (sworn before Chief Justice Sewell) identifying Charles Le François as the printer, as well as the three last numbers of the paper, were examined by the full Executive Council the next day. After discussion it agreed with Craig that the printer should be apprehended. The warrant charged Le François with 'treasonable practices' and, according to Christie, was executed with flourish: 'A party of soldiers headed by a magistrate and two constables, proceeded to the *Canadien* printing office ... where ... [they] forcibly seized the press, with the whole of the papers of every description found in the house.' By order of the full council the press and printing materials were deposited in the vaults of the courthouse. The raid produced no treasonable correspondence or subversive draft articles, although the raiders did seize an inflammatory electoral broadsheet in the press which recited Canadien grievances back to the conquest.

On 19 March the council examined this document and depositions sworn to by Le François, three of his assistants, and a medical student of Dr François Blanchet. The depositions revealed that among the owners of *Le Canadien* were MPPs Louis Bourdages, Blanchet, Bédard, Jean-Thomas Taschereau, and Joseph Borgia; that during the election Blanchet and Taschereau had been the active managers of the paper; that the notorious 'chanson' referring to Craig's advisers as scum had originally been printed at the *Le Canadien* office; and that Bédard was the author of the party's main electoral address of 1810. These were hardly startling revelations and amounted to no more than a basis for charges of seditious libel. One statement by Le François, however, banished any lingering doubts that there might not be a deeply laid plot. Dr Blanchet, it appears, had given orders to the printers that all original articles be returned to the editors or else burned, to prevent identification of the authors' handwriting. A committal warrant signed by executive councillors Thomas Dunn, François Baby, and John Young and charging Bédard, Blanchet, and Taschereau with the unknown crime of 'treasonable practices' was immediately executed. Unlike the case in 1801, the prisoners were actually detained on charges, not merely on suspicion. This minimized the chances of their successfully invoking parliamentary privilege but may well in itself have been illegal, considering the wording of the Better Preservation Act and the 1801 precedent. A similar warrant to commit three *parti canadien* activists from the Montreal District was executed and warrants against other politically prominent Montrealers such as Denis-Benjamin Viger were signed but execution suspended.

Quebec was awash with excitement, talk of plots, and stories of narrowly averted civil war. On 21 March Craig issued a proclamation explaining the purity of his motives, implying that the *parti canadien* leaders were in the pay of the French, and instructing the captains of militia and magistrates to arrest anyone spreading 'false news in any way derogatory to His Majesty's Government.' Anglican Bishop Jacob Mountain devoted his Sunday sermon to portraying Craig as the saviour of the province. general Isaac Brock shared Mountain's sentiments:

We have been in a bustle and on the alert for the last ten days ... The spirit of insubordination and revolt was advancing so rapidly among the Canadian population of the province that it became absolutely necessary for the peace to put a check to it, and fortunately a person was found at the head of Government of sufficient energy to meet and crush at once the monster who strived to draw the people ... to all the horrors of civil commotion ... I hope ... terror will prove effective ... the bubble [of conciliation] set up by Lord Dorchester and Sir. R.S. Milnes [lieutenant-governor, 1799–1805], has completely burst never to rise again.

Although confident that he had succeeded in thwarting rebellion, Craig left nothing to chance. The mails from Quebec to Montreal were briefly detained, in order, it was said, 'to get hold of the threads of the insurrectionary web ... before the news of his [Craig's] vigorous dash ... could reach their outlying fellow-conspirators.' To make sure that the democrats did not seize several dozen muskets used for training purposes, the governor had the adjutant general of the Canadien militia mount a guard over them. Until the last days of the month special military patrols marched up and down the streets of a perfectly peaceful capital. As late as July Brock found it impossible to obtain leave to visit England; the governor, still worried about insurrection, wished to retain as many experienced officers as possible in the colony. The fact that no hard evidence of a French plot was uncovered did not in the least affect the governor or his advisers, and Bédard long remained a proven traitor in their eyes.

In the Montreal District, Chief Justice James Monk, merchant James McGill, and other executive councillors examined numerous witnesses to the inflammatory electoral polemics of one François Corbeil, habitant of Île Jésus, and notary Pierre Laforce of Terrebonne. The examiners detained these two hotheads under the Better Preservation Act, having proved to their own satisfaction (for example, Laforce had received a letter from France) that they could bring 'all the facts to one single and great point of ultimate design' – that of preparing for general rebellion. Craig, in the meantime, had informed London of the arrests, referring in one dispatch to talk among Canadiens of a 'Sicilian Vespers' – a contemporary term meaning massacre of an ethnic minority – as illustrative of the agitated public mind.[38] Somewhat later, in far off Hyderabad, India, Major François-Louis de Salaberry, an anglified Canadien serving in the British army, read in a newspaper that 'there was a conspiracy discovered which was to murder all the English inhabitants.'

The Legal Aftermath

On 22 March 1810 the chief justice opened the spring assizes with a thoroughly Burkean address to the grand jury.[39] After reading Craig's proclamation verbatim – which he recommended to all who were reluctant 'to exchange the blessings of an established Government for the fruits of Anarchy' – the chief justice launched into an elaborate political/legal explanation of seditious libel. Sewell's understanding of this crime, more royalist than that prevalent in the mother country, revived the elastic concept found in the first Alien Act. The chief justice did not mention the right to criticize the government: obviously, even temperate criticism was illegal or there was a heavy presumption that any such criticism was seditious.

The function of the press, he claimed, was certainly not to advocate change. It was to aid in 'the preservation of all that is valuable to us as Men and as subjects.' The essence of any society was government and government – not the people at large – had the responsibility 'to promote and secure the happiness of the Individuals who compose it.' Any writing, therefore, which was 'detrimental to the public safety or happiness,' which raised 'discontents' against the ruling authorities, or whose 'effect is prejudicial to the public'[40] could not be tolerated by the government 'without a dereliction of its own fundamental principles.'

It followed that the abuse of the graciously conferred freedom from prior restraint on publication (dating from 1694) 'in ... the smallest Degree should be the object of legal punishment.' For the government to forgo control of the press was dangerous everywhere, particularly after the French revolution, but was especially so in Lower Canada with its simple-minded population: 'In all countries, the ignorant, the credulous and the desperate are to be found. Yet in proportion as the hearts of the Inhabitants of any Country are good and simple, in that proportion they become more readily a prey to the crafty, who in these respects have the Cruelty to deceive them – In no country therefore can attempts so to deceive, be more dangerous, than in that which we inhabit.' The governor's proclamation had taken all this into consideration and the grand jurors should do likewise in their deliberations. Leniency, when the social order was threatened with seditious publications, was 'the path that leads to Rebellion and civil War or to the subjugation of the Country by some foreign Power,' as recent events in Europe had demonstrated.

Despite Sewell's obvious invitation, the grand jury (composed mainly of English party supporters and Canadien pro-government men) indicted no one for seditious libel. Nor did it recommend indictments. It did, however, condemn recent issues of Le Canadien and some of the electoral publications struck off its press as perilous to the security of the colony. Sanctions were left to the court. The jury also censured the pro-government Mercury for exciting jealousies and distrusts among Canadiens.[41] Although the failure to indict or at least recommend prosecutions could not have pleased the administration, there were other ways to control the opposition press. In particular, Bédard and his editorial colleagues could be kept in prison almost indefinitely and the printing equipment could also remain in the court vault.[42]

While Sewell clearly wanted the editors of Le Canadien tried for seditious libel and British Attorney General Sir Vicary Gibbs suggested that such should be seriously considered,[43] the government never attempted to obtain indictments against the politicians arrested in March 1810, whether for libel or otherwise. This repeated what had happened during an earlier confrontation between the governor and his opponents: in 1808 Craig stripped parti canadien leaders of their militia commissions on the ground of their suspected ownership of a publication 'calculated to vilify his Majesty's government' in the province, but he did not instruct the attorney general to prosecute for sedition.[44] It seems likely that officials believed that Canadien juries would not convict their compatriots for non-violent, politically motivated offences unless the juries themselves were grossly manipulated – a proceeding fraught with danger to governmental legitimacy. A dozen or so Canadiens, it is true, had been found guilty of seditious offences in the 1790s but in the context of serious rioting against militia conscription (1794) or forced labour on the roads (1796–7).[45] And there is certainly evidence (such as the jailed Bédard's reelection in 1810) in this period that, already, Canadiens tended to excuse political crimes when committed to advance 'la nation canadienne.'[46]

If administration officials were indeed pessimistic about the chances of obtaining convictions, their attitude was remarkable in that Fox's Libel Act of 1792 empowering juries to return general verdicts in seditious (or criminal) libel cases was almost certainly not in force. That act had not been made applicable to the colonies. Whether it retroactively declared common law is not certain. The judges of England, during passage, advised the House of Lords that Lord Mansfield had been correct in restricting jurors to questions relating to publication and the meaning of innuendoes and reserving decisions on seditiousness to the bench. The act itself was ambiguous, referring to 'Doubts' having arisen on the issue and proceeding as follows: 'Be it therefore declared *and enacted*.'[47] There was no express assertion that the law as described had always been the correct law.[48] In any case, the highly conservative, fearful judges of Lower Canada were not likely to adopt the basic principle of the act. In addition to hampering prosecutions, such a course would mean dissociating themselves from the judges of England, almost unthinkable for a colonial bench and particularly for one that included a chief justice (James Monk) who had proclaimed in 1803 that colonial judges were *bound* by the legal opinions of the British law officers.[49] A 1795 letter written by lawyer David Ross also indicates that the question had arisen in one of Ross's cases and Monk had taken the Mansfield line, although the jury acquitted anyway.[50]

By way of epilogue, the next major seditious libel cases in Lower Canada, involving the incarceration of Montreal *patriote* editors Daniel Tracey and Ludger Duvernay in 1832, were handled not by the regular courts but by the Legislative Council (led by Speaker Jonathan Sewell), which asserted its supposed privilege to imprison for contempt.[51] Fox's Libel Act was not clearly received in Lower Canada/Quebec until 1874. In April of that year the erudite Mr Justice Thomas K. Ramsay laid down the law in no uncertain terms:

Historically it is declaratory. It will be remembered that the Judges laid down the doctrine that libel or no libel was matter of law for the Court, and they only left to the jury whether the defendant published. Juries refused to be guided by this monstrous doctrine, the object of which was really to create an exception to the general rule of the criminal law, and after a good deal of resistance Fox's libel bill was passed in 1792 to settle the difficulty. I do not intend to re-open that difficulty, which I think is settled for the whole empire, by the assertion of the true principle, and I shall leave the whole case to the jury – whether, under all the circumstances that may properly be proved there is a libel and whether the defendants published it.[52]

In the same year, the Canadian parliament enacted the principle of Fox's Libel Act for Quebec.[53]

Bédard's Application for Habeas Corpus

Bédard's application for a writ of habeas corpus was heard on 17 April by the Court of King's Bench (Quebec), which consisted of Chief Justice Sewell and puisne judges Jenkin Williams and James Kerr.[54] Defence counsel had only a slim chance of success. Appearing for the crown were Attorney General Norman F. Uniacke, Olivier Perrault, the advocate general, and Edward Bowen, who had articled with Sewell and afterwards, with his mentor's help, became acting attorney general (1808, 1810) and King's Bench judge (1812). These men were far more likely to be listened to, and they were, than the twenty-five-year-old Andrew Stuart. The latter's inexperience was manifest in his not raising a cogent argument from general principle in favour of his client. The bench, in any event, could hardly have been even remotely sympathetic to the prisoner, who was the supposed local Robespierre, the leader of the *parti canadien*, and their main political opponent. With the best will in the world, Sewell particularly could not have been impartial. As attorney general in 1797 he had drafted the Better Preservation Act to enable the government to intern MPPs without being met by valid claims to parliamentary privilege. As a member of the Executive Council, he had advised Craig to imprison Bédard under the act; he had therefore taken a position in the case that the imprisonment was not subject to privilege – which of course was the central issue.

After hearing counsels' submissions, three separate concurring judgments dismissed the application. Kerr confined himself to the technical point that there was no valid proof before the court that Bédard had been a member of the dissolved house or was a member of the present one. Williams and Sewell agreed on this point, which therefore constituted the *per curiam* ratio of the case, despite its never having been raised by the crown in argument. In a short note Williams agreed with everything said by the chief justice, who delivered the most elaborate judgment of the three (see app. 3, J, doc. 5). After disposing of the case because of the evidentiary defect, he proceeded in *obiter* (non-binding comments) to address the question in a wide-ranging hypothetical fashion. His explicit purpose was to avoid future litigation on the issue.

Sewell conceded that freedom from arrest had the same dimension in Lower Canada that it had in Britain. He therefore set out to demonstrate that in England no privilege existed in serious criminal cases. Before treating substance, the chief justice made two technical points. Citing respectable authority, he concluded that, while the privilege lasted for forty days after prorogation, it extended only to a reasonable time (to return home) after dissolution. He also accepted Bowen's argument – citing different authorities from those advanced by counsel – that being in jail at the time of the election voided the privilege, the electorate having no right to be represented by such a man. Under this doctrine Bédard and his fellow political prisoners could not claim privilege so long as they remained in jail. Potentially, where bail and the right to a speedy trial were not available, it would allow the crown to control the composition of the house simply by arresting leading opponents before the vote was completed and keeping them in prison for as long as possible.

On matters of substance, Sewell devoted considerable space to Chief Justice Charles Pratt's decision in *Wilkes* (Common Pleas, 1763), wherein he had held, accurately, that privilege had long extended to all imprisonments except those for treason, felony, and 'breach of the peace.' It followed, in his view, that it encompassed charges of seditious libel since that crime did not necessarily involve actual breach of the peace, as did some other misdemeanours (for example, assault).[55] Sewell attempted to show that, even if Pratt's judgment was correct and authoritative, it would not help the prisoner. Of the two crimes, seditious libel and treasonable practices, the former was the minor one. *Wilkes*, therefore, 'if admitted to be law, proves that the privilege ... extends thus far, that is, to *seditious acts*, but affords no proof whatever that it extends beyond them to "*treasonable practices*."' But as crown counsel had argued, the chief justice went on, the *Wilkes* decision was not law since it had been 'solemnly disclaimed by both Houses of the British Parliament.'[56] Sewell interpreted the parliamentary resolution in question as properly construing 'breach of the peace' to include all major criminal offences: 'All indictable crimes (and all treasonable practices must be indictable) are held in law to be *contra pacem domini regis*; and upon this ground, in England, it is now understood that the claim of privilege does not comprehend the case of any indictable crime.' This position was to be upheld in the future. A Commons committee of privileges in 1831, referring to the rejection of Pratt's decision, said that 'since that time it has been considered as established generally [and has remained so], that privilege is not claimable for any indictable offence.'[57]

Assessment of Sewell's Judgment

Even at the time he rendered it, Sewell's argument was highly persuasive. The parliamentary resolution, though not explicit in its scope, distinctly implied that there was no need of actual violence to disentitle from privilege. Misdemeanours such as seditious libel were indictable offences and as such were invariably described in the indictments as breaches of the king's peace. The logic of refusing privilege for all indictable offences had been accepted by the Commons as early as 1641, a position repeated almost word for word by an early post-Glorious Revolution authority, George Petyt: '*Privilege* cannot be pleaded against an *indictment* ... because all *Indictments* are contra *Pacem Domini Regis*.' Two years after the Wilkes controversy, Sir William Blackstone came down on the side of parliament: no member of either house could 'be arrested and taken into custody, unless for some indictable offence, without a breach of the privilege of parliament.'[58] Thus, even though 'treasonable practices' did not necessarily entail disturbance, the offence, being indictable, was probably exempted from the ambit of parliamentary privileges on the ground that it was, in law, a breach of the peace.

Nevertheless one can seriously question Sewell's point that, since Bédard was in jail at the time of his election, he was not entitled to privilege (assuming it otherwise existed). To say that the electors had only themselves to blame is not convincing, since the privilege of freedom from arrest, like all privileges, existed for the benefit of one or other house of the legislature, rather than the public at large, the electors, or any segment of the electors. And Sewell's use of authorities was simply not credible. He cited two precedents in support of this holding. One dated from the Tudor period, when parliament was essentially an adjunct of royal power. The other was *Sir Richard Temple* (King's Bench, 1661), which if anything proved the opposite of Sewell's contention, proceeding, as it did, on the assumption that incarceration at the time of election did not void the privilege. The same conclusion could be drawn from an 1807 precedent, which Sewell chose to ignore or which was unknown to him. A Mr Mills, while in jail, was elected to parliament. The Commons resolved that Mills was privileged and ordered him released from custody.[59]

One further question calls for answer: was Bédard entitled to his freedom on the basis of general principle, the central purpose of parliamentary privileges? The argument from general principle asks whether a member of parliament can be imprisoned, without the consent of the House of Commons, on a criminal charge where the accused has no right to a speedy trial by ordinary course of law, that is, where habeas corpus had been suspended in relation to the criminal charge in issue. A negative answer to this question involves a restrictive interpretation of the exceptions ('treason, felony or breach of the peace') to privilege, confining them to ordinary criminal cases where internment is impossible, an approach consistent with the general rule of construing exceptions restrictively and which draws support from the rationale expressed by the parliamentary resolution in the Wilkes affair that privilege ought not 'to obstruct the ordinary Course of the Laws, in the speedy and effectual Prosecution of so heinous and dangerous an Offence.'⁶⁰ Thus, the rationale of the two houses of parliament in giving breach of peace its widest possible interpretation was non-interference with speedy trials according to the common law. That rationale did not apply where the crown was able to take advantage of and had in fact taken advantage of a suspension of habeas corpus. Bédard had no way of forcing a court to order his trial, which in the ordinary course should have occurred at the March assizes of 1810. But he had not then even been indicted. Nor had the governor issued a special commission. To deny a privilege in such cases was to give the crown obvious power to coerce the Commons in England or the assembly in Lower Canada.

No clear supportive British precedent existed on this point, simply because the situation was invariably provided for in the statutes suspending habeas corpus: imprisonment of MPs and peers was prohibited without the consent of the appropriate house. But there was no negative precedent either. The provisos in the suspending acts did not deny preexisting privilege. Nor did the mere fact that protection of parliamentarians took statutory form imply there was no privilege in common law: the long established freedom of debate, for example, had been reiterated in the Bill of Rights of 1689. The provisos, then, could reasonably be interpreted as re-assertions of existing privileges, included *ex abundanti cautelâ* (from an abundance of caution). Had the draftsmen in England ever omitted the proviso, it is inconceivable that the Commons or Lords would fail to protest the crown's prolonged internment of one or more members without consent. If the question had arisen in litigation, the courts of necessity would have had recourse to the central purpose of parliamentary privilege. This was unambiguously stated by Blackstone: 'Privilege of parliament was principally established, in order to protect its members, not only from being molested by their fellow-subjects, but also *more especially from being oppressed by the power of the crown.'*⁶¹ Lord Ellenborough's dictum in *Burdett v. Abbot* (1811) is to the same effect: 'The privileges which belong to them seem at all times to have been, and necessarily must be, inherent in them, *independent of any precedent*: it was necessary that they should have the most complete personal security, to enable them freely to meet for the purposes of discharging their important functions, and also that they should have the right of self-protection.'[62] There is more: the arrests may have been illegal in the first place. In his anxiety to demonstrate that treasonable practices were more heinous than sedition and required an actual plotting against the government, Sewell inadvertently admitted that the committals had been unjustified. There had been no evidence whatever before the Executive Council of actual rebellious design. This was immediately perceived by the British attorney general, Sir Vicary Gibbs, when in 1810 he examined the proceedings of the council and the documents (including copies of *Le Canadien*) on which it had based its decisions.[63] In his report to the colonial secretary, Lord Liverpool, Gibbs allowed that the political situation in Lower Canada had probably been such as to excuse a stretching of the law. But stretched it certainly had been: 'I cannot say that the paper published in "Le Canadien" and upon which the proceedings of the Council were founded ["Chanson"?], are such as to fix upon the publishers the charge of treasonable practices, and therefore it may be difficult strictly to justify the steps which have been taken against them; but the passages which are adverted to were certainly calculated to do much mischief in the Province; they might, I think, be prosecuted as seditious libels.'[64]

Liverpool enclosed a copy of Gibbs's report in a dispatch, dated 12 September 1810, to Craig, but he did not call him or the chief justice to account or issue instructions to release any remaining prisoners.

Denouement

During the months of July and August 1810 all the prisoners except Bédard were released on bail. Some such as Blanchet and Taschereau made full confessions of wrongdoing. Others were liberated because of the danger to their health. In one case, discharge apparently came too late. Within weeks of his leaving the damp cells of the Montreal jail, François Corbeil died, a victim, according to his family, of a disease contracted in prison.[65] Bédard, who refused to confess any impropriety and demanded a trial, remained in prison for over a year. Opinion at the Château was divided as to the advisability of trying the suspects for treasonable practices or seditious libel and in the end none was prosecuted.[66] After a legislative session in which the *parti canadien* proved docile and Craig won most of the points, Bédard was released in April 1811. The governor returned to England in June. The English elite was deprived of its beloved garrison leader.

Craig's regime embittered Canadien politicians and hence made it more difficult to avoid an ultimate resort to violence, which came in 1837 and again a year later. As early as 1812 the assembly censured his conduct and in 1814 attempted to impeach Chief Justice Sewell for, *inter alia*, advising Craig to indulge wholesale in arbitrary and unconstitutional acts directed against a free press and a free political system.[67] In 1814, too, an anonymous French-language pamphlet described Craig as exceedingly vain and criticized him for having governed like an arrogant and rash grand seigneur or court favourite.[68] Three years later, the death of François Corbeil – allegedly as a result of his totally unjustified imprisonment in 1810 – was the subject of acrimonious debate in the house. A careful examination of the newspapers would likely produce many more examples of grievances related to the Craig era, which soon became known to Canadiens as the 'reign of terror,' a term remaining current at least until the 1850s. In the long run Craig indeed entered Canadien mythology. A Montreal *patriote* meeting of 1832, for example, toasted the 'memory of those who were imprisoned in 1810 for the liberty of the country,'[69] while, at one of the mass protests held on the eve of the first rebellion, Louis-Joseph Papineau pointed to 'le tyran Craig' as one of the governors who symbolized the true meaning of British sovereignty.[70] And from François-Xavier Garneau on, francophone historians often devoted considerable space in their works to the governor and his advisory entourage as the first major threat to 'la survivance.'

This long-range effect has been understood, at least in outline, by historians from the beginning. But strangely overlooked has been the dramatic impact of the 'reign of terror' on the government's emergency powers during the War of 1812.

THE NEW REGIME

I was sensible that by conciliating the Canadian Representatives I could alone hope to succeed in the accomplishment of any object I might have in view.[71]

Craig's successor as governor and commander-in-chief of British North America was Lieutenant-General Sir George Prevost, a Swiss-born officer with a distinguished war record in the West Indies.[72] The choice was made simply because Prevost was the most experienced field commander who could get to Quebec quickly, an important consideration when war with the United States appeared imminent.[73] His selection nevertheless proved to be beneficial. The new governor had successfully used conciliation and tact to deal with the French population of St Lucia, where he held office from 1798 to 1802, and in Nova Scotia, where he had governed (with a touchy assembly) from 1808 to 1811. He spoke French fluently.

Almost immediately after his arrival in the Lower Canadian capital on 13 September 1811, Prevost toured the vulnerable Montreal area to inspect its defences and observe its political characteristics. He soon concluded that the defence of the colony required conciliation of the Canadien majority. This in turn meant accommodating the Roman Catholic hierarchy and placating the leaders of the *parti canadien*. In other words, he needed to reverse Sir James Craig's policy.[74] He did not assume the leadership of the English party, dissolve the provincial parliament precipitously, or lecture or scold the assembly majority, and he exploited his limited patronage resources skilfully.

In 1811 Craig had threatened to deport summarily Bishop Joseph-Octave Plessis aboard a naval vessel if he did not accept the government's control over the church's institutional operations (for example, the appointment of curés to parishes and the naming of bishops under the Reformation doctrine of the royal supremacy).[75] Prevost, in contrast, supported Plessis's determined efforts to gain legal recognition from the imperial authorities (achieved in 1817) and obtained a raise in his governmental stipend to £1,000 per annum. With regard to the *parti canadien*, Prevost restored the militia commissions of the five leaders whom Craig had cashiered in 1808, including the influential Pierre Bédard and Speaker Jean-Antoine Panet. He promoted Louis Bourdages to colonel and the rising young political star Louis-Joseph Papineau to captain. Pierre-Dominique Debartzch (1814) and Panet (1815) were, on the governor's earlier recommendations, named to the Legislative Council. The most dramatic, and symbolic, appointment was that of Bédard as provincial judge at Trois-Rivières, an act deemed grossly irresponsible by English party leaders, who viewed Bédard as a proven traitor.[76] The governor also reversed Craig's policy by socializing with the *parti canadien* leaders.[77]

Prevost naturally distanced himself from the more aggressive of the English party, attempting to dilute the influence of the 'old gang' on the Executive Council through new appointments and consulting that body as little as possible.[78] The governor spurned the company of ecclesiastical empire-builder Bishop Mountain. Another Craig favourite, Civil Secretary Herman Ryland, lost his commodious government residence and his allowances for fuel and candles. Assistant Secretary Edward Brenton and his aide, Andrew Cochran, did Ryland's work, with the civil secretary reduced to, in Cochran's words, 'a mere cypher ... after having been so long Prime Minister.'[79] The titular secretary himself complained that he never saw a dispatch, 'incoming or outgoing.'[80] It was virtually inevitable, then, that Sewell, Ryland, Mountain, and Richardson, among others, should soon come to loathe Prevost. The English party leaders attempted to have him recalled in 1814 and that same year attacked his 'dangerous' domestic policy and his pusillanimous military stance.[81]

Prevost's policy of conciliation paid political dividends. All classes of the Canadien elite were indefatigible in their efforts to ensure the active loyalty of the people. The senior clergy took the lead, in sermons, mandements, and circular letters. They stressed the religious duty to obey the king God had placed above the Canadiens, castigated modern France as the source of all evil, and emphasized that those 'arrogant unbelievers' to the south, carriers of the impious Enlightenment with its frightful progeny of sin and bloodshed, were threatening an invasion of Catholic Lower Canada. The new mother country shone 'with a thousand rays of glory amidst all the shattered thrones' of Europe. It represented hope – the only hope – for 'untold victims of the ambition and perfidy of an insatiable conqueror.'[82]

THE LACHINE RIOT

Historians have generally affirmed the loyalty and the patriotism of the Canadiens during this period,[83] while the militia's heroics during the battles south of Montreal at Lacolle (November 1812) and Châteauguay (October 1813) have been seen as a cathartic rebirth of the *la nation canadienne* following the shock of the conquest.[84] The majority of Canadiens were in fact remarkably calm during the War of 1812 and exhibited little ill humour although there were a few instances of resistance to the mobilization to the militia. The Lachine riot, in which militiamen opposed mobilization from 30 June to 2 July 1812, was by far the most significant. This rioting and its repression were pivotal events bearing on the issue of emergency powers.

Although the United States declared war on Great Britain only on 18 June 1812, Governor Prevost had already ordered the embodiment of 2000 militiamen on 20 May. The mustering proceeded without major setbacks and in fact triggered a show of zeal, but problems such as a lack of arms and minimal accommodations gradually led to discontent.[85] Even committed officers and militiamen could not but express their dissatisfaction when for four months a large proportion still trained without proper arms and ammunition or suitable lodgings.[86]

In Lachine, the discontent ended in riot. Earlier, the habitants had asked the local captain to exempt them from the militia levy. He refused. On 29 June Major Leprohon arrested two of the more than thirty missing militiamen in the Pointe Claire district. The next day he picked up another but had to release him when faced by an armed crowd at Captain Binet's house. A group of habitants followed the officer; some asserted that they wanted to wage 'civil war' and threatened that, if Leprohon did not release the other prisoners as well as those already mustered, they would round up more than one thousand and free them by force the next day.

On 1 July hundreds of habitants, many armed with sticks or guns, poured into the area from parishes in the west and north of Montreal island as well as from Vaudreuil and Soulanges. Although the ringleaders would later assert at their trial that they merely wanted to submit an address to the authorities as to the legality of the conscription law, their behaviour at the time was quite different. On 30 June and 1 July, during exchanges with members of the Executive Council and magistrates, some claimed that they had come to rescue the mustered militiamen. Their 'peaceful' intention was also belied by the fact that many bore arms, even though some moderate participants had tried to persuade them to leave their weapons at home and the reluctant had been threatened with arson if they did not join the protest.

These hundreds of men drifted to Lachine on 1 July. Some even suggested using the government's boats to go across the St Lawrence to Laprairie and free their sons. One of the group sent two emissaries to town to ask if the new militia law was in operation. If it was not, they were to obtain the release of all militiamen; if it was, they were to convince the authorities of their compliance with it. But the executive councillors had already dispatched two justices of the peace to argue with 'those mad people, to endeavour to bring them to a sense of their duty, by delivering up the militia man who had been rescued and further to insist that four of the most forward and who appear to be rig [sic] leaders in this revolt, to deliver themselves up to Justice, failing of which to forewarn them of the consequences and that an armed force will be sent to seize them.'[87] The justices of the peace explained that the law was in force and pleaded with the habitants to lay down their arms and return home. Contradictory subcurrents were at work in the crowd, some leaders being determined to succeed in their violent endeavours and others, more moderate, insisting that they sought only information. Some even argued that Canadiens were despised and complained that they had to drill even though they were badly nourished. Soon, however, the tumult receded somewhat. Threats and guards at the back of the crowd could not stop several habitants from leaving the scene altogether.

With only 200 to 250 men remaining, Justice of the Peace John McCord, preceding the troops, threatened the habitants with the intervention of the army, read the British Riot Act of 1714, and ordered their dispersal within an hour. Failure to comply might have brought capital criminal charges.[88] Many habitants answered that they would leave if the troops retired first. A cannon shot was then fired; the habitants replied with desultory musket fire which the troops returned. One Canadien was killed; another seriously wounded. The others fled through the fields and woods in the failing light of dusk.

On 2 and 3 July about 450 soldiers and militiamen forcefully marched through the region, arresting twenty-four presumed leaders. They joined ten who had been captured on 1 July and the two others who had been arrested on 29 June. According to Prevost, on 4 July about three hundred 'of these misguided men voluntarily came in to make their submission to me, acknowledging their guilt and faithfully promising immediately to comply with the order for their being drafted and giving me the strongest assurances of their readiness in future to perform whatever service I might require of them.' The governor was satisfied that this 'riotous assembly' of 'deluded and ignorant people,' which had turned into an 'organized insurrection for the release of their quota of the militia embodied in this neighbourhood,' had been repressed by the authorities' energetic actions. Other disaffected Canadiens would be convinced of 'the futility of any future attempts to resist the laws, and [this would] ultimately ... ensure the peace and tranquillity of the Country.'[89] In fact, the governor, struck by the general loyalty and zeal shown by other mustered men across the province, expressed his 'best hopes of being able to rely upon them [the Canadiens] in the hour of trial and danger.'[90] His positive, moderate attitude contrasted sharply with that of many of his advisers, particularly the executive councillors in Quebec. The newspapers, however, tended to echo the governor. The Montreal *Herald* even found reason to predict that, if 'mistaken' rebels had faced two cannons with courage, the Canadiens would surely make fast work of invading Americans.[91]

One can in fact conclude from the evidence that the Lachine riot was not grounded in any disloyal affection for either of Britain's enemies. It was a reflection of a traditional dislike of militia duty and a fear that the 'conqueror' would oppress the conscriptees. During the militia riots of 1794 it had been widely believed in the countryside that the government would send the militiamen out of the colony to fight with the regulars, perhaps in the West Indies. The argument about legality was also traditional, having had major impact, for example, during the Road Act riots of 1796–7.[92]

At the trials held in Montreal before the King's Bench in August and September 1812, desperate pleas of pacific intentions failed, as did the claim of some rioters that they had slipped away just before the shooting. Fourteen were convicted of various offences.[93] As in the 1790s, the government, for reasons of internal security, was extremely leery of prosecuting Canadiens for high treason, although the law as then understood in the colony, in the United States, and by the British jurist Sir Edward Hyde East (1803) would have allowed such prosecutions.[94] Three men were convicted of riot and rescue; four, of having incited a seditious riot. Seven others charged with conspiracy and riot were found guilty only of having been in the riotous crowd. This leniency by the Canadien jury, which judge Pierre-Louis Panet found 'inconceivable,' did not result in milder punishments for the seven. With invasion an obvious threat, penalties were harsh for the times. Besides fines and security for good behaviour, jail sentences of one year (2), thirteen months (1), eighteen months (4), and two years (7) were meted out, averaging just under twenty months. The fifty sentences of imprisonment that had been imposed on the militia and Road Act rioters of the 1790s had averaged just over four months. The three longest terms had been for one year.[95]

As had been commonplace on the bench throughout the wars against revolutionary and Napoleonic France, Panet, in sentencing the convicted, used the trials for propaganda purposes.[96] Besides characterizing the riots as manifesting a planned 'insurrection,' he extolled the virtues of British rule for the conquered but very fortunate Canadiens, 'qui vivent si heureux ... sans taxe, sans impot, protegé dans leur religion qu'ils exercent librement.' Consult your fathers, he told the prisoners, about the miserable poverty at the end of the French regime. Today all was different, he went on, with the exaggerated fervour of the co-opted: 'Tous les habitants sont aisés, les terres bien cultivées[,] les defrichements s'accroissant d'une manière rapide-près de 50 paroisses formés depuis la Conquête, une population de 4 cent mille ames [about 275,000 in reality] de 70 mille ou elle etoit lors de la reduction de la colonie ... 600 vaisseaux qui entrent dans nos ports au lieu de 40 or 50 sous le gouvernement françois, marque sensible de notre etat florissant.' Only the most ignorant or perverse would be against the blessings flowing from the mother country.

PREVOST AND SECURITY LEGISLATION

The governor's policy of appeasing the popular politicians had impressive legislative benefits. Prevost did not, of course, value elected assemblies. They were, he thought, often perverse and almost always inconvenient. Nor did he get his way on all occasions.[97] But he did succeed in having enacted those statutes truly essential to the colony's defence. In the first session of 1812 (February to May), the legislature radically transformed the militia law, providing for the selection of 2000 young bachelors to be mustered for ninety days' training in two successive summers or for two years in case of hostilities. In the event of war, invasion, or insurrection, real or imminent, Prevost could muster the entire militia, if he thought it necessary.[98] In addition to this act, much appreciated at the Château,[99] the governor was granted lavish funds for militia drilling and other defence purposes, to be spent at his discretion. The second session produced legislation authorizing the circulation of £250,000 in army bills, a form of paper money, with £15,000 per annum for five years granted to pay the interest as it became due. At the meeting of 1812–13, a further £250,000 was authorized and, much to the governor's relief, an import tax on merchandise was adopted.[100] In 1814, £1 million more was voted. It is inconceivable that Craig would have been so successful. Despite the *parti canadien*'s good will and manifest loyalty, however, even Prevost failed in the touchy area of emergency powers.

The Fate of Habeas Corpus Suspension

In reply to Craig's speech from the throne in December 1810, the assembly had implied that it would not continue the 'illiberal' Better Preservation Act, at least without drastic alterations. Such an attitude probably convinced the Legislative Council to include in its continuation bill the standard British requirement that each house consent to the detention of its members. Leaderless and intimidated, the *parti canadien* accepted this half-loaf, without dissenting votes, much to the governor's amused delight.[101] An attempt to force the release of Bédard got nowhere.[102]

With Bédard back in the house in 1812, the majority adopted a much tougher line. Prevost opened the regular session, which began in late February, by asking, among other things, that the legislature continue the

Alien and Better Preservation acts. The *parti canadien* members agreed to consider this idea but underlined 'the repugnance we might feel from an improper use of one of them.'[103] They later characterized that 'vicious' act [the Better Preservation Act] as 'a law ever dangerous in its principles, and which may become more so in its effects if prudence is not observed, both in the passing and execution thereof.' Prevost understood the reasons for 'repugnance' and was even inclined to sympathize. After all, Sir James Craig was to blame: 'The recollection of the system of coercion exercised towards the Commons by my predecessor during the last session lay rankling in their minds, begetting irritation against His Majesty's government, reluctance to continue laws essential to the preservation of the country under the extensive operation of which several members of that body had suffered.'[104]

In accordance with its stated libertarian position, the assembly amended a council bill so as to eliminate any authority whatever to intern legislators and to make the governor solely responsible for issuing the warrants. This latter proposal aimed at reducing the incidence of internment, blaming the 'partisan' Executive Council for the 'unjustified' arrests of 1810, and, most important, provocatively moving towards genuine political independence of the judiciary. The amendments were justified as lessening any 'fears which the public would have, if they saw so extensive an authority left to individuals whom they would find in all the tribunals of the Province, and with which individuals a thousand daily occurrences may connect them ... more frequently than it would happen with the Governor.' The council refused to accept these changes, arguing that they left the province insecure and would undermine, in practice (that is, public opinion), the fundamental principle that neither the king nor his representative could do wrong. The act lapsed. Habeas corpus would not be suspended again in Lower Canada until the rebellions of 1837–8.

Despite council's position, the idea of prohibiting judges from enforcing internment legislation could be and was readily justified on the basis of removing them from political concerns, particularly in cases that could come before them as criminal trials, habeas corpus hearings, or other legal proceedings. Even some in government circles adopted this viewpoint. Chief Justice Monk, who in 1812 gave much security advice to Prevost by private letter, justified the assembly's amendment on the basis of British practice – 'the Judges are *not* [in Britain] characters of the privy council' – and stressed it was 'not necessary' that 'such commitments proceed from ... [the judicial] branch of His Majesties Government.'[105] Shortly after the session, the governor himself informed the Colonial

Office: 'The House of Assembly, in replying to the reasons offered by the Legislative Council against the innovation, with some truth and justice observed, that the Act in its operation had been found defective inasmuch as it intrusted the execution to a number of persons of whom some were Judges before whose Court every complaint of an abuse under the act must come in the first instance to be tried, and the remainder [lay executive councillors] were members of the Court of Appeal before which the cause might eventually be brought for reconsideration.'[106]

With one brief exception in Upper Canada (1814), subsequent legislation suspending habeas corpus did not permit senior members of the judiciary to participate in the internment process. Thus, the *parti canadien* had made an important contribution to judicial independence in Canada, a contribution hitherto overlooked.[107]

In the run-up to the war session of July–August 1812, the governor and his advisers examined security needs, in relation both to martial law, discussed below, and to the suspension of habeas corpus. On the latter issue, Monk saw a clear analogy between the 'Treason ... at Lachine' and the militia riots of 1794. Then, foreign 'emissaries' had been mainly French; now they were mainly American, a minor distinction. The solution was, of course, the one he had authored to 'save' the province: re-enactment of those sections of the Alien Act of 1794 expanding the definition of seditious offences and suspending habeas corpus in cases where the accused was detained on a charge or merely on suspicion of high treason.[108] Prevost was less worried about what the Lachine riot had indicated regarding potential Canadien disloyalty. An admiring Andrew Cochran, whose ideas reflected those of the governor, instructed his father early on not to believe reports of 'revolt'; he always made 'a point of laughing at it as a mere riot.'[109] Prevost, however, had some concern about possible 'troubles' if 'Yankee' spies, whom he thought were infesting the colony in shadowy droves, were not thoroughly controlled. And he had been warned in January by the British consul general at New York that in the event of war 'the Canadians will be told by French Emissaries that the American and French Interests are a part of them.'[110] Special powers were certainly needed but the governor was now thinking in terms of measures going beyond suspensions of habeas corpus.

Martial Law[111]

Earlier in this volume three usages of the term 'martial law' were identified: the governance of soldiers, now called 'military law'; military governance of occupied territory, as in Quebec from 1759 to 1764; and total governance of everyone by the military to repress rebellion or defeat invasion. These three kinds of martial law were often not clearly distinguished until the nineteenth century.[112] It is the third that concerns us here.

Speaking on the then recent rebellion in Ceylon, the Duke of Wellington told the House of Lords in 1851 that 'martial law is neither more nor less than the will of the general who commands the army; in fact, martial law is no law at all.'[113] This statement was generally accurate although somewhat too sweeping. As it developed in the nineteenth and twentieth centuries, martial law, when in force – and not restricted by statute – vested power in the military over all persons in areas where the civil authority could not operate effectively. Until the Boer War, the test for this was whether the ordinary courts were or were not functioning. The military was justified in meeting force with force and where necessary punishing civilians, even capitally, through courts martial or by less formal means, confiscating property and legislating (for example, on curfew or hoarding), or ruling through 'executive orders.' There are, however, legal rules about when martial law comes into play and the courts since the late eighteenth century have not been totally excluded from judging the military. They can decide whether or not martial law is justified by statute or, until the second third of the nineteenth century, by the royal prerogative or sheer necessity. If justified, the courts cannot interfere with military orders but, after the crisis, can punish, civilly and criminally, *clearly* excessive force or wanton cruelty. In general, even acts of indemnity, which have been common, have not removed that power.

Martial Law and the Royal Prerogative

Prevost had a strong but not conclusive basis for believing that he could bring martial law into force, although not in the conditions that existed in the summer of 1812 when he asserted his right in a message to the legislature. His commission from King George III expressly authorized him 'to declare Martial Law in time of invasion, or at other times, when by Law it may be executed.'[114] While Governor Guy Carleton's proclamation of June 1775 provided a local precedent, its legality had been vigorously denied by Francis Maseres, former attorney general of Quebec.[115] More important no doubt were the nearly identical assertions found in an Irish statute of 1799 and in an imperial act of 1803 'for the suppression of rebellion in Ireland.' Section 5 of the latter 'declared and enacted, That nothing in this act contained shall be construed to take away, abridge, or diminish the acknowledged prerogative of his Majesty, for the public safety, to resort to the exercise of martial law against open enemies or traitors.'[116] An important point to note is that parliament did not assume paralysis of the civil power to be necessary before exercising the prerogative. But neither did it assume the crown could justify its exercise on the basis of merely *apprehended* danger. The wording indicates that there had to be actual invasion or insurrection.

About 1801 the noted jurist Francis Hargrave was of the opinion that, in the absence of a statutory foundation such as the Irish Act of 1799, the prerogative of bringing martial law into force over civilians did not exist.[117] Absolute necessity was the sole basis. In fact, the authorities antedating the 1799 act tended in this direction. True, the court in the *Case of Ship-Money* (1637) had held otherwise and had also vested in the crown sole power to judge the danger, but this was a discredited Stuart precedent that had been brilliantly countered at the time by one of John Hampden's counsel.[118] The prerogative was denied also by the British law officers in 1757, by Lord Mansfield in 1781, and, quite naturally, by many of those who identified 'martial law' as essentially applicable only to soldiers.[119] These included Lord Hale, Baron Maseres, Lord Chief Justice Loughborough in *Grant v. Gould* (1792), and the Irish King's Bench in *Wolfe Tone* (1798).[120] Similar assumptions twice surfaced in Lower Canada during the 1790s. Assembly member, merchant, and constitutional expert William Grant unsuccessfully proposed a motion in 1794 that the legislature *authorize* the governor and the Executive Council to proclaim 'the Law Martial whenever the Province in his and their independent judgment and discretion is in such imminent danger of invasion, rebellion or insurrection or in such other urgent necessity as requires the same.'[121] Merchant-magistrate John Richardson, head of counter-intelligence in the Montreal District, urged the attorney general during the crisis of 1797 (when a French naval attack and Canadien insurrection were feared by officials), that if the assembly refused to suspend habeas corpus the governor, Sir Robert Prescott, should take 'upon himself the Measure of proclaiming Martial Law, and trust... to Parliament for an indemnity.'[122]

For a variety of technical reasons, the acts of 1799 and 1803 were later held to be inconclusive.[123] And beginning in the late 1830s there was a gradual but decisive move to a position that proclamations of martial law were mere announcements of fact and not instruments creating new legal relationships. They were enunciative not constitutive. In an opinion on a Lower Canadian question (1838), which would become highly influential, the British law officers advised the colonial secretary that 'the Governor of Lower Canada has the power of proclaiming, in any district in which large bodies of the inhabitants are in open rebellion, that the Executive Government will proceed to enforce martial law. We must, however, add that in our opinion such proclamation confers no power on the Governor which he would not have possessed without it. The object of it can only be to give notice to the inhabitants of the course which the Governor is obliged to adopt for the purpose of restoring tranquillity.' War had to be raging to the point where the ordinary courts were paralysed before the crown could govern civilians militarily, except if authorized by the legislature. In arriving at this conclusion, the law officers consciously disregarded a provision in the most recent Irish Coercion Act, passed only five years before, which reiterated the constitutive theory of the prerogative.[124] The 1838 opinion, qualified with relation to whether the courts had to be closed,[125] expressed the law as it came to be in the late nineteenth and twentieth centuries.[126] But all these developments were in the future. Prevost certainly had an arguable case, provided there was actual invasion or rebellion.

Martial Law before the Executive

At the end of June 1812 the Executive Council in committee of the whole assumed that, were the governor to proclaim martial law, that would be the end of the matter legally, even where invasion or insurrection was only threatening rather than actual. After all, Chief Justice Sewell, Bishop Mountain, merchant John Young, and the other members of the Executive Council, even the new ones, were men highly supportive of the royal prerogative and for almost two decades had deeply suspected Canadien loyalty. Prevost was advised 'to issue a Proclamation when and so soon as you shall see fit declaring Martial Law throughout the Province' and subjecting to it civilians as well as militiamen and the regular forces. Authority derived from the governor's commission. This opinion, delivered before any invasion took place and before the executive councillors learned of the Lachine riot, sanctioned the prerogative where the danger was but anticipated. It was essentially a return to the reasoning in the Case of Ship-Money and clearly unsupportable.

The committee did not think that 'martial Law in an unqualified degree will be necessary' and hence His Excellency should assent to any bills restricting it, on the condition that they did not undermine the defence of the colony in general or the ability of imposing on the politically disobedient penalties much heavier than the fines or short terms of imprisonment provided by the regular laws (for example, those regarding riot, militia duties, sedition). War having been declared, the legislature would likely agree in principle with the proclamation(!), but if it was refractory this would provide perfect evidence to the British cabinet that martial law was indeed vital to the survival of the imperial link.[127]

Chief Justice Monk, who had not attended the 30 June session of the council, was asked for a legal opinion on the subject. He submitted one dated 8 July in which – surprisingly – he came to conclusions different from those of his colleagues. Mere threatened invasion or rebellion, Monk thought, was not a sufficient basis on which to justify a proclamation. Justification required actual raging war to the point that the civil power, particularly the courts, could not operate. This line of reasoning distinctly implied that a proclamation of martial law was an announcement (whether thought to be a necessary one is not clear) rather than a discretionary introduction of that legal status.[128] Prevost preferred the advice of the Executive Council committee.

In a special message to the legislature at the war session (18 July), a confident Prevost sought new statutory powers 'for promptly suppressing any attempt to produce disorder or insubordination, and for the immediate punishment of whatever offences may interrupt or endanger the public tranquility.' A somewhat impolitic threat accompanied this request. As soon as war had begun and 'the country was threatened by an immediate invasion,' the governor had been vested by His Majesty with the 'power ... of making a general and unqualified declaration of Martial Law in the Province.' This declaration, Prevost seems to have assumed, with some justification in law, would have involved shutting down all the civil courts.[129] He had 'been restrained from this [extreme] measure' by the approaching legislative session, which he had hoped and still hoped would provide him with discretionary authority 'to proceed summarily against offenders of every description' and hence make total martial law unnecessary.[130]

The same day, merchant, executive councillor, and assembly member James Irvine introduced a bill 'to provide more effectually for the defence of this Province, and for the safety and protection of His Majesty's subjects therein.' A copy of this measure has not been located, but it seems almost certain to have been modelled on the Irish Coercion Act of 1803, the most recent parliamentary precedent on martial law and one that restricted its possible effects. This statute authorized the Irish authorities to issue orders providing, *inter alia*, for court-martial trials 'in a summary way' of suspected rebels and their abettors. Punishments could range up to death and habeas corpus was suspended. Such arrangements would authorize and justify internment and stiff penalties, suspend a minatory club over potential dissidents, and do away with the leniency that juries might show in political cases.[131]

Irvine's bill did not reach committee stage, being submerged by a strongly supported *parti canadien* amendment that, instead, the committee of the whole consider His Excellency's assertion of authority over martial law.[132] This came to nothing during the war session but resulted in important assembly resolutions during its successor. These contended that, according to the British constitution, martial law was applicable only to military personnel. It was regulated by the British Mutiny Act and the Militia Act of Lower Canada. The most far-reaching resolution, narrowly passed, claimed that the 'limits and operation of martial law, as above stated, could not, nor can, be legally enlarged in this Province, without the authority of the Provincial Parliament.'[133] This concept that power to institute martial law was vested, not only in the sovereign parliament but in a colonial legislature as well, would be accepted by the British law officers after the rebellion of 1837–8 in Lower Canada, but it can be challenged on constitutional principle.[134]

Governing without Habeas Corpus Suspension and Martial Law

Prevost did not refer to the need for emergency powers in his speech closing the session of 1812–13 and would not thereafter press for such.[135] The apparent reasons for this placid acceptance of the assembly's failure to cooperate are many, the most obvious being the military situation. The two American invasions (the battles of Lacolle and Châteauguay) were easily repulsed, in part by Canadien militia, and generated no 'fifth column' activity. Disturbances of any kind were rare after the Lachine riot. The most serious occurred in the remote region of La Malbaie on the eastern St Lawrence during the spring of 1813 when a Colonel Fraser and his captain, Louis Tremblay, attempting to raise a contingent, experienced severe resistance from certain militiamen who refused to go to Baie-Saint-Paul. One habitant declared that 'the orders were dirt,' and another added that 'those who ordered them were nothing but filth.' Seven of the militiamen 'responded that they did not want to leave, preferring to be killed than to leave.'[136] Finally, the leaders, Alexis, Henri, and Jean Brassard, were denounced, having harangued the villagers 'that there is no king, not any longer and we don't fight for a king and that men do not have the right to give orders, that only God can give orders ... and that the country does not belong to the English; they stole it from the French, but that they will get it back.'[137] One of the brothers was heard saying that the Canadiens 'still belonged to the French, as it was not even 50 years that the English have been in Canada, that the English orders were not to be obeyed, that they had no power.'[138] Such nostalgic sentiments had been common during the militia riots of 1794 and had occasionally surfaced during militia troubles thereafter.[139] A lenient grand jury exonerated the leaders by finding 'no true bill' in September 1813.[140]

Among the other reasons for Prevost's attitude was his perception that Craig's problems with Canadiens were the result of his authoritarian rule. To follow Craig's aggressive stand would be plainly stupid: as Cochran put it, the only way to get anywhere with this inconvenient elected body was to avoid 'scolding them and quarreling with them as his predecessor did.'[141] In any case, the assembly was highly supportive except on emergency powers and even in this area it regularly renewed the Alien Act, which permitted the internment and summary deportation of all foreigners as well as forcing them to register with the authorities.[142] The internal situation, moreover, seemed far less threatening than it had appeared to government officials over the past two decades. Napoleon was completely immersed in his disastrous Russian campaign and its aftermath and hence could not supply French troops to assist the United States. Monk was certainly not alone when in December 1812 he expressed fervent agreement with the common Canadien comment that 'heureusement les François ne se soit pas joint aux americains pour debaucher nos habitans.'[143] The English elite had long known that domestic trouble would not likely be sparked by *pure* American invasion – indeed, fierce if perhaps martially incompetent loyalty would probably be exhibited.[144] The overall success of the militia mobilization in 1812 confirmed that view and even a suspicious Chief Justice Sewell thought the Canadien masses pro-British.[145]

Nor should the potency of the ordinary criminal law be underestimated. As interpreted in the province, the substantive offences of treason and sedition were elastic.[146] Violent opposition to the enforcement of statutes could amount to treason (although Sewell in his initial wartime address to the Quebec grand jury, remarkably, required proof of some anti-government intent) and mere plotting of insurrection was certainly so.[147] Any strongly worded criticism of the government amounted to the misdemeanour of sedition. Persons charged with treason (or felony) were not bailable. Misdemeanants (for example, rioters) had a right to bail but only if the sureties offered were thought sufficient by the magistrate.

They could, if convicted, be punished by imprisonment of any length (but not transportation or death); and the Lachine rioters' sentences indicate that, despite lack of jail space, some modest increase in the normal tough sentence of one year was practical. Certainly, Prevost was pleased that the 'firmness' shown by the government during the Lachine riot trials had had a positive effect. Truly dangerous political convicts could, in small numbers, be given sentences of three or four years.[148] Dissent and espionage could be nipped in the bud by an alert magistracy, whom at the outset of the war, at least, Cochran found 'wonderfully vigilant.'[149] In September 1812 Sewell gave them a 'pep talk' in which he stressed the disasters that threatened if the common people – any common people – could be worked upon by foreign emissaries and the discontented: 'Popular tumults at this Crisis, may justly be suspected to be excited by emissaries from the Enemy and indecision may be highly dangerous – Tumults so excited are intended to lead to revolution – and revolutions should be strangled in their Birth – minds yet in amazement must not yet have time to grow familiar with their guilt – The Ringleaders must not have time to confirm their power – The People must not have time to learn to obey new masters – and the acquisition of this time must be prevented by the activity and decision of the magistrate.'[150] This perfectly enunciated the Loyalist creed of the fragility of the social order, a sense shared by a great many non-Loyalists in the English elite.

Further research will be required to assess the actual security use made of the ordinary criminal law by the Prevost administration. We do know, however, that the governor was confident he had one major trump card to play if the British connection was genuinely imperilled. Despite the assembly's assertions of January 1813, he was determined, in such a situation, to proclaim total martial law. As Cochran put it in a letter to his father, 'this knot of fools' led by James Stuart had lately resolved that Prevost 'has not the right of declaring Martial Law without the consent of the Legislature. Now these resolutions are nothing – nor will they prevent Sir George from declaring Martial Law whenever he shall deem it to be required by the circumstances of the country.'[151] As events unfolded, this ultimate card did not need to be played. The governor's confidence in his powers made special legislation far from urgent.

CONCLUSION

The Lower Canadian security crisis of 1810–11 reveals obvious facets of legal history. First, it underlines that the law does not exist in a vacuum and always requires a socio-political context to be thoroughly understood. The conflict, although legally dressed, was ultimately about power, not the meaning of law. Still, the legal materials help us understand the crisis better than if we ignored them. The long-lived anger of Canadien politicians at the judiciary, the strength of the garrison mentality in 1810, and the willingness of the imperial power to rate necessity above legality (Gibbs's opinion) are examples. The 'Baconian' bench is another.[152]

A 'Baconian' judge bent over backwards to please the executive power and, where that seemed important, paid little attention to the Cokean principle of impartial judgment. The contemporary English – even the Irish, but not the Scottish – bench was, with gross exceptions, at least mixed. The Lower Canadian judges tended in the extreme to the 'Baconian' mould, as Murray Greenwood's article in this volume on judges and treason law shows. In 1810–11 Sewell acted as Craig's 'prime minister' and security adviser, four or five years *after* the negative Ellenborough precedent. And, by 1810, extrajudicial opinions had become commonplace in Lower Canada. Sewell advised the governor on the Sulpicians' land title and the royal supremacy over the local Roman Catholic Church. Monk instructed Craig on the then very controversial problem of the Roman Catholic bishop's 'right' to define parish boundaries. One year before, the Executive Council, including the three judges, had – in a strongly royalist direction – advised on the assembly's power to exclude Jews (specifically, Trois-Rivières merchant Ezekiel Hart) and judges (De Bonne). Six years earlier all senior justices had given advice to Lieutenant Governor Robert Shore Milnes on the application of English land law in the Eastern Townships. This opinion came forty-three years after Lord Mansfield had dissociated the judges of England from such manipulation, the last known collective precedent. The Lower Canadian opinion had been initiated, not by Milnes, but by Chief Justice John Elmsley.

Except for brief periods, habeas corpus was suspended in Lower Canada from the spring of 1794 to the spring of 1812. Ironically, when the 'hot' war broke out in 1812, this power was no longer available to the governor. At that time, the submission of the bench to the colonial power was supplemented by the willingness of the executive councillors to have Prevost proclaim martial law at the very beginning of the war, when even the threat of an invasion was missing. Since the 1760–4 experience with military government, the colonial authorities had learned the advantages of adding martial law to the panoply of instruments of royal power over the people. This could not be the case in England itself, because of strong constitutional opposition that was also shared by most of the judiciary (including the conservative Mansfield). In that context, one could at the most justify suspension of a specific legal procedure such as habeas corpus, thus permitting arbitrary arrest but *not* arbitrary judgment. Adding to the suspension of habeas corpus the power of *dispensing with the courts* in security cases was possible, however, in the colonies or Ireland. Two types of emergency powers, used concurrently or alternatively, were made available to colonial powers, that is, suspension of habeas corpus and martial law. Depending on the situation, these two powers were used differently over time in Canada: martial law followed by suspension of habeas corpus in 1775–83, suspension of habeas corpus only in the wars against revolutionary/Napoleonic France, neither in the War of 1812, and both simultaneously during the rebellion period – with martial law only partially in force. The years 1812–13 saw the emergence of the concept of limited martial law, as in Ireland: essentially courts martial functioning alongside the regular tribunals. This idea would prove convenient for the governing authorities some years later. The same emergency powers would be used in conjunction with the regular functioning of the ordinary courts in non-political cases, a remarkable extension of powers previously conceived as an alternative to the total collapse of the judicial system.

The legal issue raised by Prevost's claims of being able to introduce total martial law through the royal prerogative and the assembly's adamant denial of such claims was not resolved at the time. It would arise again, in a different but much more critical form, following the 1837–8 rebellions. Indeed, twelve accused rebels of 1838 were hanged and fifty-eight other civilians transported to New South Wales by a general court martial authorized by an appointed, colonial legislature. It functioned at a time when the civil power was perfectly capable of governing and the ordinary courts were open. Such proceedings had been condemned by jurists and judges in England for centuries.

NOTES

1 G. Paquet and J.-P. Wallot, *Patronage et pouvoir dans le Bas-Canada (1794–1812): Un essai d'économie historique* (Montreal: PUM 1973), ch. 1; R.A. Musgrave, *The Theory of Public Finance* (New York: McGraw Hill 1959), ch. 1.

2 G. Paquet and J.-P. Wallot, 'Le Bas-Canada au début du XIXe siècle: une hypothèse,' *RHAF*, vol. 25 (1971), 39; 'The International Circumstances of

Lower Canada, 1786–1810: Prolegomena,' *CHR*, vol. 53 (1972), 372; 'Groupes sociaux et pouvoir: le cas canadien au tournant du XIXe siècle,' *RHAF*, vol. 17 (1973–4), 509; 'Le système financier bas-canadien au tournant du XIXe siècle,' *Annales E.S.C.*, vol. 39 (1984), 1299.

3 As it would take too long to enumerate even the main studies, only examples are provided in this and the following notes. For more details see J.-P. Wallot, *Un Québec qui bougeait: trame socio-politique du Québec au tournant du XIXe siècle* (Montreal: Boréal Express 1973), at 143ff. On the 'constitutional struggle' see, for instance, Thomas Chapais, *Cours d'histoire du Canada*, 8 vols. (Quebec: Garneau 1919/34), 2: 150–86, 218–21; H. Brun, 'La Constitution de 1791,' *Recherches sociographiques*, vol. 10 (1969), 37; L.A.H. Smith, '*Le Canadien* and the English Constitution, 1806–1810,' *CHR*, vol. 38 (1957), 93; Helen Taft Manning, *The Revolt of French Canada 1800–1835* (Toronto: Macmillan 1962), ch. 3–5; John L. Finlay, 'The State of a Reputation: Bédard as Constitutionalist,' *Journal of Canadian Studies*, vol. 20 (1985–6), 60; Fernand Ouellet, 'Bédard, Pierre-Stanislas,' *DCB* 6: 41; F. Murray Greenwood, *Legacies of Fear: Law and Politics in Quebec in the Era of the French Revolution* (Toronto: Osgoode Society/University of Toronto Press 1993), ch. 1–2, 8, 10–12.

4 On feudalism (French, Catholic, and *ancien régime*) versus capitalism (British, Protestant, and capitalist), see D.G. Creighton, *The Empire of the St. Lawrence* [1937] (Toronto: Macmillan 1956) and his *Dominion of the North: A History of Canada* (Toronto: Macmillan 1944), at 231ff. Pursuing the same theme are three works by A.R.M. Lower: *Canadians in the Making: A Social History of Canada* (Toronto: Longmans 1958), at 98, 128–9 ff.; *Canada, Nation and Neighbour* (Toronto: Ryerson 1952), at 50, passim; and *Colony to Nation*, 2nd ed. (Toronto: Longmans 1947), at 67, 155, and passim.

5 The best-known proponent of this hypothesis is Fernand Ouellet, *Histoire économique et sociale du Québec, 1760–1850* (Montreal: Fidès 1966).

6 Michel Brunet, 'The British Conquest: Canadian Social Scientists and the Fate of the Canadiens,' *CHR*, vol. 40 (1959), 108; Marcel Séguin, *L'idée d'indépendance au Quèbec, genèse et historique* (Trois-Rivières: Boréal Express 1968).

7 Gilles Bourque, *Classes sociales et question nationale au Québec, 1760–1840* (Montreal: Parti Pris 1970); S.B. Ryerson, *Le capitalisme et la Confédération – Aux sources du conflit Canada-Québec (1760–1873)* (Montreal: Parti Pris 1972); G. Bernier, 'The Rebellions of 1837–1838 in Lower Canada: A Theoretical Framework,' *Canadian Review of Studies in Nationalism*, vol. 18 (1991), 131.

8 'Problématique pour un nouvelle approche de la Constitution de 1791,' *RHAF*, vol. 27 (1973–4), 181; idem, 'La genèse et l'avènement de la Constitution de 1791,' PhD thesis, Université de Montréal 1971.

9 Greenwood, *Legacies*, passim.

10 For instance, see Craig to Liverpool, 24 March 1810, MG 11, Q series, vol. 112, NA.

11 This image or that of the interaction of different systems in the body are more relevant than those of overlays or overlapping spheres. One can think also of Kurt Lewin's 'field theory' in psychology, which takes into account 'the totality of coexisting facts which are conceived of as mutually interdependent' to explain human behaviour: Field Theory in Social Science: Select Theoretical Papers, ed. D. Cartwright (New York: Harper and Row 1951), at 240.

12 Karl Polanyi, 'The Economy as an Instituted Process,' in Trade and Markets in the Early Empires, ed. Karl Polanyi et al. (Glencoe, Ill.: Free Press 1957), at 243. On the whole question see Paquet and Wallot, 'Groups sociaux et pouvoir'; Wallot, 'Le Bas-Canada sous l'administration de Craig (1807–1811),' PhD thesis, Université de Montréal 1965.

13 See, for example, Le Canadien, June to October 1809, Jan. to March 1810, and references in n.3.

14 Wallot, Un Québec qui bougeait, at 258ff; Greenwood, Legacies, ch. 2.

15 John Henry to Civil Secretary H.W. Ryland, 26 March 1810, S series, RG 4, A 1, vol. 82, NA.

16 Craig to Liverpool, 30 March 1810, Con Docs 2: at 372ff.

17 See D.G. Creighton, 'The Struggle for Financial Control in Lower Canada,' [1931] reprinted in Constitutionalism and Nationalism in Lower Canada, ed. Ramsay Cook (Toronto: University of Toronto Press 1969), at 56.

18 Taken from Paquet and Wallot, 'Groupes sociaux et pouvoir,' as well as from their Lower Canada at the Turn of the XIXe Century: Restructuring and Modernization (Ottawa: Canadian Historical Association 1988).

19 Greenwood, Legacies, passim. See Greenwood's 'Judges and Treason Law in Lower Canada, England, and the United States during the French Revolution, 1794–1800,' in this volume.

20 Parliamentary History [hereafter, Parl. Hist.], vol. 13, col. 672 (28 Feb. 1744). Solicitor General Mansfield stated that the writ had been suspended nine times since 1688–9. Then there were the suspensions of 1744, 1777, and 1794.

21 See ibid., vol. 5, cols. 156–7 (1 March 1688/9).

22 1 Wm. and Mary, sess. 1, c. 7; 7 and 8 Wm. III, c. 11; 1 Geo. 1, c. 8 (emphases added).

23 7 and 8 Wm. III, c. 11; 34 Geo. III, c. 54.

24 For this illuminating debate see Parl. Hist., vol. 31, cols. 497–573.

25 Albert Goodwin, The Friends of Liberty: The English Democratic Movement in the Age of the French Revolution (London: Hutchinson 1979), at 334.

26 'Horne Tooke's Diary,' Notes and Queries, vol. 11, 8th series (1897), 21 at 61.

27 In re Pierre Bedard, Stuart's Reports 1. The case is included in Con Docs 2: at 379–87.

28 PC2/140: 92–3 (16 May 1794), PRO.

29 See Greenwood, *Legacies*, at 24–7, and Jean-Marie Fecteau and Douglas Hay, '"Government by Will and Pleasure Instead of Law": Military Justice and the Legal System in Quebec, 1775–83,' in this volume.

30 See Greenwood, 'Judges and Treason Law' and *Legacies*, ch. 5. The Alien Act is SLC 1794, c. 5. It is treated in detail in *Legacies*, at 119–22.

31 See ibid., at 127–31, 172–4. The Better Preservation Act is SLC 1797, c. 6.

32 Emphasis added.

33 Garner Anthony, 'Martial Law, Military Government and the Writ of Habeas Corpus in Hawaii,' *California Law Review*, vol. 31 (1942–3), 477 at 495.

34 See his address to the grand jury at Annapolis, May 1793, in *Life and Correspondence of James Iredell, One of the Associate Justices of the Supreme Court of the United States*, 2 vols., ed. Griffith J. McRee [1856 or 1857] (New York: Peter Smith 1949), 2: 386–94 at 388–9.

35 James Morton Smith, *Freedom's Fetters: The Alien and Sedition Laws and American Civil Liberties* (Ithaca, N.Y.: Cornell University Press 1956), at 72.

36 *Annals of Congress*, 1807, vol. 16 at 403–25.

37 Craig to Castlereagh, 4 Aug. 1808, CO 42/136. For this and the next subsection, see Greenwood *Legacies*, ch. 8–11; Wallot, *Un Québec qui bougeait*. Quotations are from *Legacies*.

38 The term derived from a massacre of virtually all the French in Sicily in 1282, where the first toll for vespers had been used as the signal to begin the killing.

39 A draft copy of the charge may be found in vol. 12 of the Sewell Papers, MG 23, G II 10, at 5592–600, NA.

40 These examples have been chosen to show how wide-ranging Sewell's concept was. He also classed as seditious other writings (for example, those calculated to excite disobedience to the laws) that would have been perfectly acceptable in England.

41 Montreal *Gazette*, 9 April 1810; François-Xavier Garneau, *History of Canada from the Time of Its Discovery* [1852 in French], 2 vols. trans./ed. Andrew Bell (Montreal: Richard Worthington 1866), 2: at 261. Whether this censure was made to accommodate the *ministérieliste* members or, as the historian Garneau thought, reflected 'a mere subterfuge' by a packed jury 'to give an air of impartiality' to its denunciation of *Le Canadien* has not been determined.

42 When in late April a printing press in Montreal was put up for auction, Solicitor-General Stephen Sewell acted on a directive from Craig to make sure that it did not fall 'into the hands of the Canadian gentlemen who were desirous of establishing the opposition paper in this town.' Merchant James Ogilvy attended the auction and outbid representatives of the *parti canadien*: Stephen to Jonathan Sewell, 30 April 1810, Sewell Papers, vol. 4; Craig to Liverpool, 6 Nov. 1810, Q series, vol. 113; Robert Christie, *A History of the Late Province of*

Lower Canada, 6 vols. (Quebec/Montreal: Thomas Cary *et al.* 1848–55), 1: at 346.

43 See text below.

44 Greenwood, *Legacies*, at 220–1.

45 Ibid., at 122–3, 132–3.

46 Ibid., at 88, 123, 165. Despite being imprisoned on charges of treasonable practices and despite the propaganda of Craig's proclamation and that coming from the pro-crown intervention of the Roman Catholic clergy, Blanchet, Taschereau, and Bédard were elected in rural constituencies, Bédard in two ridings: Northumberland (District of Quebec) and Surrey (District of Montreal). This attitude on the part of the voters was to become manifest several times in the future and can even be detected, in the early 1970s, in relation to the Front de Libération du Québec. See F. Murray Greenwood, 'L'insurrection appréhendée et l'administration de la justice au Canada: le point de vue d'un historien,' *RHAF*, vol. 34 (1980–1), 57.

47 32 Geo. III c. 60 (emphasis added).

48 Contrast Fox's Libel Act with the Declaratory Act of 1766 (asserting parliament's sovereign authority over the colonies): 6 Geo. III, c. 12.

49 See Monk's opinion enclosed in Milnes to Hobart, 1 July 1803, Q series. Chief Justice Sewell was always seeking guidance from British judicial authority.

50 Ross to Arthur Davidson, 9 March 1795, Arthur Davidson Letters, McCord Family Papers, McCord Museum, Montreal; Greenwood, *Legacies*, at 118–19, 124; and the introduction to this volume.

51 See F. Murray Greenwood and Barry Wright, 'Parliamentary Privilege and the Repression of Dissent in the Canadas,' in this volume.

52 *R. v. Dougall et al.* (1874) 18 *Lower Canada Jurist* 85 (QB). Ramsay had earlier made clear that prosecution counsel considered the matter unsettled. We first came across a reference to this case in a draft of Barry Cahill's '*R. v. Howe* (1835) for Seditious Libel: A Tale of Twelve Magistrates,' in this volume.

53 SC 1874, c. 38, s. 4.

54 See n.27.

55 *Wilkes v. Halifax* (1763) 19 St. Tr. 981.

56 For the resolution and proceedings thereon, see *The Law and Working of the Constitution: Documents 1660–1914*, 2 vols., 2nd ed., ed. W.C. Costin and J. Steven Watson (London: Adam and Charles Black 1961), 1: at 219–27. The Commons resolution of 24 Nov. 1763 read: 'That Privilege of Parliament does not extend to the Case of writing and publishing seditious Libels, nor ought to obstruct the ordinary Course of the Laws, in the speedy and effectual Prosecution of so heinous and dangerous an Offence.' The Lords assented to the resolution on 29 Nov. 1763. Whether the courts or the houses of parliament have

the last word on the existence of a parliamentary privilege is a thorny question which has never been satisfactorily resolved. Since in this case the houses were denying, not asserting, a privilege and the injury was suffered by an MP rather than a member of the public, we think that the resolution should be preferred on this ground as well as that of the legal logic discussed below.

57 Quoted in Sir Thomas Erskine May, *A Treatise on the Law, Privileges, Proceedings and Usage of Parliament,* 19th ed. David Lidderdale (London: Butterworths 1976), at 104. Even Justice Pratt (then Lord Camden) later recognized in passing the force of the resolution: *Entick v. Carrington* (1765) 19 St. Tr. 1094.

58 *A Treatise of the Law and Custom of the Parliaments of England* (London: Timothy Goodwin 1690; repr. 1974 by Scholarly Resources of Wilmington, Del.), at 295; Sir William Blackstone, *Commentaries on the Laws of England* [1765–70], 4 vols., ed. George Sharswood (Philadelphia: J.B. Lippincott 1859), 1: at 165.

59 1 Sid. 42 (Trinity Term, 13 Chas. II [1661], KB); May, *Privileges,* at 97; Greenwood, *Legacies,* at 241–2, 324n.36.

60 See n.56 above.

61 Blackstone, *Commentaries,* 1: 164 (emphasis added).

62 14 East 1: 137 (emphasis added).

63 That Gibbs was supplied with a full dossier of the proceedings and evidence appears from Ryland to Craig, London, 15 August 1810, Christie, *History,* 6: at 134–5.

64 Lord Liverpool to Craig, 22 Aug. 1810, report and dispatch, ibid. at 160–2.

65 Craig to Ryland, 6 Aug. 1810, ibid. at 128–9; ibid., 1: at 322–4; ibid., 2: at 159, 179.

66 Craig to Ryland, 15 Jan. 1811, Christie, *History,* 6: at 181–2; Quebec *Mercury,* 24, 31 Dec. 1810; SLC 1811, c. 7; Manning, *Revolt,* at 93–4.

67 Wallot, 'La crise sous Craig,' at 146. See also Andrew Cochran to his father, 14 Sept. 1812, Cochran Papers, MG 24 B 16, NA, and Evelyn Kolish and James Lambert, 'The Attempted Impeachment of the Lower Canadian Chief Justices, 1814–15,' in this volume.

68 *Vie politique de Mr. Ex. Membre de la Chambre d'Assemblée du B.C.* [1814], at 10–11.

69 *Vindicator,* 6 March 1832.

70 Papineau's address to the protest meeting at St Laurent, 15 May 1837, is printed in Gérard Filteau, *Histoire des Patriotes,* 3 vols. (Montreal: Éditions de L'ACF 1938–9), 2: at 106. Philippe-Joseph Aubert de Gaspé, *Mémoires* [1866 in French], trans./ed. by Jane Brierley under the title *A Man of Sentiment: The Memoirs of Philippe-Joseph Aubert de Gaspé 1786–1871* (Montreal: Véhicule Press 1988), wrote that Craig's 'memory is still odious to French Canadians after a lapse of fifty-four years' (at 265).

71 Prevost to Bathurst, 4 Sept. 1814, *Con Docs* 2: at 466.

72 The main secondary sources we have relied upon for Prevost's background and his attempts at conciliation are Manning, *Revolt*, ch. 6; Ouellet, *Lower Canada*, ch. 4; Peter Burroughs, 'Prevost, Sir George,' *DCB* 5: 693; James H. Lambert, 'Ryland, Herman Witsius,' *DCB* 7: 766. Prevost governed as administrator until 15 July 1812, although his commission was dated 21 Oct. 1811.

73 *DCB* 5: 205.

74 See, for example, Prevost to Liverpool, 20 April. 1812, CO 42/146; same to Bathurst, 4 Sept. 1814, *Con Docs* 2: at 465–8; Andrew Cochran to his father, 14 Sept. 1812, Cochran Papers.

75 *Mandements, lettres pastorales et circulaires des Évêques de Québec*, 4 vols., ed. Henri Têtu and C.O. Gagnon (Quebec: A. Coté 1877–8), 3: at 71.

76 See, for example, Jonathan Sewell's Notebook, Sewell Papers, vol. 1 (*c.* 1814–15, 75–82); Ryland to Thomas Amyot, 10 Feb. 1813, Herman Ryland Papers, MG 24, B 3, vol. 2, NA.

77 Cochran to his father, 30 Dec. 1812, Cochran Papers.

78 In January 1812 Prevost appointed at least four new executive councillors: lawyer Ross Cuthbert, judge James Kerr, merchant John Mure, and Advocate General Olivier Perrault. Although they had all supported Craig in 1810, Chief Justice Sewell thought the appointees were Prevost's men and the appointments a serious grievance: Notebook, Sewell Papers, vol. 1 (c. 1814–15), 75.

79 Quoted in Lambert, 'Ryland, Herman Witsius,' at 769.

80 Ryland to Thomas Amyot, 8 July 1812, Ryland Papers, vol. 2.

81 See references in n.72; Kolish and Lambert, 'Attempted Impeachment'; and F. Murray Greenwood, 'Richardson, John,' *DCB* 6: 643. It was not only the leaders who were enraged by Prevost but the supporting cast as well. One example was merchant James Dunlop: Dunlop to [?], 2 April 1814, Letters of James Dunlop 1773–1815, Dunlop Papers, MG 24, D 42, NA (originals in the Scottish Record Office, Edinburgh). See also Greenwood, *Legacies*, at 245.

82 Fernand Ouellet, *Lower Canada 1791–1840: Social Change and Nationalism* (Toronto: McClelland and Stewart 1980), at 100–5. The clergy quoted in translation by Ouellet (as of the latter half of 1812) were Bishop Plessis, Monseigneur Jean-Henri-Auguste Roux, superior of the Séminaire de St Sulpice, Montreal, and Abbé Jean-Jacques Lartigue, a prominent Sulpician entrusted with several delicate missions by Plessis and Roux.

83 Ibid., ch. 4. 'Their growing ethnic self-consciousness made the French Canadians more dependent upon their traditional leadership and less ready to support doctrines of a revolutionary character': S.D. Clark, *Movements of Political Protest in Canada, 1640–1840* (Toronto: University of Toronto Press 1959), at 244–5.

84 'Châteauguay was our response to Craig's, Ryland's and Sewell's accusation. Châteauguay was our vengeance. Châteauguay was the affirmation of our undeniable loyalty and our ardent patriotism. Châteauguay was the heroic illustration of the national mentality that had slowly been formed, thanks to the clairvoyant direction of our religious and civil leaders, throughout tribulations and battles of 1763 to 1813!' [trans.]: Chapais, *Cours d'histoire du Canada*, 2: at 268.

85 For the details of this levy as well as the Lachine riot, see J.-P.-Wallot's 'Une émeute à Lachine contre la "conscription" (1812),' in *Un Québec qui bougeait*, at 107.

86 Wallot, 'Émeute à Lachine,' at 109.

87 Ibid., at 115.

88 1 Geo. 1 (1714), st. 2, c. 5. This statute was one of those criminal law acts 'received' by virtue of the Quebec Act of 1774. See this volume's introduction.

89 Wallot, 'Émeute à Lachine,' at 119–20.

90 Ibid., at 120.

91 4 July 1812.

92 See Greenwood, *Legacies*, ch. 4. The legalistic emphasis was typical of popular riots in the modern era. See E.P. Thompson, 'The Moral Economy of the English Crowd in the Eighteenth Century,' *Past and Present*, vol. 50 (1971), 76. That traditional elites were also sensitive to this feeling is shown by the reaction of Roux, who regretted that the law had not been officially proclaimed in front of the militiamen and that when they arrived in Montreal they found no money, lodging, or batteaux waiting for them: draft letter by Father Roux to Prevost, St Sulpice Papers, MG 17, 1, 5, NA.

93 This and the following paragraph are based primarily on 'Jugement de Juge Panet dans une cause de mutinerie à Lachine, au sujet de l'enrôlement des miliciens en 1812,' Collection Baby, MG 24, L 3, vol. 43 (028284–98), NA, and Wallot, 'Émeute à Lachine,' at 126–33.

94 See Greenwood, 'Judges and Treason Law.'

95 See Attorney General James Monk to Dorchester, with enclosure, 15 Nov. 1794, CO 42/101; Quebec *Gazette*, 18 Sept. 1794, 26 March 1795, 6 Oct. 1796, 6 April 1797; Montreal *Gazette*, 20 March, 11 Sept. 1797.

96 See particularly Judge Pierre-Amable De Bonne's address to convicted Road Act rioters: Quebec *Gazette*, 6 April 1797.

97 For examples, see Cochran to his father, 17 Aug. 1812, Cochran Papers (regarding amendment to the Militia Bill prohibiting substitutes); Christie, *History*, 2: at 153–65; and Kolish and Lambert, 'Attempted Impeachment.'

98 SLC 1812, c. 1.

99 Cochran to his father, 17 Aug. 1812, Cochran Papers.

100 Christie, *History*, 2: at 6–8, 14–16, 63–4, 151. Cochran deemed the new tax important but had not been confident of its passage through the house, since, like all assemblies, it had a 'crossgrained notion of economy': to James Stewart, 29 Dec. 1812, Cochran Papers.

101 SLC 1811, c. 7.; Craig to Ryland, 15 Jan. 1811, Christie, *History*, 6: at 181–2; JHALC, 1810–11 (passim); Manning, *Revolt*, ch. 5.

102 Upper Canada repeated, or perhaps followed, this protection of legislative members in its suspending act of 1814: SUC 1814, c. 6, s. 6. The drafting proviso differs from the British act of 1794 (34 Geo. III, c. 54) and SLC 1811, c. 7, both of which refer in general to privileges of the two houses before dealing with the requirement of consent. The Upper Canada statute treats only the latter.

103 Quebec *Mercury*, 24 Feb., 2 March 1812.

104 'Proceedings of the House of Assembly,' 11, 16 May 1812, *Con Docs* 2: at 428–31; Prevost to Liverpool, 20 April 1812, CO 42/146.

105 Monk to Prevost, 12 Dec. 1812, S series, vol. 126. For Monk's role as security adviser see also, for example, same to same, 13, 27 July 1812, ibid., vols. 122, 123, and to ——, 8 July 1812, *Con Docs* 2: at 432–4. For recent British practice (in which judges did not participate in the decisions to intern but gave opinions in the Privy Council on the proper charges, if any), see Greenwood, 'Judges and Treason Law.' The chief justice claimed that, for his part, he would 'sincerely wish *never* to be called upon to participate in such duties.' This was a *volte face* from 1810 (to impress the new governor?): see Greenwood, *Legacies*, at 235–6.

106 Prevost to Liverpool, 8 June 1812, CO 42/146.

107 Probably of equal importance was the 1806 debate in parliament on judges sitting in the cabinet and participating in state trials. A second contribution of the *parti canadien* to judicial independence was the precedent of excluding judges from the assemblies: Greenwood, *Legacies*, at 29–31, 218, 226, 231–2, 257; SLC 1811, c. 4.

108 Monk to Prevost, 13 July 1812, S series, vol. 122.

109 Cochran to his father, 6 July 1812, Cochran Papers.

110 Same to same, 12, 23 June 1812, ibid.; Thomas Barclay to Prevost, 22 Jan. 1812, S series, vol. 117. According to Cochran, Prevost feared tampering with the Canadiens by American 'spies and secret agents introduced into this province in the guise of travellers or merchants' more than 'any open aggression of their armies.'

111 This section on martial law is based principally on the primary sources hereafter cited and the following secondary works: W.F. Finlason, *A Review of the Authorities as to the Repression of Riot or Rebellion* (London: Stevens and Sons

1868); W.S. Holdsworth, 'Martial Law Historically Considered,' *Law Quarterly Review*, vol. 18 (1902), 117; R.F.V. Heuston, *Essays in Constitutional Law*, 2nd ed. (London: Stevens and Sons 1964), at 150; George M. Dennison, 'Martial Law: The Development of a Theory of Emergency Powers, 1776–1861,' *American Journal of Legal History*, vol. 18 (1974), 52; D.A. Schlueter, 'The Court-Martial: An Historical Survey,' *Military Law Review*, vol. 87 (1980), 129; Charles Townshend, 'Martial Law: Legal and Administrative Problems of Civil Emergency in Britain and the Empire, 1800–1940,' *Historical Journal*, vol. 25 (1982), 167; Jean-Marie Fecteau, 'Mesures d'exception et règle de droit: Les conditions d'application de la loi martiale au Québec lors des rébellions de 1837–1838,' *McGill Law Journal*, vol. 32 (1987), 464; F. Murray Greenwood, 'The General Court Martial of 1838–39 in Lower Canada: An Abuse of Justice,' in *Canadian Perspectives on Law and Society: Issues in Legal History*, ed. W. Wesley Pue and Barry Wright (Ottawa: Carleton University Press 1988), 249.

112 See two essays in this volume: Douglas Hay, 'Civilians Tried in Military Courts: Quebec, 1759–64'; and Fecteau and Hay, '"Government by Will and Pleasure."' Also: F.B. Wiener, *Civilians under Military Justice: The British Practice since 1689 Especially in North America* (Chicago: University of Chicago Press 1967), passim, but particularly ch. 2.

113 Quoted in *Cases and Opinions on Constitutional Law*, ed. William Forsyth (London: Stevens and Haynes 1869), at 211.

114 Quoted in Monk to ——, 8 July 1812, *Con Docs* 2: at 433. See also Lord Dorchester's commission of 12 Sept. 1791 in ibid., at 9.

115 See Fecteau and Hay, '"Government by Will and Pleasure."'

116 Ir. 39 Geo. III, c. 11; 43 Geo. III, c. 117.

117 Printed in Forsyth, *Cases and Opinions*, at 189–92.

118 3 St. Tr. 825. For an excellent analysis see Holdsworth, 'Martial Law Historically Considered,' at 123–5.

119 With reference to Lord Hale's insistence upon its application only to the military, Dennison (n.111, at 53) stated that 'civilians within the area of combat served in defense of the realm, and thus automatically were subject to martial law.'

120 See authorities cited in n.111. *Grant v. Gould* is 2 H. Bl. 98 and *Tone* is 27 St. Tr. 613.

121 JHALC, 1793–4 (22 May 1794).

122 Richardson to Jonathan Sewell, 30 March 1797, Sewell Papers, vol. 3. There were several indemnity acts (or indemnity provisions in martial law acts; see n.111) passed for Ireland by the Irish and British parliaments in the late eighteenth and early nineteenth centuries. These legally immunized acts passed under the prerogative. Referring to such legislative provisions in general,

Holdsworth made the wise point that the 'necessity for comprehensive Acts of indemnity whenever martial law has been put in force is a strong argument in favour of this view [denying prerogative power]. Such Acts do not as a rule cover cases of wanton wrongdoing. This is the only reason for their existence' if the 'contrary hypothesis' were true: 'Martial Law Historically Considered,' at 128.

123 Ibid.; Forsyth, *Cases and Opinions*, at 212.

124 3 and 4 Wm. IV (1833), c. 4, s. 40. The law officers were perfectly aware of this Irish Coercion Act. They mentioned the act in their opinion, while Attorney General Campbell had been solicitor general and an MP in 1833.

125 According to the Judicial Committee in *Ex p. D.F. Marais* (1902) A.C. 109, the test of closed courts is not conclusive. The existence of a state of war, civil or international, is compatible in certain circumstances with the courts remaining open. Thus, the courts might be able to function 'behind the lines,' dealing with non-subversive criminal offences and civil litigation, while martial law over civilians was urgently required there and in front.

126 The opinion (Sir John Campbell, attorney general, and Sir R.M. Rolfe, solicitor general, to Lord Glenelg, 16 Jan. 1838) has been printed in the major collections of constitutional law documents: Forsyth, *Cases and Opinions*, at 198–9 (the text used here); *The Law and Working of the Constitution: Documents 1660–1914*, vol. 2, 2nd. ed., ed. W. Costin and J.S. Watson (London: Adam and Charles Black 1964), at 389–90; *Cases in Constitutional Law*, 5th ed., ed. D.L. Keir and F.H. Lawson (Oxford: Clarendon Press 1967), at 238–9. It has been cited as persusasive by a number of the leading experts on martial law. See, for example, Holdsworth, 'Martial Law Historically Considered,' at 128n.7; Heuston, *Essays*, at 152–3; Townshend, 'Civil Emergency,' at 171–2. An equally clear opinion of like import was delivered in 1857 by Attorney General Caleb Cushing of the United States: 'When martial law is proclaimed [by a governor of a state or territory] under circumstances of assumed necessity, the proclamation must be regarded as the statement of an existing fact, rather than the legal creation of that fact': quoted in Forsyth, *Cases and Opinions*, at 210.

127 Executive Council Minutes, Lower Canada, RG 1, E 1, State Book G (30 June 1812), NA. Recognizing recent political developments, the committee recommended that members and officials of the two houses of the provincial parliament be exempted during sessions.

128 Monk to ——, 8 July 1812, *Con Docs* 2: at 432–4.

129 For example, in *Wolfe Tone* (27 St. Tr. 613), heard in 1798, the Irish King's Bench accepted counsel's argument, based on long-standing authority, that when the civil courts were open there could not be a state of war justifying martial law.

130 JHALC, 1812, 2nd session (18 July). That day Prevost, writing Colonial Secretary Lord Liverpool, expressed great optimism: 'I have great reason to hope from what I see and hear of the dispositions of the House of Assembly that these measures [limited martial law and increased supply], both equally important to the present safety and welfare of the Province, will meet their concurrence': CO 42/147.

131 43 Geo. III (1803), c. 117, especially ss. 1, 4. The preamble stressed the drawbacks of using the regular courts (delays, small penalties, jury leniency): 'Whereas ... persons who may be guilty of acts of cruelty and outrage in furtherance ... of such insurrection ... may seek to avail themselves of the ordinary course of the common Law to evade the punishment of such crimes' (emphasis in original).

132 JHALC, 1812, 2nd session (20 July). The amendment passed by a vote of twenty votes to six.

133 Ibid., for 1812–13 (26 Jan. 1813). This fourth resolution passed eighteen to fifteen, which again suggests the unsettled state of the law. The interpretation of these important resolutions reveals the often summary treatment afforded the history of constitutional freedoms by historians. Thus, Helen Taft Manning attributes the resolutions to the political manoeuvres of James Stuart and comments: 'He argued with shameless sophistry that such powers were not needed, even in time of war, in view of those already granted under the militia acts and by the Governor's commission': Revolt, at 103–4.

134 See Greenwood, 'General Court Martial of 1838–39 in Lower Canada,' at 267–73. The argument is that no colonial legislature could then enact laws contravening the fundamental principles of the common law (for example, trial of civilians by courts martial where necessity did not enjoin it).

135 JHALC, 1812–13 (15 Feb. 1813); Cochran to his father, 26 (?) Jan. 1813, Cochran Papers.

136 Trans., deposition of Louis Tremblay, 28 March 1813, Ministère de justice, T0006–001/14, R. v. Alexis, Henri et Jean Brassard, ANQ; trans., deposition of Jean Filion, 28 March 1813, ibid.; trans., deposition of Joseph Lavoie, 1 April 1813, ibid.

137 Trans., ibid.

138 Trans., deposition of Baptiste Simard, 2 April 1813, who affirmed that more than seventy persons had attended the 'sermon': ibid.

139 Greenwood, Legacies, at 81, 201–2, 314n.33.

140 Bill of indictment, Ministère de justice, T0006–001/14, R. v. Alexis, Henri et Jean Brassard.

141 Cochran to his father, 26 (?) Jan. 1813, Cochran Papers. See also same to same, 14 Sept. 1812, ibid.

142 The Alien Act of 1811 (c. 3) was continued in 1812 (c. 16), 1813 (c. 5), and 1814

(c. 2). It lapsed in 1815 but a short and simple peacetime version was enacted two years later: SLC 1817, c. 20. This temporary, four-section statute (35 in 1811) did not provide for registration. It applied only to Frenchmen who had had a military or governmental connection to revolutionary or Napoleonic France. They could be summarily deported or interned, but only for two months. Christie, *History*, 2: at 6, incorrectly had the Alien Act of 1811 lapse after the first session of 1812 because of disagreements between the houses. The act of 1817 lapsed a year later.

143 Monk to Prevost, 12 Dec. 1812, S series, vol. 126.

144 See Greenwood, *Legacies*, at 212, 220–3, 318n.69. Examples of this attitude during the War of 1812 and on its eve abound. See, for example, Consul General Thomas Barclay to Prevost, New York, 22 Jan. 1812, S series, vol. 117 (regarding opinion of 'most of the British gentlemen resident in Quebec and Montreal'); Jonathan Sewell's Notebook, Sewell Papers, vol. 1 [c. 1814–15, 79–80 (a detailed analysis)].

145 See, for instance, Sewell to Prevost, 3 July 1812, quoted in Wallot, 'Émeute à Lachine,' at 134–5; Quebec *Gazette*, 24 Sept. 1812.

146 See Quebec *Gazette*, 24 Sept. 1812 (Sewell's address to the Quebec grand jury); Greenwood, *Legacies*, ch. 6, 11, 12; and, in this volume, Greenwood's 'Judges and Treason Law' and the introduction.

147 See references in the preceding note.

148 See Cochran to his father, 10 Oct. 1812, Cochran Papers; Greenwood, *Legacies*, at 123–34.

149 Cochran to his father, 23 June 1812, Cochran Papers. There are several examples of the activity of the magistrates in S series, vols. 116–23 (Dec. 1811–Sept. 1812).

150 Sewell Papers, vol. 12 (5952).

151 Cochran to his father, 26(?) Jan. 1813, Cochran Papers. See also same to Maria, 4 Feb. 1813, ibid. On 22 Nov. 1813, Major-General Francis De Rottenburg proclaimed martial law through the eastern districts of Upper Canada 'as far as relates to procuring Provisions and forage.' The assembly responded by resolving that this use of the prerogative, limited though it was, must be characterized as 'arbitrary & unconstitutional, and contrary to and subversive of the established Laws of the Land': *Con Docs* 2: at 435. For general studies see William M. Weekes, 'The War of 1812: Civil Authority and Martial Law in Upper Canada,' *OH*, vol. 48 (1956), 147, and Paul Romney and Barry Wright. 'State Trials and Security Proceedings in Upper Canada during the War of 1812,' in this volume.

152 See, on this point, Greenwood, *Legacies*, passim, but particularly 27–34, 256–60.

11

State Trials and Security Proceedings in Upper Canada during the War of 1812*

PAUL ROMNEY and BARRY WRIGHT

The war between Great Britain and the United States, which lasted from June 1812 until December 1814, gave rise to a variety of security proceedings. In addition to the prosecution of political offences according to the law of the land, two major measures were taken which originated in the fact that most of the adult population were either immigrants, or the children of immigrants, from the United States. In the early stages of the war, the government used its powers under the provincial Sedition Act of 1804, in conjunction with the militia law, to force disloyal inhabitants to leave the country. Later on, in 1814, the government procured legislation authorizing the expropriation of the estates of such persons and of those who had been convicted of high treason or had evaded prosecution for political offences by fleeing the province. In 1814, too, the government obtained the temporary suspension of habeas corpus and the passage of a statute authorizing out-of-district trial in cases of high treason.

A continuing subject of debate throughout the war was the extent to which martial law could be applied to civilians and the conditions for doing so. Limited martial law was proclaimed in different districts from time to time during the war, but there was no general province-wide proclamation and no civilians appear to have been tried by court martial. Males from sixteen to sixty years of age were liable for militia duty, a

*The authors gratefully acknowledge the valuable assistance of Beverley Boissery Greenwood.

state of affairs that made most men in the province potentially subject to military law. However, few men were harshly punished even for desertion, although avoidance of military service was rife.[1] This was probably because most recalcitrants were neutral rather than ardently pro-American. Many inhabitants were anxious to shirk their duty to the crown, but few were eager to hazard their safety in the service of the enemy.[2]

THE PURGE AND DEPORTATION OF ALIENS

Major-General Isaac Brock, commander of the forces in Upper Canada, was made civil administrator of the province and president of the Executive Council in October 1811 during the absence on leave of the lieutenant governor, Francis Gore. In February 1812, as diplomatic relations deteriorated between Britain and the United States, Brock presented intelligence to the Executive Council concerning American 'emissaries' at work in the province, and the council recommended vigilant enforcement of the Sedition Act (app. 3, K, doc. 1).

This measure had been enacted in 1804 in order to meet an apprehended danger of subversion by American and Irish immigrants, perhaps in connection with foreign invasion. It permitted the deportation of anyone who had not been an 'inhabitant' of the province for six months prior to the institution of proceedings against him, or who had not taken the oath of allegiance, if that person 'by words, actions, or other behaviour or conduct' had 'given just cause to suspect that he [was] about to endeavour to alienate the minds of His Majesty's Subjects of this Province from his Person or Government, or in any wise with a seditious intent to disturb the tranquillity thereof.' The head of government, any judge of the Court of King's Bench, or any executive or legislative councillor might order the arrest of such a person and require him to prove his innocence of the suspicions he had aroused. Should he fail to do so, the officer who had ordered his arrest might direct him to leave the province. Disobedience to such an order was made a misdemeanour, the offender to be held without bail pending trial, and a second offence was made a capital felony.

By orders in council of 24 and 25 February 1812, responsible officers were directed to enforce the act vigilantly and several special commissioners were appointed in each district for that purpose.[3] At the same time, Brock asked in vain for new security legislation, including a partial suspension of habeas corpus and the amendment of the Militia Act to require members to abjure all foreign powers.[4] The term of the House of

Assembly having expired, he hastily called a general election in the hope of obtaining a more cooperative house.

The legislature met again late in July, after the outbreak of war. At first the new assembly seemed no more amenable than its predecessor, and it did in fact refuse to suspend habeas corpus or to empower the government to issue a limited declaration of martial law to operate concurrently with the ordinary administration of justice. Brock wanted the latter measure because his official instructions authorized him in general terms to proclaim martial law 'in time of invasion or at other times when by Law it may be executed,' and he feared that this must entail the complete supersession of civil justice throughout the province. The assembly's recalcitrance was evidence of the deep unpopularity of the measure, and he had been warned that any attempt to control the militia through martial law would prompt the whole body to disperse.[5]

Although it did not give him a blank cheque, the assembly did incorporate some stringent security provisions into the militia law. Militiamen who refused to take an oath of allegiance were to be deemed enemy aliens; desertion, mutiny, and sedition were made capital offences; and procedures were established for dealing with these and lesser offences by court martial.[6] Since every male inhabitant between sixteen and sixty years of age was liable for service, the greater part of the adult male population was thereby rendered potentially subject to military justice or to the administrative measures directed against enemy aliens. One particularly important provision, which has universally been ignored by previous writers, established significant powers of preventive detention in districts subject to invasion or rebellion. It empowered military commanders to arrest any resident of such district upon suspicion of treason or treasonable practices, and to accuse him before a panel of three or more magistrates. These might, if they saw fit, imprison the suspect without bail until the end of the next legislative session.[7] This measure probably constituted the basis for the numerous preventive arrests prior to the general suspension of habeas corpus in 1814.

While the legislature was in session, Brock asked the members of the Executive Council whether they thought it expedient for him to proclaim martial law. Previously he had hesitated to do so, but the militia was showing alarming signs of insubordination and he was doubtful of the assembly's cooperation. The council advised him to proceed, and Brock consulted the governor-in-chief, Sir George Prevost, on the details of the measure. However, his victories at Detroit and Queenston Heights relieved the pressure on the province and made the question of martial law for the time being an academic one. The security provisions of the amended militia law may also have helped to avert this measure.[8]

Undoubtedly the new law made, in combination with the rigorously enforced Sedition Act, an effective purge of the population. Under their combined pressure, disloyal inhabitants began fleeing the province in large numbers.[9] In November, boards of commissioners were set up in Niagara, York, and Kingston to deal with the growing problem of men who refused both militia duty and the oath of allegiance on the ground that they were subjects of the United States. The boards were instructed to register the men for service and administer the oath of allegiance, thereby subjecting them to the militia law. Recusants who proved their status as subjects of the United States were to be deported under the Sedition Act, but those settled on lands which they had purchased, or had acquired otherwise than by grant from the crown, might be allowed to stay on passes, giving security for their good conduct. American subjects who had not reported to the appropriate board by the end of the year were subject to detention as prisoners of war.[10] Systematic deportation proceedings commenced in December.[11] Close to 400 landholders and hundreds of landless men fled or were deported as a result of these measures, but the records on the latter are less complete and there are no data on females or on males under sixteen years of age.[12] Despite the purge, disaffection among the militia and the general population remained a problem throughout the war.[13]

CRIMINAL PROCEEDINGS, 1812–13

Prosecutions for sedition and treason began in August 1812. Richard Conklin was acquitted of sedition at the Midland District assizes.[14] In the Niagara District, Joseph Bastedo pleaded guilty to the same offence and Abraham Lazatere was acquitted.[15] The details of these cases are unknown. A week later, at the London District assizes, Joseph Willcocks and John Beemer were presented for sedition. Willcocks was an MPP and leader of the Upper Canadian opposition, and the charges against him smack of a frame-up since they all related to alleged utterances in private conversation with the same person. Though he later deserted to the enemy, his activities at this time were conspicuously loyal, including service at Queenston Heights and a confidential mission to the Six Nations Indians.[16] Beemer, a justice of the peace, was one of several individuals who are stated on plausible testimony to have encouraged the Norfolk militia to disobey orders.[17] Neither man was proceeded against at the time, though Beemer was later to be detained without habeas corpus while Willcocks, having gone over to the enemy in July 1813, was to be indicted *in absentia* for high treason.[18]

The most serious cases to come before the courts during the early months of the war were those of Antoine Lafitte, Antoine Meloche, and Isaac Willet, indicted for treason at the Western District assizes of September 1812. A fourth, Allan McDougall, was presented *in absentia*. Again the details are unknown, though Willett was probably the man of that name who was captured by Brock's troops at Detroit. The three prisoners were bailed, and there is no record of subsequent process in Willett's case, but several pages are missing from the King's Bench assize minutebook at this point. While Lafitte and Meloche never came to trial, they were not discharged from their recognizances until August 1815.[19] The only other treason indictments prior to the Ancaster 'Bloody Assize' of 1814 were those of John Conner at the Midland District assizes of September 1813 and Adam Stevens and Ebenezer Ransom, indicted *in absentia* at the Home District assizes of March 1814. Conner was released on heavy recognizances (£1000 and two sureties of £500 each), and again there is no record of further process.[20]

The military vicissitudes of 1813 revealed that the defence of the province continued to be jeopardized by the disaffection of some of its inhabitants. In April, when American forces occupied the provincial capital, local residents were alleged to have pillaged the government stores and aided the enemy with information. The local magistrates, in concert with the judges of the Court of King's Bench, issued a declaration affirming that the laws of the land remained in effect and calling on 'every good subject' to aid the lawful authorities in maintaining order. The American commander, Henry Dearborn, issued an order to the same effect.[21] However, the Americans' return at the end of July evoked new demonstrations of disloyalty. Twice during the year, the ebb and flow of battle dislodged loyal forces from the Niagara peninsula, and in the autumn Joseph Willcocks and Benajah Mallory, a former MPP, began recruiting a company of Canadian volunteers to aid the invader.[22]

Under these circumstances, the continuing precariousness of the civil government prompted loyalists to canvass the virtues of martial law. While Brigadier-General Henry Procter imposed martial law in Michigan in March, there is no evidence that he imposed it in western Upper Canada as stated by Weekes.[23] Early in May a group of notables in the Niagara District petitioned the local army commander to extend such measures to the province, but Brigadier-General John Vincent refused to

proceed against persons or property without the approval of the administrator, Sir Roger Sheaffe, who had succeeded Brock upon the latter's
death at Queenston Heights. Apparently the recurrence of this question
revived the dilemma that had troubled Brock a year earlier. What followed is obscure, but it seems that Prevost commanded Sheaffe to authorize such action in his civil capacity and Sheaffe demurred in the belief
that his instructions as president and administrator did not permit anything less than a province-wide proclamation of martial law. Thereupon
Prevost ordered him to do in his military capacity what he had declined
to do as a civilian.[24] If this account is correct, the episode stands as an
early example of what was to become a standard military response to the
limits of civil authority.

There is no indication that Vincent exerted his new authority before he
was forced to abandon the peninsula about the end of May, but the victory at Stoney Creek soon permitted its reoccupation and the implementation of the new martial-law strategy. Many farmers had retreated with
the enemy, leaving large crops of grain standing in their fields. Sheaffe's
successor as commander and administrator, Baron Francis de Rottenburg, suggested that commissioners be appointed by order in council to
harvest and dispose of this grain in the public interest. The Executive
Council approved the policy but advised that it could not be implemented by order in council because it lacked the sanction of law. For this
reason, explained the chief justice, Thomas Scott, Rottenburg would have
to act in his military capacity.[25]

Scott's advice was seconded by the acting attorney general, John Beverley Robinson. 'The Council have no other means than the laws afford
them of enforcing obedience to any order, consequently if they make an
order not sanctioned by the law, they have no power of enforcing it at all,
and should a Commissioner in acting under this proclamation meet with
opposition, he must be supported by the military authorities.' For this
reason the proposed measure might more appropriately be carried out by
Rottenburg in his military than in his civil capacity. 'As president of this
Council and as an act of that Council His Honor cannot enforce that measure. As Comm[ande]r of the Forces he can.' On the advice of the Executive Council, Rottenburg's proclamation specified that the crops were
being taken by the government for the benefit of the future legal claimant
– a formula that eliminated any taint of wrongful expropriation.[26]

Prevost confirmed Rottenburg's authority under the articles of war to
proceed by courts martial against persons engaging in traitorous practices in districts under enemy occupation. He doubted, however, that the

limited martial law proclaimed in the Niagara District was sufficient warrant for such proceedings, and no action was taken, though the authorities continued to contemplate it.[27]

The conduct of some inhabitants during the occupation of York in April and July did impel the government to resort to exceptional measures against individuals suspected of treason or sedition. In August the Executive Council recommended the appointment of a secret committee of one to gather evidence of such offences, and the stationing of a detachment of troops in the capital to arrest suspects identified by the commissioner. The council justified its recommendation by referring to the large number of American settlers of doubtful loyalty, the prospect that juries would be afraid to convict offenders, the district jailer's reluctance to take custody of such offenders for fear of the vengeance of 'an exasperated banditti,' and the repeated refusal of the legislature to enact safety measures such as a suspension of habeas corpus. One member of the council, William Dummer Powell of the Court of King's Bench, recommended that Peter Robinson be appointed to conduct the investigation under the superintendence of his brother, the acting attorney general.[28]

Again the latter responded by nicely discriminating between what circumstances dictated and what the law allowed. He could not, he declared, cooperate with the military authorities in his capacity as a law officer of the crown but would gladly do so as a private individual. 'The country must not be lost by a too scrupulous attention to forms and when the civil administration of justice is found inadequate to our protection in times perilous and unusual as the present, recourse must be had to measures more efficacious and the necessity *must* and *will* justify their adoption.'[29] Rather than the single commissioner contemplated by the Executive Council, Robinson proposed a six-member committee of information, and Rottenburg duly appointed his nominees.

The record of the committee's proceedings show that sixty-four depositions were taken, forty-two suspects investigated, and thirty-two selected as serious cases warranting charges.[30] Accusations ranged from toasts 'drinking to the success of the American Fleet' and 'having all old Tories hanged' to assisting the Americans with intelligence and looting the public stores. Fourteen men were arrested and held without bail until the following spring, when four were released and the remainder either tried or held under the new habeas corpus legislation. Of these ten, three were eventually indicted for treason and five for sedition, while two were held without trial and released after the war.[31]

Of the treason suspects, one, John Chilson, was tried, rather belatedly, in March 1815 and acquitted.[32] True bills were found against the other two, but they escaped from custody before trial and fled to the United States.[33] Of the sedition prosecutions emanating from the committee, perhaps the most notable was that of Elijah Bentley, an influential Baptist preacher. Bentley was the subject of eleven separate informations, mostly for seditious words, though he was also alleged to have directed American troops to government stores. There was ample evidence of his pro-American sentiments, but the case also reflects the apprehension aroused by his status in the community. Upon his conviction in March 1814, he was sentenced to six months' imprisonment and bound over for five years in the amount of £400.[34]

Under the military exigencies of 1813, Rottenburg showed himself more willing than other generals to invoke martial law for the purposes both of security and of supply. His most controversial action of this nature, the imposition of martial law in the eastern districts in November in order to force reluctant farmers to sell supplies to the army, was censured even by the assembly of 1814, otherwise the most compliant of the war. During the ensuing row, some uncertainty arose as to whether Rottenburg had acted in his military or his civil capacity, but the institution of legal proceedings obliged Robinson to concede that both courses of action were equally unconstitutional.[35]

Although he governed the province during the darkest days of the war, even Rottenburg seems to have been reluctant to subject civilians to military trial. In August 1813 he stated his determination to proceed against the most notorious of the York sedition suspects by court martial if sufficient evidence could be obtained, but this individual, William Birdseye Peters, was a half-pay army officer.[36] Again in November, when a squad of volunteer militia under Lieutenant-Colonel Henry Bostwick captured a band of marauders in the London District, Rottenburg proposed to try some of the offenders by court martial, remarking that it 'would not only be the most summary mode of proceeding as well as the least expensive to the Public, but would be the most likely to produce their conviction.' In this case, however, the proposed recourse to military trial was based on the assumption that the persons concerned were militiamen, some of whom at any rate 'were on duty and deserted their posts to join in this act of rebellion.' For other offenders, the most that Rottenburg demanded was the earliest possible civil trial: that is, by a special commission of oyer and terminer.[37]

Rottenburg had had the idea of a special commission in mind since the summer. In July he had ordered a commission for the trial of persons accused of aiding the enemy during the first occupation of York in April. One of them was Peters.[38] Nothing had come of this when the enemy returned at the end of July, and by then the regular commissions for the annual assize circuits had been issued, precluding any trials by special commission before November. When that time came, Rottenburg gave orders for a special commission at York for the trial of the London District rebels.[39] His decision was confirmed by Sir Gordon Drummond, who succeeded him as head of government and commander of the forces in December.

According to John Beverley Robinson, the option for civil trial was prompted in part by the fear that executing traitors by military law would defeat the object the authorities hoped to attain: namely, 'to over-awe the spirit of disaffection in the Province by examples of condign punishment by the laws of the land.'[40] It also happens that, after the American victory at Moraviantown in October, Rottenburg had decided to abandon the whole of the province west of Kingston and had ordered the disbandment of the militia in the Western, London, and Niagara districts.[41] If this order was carried out, the marauders captured in November may not have been subject to military law in the ordinary way unless there was evidence that they had committed crimes prior to their disbandment. In any event, it was decided to proceed against the suspected traitors by civil process; but, since speedy punishment was still an object, Drummond decided to issue a special commission rather than await the regular administration of justice, which could not have taken effect until the late summer and fall of 1814.[42] This decision was the origin of the Ancaster 'Bloody Assize.'

THE ANCASTER ASSIZE

Despite Drummond's concern for speedy justice, more than six months elapsed between the issuing of the special commission and the sitting of the court. One source of delay was the need for preparatory legislation. The commission had been issued for the trial of all treasons committed in the London District,[43] and in the ordinary course trial would have taken place in the district where the crimes had been committed. The London District, however, was unsafe. The Americans controlled Lake Erie, and their victory at Moraviantown in October might have placed the whole southwestern peninsula in their hands had not unsustainable lines of communication forced them to withdraw. The risk of disruption by enemy action, and the prospect that jurors in a war zone might be deterred by fear if not by disaffection from judging impartially, persuaded Drummond that it was safer to try the offences out of district.

This could have been done under a statute of 1541, which allowed treason to be tried in the Court of King's Bench, sitting anywhere in England, if a prisoner had been examined by the Privy Council and 'virtually proven traitorous' in the eyes of the examining councillors.[44] Yet, apart from the question as to whether this statute could be extended to the provincial Executive Council, such executive intervention in the administration of justice was antithetical to contemporary notions of the rule of law, even in a province where two of the three judges of the King's Bench were members of the council. For whatever reason, it was judged necessary to secure a provincial statute permitting trial out of the district without recourse to this process.

With two leaders of the opposition, Joseph Willcocks and Abraham Markle, discredited by joining the enemy, the assembly was likely to be more compliant than in its two preceding sessions. When the legislature met in February, it quickly enacted measures to suspend habeas corpus (see app. 3, K, doc. 4) and to expropriate convicted traitors and others who had joined the enemy. The treason-trial legislation (see app. 3, K, doc. 6) authorized the trial of any offence of high treason, misprision of treason, and treasonable practices either by the Court of King's Bench in any district in the province or by commissioners of oyer and terminer in such district as the head of the government should appoint, without regard to the district in which the offence had been committed, and it further provided that neither grand jurors nor trial jurors need be of that district.[45] Any commission of oyer and terminer was to include the judges of the King's Bench, at least one of whom was to sit at any trial under such commission.

Even after the legal obstacle to trial out of the district had been removed, Drummond's designs continued to be impeded, and by none other than John Beverley Robinson. In Robinson's mind, the danger of enemy action in the London District was outweighed by a variety of political considerations. In order to achieve the full effect intended by the exemplary punishment of convicted traitors, it was essential that due process be followed as far as possible. Though authorized by the legislature and not unprecedented in British constitutional history, trial outside the district remained a deviation from the ordinary course and, moreover, a retroactive one in respect of the offences to be tried. 'The reason of the law in requiring trial to be had only in the District where the offence was committed is just and obvious, and whether the Jury's local knowledge of the characters and their witnesses be to the advantage of the prisoner, or against him, it is in favour of public justice that they should remain' (see app. 3, K, doc. 7). This consideration was strengthened in Robinson's mind by the belief that jurors who had been exposed to the traitors' depredations would in fact be more inclined to convict than those drawn from other districts.

This belief probably accounts for Robinson's delay in communicating with Drummond on the preparations for the assize. He had discussed the matter with Drummond before the latter left York at the end of the parliamentary session but had convinced him only to shift the venue from York in the Home District to Ancaster in the Niagara District, close by the military garrison at Burlington Heights. Ordered by Drummond to draw up the requisite commission and send it to Kingston for his signature, Robinson procrastinated for three weeks before dispatching it with the apology that he had rather 'incur the censure of a little necessary delay than hazard any measure which may involve the Government and produce difficulties which after-consideration cannot repair.' He had reviewed informations against sixty men, he reported, and had concluded that it would be possible to prefer indictments for treason against thirty of them. Most had fled, but some eight or nine remained whose conviction might reasonably be expected 'unless the Jury are at all events determined to acquit them.' He stated once more the case against extraterritorial trials, declaring in conclusion that he did so lest they be ascribed to a desire on his part to load the dice against the accused. He requested accordingly that the official order to proceed should specify the reasons that made it necessary to deviate from the ordinary course.[46]

The order was issued at once, on 5 April, but only on the 29th was Robinson able to inform Drummond that the court was to open on 23 May, nearly four weeks hence.[47] One cause of delay was probably the logistical preparations necessary for holding an assize in a place that could not easily accommodate an ordinary court, let alone one that required the assembling of many jurors and witnesses from distant parts.[48] Another was undoubtedly the legal preparations. In the ensuing weeks the number of indictments grew to more than twice the thirty mentioned in his letter of 4 April. Each case required painstaking analysis to see whether the suspect was indictable for high treason and to determine whether each specific offence was to be counted as adhering, compassing, or levying. Apart from that, it must have taken a long time simply to draft the indictments, with their extremely formal and long-winded language,[49] in multiple copies. (Under the act of 1696, each prisoner was entitled to his own copy of the indictment against him.)

It is not surprising that Drummond, impatient for action, concluded that the object of the special commission – that of exemplary punishment – had been lost by the delay and that, in view of the difficulty and expense evidently entailed in holding the court at Ancaster, the trials might as well be postponed until the regular assizes. Robinson made no objection, merely observing that further delay might afford the prisoners 'a possibility of escaping with absolute impunity' – presumably owing to their rescue by enemy action. He left it to the judges to argue that the discharge of the commission at this point, without trying the prisoners, would diminish public respect for the administration of justice.[50]

In the event, the court opened as planned on 23 May. Its proceedings fell into two phases.[51] From the 23rd to the 27th, the grand jury looked into dozens of indictments and the process of the court was instituted against the prisoners. The trials began on 7 June, while the grand jury considered more indictments. During this second phase, which lasted for a fortnight, nineteen prisoners were tried, of whom four were acquitted. Ten of the fifteen convicts belonged to the party of London District marauders whose activities had prompted the issue of the original special commission late in 1813; only one of this group was acquitted. The five other convicts, and three of the acquitted prisoners, had been indicted for offences committed on the Niagara frontier.[52]

The indictments seem to have been of two basic shapes, varying according to the nature of the offence. A surviving record of the indictment against four of the London party treats them as rebels, charging that they,

with a great multitude of traitors and rebels, against us, whose names are to the said Jurors as yet unknown did conspire, compass, imagine and intend to bring, and put us to Death, and to fulfill, perfect and bring to effect their most evil and wicked treason, and treasonable compassing and imagination aforesaid they ... with a great multitude of other traitors and rebels against us whose names are as yet unknown to the said Jurors, being armed and arrayed [etc.] did falsely and traitorously assemble and join themselves against us, and [etc.] dispose themselves against us, and [etc.] falsely and maliciously prepare, order, wage and levy a public and cruel War against us, then and there perpetrating and committing a miserable and cruel slaughter of and amongst our faithful subjects in contempt of us and our Laws ... did kill, maim and wound, divers of our good and faithful Leige [sic] Subjects then there serving in our Militia of the District of London aforesaid, and then and there marching and going under the Command of one Henry Bostwick Esquire Lieutenant Colonel in our Militia of the said District ...[53]

Here the offences charged are compassing and levying, the compassing consisting in the levying. It is likely that the indictments against the other London rebels were variants of this form, though the specific charges would have differed according to circumstances.

None of the fifteen surviving records of indictments for offences committed in the Niagara District includes a charge of compassing. They all refer not to rebellion but to some form of collaboration with the enemy, and therefore the basic charge is adhering, with the additional charge of levying in certain cases. Accordingly, they all start by averring in identical language the existence of a state of war between the king and the United States before proceeding to state, first, a general charge of adhering, and second, the specific activities in which the adhering consisted – activities that might or might not extend to the further charge of levying.[54] To incur a charge of levying, it seems to have been necessary in these cases to have committed an act of violence in immediate collaboration with the enemy. Thus, the Hartwells' attack on a militiaman with the intention of handing him over to the enemy incurred only the charge of adhering – indeed, it was only the intention that made the act treasonable at all. Likewise, the act of joining the American army amounted only to adhering, even where it was alleged that the offender had ridden with the enemy to attack British positions, unless there was evidence of actual participation in the attack. But Jacob Overholser incurred the charge of levying by accompanying American soldiers to the house of certain of his neighbours, whom they arrested and bore off to Buffalo.[55]

The record of the trials is limited to the brief minutes of the court. These show that the prisoners duly received copies of their indictment and the jury list, and that they were informed of the witnesses against them and permitted to employ one or two counsel as they chose. Most of them chose John Ten Broeck, but in at least six cases he acted in association with Bartholomew Beardsley and in at least four with William B. Peters, who also appeared as sole counsel for Noah Hopkins.[56] No prisoner seems to have been rushed to the scaffold – none was brought to trial in less than fifteen days from the time of his indictment, and as the assize advanced the interval grew to twenty-four or twenty-five days. The four acquittals, including two of the first three men to be tried, are prima facie evidence of an effective defence. Peters's status as a suspected seditionist seems not to have compromised his clients, since two of the five were acquitted.

The high rate of challenges to jurors also testifies to an energetic defence. Thirteen of the prisoners challenged more than twenty and one

(Benjamin Simmonds) as many as thirty-five. Despite his professed doubts as to the reliability of Niagara District jurors (hard to credit, since the Niagara frontier had suffered at least as much as the London District), Robinson frequently accepted the jury he was given and only twice challenged a large number. In the case of Aaron Stevens, a local man 'of respectable family' (app. 3, K, doc. 8), he went as high as sixteen; and in that of Noah Hopkins, of whose conviction he was not certain, he challenged eight.

From the standpoint of law, the trials gave rise to two interesting or curious questions. One was the vexed matter of allegiance, which arose from the uncertainty existing among English lawyers as to the status of subjects of the United States.[57] Most of the prisoners had incontestably been residents of the province at the time of the alleged offences, and so they might be supposed to owe a local allegiance to the crown which rendered them capable of treason. In at least two cases, however, that supposition was challenged.

One was that of Jacob Overholser, who had emigrated from the United States only in 1810. He raised the defence that, being an alien, he owed no allegiance to the crown once its protection had been removed by virtue of the withdrawal of British forces from the Niagara frontier. This argument was no mere formality, since the neighbours he had supposedly helped to arrest were disreputable persons who had taken advantage of the prevailing disorder in order to harass him.[58]

At issue was the question whether the subject's duty of allegiance was correlative to the crown's duty of protection or to its actual capacity to offer protection. Support for the latter position, on which Overholser relied, might have been found in William Blackstone's statement that 'allegiance is a debt due from the subject, upon an implied contract with the prince, that so long as the one affords protection, so long the other will demean himself faithfully.'[59] However, such an argument was not likely to commend itself to a Loyalist such as the presiding judge, William Dummer Powell. Overholser was condemned on the stony ground that the crown owed him a duty of protection which, even under the circumstances, exacted a reciprocal duty of allegiance. This was probably truer to Blackstone's doctrine, since the English jurist defined the fact of protection in formal terms that were unrelated to the sovereign's actual capacity to afford it.[60]

The second case in which allegiance is known to have been an issue was that of the Hartwell brothers, on whose behalf Beardsley moved for an arrest of judgment on the ground that they were aliens. No record survives of the argument, but Beardsley may have relied on the fact that the brothers had left the province upon the outbreak of war and avowed their enmity to the crown. A petition on their behalf states that they had been born in the United States since independence and had never taken the oath of allegiance. Robinson's discussion of the case (app. 3, K, doc. 8) is noteworthy for its implicit acceptance of the 'settlers and effects' doctrine, which was not made judicially binding in England until the case of *R. v. Joyce* (1946).[61] Chief Justice Scott confirmed in his report that this was the basis of their conviction.[62]

The second interesting legal question arises from the case of Robert Troup, who is said to have first pleaded guilty but then withdrawn his plea. This is the more remarkable because, upon going to trial, Troup was in fact acquitted; but we have no information as to what transpired beyond the words of a rather poor typed transcript of the rough minutes of the court: 'Pleaded Guilty the Plea Withdrawn.' The official minutes, presumably prepared from the rough minutes after the event, only add to the confusion: they state 'Pleaded Not Guilty,' but the words are crossed out. This is strange, since Troup must have pleaded not guilty in order to be tried and acquitted. Troup was indicted as one of the London District rebels, and he was the only such prisoner to be acquitted.[63] The three witnesses against him, who included Henry and John Bostwick (the latter a militia officer like his brother, and sheriff of the London District into the bargain),[64] had already testified persuasively against other prisoners. Unlike those others, however, Troup had a witness of his own, one Betsy Troup.

To plead guilty to high treason was not illegal, but it was contrary to the spirit of the procedural safeguards enacted in 1696 under the shadow of the 'Bloody Assize' of 1685, when Sir George Jeffreys, facing more than 1300 cases, had duped prisoners into pleading guilty in order to dispose of them expeditiously.[65] It was also contrary to the political objects to be served by the Ancaster trials, which required that the prisoners be condemned by their peers. In the end, the only prisoner to plead guilty was Cornelius Howey. Howey had been indicted together with Daton Lindsey, George Peacock, and Benjamin Simmonds, all of whom had already been convicted. He was suffering from what was expected to be a fatal gunshot wound, received during the affray with the Bostwicks' militia (see app. 3, K, doc. 8). Alone of the prisoners, he was not brought to the bar on 21 June to hear the sentence of death.

In the exercise of his discretion as acting head of the government, Drummond granted a reprieve of sentence to seven of the convicts and recommended to the colonial secretary that their sentence be commuted to one of perpetual banishment. The advice upon which he acted reflected the same political considerations that had governed the special commission from its inception, but it was not devoid of humanity. Chief Justice Scott recommended the execution of at least one convict from each district (London and Niagara), and preferably in the district where their crimes had been committed, but he advised in several letters that lenity would be more beneficial to the public than severity. Robinson listed seven whom he thought especially deserving of execution, considerately numbering them in order of merit in case Drummond felt inclined to hang fewer. Six of these were London rebels and the other Aaron Stevens, a spy who had traded on his standing as a former government official in order to aid the enemy. The judges made their own recommendations concerning the prisoners at whose trial they had presided.[66] Robinson's nominees went to the gallows along with Noah Hopkins.

A comparison of the cases in which sentence was executed with those in which clemency was granted suggests that the decision was influenced both by the nature of the act and by the intention with which it had been committed. Of the London rebels who survived, Garrett Neill and John Johnson were described by Robinson as 'two ignorant, inconsiderable men' and were tried in succession with much the same witnesses for the crown; Johnson was also singled out by Robinson for having been duped by his companions and for having treated their captives humanely. Robinson grouped Isaac Pettit with two others who hanged but he named these others as worse offenders; Pettit was, besides, the only Londoner to call two witnesses of his own. Cornelius Howey was recommended for mercy by Mr Justice William Campbell because he pleaded guilty and confessed in court.

Of the Niagara convicts, the Hartwell brothers, whose case Robinson discussed in detail, were minor offenders who had fallen foul of the law for not being acquainted with the niceties of the 'family and effects' rule. Jacob Overholser was convicted of relatively trivial acts on the testimony of witnesses who held a grudge against him, and he suffered the further handicap that his chief witness, a Quaker, was a non-juror and could not testify in court. Even so, the assize minutes record that the jury took an hour and a half to find him guilty, and clearly it would have been iniquitous to hang him. Unfortunately, he perished of jail fever, as did Pettit and Neill, while awaiting imperial instructions concerning the commutation of his sentence.

The guilt of those who were hanged was apparently of a different order. John Dunham, Isaiah Brink, and Adam Chrysler were named by Robinson as leaders of the London District marauders; Daton Lindsay, Benjamin Simmonds, and George Peacock had been captured in the shoot-out with Bostwick's militia. Aaron Stevens was accused of several offences, including spying for the enemy and taking part in the burning of the town of Niagara. Noah Hopkins had also given intelligence to the Americans concerning British military dispositions and had served them as a commissary.

Drummond's report on the assize to the colonial secretary, and his proclamation to the people of Upper Canada on the same subject, clearly reflect the considerations that went into the question of clemency. Citing his advisers' opinions on the benefits to be obtained by balancing severity and lenity, he referred the fate of the lucky seven to the prince regent with his personal recommendation of banishment rather than execution. In a proclamation dated 25 July, the day of the battle of Lundy's Lane, the bloodiest of the war on British soil, he warned the public that the 'forbearance' manifested in the seven reprieves would not be shown towards subsequent offenders.[67]

AFTER ANCASTER: CRIMINAL PROCEEDINGS AND THE SEQUESTRATION OF FORFEITED ESTATES

The special commission reassembled at Ancaster in August and recorded twenty-nine more true bills on indictments *in absentia* for high treason. The King's Bench minutes record eight more cases of high treason in the period from October 1814 to October 1818, but only one of them (John Chilson's) is shown to have been carried through to a verdict and that was not guilty. One prisoner escaped, another was discharged after arraignment, and two other records are of indictments *in absentia*. The conclusion of two cases is uncertain, but it is unlikely that a guilty verdict would have escaped the notice of history.[68] Two men were convicted of misprision at the London District assizes of 1814, an offence punishable by life imprisonment and forfeiture. One was sentenced to an hour's imprisonment, an hour in the pillory, and a fine of one dollar; the other sentence is not recorded.[69]

In addition to these cases, the assize minutes record several more cases of sedition, three of which attracted sentences of imprisonment and the pillory.[70] These sedition cases may have had nothing to do with the war, but in any case they illustrate the continued alarm of the authorities, which was to be further exemplified in the treatment of Robert Gourlay and in the controversy known as the alien question.[71]

In addition to summary deportation and criminal proceedings, the third major measure taken against the traitorous and disloyal was the confiscation of their estates. This reprisal required three separate legislative acts: one pertaining to convicted traitors, one to fugitives indicted *in absentia* for political offences, and one to American immigrants who, representing themselves to be British subjects, had settled in the province and taken the oath of allegiance but had voluntarily returned to the United States after the outbreak of war. In order to sequestrate the estates of convicted traitors, it was necessary to amend the British acts of 1709 and 1744 which had provided for the future abolition of forfeiture of estates upon attainder of treason.[72] The expropriation of fugitives, whether indicted or not, was a more complex matter.

Drummond first proposed to proceed by executive proclamation, but John Beverley Robinson advised him that this was illegal. Even indicted fugitives were immune from such action, for the common-law process of outlawry did not exist in Upper Canada: it could be instituted only in special county courts convenable by the sheriff, and though Upper Canada had sheriffs and counties, the latter were not administrative units and did not coincide with the sheriff's bailiwick, which was of course the district. As for fugitives who had not been indicted or subjected to any process which established their status as aliens, their title too was inviolate. Robinson offered Drummond what had become the standard alternative of acting by military command, but he pointed out that the outright sequestration of property would entail a much more far-reaching exercise of that authority than had been attempted hitherto. He recommended that the matter be left to the legislature, which he had reason to suppose would be accommodating.[73]

Drummond took his advice, and in due course the three acts mentioned above were passed: one to permit the sequestration of convicted traitors, and two others to facilitate the expropriation of fugitives. One of these introduced the English process of outlawry,[74] and the other (app. 3, K, doc. 5) dealt with persons who, having taken the oath of allegiance, had returned to the United States during the war. These were declared to be aliens and incapable of holding land, and the government was empowered to appoint commissions of inquiry to identify such persons and their landholdings, which would thereupon revert to the crown. In the case of convicted traitors and outlaws, whose identity was of course known, commissions of sequestration were issued for each individual.[75]

CONCLUSION

The outstanding security problem posed by the war arose from the American origins and doubtful loyalty of the majority of the population. The political and legal struggles to shape popular opinion, in the face of disaffection and legislative intransigence (until 1813), form an important dimension of the story. Under the circumstances the authorities, both civil and military, exhibited a striking reluctance to supersede the ordinary operation of the law where it could be avoided. The crown's legal advisers showed in addition a scrupulous concern to prevent the abuse of civil authority in the name of military necessity. Their approach was prompted in part by a lively appreciation of the value of the rule of law as a legitimating ideological sanction for the civil authority, although, as the case of Jacob Overholser suggests, this did not always prevent injustice. Still, in view of the peril confronting the colony, it can be accounted as an impressive display of procedural rectitude.

Two things helped to make it possible. One was the broad liability for militia duty, which rendered the great majority of adult males potentially subject to military law. The other was the wide scope enjoyed by the provincial legislature in the regulation of civil rights. The Sedition Act in particular, a Draconian piece of security legislation, sanctioned sweeping administrative action against individuals who could not prove that they stood beyond its reach. Added to this was wartime legislation which, even before the general suspension of habeas corpus in 1814, gave the authorities wide powers of preventive detention. However, the scope of the militia law and the resort to the Sedition Act were arguably justified by the danger of invasion, while the powers of detention, as embodied in section 39 of the Militia Act, only came into effect in the event of invasion. At any rate, although it faced alarming breakdowns of civil order in western Upper Canada, the Niagara region, and York itself, the government was able to avoid subjecting civilians to summary military trial.

NOTES

1 A list compiled by Charles Black in 1926 (MU 1368, 'Register of Persons Connected with High Treason during the War of 1812–1814 with U.S.A.,' AO) provides a useful but incomplete index of persons involved in political trials in the regular courts, habeas corpus applications, proceedings under the Alien Act, and courts martial. For courts martial see RG 8 (Militia Records), C series,

vols. 165–7, NA. Among the more notable militia cases: Amos McIntyre (desertion), sentenced to be shot, Kingston, 6 Dec. 1813; Joseph Seely (desertion and serving the enemy), sentenced to transportation for seven years, Kingston, 6 Dec. 1813 – RG 5, A 1 (Upper Canada Sundries), vol. 16: 6682–710; Uriah Kelsey and John Landries (desertion and armed in service of the enemy), sentenced to transportation for seven years, Kingston, 10 Jan. 1815; John Benedict (same offence), acquitted on the basis that he was not embodied in the militia at the time of the charge; and Isaac Simpson (desertion only), released because his imprisonment between the charge and court martial was deemed sufficient punishment – RG 8, C series, vol. 167: 14–16a. See also R.L. Fraser, 'Seely, Joseph,' *DCB* 5: 747.

2 See George Sheppard, *Plunder, Profit, and Paroles: A Social History of the War of 1812 in Upper Canada* (Montreal: McGill-Queen's University Press 1994), particularly 75–99. This book provides a useful background to several of the topics discussed in this chapter.

3 RG 1, E 1 (Upper Canada State Books), vol. 50: 32, NA; York *Gazette*, 26 Feb., 4 March, 11 March 1812. See also RG 5, A 1, vol. 15: 6060–90, and app. 3, K, doc. 2.

4 E.A. Cruikshank, 'A Study of Disaffection in Upper Canada in 1812–5,' Royal Society of Canada *Proceedings and Transactions*, 3rd series, 6 (1912), sec. 2: at 16–17, 19; William M. Weekes, 'The War of 1812: Civil Authority and Martial Law in Upper Canada,' *OH*, vol. 48 (1956), at 147, 148; and see RG 8, C series, vol. 676: 92. In March it was reported that two MHAs, Benajah Mallory and Joseph Willcocks, were assiduously promoting misapprehensions regarding the militia bills and that the proposed oath of abjuration had caused much agitation among men at the head of Lake Ontario, many of whom, like the population of the province as a whole, were American immigrants: R.L. Fraser, 'Mallory, Benajah,' *DCB* 8: 608.

5 Brock to Prevost, 28 July 1812, reproduced in Cruikshank, 'Disaffection,' at 22. Brock's doubts about martial law are explored at length in Weekes, 'Civil Authority and Martial Law,' at 149–50. Brock recommended martial law to the council on 3 August.

6 'An Act to Repeal Part of the Laws Now in Force for Raising and Training the Militia in This Province, and to Make Further Provision for the Raising and Training of the Said Militia,' 52 Geo. III, c. 1, secs. 20–24, 26, 45.

7 Act, sec. 39.

8 Cruikshank, 'Disaffection,' at 22–4; Weekes, 'War of 1812,' at 149–50.

9 Cruikshank, 'Disaffection,' at 24–5.

10 Ibid., at 27–8; RG 8, C series, vol. 688B: 152, 154–6 ('To the Boards appointed to examine persons claiming exemption from military service as being subjects of

the United States,' 9 Nov. 1812); York *Gazette,* 14 Nov. 1812; and see app. 3, K, doc. 3.

11 The proceedings of the Kingston board survive in the militia records: RG 8, C series, vol. 688B: 178–94. For a description of one case, see G.M. Craig, 'Smith, Michael,' *DCB* 5: 765.

12 There are good data on the former in the records of abandoned and confiscated lands administered under the Alien acts from 1814 on: see RG 1, A IV (Upper Canada Crown Land Office Records), vol. 16, 'Alien Estates Forfeited to the Crown (all Districts), 1819,' AO; RG 22 (Court of King's Bench), series 144, 'Alien Act Records, 1814,' AO (these records include persons convicted of treason and political offences *in absentia* as well as those proceeded against under the Sedition Act). See also RG 7, G, 16C (Letterbooks of the Civil Secretary), vol. 5, 'General return of persons possessed of lands in Upper Canada who have fled to the United States from the Districts of Newcastle, London, Home, Midland, Niagara, Johnstown and Eastern since July 1, 1812,' NA. Dated Nov./Dec. 1814, this document includes over 360 names. Cruikshank, 'Disaffection,' at 54–8, suggests 336 landowners and adds that 'it is probable that the number of landless men of whom no record has been kept, was considerably greater.' Some of the latter can be identified by cross-referencing the records cited above with more general lists of political convicts, proscribed persons, and refugees: for example, RG 8, C series, vol. 688B: 178–94; MU 1368; RG 1, E 11 ('Register of Oaths'), vol. 13, NA; and lists scattered throughout RG 8, C series, and RG 5, A 1, vol. 16: 6817–70.

13 See Sheppard, *Plunder, Profit, and Paroles,* caps. 4 and 6.

14 RG 22, series 136 (Court of King's Bench, Assizes, rough minutebooks), AO.

15 Ibid. series 134 (Court of King's Bench Assize Minutebook), vol. 4. Bastedo was sentenced to two months' imprisonment, one hour in the pillory and a fine of £5.

16 Elwood H. Jones, 'Willcocks, Joseph,' *DCB* 5: 857–8; Cruikshank, 'Disaffection,' at 22–3, 26–7, 29; Sheppard, *Plunder, Profit, and Paroles,* at 162–3.

17 Cruikshank, 'Disaffection,' at 21–2.

18 On Beemer, see RG 5, A 1, vol. 16, 6736 ('Petition of London District prisoners in York Gaol,' 14 Feb. 1814'), and RG 22, series 127 (application for habeas corpus, 13 July 1814); on Willcocks, see Jones's biography in *DCB* 5: 854; RG 22, series 134, vol. 4: 152–61 (true bill for treason), and series 127, 19 Nov. 1814 (outlawry process).

19 Cruikshank, 'Disaffection,' at 25; RG 22, series 134, vol. 4: 113 (114–22 missing); MU 1368.

20 RG 22, series 134, vol. 4: 130, 149.

21 Edith G. Firth, *The Town of York, 1793–1815* (Toronto: Champlain Society and

University of Toronto Press 1962), at 298–9; E.A. Cruikshank, 'John Beverley
Robinson and the Trials for Treason in 1814,' Ontario Historical Society *Papers
and Records*, vol. 25 (1929), at 194; Sheppard, *Plunder, Profit, and Paroles*, at 150.
22 Cruikshank, 'John Beverley Robinson,' at 194–202.
23 There is no reason to think that Procter declared martial law except in Michigan. Sheaffe wrote: 'Thinking it would be proper to transmit to Earl Bathurst
the documents received from B'Gen. Procter as explanatory of the motions for
establishing Martial Law in the territory of Michigan, I have looked for them
in vain' – Sheaffe to Freer, York, 20 March 1813 – RG 8, C series, vol. 678: 133.
Prevost's secretary wrote back: 'The papers of General Proctor explanatory of
his motives for establishing Martial Law' were passed on but 'His Excellency
does not think it necessary to refer them to the Secretary of State, as he concurs
that the B'Gen. acted with proper precaution to preserve Order in the newly
acquired Territory' – Freer to Sheaffe, 6 April 1813 – RG 8, C series, vol. 1220:
282–6.
24 E.A. Cruikshank, *The Documentary History of the Campaigns upon the Niagara
Frontier in 1812–14*, 9 vols. (Welland, Ont: *Tribune* 1896–1908), 8: at 228–9, contains a ms., said by Cruikshank to be in the handwriting of William Dummer
Powell, which notes: 'Immediately after the retreat from York, Sir Geo. Prevost
commanded Sir R.H. Sheaffe, as President, to authorize Major-Genl. Vincent
to exercise Martial Law within his district as far as related to subsistence of the
troops and protection of the Province from disaffection. This Sir R[oger]
declined to do as President, upon the ground that he had not constitutional
authority to exercise Martial Law partially and had manifested that conviction
by soliciting his Legislature to enable him to do so. The result was an absolute
military command from the Commander of the Forces to the Major-General to
authorize M[ajor]-G[eneral] Vincent, at his discretion on the ground of necessity, to exercise Martial Law as limited.'
25 RG 5, A 1, vol. 16: 6514–22 (Scott to Rottenburg, 18 July 1813; Scott to E.
McMahon, 22 July 1813; Minute of Executive Council, n.d.).
26 Robinson to McMahon, 23 July 1813, quoted in Cruikshank, 'John Beverley
Robinson,' at 196–7; RG 5, A 1, vol. 16: 6704–8 (Robinson to C. Foster, 24 Jan.
1814).
27 Prevost wrote in response to Rottenburg's request for an opinion on proceeding against inhabitants charged with treason during martial law in Niagara: 'I
conceive little difficulty which exists upon this subject, as in that case under the
15th and 16th article of the 14th section of the Articles of War, persons accused
of the crimes you write may be brought before a General Court Martial which
you are clearly authorized to convene, and may be tried and punished by it,
but I have some doubts whether Martial Law does at present exist in the Nia-

gara District to the extent that would warrant Court Martial.' He added that the district general order published by Brigadier General Vincent under the authority of Major General Sheaffe was for the limited purpose of supply for troops. Only the enemy's possession of part of the district and civilian actions which further threatened the security of the area would warrant a new martial law declaration suspending the jurisdiction of the ordinary courts. See Prevost to de Rottenburg, 28 July 1813, RG 8, C series, vol. 1221: 143–4.

28 Cruikshank, 'John Beverley Robinson,' at 197–200.

29 Robinson to Rottenburg, 20 Aug. 1813, quoted in Cruikshank, 'John Beverley Robinson,' at 200–1.

30 RG 5, A 1, vol. 16: 6536–680 ('Executive Committee to deal with reports of disloyal characters').

31 At least fifty-nine others were arrested across the province by the militia and placed into civil custody for extended periods – see MU 1368; RG 5, A 1, vol. 16, 6731–40, 6779; RG 22, series 127.

32 RG 22, series 134, vol. 4: 193. Chilson was probably the 'John Chilsom' mentioned in Sheppard, *Plunder, Profit, and Paroles*, at 150.

33 On Calvin Wood, see RG 22, series 134, vol. 4: 186; Sheppard, *Plunder, Profit, and Paroles*, at 149; and William Renwick Riddell, 'The Ancaster "Bloody Assize" of 1814,' Ontario Historical Society *Papers and Records*, vol. 20 (1923), at 114–15; on Elisha Smith, see MU 1368.

34 See RG 22, series 134, vol. 4. On Bentley, see R.L. Fraser's biography of him in *DCB* 5: 64. Andrew Patterson was also indicted in October 1813 and convicted a year later after two traverses; he was sentenced to one month's imprisonment and fined £20. Gideon Orton was indicted in March 1814, convicted a year later, and sentenced to one month's imprisonment, two hours in the pillory, and a fine of £5; on Orton, see Sheppard, *Plunder, Profit, and Paroles*, at 149. Two named men evaded warrants for their arrest while three other men, two of whom were named, were arraigned for sedition at York in October 1814. One was subsequently tried and convicted. In addition to these cases at York, the assize minutes record seven other cases of sedition from 1813 to 1815.

35 *Con Docs* 2: at 435–8; Cruikshank, *Documentary History*, 8: at 226, 227–8. It is noteworthy that the attack on the government was led by a magnate in the affected region, Levius Sherwood. As a judge of the Court of King's Bench, Sherwood was to play a leading part in a post-war controversy over civil liberties, the case of Francis Collins. On Sherwood, see Ian Pemberton's biography of him in *DCB* 7: 794.

36 Cruikshank, 'John Beverley Robinson,' at 201; on Peters, see Edith G. Firth's biography of him in *DCB* 6: 578. There is no evidence that Peters was subjected to process of any sort.

37 Robinson Papers, E. McMahon to J.B. Robinson, 26 Nov. 1813, AO.

38 Firth, *Town of York, 1793–1815*, at 315. The five also included Jesse Ketchum, later one of the most prominent townspeople.

39 RG 5, A 1, vol. 16: 6523–5 (J.B. Robinson to E. McMahon, 11 Aug. 1813); RG 8, C series, vol. 681: 108 (Rottenburg to Col. Baynes, 26 Nov. 1813).

40 Robinson Papers, Robinson to R. Loring, 25 March 1814.

41 Cruikshank, 'John Beverley Robinson,' at 202.

42 Robinson Papers, C. Foster to J.B. Robinson, 19 Dec. 1813.

43 Ibid.; and see app. 3, K, doc. 7

44 33 Hen. VIII, c. 23. See John Bellamy, *The Tudor Law of Treason: An Introduction* (London: Routledge and Kegan Paul 1979), at 106, 118, and Riddell, 'Ancaster "Bloody Assize,"' at 109.

45 A similar measure was passed to deal with the Jacobite uprising of 1745 – 19 Geo II (1746), c. 9.

46 App. 3, K, doc. 7. Robinson had drafted this letter as early as 25 March, ten days before he actually sent it: Robinson Papers, Robinson to R. Loring, 25 March 1814.

47 Ibid., Loring to Robinson, 5 April 1814, and same to same, 5 May 1814.

48 Ibid., Loring to Robinson, 8 May 1814.

49 See app. 3, K, doc. 9, part of which recites the indictment against Aaron Stevens, and the other commissions in RG 22, series 143, box 2.

50 Robinson Papers, Loring to Robinson, 8 May 1814; Robinson to Loring, 12 May 1814; T. Scott, W.D. Powell, and W. Campbell to Robinson, 13 May 1814; Loring to Robinson, 17 May 1814.

51 The official minutes of the court are in RG 22, series 134, vol. 4: 153–71. There is a typed transcript of the rough minutes in series 136, but it is of poor quality.

52 One of the acquitted prisoners, Luther McNeal, was the subject of a commission of sequestration in 1818. Apparently he was reindicted soon after his acquittal, though there is no record of the fact, but had already fled the jurisdiction of the court: RG 22, series 143, box 2, env. 1. Series 143 contains information on the charges against several of the convicts. See also L 16 (Powell Papers), untitled legal papers, vol. 2, file 27, 'Calendar of Prisoners at Ancaster,' Baldwin Room, Metropolitan Toronto Reference Library.

53 Ibid., env. 15 (Benjamin Simmonds, Daton or Datis Lindsay, George Peacock, and Cornelius Howey). The quoted passage is in the first-person plural because the source is not the indictment itself but a recital of the indictment in a royal commission. The formulaic language has been abbreviated because it is reproduced in full in app. 3, K, doc. 9.

54 See, for example, app. 3, K, doc. 9.

55 Of the commissions in series 143, box 2, those in env. 1 (L. McNeal and Abraham Harding), 2 (J. Overholser), 5 (Aaron Stevens), 7 (Joseph Lovett), 8 (Gideon Frisbee), 12 (Ira Bentley), 13 (Epaphras Lord Philps), 14 (Silas and Josiah Deane), and 16 (Samuel Thompson) recite indictments for adhering and levying; and env. 3 (Noah Hopkins), 4 (the Hartwells), 6 (Asa Bacon), 9 (Daniel Phillips), 10 (Phineas Howell), and 11 (Ebenezer Kelly and Timothy McComb) recite indictments for adhering only.

56 We cannot be entirely certain as to the appointment of counsel. The minutes (RG 22, series 134) mention no appointments for Cornelius Howey or John Dunham. Ten Broeck is listed as sole counsel for the Hartwells, but it was Beardsley who argued on their behalf for arrest of judgment (see below).

57 Paul Romney, 'Re-inventing Upper Canada: American Immigrants, Upper Canadian History, English Law and the Alien Question,' in *Patterns of the Past: Interpreting Ontario's History*, ed. Roger Hall *et al.* (Toronto: Dundurn Press 1988).

58 RG 5, A 1, vol. 16: 6865–75 (Lt.-Col. Warren to R. Loring, 26 June 1814; Thomas Moore to Drummond, 28 June 1814); and see app. 3, K, doc. 8. See also the excellent article on Overholser by R.L. Fraser in *DCB* 5: 642, reprinted in *Provincial Justice: Upper Canadian Legal Portraits from the Dictionary of Canadian Biography*, ed. R.L. Fraser (Toronto: Osgoode Society and University of Toronto Press 1992), 320–6.

59 William Blackstone, *Commentaries on the Laws of England*, 4 vols. (1765–9), 1: at 370.

60 Blackstone continues: 'As therefore the prince is always under a constant tie to protect his natural-born subjects, at all times and in all countries, for this reason their allegiance due to him is equally universal and permanent. But on the other hand, as a prince affords his protection to an alien, only during his residence in this realm, the allegiance of an alien is confined, in point of time, to the duration of such his residence, and, in point of locality, to the dominions of the British Empire.' Here the natural-born subject's duty is correlative to the prince's 'tie,' or duty, rather than his capacity to afford protection. Likewise, the alien's duty is correlative to his residence within the realm, not to the prince's capacity to afford protection. Glanville L. Williams, 'The Correlation of Allegiance and Protection,' *Cambridge Law Journal*, vol. 10 (1948), at 56–7, offers the misreading posited here.

61 [1946] AC 347. See the introduction to this volume and Williams, 'Correlation of Allegiance and Protection,' at 61–2.

62 'Excepting in the present case, the Prisoners Counsel did not bring forward Birth as a defence for their Clients – indeed it is none, while their families & effects remain in this Province': RG 5, A 1, vol. 16: 6859–64 (Scott to

Drummond, 28 June 1814). Scott was referring only to cases over which he had presided. See also ibid., 6876–7 (Petition of Samuel Hatt *et al.*, 20 June 1814).

63 Powell Papers, 'Calendar of Prisoners at Ancaster.'

64 See Alan G. Brunger's biography in *DCB* 7: 92.

65 R. Clifton, *The Last Popular Rebellion* (London: M.T. Smith 1985), cap. 8; C.C. Trench, *The Western Rising: An Account of the Rebellion of James Scott, Duke of Monmouth* (London: Longmans 1969), at 247–8.

66 RG 5, A 1, vol. 16: 6859–64 (Scott to Drummond, 28 June 1814); ibid., 6932–41 (Scott to Drummond, 5 July 1814; same to same, n.d.; same to same, 8 July 1814); ibid., 6909–12 (Report of Mr Justice Campbell, 2 July 1814); ibid., 6878–82 (Abstract of the Report of the Judges on the Convictions for High Treason, n.d.); CO 42/355/103 (Drummond to Earl Bathurst, 10 July 1814, and enclosures), PRO; and see app. 3, K, doc. 8.

67 CO 42/355/103 (Drummond to Bathurst, 10 July 1814); York *Gazette*, 24 Dec. 1814.

68 RG 22, series 134, vol. 4: Calvin Wood, Home Dist., Oct. 1814, true bill; John Chilson, Home Dist., March 1815, not guilty; Jacob Chouter, London Dist., Sept. 1815, true bill, bailed until next assizes in amount of £1000 (self) and two sureties of £500 each (the record of the next assizes is missing): William Graves, or Groves, and John Carpenter, Johnstown Dist., Sept. 1816, indicted *in absentia*; Walter Knapp, Western Dist., Aug. 1817, true bill; Jonas Seeley, Niagara Dist., Sept. 1817, true bill; William Wilson, Niagara Dist., Oct. 1818, arraigned but discharged by proclamation. The escaper was Calvin Wood. Five of the above do not appear in MU 1368 although it lists two further convictions *in absentia*: Matthias Brown, York, Oct. 1815, and Samuel Thompson, Niagara, Oct. 1816.

69 RG 22, series 134, vol. 4: Griffiths Culver; Frederick Hosie, Aug. 1814.

70 RG 22, series 134, vol. 4: Jonathan Sprague, London. Aug. 1814; Benjamin Gerow, Kingston, Aug. 1814; Graham Baytor, Niagara, Sept. 1817.

71 See Barry Wright, 'The Gourlay Affair: Seditious Libel and the Sedition Act in Upper Canada, 1818–19,' in this volume; and Romney, 'Re-inventing Upper Canada.'

72 The 1709 act provided for the future elimination of forfeiture upon the death of the Jacobite pretender while the 1744 suspended its abolition until the deaths of the pretender's sons. This legislation was repealed by 39 and 40 Geo. III (1800), c. 93 (the abolition of forfeiture was delayed in England until 1870). The 1800 act was not part of the received law of Upper Canada, and, as the 1744 rule prevailed, local legislation was necessary.

73 RG 5, A 1, vol. 16: 6704–8 (Robinson to C. Foster, 24 Jan. 1814); and see William

Renwick Riddell, 'The Sad Tale of an Indian Wife,' *Journal of Criminal Law and Criminology*, vol. 13 (1922–3), at 82.

74 54 Geo. III, c. 13 ('An Act to supply in certain cases the want of County Courts in this Province'). This inadvertently prescribed in all cases the more elaborate procedure applicable to misdemeanour, and was amended in 1815 to provide where appropriate for the briefer procedure applicable to felony: 55 Geo. III, c. 2. See also Riddell, 'Sad Tale,' at 86.

75 See app. 3, K, doc. 9 and the other commissions in the same place, some of which refer to traitors and some to outlaws.

PART THREE

c. 1814–37

12

Parliamentary Privilege and the Repression of Dissent in the Canadas

F. MURRAY GREENWOOD and
BARRY WRIGHT

In 1806 the Lower Canadian House of Assembly ordered the arrest of two Tory newspaper editors for contempt, and about a quarter of a century later the colony's Legislative Council did precisely the same thing – with momentous political fallout – to its *patriote* opponents. Similarly, Upper Canada's lower house imprisoned Joseph Willcocks, publisher of the opposition *Guardian* (Niagara), in 1808 for 'seditious' slander in his newspaper and expelled radical journalist-politician William Lyon Mackenzie five times during the early 1830s. Chapters in the evolution of a Canadian free press? Undoubtedly. Examples of Canadian state trials? Equally so.

As noted in the introduction to this volume, uses of the law for security purposes cannot be confined to the wording of legislation, criminal trials, and habeas corpus hearings. Lower Canada in 1794, both Canadas in 1838–9, the dominion in the early 1930s (section 98 of the Criminal Code and sections 41, 42 of the Immigration Act), and Quebec in 1937–9 ('Padlock Act') and 1970 (War Measures Act) experienced the repressive enforcement of legislation for security purposes. In this century, too, we have seen intrusive political espionage by the R.C.M.P., the Gouzenko royal commission of 1946 on communist espionage, and, in the 1940s and 1950s, the screening of public servants for loyalty. Here we wish to focus on a rather specialized aspect of the subject and of constitutional law: the uses made of parliamentary privilege in the context of security.

The privileges enjoyed by parliament consist of ancient rules, enforceable by each house, that emerged mainly from the thirteenth to the seventeenth centuries. Reflecting the early role of parliament as the highest court in the land, these rules have been usefully defined by the leading expert in the field, Sir Thomas Erskine May, as the 'sum of the peculiar rights enjoyed by each House collectively as a constituent part of the High Court of Parliament, and by members of each House individually ... and which exceed those possessed by other bodies or individuals.'[1]

Students of British politics tend to think of privileges as having been designed to foster the proper functioning of parliament, preserve the dignity of both houses, assert the supremacy of the Commons in matters of public finance, balance the power of the executive, and, in earlier times, defend against oppression by the crown.* Few would connect privileges and the internal security of the state. And in fact such links were tenuous, at least after the Glorious Revolution of 1688–9. The several expulsions of democratic agitator John Wilkes from the Commons (1769–74) and the detention in the Tower of radical MP-journalist Sir Francis Burdett (1810) for denying the lower house's power to incarcerate were not based on any significant security fears, except perhaps among ultra-paranoid members of parliament. The only obvious links were highly technical. In 1763 both houses resolved in another Wilkes case that freedom from arrest could not be claimed where the member had been charged with seditious libel.[2] And there was the recurrent practice from 1689 in statutes suspending habeas corpus of affording members of both houses protection against detention, except with the consent of the appropriate house.[3]

By contrast, privilege and security were often clearly and strongly intertwined in the Canadas. Before exploring that relationship, we will situate the exercise of privilege in a wider North American colonial context and then outline the murky, often controversial legal dimensions of the subject.

THE NORTH AMERICAN CONTEXT

By continual assertions of power and parliamentary privilege the lower houses of all American colonies except Georgia, Maryland, and Nova Scotia had become the dominant constitutional authorities by 1763.[4] Set-

---

*Examples include: absolute freedom of speech in debate and freedom from arrest; expulsion of members deemed unfit and arrest for contempt; exclusive rights of the Commons to initiate money bills; right of the Commons to impeach cabinet ministers before the House of Lords; and the ban on reporting debates (obsolete after 1800).

backs were rare: the occasional disallowance of legislation in London and refusals by the governors to yield the crown's theoretical right to veto the choice of house speaker, to cite two examples. Such failures were insignificant compared to the virtual legislative autonomy exercised by the assemblies and their control over public finance, which meant detailed supervision of executive officials.

These developments had been ad hoc, although by the mid-eighteenth century a vaguely defined concept had emerged from the germ idea that colonizing Englishmen carried fundamental political rights with them. From that idea many assemblymen deduced that the lower houses were more or less the equal of the House of Commons and entitled to exercise the same powers and privileges. Given this perception, the persistent attempts of parliament after 1763 to assert imperial authority over the colonies, especially in taxation, made rebellion a distinct possibility.

As historian Jack Greene has pointed out, the success of the assemblies owed much to the near-absence of countervailing forces. On many councils, which acted as upper houses and executive advisers, sat appointees drawn from the same elite that dominated the elected bodies. Such legislators often exhibited sympathy with or at least tolerance of the assemblies' claims in contests with the local or imperial executives. In other cases the councils were made up largely of officials holding office at the crown's pleasure and/or favourites and slavish supporters of the executive – men who commanded little respect in society. Governors who attempted to resist or contemplated resisting popular constitutional demands often found themselves hamstrung by the assemblies' growing financial control, isolated amidst a united elite and unsupported in London.[5]

Despite the official line that colonial legislatures were bodies thoroughly dependent on the crown, with insignificant legislative powers and no special rights in the area of money bills, imperial politicians proved largely indifferent to incremental, often disguised, encroachments on the royal prerogative. They could not, of course, rely on knowledgeable public servants (with rare exceptions) to bring these matters to their attention. Under the administrations of Robert Walpole and Thomas and Henry Pelham, moreover, policy aimed at avoiding conflict and encouraging settlement dictated that the colonials be governed with a light rein. As Greene aptly points out: 'Three times between 1734 and 1749 the ministry failed to give enthusiastic support to measures introduced into Parliament to ensure the supremacy of [royal] instructions [to the governors] over colonial laws.'[6]

Constitutional evolution in the Canadas exhibited a few similarities to the earlier colonial constitutional experience. At the opening of the first Lower Canadian legislature in 1792, lawyer-speaker Jean-Antoine Panet, an ardent Reformer and later a leader of the opposition *parti canadien* (*'patriotes'* from 1826) which controlled the assembly from 1797 to 1837, unsuccessfully laid claim to 'all the ... privileges and liberties as are enjoyed by the Commons of Great Britain.'[7] Powers similar to those of Westminster were first claimed by the Upper Canadian legislature in June 1793.[8] Under the leadership of Quebec City lawyer Pierre-Stanislas Bédard, the *parti canadien* in the years 1806 to 1810 developed a constitutional philosophy close to and possibly borrowed from that prevalent in the older colonies before 1763, namely that in local matters the assembly was to play the same role the House of Commons did in the British Isles. From this concept was deduced the right to censure or impeach local 'ministers,' control public finance, expel members as unfit legislators, and arrest outsiders for contempt.[9] In the 1820s British precedents were used by Louis-Joseph Papineau in the assembly's bitter dispute over appropriations with the Legislative Council, governor, and Colonial Office.[10] In Upper Canada matters were not as clear-cut. But from time to time, beginning in 1803 when assembly oppositionists William Weekes and Angus Macdonell sought to compel appearance of King's Bench clerk and Legislative Councillor David Burns in order to condemn government policy,[11] Reform elements in assemblies attempted to use privilege powers counter-hegemonically, legitimating such claims by citing British parliamentary practice.[12]

Similarities there were, but the differences were more significant. As noted in the introduction, the 1791 Constitutional Act was applied to the Canadas in a counter-revolutionary manner. There were two power-seeking elites in each of the Canadas which sought to exploit the constitution. In the lower province the Canadien bourgeoisie of professionals, merchants, and shopkeepers vied for political supremacy with an alliance of English merchants and professionals, senior government officials of both nationalities, and seigneurs (Canadien as well as English). To the west, an elite alliance (later called the 'Family Compact'), made up of Loyalist Tories, officeholders, and landed/mercantile interests, dominated government and were challenged by politicians of a reforming bent, professional men, and journalists drawn mainly from the middling or upper-middle ranks of society. In each case the pro-government elite dominated the Executive and Legislative councils, officialdom, and the courts. In Upper Canada, the competing political forces were sufficiently well balanced that the assembly oscillated between Tory and Reform majorities.

The assemblies' attempts at democratizing the constitution, government administration, and indeed society itself[13] were met at every point by opposition from the councils, successive governors, and the British government. The contest in Lower Canada included attempts to foster an independent judiciary (1808–10, 1814), restrict the suspension of habeas corpus (1812), and appoint an agent to Westminster (1814). Upper Canada's administrator in 1812, General Isaac Brock, denounced the assembly's use that year of its powers on contempt, and such use in 1817 was followed by the premature proroguing of the legislature in 1817 and 1818. Opposition was intense in both colonies to the elected bodies' assertions of a detailed appropriating power.[14] In contrast to the indifference exhibited by London during the first British empire, imperial officials, reacting to the American revolution, generally took pains to ensure that the Canadian assemblies remained dependent bodies. Colonial secretaries vetoed the attempt in Lower Canada (1814–15) to impeach the chief justice for alleged political offences in advising the governor, denied both lower houses' claim to disqualify an expelled member from re-election (1830s), and usually gave unreserved, often drastic, support to the Lower Canadian political establishment in the many intense conflicts involving the power of the purse (1810, 1818–37).[15] By the outbreak of the rebellions in 1837, the elected branches of the legislatures had not established their entitlement to all the privileges of the Commons and had achieved neither financial leverage nor legislative autonomy in local matters. In 1836 the Lower Canadian Legislative Council rejected, ignored, or radically amended 49 of 107 bills (including appropriations for schools) sent up by the assembly.[16]

Legal Issues

The Constitutional Act of 1791 was silent on the question of parliamentary privilege.[17] Two dramatically opposed theories developed in the void and this development in retrospect seems to have been almost inevitable.

One theory emerged from the undoubted fact that the Canadian legislatures were modelled on parliament, the 1791 act even anticipating the future creation of titled aristocracies with hereditary seats in the councils. From this basis it seemed to follow that the houses enjoyed all the privileges of the House of Commons (including in Lower Canada the right to define new ones) and the House of Lords. This was the position taken by the *parti canadien* from 1806 through the 1820s – in the next decade the *patriotes* embraced American constitutional ideals – and by the

Reform assemblies of Upper Canada from time to time. Nor were the Tories in both provinces above exercising the most extreme of the Commons' privileges when politically convenient. In 1817 and 1831 Tory-dominated assemblies in Upper Canada explicitly claimed entitlement to all privileges recognized at Westminster.[18]

The opposing theory contended that, since the Constitutional Act did not deal with the subject and the provincial legislatures had neither ancient history nor judicial functions on which to base claims, privileges of the houses were those essential to their functioning as legislative bodies. In a leading case decided by the Court of King's Bench for the District of Quebec in 1810, Chief Justice Jonathan Sewell, a principal leader of the English party, confined valid privileges of the elected branch to such as were 'indispensably necessary to the existence of a Provincial House of Assembly.'[19] Absolute freedom of speech in debate (that is, exemption from the laws of slander and sedition), freedom from arrest, and a few other privileges were considered 'indispensably necessary.' But, given this theory's heavy presumption against privilege, the right to expel members as unfit legislators (except if convicted of a serious crime) and to incarcerate persons for contempt of the house arguably were not. Such indeed were the conclusions of the British law officers in an opinion of major legal importance, an opinion that warrants analysis as the most comprehensive of the period and one conveniently forgotten by the majority of the Lower Canadian Legislative Council in 1832.[20]

The law officers' opinion originated in rumours during the summer of 1814 that both houses of the Lower Canadian legislature might shortly imprison for contempt. Justice Edward Bowen, on behalf of the judges of the King's Bench of Quebec, wrote Chief Justice Jonathan Sewell, then in London to defend himself against impeachment at the hands of the assembly.[21] (See app. 3, L, doc. 1.) Bowen asked whether the two bodies were vested with the privileges of the Commons and Lords or only 'such as are essentially necessary to their political Existence.' The latter, Bowen thought, were comprised of freedom of speech, freedom from arrest, and authority to punish contempts within the house during the session. In other words, power to intern for outside libels was not deemed 'essentially necessary.' Indeed, Bowen expressly averred that the 'Attorney General has a course [seditious libel prosecutions] to pursue in the Courts ... *amply sufficient* to check this growing Evil.' The judges, Baconian all, were nevertheless willing to abide by the law officers' or colonial secretary's political desires, viewing 'these questions to embrace Matters rather of State Policy than of Law.'

Archival evidence indicates that, with the assent of Colonial Secretary Lord Bathurst, Sewell drafted questions on privileges which were submitted to the law officers.[22] And the wording clearly invited an answer restricting the assembly to the absolutely essential.[23] He was not disappointed.

The opinion concluded that the Lower Canadian assembly was not vested with the same privileges as the House of Commons (see app. 3, L, doc. 2). The latter had derived from the 'antient law and Custom of Parliament,' particularly from its medieval role as part of the highest court in the realm. Colonial legislative bodies had no such 'history' (or judicial responsibility) on which to base claims. All valid privileges must be traced to their constitutive instruments – in Lower Canada's case, the Constitutional Act of 1791.

That instrument was silent on the point and therefore the lower house could enjoy only those privileges 'as are directly & indispensably necessary to enable them to perform the [legislative] functions with which they are invested.' The law officers cited as examples freedom of debate; freedom from arrest; 'a power to commit for such Acts of contempt in the face of the House of Assembly as produce disturbance and interruption of their proceedings'; and the right to expel 'a Member convicted by any competent Tribunal of a crime of an infamous nature.'[24] The last two examples, the only ones treating commitals or expulsions, distinctly implied that a colonial house *had no authority* to imprison for contempts committed outside the legislature or to expel on the grounds of perceived unworthiness, libel, or slander. Unfortunately for later victims of these purported privileges, the law officers' opinion was not published or communicated to the Canadian legislatures.

An Overview of the Security Dimensions of Privileges

The whole matter of parliamentary privilege in colonial legislatures is extraordinarily complex; our focus is necessarily confined to imprisonments for contempt and expulsions in a context of security concerns. The links between the enforcement of privilege and security in the Canadas were of two kinds, indirect/generative and direct.

The indirect link occurred when an assembly, controlled by anti-government politicians, asserted its supposed privileges against the executive power or its supporters *and* in so doing generated an alarmist reaction based on fear of potential rebellion. Counter-hegemonic use of privilege happened often in both Canadas, when anti-government majorities could be mustered, but did not necessarily stimulate security concerns. The multiple expulsions (1829–32) of Robert Christie from the Lower Canadian House of Assembly for having advised, as chairman of the Quebec District Quarter Sessions, the removal of several *patriote* magistrates from the commission of the peace sparked much political heat and raised serious constitutional issues, but they did not generate immediate security fears.[25] Similarly, William Weekes's 1803 attempt to use privilege powers against the Upper Canadian executive and difficulties with the assembly following the resolutions against James Durand in 1817 formed a context for later security concerns but did not give rise to them in the short term.

In Upper Canada it was the case against Robert Nichol that went farthest to generate security anxieties. By early 1812 Reformers controlled close to half the votes in the assembly. Nichol, an ally of influential Niagara merchants, complained to Administrator Brock about party faction and the bias of an assembly inquiry into his alleged misuse of provincial funds as a road commissioner. When called to the bar of the house to explain his complaints, Nichol claimed that the assembly was exceeding its privileges. The house in turn resolved that he was guilty of two counts of contempt and ordered his imprisonment for the session.[26] This prompted extensive discussion of privilege powers and the then contemporary English case of *Burdett*; after consultations in the Executive Council, Nichol successfully applied to the chief justice for habeas corpus, while the assembly declared that executive interference with legislative and judicial affairs had provoked a constitutional crisis which warranted a petition to the sovereign.[27] Shortly after, Brock observed that American sympathies among assembly members prevented passage by 'a very trifling majority' of important bills relating to the milita and habeas corpus designed to prepare the province for war.[28] These events were soon overshadowed by the actual outbreak of war but, as the essay by Paul Romney and Barry Wright in this volume illustrates, legislative intransigence continued to 1813 despite a general election in the meantime, further frustrating the government's proposed emergency measures.[29]

The most numerous and clearest examples of the indirect type are found in Lower Canada. They include the 1806 orders of the assembly to detain three outspoken English party adherents: editors Edward Edwards of the Montreal *Gazette* and Thomas Cary of the Quebec *Mercury* and Montreal merchant Isaac Todd for publicly ridiculing the *parti canadien*'s imposition of import duties, rather than land taxes, during the Gaols Act dispute. Cary, who after warrants had been issued for Todd and Edwards, had also speculated in print that Bédard and company were in league with Bonaparte, was released after apologizing at the bar of the house. The two Montrealers escaped the clutches of the sergeant-at-arms.[30] Despite its comic-opera features, English government supporters, then thoroughly imbued with a 'garrison mentality' which foresaw French invasion supported by massive and bloody Canadien insurrection,[31] took the exercise of this extraordinary power seriously. Civil Secretary Herman Ryland, for example, complained to Anglican Bishop Jacob Mountain that, if assembly encroachments were not firmly resisted, 'the Means will gradually be prepared whenever a crisis should happen, for the overthrow of His Majesty's Government in this Province.' It was to prepare the way that the *parti canadien* had revealed such an 'eager desire to exercise the high and dangerous Power of Arrest, Fine and Imprisonment.' If each new demand for privilege was not countered with vigour, it would be impossible 'for any Governor to draw forth the Energies of the Country with effect, either to repress internal Commotion or repel external attack.'[32]

Other indirect cases abound, among them the expulsion of merchant-English party politician Ezekiel Hart from the assembly because of his Jewishness in 1809.[33] Another was the assembly's vote to expel pro-government political leader judge Pierre-Amable De Bonne in 1810. To Governor Sir James Craig, this act presaged house resolutions that no officials or even ordinary English subjects could be elected and was designed to teach the people that the assembly alone governed the province, all in preparation for a hoped-for Napoleonic invasion.[34] De Bonne's expulsion precipitated the most drastic manoeuvres of Craig's 'reign of terror.'[35] Other cases were the attempted impeachment of the chief justices in 1814–15 and many incidents during the appropriations battles of the 1820s. Since the essay by Evelyn Kolish and James Lambert in this volume deals with a generative example in detail, we shall concentrate on the direct ones.[36]

Direct cases involved exercises of parliamentary privilege motivated, in part at least, by security concerns. The three cases studied in this essay featured the use of the most extreme privileges: arrest and detention for contempt, and expulsion. Editor-MHA Joseph Willcocks was jailed by the Upper Canada assembly in 1808. Twenty-four years later the Legislative Council of Lower Canada, 'tried' and jailed two outsiders of radical *patriote* persuasion: prominent Montreal journalists Daniel Tracey of the *Vindicator* and Ludger Duvernay of *La Minerve*. The supposed right to expel was used several times against William Lyon Mackenzie in the years

1831–4. All these exercises of privilege were arguably illegal and all went beyond anything conceivable in Westminster.

UPPER CANADA

As in Lower Canada, the exercise in Upper Canada of the extreme and doubtful privileges of imprisonment and expulsion were often aimed at restricting freedom of expression in the newspapers. These actions, taken by Tory assemblies in Upper Canada, reflected the prominent role of opposition newspapers in the security concerns of government. They were part of an array of measures against the 'dangerous engine' of the press that included libel prosecutions in the courts (Robert Gourlay in 1818, Bartemas Ferguson in 1819, and Francis Collins in 1828), more informal measures such as the suspension of lucrative government printing contracts (notably Gideon Tiffany in 1797 and Charles Fothergill in 1826), and forms of 'rough justice' meted out by government supporters (the destruction of Mackenzie's press in 1826).

The Joseph Willcocks case is the clearest instance of the direct security use of supposed privilege, although the repeated expulsions of William Lyon Mackenzie are probably the best known. The provincial record also reflects the limits of the measure's value as an instrument of repression, dependent as it was on the government's ability to manage assembly majorities. Willcocks's imprisonment did not diminish Reform's effectiveness in the assembly during the pre-war era, as the Nichol case highlights. And as Mackenzie's expulsions suggest, repressive uses of privilege gave a platform to the opposition cause which could be exploited to the government's detriment.

Willcocks and Contempt

Joseph Willcocks was a member of the House of Assembly from 1807 to 1813 and publisher of the *Upper Canada Guardian; or Freeman's Journal*, the colony's first dissentient newspaper. He also became the leading figure in Upper Canada's first opposition party, succeeding two fellow Irishmen: barrister William Weekes (MHA, 1804–6) and King's Bench judge and MHA (1807) Robert Thorpe. In this role he was supported by two prominent English immigrants, Surveyor General Charles Burton Wyatt and John Mills Jackson. These men were both disappointed seekers of government patronage and libertarian idealists, imbued with Irish Whig political ideology. They were loyal to crown and empire, at least until 1813, when Willcocks, disillusioned with a newly deferential assembly, joined the invading American army.[37]

Sporadic opposition to government gave way to an organized opposition movement in the assembly around the time of the passage of the 1804 Sedition Act[38] as Reform-inclined members increasingly articulated sophisticated Irish Whig arguments which emphasized that the provincial constitution should mirror the mother country's.[39] These ideas lent credibility to their demands for greater government accountability and redress of popular grievances. On the hustings, during house debate, in the *Guardian*, and at the assizes, the party stood firmly and vocally against maladminstration and the petty despotism of officials, denouncing the favouritism in appointments shown by the executive councillors ('overbearing reptiles' and 'servile instruments'), the 'tyranny' of the magistrates and the perceived tendency of sheriffs to manipulate jury panels, the pitiful state of roads and communiciations, and the costly, inefficient land-granting system. In the constitutional realm, Thorpe, Willcocks, and associates advocated greater power for the assembly and protection of constitutional liberties; they claimed all the financial powers of the Commons for the lower house, attempted to disqualify placemen from sitting in that body, and Thorpe, in particular, called for an embryonic form of responsible cabinet government. On security matters the party expressed determined opposition from the time of the passage of the Draconian Sedition Act to its successful obstruction of Brock's initiatives to suspend habeas corpus in 1812.[40]

The government's growing security concerns about foreign republican designs and the internal threat of potentially disloyal American immigrants had been first manifested in 1797 and found permanent embodiment in the 1804 Sedition Act.[41] Government circles came to think of the opposition leaders as actively disloyal, guided by veterans of the United Irish rebellions of 1798 and 1803 who had located in New York City and, through them, by the dreaded Napoleon Bonaparte. To Lieutenant Governor Francis Gore, Thorpe's flattering references to the American revolution in his electoral campaign of December 1806 were 'almost Treasonable' and the judge was certainly a strong sympathizer with, probably a member of, the United Irish.[42] His attempt to rouse popular indignation was extremely dangerous 'in this Province, where Republican Principles prevail so much.'[43] As for Willcocks, who had gone to New York to obtain his press, he too was a United Irishman in touch with his confrères in the United States. The lieutenant governor credited a report that the party aimed to 'seize upon his Excellency's

Person and the other obnoxious Officers of the Crown, and ship them off in Irons – if not worse.'[44] The plot, however, was conducted with 'such caution, that it is impossible as yet, to convict any of the parties here.'[45] It was highly likely, Gore wrote, that instructions were being sent to the plotters, including Justice Thorpe, by 'Monsieur Genet, a Frenchman employed by the Cabinet of St. Cloud.'[46]

Such exaggerations, in retrospect, were not surprising. Recently immigrated American settlers outnumbered resident Britons and Loyalists. Relations between the United States and the United Kingdom were usually tense during the century's first decade, and with the Chesapeake affair of 1807 the tension almost led to war. In the constituencies, mainly in the western parts of the province where former United States citizens were especially numerous, some Reform supporters went so far as to embrace republicanism openly and express the hope that their former country would take over the colony from Britain.[47] Despite measures to suppress the opposition movement, security concerns continued to grow; by 1811 a petition signed by nineteen magistrates and numerous other influential persons complained that 'the sudden and indiscriminate influx of foreigners, sometimes openly, at other times secretly hostile to the British Government, gives them great uneasiness' and they urged 'some check to the admission of strangers from the neighbouring States.'[48] In the assembly, the Reform members' frustration of Brock's security initiatives seemed to place the threat of subversion directly at the heart of the state itself. From 1797 to the War of 1812 the Upper Canadian equivalent of the 'garrison mentality' grew apace, a government attitude that was solidified by the wartime experience and became policy in the post-war discriminatory measures against the local 'Americans.'[49]

It must not be forgotten, either, that for centuries in England politicians favourable to the crown had, without many doubts, associated organized parliamentary opposition with disloyalty. Such a view was certainly justified during the reigns of the Stuarts and the first two Hanoverian kings. The last political grouping to be seriously tarred with this brush was the Whig rump under Charles James Fox in the 1790s. The Foxites were not, of course, in league with the French revolutionaries, but they were easily perceived in these terms since they opposed the war with France, fought against drastic security legislation, and regularly thundered against Prime Minister William Pitt's 'reign of terror.' In Lower Canada from 1794 to the War of 1812, the English elite looked upon the parti canadien as dangerously subversive. While the connection between sustained party opposition in parliament and disloyalty was being slowly undermined among British Tories during the first decade of the nineteenth century, the process would not be complete in Britain until the late 1820s when the expressive and subtle term 'His Majesty's *Loyal* Opposition' became current. In British North America, opposition remained associated with disloyalty until the achievement of responsible government in the late 1840s.

In Upper Canada, Lieutenant Governor Francis Gore's skilled subterfuge removed most of the leading opposition figures from influence.[50] Weekes was conveniently killed in a duel after criticizing the government in court. Thorpe, who had encouraged grand jurors to articulate local grievances and had advised the assembly on constitutional matters from the bar of the house, was removed from the Court of King's Bench. Willcocks and Wyatt were suspended from office. Willcocks fought on, using the platform of an opposition newspaper to attack government, and he would soon face further attempts to muzzle him.

The Niagara-based *Upper Canada Guardian; or Freeman's Journal* was established in July 1807 in response to the government's refusing Reform submissions to the *Upper Canada Gazette*. Although the *Guardian* was Irish Whig in tone rather than radical republican, Gore was convinced that it was subversive and designed to revolutionize the province. He lamented the 'vulgar attacks' by the 'Seditious Printer' which were 'relished too much, by the good people of Upper Canada.'[51] On 14 November 1807 he authorized Attorney General William Firth to prosecute the 'editor of the Jacobin paper' for seditious libel, and a warrant was issued for Willcocks to appear in York and plead before the King's Bench on 4 January 1808.[52] The matter became more urgent and complex when Willcocks announced his intention to stand for election to the assembly.

On January 4th Willcocks pleaded not guilty and was given notice of trial at the next assizes in the Niagara District.[53] He won a by-election and took his seat on 26 January. His popularity raised the spectre of an embarrassing acquittal. On 16 February the libel indictment was withdrawn and an ex officio information was issued for the same offence. Firth used the information to obtain leave to strike a special jury in York, where he intended to have Willcocks tried. Fearing a packed jury, and indeed any jury based in York, where eligible jurors were more likely pro-government and inclined to convict, Willcocks successfully applied to judge William Dummer Powell for a change of venue to the Niagara District where the newspaper was based.[54]

To reduce the risk of acquittal in Niagara, the government instigated a fall-back measure by urging parliamentary-privilege proceedings. It was increasingly confident by this point of a malleable assembly majority;

Willcocks lacked the parliamentary skills of Weekes or Thorpe and old opponents had closed ranks in support of the government. The strategy of two cracks at Willcocks was prudent. When his trial eventually came up at the Niagara assizes before judge Powell on 21 September 1808, Willcocks was acquitted, despite the attorney general's special jury and proof of publication which made him technically guilty under pre-1792 seditious-libel doctrine.[55]

In the meantime the assembly took cognizance of the editor's libel on the legislature and resolved to determine whether it constituted contempt.[56] Willcocks immediately rose to complain of the unfairness of proceeding in both the house and the courts: 'An information had already been filed against me by the King's Attorney General, for the publication of the very paragraph ... in my opinion, it would be the height of cruelty and injustice to carry on two prosecutions against me at one and the same time, for one and the same publication ... and even if I had made an assertion of this kind, the House ought not to call me to account for it, as their decision would materially influence the minds of the jury.'[57] A motion charging contempt was withdrawn and Willcocks cheekily declared that the government party was afraid to proceed, realizing its case was unfounded.[58] In reponse, a new motion was put forward that 'it is the opinion of this House that Joseph Willcocks is guilty of the charges brought against him.'[59] As Willcocks observed,

indeed there were two or three glaring contradictions in the evidence of those gentlemen, that would in a court of justice have destroyed the veracity of the whole; but in a court of parliament was considered as nothing ... I never saw a prosecution conducted with more evident disadvantage to the defendant ... I implored the House to have witnesses sworn, but this benefit was denied me as were the advantages of representation. I had but one clear day's notice of trial; and when it did commence, I was not permitted to put a single question to a witness that was at all likely to make him contradict or invalidate his testimony ... the acrimonious and personally abusive language made use of by these gentlemen, was such as we would not expect to hear in a court of justice, much less in a court of parliament.[60]

The motion was carried, the Upper Canada *Guardian* was declared 'a pestilence in the land,' and it was resolved that 'Joseph Willcocks be committed to the common gaol of the District, there to remain during the sitting of parliament.'[61] Reformer Robert Gourlay later commented: 'Had Mr. Fox [sponsor of the Libel Act in England] been still alive – Mr. Fox, who pleaded so warmly for the popular rights of Canadians, what would he have said, when he found the Representatives of these Canadians converting Parliament into a judicial court for trial of offences with which Parliament had nothing to do? ... What would Mr. Fox have said to all of this? Certainly had he moved at all in the matter, it would have been worthy of him to have gone out to Upper Canada, purposely to kick the dirty fellows of Assembly into Lake Ontario.'[62]

Gourlay cited the examples of Wilkes and Burdett to denounce the proceedings and similar ones taken against James Durand in 1817. British practice in this period was far from certain. There, the privileging of freedom of speech and the prohibition of arbitrary disqualifications of elected members were accompanied by increasely strong challenges to parliament's authority to imprison for contempt.

Even if one assumes that the provincial assembly had the jurisdiction to proceed on a contempt, and one committed outside the house, the case was indeed questionable in light of the 1763 Wilkes resolution. Members could be arrested in cases of seditious libel committed outside parliament, despite the privileging of freedom of speech within it, on the basis that the ordinary course of law could not be obstructed. Legislatures 'ought not to be allowed to obstruct the ordinary Course of the Law, in the speedy and effectual Prosecution of so heinous and dangerous an Offence.' Privilege was subordinate to the regular administration of justice and this implied that the house had no jurisdiction to treat a libel still before the courts as a contempt, as it would prejudice further legal proceedings. Willcocks's 'double jeopardy' situation, with the information remaining to be tried at the assizes, was arguably contrary to the spirit of the resolution.[63] Later, in the widely criticized *Burdett* case of 1811, Lord Ellenborough upheld the British houses' right to protect themselves from 'insult and indignity,' adding that it was beneath their dignity to await the outcome of a jury trial.[64] Ellenborough, however, did not expressly address the question of the Commons acting while a criminal charge was pending.

There were other contempt proceedings in the direct aftermath of Willcocks. John Mills Jackson, an ally of Willcocks, published a pamphlet in England on Upper Canadian misgovernment; in it, he claimed that misgovernment had reached the point where Upper Canadians were on the point of rebellion. Gore encouraged an assembly motion calling Jackson's pamphlet 'a false, scandalous and seditious libel ... tending to alienate the affections of the people ... and to excite them to rebellion.' A resolution to call Jackson to the bar of the house for trial were he to return to Upper Canada was defeated.[65]

Post-War Opposition and the Mackenzie Expulsions

Before the 1816 election the government issued orders in council to discourage American immigration.[66] James Durand, who had earlier criticized applications of martial law during the war, was one of only two members of the assembly to oppose the executive measures while other members of the Tory-dominated house even considered a bill to extend the suspension of habeas corpus. During the election Durand's opposition was attacked as disloyalty, and he responded by defending his views in a handbill and an article in the Niagara *Spectator*.[67]

A newly elected assembly convened in late February 1817 and Robert Nichol moved contempt proceedings against Durand for the publications which 'tended to bring the government and legislature into disesteem.'[68] Citing Wilkes, Nichol asserted that contempt proceedings against the author were an alternative to a seditious-libel prosecution of the editor. Requesting more time to examine the law, Durand limited his defence to the argument that Wilkes had been previously convicted and that there was no seditious intent in the statements, which were quoted out of context.[69] The house resolved the allegations proved and sentenced him to the common jail for the duration of the session. Durand evaded the speaker's warrant for arrest and the assembly expelled him *in absentia*.[70] Ironically, Nichol turned around and led an attack on behalf of Niagara area speculators on government policies which threatened to shut out Americans from the land market. The expression of accumulated grievances led to the early proroguing of the legislature in 1817 and 1818. Robert Gourlay strode into the midst of turmoil, prompting the security proceedings examined elsewhere in this volume.

Government concerns about the press only temporarily subsided after Gourlay's banishment, the seditious-libel conviction of Gourlay's publisher Bartemas Ferguson, and the demise of Ferguson's opposition Niagara *Spectator*.[71] Hugh Thomson of the *Herald* and King's Printer Charles Fothergill were targets in 1823 and 1824,[72] and the opposition newspapers in York, William Lyon Mackenzie's *Colonial Advocate* and Francis Collins's *Upper Canada Freeman*, had become the focus of official concern by the late 1820s. The destruction of Mackenzie's press in June 1826 brought the issues of government sanctioned illegality and partisanship in the administration of the law to the forefront. An assembly inquiry that followed cast doubts on Attorney General John Beverley Robinson's exercise of prerogative powers on prosecutions, and, as Paul Romney explains in this volume, the controversy formed the setting for libel charges against Mackenzie and Collins. In the end, Robinson did not proceed on the indictment against Mackenzie and Collins's conviction was to prove to be the last security-related libel case before the rebellion.

Mackenzie's repeated expulsions from the assembly (1831–4) were designed to prevent him from sitting as a member and did not result in imprisonment. Yet these incidents reflected much more than immediate partisan battles: security concerns and attempts to muzzle the press, the related controversies around the administration of justice, and the government's subsequent loss of confidence in suppressing opposition through the courts suggest a deeper security dimension. By this time the Collins case had placed the administration of criminal law under close imperial as well as local legislative scrutiny.[73] The attorney general was unwilling to risk the controversy of a special jury through the expedient of an ex officio information, and Reform popularity in York made a regular trial jury risky. Robinson's successor openly declared as much in assembly debates in December 1831.[74] Subsequent events leave no doubt that official anxiety about the colony's security played an important part in the government's campaign against Mackenzie. The motions on ineligibility were based on statements published outside the house in the *Colonial Advocate* and the offence was deemed to be one of seditous libel. By early 1832 even Collins's moderate paper, the *Freeman*, was describing Mackenzie's 'agitation and mountebank shows' as 'seditious.'[75] Magistrates, alarmed by meetings organized by Mackenzie in York and Hamilton, called upon householders to report at the police office to be sworn in as special constables. A seditious-libel prosecution against Mackenzie, based on comments in the *Colonial Advocate*, was actually contemplated by the law officers in March 1832 but the Executive Council concluded that it would not be politically expedient.[76] The courts had become an unwieldy means of repression and parliamentary proceedings for contempt appear to have filled the breach. Ultimately, however, even this alternative measure backfired on the government.

Mackenzie's encounters with privilege involved very complex political events which can be sketched only in broadest outline in an overview essay such as this. Soon after Mackenzie won a seat in the 1828 elections Lieutenant Governor Sir Peregrine Maitland warned his successor, Sir John Colborne, that 'men who were notoriously disloyal, and whose characters are really detestable are now degrading the legislature of this country by their presence.'[77] New elections following King George IV's death in 1830 resulted in a small pro-government majority in the province but a more liberal change of government in Britain. By the new year Lord

Goderich was instructing Colborne to proceed with reforms.[78] The provincial government was unreceptive and a now compliant legislature contemplated proceeding against Mackenzie in late February.[79] Between sessions Mackenzie's agitation reached new heights.[80]

Mackenzie's popular petitions to the new king were condemned when the legislature reconvened in November. The speech from the throne only hinted at Goderich's encouragement of reform. A libel bill, which would allow truth as defence, was debated and opposed by the attorney general, who, perhaps revealing the government's strategy in dealing with Mackenzie, reportedly remarked, 'There were many instances in which persons have thus been charged, and yet the juries have always acquitted the parties, declaring that the motives were not malicious.' He added, 'Look at the late trials in England of Cobbett and others, and what chance ... had a public prosecutor to convict a man even under the present law of libel.'[81] The assembly's compliance with the government caused an emboldened Mackenzie to declare in the *Advocate* that 'our representative body has degenerated into a sycophantic office for registering the decrees of a mean and mercenary executive.'[82] This was the origin of the series of expulsions that followed.

A motion was put forward to vindicate 'the independence of parliament' but Marshall Spring Bidwell's mischievous addition supporting 'a free press ... notwithstanding many different attempts to destroy its liberty' was defeated. A second amendment made the motion into a contempt proceeding. This was cast in wording that might have been, and probably was, adapted from British indictments or judgments in sedition cases: 'gross, scandalous and malicious libels, intended and calculated to bring this House and the government of this province into contempt, and to excite groundless suspicion and distrust in the minds of the inhabitants of this province as to the proceedings and motives of their representatives ...'[83] Mackenzie argued that the courts were the appropriate tribunal to resolve questions of libel.[84] It was moved that this response 'flagrantly aggravated the charge brought against him, and [he] is therefore guilty of a high breach of the privileges of this House.'[85] On 12 December he was expelled on a vote of twenty-four to fifteen and an election writ issued.

Mackenzie's famous by-election victory on 2 January 1832 included a gold-medal presentation from constituents and an escort to the polls of sleighs, one of which had a printing press mounted on it and banners reading 'Liberty of the Press' and 'A Free Press the Terror of Sycophants.'[86] He returned to the assembly sporting the medal (waggishly described as a large gingerbread by his opponents), but he was met with new charges of contempt from Solicitor General Christopher Hagerman and the Legislative Council gave notice that its privileges were also breached.[87] Hagerman moved that Mackenzie 'not only reasserted the gross, scandalous and malicious libel' of the previous expulsion, but by adding to reprinted articles a 'black list' of those who voted for expulsion and a by-election address he also 'endeavoured by false, scandalous and malicious representations, to cause his Majesty's subjects in this province to believe that the majority of their representatives should be held in abhorence by posterity as enemies to the liberties of the people they represent.'[88] Mackenzie was expelled a second time.

Mackenzie was again re-elected and expelled a third time *in absentia* at the next legislative session in November 1832. The previous two expulsion resolutions were read and the motion was simply that since he had been declared unfit he was not entitled to sit or vote and a new writ must be issued. His constituents re-elected him yet again on November 26th.[89] In the meantime Mackenzie had urged meetings throughout the province, and the result in Hamilton and York was riots. With the government now contemplating a seditious-libel prosecution,[90] Mackenzie, bypassing the legislature as Gourlay had done, collected voluminous petitions and was commissioned to present them to the British government. He was warmly received by radical British MPs and had interviews in the Colonial Office and with the secretary of state.[91]

Mackenzie had some impact and Goderich ordered Colborne to address Mackenzie's petitions. On 19 January 1833 government supporters led by Hagerman moved that the imperial instructions be simply returned with an expression of disapproval. The majority softened the motion, expressing regret that Lord Goderich had paid attention to Mackenzie's allegations when the government had majority support for its stance. The Legislative Council adopted the original motion and returned the dispatch with a protest written by Robinson. Mackenzie shrewdly thanked Goderich for the dispatch, adding that imperial instructions were bound to be frustrated without reforms.[92] Goderich had consistently expressed disapproval of Mackenzie's expulsions, calling into question the constitutionality of one house unilaterally declaring a member unfit without criminal conviction or prior statutory prohibition. He maintained that libels should be prosecuted in the courts although he would refrain from enquiring into earlier questionable prosecutions of newspaper editors.[93] Colborne does not appear to have made Goderich's concerns clear to the law officers.[94] When Goderich found out about Mackenzie's third expulsion, he instructed Colborne directly to inform Boulton and Hagerman that they would lose their appointments if their opposition to the crown continued.[95] Then, after news of the legislative reception of his instructions reached London, a furious Goderich ordered their immediate resignations, sparking a major constitutional crisis.[96]

Nothing was done about Mackenzie's seat after his third expulsion and re-election in November 1832. Over two months later, following the protest against Goderich's dispatch, an expulsion motion was carried by one vote. The majority could not be sustained on a motion for a new writ and technically, therefore, the seat was not vacated. Having greatly embarrassed the government on both the local and imperial fronts, Mackenzie returned to his seat at the next session in November 1833. The legislative clerk refused to administer the necessary oath of allegiance based on the partial vote from the previous session and the battle went outside the house with York taxpayers refusing to appoint a collector without representation. The lieutenant governor ordered the oath administered but a new expulsion vote was passed and writ issued in December. Returned by the electors by acclamation, Mackenzie again took his seat in February 1834, only to be physically removed by the sergeant-at-arms. Shortly after, York became the city of Toronto and Mackenzie was elected its first mayor.[97]

Lord Goderich recognized the doubtful constitutionality, if not legality, of Mackenzie's expulsions. After the Revolution Settlement of 1701 there was recognition that parliamentary privilege must extend to freedom of debate in order for there to be the effective functioning of parliament – an informed opposition to proposed measures was an important legislative check on government. Temporary expulsions for contempts or disruption were possible but members had immunity from prosecution for remarks in the house. With regard to outside comments, the proper forum to prosecute the alleged libels in the *Advocate*, notwithstanding *Burdett* and especially given the British law officers' 1815 opinion on the limits of the Lower Canadian legislature, was in the criminal courts. As we have seen, the government considered but was clearly mindful of the dangers of a seditious-libel prosecution. Perhaps it was also mindful of questions around the provincial legislature's jurisdiction to punish, for, unlike the cases of Willcocks and Durand, Mackenzie's contempts were dealt with by expanding expulsion privileges rather than imprisonment. Even these actions, based on a simple resolution of ineligibility, were questionable. To declare an elected member disqualified and issue an election writ required a criminal conviction, finding of election fraud, or violation of an existing statutory prohibition or equivalent joint resolution of the houses. The issues in Mackenzie's first and second expulsions, notwith-standing the government's reluctance, should have been dealt with by the law courts if they were to be pursued at all. The third and fourth expulsions were even more unfounded; with no evidence presented, they were based simply on the majority's opinion of his unfitness. In opting to suppress Mackenzie's opposition by orchestrating privilege proceedings in the legislature rather than the courts, the government was yet again attempting to be judge in its own cause.

LOWER CANADA

Robert Christie's five expulsions from the Lower Canadian house are a political inversion of the Mackenzie saga. As noted earlier, they came from a house at odds with the government, triggered by his recommendations to remove *patriote* magistrates and resistance to a select committee's attempts to establish an independent magistracy. He provoked further by suggesting that his Gaspé constituency quit the province to join New Brunswick. He was re-elected after every expulsion, with constituents demanding representation in face of arbitrary disqualifications. The matter was referred to the British government and Lord Goderich, drawing upon Wilkes, upheld Christie's right to his seat.[98] Although there are parallels to Mackenzie, his expulsions did not entail security issues. For this we must turn to another case.

The Daniel Tracey Case, 1832

From Governor Craig's era almost a generation before, the two houses of the Lower Canadian legislature had repeatedly engaged in furious combat. The issues in dispute included the barring of judges from the assembly and the suspension of habeas corpus (1808–12), control over public finances (1820s), and the right of accused felons to full defence by legal counsel (achieved in 1836). In the session that concerns us, that of 1831–2, the appointed aristocratic Legislative Council vetoed assembly initiatives to safeguard Canadien land law in the Eastern Townships and to democratize the parish vestries (*fabriques*), the intent of the latter measure being to undermine the *ancien régime* influence of the Roman Catholic clergy. The veto by the upper house of the bill concerning *fabriques* moved Daniel Tracey, editor of the Irish-Canadian, radical *Vindicator* of Montreal, to demand on 3 January 1832 'its total annihilation' as a stupid force blocking enlightened political amelioration. A similar denunciation was published by the *patriote* Ludger Duvernay in Montreal's *La Minerve* six days later.

The council ordered the arrest of both journalists on 13 January, a questionable exercise of power undoubtedly intended to counter the assembly's recent, aggressive stance on its supposed privileges. In 1826 the majority of members had asserted exclusive appropriating control over all government revenue,[99] and a year later it claimed that the authoritarian governor, Lord Dalhousie – who identified with the Stuarts – had had no right to reject the election of Louis-Joseph Papineau as speaker.[100] And as mentioned, from 1829 to 1832 it expelled Robert Christie five times for aiding Dalhousie in his attempts to purge the magistrates' bench.[101]

As a preliminary to ordering the arrest of Tracey and Duvernay, the council unanimously resolved that each of their writings 'contain a gross libel against this House and is a direct breach of its privileges.'[102] On the arrests, there was some opposition. Three members objected to the use of this unprecedented power against insignificant persons (ensuring that greater notice would be taken of them) who were, after all, answerable to the regular courts. Ultra-Tory Herman Ryland expounded on 'publications of a revolutionary tendency' aimed at changing a benevolent monarchy into an anarchistic republic, urging an address to the governor so that he, the ministry, and the general public could be better apprised of the profound dangers involved and perhaps thereby discover more drastic and hence efficient remedies. Four of the fifteen men present, while believing in '*gross* libel[s],' did not believe that the exercise of privilege in this instance was *essential* to safeguard the upper house.

Both accused, brought to the bar on the 17th, admitted publishing (and, in Tracey's case, writing) the offending articles. Asked if they had anything further to add in justification, Duvernay said nothing, while Tracey maintained the truth of his opinions. They were sentenced to remain in the common jail until the end of the current session. Neither man had access to legal counsel; they were judged not by their peers but by those attacked in the 'libels'; and in the end a serious crime was decided upon without any hearing whatsoever. Each was asked to justify himself. Obviously that could not involve denying the crime itself but was restricted to proving non-participation or repentance.

All these differences from ordinary criminal-law procedure, however, were sanctioned by British precedents. The more difficult question was whether either house had the power to imprison political opponents for supposed libel.

Precedents abounded in the two Canadas and were seemingly relevant because they involved assembly orders to arrest for libels committed outside the legislature and the Constitutional Act of 1791 governed both lower houses. In 1806 editors Edward Edwards, Thomas Cary, and merchant Isaac Todd had been ordered apprehended,[103] as was Cary again in 1813, for attacking opposition leader James Stuart in print.[104] Ten years later the editors and publishers of the *Canadian Times*, Edward V. Sparhawk and Aviel Bowman, were to be incarcerated for libelling the lower house on its 'completely anti British' opposition to the proposed union of the Canadas.[105] Upper Canada had experienced similar things in the cases of Nichol and Durand.

Only the cases of Willcocks and Nichol amount to anything resembling full precedents, since they were the only two alleged libellers actually imprisoned by either assembly. Cary (1806) was discharged. Edwards, Todd, Cary (1813), Durand, Sparhawk, and Bowman successfully evaded the sergeant-at-arms until the end of the session. There were apparently no court proceedings regarding privilege in the Willcocks case, while Nichol was released via habeas corpus by Chief Justice Thomas Scott on a technicality, the judgment not referring to the merits. Thus the local precedents, prior to 1832, determined nothing except that the assembly majorities recurrently believed they had the power to commit for libels/slanders out of doors. There was not even a significant series of actual internments, let alone judicial sanction, direct or indirect, of the legislature's claims.

The British houses, as parts of the supreme court of parliament, had imprisoned outside libellers through time (almost) immemorial. The practice was well known to Tracey's generation. In 1798, for example, the *Morning Chronicle*'s publisher was jailed by the Lords for an article spoofing that august body as a ministerial rubber stamp comically concerned about the scanty dress of ladies at the opera. A dozen years later radical MP Sir Francis Burdett was imprisoned for scandalizing the Commons in Cobbett's *Weekly Register*. In 1831 the Lords briefly incarcerated the *Times*'s printer for having suggested that the Earl of Limerick's attitude to Irish poverty was the brutal response of a 'thing.'[106]

The Burdett incident was apparently the only relevant one ever to generate judicial decision, *Burdett v. Abbot*, a judgment of Lord Ellenborough for the Court of King's Bench in 1811.[107] It is of critical importance.

The lord chief justice sanctioned the imprisonment on two bases: ancient and modern usage, but more generically, the need for each house to protect itself against dissenters who were insufficiently deferential. 'This,' he contended, was 'an essential right necessarily inherent in the supreme legislature of the kingdom.' Each house must be capable of 'protecting itself from insult and indignity.' Contemptuous libels were 'as much an impediment [through intimidation or distraction] to their efficient acting ... as the actual obstruction of an individual member by bodily force.' And it was beneath the dignity of the houses to 'wait the comparatively tardy result of a prosecution [for seditious libel] in the ordinary course of law.' Ellenborough's decision amounted to a set of unsupported assertions sanctifying political authority.

On 8 February 1832 lawyer Andrew Stuart, acting for Tracey, applied to the King's Bench for a writ of habeas corpus,[108] causing Sewell to pale visibly, it was said, and to make him attempt to have the bench dismiss the application summarily.[109] If true, the tactic did not work.

Besides celebrating a free press as essential to public enlightenment, Stuart addressed three main issues: grossly unfair procedure, inherent lack of authority, and the absence of necessity. The first hit at such oddities as councillors sitting as judges in their own cause, lack of a jury, and, above all, council's *ex parte* condemnation of Tracey: 'No human tribunal has the right to convict without hearing the party accused.' But, as mentioned, all these things, including a 'pre-trial' resolution on the offence, were commonplace in the British precedents. The second claimed that English examples had arisen in 'very remote antiquity' out of the judicial authority of parliament. Lower Canadian chambers could point to no ancient usage or judicial function but only to powers expressly granted or distinctly implied by the Constitutional Act of 1791.

Stuart conceded that in *Burdett* Lord Ellenborough had emphasized – idiosyncratically – the supposed need for self-protection. This doctrine was highly doubtful for England, given the ease with which the crown could and nearly always did prosecute such cases in the courts. It would certainly be ridiculous if this 'rubbish of a rude age' were to be applied to British North America: 'In a state of society such as that of Great Britain it is [perhaps conceivably] necessary [that] ... public authority should be armed with higher power than is required in ... new countries' such as Lower Canada. Stuart also attempted to distinguish *Burdett* on the grounds that the convicted was an MP – a difficult argument in view of the other precedents and Ellenborough's general language. Despite counsel's urging, all judges decided against Tracey. Not surprisingly.

From the beginning, chances of impartial decision had been slim. All judges were long-standing political enemies of the *patriotes*, members of the impugned council, and subordinate colleagues (on the court and/or in the house) of the main protagonist, Jonathan Sewell. One, James Kerr, was then facing multiple charges of judicial misbehaviour being prepared by the assembly and was to be judged, according to one rumour, by the council. For a generation he had looked upon people such as Tracey, Duvernay, and Louis-Joseph Papineau as representatives of blood-letting 'French democracy.' As the *Vindicator* correctly complained, Bowen was truly 'the *Own* man of the Chief Justice.' He had articled with Sewell and the latter had helped his protégé to the attorney generalship (1808) and the bench (1812). Bowen, moreover, was then financially dependent on Sewell to avoid insolvency. He was also brother-in-law to Councillor Sir John Caldwell. Taschereau, once a leader of the *parti canadien*, had become a successful seeker of crown patronage by 1815 and in the 1820s was a favoured political supporter of the authoritarian Lord Dalhousie, by whom he was appointed to the court in 1827. The *patriotes* naturally looked upon this Canadien judge as a '*chouayen*' or 'sell-out' and professed scepticism about his legal learning, he not being 'a walking library of law, the whole of which ... rests very quietly on the shelves at home, while he sits on the bench.'[110]

The main thrust of all the judgments was to accept without qualification the self-defence doctrine of *Burdett*. Kerr, for example, insisted that this summary power to imprison could not be denied the legislative councillors 'without their sinking into utter contempt and inefficiency through being exposed to derision or even intimidation.' Two judges remarked that leaving the libels to be disposed of in the courts would not work. In stark contrast to his view in 1814, Bowen noted that the house's vindication would then depend, not on itself, but 'upon the will of the crown!' Kerr adopted Ellenborough's point about the tardiness of judicial proceedings but went one better by noting that (given trial by jury) the 'uncertainty of the legal result would little conduce to maintain the dignity of these bodies.' Like Ellenborough, the Lower Canadian judges just assumed a necessity that was not there.

Bowen and Taschereau referred to the local precedents discussed above – exaggerating their scope – while all judges relied heavily on the case of *Ex Parte Samuel Wentworth Monk*, decided fifteen years before by the King's Bench, District of Quebec. Justice Taschereau went so far as to claim that the decision meant that the power of either house to imprison for contempt out of doors had 'been sanctioned by the courts of justice of this country.'[111] One of the joint protonotaries of the Montreal King's Bench, Monk had refused in 1817 to hand over certain records claimed by a special house committee investigating charges made against Mr Justice Louis-C. Foucher. For this, the assembly ordered Monk detained and he spent slightly more than a month in jail for contempt. He was released by the court after the session by means of a habeas corpus.[112]

If the judges in 1832 had wished, *Monk* might easily have been distinguished from Tracey's case. First, the issue in *Monk* did not relate to *libel* out of doors but to disobedience of the assembly's orders. And in such a case, allowing the ordinary law to take its course (for example, by prosecution for the high misdemeanour of maladministration) would certainly be tardy and quite likely amount to real obstruction of justice. Hence, in the circumstances, proceedings by means of privilege were arguably more 'necessary' than in cases of libel and the situation was closely analogous to interference within the confines of the house, which was punishable by jailing the perpetrator. Secondly, the court had not decided the merits of Monk's case. Its decision to discharge the prisoner was based on the general, well-supported principle that the orders of legislative bodies were terminated by prorogation and the committal warrant which had referred to incarceration 'during pleasure' was to that extent improper. The court had been explicit about the limits of its decision: 'Without determining therefore, whether the detention of Mr. Monk was legal or illegal ... we must discharge him upon the ground that the period for which he was [could be] committed has expired.'[113]

Stuart had emphasized the distinction between the British parliament, whose privileges were rooted in history, and its Lower Canadian counterpart, which was governed by the Constitutional Act and hence able to use only such powers as were truly *essential* to carry out its legislative functions. But the judges had paid no attention to this distinction, which created a presumption against the Legislative Council's assertion of privilege and would govern the ultimate definition of the law. That the bench ignored Stuart's argument is not surprising. What is remarkable, however, was the judges' failure to implement (or even mention) the British law officers' opinion of 1815, which clearly denied the power of imprisoning for external contempts. It is impossible to believe that Sewell, and difficult to believe that Bowen and Kerr (members of the court in 1814–16), had simply forgotten about the opinion. The limits of assembly privilege had been an intense political issue recurrently from 1806 and the precise issue had arisen as recently as 1823.

Political Aftermath

The imprisonment of Duvernay and Tracey unleashed mammoth forces of frustrated liberalism. Immense newspaper publicity was paralleled by massive demonstrations in the two cities (including receptions for the convicted men that treated them as conquering heroes) which were notable for outspoken attacks on the chief justice and the upper house.[114] Resolutions calling for the council to be elected first passed the assembly in 1832–3, putting the Papineau-led majority on a collision course with the imperial Whig government. The Tracey/Duvernay incident also provoked the first serious talk among *patriotes* of political independence and even full-scale rebellion.[115]

The arrests both revealed and reinforced profound disillusionment about the impartiality of the courts. The *Vindicator* noted that all on the *patriote* side were convinced that the council's action would be sustained, despite Stuart's unanswerable arguments: 'No one seems to think conscience or law will have anything to do in the case.' The paper went on – with prescience – to foresee possible civil unrest. 'The [popular] conclusions are all drawn from the suspicion of political or depraved motives; and the awful solemnity and majesty of justice is hardly ever thought of or mentioned. If such, in reality, be the condition of the administration of justice ... it is a most dangerous ... state of affairs.'[116] The Ninety-two Resolutions of 1834 made clear that such a perception of the bench was a truly major grievance which helped precipitate the rebellions.[117]

As for freedom of the press, it was not achieved in the wake of the arrests. Following the 1838 rebellion, for example, opposition editors were incarcerated without bail or trial for expressing dissident opinions.[118] But a free press did get its heroic martyr in Tracey – who died from cholera in July 1832. His political friends, including Louis Lafontaine, future premier of the united Canadas and one of the main founders of responsible government, erected a monument to his memory in 1832 which was replaced by one equally laudatory some eleven years after his remains were interred in the Côte-des-Neiges cemetery in 1855: 'As a public journalist and devoted patriot,' the inscription reads, 'his memory will ever be venerated by his fellow citizens.'[119]

LEGAL ASSESSMENT AND CONCLUSIONS

Later Precedents on Imprisonment for Contempt

These varied. In the Jamaica case of *Beaumont v. Barrett* (1836), involving a newspaper libel on the assembly, the Judicial Committee of the Privy Council, through Exchequer Baron Parke, upheld the power to commit. The committee followed *Burdett*, noting somewhat erroneously that the *colonial* legislature of Jamaica 'appears to possess *supreme* legislative authority over the whole of the island and its dependencies.'[120] Seven years later, in the Newfoundland litigation of *Kielley v. Carson*, the committee – one of the most prestigious boards ever struck – reversed itself, with Parke again rendering the decision.[121] Colonial legislatures held no judicial powers, unlike Westminster, which was originally a court.

Kielley involved slanders of an assembly member, both in and out of the house. Concentrating on the latter, the board held that colonial legislative bodies did not enjoy the same privileges as their equivalents in the United Kingdom where ancient history operated. Incarceration was 'by no means essentially necessary for the exercise of its functions by a local Legislature ... these ... may be performed without this extraordinary power, and with the aid of the ordinary tribunals.' Reversal was justified on several grounds, for example, that judgment in *Beaumont* had been rendered immediately after argument. On this score, their Lordships were mesmerized by Ellenborough's widely phrased *dictum* in *Burdett*: 'which *dictum* ... cannot be [taken as] ... authority ... that every Legislative body has the power of committing ... The observation was made ... with reference to the *peculiar* powers of Parliament, and ought not, we all think, to be extended any further.' *Kielley* became the definitive decision on the power of colonial houses to commit and indeed settled the general point that any privilege had to be 'essentially necessary' rather than merely useful or analogous to British practice.[122] The presumption was strongly against the validity of any debatable power claimed by one house, unsupported by constitutional or special statutory grant.

The Power of Expulsion

In both Mackenzie's and Christie's cases, the assemblies claimed a privilege to disqualify sitting members from re-election. This interference by a single house with the rights of the electorate, through the creation of a disability unknown to law, ran contrary to the ultimate and permanent resolution by the House of Commons in the Wilkes affair in 1782. That resolution (passed by a margin of 115 to 47) had condemned any unilateral creation of incapacity 'as being subversive of the rights of the whole body of electors of this kingdom.'[123] It was therefore not surprising that the colonial secretary reprimanded both lower houses in the Canadas for having gone beyond even imperial precedent, let alone the restricted scope enjoyed by colonial houses.[124]

They had also gone beyond a clear Lower Canadian precedent. In

March 1799, country merchant Charles-Baptiste Bouc had been convicted in the King's Bench, Montreal, of defrauding a Terrebonne farmer in a wheat deal and sentenced to three months' imprisonment.[125] Expelled from the assembly by simple resolution in 1799, 1800, and 1801 (twice), he was three times re-elected. The assembly did not claim the right to disqualify Bouc and indeed, following the last re-election, it was unanimously agreed that Bouc 'is duly elected a Knight to serve in this present Provincial Parliament.' In 1802 permanent exclusion was achieved by local statute applying strictly to Bouc.[126] The Mackenzie/Christie precedents would not be followed after confederation by parliament, even though that body was *not a colonial legislature* in matters of privilege.

Another question is whether a colonial house enjoyed even the simple power to expel based on the majority's view that a member was unfit to act as a legislator. The British Commons was certainly vested with such a privilege, as was the Canadian house after 1867 by virtue of section 18 of the British North America Act. As opposed to mere suspension, expelling a member (who did not wish to retire) forced him to seek re-election.[127]

In the Canadas, at least three expulsions other than Mackenzie's raised the issue but they all ended in ambiguity.[128] The only clear, reasoned precedent is the law officers' opinion of 1815, which leads to the conclusion that mere perceived unworthiness or libellous statements were not sufficient grounds for expulsion. This also emerges from three non-Canadian decisions rendered by the Judicial Committee in the latter half of the nineteenth century.

The cases all accepted *Kielley v. Carson* as authority, not only in its specific result, but also for the generalizations that the 'lex et consuetudo Parliamenti' did not extend to colonial legislatures and privileges could be exercised only when demonstrably essential. How stringent this test was became apparent in the concrete instances adjudicated. In *Fenton v. Hampton* (Van Diemen's Land, 1858), the board held that refusal to cooperate with one of its committees did not entitle a colonial council to imprison the offender, thus casting retrospective doubt on the decision in *Monk*.[129] Eight years later (*Doyle v. Falconer*) the committee laid down that the Legislative Assembly of Dominica had no power to incarcerate for contempts, even those committed in the house (a member had refused the speaker's order to cease debating), a conclusion more restrictive than that of the law officers in 1815.[130] The third decision was *Barton v. Taylor* (New South Wales, 1886), which held that for colonies 'protective and self-defensive powers only, and not punitive are necessary.' It therefore followed that, while an obstructive legislator could be suspended for a brief time or until he apologized, suspension for an indefinite period at the assembly's discretion was *ultra vires*. *Barton* was the only case to mention expulsion. The house had the right 'to expel for aggravated or persistent misconduct [obstruction].'[131]

Thus the authorities indicate that the assemblies of Lower Canada and Upper Canada had not acted legally in the Christie and Mackenzie cases. Neither man had been convicted of any crime in a court of law and neither had been guilty of aggravated or persistent obstruction, the only instances in which expulsion was permitted. The same generalization can be made about the Lower Canadian house's decisions to expel Ezekiel Hart for being a Jew and Pierre-Amable De Bonne for being a judge.

The cases analysed here demonstrate one of the curious byways where Canadian state trials can be found: when legal proceedings failed, or held uncertain prospects for the government, supposed privilege powers were sometimes resorted to. These cases reflect the partisan extremes to which colonial legislative houses could go to suppress freedom of the press and deal with broader security anxieties. The activities of Reform politicians and their 'dangerous engine,' opposition newspapers, were considered 'seditious,' and, unlike the courts, the houses acted as judges in their own causes. With the possible exception of the Duvernay/Tracey detentions, the positions taken by the houses exceeded the partiality of the colonial courts. It cannot be imagined that the Commons or Lords would have conducted themselves in the same manner in this period, despite their greater powers under constitutional law. One cannot conceive that the House of Lords, for example, would have ordered a person detained when the lord chancellor knew of a law officers' opinion denying power in such a case. Imprisoning editors for published opinions when recourse had already been had to the courts, thus placing them in double jeopardy, and arbitrary disqualifications certainly violated the law and exceeded claims accepted in the mother county. These excesses were arguably known to be questionable, but Reformers also exploited supposed privilege, using the powers as a means to pressure governments before responsible government came into existence. The security concerns triggered by such counter-hegemonic uses of privilege powers are examined in detail in the essay that follows.

NOTES

1 Erskine May, *A Treatise on the Law, Privileges, Proceedings and Usage of Parliament*

(19th ed.), ed. David Littledale (London: Butterworths 1976), at 67. We have used May as our principal secondary guide to the law governing privileges.

2 See Jean-Marie Fecteau, F. Murray Greenwood, and Jean-Pierre Wallot. 'Sir James Craig's "Reign of Terror" and Its Impact on Emergency Powers in Lower Canada, 1810–13,' in this volume.

3 Ibid.

4 The following paragraphs are based primarily on A.B. Keith, *Constitutional History of the First British Empire* (Oxford: Clarendon Press 1930); Mary P. Clarke, *Parliamentary Privilege in the American Colonies* (New York: Da Capo 1943); Alfred H. Kelly and Winfred A. Harbison, *The American Constitution: Its Origins and Development*, 3rd ed. (New York: W.W. Norton 1963), at 28–32; and especially Jack P. Greene, *Negotiated Authorities: Essays in Colonial Political and Constitutional History* (London: University Press of Virginia 1994), ch. 7 ('The Role of the Lower Houses of Assembly in Eighteenth-Century Politics,' 163–84). By 1776 Maryland had joined the club. In 1763 Georgia and Nova Scotia had less than a decade of experience with representative government.

5 Greene, *Negotiated Authorities*, at 167; [Secretary of State Lord Grenville], 'Discussion of Petitions and Counter Petitions re Change of Government in Canada,' Aug.–Oct. 1789, *Con Docs* 1: at 978–9. Councillors held their seats at the crown's pleasure. Besides their legislative and executive functions, most councils acted as courts of last resort in the colonies.

6 Greene, *Negotiated Authorities*, at 174.

7 Quoted in Lawrence A.H. Smith, '*Le Canadien* and the British Constitution, 1806–1810,' *CHR*, vol. 38 (1957), 93 at 98. The acting governor, Sir Alured Clarke, granted the assembly only its 'just Rights and Lawful Privileges' (ibid.).

8 The assembly condemned Sheriff W.B. Sheehan's conduct when he attempted to serve a writ on a member. See W.R. Riddell, 'The Legislature of Upper Canada and Contempt: Drastic Methods of Early Provincial Parliaments with Critics,' *OH*, vol. 22 (1925), 186 at 186–7.

9 See Smith, '*Le Canadien* and the British Constitution'; Helen Taft Manning, *The Revolt of French Canada, 1800–1835* (Toronto: Macmillan 1962), ch. 5; John L. Finlay, 'The State of a Reputation: Bédard as Constitutionalist,' *Journal of Canadian Studies*, vol. 20 (1985–6), 60; Fernard Ouellet, 'Bédard, Pierre-Stanis-las,' *DCB* 6: 41; F. Murray Greenwood, *Legacies of Fear: Law and Politics in Quebec in the Era of the French Revolution* (Toronto: Osgoode Society/University of Toronto Press 1993), ch. 10, 11.

10 See Robert Christie, *A History of the Late Province of Lower Canada*, 6 vols. (Quebec/Montreal: Thomas Cary et al. 1848–55), 2–4: passim.; Donald Creighton, 'The Struggle for Financial Control in Lower Canada, 1818–1831,' *CHR*, vol. 12 (1931), 120; Manning, *Revolt*, passim.

11 Burns refused to appear on the advice of the Executive Council, leading a house committee to declare, 'The House of Assembly of the Province of Upper Canada is a Superior Court of Record and that every disobedience of the orders thereof is high contempt and misdemeanour punishable at its own discretion.' No motion followed. See Riddell, 'Drastic Methods,' at 189, 191–2.

12 See also the following accounts of confrontations over government finance in 1806 and 1816: Gerald M. Craig, *Upper Canada: The Formative Years, 1784–1840* (Toronto: McClelland and Stewart 1963), at 58; Aileen Dunham, *Political Unrest in Upper Canada 1815–1836* [1927] (Toronto: The Carleton Library/McClelland and Stewart 1963), at 49–51. Important in this regard, too, is the case of Robert Nichol, discussed below.

13 In the 1820s and 1830s, for example, the Lower Canadian Legislative Council blocked assembly initiatives to entitle accused to a full defence by counsel (from 1824 until 1835–6), to democratize the parish *fabriques* or vestries (1831), and to impose more stringent penalties on those who engaged in the 'aristo-cratic' practice of duelling (1836). In Upper Canada, from 1825 on the council vetoed regular assembly attempts to abolish the land-inheritance rule of primogeniture.

14 See Robert Christie, *History*, 2: at 151–2, 167–71; R.L. Fraser, 'Nichol, Robert,' *DCB* 6: 539 at 540; Greenwood, *Legacies of Fear*, ch. 10, 11; and nn.9, 10, and 12.

15 See n.10.

16 Edmund B. O'Callaghan, *The Late Session of the Provincial Parliament in Lower Canada* (Montreal: 1836).

17 31 Geo. III, c. 31.

18 See the discussion of James Durand below. On the assembly's action in 1831, see Charles Lindsey, *The Life and Times of Wm. Lyon Mackenzie*, 2 vols. [1862] (Toronto: Coles Canadiana Collection 1971), 1: at 209–10.

19 *In the Case of Pierre Bedard* (1810), Stuart's Reports 1. Sewell's judgment is found at 13–19.

20 Attorney General Sir William Garrow and Solicitor General Samuel Shepherd to Colonial Secretary Lord Bathurst, 30 Dec. 1815, *Con Docs* 2: at 480–3.

21 2 Aug. 1814, Sewell Papers, MG 23, G II 10, vol. 5, NA.

22 The original text of the questions (CO 42, MG 11, vol. 164, 194–5, NA) is defi-nitely in Sewell's handwriting. See also Henry Goulburn (under-secretary of state) to Sewell, 14 Nov. 1815, Sewell Papers, vol. 5.

23 Sewell cited three sections of the 1791 act dealing with legislative power as the only 'clauses of the Statute that relate ... to the Authority ... of the Assembly of Lower Canada' and noted that the latter nevertheless claimed *all* the privileges of the House of Commons.

24 See the description of the Bouc expulsions (Lower Canada, 1799–1802) in the text below.

25 See Christie, *History*, 3: ch. 28–31, 33; Shirley Sprague, 'Christie, Robert,' *DCB* 8: at 154–5.

26 RG 1 E 3, Submissions to the Executive Council, N5, vol. 56, at 40, NA; *Con Docs* 2: at 425–7; and R.L. Fraser, 'Nichol, Robert,' 539 at 540.

27 The chief justice granted the application on the basis that the commitment failed to show cause and indicate the resolutions of the house or a sentence. Legislative Council committee, 2 March 1812, RG 1, E 3, N 5, vol. 56.

28 E.A. Cruikshank, 'A Study of Disaffection in Upper Canada in 1812–15,' *Royal Society of Canada, Proceedings and Transactions*, 3rd ser., 6 (1912), 1 at 16–17.

29 By 1814 the opposition presence in the assembly had been reduced by the defection of Joseph Willcocks, Benajah Mallory, and Abraham Markle to the U.S. side and the marginalization of others such as David McGregor Rogers. Nichol, elected in 1812, became the government's house leader, introducing the emergency measures in 1814.

30 For a detailed study see Jean-Pierre Wallot, 'La querelle des prisons dans le Bas Canada (1805–1807),' in his *Un Québec qui bougeait: trame socio-politique au tournant du XIXe siècle* (Montreal: Les éditions du Boréal Express 1973), 47.

31 See Greenwood, *Legacies of Fear*, passim, but particularly ch. 5, 9–11.

32 Ryland to Mountain, 27 April 1806, Mountain Papers, series C, vol. 5, Quebec Diocesan Archives (Lennoxville, Quebec). See also Quebec *Mercury*, 10 March 1806.

33 See *Con Docs* 2: at 351–4; B.G. Sack, *History of the Jews in Canada* [c. 1945] (Montreal: Harvest House 1965), at 69–79; Greenwood, *Legacies of Fear*, at 216–18, 226, 229–30.

34 Ibid., ch. 10, 11.

35 Ibid. See also the essay by Fecteau, Greenwood, and Wallot, 'Sir James Craig's "Reign of Terror."'

36 See also n.9.

37 See Elwood Jones, 'Willcocks, Joseph,' *DCB* 5: 854.

38 44 Geo III c.1, discussed at length in the following essays in this volume: Paul Romney and Barry Wright, 'State Trials and Security Proceedings in Upper Canada during the War of 1812'; Barry Wright, 'The Gourlay Affair: Seditious Libel and the Sedition Act in Upper Canada, 1818–19'; and Paul Romney, 'Upper Canada in the 1820s: Criminal Prosecution and the Case of Francis Collins.'

39 Prior to the legislation Weekes attempted to use privilege powers against the executive and in the session following the passage of the legislation he

stepped up a principled attack, drawing parallels with colonial rule in Ireland, where grievances had led to rebellion, repression, and union with Great Britain.

40 See 'Political State of Upper Canada,' *PACR*, 1892, 32; G.H. Patterson, 'Weekes, William, *DCB* 5: 844; Jones 'Willcocks, Joseph'; R.L. Fraser, 'Jackson, John Mills,' *DCB* 7: 438; G.H. Patterson, 'Thorpe, Robert,' *DCB* 7: 864; Elwood H. Jones, 'Wyatt, Charles Burton,' *DCB* 7: 929; S.D. Clarke, *Movements of Political Protest in Canada, 1640–1840* (Toronto: University of Toronto Press 1959), at 213–22; H. Guest, 'Upper Canada's First Political Party,' *OH*, vol. 54 (1962), 275; Craig, *Upper Canada*, at 58–65; G.H. Patterson, 'Whiggery, Nationality and the Upper Canadian Reform Tradition,' *CHR*, vol. 56 (1975), 25; R.L. Fraser, 'All the Privileges Which Englishmen Possess: Order, Rights, and Constitutionalism in Upper Canada,' in *Provincial Justice: Upper Canadian Legal Portraits from the Dictionary of Canadian Biography*, ed. R.L. Fraser (Toronto: Osgoode Society/University of Toronto Press 1992), xxi.

41 See Enemy Aliens Act (1797) 37 Geo. III c. 1; *R. v. Tiffany*, RG 22, series 125, Court of King's Bench Term Book, AO; D.J. Brock, 'Tiffany, Gideon,' *DCB* 8: 887; D.G. Lochhead, 'Tiffany, Silvester *DCB* 5: 814.

42 S.R. Mealing, 'Gore, Francis,' *DCB* 8: 336 at 339.

43 Quoted in Craig, *Upper Canada*, at 62 [Jan. 1808]

44 —— to McGill, 17 June 1807, 'Political State of Upper Canada,' at 85–6.

45 Gore to under-secretary of state, 4 Oct. 1807, ibid., at 113. See also —— to Gore, 21 Aug. 1807, ibid., at 86.

46 See Gore's marginal note in the letter cited in n.44. Genêt was probably Citizen Edmond Genêt, ambassador to the United States from revolutionary France in 1793–4. In that office he had attempted to foster a rebellion in Lower Canada that would be coordinated with a French naval invasion and supported by a land attack from Vermont. In 1807 Genêt was living in New York state. See Greenwood, *Legacies of Fear*, ch. 4.

47 See Clark, *Political Protest*, at 218 (citing travel writer Christian Schulz in 1807).

48 Cruikshank, 'Disaffection,' at 15–16.

49 See, for example, Craig, *Upper Canada*, at 47–9, 58–65, 70–7, 101, 111, 116–18, 166, 173, 178, 182, 198–201, 207, 221, 229, 241, 246.

50 See correspondence reproduced in 'Political State of Upper Canada.'

51 Gore, through paid agents, kept close watch on Willcocks as he left for the United States to obtain a press. Anonymous informants wrote from New York that he kept company with 'both foreigners and natives residing in this City and in the Western part of this State, [who] contemplate a *Reform* in the Government of the Upper Province. The Person alluded to returned a few weeks ago to the Upper Province with a Printing Press and Press Men; a committee

of correspondence is formed, which is to prepare the *minds of the People* for some great *change.'* Another note read that 'they are nothing less than an attempt to *revolutionize* the Province. The Engine to be made use of to carry this object into effect is a free Press as it is called.' See Gore to Castlereagh, 21 Aug. 1807, 'Political State of Upper Canada, at 81, 85–6.

52 RG 22, series 125/127 Court of King's Bench Termbook, Michaelmas Term, 14 November 1807, AO. See Gore to Watson, 4 Oct. 1807, 'Political State of Upper Canada,' at 113 and 115. Also: W.R. Riddell, 'The Information Ex Officio in Upper Canada' *Canadian Law Times*, vol. 41 (1921), at 91–2; Paul Romney, *Mr Attorney: The Attorney General for Ontario in Court, Cabinet and Legislature, 1791– 1899* (Toronto: Osgoode Society/University of Toronto Press 1986), at 44.

53 RG 22, series 125/127, King's Bench Termbook, Hilary Term, 4 Jan. 1808, AO. Willcocks was obliged to provide securities.

54 Ibid., 16 Feb. 1808; see also Riddell, 'Information Ex Officio,' at 91–2. Powell's decision to approve Willcocks's request appears to have surprised the government.

55 RG 22, series 134, Court of King's Bench Assize Minutebook, vol. 3, 296, AO. Willcocks objected to Firth calling a special jury on the information and conducted his own defence. Joseph Waters was called by the crown to prove publication, which Willcocks acknowledged. The question of the applicability of Fox's act was not explicitly raised but the jury gave a general verdict which was likely influenced by Willcocks's previous punishment for contempt. See discussion of Fox's act in the introduction to the volume.

56 Captain Cowan proposed the motion based on a 'slanderous' paragraph which implied that members of the house had been bribed by the governor with land to vote against the interests of their constituents. See 'Address to the Electors of the West Riding of the County of York, the first Riding of the County of Lincoln, and the County of Haldimand' (by Willcocks from the Home District jail, 6 March 1808), *Upper Canada Guardian*, Friday, 18 March 1808. Reproduced in Robert Gourlay, *Statistical Account of Upper Canada*, vol. 2 (New York: East Eardsley, repr. 1966), notes at 656–62.

57 Ibid.

58 Ibid., at 657.

59 Ibid., at 657–8.

60 Ibid., at 655, 658–9.

61 Ibid., at 655.

62 See Gourlay, *Statistical Account*, at 650–1.

63 The Wilkes resolution did not explicitly say that the houses could not punish contempt while a prosecution was pending in the courts, athough Gourlay's extrapolation of the resolution that the ordinary course of justice should not be

obstructed was a sound one (see Gourlay, *Statistical Account*, 2: at 650n.). For discussion of the incident, see Greenwood, *Legacies of Fear*, at 129–30, 242.

64 See *Burdett v. Abbot* (1811) 14 East 1, 136–58. Ellenborough's confirmation that the high court of parliament had analogous powers to those of the courts of law, including the right to commit for contempt to vindicate its dignity, was not expressed as an unqualified carte blanche for parliament's disciplinary powers. He added that the courts have jurisdiction to enquire into a committal if the contempt was an offence at law and if the matter appearing on the return (for habeas corpus) was arbitrary. The authors' review of procedural deviation on committals is taken from *Stockdale v. Hansard* (1839) 9 Ad. and E., 1.

65 MG 11, Q series, Upper Canada State Papers, Gore to Liverpool, 9 Aug. 1810, 313 at 316, NA; JHAUC, AO *Report*, 1911; Riddell, 'Contempt,' at 194. Further attempts were made to counter Jackson's *A View of the political situation of the province of Upper Canada* (London: 1809). See John Strachan, *A Discourse on the Character of King George the Third Addressed to the Inhabitants of British America* (Montreal: 1810), and Richard Cartwright, *Letters, from an American Loyalist in Upper Canada, to His Friend in England, on a Pamphlet Published by John Mills Jackson, Esquire: Entitled, A View of the Province of Upper Canada* (Halifax: 1810).

66 The measures restricted landholding by Americans and was supported by the sanctions of the Sedition Act: the Executive Council prohibited the administration of the oath of allegiance to American immigrants (which by legislation was a precondition to holding land) and authorized magistrates to report all suspicious Americans. See RG 1, E 1, Minutes of the Executive Council, 7 Oct. 1815, NA; Report, Gore to Bathurst, 17 Oct. 1815, reproduced in E.A. Cruikshank, 'The Government of Upper Canada and Robert Gourlay,' *OH*, vol. 33 (1936), 65 at 108–9.

67 See Gourlay, *Statistical Account*, 2: at 631–2; J.C. Weaver, 'Durand, James,' *DCB* 6: 228–30.

68 The proceedings are reproduced in their entirety in Gourlay, *Statistical Account*, 2: at 628–65.

69 Ibid., 633, 635–9.

70 Ibid., 640–4. Gourlay suggests (at 654) that if Burdett or Hobhouse had escaped the speaker's warrant they would not have been similarly expelled.

71 The Kingston *Chronicle*, which had been sympathetic to Gourlay, came under the control of conservative owners who were associated with Robert Stanton.

72 Thomson became an advocate of the Reform cause, and his reference to Robert Stanton's action in prematurely closing the polls to the detriment of Marshall Spring Bidwell was made in the course of comments on Stanton's involvement with a legislative committee on the Bank of Upper Canada. He was summoned to appear at the bar of the assembly in 1823 on charges of contempt, repri-

manded by Speaker Sherwood for printing a 'false, scandalous and malicious libel,' and warned that he would be prosecuted and punished if it continued See JHAUC, 1823; H.P. Gundy, 'Thomson, Hugh Christopher,' *DCB* 5: 773. King's Printer Charles Fothergill was dismissed from the position after his 1824 election and involvement with Reform, to be succeeded by none other than Robert Stanton. See Paul Romney, 'Charles Fothergill,' *DCB* 7: 317.

73 See Romney, 'The Collins Trials'; JHAUC, 1829, Appendix, 'Report of the Select Committee on the Petition of Francis Collins.' The British government considered Collins's punishment excessive: Scarlett and Sugden to Murray, 30 June 1829, CO 42/390/49–50, NA.

74 The prevailing controversy over the crown's monopoly explains why Attorney General Robinson had resisted informations and proceeded against Mackenzie and Collins by indictment in the 1828 prosecutions (see especially Robinson to Maitland, 10 May 1828, reproduced in CO 42/386, 'Papers Relating to the Removal of the Honourable John Walpole Willis,' printed by British House of Commons, 1829, at 24–5, NA). The earlier trial of Gourlay's publisher Ferguson in 1818 by ex officio information had been criticized because the British Six Acts restricted the information.

75 Collins opposed suggestions that Mackenzie ought to be tried in the courts, saying that such charges should be brought only against a man of sane mind and that, like Gourlay, Mackenzie had become completely beside himself. See *Canadian Freeman*, 3 and 26 Jan., 22 and 29 March 1832.

76 See two documents in RG 1, E 3, Submissions to the Executive Council, vol. 16, file C 6: Opinion of the Law Officers of the Crown, 16 March 1832, which affirmed that articles in the *Advocate* had a seditious tendency; and the conclusion of the Executive Council on 17 March that a prosecution would not be politically expedient. The government had also considered prosecuting Captain John Matthews for seditious words for asking a group of travelling American actors to sing 'Yankee Doodle' and 'Hail Columbia' at a party. The government withdrew his pension instead. See William Kilbourne, *The Firebrand: William Lyon Mackenzie and the Rebellion in Upper Canada* (Toronto: Clarke Irwin 1956), at 52, 75–6, 81.

77 Quoted in ibid., at 52. The assembly's Reform majority continued to expose abuses through investigative committees. Mackenzie presided over five, tackling a huge range of issues, and his *Colonial Advocate* made repeated appeals for legislative and judicial reform.

78 The British government's committee on the Canadas recommended in 1828 that judges be removed from councils and that legislative councils be made more popularly representative and independent of the executive. In a dispatch to Colborne (8 Feb. 1831) Goderich indicated that judicial tenure be changed

from royal pleasure to good behaviour, reiterating that judges should not sit in council. See W.D. LeSueur, *William Lyon Mackenzie: A Reinterpretation* (Toronto: Macmillan, repr. 1979), at 146–7, and Dunham, *Political Unrest*, at 115–22.

79 A motion, put forward by Allan MacNab, alleged that parliamentary journals printed by Mackenzie – extra copies without the appendix were distributed free – constituted breach of the privileges of the house. The law officers concurred but the motion was defeated when put to a vote. See LeSueur, *Mackenzie*, at 150.

80 See, for example, *Colonial Advocate*, 10 March 1831. He focused on law reform, with proposals ranging from Legislative Council membership (judges were to be excluded from council) and security of judicial tenure to the quarter sessions, local government, and juries.

81 Reported in the *Canadian Freeman*, 2 Dec. 1831.

82 The assembly's refusal to refer one of Mackenzie's petitions to a committee was the direct cause of the declaration: see *Colonial Advocate*, 24 Nov. and 6 Dec. 1831; LaSueur, *Mackenzie*, at 159–60, 163.

83 JHAUC, 6 Dec. 1831.

84 Ibid.

85 Ibid., 12 Dec. 1831.

86 LeSueur, *Mackenzie*, at 173.

87 *Colonial Advocate*, 2 and 5 Jan. 1832.

88 On 7 January the assembly voted twenty-seven to nineteen that Mackenzie was 'unfit and unworthy' to hold a seat. Bidwell's motion that the expulsions had caused so much excitement that it was necessary to vindicate the assembly's actions by a general elections was rejected. See Appendix, JHAUC, 1832.

89 LeSueur, *Mackenzie*, at 196.

90 See n.76.

91 See RG 7, G 1, vol. 69, NA; LaSueur, *Mackenzie*, at 187.

92 Ibid., at 198–205.

93 Stanley to Colborne, 2 April 1832, in acknowledgment of Colborne's letter of 31 Jan. 1832, RG 7, G series, G 1, vol. 68, NA; LaSueur, *Mackenzie*, at 209.

94 LeSueur, *Mackenzie*, at 197.

95 RG 7, G 1, vol. 70, Goderich to Colborne, 6 March and 30 April 1833; LaSueur, *Mackenzie*, at 209–10.

96 RG 7, G 1, vol. 70, Goderich to Colborne, 26 March 1833. This dispatch authorized the appointment of Reformer John Rolph as solicitor general and English barrister R.S. Jameson as attorney general. Goderich's replacement by Stanley, representations from the province, and Boulton's pleading in London resulted in the restoration of Hagerman to his office and the appointment of Boulton to the chief justiceship of Newfoundland.

97 Kilbourne, *Firebrand,* at 96–7; LeSueur, *Mackenzie,* at 216–20.

98 Christie, *History,* 3: ch. 28–31, 33; Sprague, 'Christie, Robert.'

99 Christie, *History,* 3: 107.

100 *Con Docs* 3: at 416–19.

101 Christie, *History,* 3: at 240–4.

102 This and the next two paragraphs are based on JLCLC, 1831–2 (13, 17 Jan. 1832); *Vindicator,* 20 Jan. 1832.

103 See Donald Creighton, *The Empire of the St. Lawrence* [1937] (Toronto: Macmillan 1956), at 155–65; Wallot, 'Querelle des prisons,' at 63–8; Greenwood, *Legacies of Fear,* at 190.

104 Montreal *Gazette* (reprint from the Quebec *Mercury*), 23 Feb. 1832.

105 Ibid.

106 *Parliamentary History,* vol. 33 (21, 22 March 1798), cols. 1310–13; *Parliamentary Debates,* 3rd series, vol. 3 (18, 20, 21 April 1831), cols. 1701–19, 1748–84; *Burdett v. Abbot* (1811 – KB), 14 East 1 (Lord Ellenborough's judgment at 131–63).

107 Ibid. See also Erskine May, *The Law, Privileges, Proceedings and Usage of Parliament* (21st ed.), ed. C.J. Boulton (London: Butterworths 1989), at 103–9.

108 *In the Case of Daniel Tracey,* Stuart's Reports 478.

109 *Vindicator,* 17 Feb. 1832.

110 See the letters from Bowen to Sewell, Jan.-April 1832, in the Sewell Papers, vols. 6 and 7.

111 At 515. The *Monk* case is found in Stuart's Reports 120.

112 JHALC, 1817 (19, 21 Feb.)

113 At 121.

114 See, for example, the issues of *La Minerve* and the *Vindicator* from mid-January to mid-March.

115 *La Minerve* , 13 Feb. 1832 (quoting Papineau on non-violent separation); ibid., 16 Feb. 1832.

116 *Vindicator,* 17 Feb. 1832.

117 See Greenwood, *Legacies of Fear,* at 330n.52.

118 See Greenwood, 'The General Court Martial of 1838–39 in Lower Canada: An Abuse of Justice,' in *Canadian Perspectives on Law and Society: Issues in Legal History,* ed. W. Wesley Pue and Barry Wright (Ottawa: Carleton University Press 1988), 249 at 256.

119 Emmet J. Mullally, 'Dr. Daniel Tracey, a Pioneer Worker for Responsible Government in Canada,' Canadian Catholic Historical Association *Report* (1934–5), 33 at 34.

120 1 Moo. P.C. 59.

121 (1842–3) 4 Moo. PC 63. The board consisted of John Copley, Lord Chancellor Lyndhurst; Vice-Chancellor Lancelot Shadwell; Dr Stephen Lushington;

Thomas Erskine; James Scarlett, Lord Abinger; Henry Peter, Lord Brougham; Thomas, Lord Denman; Sir Nicholas Conyingham, Lord Tindal; John, Lord Campbell; Charles Christopher Pepys, Lord Cottenham; and John Parke, Lord Wensleydale. Three – Parke, Erskine, and Shadwell – had sat on *Beaumont*.

122 See, for example, the Judicial Committee cases discussed in the text below; *The Annotated Constitution of the Australian Commonwealth* [1901], ed. John Quick and Robert R. Garran (reprint, Sydney: Legal Books 1976), at 503–4; Sir Kenneth Roberts-Wray, *Commonwealth and Colonial Law* (New York: F.A. Praeger 1966), at 383–7.

123 3 May 1782, quoted in *Law and Working of the Constitution: Documents 1660–1912*, 2nd ed., 2 vols., ed. W. Costin and J.S. Watson (London: Adam and Charles Black 1961/64), 1: at 235. See also May, *Parliamentary Practice*, at 112–13.

124 Goderich to Aylmer, 26 Jan. 1832, quoted in Christie, *History*, 3: at 441–2; same to Colborne, 8 Nov. 1832. In the January dispatch, Goderich wrote that he found it inconceivable that the Lower Canadian assembly would maintain its illiberal position in view of the denouement to the 'well known conflict between the electors ... of Middlesex and the house of commons' in 1782.

125 Jonathan Sewell to his wife, 4 March 1799, Sewell Papers, vol. 3; Richard Chabot, 'Bouc, Charles-Jean-Baptiste,' *DCB* 6: 77 at 78.

126 'Proceedings Relating to the Expulsion of Mr. Bouc from the House of Assembly, Lower Canada,' *Con Docs* 2: at 285–91; SLC 1802, c. 7.

127 Section 18 conferred on the Commons and Senate such privileges as were declared by Canadian statute provided that they did not exceed those enjoyed by the British House of Common in 1867. This was later expanded (1875) by imperial amendment to those enjoyed by the British House at the time of the Canadian act. SC 1868, c. 23, s. 1 conferred on the Senate and Commons the British privileges. Examples of expulsion include Louis Riel in 1874 (re-elected but again expelled in 1875) for being a fugitive (unconvicted) from justice (there were British precedents) and for disobeying an order of the Commons to appear in his place. In 1891 Conservative Party treasurer Thomas McGreevy was expelled for suspected corruption. Re-elected in 1895, he was allowed to take his seat. In neither case was an attempt made to incapacitate the member from being re-elected. See George F.G. Stanley, *Louis Riel* (Toronto: Ryerson Press 1963), at 201–5, 208, 220; Canada, House of Commons *Debates*, vol. 33 (29 Sept. 1891); Michèle Brassard and Jean Hamelin, 'McGreevy, Thomas,' *DCB* 12: 626 at 30.

128 In his 1832 dispatch to Aylmer on the Christie affair (n.124), Goderich's position on expulsion was not clearly expressed. For the Lower Canadian cases of

Ezekiel Hart (1808, 1809) and judge Pierre-Amable De Bonne (1810), see Greenwood, *Legacies of Fear*, at 216–18, 226, 229–31.

129 11 Moo. P.C. 347.

130 LR 1 PC 328.

131 11 AC 197 particularly at 203–5. It is clear from the context and other wording that 'misconduct' meant 'obstruction.' There was, read the judgment at 203, an inherent power 'in every Colonial Legislative Assembly to protect itself against obstruction, interruption, or disturbance of its proceedings by the misconduct of any of its members in the course of those proceedings.'

13

The Attempted Impeachment of the Lower Canadian Chief Justices, 1814–15

EVELYN KOLISH and JAMES LAMBERT

Saturday, 26 February 1814. James Stuart rose in the House of Assembly of Lower Canada to state that the 'committee appointed to prepare Heads of Impeachment against Jonathan Sewell, Esquire, Chief Justice of the Province and James Monk, Esquire, Chief Justice of the Court of King's Bench for the District of Montreal,' which he chaired, had completed its work. He then read twenty-five charges. Against Sewell, it was alleged that he 'traitorously and wickedly endeavoured to subvert the Constitution and established Government' of Lower Canada and 'introduce an arbitrary, tyrannical Government against Law, which he hath declared by traitorous and wicked opinions, counsel, conduct, judgments, practices and actions.' More specifically, the report asserted that:

- as a chief justice, Sewell had 'usurped' legislative authority through his judgments and the adoption of certain regulations published as *Rules and Orders of Practice;*
- as speaker of the Legislative Council and chair of the Executive Council, he had poisoned the mind of Governor Sir James Craig against the Canadien population and the House of Assembly by proffering 'false and malicious slanders' and had misled Craig 'to dissolve the Provincial Parliament, without any cause whatever' in May 1809;
- as Craig's adviser he had persuaded the governor to dismiss unjustly loyal officeholders, notably Jean-Antoine Panet, speaker of the assembly, as lieutenant-colonel of militia;

- as a government official, he had facilitated establishment of the newspaper *Vrai-Canadien* 'for the purpose of calumniating and vilifying' the Canadiens and certain members of the assembly;
- he had sought 'to extinguish all reasonable freedom of the Press, destroy the rights, liberties and security of His Majesty's Subjects in this Province, and suppress all complaint of tyranny and oppression' by advising seizure of the printing press of Charles LeFrançois and LeFrançois's imprisonment;
- he had counselled Craig to arrest Pierre Bédard, François Blanchet, and Jean-Thomas Taschereau, members of the assembly, 'upon the false and unfounded pretext of their having been guilty of Treasonable Practices,' and had had them held without bail for a long period and without bringing them to trial in order to prevent their re-election;
- he had used his office 'to mislead the Public, deceive His Majesty's Government, and obtain pretexts for illegal and oppressive measures, instigated and promoted various acts of tyranny and oppression ... in other parts of the province, whereby divers individuals upon the false pretext of having been guilty of treasonable practices were exposed to unjust prosecutions, imprisoned and oppressed';
- he had induced Craig, on 21 March 1810, when 'profound tranquillity prevailed in the province,' to issue a proclamation implying the guilt of Bédard, Blanchet, and Taschereau and 'a state approaching open insurrection' in the colony, thus calumniating the Canadiens and encouraging the Americans to invade, and then he himself read the proclamation in open court with a view to influencing the jury;
- he had endeavoured to 'favour the progress of American influence' in the colony and 'traitorously' abused his authority 'to promote the advantageous establishment of Americans ... and to pave the way for American predominance therein' at the expense of the Canadiens and 'with a view to subversion of His Majesty's Government';
- he had, influenced by a desire 'to accelerate a political connexion of this Province, with part of the United-States of America,' plotted with 'an adventurer,' John Henry, to promote rebellion among the Americans and dismemberment of the union, placing Britain in a potentially compromising position;
- and, finally, as speaker of the Legislative Council, he had promoted animosity towards the assembly, fomented division in the colony, undermined confidence in the loyalty of the Canadiens, and produced 'a want of confidence in the administration' of the colony, thus weakening its 'exertions.'

At Monk, the report levelled the first few accusations made against Sewell and then added that Monk had, as judge, 'publicly ascribed to the

... Court of King's Bench, the power of altering, changing and modifying' provincial laws; denied writs of habeas corpus to eligible persons; and, in some cases, 'advised Criminal Prosecutions' and then sat in judgment on them.[1] (See app. 3, M.)

The litany of charges brought against Sewell and Monk, and the very tone, mode, and context of their presentation, crystallize virtually all the elements that conditioned the administration of justice in early-nineteenth-century Lower Canada: personal ambitions and animosities, judicio-cultural differences, political conflict, and ethnic suspicions. That the assembly's attack was spearheaded by Stuart and aimed personally at Sewell and Monk emphasizes that, in the small world of Lower Canada, personal relationships had a significant impact on public life. That the attack focused in part on Sewell's and Monk's adoption of rules of practice reflects a long-standing judicio-cultural controversy that pitted English civil law against French civil law. That Sewell was charged with fomenting division between the assembly and certain of its members on the one hand and the governor and Legislative Council on the other demonstrates how closely the judicial system was integrated into the confrontational politics of the time. Finally, that Sewell was charged with attempting to undermine British confidence in Canadien loyalty and strengthen American influence in the colony underscores the ethnic and national tensions that were never far from the surface of Lower Canadian society. Each of these elements alone was sufficiently powerful to hamper the administration of justice; when combined they reinforced each other, as they did in the attempt to impeach the chief justices, and could throw the judicial system into a crisis while reflecting how that system formed a part of the broader socio-political struggle for control of the institutions regulating Lower Canadian society. This essay will examine the personal, judicial, political, and social dimensions of the attempt to impeach the chief justices in order to determine its significance for an understanding of the dynamics of Lower Canadian society and for the course of that society's subsequent development.

The use of impeachment as a weapon in constitutional battles has played a much less prominent role in Canadian than in American history. Nonetheless, the perceived importance of the judiciary in the maintenance of order, as a bulwark against chaos and social upheaval, made judges tempting targets both for security-minded executives, as in the cases of the removal of Robert Thorpe and John Willis in Upper Canada for example, or for reformist factions in assemblies attempting to strike a blow at the executive, as in the situation examined here. More particularly with respect to security, although the attempt to impeach did not itself constitute a menace, the mere fact that each side pointed strongly and frequently to alleged threats to security in the demands and actions of the other underlines the extent to which that issue was still, in the years immediately following the War of 1812, politically potent. The success of the chief justices in presenting the process of impeachment itself as a threat to security, whatever the reality, was central to their ultimate vindication by the imperial authorities.[2]

THE PERSONAL CONTEXT

Historians rooted in the complex, mechanized, institutionalized, and impersonal society of the late twentieth century have difficulty grasping the extent to which Lower Canada was still largely a society of personal relations. In the attempt to impeach the chief justices, the relations between Stuart and Sewell on the one hand and between Sewell and Monk on the other demonstrate how personal relations, in combination with other factors, could affect colonial developments.

It was no accident that the charges brought against the chief justices were read by Stuart. For Governor Sir George Prevost, 'Stuart's personal animosity towards the two Chief Justices, and particularly towards Mr. Sewell, has shewn itself too strongly in the course of the proceedings against those Gentlemen to leave a doubt upon the mind of any unprejudiced person with regard to his motives on this occasion.'[3] Prevost's opinion was echoed by Pierre Bédard, a contemporary from the opposite end of the spectrum, whose reflections on the issue of rules of practice show a genuine attempt to weigh both sides of the question with a minimum of personal involvement.[4]

In keeping with his conservative Loyalist family background and education, Stuart was a natural candidate for officeholding and government service.[5] His talent as a young lawyer had favourably impressed Lieutenant Governor Sir Robert Shore Milnes, who had employed him as a personal secretary and then named him solicitor general in 1805. Frustration of Stuart's ambitions after Milnes's departure began his 'detour' into the role of leader of the opposition.

Arrogant, sensitive, and choleric, Stuart took Governor Craig's preference for Edward Bowen as attorney general in 1809 as a personal affront. He deliberately snubbed the new governor by failing to pay his respects socially and by occasionally voting with the opposition in the assembly – inappropriate behaviour for a solicitor general in a world of patronage politics. He shortly paid the price by losing his post, which Craig granted to Stephen Sewell, brother of the chief justice. Insult was added to injury when Stuart lost his seat in the assembly to Stephen Sewell in the election of 1810. Stuart's fierce sense of grievance seems to have focused on Jonathan Sewell, doubtless both for Sewell's probable influence in his brother's advancement[6] and for his close association with Craig throughout that governor's tenure.

There are no similarly clear grounds for Stuart's animosity towards James Monk, who was a rival rather than a supporter of the chief justice. However, Monk had been on poor terms with Stuart's former patron, Milnes,[7] and had favoured Craig's hard-line stance against the Canadien party, so that Stuart might well have deemed him guilty by association. He was also chief justice of Montreal and therefore prominent in the colonial officialdom to which Stuart aspired and from which he had been excluded.

Sewell's relations with Monk were only marginally better than those with Stuart and for the same reason: ambition. The two first met, probably in 1789, after Sewell's arrival at Quebec from New Brunswick to start a career in law. Monk, who had been dismissed as attorney general in April, undoubtedly looked askance at the new arrival's efforts to cultivate favour with Governor Lord Dorchester and Chief Justice William Smith, both of whom Monk blamed for his dismissal. In November Monk sailed for England to try to recover his position; after much frustration he succeeded and returned triumphant to Quebec in October 1792 to take over the duties from the acting holder of the office, Jonathan Sewell himself, who had been appointed by Dorchester. In October 1793 Dorchester and Smith obtained for Sewell the position of solicitor general, which deprived Monk of some fees for government business.[8] Sewell, Monk wrote to his patron in England, was 'a Going Man.' 'A Bostonian Lad, Son of the Judge of Admiralty, he has some parts,' Monk acknowledged, but, fearing Sewell's rise, he added that Sewell was 'without much experience, and in my mind not adequate to the duties required of Attorney General.'[9]

Monk and Sewell necessarily collaborated in 1794 to suppress successfully a budding movement of protest against the colony's Militia Act. Monk was rewarded for his role that year when, although passed over for the post of chief justice at Quebec, he was given the new but more junior position of chief justice of the Court of King's Bench at Montreal. To Monk's dismay, Sewell succeeded him as attorney general.

Sewell had no great regard for Monk. A staid family man, Sewell once remarked drily to his wife: 'The Chief Justice will not, I apprehend give above seven public dinners a week during term, at least he has not hitherto exceeded that number.'[10] Thereafter, efforts by both to trip up the other on certain political and legal matters were barely modulated by a general agreement on the broader issues of British colonial administration. Monk, however, was on the margins of British official society, whereas Sewell was a rising star.[11] Resentment smouldered in Monk; disdain grew in Sewell. After he was twice passed over for the ultimate prize of chief justice at Quebec, Monk was mortified in 1808 to see his rival promoted to that post.[12] In short, according to a contemporary observer, Sewell and Monk 'entertained a most perfect and cordial hatred for each other.'[13]

Had Stuart attempted to topple Sewell on political grounds only, it is doubtful that Monk would have intervened. However, by including charges that rules of practice Sewell had published in 1809 were 'repugnant and contrary to the Law,' Stuart also attacked Monk, whose own rules of practice, published two years later, were inspired by Sewell's. This was a tactical error because Monk could bring to the defence of the judges three invaluable qualities: experience of a similar situation in 1787 (in which he had lost but learned), intimate knowledge of the workings of the imperial government, and steady nerves. According to a contemporary, Sewell, 'a man of great talent' but 'fine' feelings and 'weak' nerves, was thrown by the assembly's charges into 'a state of pitiable distress'; however, Monk, 'who is pretty well case hardened,' was singularly unaffected. It may well be that the sang-froid of his long-time rival more than the encouragement of his political friends emboldened Sewell to resist rather than seek a compromise, which was always his tendency in situations of confrontation (resignation being out of the question).[14] This was important because Sewell, probably more than anyone else in the colony, could turn the tables politically on the Canadien party.

Although the context of interpersonal relationships should not be underestimated, so obvious were Stuart's motives for leading the assembly's attack on the chief justices, both to contemporaries and to historians, that they have contributed to obscuring the importance of the rules-of-practice controversy in historical analysis until recently.[15] A glance at the judicial background of rules of practice in Quebec is necessary to put the impeachment attempt into perspective.

THE JUDICIAL CONTEXT

The lack of printed rules of practice had long been felt in the colony. The Quebec Act's reintroduction of French and Canadien civil law in 1774 had failed to define clearly the sources of that law and the limits that the English court structure might impose upon it. This ambiguity, combined with a bench that had few members with legal training and even lacked a chief justice for a long time, had already resulted in confusion and irregularities in the practice of the courts in the late 1770s and the 1780s, culminating in a major inquiry into the administration of justice in 1787. That year, with the ordinance governing the administration of justice about to expire, Chief Justice William Smith seized the opportunity to propose an ordinance designed to extend the use of English civil law and legal practices. It was immediately countered by the French party, which put forward a proposal intended to extend the use of French law. The British merchants in the colony, who supported Smith, hired Monk as a private attorney to present their views in the Legislative Council.

During his presentation, Monk urged 'the propriety of restraining the judges to more fixed and determinate rules of conduct, with regard to the practice of the courts, and to the laws and maxims which ought to govern them in their decisions.'[16] So effective was Monk that Dorchester was induced to open an inquiry into the administration of justice. In it, the merchants claimed, Monk would be able 'to shew the want of *order, rule, regularity,* certainty, and the great delays and *procrastination'* in the courts of common pleas.[17] Indeed, although during the inquiry he attacked many aspects of the administration of justice – including the alleged indiscriminate use of English law, French law, or equity, which meant that the judges were in effect 'assuming the powers of Legislators'[18] – he returned regularly to the lack of rules of practice, which allowed defendants unlimited delays in presenting their cases.[19] Monk argued that eliminating exaggerated delays through the use of proper rules of practice was the judges' responsibility, that the ordinance of 1777 did not provide sufficient rules, that no legislature could,[20] and that the form of proceedings used prior to the conquest in situations not foreseen by the ordinance of 1777 was insufficient and inappropriate.[21]

Years later, in 1814, Stuart acknowledged in the report of the assembly's committee to examine the published rules of practice that 'the alterations made in the Judicature of the Country, and the English Forms of Judicial proceedings introduced subsequent to the Conquest, having made many of the Regulations of the French Law inapplicable, some Rules became necessary to settle points of Practice not regulated by the existing Law.'[22] Indeed, in 1787, the very year of the inquiry, an ordinance had been adopted that stated: 'It shall henceforth belong to the provincial court of appeals ... to make rules and orders to regulate, effectuate and accelerate the proceedings in all causes of appeal, for the advancement of justice, and to prevent unnecessary delays and expense in the same.'[23] Monk had apparently won his point; the clause, however, may have remained a dead letter. Monk claimed victory again in successfully defending before the new colonial legislature in 1793 a judicature bill, which he had largely inspired, and which included a clause, he said, obliging the judges and crown officers to submit rules of practice and suitable lists of fees.[24] In fact, the Judicature Act of the next year merely maintained in force all previous laws constituting rules of practice and those giving authority to the courts to establish rules.[25] In 1801 yet another act gave 'the different Courts of Civil judicature in this province ... power and authority to make and establish such Orders and Rules of practice in the said Courts in all Civil matters, touching all services of process, execution and returns of all Writs, Proceedings for bringing causes to issue, as well in Term time as out of Term, and other matters of regulation within the said Courts.'[26] Stuart argued that these passages severely limited the courts' prerogative of making rules.[27] This hardly seems true, since their language offered the courts considerable scope.[28]

The hostility to judges using personalized rules of practice contrary to colonial legislation was expressed in the context of a bench that was pro-French. The gradual elimination of the French-party judges made the question of rules of practice less important for the British merchants and bureaucrats that Monk had represented. But complaints about the arbitrariness of the judges then became commonplace on the other side of the political and legal fence, among Canadien lawyers and litigants, who grew more and more persuaded, in the first decade of the century, that the predominantly English bench was undermining Canadien law and procedure and more or less systematically introducing English legal notions in cases that should have been governed by Canadien law.[29] The charge that rules of practice were being used in this way, and usurping the role of the legislature to boot, appears in the press as early as 1807.[30]

Since the argument that rules of practice were being used to undermine the civil law was a central issue in the impeachment attempt, a few comments are in order concerning the attitudes of the two chief justices and their opponent to the status of the civil law in a British colony. To begin with Monk, he was well versed in the French civil law and perceived its maintenance in some respects as just and necessary to obtain the allegiance of the Canadiens. He favoured its retention for real estate, marriage, and inheritance, in Canadien-inhabited areas; argued for its application on socage lands (contrary to all his English-language colleagues on the bench) in 1803; and defended the right of the habitant to concessions of seigneurial land on demand and at reasonable rates, and of the Roman Catholic Church to the *pain béni*.[31] That said, however, Monk was not committed to the French civil law either intellectually or socially. In 1787 he affirmed that 'the Constitutional principle of Colonization in every modern empire is the extension to Such Colony of the National Laws for securing personal rights of the National born subjects.' As well, he continued, in policy the granting of English civil law would help populate the colony, encourage commerce, and reinforce ties to Britain.[32] The following year he drafted a proposed constitutional bill designed in part to assimilate Quebec to the other British colonies 'in Laws and Government, manners & customs.'[33] And in 1811, as he published his rules of practice, he felt that the laws of the colony had to be amended to bring them into conformity with a new socio-economic context if the current reform of the administration of justice, of which the publication of the rules was a step, was to continue. To Prevost he wrote in December that 'much remains to be done, to improve the Administration of the Laws, to the actual and growing state of the Colony,' that the provincial statutes 'have fettered the Courts of Law,' and that the French laws in force in the colony should be amended in the directions they gave for their execution and their administration by the courts.[34]

Like Monk, Sewell manifested an ambivalent attitude towards the French civil law, but he had an even firmer grasp of it.[35] Contrary to Monk, he argued in 1795 that it was 'an established Principle that in Conquered or ceded Countries, the ancient Laws remain, until the King or Parliament shall have actually set them aside.' This not having been done, 'the antient Law still Subsists and is in fact the Common Law of the Province under a declaratory Act of Parliament.'[36] He felt that the British government had been remiss politically in maintaining French civil law, but he acknowledged that its action had merit. Nevertheless, as attorney general, Sewell was vigilant in his efforts to influence legislation in a way that would weaken those parts of Canadien law that he saw as obstacles to anglicizing Canadien society – for example, seigneurial tenure or the matrimonial regime of community of property.[37]

Yet there is little evidence that Sewell was seen as an enemy of the civil law tradition or that his 1809 rules of practice were interpreted as an attack on that tradition. Hitherto, and notwithstanding an assertion by Stuart to the contrary, previous practices of the courts had given so little satisfaction that *Le Canadien*, on Sewell's appointment to the bench in 1808, had expressed hope that he would draft satisfactory rules.[38] Moreover, that same year, Justin McCarthy dedicated his *Dictionnaire de l'ancien droit du Canada* to the new chief justice, 'jouissant de l'estime entière du Public.'[39]

Stuart's views on Canadien civil law were less ambiguous than those of Sewell or Monk. His defence of Canadien law during the effort to impeach his rivals for judicial office was the sole time in his legal and political career that he adopted a position in favour of the civil law tradition. As a lawyer and later a judge, he was a sufficient master of both legal systems to navigate in the confused waters of Lower Canadian courts, but the lack of published reports in this period makes it difficult to evaluate whether he adhered to any consistent line of interpretation, either for or against Canadien law. By the 1820s, after returning to the English party, Stuart was a prominent opponent of existing real estate law, especially seigneurial tenure,[40] and such aspects of the Canadien law of hypothecs as customary dower. As a final indication that his arguments in 1813–14 were opportunistic, as chief justice in 1850 he maintained several of the rules of practice that he had earlier attacked. Thus, ironically, the two chief justices charged with using the rules of practice to undermine French law were arguably less hostile to the civil law over the entire course of their careers than was their principal accuser.

However, what was initially to have been an impeachment of Sewell and Monk on judicial grounds took on a new dimension when, on 18 February 1814, the assembly authorized a committee, led by Stuart and including Louis-Joseph Papineau, 'to add such Heads of Impeachment as may appear just and proper.'[41]

THE POLITICAL CONTEXT

In a startling development, Stuart's committee introduced twelve 'political' heads of impeachment against Sewell (none was brought against Monk), so that nearly two-thirds of the charges condemned his political views and actions. The reason is that the courts were widely perceived to be an arm of government and this perception made judges vulnerable to political attacks.

The British government institutionalized the close relationship between the judiciary and the provincial government by appointing judges – such as Adam Mabane – to the Legislative Council, a practice it maintained after the adoption of the Constitutional Act of 1791. As attorneys general successively in the 1790s and early 1800s, Monk and Sewell reinforced the identification of the courts with the government by judicializing the repression of movements of protest and dissent. Sewell continued to pursue this practice after he became chief justice in 1808, which gave rise to heads of impeachment 10–14.[42] In official circles, both in the colony and in London, the administration of justice generally, and the bench specifically, were deemed to be instruments of social and political regulation of a foreign culture that, if not openly threatening to British colonial government and the British colonial minority, was at least sullenly hostile and in need of control.

The relationship between the judiciary and the provincial administration was not seen in the same light by the Canadien party in the House of Assembly. This was made clear in 1808 when it sought to expel from the assembly one of its most effective and hated opponents, Pierre-Amable De Bonne, a judge on the Court of King's Bench for the District of Quebec since 1794. Although its action was probably primarily tactical, the Canadien party grounded its justification in principle: judges, because of the judicial power they possessed, should be excluded from the legislative process. A bill disqualifying judges from sitting in the assembly (De Bonne was the only one) was about to be passed when Governor Craig stepped in to dissolve the legislature. The British government rebuked Craig, and the governor was resigned to accepting, from the succeeding assembly, another bill disqualifying judges. However, the Canadien party, impatient with such formalities and determined to be rid of De Bonne, carried a simple resolution to exclude him, and in doing so it provoked another dissolution by Craig.[43]

Four years earlier, in 1806, during a debate over the appointment of Lord Chief Justice Ellenborough to the cabinet, all parties in the British parliament had condemned as unconstitutional any clear mixing of politics and judicial administration, and it was possibly in part for that reason that Craig had been rebuffed over De Bonne's exclusion. Yet neither this debate nor the British government's acceptance of the assembly's desire to exclude judges from its midst signalled acquiescence in the principle that judges should be excluded from the legislative process; in 1808, the same year that the assembly moved against De Bonne, Sewell was named president of the Executive Council and the following year he was made a member of the Legislative Council. The Canadien party's efforts to exclude judges from the assembly because of their judicial influence (successful in 1811) finds echoes in heads of impeachment 11, 13, and 14. Rather raggedly, they condemned Sewell for, first, having participated in putting into place the political conditions that enabled Craig in March 1810 to order the arrest of certain members of the Canadien party, Pierre-

Stanislas Bédard, François Blanchet, and Jean-Thomas Taschereau, and then, secondly, having presided over the court in which the judicial consequences of those same political acts were considered and Bédard was refused a writ of habeas corpus.

The political heads of impeachment introduced by Stuart and his committee reflected major themes of a program developed by the Canadien party over the previous decade. Those themes were judicial, social, and economic as much as political, but they all came back to a political centre, the House of Assembly, which the party dominated and from which it hoped to control the evolution of Lower Canadian sociey. To reach this goal, however, required a restructuring of power within the colony.

The Canadien party had emerged from the reform movement of the 1780s, which had to a large extent forced the inquiry into the judiciary in 1787. That movement became a fragile, strategic alliance between, on the one hand, British merchants and some British officeholders (such as Monk) and, on the other, Canadien professionals (notaries, lawyers, and doctors) and small businessmen. Their only common objectives were to rid the colony of the officeholding oligarchy in the Legislative Council and to introduce British parliamentary government, in particular an elective assembly, which both groups expected to control. Each side then intended to introduce, maintain, or reinforce the practices and institutions that reflected its aspirations. The British merchant class, which dominated the British side of the alliance, hoped to use the new legislature to reproduce the legal, social, and economic institutions of commercial Britain. Their officeholding allies agreed on the necessity to reproduce British institutions of social regulation but, often disdainful of the commercial mentality, were far less committed to measures favouring commercial growth.[44] They largely shared with the predominant Canadien element in the reform movement a preoccupation with the ownership of land (which even the British merchants had to a lesser extent and in a different way). What separated British officeholders from Canadiens, however, was the legal framework regulating land ownership; the former wished to introduce as widely as possible British free and common socage, while the latter was determined to maintain French seigneurial tenure. Since each system was rooted in the civil law of its country of origin, a clash over land tenure was necessarily accompanied by conflict over that law. On this matter the British officeholders found themselves in agreement with the British merchants and in opposition to both Canadien elements of the reform movement.

After passage in 1791 of the Constitutional Act granting an assembly, the reform alliance broke up into its two major components – the Canadien liberal-professional bourgeoisie on the one hand and the British merchant class on the other – with a minority from each ethnic group joining the camp of the other on the basis of personal, class, or philosophical interests. These two groups contended for control of the assembly and victory ultimately went to the Canadien professionals who capitalized on a nationalist appeal to the electorate. Control of the legislative process still escaped them, however, because the Legislative and Executive councils, to which the English party had retreated, as well as the governor himself, were independent of the assembly. After about 1805 Pierre-Stanislas Bédard began to develop the theory of ministerial responsibility as a means of bringing these elements under assembly control. This theory posited a governor representing the monarch – and as such responsible only to London – and local 'ministers' advising the governor who were accountable, in some ill-defined way, to the assembly. The political problems in the colony, it was argued, stemmed from the governors acting on advice from ministers who did not enjoy popular support and were often antipathetic towards the Canadiens, whom they misrepresented to the governor. In 1809 Bédard had insisted that the 'ministers' of the governor be identified so that they could be brought to account. This demand foreshadowed a claim by the assembly to be able to impeach ministers lacking popular support and laid the groundwork for a demand that some ministers at least be drawn from the majority party in the assembly in order to guarantee their popular support.[45]

Through the impeachment charges against Sewell, Stuart and his committee in effect identified the chief justice as a minister who ought to be removed on the grounds that he was antipathetic to the people and was misusing his position. Such is the political foundation at the basis of heads of impeachment 6–17 in which Sewell is generally accused of having either 'advised,' 'counselled,' and 'induced' the governor to undertake an unwise or unjust action or 'poisoned' the mind of the governor against the Canadiens by maliciously slandering them. These charges constituted a practical test of the theory worked out mainly by Bédard, although Bédard himself seems not to have participated in process.[46] (No 'political' charges were brought against Monk because he could not credibly be identified as a minister in the government; he had clearly been consigned to the fringes of political life.)

The 15th head, charging Sewell with promoting American influence in the colony, reflected another theme developed by the Canadien party in the previous decade. Aware that ethnic and cultural affinities would give the colony's English party more credibility than itself in London, the Canadien party sought to undermine its rivals by charging that their attempts to overwhelm the peaceable and loyal Canadiens facilitated a dangerous introduction of Americans and American influence. The Canadiens, antipathetic to American religion, culture, and institutions, constituted a bulwark against the 'Yankees.'

By 1810 Bédard and the Canadien party were expressing their views with increased vehemence in the pages of the party's newspaper, Le Canadien. In March Sewell was among the members of the Executive Council who advised Craig to seize the paper's press and detain Pierre-Stanislas Bédard, François Blanchet, Jean-Thomas Taschereau, and others connected with the newspaper on suspicion of treasonable practices under the Better Preservation Act. These were the grounds for heads of impeachment 10–14.

For his part, Jonathan Sewell was the quintessential representative of the British officeholding class that, on most issues (taxing land being the notable exception), allied itself politically with the British merchant class following the split in the reform movement after 1792.[47] A full understanding of the political views that ultimately made him the target of impeachment proceedings must take account of certain fundamental facts. First, Sewell was eminently comfortable in both the French language and the French civil law. His efforts to anglify Lower Canada did not stem from any personal fear of French culture; he was anything but culturally narrow-minded. Sewell's visceral fear was rather of the masses. As a boy of eight during the American revolution he had been marked for life by the sacking, before his very eyes, of the family mansion in Cambridge, Massachusetts, by a patriot mob. Later, during the French revolution, stories of havoc wreaked by mobs on the persons and property of the upper classes were not distant reports to him; they were a reminder of what may have been the most terrifying experience of his life. In a period of social transition,[48] Sewell wanted above all to buttress the institutions that would regulate the masses, the greatest potential threat to social order. In Lower Canada those masses were cultural cousins of the very mobs who had brought France to anarchy and paved the way for the accession of Europe's greatest despot, Napoleon Bonaparte, and the subsequent war against Great Britain and her colonies. In lengthy strictures which he added to his reading of Craig's proclamation at the assizes of March 1810, Sewell justified the arrest of the owners of Le Canadien by asserting that the mob violence of the French revolution had demonstrated the destructive potential, in an overwhelmingly uneducated population, of a so-called free press. Calumnies and seditious writings, he warned, 'provoquent et soulèvent les Passions du peuple contre ceux qui les gouvernent, et très souvent celles de ceux qui gouvernent contre le peuple, et en détruisant ainsi cette confiance mutuelle qui est le grand soutien des États, Elles ouvrent le chemin qui conduit à la rébellion et à la Guerre Civile ou à la subjugation du Pays par quelque pouvoir étranger.'[49]

Sewell's intelligence, cultured manner, and practical (if not ideological) moderation ensured that his views were listened to by both Milnes and his successor, Craig. After 1808 his official positions as chief justice of Lower Canada, chairman of the Executive Council, and speaker of the Legislative Council lent credence to his identification by the Canadien party as a minister. In responding in 1810 to a request from Craig for an analysis of the ills of the colony, Sewell unwittingly substantiated the Canadien party's portrayal of a minister advising the king's representative on policy. At the very least his response contained many elements condemned in the heads of impeachment charging him with misrepresenting the Canadiens, poisoning Craig's mind against them, and favouring American influence. The problems in Lower Canada arose from two sources, Sewell told Craig: '1st From the French predilections in the great Mass of the Inhabitants, and 2ly From want of influence and power in the Executive Government.' He added that 'the great links of connection between a Government and its subjects are religion, Laws and Language' and that in Lower Canada those links were non-existent and could not be forged because of 'national antipathy' as long as the colony maintained its French institutions and culture. If Britain was to retain Lower Canada and the British population there to live in security, the French-speaking population would have to be anglified by measures designed either to reduce the influence of French institutions or to transform them into British institutions. To tolerate the existing situation was to court a repeat of the French revolution by the 'French' masses of Lower Canada.[50] To facilitate instead the reproduction of English society in Lower Canada, Sewell recommended measures he had been proposing over the past decade, among them control of the Roman Catholic clergy, conversion from seigneurial to freehold tenure, government-controlled education financed by confiscation of the Sulpician estates, and encouragement of American immigration. Since the English were unlikely to immigrate in large numbers, the Americans would make honourable substitutes. Being descendants of Englishmen and possessing the same language and religion, Americans would be 'more easily assimilated, and become better subjects than those which we now possess.'[51] This was the position for which he was attacked in head of impeachment 15.

Such, then, was the political context for the the attacks on Sewell and Monk generally and more specifically for the political heads of impeachment, 6–17, brought against Sewell. It is now necessary to analyse in more detail the charges themselves in order to determine, given the personal, judicial, and political contexts, the extent to which, and the manner in which, they could be advanced or refuted with success before the court of imperial authority.

THE HEADS OF IMPEACHMENT

The attempt to impeach began on 27 January 1813 with the creation of a committee of inquiry into the rules of practice published in 1809 and 1811. This committee's report, heavily inspired by its president, James Stuart, was the springboard from which the heads of impeachment were subsequently launched. A brief comparison of the thrust of the report on the rules of practice with the heads of impeachment should help to determine to what extent genuine problems in the functioning of the judicial system were at stake.

The central argument of the committee's thirty-six-page report is quite simple: the judges were usurping the role of the legislature by amending civil procedure through rules of practice. Such an approach was contrary to the spirit of the civil law system and the sphere of rules of practice should have been strictly limited to adjusting the French code of procedure when it was rendered inapplicable by the introduction of English court structures and some specific English forms of procedure. A lengthy analysis of specific rules provided clear examples of this judicial encroachment on the legislature's domain. For instance, the rules of practice published by Sewell and Monk reduced the number of witnesses allowed to establish a specific fact and gave judges discretionary powers in allocating expenses.[52] Other rules imposed fixed forms of procedure on the English model.[53] However, the detailed critique of these rules often loses sight of the general argument in a welter of secondary considerations, or sees the roots of tyranny in matters that fairly clearly do lie within the purview of rules of practice, such as readjusting court fees and requiring the deposit of a sum to cover the administrative costs of appealing interlocutory judgments.[54] Other accusations, such as those castigating the heavy-handed recourse to contempt of court to ensure the payment by lawyers of the fees of the court clerks, added little or nothing to the central argument and principally provided an occasion to accuse the judges of authoritarian and tyrannical impulses.

While Stuart had put his finger on a genuine problem in the evolution of Lower Canada's legal system, he clearly was unconcerned with solving that problem and refused to admit that the judges were acting in good faith and with the intent to lessen the confusion in the administration of justice. Pierre Bédard, former leader of the Canadien party and provincial judge at Trois-Rivières, saw both these aspects of the issue, and in his letters to his friend John Neilson he provided a uniquely balanced contemporary view. As he put it, 'Si le juge en chef pouvait bien représenter l'état où était la procédure avant lui à Québec, il paraîtrait avoir fait un grand bien par ses règles, quoi qu'elles aient des défauts, et je crois sincèrement qu'elles sont plutôt matière à lui faire donner des éloges que du blâme.'[55] Although he disapproved both of the personal motives and of the excessive, negative nature of the attack on the rules of practice, Bédard did agree with the underlying arguments of the committee – or rather, he perceived, probably more acutely and with greater intellectual conviction than even Stuart did, both the roots of the difficulty and the potential remedies for it. For Bédard, the rules of practice exemplified two principal problems: first, the replacement of French laws of procedure by incomplete and inadequate provincial statutes that required judges to fill the vacuum with rules of practice; secondly, the active involvement of the judges in the legislature, which he felt undermined their respect for the law they were called upon to apply.[56] Thus, although he did not support the impeachment of the chief justices, he did support the assembly's efforts to effect a separation of judicial and legislative powers, a stance entirely in keeping with his advanced constitutional views.

James Monk and Jonathan Sewell could hardly be expected to see things from Bédard's perspective. For them, the virtual abrogation of French civil procedure was implicit in the establishment of British courts, and the introduction of rules of practice similar to those applied in courts in England was a natural and positive development. Monk found the very notion of following the spirit of the French procedural system 'absurd and impossible.'[57]

Without being quite so categorical, Sewell believed in creating a new, blended 'code of practice' suitable for courts that had to administer 'two opposite systems of Jurispudence.'[58] This could scarcely be accomplished if *ancien régime* French civil procedure was still in force, and under his influence and that of Monk the Court of Appeals would, in the years immediately following the impeachment attempt, treat the *ordonnance civile* like a 'dead letter rule of practice' made obsolete by the 'change of the constitution of the courts.'[59] Nor could Sewell envisage the pursuit of his goal of a hybrid procedure with a legislature dominated by the Canadien party. In fact, he briefly contemplated recourse to imperial legislation as the only 'means to saving the judicature of the colony.'[60] In other words, Monk and Sewell were intellectually and politically convinced of the need to replace the old law of procedure with rules of practice and to maintain if not strengthen the political role of a predominantly British judiciary.[61]

A perusal of the heads of impeachment shows that the assembly was much less concerned with the problems raised by its inquiry into rules of practice than with the constitutional question of the judges' role – particularly Sewell's – in colonial politics. Of the twenty-five heads of impeachment, only eight concern the rules of practice, and in fact, because of repetition, these could be reduced to four. All thirteen remaining charges against Sewell are of a political nature and resulted directly from his role as Craig's adviser.

The heads of impeachment begin with the vague but violent charge, already quoted, that Sewell had 'traitorously and wickedly endeavoured to subvert the Constitution and established Government' of Lower Canada and 'introduce an arbitrary, tyrannical Government against Law.' Following this are the four counts touching rules of practice, the essence of which was that the rules exceeded the authority of the courts and thereby usurped legislative powers. Then the indictments get to the heart of the matter, crucifying Sewell for Craig's actions against the assembly, its leaders, and its policies. Behind the purple prose of the heads of impeachment, couched in the formalized hyperbole so typical of common-law indictments, there is a very large kernel of truth in each political accusation.

Sewell did indeed counsel Craig in such actions as the decision to dissolve the assembly and to dismiss the more vocal Canadien party members from positions in the militia. He concurred with the seizure of the press and papers of the printer of *Le Canadien* and the imprisonment of the publishers of the same newspaper – Pierre Bédard, François Blanchet, and Jean-Thomas Taschereau – on charges of treasonable practices and was perfectly content to let them rot in prison and then discharge them without bringing them to trial. He probably counselled the governor to issue a proclamation referring to the foregoing imprisonments in a way that implied guilt and contribution to a state of near insurrection. He believed in encouraging American immigration and the establishment of a partisan newspaper opposed to the Canadien party. Sewell also read the governor's proclamation in open court to influence the grand and petit juries and used his influence as speaker of the council to block laws passed by the assembly. There is also no doubt that Sewell made his own distrust of the Canadien population known to Craig.

Yet the indictments fall wide of the mark both in their explanation of Sewell's motives and objectives and in their attempt to render him solely responsible for the governor's political agenda. On the question of intent, it seems clear that all these various activities naturally grew from Sewell's devotion to empire, his fear of social disorder, and his obsession with security issues, all in the context of what Murray Greenwood has called the 'garrison mentality.' As respectful of the law as he was in most instances, Sewell was ready to pervert justice in the interests of security. He genuinely believed that the Canadien population was not to be trusted and could readily be led into revolt by demagogic politicians or over-zealous clerics. He was firmly convinced that the colony could be saved for the empire and its British subjects only by anglicizing it, by protecting the king's prerogative and opposing the growing influence of the Canadien-dominated assembly, and by filling the province with English and American settlers who would leaven the untrustworthy Canadien masses. Hence the absurdity – for the outside observer – of the charges that what he did was wicked, malicious, treacherous, false, deceitful, with intent to oppress and install tyrannous and arbitrary government, and so on.

On the question of responsibility, the charges were bound to fail, both because Craig had in fact been an active and strong-minded governor who pursued courses in which he firmly believed, and because the Colonial Office was still a long way from being able to see the governor in the same light as a king who reigns but does not govern. Moreover, Sewell was far from alone in his perception of the Canadiens as disloyal and in dire need of anglicization. One has but to read the Quebec *Mercury*, or the opinions of Herman Witsius Ryland, to see that the chief justice was more nuanced and supple than many other spokesmen of the English community.

Since the Canadien members of the assembly were the targets, sometimes victims, of Craig's and Sewell's actions, their perceptions of the malicious, oppressive aims of the English party are entirely understandable. However, imperial officials were unlikely to see malice, treason, and oppression lurking; indeed, they would credit their colonial compatriots with loyalty and honest motives, and possibly share their distrust of the Canadien population, albeit with less conviction and anxiety. That the assembly could be led to vent its frustrations in such terms by a skilled and unscrupulous man bent on personal revenge testifies to the intensity of a political polarization that was both partisan and ethnic in nature.

STRATEGIES AND TACTICS

Had the driving force behind the attempt to impeach Sewell and Monk been primarily judicial, the terrain on which the battle was fought would also have been primarily judicial. Such was not the case. The importance of the role played by political strategies and tactics indicate that the impeachment proceedings were essentially political. As early as January 1813, when Stuart first proposed that the assembly examine the rules of practice published by the judges years earlier, Monk had already half divined the political intent behind the judicial façade. He wrote to his arch rival, Sewell, that if the judges had erred in adopting rules in direct violation of a positive law, the appropriate remedy was correction on appeal. If the judges had misconstrued an act of the legislature, the correction lay in an act declaratory of the law or restrictive in interpretation. It was unheard of that judges could be impeached for error of judgment; impeachment was the appropriate response only to 'the wilful perversion of power.'[62] That was exactly the strategy that Stuart and the assembly adopted: prove 'wilful perversion of power.'

In examining the 'impeachers,' one confronts two major questions: first, how much of this strategy arose from Stuart's personal vendetta and how much was consciously supported by the assembly; secondly, what was the real objective – was it the sacking of the chief justices, or punishment by harassment? The very choice of impeachment suggests that Stuart was following this route because it was readily open to *him* to initiate and because it fit in well with the overall direction of the assembly's constitutional position, thus making it relatively easy to win enough support for his propositions.

It is not clear that the assembly would have thought of using these tactics without Stuart's guidance. He had laid the basis for recourse to extraordinary procedures in the conclusion of the report on the rules of practice, in which he emphasized that since the colony's constitution did not include a court empowered to deal with abuses of judicial power, the assembly must in its wisdom find an appropriate way to submit the problem to the imperial government.[63]

Why impeachment? Impeachment had emerged in the fourteenth century as one of parliament's weapons in the struggle to prevent royal officials and favourites from breaking the law with impunity. It became a measure of major constitutional importance in the seventeenth and the early eighteenth centuries and was of particular service during parliament's struggles with the Stuarts, before and after the Restoration, resulting in the establishment of the principle that even the greatest ministers of the crown were all subject to the law. The process requires cooperation between the two houses of parliament, with the Commons accusing and the Lords sitting in judgment. Consequently, William Holdsworth points out, as the aim of the Commons gradually came to be the removal from office of ministers of whose programs and policies it disapproved, impeachments became less and less effective constitutional weapons and in the early nineteenth century gave way to the unwritten conventions of ministerial responsibility.[64]

Impeachment in England had thus generally been applied not to judges for abuse of judicial power but to the king's ministers, and often for clearly political motives. However, in a colony where judges still held their commissions during pleasure, were regular members of the Executive and Legislative councils, and had recently been close advisers of a governor whose policies had been deeply offensive to the assembly, the parallels are not hard to draw. The fact that the heads minimized the charges of usurping legislative power to concentrate instead on those against a governor's adviser (so similar to a king's minister) makes the procedure quite similar to seventeenth-century English precedents.

The advantage of impeachment, from the point of view of a colonial assembly, was that it allowed assembly members to take the initiative by using a form of criminal accusation reserved to the elected branch of the legislature. By so doing, the assembly could imply that its enemies were criminals and force them to defend themselves and prove their innocence. While it might not succeed in having them condemned and dismissed, it could make its dislikes and the dangers of crossing its will more clearly apparent. This also dovetailed with the strategy of imitating positions taken by the Commons in England in that house's historic efforts to establish legislative dominance.

There were, of course, inherent constitutional problems in using the impeachment procedure. A colonial assembly was not the House of Commons and a legislative council did not have the judicial powers of the House of Lords. Not that the Lower Canadian assembly would have wanted to see its upper house judge this case, considering the political stance of the council and the fact that Sewell was its speaker. The assembly thus distorted the procedure, using it to attempt to force a trial of the chief justices by authorities in London and, in light of the gravity of such extraordinary criminal accusations, to oblige the current governor to suspend the accused during the interval.

Prevost did not fall into this trap. Recognizing the weakness of the assembly's constitutional position, he refused to suspend Monk and Sewell. He insisted that, for such drastic measures, the charges would have had to be made jointly by both legislative chambers, and he was able to point to the council's vehement disagreement with the assembly's action. He did, however, feel compelled to transmit the heads of impeachment to London.

The differences between the assembly's position and that of the Commons further handicapped its efforts to carry through with the impeachment procedure by acting as the prosecutor. The assembly did indeed designate Stuart to present its case against the judges but was unable to send him to London, because the council refused to sanction its allocation of funds for the purpose. The assembly later tried to name judge Bédard as an agent to represent the colony in England. But the council would not countenance this measure either and torpedoed the assembly's plans by simply refusing to pass the bill.

The strategy of the chief justices was probably mapped out mainly by James Monk on the basis of his experience of attacking the judicial system in 1787. He drew from it a bitter lesson: 'Never use uncommon ardor but where the policy of St James [the imperial government] is incontrovertibly clear. The ... Tranquility of the Colony is the object here [London], and no Consideration should hazard that object with a politic Man.'[65] Stuart had used 'uncommon ardor'; the assembly had disturbed the 'Tranquility of the Colony.' Both had erred politically, Monk believed, and were vulnerable to counter-attack. 'The [political as opposed to legal] Character of the impeachm^t should surely be made to strike every person who reads such charges,' he wrote to Sewell in May 1814. Asked by the latter for comments on his draft responses to the accusations, Monk replied that 'however ample & sufficient they are ... for the sedulous consideration of a leisured jurist,' they ought to be severely contracted and presented more politically. The strategy, then, that had been suggested by the assembly's addition of political charges was to fight fire with fire by turning the accusers into the accused and portraying the judges as bulwarks of the imperial connection against the destructive forces of democracy.[66] The tactics employed, which Monk had worked out by early

1813,[67] were: respond directly to the imperial government rather than to the assembly, while using the Legislative Council to prevent the assembly from presenting its case in England; portray the assembly as a popular body inspired by French revolutionary thought which aimed to overthrow the balanced constitution of the colony and British rule by profiting from the war with the United States; describe the attack on the chief justices as an attack on the judiciary, which, in Lower Canada as elsewhere, was a guardian of British constitutional government; exploit Sewell's abilities and the English party's connections in England; paint the attempts of Craig's successor, Prevost, to win the support of the assembly as a vain and dangerous appeasement of suspect popular leaders which would encourage dissent.

The thrust of the first tactic was to have the Legislative Council block the road.[68] Monk argued that it would be constitutionally dangerous to admit that the popular branch of the legislature could act without the concurrence of the appointed upper house: 'The component parts must use extreme caution, in preserving the right of each; or in the conflict those seperate powers will be arrogated and consolidated into one.'[69] The council denounced the attempt to impeach unilaterally as an 'illegal and alarming assumption of power.'[70] The same strategy of obstruction underlay the council's decision to refuse the funds that would have enabled Stuart and Bédard to defend the assembly's case in London.[71] It was a tactic justified by Monk nearly a month earlier on the ground that such an agent would usurp the constitutional role of the governor.[72]

In January 1813 Monk traced for Sewell the arguments of a potential counter-attack which constituted the judges' second tactic. By its action, the assembly threatened to take control of the entire legislature, the judiciary, and, if it succeeded, the executive, which would also be subject to threat of impeachment. 'If the boundaries of power are not distinctly drawn on every constitutional question,' he wrote, 'we shall inevitably expose the order and existence of Gov't to every demagogue that can seduce poor uninformed, easy, or seditious, and designing Men.'[73] Late in 1814 Sewell would argue in defence of the judges that the assembly's action 'assumes rights in the Legislative power the most dangerous to tranquil, constitutional, and good Government'; its 'nefarious' objective was 'that of transferring the Executive Power, and Prerogative of the Crown, to the Legislative: the representatives of the People.'[74]

Monk's and Sewell's comments indicate the third tactic in the chief justices' strategy: treat the attempt to impeach the chief justices as an attack on the judiciary and, through it, on the government. Judges must be accountable for their judicial conduct but only according to strict legal procedure, Monk told Sewell in January 1813. 'Can they be sacrificed to popular clamor, without destroying the Royal Government,' he asked. 'Lord Kenyon would answer no. That this is the beginning. Meet and resist it, or perish in the consequences!'[75] A year later, no doubt recalling his painful experience of 1787, Monk reminded Sewell of the argument: 'Impeach. cannot go against judges,' especially in the colonies, 'without – more or less – implicating the Power that created and upholds them.'[76] The government, if the judges organized their arguments properly, would be obliged to protect them. To this end he sought from his brother, George Henry in Nova Scotia, information on an unsuccessful attempt in 1790 by the Nova Scotia House of Assembly to impeach judges James Brenton and Isaac Deschamps.[77] He also argued that those who had opposed the Militia Act in the War of 1812 sought now to emasculate the judiciary, which had effectively defended royal authority then by punishing offenders against the act.[78] More generally, he contended that the judges' efforts to marry French and English legal practices had strengthened British rule and marked them for attack. 'I will be bold to say – It has been the Judicious, temperate Amalgamation (if the word can be used) of the French general Jurisprudence, with English legal principles ... that sedulously have sought for and applied from the Civil Law, reciprocally aided and strengthened by the Rules of Practice that, in Judging ... Seven thousand Causes, has produced known principles of Right & Justice ... that has maintained the King's Government with internal tranquility through all the trying days of French revolutionary effervescence, since the establishment of the present constitution.'[79]

The chief justices did not constitute the entire judiciary, and again Monk was probably behind the tactic to include the other judges in the charges. The Executive Council being the final court of appeals in Lower Canada, he warned John Richardson, an executive councillor, that the resolutions of the assembly were in fact 'against the King's Governm^t in its whole judicial functions, and implicate ... the Executive Council.'[80] Less than two weeks later, on 26 February 1814, the members of the Executive Council and the puisne judges of the courts of King's Bench at Quebec and Montreal petitioned to be included in the charges respecting the rules of practice since they had all been consulted and had all approved them.[81] The assembly's effort to isolate the chief justices had failed; it became possible to argue that the assembly was attacking another branch of the balanced constitution of the colony, the judiciary, one of the principal safeguards of British rule in Lower Canada.

Although Monk seems to have proposed the strategy and tactics, with Richardson's participation, it was Sewell, whose intellectual abilities and legal erudition were widely recognized, who prepared the defence.[82] He marshalled numerous references behind his main argument that the crown must protect its officers if it was to maintain its authority in the colony. Lord Kenyon was quoted as having said in 1799, during the French revolution, that 'if ever the time shall come when factious men will overturn the Government of the Country They will begin their work by *calumniating the Courts of Justice* and both Houses of Parliament.'[83] Sewell appears to have argued that the assembly could not speak for the entire legislature, particularly in asserting that the legislature had not intended to give the judges authority to make rules of practice; that law was distinct from practice and, although law emanated from the legislature, practice was a prerogative of the crown, established through the judges it appointed and not, therefore, subject to censure by the assembly; that it was extremely difficult to frame rules of practice that would encompass both French and English legal systems, and that only 12 of 246 rules were contested and those were invariably 'rules which affect the pockets of the Attornies or their Interest in some other respect'; and that the assembly had chosen not to inquire into the rules of practice employed in Trois-Rivières, where Bédard, an ally, was judge.[84]

Sewell decided to go to England to defend himself and was mandated by all the judges to defend them.[85] He was to take addresses from both councils and the 'principal Inhabitants' of Quebec and Montreal[86] and letters of introduction from judges, officeholders, and merchants to influential men in England.[87] In order to embark on this mission, he required a leave of absence from Governor Prevost, who was the target of the final tactic in the judges' strategy.

Prevost's policy of conciliating the Canadien party had earned him the disdain of many adherents to the British party.[88] Also, his forwarding to London of the assembly's charges without the concurrence of the Legislative Council and his initial reluctance to grant Sewell leave of absence heightened resentment.[89] Yet Prevost ultimately supported the chief justices. He incurred the assembly's wrath by refusing its advice to suspend them. He affirmed of Monk and Sewell that he had never 'heard a suggestion against their integrity or ability' in their offices.[90] He even provided Sewell with free passage on a government transport and a letter of introduction to Bathurst.[91]

In spite of this support and notwithstanding the misgivings of friends that he would seek reconciliation with Prevost,[92] Sewell faithfully carried out the final tactic of the judges' strategy: portray Prevost's attempts to conciliate the assembly as dangerous and likely only to encourage its ambitions, and obtain a return to Craig's hard-line approach. Sewell argued that Craig had restored in the Canadien party a healthy respect for imperial authority. Prevost, to win Canadien support for the war effort (a senseless policy, Sewell argued, because the religious and national loyalties of the Canadiens made them natural enemies of the Americans), had undone Craig's work and unwittingly rendered his administration 'republican.' He had promoted to office men such as Bédard, whom Craig had imprisoned for treason, and emboldened leaders of the popular party to wreak vengeance on loyal officers. 'They have assumed to themselves the control of the King's Courts of Justice – and described his justices as enemies to the Constitution and as promoters of Arbitrary Government – and yet they call themselves his most loyal & affectionate subjects. Can it be a justifiable procedure to foster and to encourage the very men who have been declared traitors, to put them not only into office but into offices of the highest Trust? To hold out rewards to the discontented to cast off the oldest and most faithful Servants of the Crown without a Cause and thus to nurse up dissatisfaction into Mutiny and Rebellions.' Prevost had lost control to the assembly and had himself fallen victim to its censures. Maintenance of British rule in Lower Canada now rested on maintaining in office those who in the past had supported Craig. This alarmist vision, greatly reinforced by Prevost's stance in the impeachment affair, was shared not only by all the English party's leaders but by virtually all its supporters, including, for example, the Montreal *Herald*, young lawyer Samuel Gale the younger, and Montreal merchant James Dunlop.[93]

The strategy was complete. Gradually, the party of the chief justices had moved from a defensive tactic of containment to an offensive tactic of charging the assembly with plotting to take control of government through manipulation of Prevost. The accused had become the accusers; it was no longer the chief justices who were on trial but the assembly and Prevost.

THE BRITISH REACTION

Sewell arrived in London on 21 July 1814.[94] He immediately visited the people for whom he had been given letters of recommendation and sounded out the Colonial Office. Under-Secretary Henry Goulburn reassured him that Colonial Secretary Lord Bathurst would not consider the political charges since 'it would be to admit that a councillor was responsible for the acts of a Governor contrary to every principle.' The charges concerning the rules of practice would be submitted to the Privy Council, which, it was fully expected, would quash them.[95] Sewell waited to present his case,[96] but the decision was a foregone conclusion. Long before it was rendered, Monk had written: 'The Justification of the Chief Justices and Courts of Judicature in this Colony was easy to apprehend.'[97] Not until the spring of 1815 was Sewell invited to present his case; the delays were probably bureaucratic rather than due to political hesitation. Resolutions from the House of Assembly sent in March 1815, reaffirming its determination to proceed and naming Stuart its agent for the presentation of its case,[98] although considered, did not affect the Privy Council's deliberations.

Under instructions from Bathurst, those deliberations were limited to investigation of the charges respecting the rules of practice.[99] The attorney and solicitor generals had opined that the assembly had not taken 'the distinction between an alteration of the general rules of law by which Justice is to be administered, and an alteration of mere rules of practice for regulating the mode of proceeding in the Courts.' If judges did not have the latter power, asserted the law officers, they would be unable to administer the courts effectively 'and therefore such alteration of former rules or addition or substitution of new rules cannot be deemed an assumption of legislative authority.'[100] Although the law officers found some rules unnecessary, they found none to be in excess of the judges' jurisdiction. They pointed out the praiseworthy objectives of most and observed that similar ones were applied in England.[101]

The real problem of conflicting English and French legal models had failed to emerge clearly in the welter of violent language and tendentious phrasing. Even had this problem been properly expressed, in the way in which Bédard put it in his letters to Neilson, it seems likely that the law officers would have found the presumed abrogation of pre-conquest civil procedure – as well as the use of English models – to be entirely appropriate and desirable.

On 29 June 1815 the investigating committee of the Privy Council concluded that the rules of practice 'were not made by the said chief justices, respectively, upon their own sole authority, but by them, in conjunction with other judges of the respective courts, and within the scope and power of that jurisdiction with which, by the rules of law, and by the colonial ordinances and acts of the legislature, these courts are invested, as consequently that neither the said chief justices, nor the courts in which they preside, have, in making such rules, exceeded their authority, nor have been guilty of any assumption of legislative power.'[102] The complaints were dismissed. Foreseeing resistance on the part of the Lower Canadian assembly and wanting to impress upon it the solemnity of the inquiry and the weight of the decision, the Privy Council, exceptionally, published the names of the members of the committee of investigation: the Prince Regent, the Duke of York, the Duke of Cumberland, the Archbishop of Canterbury, the Lord Privy Seal, Viscount Castlereagh, Bathurst, and the Chancellor of the Exchequer. This aristocratic approach, typical of the *ancien régime*, had no effect on the assembly, whose roots were in more democratic values.[103]

DENOUEMENT AND SEQUEL

Two weeks after the Privy Council rendered its decision Bathurst transmitted it to Sir Gordon Drummond, who had replaced Prevost. All charges that Sewell had poisoned Craig's mind or had committed illegal acts in the Henry affair had been rejected out of hand. What Craig did was not illegal, required no vindication, and was his own, not Sewell's, responsibility in any case. Bathurst found it curious that those charges had not been made during Craig's administration but held back 'until it was thought that they might be brought in aid of an accusation against the Chief Justice arising out of circumstances totally distinct.' Drummond was to express the British government's regrets respecting such purely political tactics because of their 'tendency to disparage in the Eyes of the inconsiderate and ignorant their [the chief justices'] Character and Service' and diminish their influence.[104]

The Privy Council's decision was widely publicized in Lower Canada by Sewell's friends. Anglican bishop Jacob Mountain informed Sewell that the leaders of the assembly 'do not hang down their heads like bulrushes but still walk erect,' considering that they had won popular support and made a strategic gain. In examining their charges, the Privy Council had established their right to initiate proceedings without the concurrence of the Legislative Council. Only the council's refusal to allow them to send an agent had saved Sewell and Monk, they asserted.[105]

On 2 February 1816 Drummond informed the assembly of the Privy Council's decision and of the imperial government's disapproval of the assembly's proceedings. When the house determined to petition for reconsideration, Drummond, as instructed, dissolved it.[106] According to Drummond, Stuart's insistence alone explained the assembly's persistence.[107]

Sewell arrived back at Quebec with his family in July 1816 to a salute from the citadel, a compliment rarely accorded a civilian and even less to a colonial official.[108] In a letter introducing Sewell to the new governor at Quebec, Sir John Coape Sherbrooke, Bathurst recommended the chief justice as someone with 'both the means and the disposition to afford you every assistance,' the colonial secretary having formed 'an opinion that his judgement and discretion are in no degree inferior to his talents and general information.'[109] This injunction placed Sherbrooke in a difficult position. He believed that 'the feeling of hostility against that gentleman [Sewell] pervades all classes, and prevails with violence even in the obscurest parts of the Province.' Sherbrooke felt that it would have been conducive to peace in the province to have let the assembly's agent go to England, for that would have deprived the Canadien party of its argument that the people's case had not been heard. In 1817 the assembly petitioned Sherbrooke for a salary of £1,000 for its speaker, Louis-Joseph Papineau. Sherbrooke agreed, but in return for a salary for the speaker of the Legislative Council, Sewell himself. The deal was done. When, shortly after, the assembly took up Drummond's message of the previous year announcing Monk's and Sewell's exoneration, a violent debate occurred during which many of Stuart's friends abandoned him in order not to jeopardize the arrangement.[110] Furious, Stuart ceased to attend the assembly.[111]

The assembly gradually moved away from impeachment in its constitutional struggles. While there was another attempt to impeach a judge in 1817,[112] it petered out after a two-year process of written charges and counter-charges. In the late 1820s and early 1830s the assembly switched its tactics. On the one hand, it held inquiries into the behaviour of four 'anglicizing' judges and recommended their dismissal to the governor, who dismissed none of them.[113] On the other hand, it repeatedly and unsuccessfully attempted to adopt legislation to ensure the independence of the judiciary.[114] The final stage in the evolution of this ongoing constitutional battle was the attempt to obtain an elected council – a pattern similar to that found in Upper Canada.[115]

CONCLUSION

An overall assessment of the impact and importance of the impeachment proceedings must look at both the political and judicial aspects as well as the evolution of the principal protagonists. As to the three principal figures in this drama, James Monk retired four years after his vindication and may well have felt the impact most severely, since the assembly would vote him only a half-pay pension for his retirement. Sewell became more moderate and less interested in anglicizing the Canadiens, but this was arguably less a result of the highly stressful experience of impeachment than of the events of the War of 1812, which had disproven some of his worst fears about the disloyalty of the population. Stuart turned his back on his erstwhile political bedfellows and reverted to the more profitable role of government supporter and officeholder. Perhaps his attacks on Canadien law as attorney general were more vehement than they otherwise might have been, fuelled by his sense of betrayal.

What then, of the judicial question that provided the initial pretext for impeachment? In the short term, the rules of practice were upheld, and Monk and Sewell renewed efforts to improve and regularize procedures through such rules. Those criticized in the impeachment were maintained for some forty years. Ironically, the next major revision of the published rules would come from James Stuart in 1850, after he became chief justice, and, as noted earlier, he would retain several rules that he had attacked so vehemently in 1813.[116]

The underlying problem of clarifying civil procedure and especially the limits of its French content was not addressed, however, and confusion and contradictions continued to reign even after promulgation of the code of civil procedure in 1867.[117] The failure to impeach was probably not a factor in this result. Paralysing the judges' use of rules of practice would not have cleaned up the judicial mess – legislative clarification was needed and the assembly had shown no interest in a legislative remedy, such as codification.

As a political strategy, impeachment had failed to achieve the assembly's immediate objectives inasmuch as both judges were vindicated and remained in office and in the councils. It had succeeded, however, in undermining the reputation of the chief justices and, by ricochet, of the administration of justice among the Canadien population (at least, such observers as Herman Ryland and Sir John Sherbrooke believed so).[118] Although there is no evidence that the judges were corrupt or unjust, they were clearly perceived to be partisan, which weakened the judiciary's moral authority and usefulness as an instrument of legitimization of power. Yet it is difficult to measure how widespread hostility towards the judges was.

Politically, the impeachment attempt and its failure were neither a turning point nor a cul-de-sac but rather a single exchange in an ongoing dialogue of the deaf. Born of anger and resentment over previous political events, the episode seems, at most, to have served as a lesson to Canadien nationalists that more general, less personalized tactics might bear fruit. The experience of defeat did not prevent the assembly, a decade or so later, from returning to the strategy of attacking individual judges who, among other defects, were partisan and anti-Canadien. It merely reinforced the conviction of Canadiens that the ethnic composition of the judiciary was unjust and guaranteed to undermine Canadien civil law. It certainly did nothing to stem the growing conviction among Canadiens that judges as a class had to be removed from the political arena.

On the government side, the impact is not clear-cut either. Governor Sherbrooke seems to have been confirmed in his determination to use conciliatory tactics to persuade the assembly that cooperation was more profitable than confrontation, but imperial officials did not necessarily share his views. Both the local oligarchy and the British government doubtless became more convinced that the judiciary's vital role in maintaining the political status quo could not be compromised. One can see the reaction to the impeachment attempt as a 'legacy of fear,'[119] yet another illustration of the garrison mentality that had first given rise to Craig's 'reign of terror.'

Hence, although the rules of practice illustrated a genuine judicial problem, the impeachment controversy was not a decisive moment in the evolution of the judicial system. Its roots lay in the long-term obsession on the part of the colonial oligarchy and the imperial government with security issues and in the contending parties' growing awareness that the law and the judiciary were important weapons in the larger political and constitutional battle. Before any significant legal reform could take place, the conflict between two opposing political visions had to be resolved.

NOTES

1. *Proceedings in the Assembly of Lower Canada on the Rules of Practice of the Courts of Justice and the Impeachments of Jonathan Sewell and James Monk Esquires* (n.p.: 1814), at 46–57.
2 Other actions emanating from the legislature that are related, indirectly as well as directly, to security are examined in F. Murray Greenwood and Barry Wright, 'Parliamentary Privilege and Repression of Dissent in the Canadas,' in this volume.
3 *Con Docs* 2: at 462.

4 Bédard to Neilson, 3 Nov. 1814, Neilson Papers, MG 24, B1, NA. According to Bédard, 'Mr. Stewart ne travaille que pour sa propre satisfaction.'

5 See Evelyn Kolish, 'Stuart, Sir James.' *DCB* 8: 842.

6 Stuart had served the last two years of his legal apprenticeship with Jonathan Sewell and thus might well have expected the latter's support. This previous association probably made his resentment of Sewell's nepotism much stronger than it might otherwise have been.

7 See James H. Lambert, 'Monk, Sir James,' *DCB* 6: 511.

8 Ibid.

9 Monk to Nepean, 24 Oct. 1793, CO 42/97, PRO (copies at NA).

10 Sewell to Harriet Sewell, 27 Feb. 1798, Sewell Papers, MG 23, GII, 10, vol. 3, NA.

11 Following the death of John Elmsley in 1805, for example, the establishment at Quebec, almost to a man, supported Sewell's bid to succeed him and even warned against an appointment of Monk. See T.R. Millman, *Jacob Mountain, First Lord Bishop of Quebec: A Study in Church and State, 1793–1825* (Toronto: University of Toronto Press 1947), at 115; R.S. Milnes to Lord Camden, 13 May 1805, CO 42/127. The situation repeated itself following Allcock's death in 1808.

12 Monk to George Henry Monk, 20 April 1808, Monk Papers, MG 23, GII, 19, vol. 3, NA.

13 RG 4, S series, A1, vol. 166 [14 July 1817], NA.

14 See F. Murray Greenwood and James H. Lambert, 'Sewell, Jonathan,' *DCB* 7: 782.

15 Contrast Helen Taft Manning, *The Revolt of French Canada (1800–1835)* (Toronto: MacMillan 1962), at 106–8, Thomas Chapais, *Cours d'histoire du Canada*, 8 vols. (Montreal: Boréal Express 1972), 3: at 17–30, or Fernand Ouellet, *Histoire économique et sociale du Québec 1760–1850*, 2 vols. (Montreal: Fides 1971), 1: at 228 with Evelyn Kolish, 'Changements dans le droit privé au Québec/Bas-Canada entre 1760–1840: attitudes et réactions des contemporains,' PhD thesis, University of Montreal 1980.

16 James Monk, *State of the Present Form of Government of the Province of Quebec ...* (London: J. Debrett 1787), at 39–40.

17 The British merchants in the province of Quebec to Dorchester, 30 April 1787, CO 42/50.

18 Ibid., vol. 54.

19 Ibid.

20 Examination of Alexander Gray, 14, 16 June 1787, ibid.

21 Monk's response to the judges' summary of the inquiry, early November 1787, ibid.

22 *Proceedings*, at 7.

23 SOQ, (1787) 27 Geo. III, c. 4.

24 Monk to Henry Dundas, 30 May 1794, CO 42/100.

25 SLC, 1793, c. 6.

26 SLC, (1801) 41 Geo. III, c. 7, art. 16.

27 *Proceedings*, at 7.

28 Evelyn Kolish, *Nationalismes et conflits de droits : le débat du droit privé au Québec, 1760–1840* (Montreal : Hurtubise HMH 1994), at 99.

29 See Jean-Pierre Wallot, 'Plaintes contre l'administration de la justice (1807),' *RHAF*, vol. 19 (1965–6), 551, and vol. 20 (1966–7), at 28–43, 281–90, 366–79. See also Kolish, *Nationalismes*, at 107–25.

30 See article signed 'un amateur de justice,' *Le Canadien*, 13 Nov. 1807.

31 Monk to Lord George Germain, 20 Oct. 1779, Germain Papers, MG 23 A6, NA; Monk, *State of the Present Form of Government*, at 69–70; Kolish, 'Changements,' at 302–8; Monk and Pierre-Louis Panet to Robert Shore Milnes, 20 June 1803, CO 42/122; Monk to Henry Dundas, 6 June 1794, ibid., vol. 100; *Con Docs 2*: at 118; Ivanhoë Caron, 'Inventaire de la correspondance de Mgr Joseph-Octave Plessis, archevêque de Québec,' *Rapport de l'Archiviste de la Province de Québec pour 1932–33* ([Quebec] : King's Printer 1933), at 56.

32 Memorandum by the merchants to the Legislative Council, 18 April 1787, CO 42/52.

33 Monk to Brook Watson, 25 Oct. 1788, Monk Papers, vol. 2.

34 Monk to Prevost, 9 Dec. 1811, RG 4, A1, vol. 70, NA.

35 Greenwood and Lambert, 'Sewell, Jonathan,' at 783.

36 Sewell to Dorchester, 10 June 1795, CO 42/104.

37 Kolish, 'Changements,' at 296–338.

38 *Le Canadien*, 27 Aug. 1808.

39 Justin McCarthy, *Dictionnaire de l'ancien droit du Canada ou compilation des édits, déclarations royales et arrêts du Conseil d'État des rois de France concernant le Canada &* (Quebec: John Neilson 1809). Two cases illustrate Sewell's impartial use of French law and practice: *Pozer v. Meiklejohn*, 14 April 1809, and *Hunt v. Bruce*, 13 Feb. 1810, reported in *Pyke's Reports of Cases Argued and Determined in the Court of King's Bench for the District of Quebec and the Province of Lower Canada, in Hilary Term in the 15th Year of the Reign of George III* (1811).

40 See Stuart's report to Kempt on a bill recognizing the validity of hypothecs on socage lands, 10 April 1829, MG 11, Q series, A 188–2: 406, NA.

41 *Proceedings*, at 7.

42 On this question generally see the biographies of Monk and Sewell in the *DCB*, the bibliographies of which refer to works more specifically devoted to the use of the judicial process to suppress protest and dissent prior to the War of 1812.

43 Pierre Tousignant and Jean-Pierre Wallot, 'De Bonne, Pierre-Amable,' *DCB* 5: at 235.

44 Both Monk and Sewell sought to discourage their charges (Monk his nephews and Sewell his sons) from adopting a career in commerce. See their biographies in the *DCB*.

45 Fernard Ouellet, 'Bédard, Pierre-Stanislas,' *DCB* 6: at 45–6; Manning, *Revolt*, at 69–71.

46 For a fuller discussion of this question, see Ouellet, 'Bédard, Pierre-Stanislas,' at 45–6.

47 On Sewell generally, see Greenwood and Lambert's biography of him in *DCB* 7: 782.

48 There is a now a vast literature on the question of the economic and social transition from a feudal to a capitalist society in Lower Canada. For the most important sources, see James Lambert, 'Quebec/Lower Canada,' in *Canadian History: A Reader's Guide, Volume 1: Beginnings to Confederation*, ed. M. Brook Taylor (Toronto: University of Toronto Press 1994).

49 Sewell's charge to the grand jury, March 1810, Sewell Papers, vol. 5.

50 Sewell to Craig, *c.* May 1810, CO 42/141.

51 Ibid.

52 Section 27, articles 1 and 18, and section 40 of the rules of practice of the Court of King's Bench, District of Montreal.

53 Section 12, articles 6, 7, and 9 of the rules of practice of the Court of King's Bench, District of Montreal.

54 For more details on these rules, see Kolish, 'Changements,' at 367–83.

55 Bédard to Neilson, 3 Nov. 1814, ibid.

56 For his explanation of the first aspect, see Bédard to Neilson, 23 Feb. 1814, and for the second, Bédard to Neilson, 8 March 1814, ibid.

57 For example, see Monk to Sewell [? date], Sewell Papers, vol. 16 [5?].

58 'Notes on the Impeachment', ibid., vol. 10.

59 Bédard to Neilson, January 1815 [1816], Neilson Papers.

60 Journal of Sewell's trip to England to defend the judges against the heads of impeachment, entry for 1 June, Sewell Papers, vol. 10.

61 Sewell, like Governor Matthew Aylmer in the 1830s, saw the 'ascendancy of British Interests at the Bench' as imperative. See Aylmer to Spring Rice, 28 Nov. 1834, MG 11, Q series, vol. 217.

62 Monk to Sewell, 22 Jan. 1813, Sewell Papers vol. 5.

63 *JHALC*, 1814, Appendix E, at 41.

64 William Holdsworth, *A History of English Law*, 16 vols. (London: Methuen 1966), 1: at 379–85; 6: at 259–62.

65 Monk Papers, vol. 3.

66 John Richardson to Sewell, 7, 14 Feb. 1814, Sewell Papers, vol. 5.
67 Monk to Sewell, 22 Jan., 4 Feb. 1813, ibid.
68 Executive Councillor John Richardson opposed this strategy, at least initially. Richardson to Jonathan Sewell, 14 Feb. 1814, ibid.
69 Monk to Sewell, 22 Jan. 1813, 10 Feb. 1814, ibid.
70 JLCLC, 1814 (2 March), at 73.
71 Manning, *Revolt*, at 107–8.
72 Monk to Sewell, 10 Feb. 1814, Sewell Papers, vol. 5.
73 Monk to Sewell, 22 Jan. 1813, ibid.
74 Memorandum by Sewell, *c.* November 1814, ibid.
75 Monk to Sewell, February 1814, ibid.
76 Monk to Sewell, 7 Feb. 1814, ibid.
77 Monk to George Henry Monk, 30 March 1813, 15 March 1814, Monk Papers, vol. 3; Sewell to Prevost, 8 March 1814, CO 42/159; Allan C. Dunlop, 'Brenton, James,' *DCB* 5: 108; Grace M. Tratt, 'Deschamps, Isaac,' *DCB* 5: 250.
78 Monk to Sewell, 30 Jan. 1814, Sewell Papers, vol. 5; Monk to Lord Bathurst, 5 July 1821, CO 42/189.
79 Monk to Sewell, 28 Feb. 1814, Sewell Papers, vol. 5.
80 Monk to Richardson, 7 Feb. 1814, ibid., 2174.
81 CO 42/156.
82 Notebook beginning 'Journal of my proceedings in consequence of the Impeachment preferred against me by the Assembly of Lower Canada' (hereafter Notebook, Journal) [*c.* 15 June 1814–20 June 1815], Sewell Papers, vol. 1, Journals and notebooks, 1[a].
83 Notebook of Jonathan Sewell beginning 'Agenda London, 29 Sept. 1814' (hereafter Notebook, Agenda), Sewell Papers, vol. 1, Journals and notebooks, 1[b]: at 90, 93–5.
84 Ibid., at 86–92.
85 Monk to Sewell, 29 June 1814, Sewell Papers, vol. 5.
86 Notebook, Journal; Robert Christie, *A History of the Late Province of Lower Canada* ..., 6 vols. (Quebec: Thomas Cary 1848–54), 2: at 166–8.
87 Notebook, Journal.
88 On Prevost's administration and policies, see Peter Burroughs, 'Prevost, Sir George,' *DCB* 5: 693, and Manning, *Revolt*, at 93–108.
89 Notebook, Journal, 8 March 1814.
90 Prevost to Bathurst, 18 March 1814, CO 42/156. Prevost's reduction of the origins of the heads of impeachment to a matter of 'personal pique and party spirit,' however, confirms Monk's suspicion that he did not consider the charges to be of much constitutional significance. His endorsement of the chief justices is noticeably reserved, reflecting his knowledge that they were not his allies.

91 Notebook, Journal, June 1814.

92 Jacob Mountain to Sewell, 15 June, 7 Oct. 1814, 123, case 1, folder Mt-Sewell corr., 1798–1823, Quebec Diocesan Archives; Mountain to Sewell, Stephen Sewell to Jonathan, 3 Nov. 1814, Sewell Papers, vol. 5.

93 This paragraph is principally a résumé of notes made by Sewell for the presentation of his case to the British government. See Notebook, Agenda. For the *Herald* and Gale, see the issues of that paper for 1814–15 and J.-C. Bonenfant, 'Gale, Samuel,' *DCB* 9: at 297. Dunlop thought the public was out of control because of Prevost's conciliation and hoped the imperial government would quickly send about 15,000 troops to the colony: Dunlop to [?], 2 April 1814, 'Letters of James Dunlop 1773–1815,' MG 24, D 42, NA.

94 Notebook, Journal, 17 July 1814.

95 Ibid., 25 July 1814.

96 Sewell to Bathurst, 16 Sept. 1814, ibid.; CO 42/159.

97 Monk to Sewell, 4 Nov. 1814, Sewell Papers, vol. 5.

98 *JHALC*, 1815, at 584; Quebec *Gazette*, 30 March 1815; Prevost to Bathurst, 21 March 1815, CO 42/161.

99 Report of the committee of the Privy Council investigating the heads of impeachment, 29 June 1815, Sewell Papers, vol. 16.

100 'Extract of a report of Mr Attorney and Solicitor general, 20 May and 20 June 1815, ibid.

101 Ibid.

102 *Gazette*, 7 Dec. 1815.

103 Ibid.

104 Bathurst to Drummond, 12 July 1815, Sewell Papers, vol. 5.

105 Ibid., Mountain to Sewell, 23 Dec. 1815.

106 *JHALC*, 1816, at 338–44.

107 Drummond to Bathurst, 27 Feb. 1816, CO 43/24, PRO (copies at NA).

108 Index to the Quebec *Gazette*; P319/1, anonymous nineteenth-century manuscript biography of Sewell, at 24–5, ANQ.

109 Bathurst to Sherbrooke, 10 May 1816, CO 43/24.

110 Sherbrooke to Bathurst, 27 March 1817, CO 42/173.

111 Kolish, 'Stuart, Sir James,' at 843–4.

112 The 1817 attempt was directed against Louis-Charles Foucher.

113 The judges in question were James Kerr, John Fletcher, Samuel Gale, and John Gawler Thompson.

114 See Kolish, *Nationalismes*, at 149–51.

115 G.M. Craig, *Upper Canada: The Formative Years, 1784–1841* (Toronto: McClelland and Stewart 1963), at 203–6.

116 Chapais, *Cours d'histoire*, 3: at 27–8.

117 On the hybrid nature and confused state of civil procedure in Quebec up to

codification, see J.-M. Brisson, *La formation d'un droit mixte: l'évolution de la procédure civile de 1774 à 1867* (Montreal: Editions Themis 1986).

118 See H.W. Ryland, 'A Brief Review of the Political State of the Province of Lower Canada during the Last Seven Years,' Ryland Papers, MG 24, B3, NA, and Chapais, *Cours d'histoire*, 3: at 49.

119 See F. Murray Greenwood, *Legacies of Fear: Law and Politics in Quebec in the Era of the French Revolution* (Toronto: Osgoode Society/University of Toronto Press 1993).

14

The Gourlay Affair: Seditious Libel and the Sedition Act in Upper Canada, 1818–19

BARRY WRIGHT

The post-war resurgence of the Reform movement in Upper Canada owed much to the tireless leadership of Robert Gourlay, a Scottish radical active in England who had left for North America just prior to a spate of sedition prosecutions. The main events of the subsequent story – Gourlay's arrival in Upper Canada in 1817, twenty-seven-month stay followed by banishment in 1819, and forty-year campaign for vindication – have been thoroughly examined elsewhere and so are presented only in briefest outline here.[1] What has been largely neglected, however, is the legal significance of the Gourlay affair. His trials are arguably Upper Canada's equivalent to the celebrated trial of Joseph Howe and would have attracted similar attention had he not been banished from the province. Moreover, the measures taken against Gourlay and Bartemas Ferguson, editor of the Niagara *Spectator*, reflect the full range of sedition laws and their administration in the province.[2]

Gourlay's encounters with the law fell into two broad stages. The first involved two prosecutions by indictment against him for seditious libel. The second entailed an array of measures: the direct suppression of Gourlay's 'constitutional meetings' with the passage of the Seditious Meetings Act, the issuing of a remarkable extrajudicial opinion on the applicability of the Sedition Act of 1804 to Gourlay and his subsequent deportation under it, and a prosecution for seditious libel by the procedural expedient of an ex officio information against Gourlay's editor, Ferguson.

The election of late 1816 and the following sessions of the House of

Assembly revealed deep divisions over post-war government policy, especially concerning aliens. Executive orders were issued to limit American immigration; magistrates were directed to stop administering the oath of allegiance, register all American residents, and use the Sedition Act to deport any deemed a security threat.[3] As noted by Murray Greenwood and Barry Wright in the essay on parliamentary privilege, contempt proceedings were taken against James Durand for his criticism of these measures and of bids to suspend habeas corpus. Soon after, assembly supporters of Niagara land speculators also began to condemn government policies. Calls for a general committee on the state of the province led to the premature proroguing of sessions in 1817 and 1818.[4] Gourlay entered the province in the midst of this political turmoil.

Lukewarm official support for Gourlay's statistical accounting quickly dissipated when he released an 'Address to the Resident Landholders of Upper Canada' calling for meetings to collect local grievances.'[5] Another address, published in the Niagara *Spectator*, openly denounced the government and supported assembly calls for a general commission of inquiry.[6] The abrupt ending of the assembly session in 1818 led Gourlay to declare in his third address that 'parliament is broken up and the Constitution is in danger' and to propose that township meetings elect delegates to a constitutional convention in York empowered to send popular grievances direct to the sovereign.[7] His advocacy of potentially revolutionary meetings caused Gourlay to be placed under close surveillance.[8]

The government was cautious about heavy-handed repression which would create a popular platform for the opposition cause. As Attorney General John Beverley Robinson astutely observed: 'It requires undoubtedly to be well considered in cases of this kind how far it may be expedient to commence prosecutions, for however unquestionable the law may be, the improper lenity, or worse conduct of Jurors frequently screens the offender from punishment. This gives importance to what otherwise might perhaps have sunk into contempt, and the acquitted libeller is immediately elevated into a Champion for liberty and against imaginary oppression.'[9] Despite the risks of a jury trial, however, Robinson concluded that the only legitimate legal option was a seditious-libel prosecution. After soliciting judicial opinion, a practice he would later rely heavily on, he decided that the prohibition of popular conventions would have to be legislated.[10] The equation of criticism of the government with disloyalty quickly led Gourlay's more powerful supporters to abandon him as they realized that their interests would be best served by backing the government's campaign of repression.

GOURLAY'S TRIALS FOR SEDITIOUS LIBEL

The prosecutions that followed confirmed Robinson's fears of creating publicity for the Reform cause. Gourlay's arrest was ordered in June 1818 on a government warrant for libel supplemented by a private complaint for sedition from Jonas Jones and Duncan Fraser.[11] The government had two charges against the man described by newly arrived Lieutenant Governor Sir Peregrine Maitland as 'half-Cobbett, and half-Hunt,' one to be tried at the Midland assize in Kingston and the other at the Johnstown assize in Brockville.[12] Copies of the indictments were witheld from Gourlay when he requested them, obliging him to prepare a defence based on arrest warrants that simply referred to 'false, wicked and seditious libel styled Principles and Proceedings of Inhabitants of the District of Niagara and Petition to the Prince Regent.' His defence was further compromised when he found out at the last moment that the Midland assize was scheduled weeks earlier than usual.

The trial in Kingston was held on August 15th and was prosecuted by acting solicitor general Henry Boulton before judge William Campbell.[13] Boulton identified Gourlay's authorship of the libel and suggested that he was hiding behind a printer in the manner of the vilified Joseph Willcocks, a leader of the pre-war opposition who died fighting for the American side during the War of 1812. He suggested that the constitutional meetings promoted in the libel were prohibited in Britain and their effect would be to overturn the constitution. If Gourlay was responsible for the publication in question the jurors must find him guilty.[14] Boulton's argument, with the question of seditious effect withheld from the jury, reflected the state of the doctrine before Fox's Libel Act of 1792.

As Howe was to do later, Gourlay defended himself, although it appears that he was assisted by former Massachusetts attorney general Barnabas Bidwell.[15] His legal arguments probed the contestable elements of libel proceedings and were informed by Whig constitutional understandings and contemporary English cases. (See app. 3, N, doc. 1.)

Gourlay opened by suggesting that the pre-trial procedural decisions noted above reflected a vindictive government bent on repression. The early scheduling of the assizes nearly resulted in his being found in contempt and the refusal of a copy of the indictment compromised his ability to mount a defence.[16] The court's discretion on this and on other matters, such as the defendant's right to counsel, had been successfully contested and limited in Britain. The crown had also refused him the right to examine all the witnesses he called.[17] Such procedural discretionary powers frustrated and eroded the constitutional rights that, according to governments, all British subjects held.[18]

Gourlay's substantive arguments exposed the real weaknesses of the crown's case. British subjects enjoyed the constitutional right to petition and could not be charged with sedition or libel in exercising that right.[19] Gourlay admitted that under libel doctrine 'the lowest drudge employed to give it circulation is actionable,' but even under this arbitrary rule he was an accessory rather than a principal to publication.[20] The prosecution's burden of proof in criminal trials included proof of intention. Far from establishing criminal intent, the solicitor general had simply declared seditious innuendo and proved nothing more than publication of a pamphlet.

On this last point Gourlay drew from Thomas Erskine's famous seditious libel defences before Fox's act, thus opening the way for his constitutional arguments on the jury.[21] Gourlay noted that the sheriff, under the attorney general's instruction and in accordance with provincial practice, had chosen jurors exclusively from Kingston rather than impartially from the whole district. This method of proceeding contained the potential for executive abuse and assembly bills had unsuccessfully attempted to end it.[22] Gourlay then moved on from questions of composition to the jury's power to resist judicial instructions and the law in delivering its verdict. Juries had the right to give a 'free verdict according to conscience' to nullify oppressive laws or prosecutions. As Erskine asserted, jurors were entitled to reflect on whether there was seditious intent underlying the publication, a position that, after long struggle, had resulted in the British legislative vindication of popular rights in the face of common law that was biased in favour of the executive[23]: 'It had been long inflicted that juries should give their verdict, in cases of libel *only* as to the fact of publishing ... The present Lord Erskine gained immortal honour by overturning this rule ... and as it was of infinite consequence to the liberty of the Press – Mr. Fox, and he, introduced a bill into Parliament, and had it enacted, that in cases of libel, jurors should be free to decide for themselves upon the whole matter ... It is now the undeniable right of jurors ... to give the verdict at their own discretion on the whole matter in issue.'

As noted in document 1 (app. 3, N), Fox's act was erroneously understood *not* to be part of the received law in Upper Canada. Gourlay was thus forced to resurrect Erkine's pre-reform arguments against the common-law doctrine of seditious libel which artificially converted factual questions of intent into questions of law.[24] The jury could nullify this archaic law by exercising its constitutional right to a verdict according to conscience; indeed, said Gourlay, 'to leave this to the dictum of the bench would be a dangerous sacrifice of liberty.'[25] The jury heeded Gourlay. After Boulton exercised the crown's controversial prerogative right to make the final statement, they returned a verdict of not guilty.[26]

Victory celebrations were short-lived as it became clear that Gourlay still had to face another trial in Brockville at the Johnstown assizes beginning on August 25th. When questioned about the trial date, Boulton suggested that the trial might be postponed to the next assizes. Gourlay demanded a discharge on the grounds that he had already been acquitted, but a true bill was then returned on an indictment charging him with 'diffusing discontents and jealousies and raising tumults' and setting a trial date of 31 August.[27]

The original warrant, which was the only document Gourlay had access to, had suggested a charge of seditious words rather than seditious libel. The complaint of Jones and Fraser related to Gourlay's reading of the address in Johnstown rather than the libel settled by the jury in Kingston. However, the crown's pleadings focused on libel based on passages in his third address not submitted as evidence in Kingston.

Gourlay therefore had good grounds for an *autrefois acquit* defence. If raised, it was certainly brushed aside. He again stressed the constitutionality of his addresses and actions and reasserted the crown's failure to demonstrate intent. His attempt to call witnesses to testify that the address in question did not cause tumults (except among government supporters) was refused. Nonetheless, he successfully admonished the jury to consider the whole matter in its verdict, and, despite Boulton's resort to the crown's prerogative of final reply, he received a second acquittal.[28]

LEGISLATIVE RESPONSE, EXTRAJUDICIAL OPINION, AND EXECUTIVE MEASURES

The government's response to the embarrassing acquittals was to resort to legislative measures, namely a new law to suppress further political meetings and use of the 1804 Sedition Act. Gourlay's banishment under the 1804 act entails numerous legal points of interest: an extrajudicial opinion on the act's applicability to British subjects, a summary hearing, and a deportation order, the disobedience of which led to Gourlay's arrest and detention without bail. At his eventual trial Gourlay received a judicial banishment order, which, if disobeyed, would be treated as a capital offence. A seditious-libel prosecution was also taken against Gourlay's publisher, Bartemas Ferguson of the Niagara *Spectator*, by ex officio information rather than an indictment.

The Seditious Meetings Act was designed to prohibit further political meetings and thus close the legal lacuna noted earlier by Robinson. The prematurely reconvened assembly quickly passed the government's bill in late October.[29] Popular conventions deliberating on public issues, grievances, or petitions were forbidden on the basis that they encouraged tumult and riot and usurped the functions of the legislature. Persons who organized or attended such meetings were guilty of a high misdemeanour. The law appears to have deterred further assemblies and did not result in prosecutions, but as we shall see, it did trigger other events.[30]

Meanwhile, the government turned to consideration of the Sedition Act, passed in 1804, ostensibly in response to imperial encouragement of a *temporary* measure to contend with foreign intrigues against British rule in North America. (See app. 3, K, doc. 1.) Its legislative history reveals that the main government concern underpinning the *permanent* act was disloyal disaffection stemming from American immigrants and Irish and British reform influences.[31] It came to stand as a symbol of official intolerance of aliens and oppositionists alike, delineating the loyal community and the presumed disloyal element to be excluded if possible. The struggle to repeal the act in the 1820s, with majority bills in the assembly struck down by the upper house, made it a central cause in the battle for responsible government.[32] As noted in the essay by Paul Romney and Barry Wright on security proceedings in the War of 1812, the Sedition Act authorized the deportation of persons who were not permanently resident in the province six months before proceedings were initiated or who had not taken a provincial oath of allegiance. Such persons, allegedly engaged in seditious activity or intending to alienate subjects from the government, could be arrested on a warrant of the lieutenant governor, a judge of the Court of King's Bench, or executive or legislative councillor and brought before a summary hearing (without counsel or jury), where they would bear the burden of proof to show that they did not come within the terms of the legislation. If this was not done they could be ordered deported immediately or to submit security for good behaviour until they left. Refusal to leave constituted an offence for which the accused would be arrested and held without bail until trial at the crown's discretion. Upon conviction, the accused could be deported immediately or after a term of imprisonment, with further refusal to leave being a capital offence. As Chief Justice Powell observed: '[The act] subjects the Earl

[of] Bathurst if he should pay a visit to this Province and his Looks should offend Isaac Sweezy [who had informed against Gourlay] to be ordered out of the Province by the enlightened Magistrate, and if that disobedience which constitutes the offence is found by a jury, to be banished, under penalty of Death, should he remain ... without the Slightest Enquiry into the Cause or Justice of the worthy Magistrate's suspicion that he was a Suspicious Character.'[33]

The Sedition Act was submitted to the judges of the Court of King's Bench, secretly assisted by Attorney General Robinson,[34] for an extrajudicial opinion on its applicability to Gourlay. (See app. 3, N, doc. 2.) This remarkable exercise of soliciting judicial opinion before trial was of doubtful constitutionality. A favoured means of manipulating the bench in politically sensitive cases under the Stuarts, the practice had fallen into disuse by the 1760s and was heavily criticized thereafter in Britain, although it became commonplace in Lower Canada.[35] On November 10th the King's Bench reported, resolving every ambiguity in favour of the crown. It ruled that the oath of allegiance referred to in the Sedition Act had to be taken in the province and that the legislation itself had 'originally [been] enacted to guard against the seditious practices of natural-born [British] subjects as well as aliens.' The judges added that 'in the sound Construction of that Act' the reference to 'inhabitant' was to be given the meaning of 'any Person living in this Province for the continued term of six months.'[36] Gourlay had taken the oath of allegiance in the United Kingdom but not the province, and within six months of doing so he had visited the United States without establishing a permanent residence in Upper Canada.

Sedition Act proceedings against Gourlay were triggered by his famous 'Gagg'd, by Jingo' response, printed in the *Spectator*, to the seditious meetings legislation. This was also the pretext for actions against Ferguson, who, with co-editor Benjamin Pawling, was arrested on December 16th and, after some initial confusion, proceeded against for seditious libel by ex officio informations.[37] The prerogative gave the crown full discretion to decide when it would proceed to trial and Robinson warned that the subsequent conduct of the newspaper would determine the matter.[38] Two days later Gourlay was arrested and on the 21st he was brought before a hearing headed by William Dickson and four others sitting as commissioners.[39]

Gourlay's claim that the legislation did not apply to British subjects was quickly dismissed by the commissioners, armed as they were with the extrajudicial opinion. They questioned him about his connections with

William Cobbett, Henry Hunt, and the Spa Fields riots as well as his visits to Ireland and the United States. When Gourlay failed to prove satisfactorily that his words and conduct were not intended to promote disaffection against the government, the commissioners issued an order declaring him a seditious alien and stated that he must leave by January 1st.[40]

Gourlay refused to leave on the basis of his previous acquittals on sedition charges and his constitutional right to be held innocent until convicted by a regular jury. As provided for under the Sedition Act, he was arrested on 4 January 1819 and committed to the district jail of Niagara without bail for an indefinite term; his petition to Chief Justice Powell for a writ of habeas corpus was denied (after Powell's consultations with the attorney general on the legislative provisions).[41] He was confined for eight months before the crown decided to put him on trial. His contributions to the *Spectator* continued until June, when he was ordered into solitary confinement in a poorly ventilated cell.[42] As for Ferguson, Robinson, supported by resolutions in the assembly and by Lieutenant Governor Maitland, proceeded against him under the information from the previous December.[43]

Gourlay and Ferguson were tried at the Niagara assizes, which began on 16 August. Robinson came well prepared for the trials, having ascertained in advance Chief Justice Powell's compliance with the exceptional procedures taken under the Sedition Act and the crown's information.[44] Moreover, both cases were to be tried by what appears to have been carefully packed juries. In Ferguson's case, the crown called a special jury under the ex officio prerogative.[45] Gourlay, unfit to stand trial, was incapable of challenging the sheriff's selection.[46] Unlike the juries of the previous year, neither the jury in Gourlay's case nor that in Ferguson's was inclined to exercise a verdict according to conscience in order to nullify an oppressive law and prosecution.

Ferguson's trial was on August 19th. Although the details are sketchy, it appears that, despite what was described as 'an able defence' by his counsel, Robinson successfully prevented the arguments from going beyond the fact of publication.[47] The jury, not disposed to delivering a general verdict in any event, quickly found Ferguson guilty. He was returned to jail, and, as was possible under ex officio procedure, sentencing was postponed beyond the end of the assizes to the next term of the Court of King's Bench in early November. The sentence would be determined by the legal outcome of Gourlay's trial the next day and its political fallout.[48]

In Gourlay's trial, Robinson needed only to prove an order to leave the province and Gourlay's disobedience of it[49]; he did not have to establish the existence of sedition nor was the jury entitled to inquire into it. If Gourlay conceded his refusal to be deported, all other issues were a question of law and the jury was directed by the law to convict. After examining the commissioners to establish the regularity of the hearing under the terms of the act, Robinson put the simple question to the jurors.[50] Gourlay again insisted on defending himself, but as the result of his extended confinement he came under the confused impression that he was being tried for seditious libel. Instead of protesting the charge as he had originally intended, he pleaded 'not guilty' and the trial proceeded. He rambled on about his previous acquittals and his defence, as the Kingston *Chronicle* noted, was 'idle and absurd to the extreme.'[51] Any remote possibility of persuading the jury to exercise a wider verdict was lost. Chief Justice Powell's charge to the jury narrowly followed the letter of the law. It was a law that invariably favoured the crown's position, and a guilty verdict was returned. In sentencing, Powell stressed the importance of the integrity of law and its consistent application, expressing none of his private concerns about the Sedition Act's constitutionality. Gourlay was told to put his formidable energies to more positive ends and directed to leave the province within twenty-four hours or face a capital charge. Following the trial, he returned to Britain via the United States and began his life-long campaign for vindication.[52]

At Ferguson's 'sentence hearing' months later, favourable affidavits were countered by Robinson, who stressed Ferguson's ample warning from the crown nearly a year earlier, his support of the imprisoned Gourlay's continued sedition, and the disaffection generated by the dangerous engine of a press controlled by irresponsible editors. He also referred to the gravity with which the offence was then regarded in England. On 8 November Powell, Campbell, and Boulton delivered what Riddell called a 'scandalous' and 'atrocious' sentence: imprisonment, the pillory, and fines which proved ruinous for his newspaper.[53]

At the lieutenant governor's suggestion, the seditious meetings legislation was repealed at the next legislative session in early 1820.[54] Ferguson's petition pleading for remission of the remainder of his sentence narrowly passed in the assembly, but a motion to repeal the Sedition Act was defeated. This was the first of numerous repeal attempts which, along with bills to reform jury selection, were to be rigorously pursued as the 1820s progressed. Far from quelling the fires of opposition, Gourlay's mistreatment set off a resurgent opposition movement fuelled by further discriminatory measures against aliens. The subsequent repressive measures against Reform are examined by Paul Romney in the chapter that follows.

Legally, the Gourlay affair illuminates a range of issues related to the partisan manipulation of the administration of criminal law which were to be further played out in the 1820s. At the root of the problem was a colonial legal system which was much more dominated by the executive than its British counterpart. The attorney general's monopoly over prosecutorial authority resulted in freer resort to ex officio informations, a controversial prerogative in Britain. As well, the extrajudicial opinion from King's Bench on the applicability of the Sedition Act and consultations with the attorney general on Gourlay's application for habeas corpus reflected a colonial legal culture where judges were leading members of executive councils and where their compliance was ensured by their tenure according to royal pleasure rather than good behaviour. Executive influences even extended to the local administration of justice, as highlighted by the management of jury selection. Although the power of the jury's free verdict was evident in the Kingston and Brockville trials, this unpredictable element of the process could be managed by jury packing, facilitated either by a special jury under ex officio information or through influence on the executively appointed sheriff and his selection of jurors. The sweeping provisions of the Sedition Act were unprecedented in the empire in this period. Although the opinions Gourlay received as to its suspect legality and constitutionality proved of little immediate help, the long struggle to repeal the legislation underlined the lack of accountability of the appointed legislative and executive councils to the elected assembly, a legacy of the Constitutional Act of 1791 and a glaring instance of the province's divergence from the 'very image and transcript' of the British constitution.

NOTES

1 I am indebted to Lois Darroch for her helpful comments on an earlier version of this essay. The long-lived Gourlay wrote prolifically. See especially his *Statistical Account of Upper Canada*, 2 vols. (London: 1822; repr. New York: East Ardsley 1966), and *The Banished Briton and Neptunian* (Boston: S.N. Dickinson 1843). Also valuable are Lois Darroch Milani, *Robert Gourlay, Gadfly: Forerunner of the Rebellion in Upper Canada, 1837* (Toronto: Ampersand Press 1971); W.R. Riddell, 'Robert (Fleming) Gourlay, As Shown by His Own Records,' *OH*, vol. 14 (1916), 5; E.A. Cruikshank, 'The Government of Upper Canada and Robert

Gourlay,' *OH*, vol. 33 (1936), 65; S.F. Wise, 'Gourlay, Robert Fleming,' *DCB* 9: 330.

2 See Barry Cahill, '*R v. Howe* (1835) for Seditious Libel: A Tale of Twelve Magistrates,' in this volume, as well as my essay 'Sedition in Upper Canada: Contested Legality,' *Labour/Le Travail*, vol. 29 (1992), 7, which offers an overview of the provincial record of sedition prosecutions and explores their repressive and counter-hegemonic dimensions. A re-examination of RG 22, series 134, Court of King's Bench Assize Minutebook, AO, and various records related to the War of 1812 indicates a dozen more cases in addition to the thirty-four listed in my 1992 article.

3 The oath of allegiance was made a prerequisite to holding provincial land and the orders cast in doubt the titles of 'late Loyalists' who had migrated to Upper Canada after American independence. The executive's reading of the peacetime scope of the Sedition Act paved the way for the creative application of the legislation to Gourlay. See JHAUC, 1816; RG 1, E 1, Minutes of the Executive Council, 7 Oct. 1815, NA; and Gore to Bathurst, 17 Oct. 1815, reproduced in Cruikshank, 'Government,' at 108–9.

4 See JHAUC, 1817, 1818. The aliens policy threatened the land market for speculators. The policy was eventually found to contradict the Treaty of Paris of 1783, imperial legislation of 1790, and the Constitutional Act of 1791. See Paul Romney, *Mr Attorney: The Attorney General for Ontario in Court, Cabinet, and Legislature, 1791–1899* (Toronto: Osgoode Society/University of Toronto Press 1986), at 83–4; Aileen Dunham, *Political Unrest in Upper Canada, 1815–1836* (Toronto; repr. McClelland and Stewart 1963), at 49.

5 *Upper Canada Gazette*, 30 Oct. 1817. On Gourlay's falling out with leading officials, see Riddell, 'Gourlay,' at 16; Strachan to Harvey, 22 June 1818, reprinted in *John Strachan: Documents and Opinions*, ed. J.L.H. Henderson (Toronto: McClelland and Stewart 1969), at 67.

6 *Spectator*, 5 and 12 Feb. 1818.

7 Ibid., 2 April 1818 (reprinted in Cruikshank, 'Government,' at 134–8). See also Riddell, 'Gourlay,' at 24–5. British constitutional convention was that the crown's prerogative was to be exercised circumspectly.

8 Administrator Samuel Smith wrote to Bathurst on 18 April: 'I have ... directed the Attorney General to watch the progress of this person and his employees in order to seize the first proper occasion to check by criminal prosecution the very threatening career now entered upon.' Robinson arranged for close surveillance and interception of Gourlay's mail. See Smith to Bathurst, 18 April 1818, reprinted in Cruikshank, 'Government,' at 139–41; Strachan to Harvey, 22 June 1818, reproduced in Henderson, *Strachan*, at 68, and Gourlay, *Chronicles of Canada; Being a Record of Robert Gourlay* (St Catharines: *Journal* 1842).

9 Robinson added: 'No time more than the present ever afforded stronger evidence of this truth in the experience of the Mother Country.' See Robinson to Jarvis, 13 June 1818, reproduced in Cruikshank, 'Government,' at 145–6. On the British government's approach to seditious-libel prosecutions in 1817 and 1818, see Michael Lobban, 'From Seditious Libel to Unlawful Assembly: Peterloo and the Changing Face of Political Crime, *c.* 1770–1820,' *Oxford Journal of Legal Studies*, vol. 10 (1990), 305 at 327.

10 Robinson wrote: 'The only Law I know of, under which these meetings ... might be suppressed is the British Act of 13 Charles 2d Stat. 1. Ch. 5th against tumultuous petitions. It has indeed been asserted that this act is virtually repealed by the Bill of Rights ... nothing certainly would give more consequence and popularity to Mr. Gourlay's wild measures than to attempt to suppress these meetings by any harsh construction of Law ... But as there can be no doubt that Mr. Gourlay's publications are gross libels on the administration of the Government, I apprised Your Honour of my intention of adopting the only course sanctioned clearly by the Law' (Robinson to Smith, 29 June 1818, reproduced in Cruikshank, 'Government,' at 150–2). In a further letter Robinson solicited an opinion from the Court of King's Bench on prohibiting the meetings; see Robinson to Smith, 4 July 1818, and Powell to Smith, 7 July 1818, reproduced in Cruikshank, 'Government,' at 153–4). Robinson's British counterpart, Sir Vicary Gibbs, failed in the 1817 case of *Wooler* to have discussion of petitions considered sedition, but under legislation passed shortly afterwards political assemblies were limited to fifty persons (57 Geo. III c. 19, s. 23).

11 Jones was given the task of following Gourlay's movements. On 25 June in Johnstown, Jones convinced magistrate Fraser to lay an information against Gourlay for his 'seditious words' during the recruitment of representatives for the York convention. See Gourlay, *Statistical Account*, 2: at 665, and Riddell, 'Gourlay,' at 28–9.

12 See Maitland to Bathurst, 19 Aug. 1818, reproduced in Cruikshank, 'Government,' at 156–7.

13 It is unclear why Boulton rather than Robinson prosecuted since the former's appointment was confirmed only in 1819 and questions surrounded his involvement in the 1817 duel between Samuel Peters Jarvis and John Ridout that had resulted in the latter's death. The Gourlay proceedings were omitted from the assize minutebooks (5:22); the clerk's entry reads, 'The minutes of Proceedings for the Eastern, Johnstown and Midland Districts were taken away from the Crown Office by Henry John Boulton Esquire, Solicitor General, *personally*, and never returned, although often asked for, for want of which, they are not recorded' (see also Milani, *Gadfly*, at 178). Fortunately, a

record of the Kingston trial survives in the form of the pamphlet published by the Kingston *Gazette* (RG 1, Pamphlet collection 1–1051), *Address to the Jury, at the Kingston Assize, in the Case of the King v. Robert Gourlay*, NA), reproduced in part in this volume as doc. 1, app. 3, N. See also Gourlay's, *Chronicles of Canada*, at 23, and *Banished Briton*; and Robinson's report (unsigned) on the Gourlay affair in CO 42/368/161–7, NA.

14 *Address to the Jury*, at 4.

15 Riddell, 'Gourlay,' at 34. Although the most notable of the pre-revolutionary American seditious libel cases involving jury nullification, *Zenger* [(1735) 17 St. Tr. 675], influenced the 1820 Nova Scotia case *Wilkie*, Gourlay did not refer to it despite Bidwell's probable assistance.

16 *Address to Jury*, at 19–20. This was likely an attempt to prevent his return to the province. In scheduling the proceedings a month early when Gourlay was expected to be in New York, the government could prevent his return to the province by a finding of contempt of court. On application to the court after the trial, a copy of the indictment was still refused (see *Address to Jury*), suggesting that the crown possibly feared an action for malicious prosecution. Both in Britain and the Canadas, the legal right to counsel on felony charges (they were in fact allowed for treasons and misdemeanours) came only with the Prisoner's Counsel Act of 1836. See J.M. Beattie, 'Scales of Justice: Defence Counsel and the English Criminal Trial in the Eighteenth and Early Nineteenth Centuries,' *Law and History Review*, vol. 9 (1991), 221, and Milani, *Gadfly*, at 166.

17 *Address to the Jury*, at 6.

18 Ibid., at 21.

19 Ibid., at 13–16. Gourlay stressed that the right to petition was upheld by the Revolution Settlement, as Attorney General Robinson had earlier acknowledged, and was privileged no matter how controversial it was. See nn.9, 10.

20 *Address to Jury*, at 5.

21 Fox's act vindicated the right of the jury to a general verdict, which Thomas Erskine had argued for earlier in defiance of the prevailing opinion among judges. Clarification of the burden of proof on the prosecution (and the elaboration of other procedural and evidentiary rules) developed with the increased involvement of lawyers in criminal trials, a process in which Erskine and William Garrow played leading roles and in which the protections of the Treason Act of 1696 served as an important model. See Beattie, 'Scales of Justice.'

22 *Address to Jury*, at 20. In 1811 and 1812 Joseph Willcocks brought forward the first bills to restrain the executively appointed sheriffs from packing juries. William Lyon Mackenzie initiated debate on a new series of bills (*Colonial Advocate*, 1 July 1824) and such measures were passed by majorities in the

assembly thoughout the remainder of the decade, only to be terminated in council.

23 *Address to Jury*, at 21.

24 Ibid. As noted in the introduction to this volume, Fox's Libel Act was seen by many to be declaratory, passed to correct a judicially manufactured distortion of the doctrine. The pamphlet trial report notes that, since Fox's act had been passed after the Constitutional Act of 1791, the jurors' rights remained within the arbitary discretion of judges in the province and it was recommended that Fox's act be expressly adopted by the provincial legislature. However, the act did indeed apply in the province because it was passed (31 Jan. 1792) and proclaimed (15 June 1792) before the reception date specified in (1800) 40 Geo. III, c. 1 – 17 Sept. 1792. Following the conviction of Francis Collins, John Beverley Robinson accepted that the legislation applied in the province (see Robinson's statements to the select committee on the petition of Collins, JHAUC, 1829, Appendix; judge Sherwood did not concur – Sherwood to Colborne, 26 March 1829, CO 42/388/134–41, NA). Its applicability was further confirmed by the attorney general in assembly debates on libel law in December 1831.

25 *Address to Jury*, at 21.

26 Kingston *Gazette*, 18 Aug. 1818; *Address to Jury*, at 22. In private prosecutions, which were the norm in England during this period, the defence was given the last word to the jury.

27 Gourlay, *The Banished Briton and Neptunian*, no. 12:112; Kingston *Gazette*, 2 Sept. 1818; Riddell, 'Gourlay,' at 35; Milani, *Gadfly*, at 177–8.

28 The assize court records for Johnstown assizes are also missing (see n.13) but, unlike the Kingston assizes, there is no outside report. The crown had evident difficulty with the wording of the indictment and the Johnstown evidence was complicated by Gourlay's action against Fraser for assault. As noted earlier, the government may have feared an action for malicious prosecution, and Boulton may have been anxious about the permanency of his appointment. Gourlay managed to secure Fraser's conviction for assault at the Quarter Sessions and to extract a public apology from Stephen Miles, editor of the Kingston *Gazette*, who had been pressured to publish government propaganda under his own name. See Riddell, 'Gourlay,' at 28–9; H. Pearson Gundy, *Early Printers and Printing in the Canada* (Toronto: Bibliographical Society of Canada 1957), at 26–7.

29 58 Geo. III c. 11. Legislative compliance reflected the restoration of the alliance between the Niagara and governing elites. Although the early recall was obstensibly due to fiscal concerns, Maitland's throne speech of 12 October emphasized, '[We] feel a just indignation at the attempts which have

been made to excite discontent and to organize sedition.' After Maitland offered concessions on the economic matters at issue, the assembly apologized for its previous lack of cooperation and ordered minutes referring to the recent struggles between the houses expunged. Robinson brought forward the legislation he had drafted with the assistance of the judges. The bill was opposed by only one member. See *Debates*, House of Assembly, 21, 22, 23, and 31 Oct. (reproduced in Gourlay, *Chronicles of Canada*, at 30–4); also, Robinson to Hillier, 18 Nov. 1818, reproduced in Cruikshank, 'Government,' at 165.

30 See n.10. In the debates it was claimed that the act was based on similar British legislation (Pitt's 'seditious meetings' act [36 Geo. III c. 8] was a temporary measure and the 1817 legislation referred to in n.10 simply limited meetings to fifty delegates). The Six Acts were not passed until the next year. Dunham suggests that the legislation went no farther than the contemporary British measures (*Political Unrest*, at 59), but the Six Acts, unlike the Seditious Meetings Act, were temporary measures that had to be renewed every legislative session. Also, the Six Acts explicitly restricted the use of ex officio informations, which were resorted to against Ferguson. On Gourlay's view of the legislative history, see 'Recapitulation and Conclusion, Concerning the Convention and Gagging Law,' *Chronicles of Canada*, no.1: at 38–40.

31 'An Act for the Better Securing This Province Against All Seditious Attempts or Designs to Disturb the Tranquillity Thereof' [(1804) 44 Geo. III c. 1]. The act was flexible enough to apply to British subjects and so reflected concerns about the arrival of Irish in the province after the rebellion. Reference to the legislation as the Alien Act is a misnomer and creates confusion with the Alien Acts passed from 1814 onwards to confiscate and sell properties left by Americans who had been convicted of treason or outlawry or who had been deported or had fled during the war. The 1804 measure was introduced in the Legislative Council; only two members of the assembly attempted to limit it to a temporary war measure, although William Weekes vigorously attacked it in his election broadside following its passage as an infringement on the ancient English liberties and an example of need of vigilant legislators to check executive and judicial abuses (*Upper Canada Gazette*, 25 Jan. 1805, as quoted in G.H. Paterson 'William Weekes,' *DCB* 5: 844–5). Both Gourlay and Riddell suggested a primary British role (Gourlay, 'General Introduction,' *Statistical Account*, 1:lxiv; Riddell, 'Mr. Justice Thorpe: Leader of the First Opposition in Upper Canada,' *Canadian Law Times*, vol. 40 (1920), 912, and 'Gourlay,' at 41). However, councillors Richard Cartwright and Samuel Street (quoted in Riddell, 'Gourlay,' at 63n.107, and Cruikshank, 'Government,' at 133) indicated that the temporary enemy aliens act [(1797) 37 Geo. III c. 1] was used as a

model and extended to cover local concerns about immigration after Lieutenant Governor John Graves Simcoe's 1792 proclamation, applicable not only to aliens but all 'strangers.' See *Journals*, House of Assembly and Legislative Council, February-March 1804, reproduced in *Sixth Report of the Archives for the Province of Ontario* (Toronto 1911).

32 Attempts to repeal the Sedition Act extended from 1819 to 1829; eight of the repeal bills were passed by majorities in the assembly, only to be struck down in the upper house. The last bill, which was opposed by only one member of the assembly, the attorney general, became law after the matter was included in a petition to the British government.

33 Powell to Gore, 18 Jan. 1819, quoted in Riddell, 'Gourlay,' at 41.

34 For Robinson's report on the Sedition Act and its application to Gourlay, see CO 42/368/153–9, 161–7, NA.

35 On the practice of extrajudicial opionions and their reflection of a 'Baconian' judiciary, see F. Murray Greenwood, *Legacies of Fear: Law and Politics in Quebec in the Era of the French Revolution* (Toronto: Osgoode Society/University of Toronto Press 1993), at 32–4.

36 Report of the judges to Sir Peregrine Maitland, 10 Nov. 1818, reproduced in app. 3, N, doc. 2.

37 Sworn informations against the accused were given by Issac Swayze, who, many years earlier, had been the second person in the province to be prosecuted for sedition and since the time of the war had ingratiated himself with the government. See Swayze to Hillier, 16 Dec. 1818, reproduced in Cruikshank, 'Government,' at 165. See also Gourlay, *Banished Briton and Neptunian*, no.16: at 163, and no.22: at 263; *Statistical Account*, 'General Introduction,' 1:lxviii; 2: at 498.

38 The procedural advantages of ex officio information allowed for this 'hanging threat' and bypassed the grand jury required for indictments. The crown could call a special jury and the sentence could be determined well after trial. The prerogative was controversial in Britain, so much so that when the Six Acts were passed its use was explicitly restricted. The provincial crown's prosecutorial powers were at this time under imperial scrutiny as a result of the fallout from the controversy involving Lord Selkirk and the Hudson Bay and North West companies. See RG 7, vol. 59, and CO 42/362.

39 See 'Order to Commit Robert Gourlay, 4 Jan. 1819,' *Con Docs* 2: at 14. Gourlay claimed to have had no previous idea of the existence of the legislation (Milani, *Gadfly*, at 184–5).

40 Gourlay had resided in the province for the past year and a half and owned property, but the technical interpretation of the legislation by the judges meant that temporary absence without a permanent residence sufficed (he

stayed at hotels and with supporters). See 'Order to Commit,' at 14–15; Gourlay, *The Banished Briton and Neptunian* no. 16: at 165; Cruikshank, 'Government,' at 97; and Milani, *Gadfly*, at 187–8.

41 See petition of 13 January in Gourlay, *Statistical Account*, 'General Introduction,' 1:xl. On 20 January Powell endorsed the writ and ordered Gourlay delivered to his chambers in York, where Gourlay demanded an immediate hearing before the King's Bench. Powell left to consult with the attorney general and returned declaring that the act allowed neither a hearing nor bail. See Gourlay, *The Banished Briton and Neptunian*, at 189; Gourlay, *Statistical Account*, 'General Introduction,' 1: at x, xli–xliii.

42 Riddell, 'Gourlay,' at 65, provides a grim contemporary description of the jail and Milani, *Gadfly* (at 199) describes Gourlay's ordeal in detail.

43 The information was triggered by a libel in the 28 June issue. See JHAUC, 5 July 1818, at 173; RG 5, B 3, vol. 21, NA. (His co-accused, Pawling, died shortly after the initial arrests in December.) As a result of the ex officio procedure, Ferguson's pre-trial proceedings were limited to his exceptional appearance before the full King's Bench in York (the prerogative bypassed the grand jury). He was remanded for trial at the next assizes in Niagara. See Riddell, 'Gourlay,' at 51; Riddell, 'The Information Ex Officio in Upper Canada,' *Canada Law Times*, vol. 41 (1921), at 93–4; *Spectator* 29 July 1819; Gourlay, *The Banished Briton and Neptunian*, no. 34: at 476.

44 Powell's private reservations about the Sedition Act (see n.33) were belied by his public actions, the extrajudicial opinion, and consultation with the attorney general on Gourlay's application for habeas corpus. As for the mode of prosecuting Ferguson, Powell privately noted, 'What is laughable in this is that the Gov't. in Compliance having ordered the Att. to prosecute, is now condemned, by themselves for the mode adopted by that officer, by Information instead of Indictment' (Powell to Gore, 11 July 1819, quoted in Riddell, *The Life of William Dummer Powell* (Lansing, Mich.: 1924), at 119. On Powell's dilemmas, see Milani, *Gadfly*, at 202, 208–9; Riddell, 'Gourlay,' at 53.

45 The crown's selection rights exceeded the defendants' under the information. See Gourlay, *The Banished Briton and Neptunian* no. 34: at 477.

46 See n.22. Gourlay later claimed that the sheriff's selection resulted in a notoriously packed jury. See Gourlay, *Statistical Account*, 'General Introduction,' 1: at xv (note); *Statistical Account*, 2: at 342; and Milani, *Gadfly*, at 200–1.

47 R.L. Fraser, 'Ferguson, Bartemas,' *DCB* 6: 247. The record of Ferguson's trial in RG 22 lacks important information because Ferguson was not indicted by a grand jury. Ferguson had the right to counsel because seditious libel was a misdemeanour.

48 See Milani, *Gadfly*, at 199; Dickson to Hillier, 23 Aug. 1819, reproduced in

Cruikshank, 'Government,' at 172. The crown may have had reservations about Powell's willingness to impose a heavy sentence on his own, given that he was privately uncomfortable with the repressive measures.

49 See Riddell, 'Gourlay,' at 52. Gourlay's indictment can be found in RG 22, series 138, 'Criminal Filings,' box 1, AO.

50 See Milani, *Gadfly*, at 203; Patrick Brode, *Sir John Beverley Robinson: Bone and Sinew of the Compact* (Toronto: Osgoode Society/University of Toronto Press 1984), at 56–7.

51 Reproduced in Gourlay, *Statistical Account*, 'General Introduction,' 1: at ccclvi. He argued a difference of opinion with Cobbett and Hunt and the illegality of his imprisonment. Later, he admitted that he was temporarily incapable of reason. See Gourlay, *Statistical Account*, 'General Introduction,' 1: at xiv–xv; *Statistical Account*, 1: at ccciv. Gourlay's condition was verified by various witnesses who testified at an 1841 assembly committee inquiry into the affair.

52 After Gourlay's return to Britain he was imprisoned for horsewhipping Lord Brougham in the lobby of Westminster, an incident sparked by the future lord chancellor's failure to press a petition concerning Gourlay's treatment in Upper Canada. Gourlay continually petitioned Canadian legislatures for redress until the 1860s. After the findings of the legislative committee in 1841, the government offered a pardon but no compensation. In 1856 a free pardon was granted along with a small pension (registered 14 May 1857: RG 68, 273, NA), both of which he rejected. In 1858 he asked to be heard at the bar of the house and left the province later that year, dying in Edinburgh in 1862. See Milani, *Gadfly*.

53 RG 22, series 125, Michaelmas Term; Riddell, 'Gourlay,' at 51; Riddell, 'Information Ex Officio,' at 94–5. The sentence included a fine of £50, imprisonment for a year and a half, and the pillory for one hour daily during the first month of the sentence. Once his term of imprisonment was over, Ferguson would have to secure his release with £500 in personal sureties and two further sureties of £250 each for his good behaviour over a term of seven years. The pillory and half the term of imprisonment were commuted by Powell upon Maitland's instructions. See Powell to Maitland, 17 Nov. 1819, RG 5, A 1, Upper Canada Sundries, 44: 21683–6.

54 60 Geo. III c. 4; JHAUC, 21 Feb. 1820. See also Maitland to Bathurst, 7 March 1820, reproduced in Cruikshank, 'Government,' at 174.

15

Upper Canada in the 1820s: Criminal Prosecution and the Case of Francis Collins

PAUL ROMNEY

After the Gourlay affair, the administration of justice in Upper Canada became a leading target of political discontent. One subject of complaint was the system of trial by jury. Its critics deprecated the domination of assize grand juries by the district magistrates; they inveighed against the sheriff's influence on the selection of juries in trials both criminal and civil; they resented the fact that, in civil matters, a jury's verdict could be reversed on appeal by the Court of King's Bench.[1] Another, more obviously political controversy blew up in 1828 over the role of the law officers of the crown in criminal prosecutions.

The years 1826–8 had been particularly difficult for the provincial government, with the alien question in particular causing it much unpopularity and embarrassment. The humiliating rejection of Attorney General John Beverley Robinson's naturalization bill by the House of Assembly in December 1825 was capped in 1827, when the imperial government disallowed a subsequent bill apparently in response to a public petition got up by opposition politicians and promoted by the anti-government press. The government and its supporters reacted to these embarrassments with vituperative denunciation and assorted acts of repression, not stopping short of physical violence. The law officers' seeming complaisance towards this violence focused attention on their claim to a monopoly of the conduct of prosecutions at the assizes. That claim was the nub of the controversy in 1828.

Among the weapons wielded against the opposition in 1828 was the law of libel. The attorney general tried to subdue the press by instituting libel proceedings against opposition journalists and suspending the prosecution in consideration of the defendant's good behaviour. This standing threat was reinforced by requiring the defendant to give sureties for his good behaviour, which were to be forfeited in the event of his subsequent conviction for libel. These tactics further discredited the government. Critics perceived a stark contrast between the government's tolerance of the vituperation and violence directed against the opposition and its alacrity in instituting proceedings for seditious libel when there was no threat of civil unrest.

Both issues – the libel prosecutions and the law officers' monopoly – crystallized in the case of the journalist Francis Collins, a leading critic of the administration of justice. Finding himself the object of four such prosecutions, he challenged the law officers' monopoly, and their partiality in the administration of justice, in open court.

THE CONTROVERSY OVER ASSIZE PROSECUTIONS

In England the attorney general and solicitor general had nothing to do with ordinary criminal prosecutions. These were conducted by counsel specially retained by some interested member of the public.[2] In Upper Canada, however, it was usual for criminal prosecutions in the Court of Oyer and Terminer and General Gaol Delivery to be conducted by the attorney general or solicitor general. This function was a valued perquisite of both offices, especially in the early decades, because the incumbents received a fee from the public purse for each such prosecution, and it quickly acquired in the minds of its defenders the status of a right. The claim of right was officially dismissed in 1811 by the provincial Executive Council when the lieutenant governor barred his attorney general, William Firth, from travelling the assize circuits, but with Firth's departure from the province the question was left unresolved.[3]

It was revived in the 1820s as part of a broader controversy over the alleged unfairness and partisan bias of the province's legal system. The heightened vehemence of political controversy after the War of 1812 gave rise to several causes célèbres which called in question the law officers' capacity to act impartially as public prosecutors. The most notorious was the so-called types riot of June 1826, when articled clerks of both law officers took part in the destruction of the printing office of William Lyon Mackenzie, the radical journalist, at York by a gang of young patricians after he had subjected the law officers themselves, and other leaders of the legal profession, to vituperative criticism.[4] Mackenzie sued his attackers and won heavy damages, but later he declared that his legal advisers had dissuaded him from prosecuting the culprits because of Attorney General Robinson's supposed bias in their favour.[5] The attorney general normally prosecuted at the assizes for the Home District, where the offence had been committed.

Another affair that cast doubt on the law officers' impartiality was the tarring and feathering of George Rolph at Ancaster, near Hamilton, a few days before the types riot. The victim's brother was John Rolph, a leader of the provincial opposition, and the attack was traced to several prominent supporters of the government, including two magistrates and the sheriff. Instead of instituting a criminal prosecution against his suspected assailants, George Rolph too proceeded against them by civil action. At the trial the defendants were represented by the solicitor general, Henry John Boulton, acting in his private capacity.[6] There was nothing illegal in this, since at that time both law officers, like their English counterparts, conducted an extensive and lucrative private practice,[7] but the solicitor general normally prosecuted at the local assizes and did so on this occasion (or he could not have been on hand for the civil trial). Rolph could hardly have trusted Boulton to prosecute men whom he was representing in the civil action.

Early in 1828 the question of the law officers' duty was brought before the House of Assembly in connection with a third scandal, the so-called Niagara Falls Outrage. This concerned the military eviction of an innkeeper, William Forsyth, from land overlooking Niagara Falls which he had enclosed but which the government claimed as a military reserve. Like Mackenzie and Rolph, Forsyth proceeded against the culprits by civil action, but he also complained to the House of Assembly of his inability to obtain justice in the criminal courts. He considered the offence against him as a fit subject for criminal prosecution in addition to the civil proceedings, he declared, but had been deterred by the defendants' retention of both the attorney general and the solicitor general as counsel in the latter. The law officers' claim of an exclusive right to conduct assize prosecutions had precluded him from employing counsel of his own to act for him.

The assembly appointed a select committee to inquire into the law officers' duty with respect to the administration of criminal justice.[8] In its report, the committee pointed out the conflict of interest produced by the law officers' monopoly, but its inquiry into the legality of their claim was inconclusive. John Walpole Willis of the Court of King's Bench, who had arrived from England less than six months previously, gave an authoritative account of the English practice and stated his belief that there any barrister was entitled to be employed to conduct any ordinary prosecution. He defined two classes of exceptions: first, 'all matters of revenue, treason, and personal rights of the crown, and those under its immediate protection, as the affairs of lunatics and charities,' and second, misdemeanours prosecuted in the crown office or by ex-officio information (political offences in respect to which the government chose to avoid the normal procedure of indictment before a grand jury). When it came to Upper Canadian practice, however, the witnesses were all but unanimous in declaring that the monopoly had always been upheld, but no explanation was advanced beyond the assumption that the Court of King's Bench had always sanctioned it and always would.[9]

The only shadow of an exception was the case of *R. v. Elrod* (1824).[10] The defendant having failed to appear in answer to the indictment, a leading barrister, William Warren Baldwin, moved for a writ of outlawry to compel his appearance and the court asked the crown officers if they consented to Baldwin's right of motion. At first the attorney general raised a doubt on the ground that the alleged offence was a capital crime and all such prosecutions in Upper Canada were conducted by the crown lawyers. When the motion was renewed, however, Robinson informed the court that he could find no authority against Baldwin's right to move. The case led Baldwin's son Robert, testifying before the select committee four years later, to infer that the court and the attorney general had not been entirely sure of the crown officers' right to monopolize prosecutions at the assizes. But the matter had been one of instituting process rather than conducting a prosecution, and the younger Baldwin soon turned out to be mistaken in his understanding of Attorney General Robinson's position at any rate.

At the Home District assizes of April 1828, Robinson brought four indictments for libel – the first since the prosecution of Bartemas Ferguson in 1819 – against an anti-government journalist, Francis Collins. Two of the indictments were requested by Solicitor General Boulton and another official, Samuel Peters Jarvis, for remarks on a fatal duel of 1817, in which Boulton had been Jarvis's second. Jarvis had also played a leading part in the types riot and had published a pamphlet justifying it,[11] and Collins's strictures on him had appeared in a discussion of either the riot or the pamphlet. Another indictment arose from remarks on the assize grand jury, of which Jarvis happened to be a member, as were Boulton's brother and several others who had been involved in either the riot or the duel or were intimate with those who had.[12]

When, therefore, Robinson moved to arraign Collins on the fourth indictment, which concerned an attack upon the lieutenant governor, Sir Peregrine Maitland (app. 3, O, doc. 1), Collins complained of the injustice of indicting him for his remarks on notorious outrages while most of the participants in those outrages had escaped prosecution. He insisted on prosecuting the types rioters and both seconds in the duel in order (he said) to compel Robinson to do his duty by conducting the proceedings. The presiding judge, Mr Justice Willis, had fallen out with the attorney general and most of York's high society. Willis heard Collins despite the attorney general's objections. When Collins doubted that either the grand jury or the law officers could be trusted to do their duty impartially, the judge assured him that he, Willis, would see that everyone did his duty.

Robinson thereupon drew up indictments and presented them with supporting evidence to the grand jury, which found a true bill in each case. When the first came up for trial, however, Collins applied for leave to have the proceedings conducted not by Robinson but by his own counsel, Robert Baldwin. Thereby he contrived to attack the law officers' monopoly in both its legal and its constitutional aspects. Was the monopoly legal? Even if it was, did it not, in the circumstances prevailing in Upper Canada, create an unconstitutional impediment to the politically impartial administration of justice? Robinson had to defend it on both grounds.

He excused his failure to proceed against the types rioters by asserting that in such cases, where the culprits were open to both criminal and civil proceedings, it was usual to allow the victim to choose his mode of action. Mackenzie had opted for civil proceedings, and Robinson, had he instituted a prosecution on his own initiative, might have been accused of pursuing a criminal penalty in order to reduce the damages Mackenzie was likely to obtain; indeed, friends of the types rioters had asked him to institute proceedings with just that end in view. After the civil trial, however, he had urged the grand jury to ask Mackenzie whether he wished to press criminal charges as well, and Mackenzie had declined to do so. Robinson noted that in England, when an individual was subjected to criminal proceedings for an act which had already incurred a civil penalty, it was usual for him to apply to the attorney general to exercise his discretionary power of staying the prosecution by entering a *nolle prosequi*.[13] Robinson had contravened that practice in the present case in order to protect the grand jury from subsequent accusations of bias in favour of the rioters.

The larger question – that of the law officers' monopoly – was one on which Robinson had already given his opinion at least twice, though never in public. In 1818 a Scottish colonizer, the Earl of Selkirk, had complained of Robinson's refusal to prosecute an imperial official who had allegedly mistreated a party of Selkirk's settlers. Robinson had replied that, in such a case, a prosecutor was at liberty to employ private counsel: the crown officer's abstinence meant only that the costs of the prosecution would not be borne by the government. Thus the law officers' inaction could not entail a failure of justice. On the other hand, Robinson insisted that the attorney general had a legal right to assume the conduct (personally or by delegate) of any prosecution; the English officer's customary abstinence from the conduct of ordinary prosecutions represented an exercise of official discretion, and a prosecutor's right to choose counsel was subject to that discretion. Now, in 1828, Robinson reiterated these arguments in court and acted accordingly. Declining to act on the murder indictment because he thought it groundless, he let Robert Baldwin conduct the proceedings. But since it was the law officers' duty and right 'to conduct all Criminal Prosecutions for which they thought there was Ground,' he insisted on prosecuting the types rioters himself.[14]

After the April assizes and the critical report of the assembly select committee, Robinson sent a circular to the provincial bar asking its members to state any instance in which they thought him to have failed in his duty with respect to criminal prosecutions. This circular evoked a swingeing rebuke from William Warren Baldwin, who cited four cases, including the types riot and the attack on George Rolph. Much of Baldwin's rebuke went beyond the matter of criminal prosecutions to condemn Robinson for failing, as head of the bar and a master of articled law students, to insist on proper standards of professional decorum, but he censured the law officers and the government for failing to uphold standards of public decorum by acting aggressively against Mackenzie's and Rolph's assailants, and he blamed Solicitor General Boulton in the latter case for representing individuals whom he should have been prosecuting.[15]

Baldwin's other examples were cases of misconduct by magistrates. One involved Singleton Gardiner, whose outspoken criticism of the London District magistrates had subjected him to judicial harassment and wrongful imprisonment.[16] Gardiner had won a verdict for trespass and false imprisonment against two of his persecutors at the assizes, but this had been reversed on a technicality in the Court of King's Bench, Robinson defending. Baldwin condemned Robinson for his failure to vindicate the rule of law by instituting criminal proceedings against the two magistrates: 'I thought the defendants fit subjects for a criminal information at the instance of the Attorney General or at least they should have been omitted in the Commission of the Peace. I felt the whole matter highly discreditable to the jurisprudence of the Country; whether you knew all the facts I will not say; but sufficient must have come to your knowledge to have made your official interference both proper and necessary.'[17] The second case concerned Boulton's failure to institute proceedings against certain Gore District magistrates for neglecting to arrest two perpetrators of a brutal rape, presumably (wrote Baldwin) because the culprits had also been complicit in the tar-and-feather outrage.

THE TRIAL OF FRANCIS COLLINS

According to Collins himself, his conduct at the York assizes was prompted by the four indictments, which he cited as evidence of his enemies' intention to wage a 'war of extermination' against him.[18] Collins's assertion may well have been correct, given his record of hostility to the government, but the war could only have been intensified by his collaboration in the attack on the administration of justice. Although there is no direct evidence, there can be little doubt that the controversy of 1828 was engineered by leaders of the provincial opposition – principally John Rolph and the Baldwins – with the connivance of Forsyth, Collins, and perhaps Willis, among others; the two laymen, at any rate, are unlikely to have acted as they did unless instigated by their legal and political advisers.[19] A revealing letter from George Rolph to Dr Baldwin expresses the wish that Collins should attend the next Gore District quarter sessions in order to report the proceedings.[20] The letter is undated, but the sessions may have been those of April 1828, when the grand jury, apparently unprompted, presented ten men for their part in the attack on Rolph and declared that the circumstances of the crime and the stature of the accused convinced them that the offence ought to be tried in the Court of King's Bench. When the magistrates declined to cooperate, John Rolph produced a writ of certiorari, signed by Willis, commanding the magistrates to stay the proceedings and transfer the indictments to the King's Bench. This episode was not reported in the *Canadian Freeman*, perhaps because Collins was detained at York by the libel indictments, but his collaboration with the opposition probably influenced the attorney general's attitude towards him from the time of the April assizes if not earlier.[21]

Indeed, Robinson scarcely tried to mask his animosity. After the attorney general's ritual subjection to the rule of law in April, Willis suggested that Robinson drop the libel prosecutions in order to restore harmony. Robinson would not do so, consenting only to hold the proceedings over to the next assizes 'in order to see if there would be any improvement in the conduct of the Press, of which he had but little hopes.' Robert Baldwin condemned this as an unconstitutional infringement on the liberty of the press, but Robinson held fast. That very day William Lyon Mackenzie was presented for a libel on the House of Assembly, allegedly uttered in an article on the select committee's report on the law officers' monopoly. He and Collins were bound over to appear at the next assizes, the latter on the charge of libelling the grand jury. For his part, Collins 'assured the court and the Attorney General that if they wished to soften down his editorial conduct by keeping indictments of this kind hanging over his head *in terrorem*, they were never more mistaken in their lives, as it would only cause him to bring out his remarks with increased severity.'[22]

Throughout the summer Collins kept his word, reporting generously on subsequent developments in the tar-and-feather outrage and on the controversy caused by the suspension of judge Willis in June. During the autumn assizes he contrived to insult two judges of the King's Bench: Christopher Hagerman, who had been appointed temporarily to replace Willis, for his handling of Michael Vincent's trial for murder,[23] and Levius Peters Sherwood for his conduct at the arraignment of the editor of the *Upper Canada Herald*, Hugh Thomson, on a charge of libel against the lieutenant governor. Thomson, a member of the House of Assembly, was required to give bail not only for his appearance at trial but also for his good behaviour, a proceeding that Collins denounced as 'an act of open tyranny – subversive alike of the freedom of the Press and the liberty of the subject. It is a stretch of arbitrary power that dare not be attempted in England, where in all cases of ordinary libel, the person indicted is merely bound over, *on his own recognizance*, to take his trial ... In Ireland, too, even in rebellion ... no such measure was resorted to. – No, this violation of British rights was left to be introduced into British jurisprudence by some of the agents of mis-rule in Lower Canada, and then by Judge Sherwood ... into this colony.'[24] Besides attacking the administration of justice, Collins expressed himself freely on other political topics.

At the Home District assizes in October, Robinson duly summoned Collins to answer for his alleged libel on the lieutenant governor, on which he had evaded trial in April. To Robinson's chagrin, Collins proved from the record that he had not been arraigned on this charge in April and vindicated, against the attorney general's strenuous opposition, his right to traverse to the next assizes. On being required, like Thomson, to give bail for good behaviour, however, Collins opted to go to trial at once. He was acquitted, Robert Baldwin defending in John Rolph's absence, only to be arraigned on new charges arising from his comments on the foregoing proceedings and on an apparent breach of duty by Robinson in his capacity as legislative draftsman (see app. 3, O, docs. 2, 3). The impugned matter referred solely to Robinson and included only fleeting references to Boulton and Hagerman, yet the indictment (presumably authored by Robinson) alleged a libel upon them too, also in their official capacities, and hence upon 'the administration of justice in this province.'[25]

Both John Rolph's address to the jury and the controversy surrounding the verdict illuminate the trial's significance. Rolph placed it squarely in the context of the larger scandal over political partiality in the administration of justice by reading attacks on the anti-government majority of the House of Assembly that had appeared in the official *Upper Canada Gazette* and the subsidized Kingston *Chronicle*. These offences had passed unprosecuted while Collins was pursued with 'charges more of a ludicrous than of a serious character, in the apparent hope, deduced from the doctrine of chances, of insuring success with one out of so many.'[26] Robinson's inconsistency proved (said Rolph) that his pursuit of Collins originated not in an impartial concern for the public peace but in a desire to overawe the anti-government press.

When Rolph came to the details of the indictment, he seems to have concentrated almost entirely on Collins's allegation that Robinson had uttered an 'open and palpable falsehood' concerning his arraignment.[27] He suggested that the word *falsehood* meant an untrue statement but not, like *lie*, one that was intentionally untrue. He maintained, however, that Collins had had ample cause to suspect that Robinson had been lying and to complain bitterly of the attorney general's dangerous errors. Rolph said little or nothing about the charges relative to Hagerman, Boulton, and the Burlington Bay Canal Act, probably counting on the jury to dismiss the first two as trivial and accept Collins's remarks on the act as fair comment. He also ignored the words 'native malignancy,' perhaps hoping that these too would pass for fair comment in view of Robinson's persecution of Collins and the pertinacity with which he had denied the latter's right to traverse.

If so, Rolph was disappointed. After five hours, the jury returned with a verdict of 'guilty of a libel upon the Attorney General only.' What happened next is unclear. According to Collins and his supporters, Hagerman, substituting for the sick Sherwood, refused to receive the verdict and insisted that the jury bring in a verdict on the indictment as a whole, whereupon they retired again and returned with a verdict of guilty.[28] Hagerman explained that he would have received the first verdict had not Rolph insisted that the indictment contained only one count – that of a libel on the administration of justice – and that the jury's return amounted, therefore, to a verdict of not guilty. He, Hagerman, had replied that he did not think that the jury intended to acquit Collins, but rather to indicate that the libel was contained only in the words referring to Robinson; accordingly, he had told the jury that they might find a general verdict of guilty if they found that any part of the article constituted a libel on the administration of justice. These instructions had formed the basis of the jury's general verdict.[29] Hagerman's account is plausible, but it runs against testimony elicited by a select committee of the assembly. This indicates that the only words upon which Collins was convicted were 'native malignancy,' not 'open and palpable falsehood' or his substantive strictures on Robinson's official conduct.[30]

What really made the case notorious was the sentence imposed by Sherwood and Hagerman, sitting together. They condemned Collins to a year's imprisonment and a fine of £50, and further required him to give personal bail in the amount of £400 and two sureties in the amount of £100 each for his good behaviour for three years from the end of his sentence. The prisoner was to remain in prison until he complied with these conditions. The blatantly repressive, not to say vindictive, nature of this punishment brought every part of the proceedings into question, leading to the appointment of the assembly select committee and the adoption of strong resolutions by the house. These impugned Sherwood's charge to the jury, with some justice, as a prejudicial deviation from the record and accused Hagerman of acting as judge in his own cause. The latter's insistence on a general verdict was denounced as making Collins appear guilty of charges of which the jury had acquitted him, 'whereby false grounds were afforded upon the record for an oppressive and unwarrantable sentence.' The amount of the bail was condemned as amounting in practice to a sentence of imprisonment for life (app. 3, O, doc. 7).

Collins himself remarked that, a year earlier, a man convicted of beating and kicking another to death had been sentenced to the same term of imprisonment, fined £10, and released without sureties.[31] But as Sherwood admitted (app. 3, O, doc. 5), Collins's sentence had been estimated not according to any abstract ideal of just punishment but with a view to deterrence. Whether the offence to be deterred was that of which the jury

had intended to convict Collins, Sherwood did not say. The vindictiveness of Sherwood's charge, and the tenor of his explanation to Lieutenant
Governor Sir John Colborne, lent colour to the notion that Collins had
been punished for offences that did not appear on the indictment, such as
his pertinacity in prosecuting the judge's son Henry for riot and his
brother-in-law, Solicitor General Boulton, for murder. At any rate the
English law officers, when the matter was referred to them, reported that
the punishment was excessive by English standards and recommended
that both sentence and bond be reduced to one half.[32]

POLITICS AND THE LAW OF LIBEL

The prosecution of Collins, and the indictment of Mackenzie and Thomson, illustrate the character of British and Upper Canadian constitutionalism in the 1820s. The civil commotions of the seventeenth century had
established the principle that the monarch could do no wrong and that
the faults of his government were those of his advisers, who accordingly
were answerable to parliament for the administration of the realm. Originally this accountability was confined to illegal or unconstitutional conduct, but during the eighteenth century it was increasingly extended to
political matters. However, even this enhanced conception of responsible
government advantaged only that small minority of British subjects
which was actually (as distinct from formally) enfranchised by an inegali-
tarian constitution. The great majority even of adult males remained dis-
enfranchised, and their political disabilities were reinforced by an array
of legal or quasi-legal impediments to the free expression of political
opinion. In the interval between the Seven Years' War and the War of
American Independence, some of these impediments were judicially dis-
countenanced, but new sanctions were taking shape all the time. One was
the doctrine of scandalizing the court, which authorized a judge to punish criticism of his judicial conduct as a contempt of court.[33]

   As Philip Hamburger has demonstrated, the whole law of libel as it
existed at the end of the eighteenth century was a coinage of this nature.
Originally confined to manuscripts that, by virtue of their defamatory
nature, were deemed liable to cause a breach of the peace, it was judicially extended in the eighteenth century to printed publications that criticized the government and its officers. By this means the judges made up
for older methods of controlling the press which had become unusable in
the wake of the Glorious Revolution.[34] Fox's Libel Act of 1792 redressed
the balance somewhat in favour of liberty of expression, but over the next

thirty years judges did their best to construe the act narrowly, preserving what they could of that power to determine libel of which parliament had intended to deprive them.[35]

The array of repressive doctrines that made up the law of libel was supplemented by procedural expedients which allowed the government or the courts to inflict 'punishment before trial.'[36] The chief of these was the ex officio information, which Robinson employed against Bartemas Ferguson in 1819 but – recognizing its unpopularity[37] – abstained from using in 1828. Instead he resorted to the procedure of binding to good behaviour, whereby the defendant was obliged upon indictment to post bond in the amount determined by the court and ran the risk of forfeiting it should he subsequently utter a libel. This procedure was condemned as inappropriate to the crime of libel, a uniquely indeterminate offence in that it depended on a jury's judgment as to whether the words constituted an offence or not.[38] Apologists for the procedure traced it back to a fourteenth-century statute, ignoring the fact that the statute had nothing to do with libel (app. 3, O, doc. 6). It was in fact enacted to control the lawlessness of soldiers returned from King Edward III's wars with France, and its extension to the crime of libel was but one of several judge-made applications with which it had become encrusted over the centuries.[39] Touching libel in its traditional form – that of a defamatory writing tending to a breach of the peace – the extension may not have been unjustified, but the use of a medieval statute to constrain the press was quite antithetical to what libertarian Whigs supposed to be the spirit of the Glorious Revolution, and the words of Lord Ashburton (the eminent eighteenth-century lawyer John Dunning)[40] quoted by the House of Assembly (app. 3, O, doc. 7) vividly express their resentment of the novelty. As Robinson noted, however (app. 3, O, doc. 9), Dunning's scorn had not sufficed to outlaw it, and it was employed in the United States as well as England.[41]

Such was the law of libel as received in Upper Canada. According to judge Sherwood (app. 3, O, doc. 5), it permitted 'proper and decent' criticism of public men and measures while discountenancing 'calumny and abuse'; according to its critics, it permitted calumny and abuse against opponents of the government while denying them the right to reply in kind. Certainly, if tone was the criterion, there is nothing to distinguish the indicted words of Mackenzie, Thomson, and Collins from a hundred other articles on both sides of the political debate. Mackenzie's offence was little more than an injunction to his readers to 'turn the rascals out' at the approaching general election; the 'communication' for which Thomson was indicted was a virtual reiteration of a report of a committee of the House of Assembly, albeit one that Thomson himself had initiated and chaired[42]; in both of Collins's trials, the matter at issue was arguably fair comment.

Of course, the law cared nothing for the truth of the objectionable words, as Sherwood informed the convicting jury; it cared only that they conduced to a breach of the peace (app. 3, O, doc. 4). Ostensibly, it did not matter whether the likely target of violence was the victim of the libel or the libeller himself. The prospect that Sherwood conjured up in his charge was that of violence against Collins; and it was no idle prospect, for the tendency of criticism of the attorney general to provoke a breach of the peace had been amply demonstrated by the types riot of 1826, and Sherwood's own son had been one of the rioters. But this specious even-handedness masked a strong bias in favour of the crown and its high officers, any criticism of whom, no matter how accurate, could be impeached as a danger to peace, order, and good government. That danger could fall far short of any immediate prospect of violent disorder, let alone an intention on the author's part to promote such disorder. Collins's exposure of the attorney general's animosity towards him, admittedly expressed in language coloured by months of legal harassment, was deplorable in Sherwood's eyes, not merely as an offence against John Beverley Robinson but as 'tending to the obstruction of Justice, the deterioration of a fair and unbiassed trial by Jury, and the consequent taking away from all Courts a proportion of their power to do justice' (app. 3, O, doc. 8).

S.F. Wise has drawn attention to the way in which the Upper Canadian constitution allowed the administrative elite to act as a political party while pretending to be above politics. As a party of officeholders who were not constitutionally accountable to colonial public opinion, they were able to pursue their political ends through their performance of the ostensibly non-partisan function of administering the king's government. Not only the ideology of loyalism but the very structures of government abetted the elite's propensity to identify their private interests with the public interest and themselves with the state.[43] Collins's case shows how the law of libel worked to the same effect by defining the sphere of politics in such a fashion as to accord public men, at the discretion of the attorney general, a partial immunity from hostile criticism.

Sherwood's vindication of his and Hagerman's conduct was redolent of the premise that Upper Canadian justice was neutral and the judges impartial servants of the public interest. 'The Judges have never interfered in the least with politics,' he wrote, 'and the libel in question has no allusion to politics, yet all attacks on the Court of King's Bench seem to have originated with a political party' (app. 3, O, doc. 8). Who would guess from this that a political bias in the administration of justice was one of the fundamental issues between Robinson and Collins? Or that Robinson's prosecution of Collins was arguably an example of such bias? Or that Mr Justice Sherwood had recently been a plaintiff before Mr Justice Hagerman in a civil action which had been a cause of scandal both in its own right and by virtue of its connection to another scandal in which Sherwood's brother-in-law, Solicitor General Boulton, was the chief object of complaint?[44] Sherwood's remarks inhabit a universe of discourse in which a judge might be supposed to feel less animosity towards a man who had been acquitted of libelling him than one who had been convicted of doing so (doc. 8). More perniciously still, for all Sherwood's lip-service to the ideal of free speech (doc. 5), the law of libel embodied the principle that, so far as the press was concerned, neither the monarch, nor his advisers, nor any high officer of the government could do wrong.

Granted, the operation of the law was subjected to public opinion as expressed by grand and petty juries. In Upper Canada, however, it was a leading complaint against the administration of justice that assize grand juries were dominated by the local magistrates and the selection of petty juries subject to the influence of the sheriff. In Canada, as in England, it was not until government itself was acknowledged as a legitimate object of party-political competition, and subjected to public opinion by political means, that the eighteenth-century conception of criminal libel was finally undermined.

NOTES

1 Paul Romney, *Mr Attorney: The Attorney General for Ontario in Court, Cabinet, and Legislature, 1791–1899* (Toronto: Osgoode Society/University of Toronto Press 1986), at 107, 114, 137, 290–6; Paul Romney, 'From Constitutionalism to Legalism: Trial by Jury, Responsible Government, and the Rule of Law in the Canadian Political Culture,' *Law and History Review*, vol. 7 (1989), 130.

2 Douglas Hay and Francis Snyder, 'Using the Criminal Law, 1750–1850: Policing, Private Prosecution, and the State,' in *Policing and Prosecution in Britain, 1750–1850*, ed. Hay and Snyder (Oxford: Clarendon Press 1989), 16.

3 Romney, *Mr Attorney*, at 46–8, 122–3.

4 Paul Romney, 'From the Types Riot to the Rebellion: Elite Ideology, Anti-legal

Sentiment, Political Violence, and the Rule of Law in Upper Canada,' *OH*, vol. 79 (1987), 113.

5 *The History of the Destruction of the Colonial Advocate Press by Officers of the Provincial Government of Upper Canada and Law Students of the Attorney and Solicitor General* (York, U.C.: 1827), at 14.

6 Romney, *Mr Attorney*, at 109–11.

7 Ibid., at 50, 75, 81; J.Ll.J. Edwards, *The Law Officers of the Crown* (London: Sweet and Maxwell 1964), passim.

8 Romney, *Mr Attorney*, at 115–22.

9 Ibid., 128–9.

10 Taylor's King's Bench Reports 120.

11 *Statement of Facts Relating to the Trespass on the Printing Press in the Possession of Mr. William Lyon M'Kenzie in June 1826* (York, U.C.: n.d.). There is a copy in CO 42/385/52–68.

12 *Canadian Freeman* (York), 17 April 1828. On Collins, see H.P. Gundy's biography of him in *DCB* 6: 164. The number or numbers in which the libels appeared are not extant.

13 Romney, *Mr Attorney*, at 130–2.

14 Ibid., at 123–8, 132–3 (quotation at 133).

15 Romney, *Mr Attorney*, at 133–5; Romney, 'From the Types Riot to the Rebellion,' at 130–1.

16 Romney, *Mr Attorney*, at 107–9.

17 MTRL, Baldwin Room, William Warren Baldwin Papers, B 103, Baldwin to Robinson (draft), 31 May 1828.

18 *Canadian Freeman*, 1 May 1828.

19 The likelihood of Willis's participation has recently been questioned, but not convincingly: see Leo A. Johnson, 'John Walpole Willis's Judicial Career in Upper Canada, 1827–28: The Research Impact of Computerized Documentation on a Non-controversial Theme,' *OH*, vol. 85 (1993), 154 and passim.

20 William Warren Baldwin Papers, unbound misc. papers, file 'miscellaneous,' G. Rolph to Baldwin, n.d.

21 Romney, *Mr Attorney*, at 111–13; and see *Canadian Freeman*, 22 May 1828.

22 *Canadian Freeman*, 24 April 1828.

23 *Canadian Freeman*, 2 Oct. 1828; see also ibid., 11 Sept., 18 Sept. 1828.

24 Ibid., 18 Sept. 1828. For Thomson's indictment, see *Upper Canada Herald* (Kingston), 17 Sept. 1828.

25 *Canadian Freeman*, 16 Oct., 23 Oct. 1828.

26 'You heard the learned council for the crown (the zealous prosecutor in his own case, and the supine observer of the most glorious libels against others,) expatiate upon the dreadful crime of libelling a court of justice. Strange it is

that the learned gentleman never had the horrors against libelling the high court of parliament, or attempted to prosecute those who were branding it with infamy': ibid., 6 Nov. 1828.

27 Rolph's address is printed apparently in full, as though, like Sherwood's charge (app. 3, O, doc. 4) it was taken down in shorthand by Collins and transcribed by him for the typesetter. My discussion of his argument is based on that surmise. In his charge, however, when discussing the words 'this we view,' Sherwood quotes Rolph as making a remark that does not appear in the reported speech.

28 *Canadian Freeman*, 30 Oct. 1828; ibid., 25 Dec. 1828; JHAUC, 1829, Appendix, 'Report in Collins' Case,' evidence of James Small and Bradshaw McMurray. See also doc. 10 in app. 3, O.

29 CO 42/388/142–9 (Hagerman to Sir John Colborne, 26 March 1829). See also Sherwood's remarks on the subject: ibid., 108–9.

30 'Report in Collins' Case,' evidence of Patrick Kenny and Bradshaw McMurray; *Canadian Freeman*, 30 Oct. 1828.

31 *Canadian Freeman*, 27 Nov. 1828.

32 CO 42/390/49–50 (J. Scarlett and Edward B. Sugden to Sir George Murray, 30 June 1829). See also app. 3, O, doc. 8.

33 Douglas Hay, 'Contempt by Scandalizing the Court: A Political History of the First Hundred Years,' *Osgoode Hall Law Journal*, vol. 25 (1987), 431; Robert R. Rea, *The English Press in Politics, 1760–1774* (Lincoln, Neb.: University of Nebraska Press 1963).

34 Philip Hamburger, 'The Development of the Law of Seditious Libel and the Control of the Press,' *Stanford Law Review*, vol. 37 (1984–5), 661; and see the introduction to this volume.

35 Thomas Cooper, *A Treatise on the Law of Libel and the Liberty of the Press* (New York: G.F. Hopkins and Son 1830; repr. Arno Press 1972), at 73–5, 77–8.

36 William H. Wickwar, *The Struggle for the Freedom of the Press, 1819–1832* (London: George Allen and Unwin 1928; repr. New York: Johnson Reprint 1932), at 37–40.

37 Romney, *Mr Attorney*, at 329–30.

38 *Canadian Freeman*, 18 Sept., 20 Nov. 1828.

39 Richard Burn, *The Justice of the Peace and Parish Officer*, 22nd ed., 5 vols. (London: 1814), 5: at 250, cites the early-seventeenth-century jurist Michael Dalton as authority for the application of the proceeding to libellers. Burn's account of the proliferation of the offences to which the proceeding was applicable was cited in the Upper Canadian press in support of the contention that this application was illegal: *Canadian Freeman*, 20 Nov. 1828, quoting *Brockville Recorder*.

40 See DNB 6: 213 and Rea, *English Press in Politics*, passim.

41 On the United States see Norman L. Rosenberg, *Protecting the Best Men: An Interpretive History of the Law of Libel* (Chapel Hill, N.C.: University of North Carolina Press 1986), at 94–6, 106–7; on England see Wickwar, *Struggle for the Freedom of the Press*, at 39.

42 H. Pearson Gundy, 'Hugh C. Thomson: Editor, Publisher and Politician, 1791–1834,' in *To Preserve and Defend: Essays on Kingston in the Nineteenth Century*, ed. Gerald Tulchinsky (Montreal: McGill-Queen's University Press 1976), at 216–17.

43 S.F. Wise, 'The Reform Tradition in Upper Canada,' in Wise, *God's Peculiar Peoples: Essays on Political Culture in Nineteenth Century Canada*, ed. A.B. McKillop and Paul Romney (Ottawa: Carleton University Press 1993), at 176–9.

44 Romney, *Mr Attorney*, at 71–82, 142–5, 151.

16

Liberty of the Press in Early Prince Edward Island, 1823–9*

J.M. BUMSTED

The development of the concept of liberty of the press in early British North America is a topic that has a certain old-fashioned liberal ring to it. Predictably, then, it has not drawn enormous attention from Canadian scholars in recent years, although it has not entirely disappeared from consideration. Liberty of the press was the theme of a 1974 article by H.P. Gundy entitled 'Liberty and Licence of the Press in Upper Canada.'[1] In 1982 J. Murray Beck devoted a chapter of the first volume of his biography of Joseph Howe to the 1835 trial for seditious libel, probably the most famous single court case on the subject in Canadian history.[2] Two years later, Gwendolyn Davies offered a study of libel outside a national-security context, focusing on Halifax newspaper editor Edmund Ward who was convicted for libelling one of his contributors, James Irving.[3] In 1994 Barry Cahill analysed the case of William Wilkie of Halifax, convicted of seditious libel in 1820, and in this volume he revisits the Howe case.[4] Sedition and libel trials in Upper Canada, based on common-law doctrines and the province's Sedition Act of (1804), were examined by Barry Wright in an article published in 1992.[5] A number of other early trials have been recently discussed more briefly in *Dictionary of Canadian Biography* sketches of pioneering editors and printers who tested the law (principally concerning contempt and libel) in the years before 1843,

*The author wishes to acknowledge the financial assistance of the Social Sciences and Humanities Research Council of Canada, which made possible the research on which this article is based.

when the British parliament passed a statute allowing truth as a defence in such court actions.[6]

Before 1843, the law concerning libel and contempt was most unclear and quite variable from one British North American colony to another, depending on the way it had been tested and interpreted within the local court system.[7] Colonial American modifications of earlier English principles in favour of editorial freedom did not appear to extend to remaining British colonies after the revolution.[8] The English legislative reforms of the law of libel at the end of the eighteenth and the beginning of the nineteenth century, notably Fox's Libel Act of 1792, had come too late to be received routinely into the various provinces of British North America as part of the inheritance of English statutes. The statute post-dated most colonial reception dates for English legislation. Wright argues that, on the basis of reception, Fox's act was erroneously excluded on occasion in Upper Canada.[9] As noted in the introduction to this volume, the act provided that in the trial of a libel the jury could give a general verdict upon the entire issue and would not be required by the court to find the defendant guilty simply on the basis of proof of publication. The act continued to allow, as in other criminal cases, the court to direct the jury on the matter in issue between the crown and the defendant or defendants, and the jury to find a special verdict. It appears that colonial judges who applied Fox's principles did so largely at their own discretion.

The most typical sort of case involved an editor or printer publishing an anonymous article or letter to the editor that was highly critical of the government; he would then be summoned to court to respond to an action for libel initiated by a colony's attorney general or solicitor general on behalf of a member or members of the elite 'compacts' that dominated most of the colonies of British North America before the introduction of responsible government. The action might be for seditious libel, for criminal libel, occasionally for civil libel, and for contempt in a legislature. The number of prosecutions varied in the provinces; there appears to have been only two seditious libel cases in Nova Scotia between 1794 and 1835, while in Upper Canada there were well over thirty common-law sedition prosecutions between 1794 and 1829, in addition to summary deportations under the Sedition Act and parliamentary-privilege actions for contempt.[10] In 1820 in Nova Scotia, William Wilkie – who had written an attack on Halifax's civil authorities published in Anthony Holland's *Acadian Recorder* – was tried for seditious libel.[11] The judge charged the jury that they should acquit if they honestly thought that the author had written with an eye to the public good. Wilkie, who had not only acknowledged the libel in court but had expanded upon it 'in terms so much more offensive than the language of the libel itself,' got no sympathy from the jury, which convicted after only a five-minute deliberation.[12] He was summarily sentenced to two years at hard labour in the local workhouse. On the other hand, as Barry Cahill's essay in this volume indicates, Joseph Howe was acquitted by his jury after defending himself without legal counsel.[13]

Although the oppressive behaviour of the officeholding oligarchies was indisputable, the assemblies that often opposed them were little better. It was an open question whether a critical editor (or author) received worse treatment before the bar of a court of law or before the bar of a House of Assembly, as more than one editor could attest. The essay by Murray Greenwood and Barry Wright in the present volume examines the 1808 case of Joseph Willcocks, who was thrown into jail by the Upper Canadian legislature for contempt of the privileges of the house, and other contempt cases.[14] In a second contribution to this volume, Barry Wright studies Bartemas Ferguson's heavy punishment on a conviction for seditious libel in connection with Robert Gourlay's reform agitation.[15] The worst treatment of all was extralegal, coming at the hands of anonymous mobs. These tactics were employed in Newfoundland and Upper Canada, although they were not common. In Newfoundland, Henry Winton, editor of the *Public Ledger and Newfoundland General Advertiser*, lost his ears to assailants unknown in 1835.[16] The destruction of William Lyon Mackenzie's printing presses and other forms of 'rough justice' have been documented by Paul Romney and forms a context to his essay in this collection on criminal prosecution in the Upper Canada of the 1820s.[17]

As has already been suggested, no two prominent 'liberty of the press' cases, much less the cases in any single province of British North America, were exactly alike. Some editors and authors had legal counsel and others defended themselves; some were charged under criminal law and some under civil law; some were found guilty and others innocent; some were let off lightly and others received what today seem like cruel sentences, often actually carried out. By the 1820s most provinces in British North America had accepted the recently emerging English doctrine that editors could report with relative impunity upon legislative debates and court proceedings, even reproducing potentially libellous statements issued under parliamentary privilege in the course of debate.[18] In 1826 a legislative committee in Upper Canada headed by John Rolph reported that 'in every free country the public have given every encouragement to the reporting of legislative proceedings; and the English house of commons has in no case, attempted with success to embarrass or suppress their publication. Some of the most valuable sources of parliamentary history, relating to the usage and privileges of parliament and the liberties of the people have been derived from the direct encouragement of such publications by the public, and the tacit consent of the legislative assembly.' In most provinces, therefore, cases after 1820 did not normally involve the reporting on or reprinting of official proceedings, but rather editorial comment upon those proceedings or upon the character of officials of the government.

To almost any generalization an exception can be found, and the absence of cases challenging official reporting does not apply to the tiny province of Prince Edward Island. Perhaps no province had a stranger history with regard to liberty of the press than that isolated but tumultuous colony in the Gulf of St Lawrence. But no province had a more curious history, period, or stranger legal affairs. The editor involved was James Douglass Haszard of the *Prince Edward Island Register*, and, in contrast to the more notorious trials of the time in other provinces, the issue on the Island was indeed the right of an editor to reprint verbatim and without editorial comment a true record of certain public proceedings, particularly petitions to the crown complaining of official malfeasance, debates in the House of Assembly, and transcriptions of court cases.[19] There were two separate rounds of litigation, one in 1823 in the Court of Chancery and one in 1829 in the Supreme Court. In neither case was Haszard prosecuted by official request. In both instances prosecution was undertaken by injured parties ostensibly acting privately. Beyond these similarities the two rounds of cases were quite different, and they had quite different results. Together, they tell us a good deal both about colonial awareness of the current state of English law and about local legal practice. They also remind us that the history of the Canadian law must be approached on a province-by-province basis, for each province has its own law and its own legal history.

The 1823 case was, in its own way, unprecedented in either English or colonial jurisprudence in the nineteenth century. The offence was the editorial reprinting in the *Prince Edward Island Register* of a petition to the crown for the recall of the province's lieutenant governor, Charles Douglass Smith.[20] The case was tried in the province's Court of Chancery, upon complaint of the court's master-in-chancery, Ambrose Lane (also Smith's son-in-law), before the chancellor (who just happened to be Smith himself).[21] The charge was not libel, either criminal or civil, but contempt of a prerogative court not governed by the common law. The subsequent trial was the only liberty of the press case in British North America heard in a chancery court, although such courts were more numerous in early British North America than is typically appreciated.[22]

LANE v. HASZARD (1823)

The Political Background

Prince Edward Island's chancery court had been established in the late 1780s by Lieutenant Governor Edmund Fanning.[23] A Loyalist, Fanning had served as a colonial official in North Carolina and New York. Especially in the latter colony, a chancery court had been in operation for many years, at least in part acting as an important political arm of the governor's authority in opposition to the legislature. On the Island, as in the American colonies, chancery had proved a powerful weapon in the hands of a prerogative-conscious governor. In Haszard's case, the charge could have been brought as libel in the Island's Supreme Court of Judicature, where it would have been heard by a jury. Instead, the contempt charge was heard only before the chancellor of the court involved. Since the court involved was not a common law court, and the charge was technically not libel, little of what happened tested normal libel law in the province. Both the petition against Smith and the employment of the Court of Chancery were related, but the connection requires some explanation.

Charles Douglass Smith had been appointed lieutenant governor of Prince Edward Island to succeed J.F.W. DesBarres in 1812, apparently as a client of Lord Grenville, to whom he was distantly related by marriage.[24] His two brothers were both political figures prominent in the government of the time, and Smith had some extremely high Tory notions about the use of the prerogative to achieve his goals.[25] In Prince Edward Island, Smith had quickly recognized that the notorious 'land question' (the entire land surface of the colony had been originally awarded by lottery to private proprietors in 1767) was deeply enmeshed in local politics. There were two parts to the land question after 1813: the forfeiture of township and other lands for failure to fulfil the terms of their allocation, and the question of payment of quitrents to the crown. Smith saw quitrents as an alternate source of revenue for the colony to taxation voted by a legislative assembly with which he was in conflict, and the forfeiture of lands as a way to court popular favour as well as to obtain a source of patronage and influence. Smith did not find an assembly a legislative necessity, insisting that 'the Constitutional Laws of England are the Laws of its Colonies unless & Until modified by Colonial Legislation.'[26] This doctrine in Smith's hands meant that the colony could employ (and even modify) English law by executive fiat to suit its own purposes without requiring local legislation.

As is usually the case in such situations, Smith's despotism was neither totally benevolent nor altruistic. He practised nepotism of the worst kind, was totally paranoid about opposition to his policies, and was quite capable of the most flagrant sort of manipulative behaviour. But at the same time, he did have some notion of the baneful machinations of the local elite, and many of his policies were designed to circumvent the elite's self-interested behaviour, indisputably devoted to the acquisition of land and power. In his own way, Smith was a straightforward man. He broke in horror with Attorney-General William Johnston in 1820 when it became clear that Johnston had been systematically bilking his overseas clients while serving as their agent, although such behaviour had long been standard practice on the Island.[27] In any event, by 1823 the opposition to Smith had grown to include almost the entire political universe of the colony. It began assiduously circulating among the electorate petitions to the crown calling for Smith's recall. This chorus of hostility was orchestrated by Captain John Stewart, who as receiver general of quitrents had earlier made a small fortune by playing the British government off against the proprietors.[28]

One of the major grievances against Smith was his control of the judicial system of the colony. Shortly after his arrival, Smith had decided that the Supreme Court of the colony was part of the elite conspiracy against justice, and he had responded by continuing and even expanding his predecessors' practice of employing the Island's chancery court – in the eighteenth-century American colonial tradition – as a counterweight to the Supreme Court.[29] While Smith's employment of chancery had a certain plausible air of righteousness about it, he was also capable of using that court to settle personal vendettas, however much he insisted on the coincidence of his public and private actions. In 1816 Smith as chancellor had heard complaints of professional misconduct against the Island's leading attorney, James Bardin Palmer, which had resulted in Palmer being disbarred for several years from the chancery court and ultimately from all other Island courts.[30] Not surprisingly, Smith had long regarded Palmer as one of the leaders of opposition to his government. In 1819 crown legal adviser James Stephen, Jr, was highly critical of this disbarment, insisting that Smith's judicial behaviour was not consistent with legal proceedings in England and that his refusal to allow appeal to the Privy Council was both without grounds and unprecedented. Not a single one of the ten charges directly involved Palmer's behaviour before the Court of Chancery, insisted Stephen, and not one had been proved beyond doubt because all rested on unsubstantiated affidavits.[31] Smith dodged a potential bullet by reinstating Palmer, partly because he and that worthy had come to a political understanding.

The Palmer case provided a precedent of sorts, one of employing the chancery court to do political business on behalf of the Smith interests. Thus, it was to be expected that the Smith family would turn to chancery again in 1823, when *Prince Edward Island Register* editor James Douglass Haszard published without editorial comment the petition to the crown of voters from Queen's County calling for Smith's recall. The petition, which had been generated by a committee of seven who had submitted it in writing to the newspaper, was highly critical not only of Smith but of his entire administration. Among other charges it accused Master-in-Chancery Ambrose Lane of levying unwarranted and illegal fees in his official court capacity. Smith had permitted these oppressive and illegal charges and fees, far in excess of those charged by his predecessor and unauthorized by the act of the assembly regulating fees of office, declared the petition, which also complained of informations filed in chancery against supposed trespasses on ungranted lands, a judicial procedure that it claimed was legally unnecessary and ruinously expensive. As we shall see, these criticisms, while plausible and illustrative of impolitic behaviour, were of actions that could not be proved to be illegal. Further, complaints of nepotism could hardly be regarded as even improper, given standards of the time.

The Chancery Trial of 1823

Lane employed James Bardin Palmer as his attorney and brought a civil charge of contempt of court before the chancellor, which was heard beginning on 14 October 1823. This case was an important one for the Island, and it is one of the best documented in the province's early legal history – and probably that of the entire Maritime region. We have two independent sets of law reports, one from the prosecution and the other by defence attorneys Charles Binns and Robert Hodgson. The two reports are not directly at variance but they offer quite different perspectives. The set in the Colonial Office papers offers detailed summaries of Palmer's arguments and little of the defence.[32] The other set, some of the earliest reports published in the region, provides much more detail of the defence and more legal citations offered by the two sides, and it also quotes several interjections from Chancellor Smith which anticipated Gilbert and Sullivan.[33] The main problem with reconciling the two sets of reports is in terms of chronology, a point made by James Stephen in his official report to the Colonial Office on the case.[34] There is also a post-trial 'statement of defence in the form of a law case' from Chancellor Smith to the secretary of state for the colonies, and further details in documents by the Island's attorney general, William Johnston.[35]

With the court's encouragement, a very young and thoroughly intimidated editor, having consulted lawyer Binns, escaped punishment by acknowledging his error and disclosing the names of those responsible for circulating the petition. Neither the newspaper nor its editor was the target of this action. The chancellor remarked as he discharged James Douglass Haszard from the bar, 'I compassionate your youth and inexperience, did I not do so, I would lay you by the heels long enough for you to remember it,' adding later, 'You have delivered your evidence fairly, plainly, clearly, and as became a man, but I caution you, when you publish any thing again, keep clear Sir, of a Chancellor, beware Sir, I say of a Chancellor.'[36]

James Bardin Palmer, on behalf of the plaintiff, insisted that the offending paragraphs in the newspaper were 'libellous & contemptuous reflections on this Court and on the Officer who now complained.' When the chancellor pointed out the trial was not for libel, since chancery was not a court of criminal jurisdiction, Palmer responded that it was important to show the nature of the complaint.[37] He cited Serjeant Hawkins on libel and William Blackstone on contempt:

A contempt may be committed by disobeying or treating with disrespect the Kings writ, or the rules or process of Court by speaking or writing contemptuously of the Court or Judges acting in their judicial capacity by printing false Accounts (or even true ones without proper permission) of causes then depending in Judgment, and by any thing in short that demonstrates a gross want of that regard and respect, which when once Courts of Justice are deprived of their Authority, (so necessary to the good order of the Kingdom) is entirely lost among the People, a Power (says that learned Judge) in the Supreme Court of Justice to suppress such contempts by an *immediate Attachment* of the offender results from the first principles of the judicial establishments, and must be an inseparable attendant upon every superior tribunal.[38]

Such was the law, said Palmer, and it was often applied. This case was flagrant, the motives without mitigation. He could anticipate no defence. The Bill of Rights allowed subjects to petition the king, Palmer argued, but petitioning the monarch and publishing paragraphs in newspapers 'are two very different and distinct acts, though they may relate to the same subject matter.' He intended to move for attachments (arrests for contempt of court) absolute against the seven persons named as the committee. At this point the hearing adjourned.

When the hearing resumed on 16 October, a great crowd pressed to gain admittance to the Court of Chancery. The contempt trial had become high political drama and a major public event. Charles Binns appeared for three of the defendants.[39] Binns, one of the unsung legal heroes of early British North America, insisted that Britons had a constitutional right to petition and to protest against grievances. He admitted that certain passages of the petition 'bore heavily' – the phrase is probably Palmer's since the quotation is from his report on the case – but maintained that people could not be held in contempt merely for printing a petition in a newspaper. The Bill of Rights, insisted Binns, was the rock that his clients stood on, and it could not be discarded. His Majesty's subjects had a right to animadvert with force and strong language in the petitions, and courts had always construed that right generously.[40] Only publication independent of the matter of the petition could be contemptuous, and he cited a case, *Dr. Lake v. King*, which he insisted was a full precedent.[41] This case involved a petition to a committee of the House of Commons, printed by the defendant and circulated among the committee's members, and judgment had been given for the defendant. He also cited *King v. Wright*, where a bookseller defended himself against libelling Horne Tooke by claiming that the paragraph in question was taken from a secret report of a committee of the House of Commons.[42]

Charles Binns went on to insist that it was also legal to publish proceedings of parliament, and here he was immediately contradicted by both the chancellor and Palmer. The chancellor said, 'I will answer you, Sir, at once – it is not lawful to do so.' Binns amended his remarks to state that even if not strictly legal the daily practice still implied assent.[43] The chancellor queried what proceedings in parliament had to do with the subject before the court, demonstrating his tendency to construe precedents most narrowly. Binns continued to insist that it was the birthright of a British subject to state grievances in a petition to the crown. The defence attorney maintained that the publication had been made 'by the committee for the information of those interested, who as yet had not signed the petition, nor given their evidence.' The learned counsels debated the important point of whether or not the petition had been completed. The chancellor insisted that 'it is not this Court that prosecutes at all – it is not the Court, but other persons, bear that in your recollections,' thus emphasizing that this was a private rather than a public complaint.[44]

James Bardin Palmer rose to answer the opposing arguments. The intent of the publication, he maintained, was to rouse the country, and therefore it was not justifiable. The *Dr. Lake v. King* case actually worked against Binns's position, for only part of it had been stated. In that instance, said Palmer, the court had found for the defendant, but solely because he had delivered the printed copy only to members of the committee. 'I may insert slanderous matter in a petition to the House of Commons and present it without prosecution, but if I show this petition to anyone else, I have published a libel.' Such facts were well known, having been published in the Halifax newspapers, presumably in the reports on earlier libel cases. Moreover, Blackstone was improperly cited. That worthy had insisted on the liberty of the press, argued Palmer, but he had gone on to note that this liberty consisted in laying no previous restraint on publication, not 'as foolishly imagined, in a freedom from all censure for criminal matter when once published.' While he had sought to avoid the question of truth, added Palmer, it was nonetheless the case that the paragraphs contained many falsehoods and inaccuracies.

Charles Binns asked the court to refer the matter to some other authority. He insisted that, although Palmer had tried to introduce the doctrine of truth, this was not really at issue. His clients had done nothing but publish their resolutions and what was necessary to introduce them. The chancellor rejected the application for referral. He asked why the resolutions had been published at all, given that publication was not petitioning. Even if one gave full scope to the petitioners, Smith noted, they had brought local government into odium and contempt, and his bounden duty was to punish all contempts. His Excellency went on to note that 'the paragraphs alluded to reflected on the Officer of the Court, and the Court,' and he pronounced their publication to be 'a flagrant contempt of this court . . . leaving all other Matters to be adjudicated by a Criminal Court.' He thus heard Palmer's motion for attachments against all seven defendants and granted them, giving credit to Binns for an able defence 'on the slight and flimsy grounds he had to rest upon.'[45] Smith was quite unnecessarily patronizing in this left-handed compliment, which demonstrated a distinct unwillingness to recognize the force of Binns's arguments. Although both sides had cited a substantial number of precedents in English case law, most of Palmer's precedents had come from the eighteenth century, while Binns had offered more recent English law. The court was then adjourned for ten days; it met again on 27 October.

This final session was again a tumultuous one, attended by a large number of unruly spectators. The court heard motions from Palmer to commit the gentlemen present on attachment (that is, to jail them), and so ordered. At this point the question of which defendants were before the bar was discussed. Palmer presented to the court an affidavit that a constable had particularly sought John Stewart at Mr Sims's house, where he usually lodged when in town, and then had gone to Mr McGregor's house, where he was forcibly denied entry, although he could see McGregor and Stewart through the window and hear their voices, especially Stewart's, which was 'quite remarkable.'[46] The attorney general, William Johnston, at this point stepped forward to deny the constable's affidavit, insisting that he was in the McGregor house himself at the time and Stewart was not present. The entire Island was aware that Stewart was preparing to depart for London to deliver the various petitions against Smith to the crown, were he not apprehended by the sheriff before he could get away. Many suspected that detaining Stewart was behind the entire contempt action. When Palmer subsequently insisted that registrar's fees had not been altered since Johnston had filled that office, the attorney general again rose to contradict the assertion. The chancellor was about to order the court adjourned, and the crier had begun the usual proclamation, when Robert Hodgson begged that His Excellency would delay a few minutes to allow Charles Binns, not yet in court, to be heard. Palmer attempted to argue against such a delay, but Johnston rose yet again, desiring to know if it was being maintained at law that a person in custody under an attachment for contempt could not be heard at the bar. At this point a violent commotion occurred below the bar, with much shouting and clapping of hands. Johnston, after restoring order, threatened to commit the first man who made such noises again.

Charles Binns finally arrived and said that one of the defendants wanted the final judgment on motion rather than on petition, adding that the defendants did not seek to mitigate but wanted to hear sentence of the court immediately before being placed in custody. The chancellor responded, 'Words are but wind, Sir, remember I have a record, Sir, let them petition.' When Binns went on to insist that his clients denied wrongful action, the chancellor responded, 'You plead that do you Sir? Caro bono malas.[47] The attorney general rose as a friend of the court to observe that the whole proceedings were unprecedented, to which the chancellor responded, 'Things occur here [on the Island] every day that never occur elsewhere.' The attorney general replied, 'In that I do most cordially concur,' and the chancellor added, 'And there are assumptions and presumptions which would be suffered nowhere else.'[48] The attorney general maintained that he had no notion of raising a popular commotion. He was 'as much averse to courting popular applause as he was to truckling to arbitrary power or tyranny.' This remark provoked much huzza-ing from the spectators, and the chancellor asked, 'Whence this acclamation Sir?' When order was restored, the attorney general denied imputing to the court the exercise of tyranny and arbitrary power.

According to the later report of Chancellor Smith, the court was continually interrupted by 'huzzas, acclamations, and clapping of hands.' There was not a sufficient force present to place the defendants in custody, he insisted. Outside the courtroom the defendants – linked arm-in-arm and surrounding the chancellor, one of them reading from a written paper – proclaimed that 'we refuse to be delivered to the sergeant at arms and we will pay no costs.'[49] If a court could convert every action of political complaint by construction into a contempt of its authority, argued Charles Binns at the conclusion of his published report, the English constitution was at an end.[50] Attorney General Johnston concurred on perhaps more narrow grounds, subsequently offering as a legal opinion to Lieutenant Governor Smith his view that 'the Cause of proceedings in Chancery summarily to punish for a contempt' in 'this case is erroneous.'[51]

The six defendants attached remained at liberty for some days and then surrendered themselves. By this point John Stewart had managed to get away to England from Pictou, Nova Scotia. Whether Stewart had actually earlier escaped the Island concealed in a cask of fish is not clear, although it remains part of Island legend. His colleagues petitioned the chancellor on 30 October for a final judgment. Smith replied, 'From the Gross Manner in which the *Court* was insulted on the last Court day he does not intend to go there again upon the point in Question until he can be assured that no return of the like conduct will be resorted to.'[52] At the same time, he set the petitioners at liberty until the time of judgment. The whole case, Smith maintained, was an '*unexpected avowal of intended Resistance*' which 'made the matter shoot up into a *Political* Question in consequence of which the advice of the Council was taken.'[53] The government had been vilified, but Smith maintained that he had stayed the judgment for contempt in order to receive instructions from home on this surprisingly contentious case.

The Aftermath of the Trial

While the entire Island awaited the British government's response to the case and to the petition that had sparked it, the case itself and its issues were kept before the public, both in the tiny colony and beyond. James Douglass Haszard made some amends for his pusillanimous behaviour before the bar of chancery by printing the full law reports of the case by Charles Binns in his newspaper. He went even farther by printing a letter to the editor signed by Binns and dated 25 October 1823 (see app. 3. P, doc. 1) which opened, 'There is perhaps nothing more dear to the hearts of British subjects, than the legitimate freedom of the press, and as you have been pleased to suggest a wish, that I would give my best advice for your future government in regard to the insertion of public proceedings in general in your paper, I feel it my bounden duty as a small return for your many acts of kindness, at once to commence my compliance with your wish.'[54] Binns then proceeded skilfully to summarize a progressive view of the current English law on liberty of the press.[55] He did not base his argument on any abstract philosophies about freedom of speech, however, but instead entirely on what he insisted the English law permitted.

Binns began by quoting the recently published opinion of jurist Francis Ludlow Holt on libel, which held that the best interest of the magistracy was truth and that the people had a right to petition and remonstrate with the crown and parliament providing they did '*not provoke the passions of populace to overawe the Laws*' – the emphasis was Holt's – and concentrated on making the truth known.[56] According to the Charlottetown lawyer, Holt had then added that 'the right *claimed by the Press*, to examine and censure the conduct of public men is partly made up of the natural right of thinking and speaking, *and is a peculiar right expressly recognized by the British Constitution* under the form of petitioning.' For Binns, this assertion went considerably beyond the right to publish petitions. He offered detailed discussions of several cases which suggested that there was no offence in an editor publishing a true copy of official proceedings, while those responsible for statements made in those proceedings were governed by the doctrine of malice. Binns added, 'Liberty has expanded in *England* as the time became more modern,' and it was perfectly safe to publish true reports of parliamentary and legal proceedings provided there was no order to the contrary. He was, moreover, entirely convinced that the right of petition fell under the same rules of truth and malice. While Binns accurately quoted from his authorities, in failing to discuss the many exceptions and caveats presented by Holt he did manage to make the English law sound more clear-cut than it actually was. And he offered no abstract principles.

James Bardin Palmer soon responded in the *Register* to the Binns letter and law reports, arguing that 'I have thought it probably no disadvantage to our public character for talent, that we can at least write a speech, whether we made it in court or not.'[57] He added, 'I have heard words put into my own mouth, which God knows I never uttered.' Palmer was notorious throughout his career for complaining about the inventiveness of court reporting on the Island. He insisted on this occasion that there was a respectable bar in the neighbouring colonies that would find Binns's arguments 'extravagant,' and he promised to answer them in a future issue of the newspaper. Editor Haszard added a commentary upon the Palmer letter, insisting that the reports of Binns and Hodgson were accurate. Palmer did respond briefly to the substance of Binns's position a few weeks later, summarizing it as stating that 'all proceedings in Courts of Justice, in Parliament, or resolutions at public meetings constitutionally assembled to petition the King, may legally be published in a newspaper; and that it lies with a prosecutor or plaintiff suing at law for such publications, to prove malice against the printer.'[58] Palmer, of course, disagreed with such a view, although he admitted that 'such things have happened without prosecution.' Deliberately arguing without 'law authorities,' he maintained that it would be unreasonable to put the onus of malice on the prosecutor. He might have gone farther had he read Holt carefully.

In the same issue of the *Register*, a pseudonymous letter from a 'Country Schoolmaster' observed that until lately newspapers from other colonies had ignored Prince Edward Island but now they 'contain something respecting this Colony,' presumably a reference to reports of the great chancery case published abroad.[59] There is no evidence that Halifax newspapers printed anything about this Island case. However, Binns had offered advice and references which Howe might have found useful in his own libel trial of 1835. Although the Howe case went far beyond editorial reprinting of official documents, Binns's reliance on Holt emphasized the twin legal doctrines of truth and malice that would serve as the basis of the modern law on the subject of libel.

An English legal opinion on the P.E.I. chancery case was prepared with unusual alacrity by James Stephen, Jr, who reported from Lincoln's Inn to the colonial undersecretary, Robert Wilmot Horton, on 31 December 1823, only two months after the final tumultuous session of the court.[60]

Stephen acknowledged that from the documents available he had some difficulty in constructing a narrative or in understanding some of the legal points, but he saw two distinct questions. First, had a contempt of court been committed to justify the summary proceedings of the chancellor? Secondly, were the proceedings regular and legal? Stephen had already had experience in the Palmer disbarment case with the legal pronouncements of Chancellor Smith, and he had not then been impressed. This case would be no different.

Stephen turned to the second question first, claiming that the court could not make the order for attachment absolute on the testimony of only one witness (Haszard), particularly one it had threatened into cooperation. The court was equally irregular in freeing the parties without responding to their petition to do so. Stephen reserved the question of whether Smith was correct in his apprehension of sufficient danger to convoke his court in the first place. As for the rules of law, wrote Stephen, they had been stated by Lord Hardwicke in *Read*. It was important to remember that only the contempt and not the libel was relevant. According to Hardwicke, three species of writing alone constituted contempt of court: scandalizing the court, abusing parties concerned in causes there, or prejudicing mankind before the cause was heard. After examining Hawkins's *Pleas of the Crown* and Blackstone's *Commentaries*, Stephen doubted that the publication in question was a contempt, although it might well be libellous. The resolutions were adopted for the lawful purpose of forming the groundwork for a petition to the crown, at a legal meeting, and it was quite impossible to decide whether their publication was essential to the act of petitioning.

For Stephen, in the end the most important question was whether the judge had acted with temper, discretion, and propriety. Here he was quite categorical and scathing. No instance in modern times could be found where an English judge had committed on such a contempt or had sat in judgment on a case so close to himself. 'Instead of preferring an Indictment at Common Law,' argued Stephen, Smith had 'chosen to act as Judge in his own cause!' Since the publication involved was connected with a petition to the crown against Smith himself, the chancellor had another reason to hesitate to employ the power of commitment. 'It would hardly seem consistent with the decorum of the Chancellor's high station, to have adopted such a measure, which has the appearance of an attempt to silence such an imputation as this.' Even if the language of the legal authorities gave the chancellor the discretion to commit, the court in propriety should have refused to exercise its power. It was not clear whether

Stephen was prepared to deny Smith the legal right to commit or to charge him with serious legal error, but he was quite definite on the impolitic nature of the action. Even Smith acknowledged that he had been wrong in pursuing this case, writing pathetically to Lord Bathurst in May 1824, 'I should never have dreamt of going to Law with people prepared to go to War had I been aware of that being the Case, that disposition appear'd suddenly & unexpectedly.'[61]

In many respects, *Lane v. Haszard* was unsatisfactorily inconclusive, particularly since the chancellor did not allow the case to be completed. John Stewart was never arrested and the remaining defendants were released indefinitely. Smith's conduct of the trial – and especially his willingness to allow the charge of contempt to be heard – doubtless damaged him in the eyes of the British government, contributing to his recall in 1824. At the same time, there were so many charges against Smith from so many quarters that his demise was almost inevitable. Perhaps the individual most directly injured by the trial was John Stowe[62] of Charlottetown, the constable who had testified in court that John Stewart was hiding behind locked doors in the house of John MacGregor. Stowe was charged in the Island Supreme Court by Attorney General Johnston (in his official capacity) with malicious perjury, the grand jury found a true bill, and the hapless constable was tried and convicted on 25 February 1824.[63] The chief witness for the prosecution was Johnston himself, and the foreman of the grand jury was one of the seven chancery defendants. Stowe complained to Smith about his treatment, arguing that because of the present state of public opinion on the Island he could not get a fair trial.[64] He noted that two of his cases as constable were returned by the grand jury as 'not found,' including a charge of assault against an individual who had knocked out three of Stowe's teeth. The chief justice reserved judgment in *Rex v. Stowe*, and it too appears never to have been completed.

Lieutenant Governor Smith wrote to the Colonial Office in March 1824, enclosing a petition from Stowe and a comment that 'where Party runs high in England a Trial may be carried into another (if impartial) County,' but the petitioner had no such refuge on the Island.[65] Stowe's affidavit, even if it did include erroneous information about Attorney General Johnston, was made without malice or corruption, argued Smith, and had had no effect on the chancery case whatsoever. In yet another hurried report on an Island legal incident, James Stephen wrote that under ordinary circumstances the British government did not interfere in cases of perjury, and he complained that the court documents had not been included in Smith's report on the case. Though he believed that the proceedings against Stowe had been illegal and unjust, Stephen added that there would be great constitutional objection to any government interference on Stowe's behalf. And so Smith had to be informed that he could not employ the royal prerogative to protect the defendant; instead he would have to search for every other possible method of redress.[66]

Charles Douglass Smith's generally impolitic and imprudent behaviour over the years served as the reason for the eventual British decision to recall him. It is not clear how the lieutenant governor's position was affected by an investigation by a justice of the Nova Scotia Supreme Court into the matter of the authorization of unusual fees in the Court of Chancery, although in his report Mr Justice Brendon Halliburton acquitted Smith of any improper behaviour.[67] 'I feel . . . no hesitation in reporting that His Excellency Lieutenant Governor Smith has not established any fee table which authorizes charges far exceeding in amount whatever was exacted by his Predecessor and totally unauthorized by the Act of Assembly, for regulating the fees of Office.' In short, the charges of the petition in this respect could not be sustained. On the other hand, wrote Halliburton, the practice of law officers under that table – while not illegal – was excessive. Lane – unlike those before him – charged every fee he was authorized to take. Practitioners before the court complained that they had to pay for copies of their own documents if they wished to use them in court, an unusual practice that might well be discontinued. Although Halliburton did not make the point, the fee structure of the Court of Chancery was doubtless one of the major reasons why this body was not much employed for legitimate equity purposes.

Halliburton noted one other nasty and costly practice involving the Island chancery court. In most jurisdictions, attachments for contempt were considered as civil process, but on the Island they were treated as criminal offences. In the case of *Smith v. McAuslane*, for example, Attorney General Johnston, acting for the complainant, got an order for attachment for non-payment of costs, and the defendant was taken into custody late in 1822 while drinking in a public house at the same time that another constable executed a civil attachment for small debt. In the morning James Bardin Palmer moved for contempt of chancery against the constable with the civil writ, one Collins, a poor man, and refused to let him be heard in court without the payment of substantial fees. This case, opined Halliburton, involved an illiterate man in considerable expense for the performance of his duty in an office he was compelled by law to fill, suggesting that the officers of the court were occasionally 'overzealous.' But

Smith was not involved in such business. Mr Justice Halliburton would subsequently preside at the Joseph Howe libel trial. Perhaps he had learned from *Lane v. Haszard* and its fallout some of the dangers of impolitic behaviour by judges in cases involving liberty of the press.

In his comments on the battery of charges alleged against Smith, James Stephen, Jr, insisted that he had no opinion on the question of whether they were so grave and weighty as to warrant immediate recall.[68] But Stephen's summary of the accusations was hardly dispassionate and his use of evidence highly selective. On the charge related to the enforcement of the quitrent act of 1802, for example, Stephen wrote that the affidavits attached in support of this charge 'indeed disclose a scene of extortion, injustice, and abuse of the process of the law, which would have been incredible, had it not been stated on the concurrent testimony upon oath of no less than twenty-six different persons.' Such an assessment was by itself sufficient to cook Smith's goose. But in this instance and elsewhere, Stephen accepted the principle of substantiation by voluntary affidavit, thus ignoring what every Islander at the time (and subsequent historians) accepted as given: on the Island, voluntary affidavits were often collusive and frequently perjured. Had he thought back to the charges that had led to the disbarment of Palmer, which were almost entirely based on voluntary affidavit, Stephen might have been more suspicious. Still, Smith had behaved badly and richly deserved to be recalled. It was perhaps only justice that he was in effect condemned by the British government almost entirely upon voluntary affidavit without being heard in his defence. He was swiftly replaced as lieutenant governor and summoned home to answer the charges against him.

PALMER v. HASZARD (1828)

Although Smith went home in disgrace late in 1824, several of the protagonists in *Lane v. Haszard* reappeared in another press case in 1829. This case did involve libel. A year earlier, the Island's House of Assembly had refused to allow James Bardin Palmer to take his seat after a by-election, resolving that he was 'unworthy and unfit' to be admitted to the House. The principal speech against Palmer had been delivered by his old adversary William Johnston, who had charged Palmer with 'corrupt conduct in the Court of Chancery' and 'illegal and oppressive practices.' This speech was full of attacks on Palmer's character and behaviour and was reported in full in Haszard's *Prince Edward Island Register*.[69] Palmer brought a civil suit for libel against Haszard, claiming £5000 damages, and the case was heard in July 1829 in the Island's Supreme Court before Mr Justice Edward Jarvis and a special jury.[70] In contrast to his behaviour in 1823, the printer took full responsibility for the publication. Palmer conducted his own case, insisting that any damages awarded would be used to establish a truly independent newspaper on the Island and maintaining that the charges made by Johnston against him in the legislature were false and libellous, maliciously intended to injure his reputation. In defence was attorney John Lawson, the Island's solicitor general who in this case was apparently acting in a private capacity. Lawson contended that 'a fair report of the proceedings of a Court of Justice or of Parliament was perfectly legal, although containing passages which, if published under other circumstances, might be libellous.' Palmer denied not only the publication's accuracy but also the applicability to the Island of the English precedents cited by Lawson. In England, he argued, 'where none but men of Education get into Parliament, and where no language was used but such as befitted men of rank, the publication of debates could do little harm; but were such a practice tolerated here, what would be the consequence?' An illiterate person could get into the Island house and make abusive speeches of all kinds, Palmer insisted. Nobody would be safe.

In his summation to the jury, Chief Justice Jarvis said that the first question to be decided was whether a libel was involved. This approach suggests an acceptance of Fox's Libel Act, although nobody in 1829 cited or mentioned it. Jarvis went on to say that he thought the words as stated were libellous, injurious to Palmer's reputation. What a member of parliament may say he could not be held responsible for, but reporting out of doors was different. Liberty of the press could not be used to defame individuals. Echoing Blackstone, Jarvis allowed that publishing reports of courts or legislatures that contained injurious material could not be prevented in advance, but he insisted that such reporting was liable to prosecution. If the jury 'were of the opinion that the article complained of was a fair report of a debate in the House of Assembly, and that there was no express malice on the part of the Defendant, although legal malice was implied, that would weigh with the jury in mitigation of damages.'[71]

The jury deliberated for an hour and a half and returned a verdict of guilty without malicious attempt. They were sent back to come up with an unqualified verdict. Had the jury returned a verdict of not guilty, we might have some better idea whether Fox's act had been extended by the court to the Island. Instead, the jury returned in twenty minutes with a new verdict: 'We find the Defendant guilty – Damages, ONE SHILLING!'

The plaintiff moved for arguments for a new trial because of jury prejudice against him. It goes without saying that there would have been no appeal from a jury decision that had dealt with both law and fact. The motion was granted and the cause argued. Justice Jarvis admitted surprise that the motion for a new trial had come from the plaintiff rather than the defence, since Lawson had admitted that he was unhappy with the law laid down by the court. Lawson insisted that, despite this case, the principle was yet unshaken that 'an editor of a public newspaper publishing a *true* account of what passed either in Parliament or in a Court of Justice, though it may reflect on the character of an individual, is not guilty of libel.' The chief justice stood by his view of the law but added that it would be hard to find another jury. In England venue could be moved, but 'he must take the country as he found it.' He denied the motion.

From our perspective, the jury charge of Chief Justice Jarvis certainly emphasized the extent to which colonial jurisdictions could ignore the latest English precedents, as well as the variations possible from one colony to another. Haszard himself, in editorial comments at the end of the law report he published in his newspaper, admitted that he found 'the extraordinary view of the law as laid down by the Chief Justice' to be 'dangerous doctrine.' But at the same time, he found some encouragement in the decision. 'Thanks ... to the free constitution which guards the British Press, it is beyond the power of any judge whatever, to controul its mighty energies, provided juries prove faithful to the sacred trust reposed in them. They alone are the Constitutional judges of the law as well as the fact in actions for libel.' *Palmer v. Haszard* enunciated perhaps the most important pre-1843 principle of all regarding liberty of the press in British North America, that in the end the jury was responsible for both law and fact in libel cases, however double-edged that principle was. Certainly Mr Justice Halliburton in the Howe case of 1835 accepted this principle, which permitted the jury to acquit the defendant. While it was impossible to tell what a jury might do, and equally impossible to appeal to a higher court a jury decision on both fact and law, the common law of libel had by the 1820s advanced well beyond the point where truth and motive were unknown to it. Attorney General S.G.W. Archibald would attempt to argue the contrary in the Howe case, but with no success.[72]

The two Prince Edward Island cases on the question of liberty of the press may or may not have resulted in either 'good law' or precedents carried forward to other jurisdictions. What they do demonstrate, however, is that colonial knowledge of the current state of the English common law on the subject was substantial. Moreover, the common law on libel and contempt had changed significantly since the days of Blackstone and Serjeant Hawkins. At least on Prince Edward Island, the principle that a jury decided both fact and law provided a considerable measure of potential protection for a newspaper editor.

NOTES

1 H. Pearson Gundy, 'Liberty and Licence of the Press in Upper Canada,' in *His Own Man: Essays in Honour of Arthur Reginald Marsden Lower*, ed. W.H. Heick and Roger Graham (Montreal and Kingston: McGill-Queen's University Press 1976), 71.

2 J. Murray Beck, *Joseph Howe*, 2 vols., 1: *Conservative Reformer, 1804–1848* (Montreal and Kingston: McGill-Queen's University Press 1976), 129. This chapter reprinted Beck's earlier article '"A Fool for a Client": The Trial of Joseph Howe,' *Acadiensis*, vol. 3, no. 2 (1974), 27.

3 Gwendolyn Davies, 'James Irving: Literature and Libel in Early Nova Scotia,' *Essays in Canadian Writing*, vol. 29 (1984), 48.

4 Barry Cahill, 'Sedition in Nova Scotia: *R. v. Wilkie* (1820) and the Incontestable Illegality of Seditious Libel before *R. v. Howe* (1835),' *Dalhousie Law Journal*, vol. 18, no. 2 (1994), 459.

5 Barry Wright, 'Sedition in Upper Canada: Contested Legality,' *Labour/Le Travail*, vol. 29 (spring 1992), 7. This piece overviews the record of such trials in the province, focusing on their repressive and 'counter-hegemonic' dynamics. The Robert Gourlay affair gave rise to the most prominent cases and is the focus of an essay in this volume.

6 See the following articles in the *DCB*: D.A. Sutherland, 'Wilkie, William,' *DCB* 5: 853; Elwood H. Jones, 'Wilcocks, Joseph,' *DCB* 5: 859; Fernand Ouellet, 'Bédard, Pierre-Stanislas,' *DCB* 6: 41; J. Donald Wilson, 'Cockrell, Richard,' *DCB* 6: 158; H.P. Gundy, 'Collins, Francis,' *DCB* 6: 164; John C. Weaver, 'Durand, James,' *DCB* 6: 228; R.L. Fraser, 'Ferguson, Bartemas,' *DCB* 6: 247; Gertrude Tratt, 'Holland, Anthony Henry,' *DCB* 6: 321; Elizabeth Waterston, 'Waller, Jocelyn,' *DCB* 6: 801; Jean-Marie Lebel, 'Duvernay, Ludger,' *DCB* 8: 253; George L. Parker, 'Ward, Edmund,' *DCB* 8: 922; W.S. MacNutt, 'Hooper, John,' *DCB* 9: 399; Ian Ross Robertson, 'Haszard, James Douglas,' *DCB* 10: 339. A number of these figures are examined in this volume.

7 Generalizations in such works as W.H. Kesterton, *A History of Journalism in Canada* (Toronto: McClelland and Stewart 1967), at 20–5, are typically overstated.

8 Leonard W. Levy, *The Emergence of a Free Press* (New York: Oxford University Press 1985).

9 Wright, 'Sedition,' at 17.

10 Ibid., at 23. Wright estimated thirty-four prosecutions based on the Court of King's Bench assize minutebook. His subsequent review of court records during and immediately after the War of 1812 suggests closer to forty prosecutions.

11 G.V.V. Nichols, 'A Forerunner of Joseph Howe,' *CHR*, vol. 8 (1927), 224.

12 Sutherland, 'Wilkie, William.'

13 Cahill, 'Sedition in Nova Scotia.'

14 Jones, 'Willcocks, Joseph'; Gundy, 'Liberty and Licence'; J.S. Martel, 'The Press of the Maritime Provinces in the 1830s,' *CHR*, vol. 19 (1938), 24; W.R. Riddell, 'Joseph Willcocks, Sheriff, Member of Parliament and Traitor,' *OH*, vol. 24 (1927), 475.

15 See also Fraser, 'Ferguson, Bartemas'; W.R. Riddell, 'The First Law Reporter in Upper Canada,' *Canadian Bar Proceedings*, vol. 2 (1916), at 139–40.

16 Patrick O'Flaherty, 'Winton, Henry David,' *DCB* 8: 947.

17 Paul Romney, *Mr Attorney: The Attorney General for Ontario in Court, Cabinet and Legislature 1791–1899* (Toronto: Osgoode Society/University of Toronto Press 1986); Patrick Brode, *Sir John Beverley Robinson: Bone and Sinew of the Compact* (Toronto: University of Toronto Press 1984), at 133.

18 Mary McLean, 'Early Parliamentary Reporting in Upper Canada,' *CHR*, vol. 20 (1939), 378; H.G. Jordan, 'The Reports of Parliamentary Debates, 1803–1908,' *Economica*, vol. 11 (1931), at 437.

19 James Douglass Haszard (1797–1875) was the son of Rhode Island Loyalists who established the *Prince Edward Island Register* in 1823. He later published the *Royal Gazette* and *Haszard's Gazettte*. He was not known for his crusading zeal.

20 *Prince Edward Island Register*, 13 Sept. 1823. The *DCB* sketch of Haszard has the date wrong. Charles Douglass Smith (1761–1855) was born in England. After a less than spectacular army career he took early retirement in 1798. In 1812 he was appointed lieutenant governor of Prince Edward Island, a post he held until 1824.

21 Ambrose Lane (1791–1853) was born in Ireland and served in the British army before retiring in Charlottetown in 1819, where he married a daughter of C.D. Smith. He was a member of council until his death and later served on the Supreme Court.

22 Stanley Katz, 'The Politics of Law in Colonial America: Controversies over Chancery Courts and Equity Law in the Eighteenth Century,' in *Perspectives in American History*, vol. 5 (1971), 257.

23 For Fanning, see my sketch in *DCB* 5:308.

24 Grenville Papers, Additional Manuscripts, 59004, BL.

25 Phillip Buckner, 'Smith, Charles Douglas,' *DCB* 8: 823; Sir William Sidney Smith (1766–1840) was a British admiral and member of parliament; John Spencer Smith (1770–1845) was a diplomat at Constantinople and Munich. For the family, see John Barrow, *The Life and Correspondence of Admiral Sir William Sidney Smith, G.C.B.*, 2 vols. (London: Richard Bentley 1848).

26 Smith to Lord Bathurst, 23 March 1815, CO 226/30/3–15, PRO.

27 William Johnston (1779–1828) was born in Scotland, came to the Island in 1812, and was appointed attorney general in 1813. See M. Brook Taylor's sketch in *DCB* 6: 359.

28 John Stewart (1758–1834) was born in Scotland and had come to the Island with his father (who was appointed as chief justice) in 1775. He spent his lifetime in political controversy. In 1806 he published the first history of the Island. See F.L. Pigot's article in *DCB* 6: 735.

29 H.T. Holman, 'The Early History of the Court of Chancery on Prince Edward Island,' unpublished manuscript in author's possession.

30 James Bardin Palmer (1771–1833) was born in Dublin. Trained as a lawyer, he came to the Island in 1802 and soon became its leading legal practitioner. He also became the leading advisor of J.F.W. DesBarres and was stripped of his offices in the Loyal Elector debacle of 1812. He fought for reinstatement and was readmitted to the bar, but was disbarred by Smith in 1816. See H.T. Holman's biography in *DCB* 6: 565.

31 James Stephen to Lord Bathurst, 20 Aug. 1819, CO 226/35/304–44.

32 CO 226/39/167–79.

33 *Prince Edward Island Register*, 25 Oct., 15 Nov., 20 Nov. 1823.

34 James Stephen to R.W. Horton, 31 Dec. 1823, CO 226/39/232–44.

35 Smith to Lord Bathurst, 17 Dec. 1823, CO 226/39/201–31; same to same, CO 226/39/264–86.

36 'First Day's Report Communicated by Mr. Binns Contempt in Chancery Charlottetown October 14 1823,' *Prince Edward Island Register*, 1 Nov. 1823.

37 'Law Report Contempt in Chancery Tuesday October 14 1823,' CO 226/39/347–63.

38 William Hawkins, *A Treatise of the Pleas of the Crown* (seven editions in the eighteenth century) and Sir William Blackstone, *Commentaries on the Laws of England* (five eighteenth-century editions), although old, remained the standard textbooks for most lawyers of the early nineteenth century.

39 Charles Binns (c. 1786–1847) was born in England and came to the Island in 1808, originally to work with James Bardin Palmer. He was a leading advocate of accurate court reporting and of law reform on the Island. See M. Brook Taylor's biography in *DCB* 7: 76.

40 'Second Day's Report Court of Chancery 16 October 1823,' *Prince Edward Island Register*, 8 Nov. 1823, CO 226/39/347–63.

41 1 Saunders Report at 120.

42 8 Term Reports at 293.

43 *Prince Edward Island Register*, 8 Nov. 1823.

44 'Second Day's Report Court of Chancery 16 October 1823,' *Prince Edward Island Register*, 15 Nov. 1823.

45 *Prince Edward Island Register*, 15 Nov. 1828.

46 'Third Day's Report Contempt in Chancery 27 October 1823,' CO 226/39/176–85.

47 *Prince Edward Island Register*, 15 Nov. 1823.

48 CO 226/39/281–6.

49 Smith to Sir James Kempt, 29 Oct. 1823, CO 226/39/157–61; Smith to Lord Bathurst, 17 Dec. 1823, CO 226/39/201–32.

50 *Prince Edward Island Register*, 15 Nov. 1823.

51 'Opinion of William Johnston, 11 Nov. 1823,' CO 226/30/270–3.

52 A. Lane to Charles Binns, 30 Oct. 1823, CO 226/33/163–5; same to same, CO 226/30/180–3.

53 Smith to Bathurst, 1 Dec. 1823, CO 226/39/191–6.

54 *Prince Edward Island Register*, 8 Nov. 1823.

55 See app. 3, P.

56 See Francis Ludlow Holt, *The Law of Libel, in Which Is Contained a General History of This Law in the Ancient Codes, and of Its Introduction, and Successive Alterations, in the Law of England* (London: J. Butterworth 1816).

57 *Prince Edward Island Register*, 20 Nov. 1823.

58 Ibid., 20 Dec. 1823.

59 Ibid.

60 CO 226/39/232–44.

61 Smith to Bathrust, 29 May 1824, CO 226/40/60–3.

62 Stowe (1760–1850) was elected to the assembly for one term in 1806.

63 RG 6, Supreme Court Records, Supreme Court Minute Book, February 1824, PARO.

64 Petition of John Stowe, 28 Feb. 1824, CO 226/40/38–40.

65 Smith to R. Wilmot-Horton, 15 March 1824, CO 226/40/52; Observations by Smith on Stowe Case, 28 Feb. 1824, CO 226/40/41–2.

66 James Stephen to Wilmot-Horton, 5 May 1824, CO 226/40/191–7.

67 Brendon Halliburton to Sir James Kempt, 23 May 1824, CO 226/40/324–52.

68 James Stephen to Wilmot-Horton, 27 March 1824, CO 226/40/421–40.

69 *Prince Edward Island Register*, 23 March 1828.

70 Ibid. For Jarvis (1788–1852), appointed Prince Edward Island Supreme Court

chief justice in 1828, see the biography by the author and H.T. Holman in *DCB* 8: 428.

71 This was probably not an unreasonable statement of Holt's chapter entitled 'Of Libels Against a Man in Respect to His Profession and Calling' (at 199). Holt emphasizes: 'In cases of this kind the law will always distinguish between the spirit and liberal freedom of criticism and the malice of a libel' (at 203).

72 Beck, *Joseph Howe*, 1: at 146.

17

R. v. Howe (1835) for Seditious Libel: A Tale of Twelve Magistrates

BARRY CAHILL

'It was my fortune to study the law of libel once, and in three weeks I think I read more of it than any lawyer ever did in Nova Scotia ... And while my law was accepted as sound, the law of the bar, and of the judges too, was voted absurd by the jury.'

– Joseph Howe, 1850

'He [Howe] had seen the Family Compact strike down one reformer after another in Canada, New Brunswick, Prince Edward Island and Nova Scotia, by means of an indictment for criminal libel.'

– D.C. Harvey, 1939

In a seminal article published in 1974, Kenneth McNaught described *R. v. Howe* as one of Canada's 'two most significant cases involving political freedom of the press' – the other being *R. v. Dixon* for seditious libel (1920), arising from the Winnipeg General Strike of 1919. An equally influential article published the same year by Joseph Howe's biographer, Murray Beck, claimed: 'It is often stated that Howe established the freedom of the press through his acquittal in 1835. This is a myth that has little basis in fact.'[1] Such words from such an authority should give one pause. Yet none of the existing scholarship on *R. v. Howe*, including – one might even say, especially – Beck's, has offered a politico-legal analysis of a proceeding that was in fact (though not in myth) a trial for sedition, an alleged crime against the state bearing far more fundamentally on the constitutional liberty of the subject than any mere criminal defamation.[2]

Nova Scotian politics in the period 1830 to 1835 were in a state of ferment and flux.[3] The Tory-Loyalist ascendency, which had endured for nearly forty years, crashed in electoral flames in 1830 but no new consensus emerged to replace, much less revive, the *ancien régime*. The progression of Joseph Howe, the Tory son of a Tory-Loyalist, from Conservative to Reformer climaxed in the seditious-libel trial of 1835, which historian-archivist D.C. Harvey viewed as the culmination of Nova Scotia's twenty-year-long intellectual 'Great Awakening.' But the mere coincidence that Howe, editor of 'the leading newspaper in British North America,' was acquitted for having published an alleged seditious libel does not mean that through 'the favourable result of the libel action in 1835' – as Harvey styled it – the *Novascotian* 'succeeded in establishing the freedom of the press.'[4]

This inquiry argues that there was no perceived difference, legal or otherwise, between sedition and the defamation of public officials when Joseph Howe was tried for seditious libel in Canada's oldest common-law jurisdiction. Nova Scotia, unlike Britain and Upper Canada, never imposed the oppressive burden of a Sedition Act, instead relying exclusively on the double-edged sword of the common law to repress political dissent.[5] Though actions for slander were routine in the civil-justice history of colonial Nova Scotia, the only prosecution for seditious libel known to have antedated *Howe* was *R. v. Wilkie* (1820), before which 'a prosecution for a Public Libel ha[d] been almost unknown here.'[6] There was a distinction between private- and public-criminal defamations, but the distinction between public-defamatory libel and seditious or blasphemous libel had not yet even crystallized in England by 1819, when parliament passed 'An Act for the More Effectual Prevention and Punishment of Blasphemous and Seditious Libels'[7]; the act did not extend to Nova Scotia, nor was it ever enacted there. Despite the uncertain doctrinal context, however, various aspects of the proceedings as instituted suggest that the prosecution was malicious; that hostile influence was likely employed; and that Howe was forced by the Halifax grand jury to submit to a political show trial, when they might otherwise have quashed the indictment on legal grounds.

Though seditious libels in England and Upper Canada were often prosecuted by way of the attorney general's ex officio information, rather than indictment before the grand jury, the use of indictment in *Howe* does not mean that any practical distinction between public-defamatory and seditious libel existed in the criminal-justice system of Nova Scotia, only that the ex officio information was almost completely unknown to criminal procedure in the colony. Scholars of the historical development and implementation of procedural law stand to learn from *Howe* important lessons about the administration of the unreformed criminal-justice system – chiefly that the attorney general's 'ex officio' indictment (so to speak) served the same purpose as the attorney general's ex officio information did elsewhere. Whether use of the indictment as a prosecutorial instrument stated anything about the specific nature of the libel charged, or simply about the narrow range of prosecutorial options available to the crown in Nova Scotia, intrudes on larger debates over criminal procedure. It will be seen that there was sharp disagreement between Beamish Murdoch ('Nova Scotia's Blackstone') and the upper echelons of the bench and bar over the legality of ex officio informations.

Other questions that must be posed are whether the criminal law – substantive, procedural, or both – was more honoured in the breach than the observance; and whether the prosecution of Joseph Howe for libel would have taken place at all had Howe's newspaper not been the voice of radical opposition to Halifax's appointive municipal government. Corrupt, inefficient, and unreformed – this self-perpetuating gerontocracy of justices of the peace on the old English model had ruled Halifax since its founding in 1749 and had been resisting any and all attempts at civic incorporation since 1785. More to the point, direct criticism of the magistrates was construed as implied criticism of the lieutenant governor and Council, who 'were equally supreme in the control of town affairs as those of the province at large.'[8]

ATTACK ON MAGISTRATES IN THE *NOVASCOTIAN*

'These irregularities [in the administration of justice in the Commissioners' Court],' Howe was to assert in his defence,[9] 'formed a part of the general system, which justified the charges of grand juries, the surprise of the executive, the investigations of the Council, and the publication of the alleged libel.' Such was the political context of the prosecution; the legal context was quite another matter.[10] At a special sessions held on 8 January 1835 the *custos rotulorum* [chief magistrate] of the District of Halifax, the opulent merchant James Foreman,[11] informed his fellow magistrates[12] that they had been asked – by whom is not recorded – to take into consideration a letter signed 'The People,' published in Joseph Howe's *Novascotian* on New Year's Day,[13] which reflected ill on the magistrates.[14]

Rather than consult in the first instance with the attorney general, as the chief justice was later to suggest they should have done, the magistrates went over the heads of the law officers by taking their complaint directly to Lieutenant Governor Sir Colin Campbell, who, ironically, had been praised by 'The People' as the political messiah of Nova Scotia – the reincarnation of the late, lamented Sir John Coape Sherbrooke.[15] The lieutenant governor, whom the subscribing magistrates asked 'to direct the Crown officers to take immediately the necessary steps for prosecuting the party who has made them [the charges],'[16] 'referred [the complaint] to His Majesty's Attorney General, who will forthwith take the proper steps for prosecuting the party complained of, as herein requested.' Attorney General Samuel George William Archibald thereupon enquired 'whether the Magistrates wish the Publisher or Author of the Publication in the Nova Scotian of the 1st Instant signed "The People" to be prosecuted.' The magistrates returned no answer; having already stated their position clearly in the complaint,[17] they saw no need to indicate whom to prosecute 'for a libel.' The 'party complained of' was the writer of the letter, not the editor of the newspaper who had published it, though the editor could be held liable. The attorney general nevertheless feigned ignorance of the magistrates' request. Though Archibald was afterwards to admit during the trial that the name of the author had never been demanded, he insisted that 'had the author been given up,' he 'would not have proceeded against the publisher.'[18]

The magistrates accepted the high-prerogative lawyer's view of libel, which had obtained in England since Lord Chief Justice John Holt's time in the early 1700s: a defamatory libel against crown servants was *ipso facto* seditious.[19] The question of imputing criminal responsibility was one that the magistrates were willing to leave to the attorney general, having succeeded in their primary aim of soliciting a prosecution from the well-intentioned but inexperienced lieutenant governor.[20] As there were no lawyers among the magistrates of the Court of Session, there was no mention of 'libel' and consequently no recognition of the fact that either publication or authorship might create liability. The magistrates, moreover, retained legal advice only after the government had ordered the prosecution of Howe. The fact that the justices had not been libelled in their judicial capacity, and that neither the pseudonymous author of the offending letter nor the editor-proprietor-printer of the newspaper in which it was published had had any formal dealings with the Court of Session which might have given rise to the alleged libel, were not taken into consideration.

It must be borne in mind that the context of both the writing and the publication of the letter signed 'The People' was ongoing complaints by the Halifax grand jury of 1834 – a more popular and representative body than the magistrates[21] – against misgovernment by the JPs of the largest of the three municipal districts comprising greater Halifax County before 1836. Howe had been successfully waging a war of words against the magistrates in the columns of the *Novascotian*, with the help of official grand jury documents supplied him by the foreman. By the end of the grand jury's term of office, the magistrates had had enough. Though they were losing the war of words in the press, it required a degree of brazenness to allege libellous a letter in which the new lieutenant governor of the province was obsequiously praised – not as chief *executive* but as 'Chief *Magistrate*' [italics added]. The grand juries of the years 1832 through 1834 had been of a progressive 'radical Whig' tendency.[22] The magistrates thus chose the interregnum between the retirement of the old year's grand jury and the summoning of the new to solicit a public prosecution from the only high officer of state with power enough to order it. They were doubtless aware that at common law a prosecution precluded any inquiry into the truth of the libel. Howe later observed in his address to the jury, 'The truth would be no defence in a criminal action [*sic!*], as the magistrates very well know or they would not have brought it.'[23]

The magistrates, stung by the grand jury's publication of presentments and other offical documents critical of the Court of Session, plainly viewed the libel prosecution as a strategic imperative, not as a tactical alternative to a civil action. The very fact that the magistrates retained counsel – after the indictment was safely preferred by the crown, on behalf of the government, and accepted by the grand jury – suggests that civil action might have been under consideration as a contingency, should the prosecution fail. The prosecution did go forward and fail, but no actions for civil defamation were brought as a result: 'Some of them [the magistrates],' Howe was to write to his sister, 'are blustering about private actions, but they won't meddle with me in a hurry.'[24]

The letter from 'The People' that triggered the indictment was no more than a *casus belli*; an earlier one bearing the same signature – of a significantly more radical cast and militant tendency – published in the *Novascotian* in November 1834 had been met with deafening silence. Had the magistrates been exercised by the letters per se, they would have solicited the prosecution two months earlier, when they would nevertheless have had to negotiate a grand jury 'which was no less militant than that of 1832 on which he [Howe] had sat.'[25] The real reason was magisterial spite and spleen at the fact that the old grand jury had gone over the heads of the Session – their nominal superiors – in order to carry their grievances directly to the lieutenant governor. 'By mid-January the Committee of the Council had confirmed many of the charges of the grand jury.'[26] Howe, for his part, had printed in the *Novascotian* every official grand jury document with which the foreman supplied him, including not only the address to the lieutenant governor but also the various presentments.[27]

JOSEPH HOWE INDICTED

Libel, then as now, might be a crime or a tort or both and it was difficult for prosecutors to determine where criminal responsibility and civil liability bifurcated or converged. While Howe as proprietor of the *Novascotian* was responsible for any libel published in his newspaper, there was no legal reason why he alone should have been prosecuted, had not the overarching political purpose been to silence him rather than 'The People,' a mere ghost writer. Indeed the restrictive precedent suggested by *Wilkie*, which Archibald also prosecuted, was that the author rather than the publisher be prosecuted for a seditious libel.[28]

The most important decision that had to be made by the crown after whether, and whom, to prosecute was how to prosecute. No attempt had been made by author or publisher to deny or disavow responsibility for the alleged libel; yet the complainant magistrates themselves had impliedly inculpated the author, not the publisher. It is therefore probable that the decision to prosecute Howe, and Howe alone, was dictated by political considerations: the executive[29] seized the opportunity to rid themselves of a meddlesome newspaper editor.[30] It is unlikely that Attorney General Archibald, whose sympathies lay with neither the Council nor the magistrates, would have invited further controversy by filing an ex officio criminal information.

In England 'the Attorney General himself usually prosecuted [public libels],' writes J.R. Spencer.[31] 'The prosecution was nearly always begun on the Attorney-General's *ex officio* information – a procedure which short-circuited the preliminary stages through which prosecutions ordinarily had to go, and so obviated the risk of an independently-minded [grand] jury refusing to find a true bill against the accused.' The only ex officio information known in practice to Nova Scotia's criminal procedure was that authorized by provincial statute for a breach of the revenue laws.[32] An ex officio information had not been filed in *Wilkie*, which certainly met Murdoch's criteria for use 'in cases of sedition, riots of a public nature, and libels against the executive government.'[33] Perhaps the reason why Attorney General Archibald refrained from laying an information was that he wished to emphasize his restrained and dispassionate exercise of prosecutorial discretion. 'I could have proceeded by that mode [ex officio information],' Archibald was to hyperbolize during his summation, knowing full well that he could only have done so according to English practice, 'but I have never been inclined to ride upon the prerogative of the Crown, and I therefore laid the matter before the grand inquest [jury] of the county ... One gentleman [*who?*] named the other course to me, but I said No; I will proceed by a fairer mode of indictment.'[34] Archibald tactically chose to proceed by way of indictment in order to give the grand jury the opportunity of quashing the bill. Unfortunately for Archibald, and more so for Howe, the grand jury was adhering to a different agenda. The attorney general's strategy depended on the grand jury's willingness to return a 'No True Bill'; had they thrown out the indictment, he would not file an ex officio information in order to sustain the prosecution. Preferring an indictment, in any case, was the lesser of two evils – it imparted the reality as well as the appearance of due process – and held out the possibility that the grand jury might refuse to find a true bill against the accused. Though the attorney general had no choice but to institute proceedings, he could nevertheless exercise official discretion by choosing the less oppressive mechanism for driving the prosecution.

On 4 February 1835 Joseph Howe received from Attorney General Archibald an official letter informing him that the crown intended to prosecute him for libel at the next term of the Supreme Court, which was six days away. Howe published the full text of the letter in the following day's edition of the *Novascotian*; it was already the worst-kept secret in Halifax that the crown intended to proceed by way of indictment. The accused was concerned, understandably, that the crown might proceed by way of ex officio information rather than run the risk of the grand jury's quashing the indictment. Hilary Term 1835 had to be statutorily delayed by one month, owing to the overlong legislative session.[35] It finally commenced on 10 February but was immediately adjourned for a week, there being no criminal business other than the indictment against Howe for libel,[36] which the attorney general stated he would be prepared to submit to the grand jury on 17 February.

The grand jury for the year had been impanelled on the opening day of term, in order to be formally charged by the chief justice.[37] The date was later than usual but in good time for the spring sitting of the Quarter Sessions on 3 March. For obvious reasons, both Howe's half-brother Joseph Austen and the two magistrates, James Noble Shannon and John Leander Starr,[38] sought and received permission to withdraw when the attorney general, on 17 February, came to the grand jury room in the courthouse and presented to the foreman an indictment against Joseph Howe for libel. Howe's speech in his own defence at the trial, which is almost the only source of knowledge of the text of the lost indictment, quotes a few passages from it which suggest that the charge, in substance though not in form, was more sedition than defamation, in other words, seditious libel. The crown's only witness was Hugh Blackadar, editor of the principal Tory organ, the Halifax *Journal*,[39] the proprietor of which, John Munro, was also a member of the grand jury. The second letter from 'The People,' which formed a part of the indictment, was ordered read. 'After much discussion,' a consensus not having been reached, and the Supreme Court having already adjourned, the grand jury also adjourned for three days. When it resumed deliberations on 20 February, three members being absent without leave and the same three members again being excused, the eighteen present returned the indictment endorsed 'A True Bill.'[40] Monday, 2 March 1835, was thereupon fixed by the attorney general as the trial date. 'Previous to the Grand Jury coming to a decision,' reported the *Novascotian* on 26 February, 'the Box containing the bill, and all their Records, was found to have been taken from the Jury Room – and no little confusion arose in consequence. It was finally discovered in the Treasurer's Office,[41] whither it had been carried by the Messenger of the House of Assembly, who presumed that it belonged to some of the Committees which usually occupied the room.'

On 24 February 'the Body of the Magistrates entered [the Supreme Court], and demanded an interview with the Chief Justice,' which was granted. Speaking on behalf of his colleagues, Richard Tremain, the senior magistrate,[42] read a resolution

which he stated had been passed at a meeting of the magistrates convened that morning [24 February], to the effect, 'That it was resolved unanimously, that leave be asked of this Honorable Court to grant to Mr Joseph Howe, in his defence at the approaching trial, every facility for substantiating, and proving the charges made by him [*sic*!] in the Novascotian of the 1st Jan. last.' His Lordship said, that such interference was out of the usual course, that he considered it extra-judicial, and that he could take no notice of it. He referred them, however, to their counsel, the Attorney General, with whom they might consult upon the course to be adopted.[43]

This bizarre request contains the germ of Howe's successful self-defence and suggests that the magistrates misconceptualized *Howe* in terms of civil action, to which the truth of the alleged libel would have formed a total defence. Had the request been granted, and by the same judge who was scheduled to preside at the spring criminal assizes, the whole course of provincial common law might have been changed.

At the same meeting of the Court of Session, another of the magistrates who had signed the complaint successfully moved a resolution that a retainer be paid out of the police magistrates' budget to barristers Charles Twining and James F. Gray (the crown attorney) as attorneys for the prosecution.[44] It was further resolved that magistrates Dr Samuel Head and Richard Tremain, both of whom had signed the complaint, and David Shaw Clarke, clerk of the peace, 'be a Committee to superintend the progress of the Trial of the Indictment against Mr Joseph Howe for a Libel upon the Magistrates.' The twelve magistrates were nothing if not well organized and well prepared.[45] 'They [the magistrates] have taken six weeks to determine on this prosecution,' Howe was to complain in his defence,[46] 'leaving their adversary but a few days to prepare; and finally, they have brought their action by indictment, well knowing that the court could not admit evidence but on the side of the Crown.'[47]

Though Attorney General Archibald's reasons for proceeding as he did, in full conformity to Nova Scotia criminal procedure, seem clear enough, the grand jury's reasons for proceeding as they did are obscure by comparison. Moreover, if the petit jurors were to be the heroes of the piece,[48] the grand jury were the villains – or at least the anti-heroes. A body that, when Howe was a member in 1832, could be described as politically 'militant,'[49] had clearly undergone a sea change. The role of the grand jury is the most impenetrable mystery of the Howe libel trial, because the political reasons for committing the accused for trial were easily obscured by the legal grounds, which were themselves suspect and questionable. The indictment is no longer to hand, and so it is impossible to know exactly what offence was charged. If there was connivance between the magistrates and the government,[50] which led to the lieutenant governor's ordering the attorney general to prosecute – certainly against Archibald's judgment and perhaps also against his advice – then perhaps there was also connivance between the magistrates and the grand jury which led to acceptance of the indictment.

It is a salient fact that the same two magistrates who were also members of the grand jury had put their names to the request for a prosecution. It is for reasons such as this that students of the Howe libel trial have forborne to investigate the pivotal role of the grand jury, who concluded that (in Howe's words) the 'indictment in which I am charged with sedition and rebellion'[51] was fully supported by the crown's evidence. The grand jury could have quashed the indictment on evidentiary grounds. They might have insisted that the author of the alleged libel be charged, instead of or in addition to the publisher, and that the indictment be redrawn accordingly; they might have denied the innuendo (the construction placed by the crown on the alleged defamatory words); they might have concluded that the publication of the alleged libel was immaterial, because the statements made in 'the letter, as contained in the indictment' were not defamatory on the face of them; they might have concluded that, since an action for libel lay where an indictment was maintainable, a private action rather than a public prosecution should have been brought. The grand jury were clearly under no legal obligation to return a true bill.

On the assumption that presenting the weakest, most perfunctory case possible was a rather unsubtle appeal by the attorney general to quash the indictment, the grand jury chose not to run the risk of antagonizing government by quashing the bill. These indeed were the principal grounds on which the Halifax bar declined en masse to accept Howe's brief, not to mention the fact that two earlier libel prosecutions, *Wilkie* (1820) and *Forrester* (1825) – the former seditious, the latter defamatory – had resulted in convictions. The grand jury's returning a true bill suggests, at the very least, timidity in the exercise of their inquisitional function, where political trials in the Supreme Court were concerned, and their behaviour by no means matched the independence and self-assertiveness of their recent predecessors. If the grand jury of 1835 had been of the same political stripe as the one of 1834, the indictment would doubtless have been quashed. *Everything turned on the composition of the new grand jury*: whether to prosecute; whom to prosecute; by what means – indictment or (in theory) ex officio information – to prosecute. The attorney general, having given the new panel ample opportunity to quash the indictment, was at the same time appearing to carry out dutifully the government's instructions. Yet the grand jury's finding was a foregone conclusion; the panel was 'packed' as effectively as special juries for libel trials were in England before the passage of the Juries Act of 1825.[52]

Prosecution by means of indictment involved other risks; elsewhere, this mode in such cases 'was often interpreted as a tacit admission of the truth of the accusation.'[53] Archibald would not have wished to emulate the example of the attorney general of England, Sir James Scarlett, who a few years before had been carrying on a series of public-libel prosecutions which 'roused considerable resentment and were generally thought to have been a mistake.'[54] Taking a longer and more realistic view of the political implications, 'Archibald was deliberately moderate, fully realizing that this was one jury trial he could not possibly win.'[55] Though he may have enjoyed 'the freedom to stay any private prosecution potentially embarrassing to the authorities,'[56] Archibald did not want to stretch this prerogative on a prosecution requested of, agreed to, and ordered by the authorities. The attorney general's freedom of action was circumscribed less by the narrow range of prosecutorial options available to him than by government's political will to prosecute.

Whether to institute criminal proceedings for a public libel was a decision for the executive, not the law officers. The well-meaning, though badly informed and worse-advised, lieutenant governor would have been justified in rejecting the advice he received – to grant the magistrates' request for a prosecution – and would thus have avoided the contradiction between his enlightened response to well-founded complaints by the former grand jury against the Court of Session and his credulous acquiescence in the magistrates' heavy-handed attempt to silence their political opponents. The grand jury could not be silenced, but – unlike Howe and the *Novascotian* – they could be ignored; all the magistrates had to do was wait until their annual term was up. Unlike the Court of Session, to which retiring grand jurors often sought and occasionally received promotion, the grand jury was not a self-perpetuating, self-referential gerontocracy. Yet the very success of the 1834 grand jury in bringing long-standing grievances to the attention of government, and the *Novascotian*'s popular advocacy of the grand jury's agenda, forced the sessions to respond to the press campaign against them. The intention was to nullify the effects of the former grand jury's 'public relations blitz' by depriving them of their mouthpiece.[57]

The new grand jury appear to have done what the government expected of them; an indictment for public libel had been preferred, and so they were to rubber stamp it. Both the magistrates and the attorney general were thus dependent on the cooperation of that popular body, which had greater room to manoeuvre than either of them, in order to achieve their respective aims. While Archibald's sympathies lay with the accused, the sympathies of the grand jury seem to have lain with the invisible prosecutors – whose vendetta against those reformers for whom Howe spoke could not be resisted by the attorney general.[58]

TRIAL BY JURY

J.R. Spencer's evocation of 'the machinery by which political libel trials used to be stage-managed [in England] – *ex officio* criminal informations and special juries'[59] – applies in the latter, though not the former, respect to Nova Scotia, which held its first and only public-libel prosecution against a newspaper when such proceedings 'had largely died out in England.'[60] On Monday, 2 March 1835, *R. v. Howe*, for libel, came to trial in the Supreme Court before Chief Justice Brenton Halliburton and a special jury. 'The trial was further stage-managed in that a special jury was summoned to hear it' – on the usually correct hypothesis that a handpicked or packed jury would 'have little sympathy with radicals.'[61]

Indeed, the very fact that a special jury was empanelled, in term time, to try an indictment highlights the extreme anomalousness of the prosecution; it was only possible because there was no other criminal business on the docket. (This happenstance effectively – and, from the attorney general's perspective, ironically – replicated one of the procedural advantages of the ex officio information.) Howe, like a subsequent editor of the *Novascotian*, 'laboured ... under the difficulty that the special juries in libel cases were chosen from the grand jury panels, whose members, because of large property qualifications, were likely to be heavily tory in complexion.'[62] The petit jury, five of whom had served with Howe on the 'militant' grand jury in 1832, and three others of whom had served on it the following year, consisted largely of merchants and tradesmen.[63] The court-appointed foreman was Charles John Hill, a failed auctioneer and former business partner of police magistrate John Liddell, one of the twelve magistrates who had signed the complaint. The accused Joseph Howe was arraigned and pleaded 'Not Guilty'; he was not represented by counsel. 'This was an action [*sic*] for libel,' announced the conservative *Times* on the second and final day of the trial, 'brought at the suit of the Magistrates of Halifax on the Part of the Crown against the Printer and Editor of the *Novascotian*, and contained in that paper of the 1st of January'[64] – a masterpiece of opacity and refraction, tending to disguise the fact that *Howe* was a public prosecution for libel instituted by the crown at the behest of the magistrates of Halifax.

THE VERDICT[65]

As the first acquittal of an accused under the Libel Act of 1792 in Nova Scotia, *Howe* was a perfect example of a case that became a precedent the moment the verdict was announced. 'Your verdict will be the most important in its consequences ever delivered before this tribunal,' Howe admonished the jury in his defence, implying broadly that the liberty of the press might be in jeopardy if they were to find against him.[66] A week before the trial commenced, Howe had confided to his wife his belief that if the jurors 'were fair and rational men, they must acquit me.'[67] In the event, the jury took all of ten minutes unanimously to find the accused not guilty. Following the direction of Chief Justice Halliburton, presiding, that they were to state by their verdict whether the letter published in the *Novascotian* was a libel, they concluded that it was not and found accordingly. (See app. 3, Q.)

No defence that induced a libel jury, in the wake of Fox's act of 1792, to return a unanimous verdict of not guilty could reasonably be described as 'from the point of view of the law ... magnificently irrelevant.'[68] Such an interpretation ignores the practical fact that the jury was ultimately judge of both law and fact; the judge could only advise and warn, direct and instruct – and then consent to the verdict, whatever it was. The jury's responsibility was greater still because there was no clear 'positive law' defining libel either as tort or as crime[69]; that was for the courts to determine by reference to accumulated case law, each case being decided on its own merits. Howe himself – not to mention one of the magistrates' two retained counsel who was 'moonlighting' as crown attorney – adduced Fox's act and expounded its pertinence to the case; Howe, adverting to its common-law aspect, styled it the 'Declaratory Act.' As part of formally received English criminal procedure and applicable as an imperial statute, therefore, Fox's act was in force and enforceable in Nova Scotia's King's Bench. To be sure, Attorney General Archibald passed over in silence an act that he knew to be the strongest legal weapon in Howe's tiny arsenal, but the crown attorney had already elucidated it in his opening while the accused Howe reprised the theme in his defence and Archibald lazily declined to recapitulate it in his reply. Nevertheless, even a scholarly biographer, such as Beck, is content to accept the attorney general's non-statement as an authoritative chief source of information about the law of libel as it then stood. Archibald said nothing about Fox's act; ergo, neither does Beck. Howe's exposition of the law, in which he dwelt with the implications of Fox's act, was more satisfactory because he had closely studied the treatise-writers in preparation for conducting his own defence.[70]

A likewise fallacious rationalization is to suggest, as did *Howe* centenary scholar J.A. Chisholm, that the law was disregarded by the jury in their verdict.[71] *Pace* Chief Justice Chisholm, the law was changed by the verdict of the jury precisely because the latter observed the law as it then stood with the most literal strictness, exercising their prerogative under Fox's act to 'give a general verdict upon the whole matter in issue.' They found that there was no libel, not necessarily because the charges were true or because their publication had been for the public benefit, but because there was no seditious intention. Howe was 'technically guilty'[72] of the offence only inasmuch as the pre-Fox's act common-law rule enabled the crown to infer malice, and hence guilt, from the mere fact of publication and forced the jury to concur in the innuendo ascribed by the crown. As a result of Fox's act, the jury *might* concur but was not obliged to. Howe took matters a step farther by asking the jury to infer absence of malice from truth and public benefit, these being the two elements that would afterwards combine in the Libel Act of 1843 ('Lord Campbell's Act') to form the modern defence of justification. The fact that the crown inferred malice, without having to prove the seditiousness of the published matter, was an attempt to presume the accused guilty, as it were, until he could prove himself innocent.[73]

The verdict in *Howe* demonstrates not only that Fox's act was in force in Nova Scotia, but also that it could and did redound to the benefit of the accused in libel. Howe correctly showed that Fox's act was passed 'in amelioration of the common law and increased the liberty of the subject,'[74] which provided the grounds for its reception. By rebutting the legal inference of malice, which operated as a presumption of guilt, Howe destroyed the crown's case against him and pointedly gave the jury that 'clear and distinct direction' which the bench should have done but failed to do: 'Their lordships [*sic*: his lordship] will tell you that you are the sole judges of the fact and of the law; and that although every word of what I have published were false, and its tendency most injurious, that you are to try me solely by the motive and intention by which I was controlled.'[75] By such muscular admonitions, Howe galvanized the jury to the full exercise of their powers on the verdict, powers that had been confirmed by Fox's act. The attorney general and the chief justice, for their part, supposed wrongly that given enough rope Howe would undoubtedly hang himself, as William Wilkie had done fifteen years earlier. The spirit of condescension wrought by age and professional vanity, joined to the comparative youth and social and occupational status of the accused, blinded both Archibald and Halliburton to the possibility that a mere tradesman, however intelligent, studious, and articulate, could mount a legally effective defence to a charge of seditious libel.[76]

Howe was very far from either being a lawyer or thinking and behaving like one, but he had studied intensively both the pertinent case law and the treatises. By no means 'magnificently irrelevant' from the point of view of law, moreover, Howe's defence exploited to the full the resources of English criminal law. Though the accused may well have 'stated a great variety of things which could not be evidence,'[77] he had also stated more law than either the attorney general in his summation or the chief justice in his charge. To the extent to which doubts in the common law respecting the function of juries in cases of libel were removed by Fox's act, Howe construed the remedial statute liberally.[78] Hence the astuteness of the jury's decision 'to take its view of libel, not from Archibald, not from Halliburton, but from Howe, and bring in a verdict of not guilty.'[79] Despite the irresistible brilliance of his oratory, Howe's triumph was more forensic than oratorical in character. To paraphrase Beck,[80] the accused had in effect convinced the jury that the procedural law applicable to their function in a libel case empowered them honourably to acquit him.

CONCLUSION

The question of criminal responsibility had been settled; civil liability was another matter. Spencer points out that a libel prosecution was not necessarily an alternative to civil action but could be pursued before, after, or concurrently with such action.[81] He also argues, however, that 'a large number of [private libel] prosecutions took place in situations where a civil action for defamation was not really a practicable or adequate alternative.' A class of action 'where the civil law would have been inept involves libels upon magistrates in the execution of their duties'[82] – presumably whether administrative or judicial. *Howe* may be considered to have involved both aspects: the magistrates of Halifax, not to mention the trial judge, certainly considered that the complainants were being libelled in the performance of their official duties.

Two days after the verdict, ten magistrates, including eight of the twelve and three of the magistrates whom Howe had criticized by name in his defence, met to consider their response to Howe's acquittal; a resolution to 'institute proceedings' for private-defamatory libel was tabled but voted down by a margin of four to three, three of the magistrates abstaining.[83] (Subsequent prosecutions would have been barred by *autrefois acquit*, if the attorney general failed to enter *nolle prosequi* on the indictment.) There were also legal ramifications over the long term; *Howe* certainly discouraged any further libel prosecutions.

In other respects, the trial *in toto* – not merely 'the events of March 3'[84] (crown's closing, judge's charge, and jury's verdict) – was pure anti-climax; Howe had already won the political struggle before the legal battle was even joined. Nevertheless, consigning the activist grand jury to oblivion in December 1834, while its organ the *Novascotian* went from strength to strength in January 1835, made certain that Howe would be the target when the inevitable counter-attack occurred. He would answer for the *lèse-majesté* of the old grand jury, while the government bided its time, taking 'six weeks to determine upon this prosecution.'[85] The trial was not really about law enforcement or the administration of criminal justice, but about official repression and prescribing the outer limits of political dissent. The municipal-government reforms that the three previous years' grand juries had so persistently sought were well in train before criminal proceedings against Howe as publisher of the alleged libel were instituted.[86] This fact perhaps weakens David Sutherland's contention that 'Joseph Howe, in his defence speech, argued that certain members of the magisterial board [that is, the twelve subscribing complainants] and Grand Jury had supported the prosecution in the expectation that a libel trial would force reform of the municipal government.'[87] Clearly, a plurality of the members of the grand jury had had to approve the indictment in order for it to proceed to trial, but Sutherland goes rather too far by suggesting that Howe himself thought that the case against him was the work of agents provocateurs. The preponderance of evidence suggests rather that the prosecution was a desperate rearguard action taken in order to quash the municipal-government reform movement being carried forward by the grand jury with the cooperation of Howe, a crusading editor who placed his newspaper at the disposal of the foreman.

Perhaps the most unsatisfactory aspect of Beck's restrictive, politico-biographical approach to *Howe* – the quintessential show trial – is that, while he is prepared to characterize as 'political' or even as 'state' trials the successful civil actions for private-defamatory libel brought against the radical reformer Richard Nugent, Howe's successor at the *Novascotian*, he withholds such apt characterizations from the unsuccessful public-libel prosecution of the 'conservative reformer' Howe, to whose trial for seditious libel they are far more applicable. What was true of

Richard Nugent in 1843 had been true, a fortiori, of Howe eight years earlier: he appeared to be the target 'of political enemies who, unable to contend effectively with the chief reform organ, sought to get rid of its ... editor by pursuing him mercilessly.'[88]

In terms of colonial legal history the significance of *Howe* lies in the fact that it was a long delayed replay of *Zenger*, 'the famous case that established the first important victory for freedom of the press in the colonies.'[89] George Farquhar, a centenary student of *Howe*, is the only one to have drawn the comparison with *Zenger*, which took place in New York exactly one hundred years previously.[90] Among Howe's contemporaries, not even those expatriate Nova Scotians resident in New York who presented Howe with an inscribed silver pitcher commemorating 'his eloquent and triumphant defence in support of the freedom of the press' made the obvious parallel. Like Howe, Zenger was a newspaper editor charged with publishing a seditious libel; unlike Howe, he was tried on an ex officio information after the grand jury refused to find a true bill on the indictment.[91] Just as counsel's successful defence of Zenger articulated the principles later to be entrenched in Fox's act, so Howe's successful defence of himself a century later, employing Fox's act, enabled him to disprove seditious intention to the jury by destroying the innuendo. The prosecution of Howe could have succeeded if Fox's act had not been passed or if it had not been in force in Nova Scotia; however, both of these conditions, essential to Howe's defence, were fully met. Howe, though without a lawyer to defend him, had as his allotted guardian counsel the shade of Thomas Erskine, owing to 'whose exertions,' declaimed Howe, 'the Declaratory Act [the Libel Act of 1792] was passed, confirming the right of juries to decide on the law and the facts, and whose views of the true bearing of the law of libel are now generally recognized.'[92] *Howe* – unlike *Zenger* – was able to become a 'legal precedent' precisely because the statutory lacuna had been filled in the interim. The myth that Howe established freedom of the press, which can be traced back directly to Howe's own first post-acquittal editorial in the *Nova-scotian*, subsisted continuously until Beck's ground-breaking 1974 article in *Acadiensis*.

Though *Howe* was indisputably a political trial, it was by no means the first instance of 'sedition in Nova Scotia'; excluding the eighteenth-century cases – *Hoffman* (1754), *Salter* (1777), and *Houghton* (1777) – pride of place belongs instead to *Wilkie*, the subject of which fared much worse when indicted and tried by Chief Justice Sampson Salter Blowers for seditious libel in 1820. Much the same can be said of another instance of postbellum reflex authoritarianism – *R. v. McLachlan* (1923), for seditious libel, arising out of working-class radicalism in industrial Cape Breton – which is the only later prosecution (other than *Dixon*) with which *Howe* is remotely comparable.[93]

From the point of view of the administration of criminal justice, the most interesting feature of *R. v. Howe* is that an anomaly in Nova Scotia's criminal procedure was used to explain the difference between private and public libel and to justify the prosecution. If the alleged libel was not prosecutable by private information, as criminal defamation – which the crown argued – how then could it be prosecutable by indictment, except as sedition?[94] No formal request for a *public*-libel prosecution should have been made; the lieutenant governor should have sought guidance from his chief law officer, rather than from his confidential advisers, before granting the magistrates' request; the attorney general should not have been ordered to institute proceedings without being specifically instructed by the government against whom he was to institute them. To this day, notwithstanding the dissimulation of crown counsel during the trial, it remains unclear who made the decision and who gave the order to prosecute Howe. Once the die was cast, however, Archibald could only feign to choose between prosecuting by indictment and prosecuting by ex officio information, thus placing the responsibility for the trial squarely on the backs of a compliant grand jury. He then had to prepare the indictment and present it to the grand jury, in the forlorn hope that they would recognize it for what it was – a shameless act of political brinkmanship – and quash it accordingly. Instead the grand jury, in their zeal to collaborate with government, committed the accused for trial, thereby trapping the attorney general in the invidious position of conducting the prosecution – against his inclinations and better judgment and towards probable failure. However much sympathy one feels for Howe, maliciously (though ineptly) prosecuted, one cannot help feeling some for Archibald, a great and honest lawyer compromised in the execution of his onerous official duty by a neophyte lieutenant governor's influence-peddling political advisers.

As an episode in the history of Canadian law – not merely one in the political career of Joseph Howe or even in the politics of Nova Scotia – the case of *R. v. Howe* clearly demonstrates the broad applications of a loosely defined political offence such as sedition.[95] The misdemeanour of seditious libel was doctrinally complicated by the fact that sedition and libel were separate offences, between which seditious libel was the judicially manufactured interface.[96] Sedition, like defamation, was one of the forms that criminal libel might take. Howe nevertheless was charged with 'libel,' and seditious libel thus represents an historical reconstruction, *faute de mieux*, of the legal heart of the lost indictment. Though it was in the interest of J.B. McLachlan's counsel, in 1923, to refer to Howe as a 'seditionist,' no one in 1835 – except Howe himself, and that only when straining for rhetorical effect – thought that he had been charged with sedition.[97] Few admirers of Howe would feel the force of G.S. Harrington's comparison of the radical reformer McLachlan to the 'conservative reformer' Howe, or agree that the government's motive in maliciously prosecuting McLachlan was really the same as its motive in maliciously prosecuting Howe.[98] Like the Upper Canada sedition cases analysed by Barry Wright, the Nova Scotia sedition cases 'suggest the importance of law both to the government and to the experiences of opposition figures.'[99] Whatever the long-term historical significance of *Howe* for the development of sedition law, its short-term legal effect was to decriminalize libel in pre-confederation Nova Scotia. Though political libel cases were common in subsequent years, they were all private actions not public prosecutions. As a result of *Howe*, the crime of libel had been temporarily transformed into the tort of defamation. Not until *McLachlan*, eighty-eight years later, was sedition in Nova Scotia heard of again: *Howe redivivus*.

NOTES

1 Kenneth McNaught, 'Political Trials and the Canadian Political Tradition,' *University of Toronto Law Journal*, vol. 24 (1974), 149 at 164 [repr. in *Courts and Trials: A Multi-disciplinary Approach*, ed. M.L. Friedland (Toronto: University of Toronto Press 1975), at 137]; J.M. Beck, '"A Fool for a Client": The Trial of Joseph Howe,' *Acadiensis*, vol. 3, no. 2 (1974), 27 at 39 [repr. in *Atlantic Canada before Confederation. The Acadiensis Reader: Volume One*, 2nd ed., comp. and ed. P.A. Buckner and David Frank (Fredericton: Acadiensis Press 1990), 243; repub., in lightly rewritten form, as chapter 9 of J.M. Beck, *Joseph Howe* (2 vols.), 1: *Conservative Reformer, 1804–1848* (Kingston and Montreal: McGill-Queen's University Press 1982), at 129]. See G.A. Rawlyk, 'J.M. Beck's *Joseph Howe*,' in *The Proceedings of the Joseph Howe Symposium: [1983] Mount Allison University* (Sackville N.B.: Centre for Canadian Studies, Mount Allison University; and Halifax: Nimbus 1984), 117 at 122.

2 *Howe* was not reported in 1 NSR [1 Thom. 2nd] and was therefore not cited in what is still 'the only Canadian text on criminal libel': J. King, *The Law of Crim-*

inal Libel (Toronto: Carswell 1912). The criminal-case file, which may have been consulted by William Annand for his *editio princeps* of 1858, was not known to exist at the time of the centenary in 1935. An informal stenographic report formed the basis of the imprint, *Trial for Libel | on the | Magistrates of Halifax, | The King vs. Joseph Howe, | Before the | Chief Justice and a Special Jury | Supreme Court – Hilary Term* (Halifax: [Joseph Howe] 1835), CIHM #62316; reprinted in *The Speeches and Public Letters of the Hon. Joseph Howe*, 2 vols., ed. William Annand (Boston: John P. Jewett 1858), 1: at 14, and thence in *The Speeches and Public Letters of Joseph Howe* ..., 2 vols., rev. and ed. J.A. Chisholm (Halifax: Chronicle Publishing 1909), 1: at 22.

3 J.M. Beck, *Politics of Nova Scotia* (2 vols.) vol. 1: *1710–1796* (Tantallon, N.S.: Four East 1985), at 101. *Howe* is indisputably 'the most celebrated of all Nova Scotian trials': ibid., at 109.

4 D.C. Harvey, 'The Intellectual Awakening of Nova Scotia,' *Dalhousie Review*, vol. 13 (1933), 1 [repr. in *Historical Essays on the Atlantic Provinces*, ed. G.A. Rawlyk (Toronto: McClelland and Stewart 1967), 99 at 99, 117]. See also *The Heart of Howe: Selections from the Letters and Speeches of Joseph Howe*, ed. D.C. Harvey (Toronto: Oxford University Press 1939), at 89–91 ('No sacrifice too great for freedom of the press').

5 On this subject see Barry Wright, 'Sedition in Upper Canada: Contested Legality,' *Labour/Le Travail*, vol. 29 (1992), 7; there is no reference to either *Wilkie* or *Howe* in that study.

6 *Nova Scotia Royal Gazette* (Halifax), 19 April 1820, at 3; G.V.V. Nicholls, 'A Forerunner of Joseph Howe,' *CHR*, vol. 8 (1927), at 224–32. David Sutherland takes the view that 'Nova Scotia had a parallel to Gourlay in the person of William Wilkie': D.A. Sutherland, 'Wilkie, William,' in *DCB* 5: 853; see also the author's article, 'Sedition in Nova Scotia: *R. v. Wilkie* (1820) and the Incontestable Illegality of Seditious Libel before *R. v. Howe* (1835),' *Dalhousie Law Journal*, vol. 17, no. 2 (fall 1994), 458. For the relationship between *Wilkie* and *Howe* as exercises in the official repression of political dissent, see J.S. Martell, 'Origins of Self-Government in Nova Scotia, 1815–1836' (PhD thesis, University of London 1935), at 375–6.

7 (1819) 60 Geo. III, c. 8 – one of the 'Six Acts,' a series of repressive measures enacted in the wake of the Peterloo Massacre; see J.R. Spencer, 'Criminal Libel – A Skeleton in the Cupboard,' in Crim. L.R. [1977], 383 at 384 and 386. On the English legal background to sedition and seditious libel, see this volume's introduction.

8 T.B. Akins, 'History of Halifax City,' *Nova Scotia Historical Society Collections*, vol. 8 (1895), at 88.

9 Chisholm, *Speeches*, 1: at 58. The Commissioners' Court was 'a court for the

summary trial of actions' – a prototype of the modern small-claims court – unique to Halifax township. It was established by act of the legislature in 1817, about two years after the Police Court came into being.

10 See generally D.A. Sutherland, 'The Merchants of Halifax, 1815–1850: A Commercial Class in Pursuit of Metropolitan Status' (PhD thesis, University of Toronto 1975), at 244–52.

11 See D.A. Sutherland, 'Foreman, James,' *DCB* 8: 299. Lending both his signature and his prestige to the magisterial request for a public prosecution was to be among Foreman's final acts as *custos*; before the end of January he had resigned, pleading old age: Minutes of Council, 26 Jan. 1835: RG 1, vol. 196: 115, PANS.

12 That is, twelve of those justices of the peace (out of a total of about thirty-two) who acted as magistrates; in other words, the active judicial bench, over which the *custos* of the district presided ex officio as the chief (though not necessarily the most senior) JP. At least three of the current active magistrates did not sign the complaint.

13 The bearer of the nom de plume was George Thompson (1800–56), an old friend of Howe's: Beck, *Howe*, 1: at 133.

14 'Sessions/1834' : RG 34–312, series P, vol. 11, PANS.

15 This, of course, was because Campbell cooperated with the old year's grand jury by expeditiously referring their complaints about the Court of Session first to the Council and then to the legislature: JHANS, 2 February 1835 and passim. On Campbell's administration (1834–40) see S.W. Spavold, 'Nova Scotia under the Administration of Sir Colin Campbell' (MA thesis, Dalhousie University 1953), and P.A. Buckner, 'Campbell, Sir Colin,' *DCB* 7: 142.

16 James Foreman *et al.* to Colin Campbell, 8 Jan. 1835: MG 20, vol. 700, file 49 (Royal Nova Scotia Historical Society fonds), PANS. All but two of the signatories – Samuel Head and John Howe, Jr (a printer) – were merchants; one of them was also a member of the grand jury for 1835; and four were to resign in consequence of the verdict in *Howe*. On the invidious position in which adjunct king's printer John Howe *fils* (1784–1843) – half-brother of Joseph – found himself, see Beck, *Howe*, 1: at 341n.28.

17 'Sessions/1834,' date 24 Jan. 1835.

18 Chisholm, *Speeches*, 1: at 77.

19 Wright, 'Sedition in Upper Canada.'

20 Campbell had taken office only the previous July.

21 The grand jury was the municipal-government watchdog; though both it and the Court of Session simultaneously performed judicial functions, they did not do so exclusively in relation to each other.

22 Beck goes so far as to state that 'the grand juries of the 1830's ... provided the

political education for the leading Reformers of Halifax, Howe included':
Howe, 1: at 29.

23 Chisholm, *Speeches*, 1: at 36; from this it is clear that Howe conceptualized the proceeding as a private prosecution for defamatory libel. It also explains Howe's emphasis on the priority of the private action, which would have brought the defence of justification within the ambit of procedural law, and suggests that Howe may have underestimated the depth of the government's interest and involvement in the prosecution.

24 J.A. Chisholm, 'More Letters of Joseph Howe,' *Dalhousie Review*, vol. 12 (1933), 481 at 483.

25 Beck, *Howe*, 1: at 30.

26 Ibid., 1: at 33. Howe was to quote the committee's report in the course of his defence speech; it remains unclear how he obtained a copy. Perhaps the source of it was Mrs Joseph Howe's paternal uncle, Peter McNab II (1767–1847), a prominent merchant who had been appointed to the Council in January 1832 and who was a member of the committee reporting on the grand jury's address.

27 Howe remarked to the trial jury that the old grand jury's final presentment 'at the close of the December term is a grosser libel than this letter [from "The People"]': Chisholm, *Speeches*, 1: at 60. Of course, it was a privileged communication, for publishing which Howe (or the foreman who supplied the copy) might conceivably have been prosecuted for criminal contempt towards the Court of Session.

28 For a revealing exchange between Archibald and Howe on this subject during the former's 'reply,' see Chisholm, *Speeches*, 1: at 77.

29 Chief Justice Halliburton, who presided at Howe's trial, had been a member of Council for twenty years and – since 1833 – its ex officio president. On the routine practice of senior colonial judges holding executive office, see this book's introduction. Lawyer-newspaper editor George Farquhar is the only student of *Howe* ever to have drawn attention to the anomalous position of Chief Justice Halliburton as trial judge; his conflict of interest 'was certainly in violent contradiction to every principle of justice': 'Howe's Great Victory Marked Beginning of New Era For The Press ...,' Halifax *Chronicle*, 4 March 1935, at 10.

30 Howe implied broadly that the committee of Council appointed to investigate the charges of maladministration against the Court of Session sided with the magistrates against the grand jury: Chisholm, *Speeches*, 1: at 61–3.

31 'Criminal Libel,' at 384.

32 Beamish Murdoch, *Epitome of the Laws of Nova-Scotia*, 4 vols. (Halifax: Joseph Howe 1832–3), 4: at 181–2.

33 In Nova Scotia the ex officio information was treated as if it were a high-

prerogative writ; it was rarely applied for and even more rarely issued – out of the Court of Chancery. In Upper Canada, on the other hand, the ex officio criminal information 'was widely resorted to': Wright, 'Sedition in Upper Canada,' at 18.

34 Chisholm, *Speeches*, 1: at 74.

35 (1834–5) 5 Wm. IV, c. 1: 'An Act to Alter the Sitting of the Next Ensuing Term of the Supreme Court at Halifax' (passed 29 Dec. 1834).

36 *Howe* does not appear on the attorney general's docket of causes for Hilary Term 1835: MG 1, vol. 89, doc. 250 (S.G.W. Archibald fonds), PANS.

37 'Extracts from the Minutes & proceedings of the Grand Jury for the County of – Halifax – Supreme Court/Hilary Term' [1835]: RG 34–312, series P, vol. 14, PANS. Five of the grand jurors were afterwards appointed magistrates to fill vacancies arising from the verdict in *Howe*: Stephen Newton Binney, William Anderson Black, Edward Cunard, Lawrence Hartshorne, and John Williamson; four of the five, however, excluding only the arch-Tory Binney, declined to serve.

38 Despite the fact that Starr had signed his name to the magistrates' complaint, in his capacity as grand juror he appeared to want no part in the prosecution of Howe: Starr's 'credibility as a reformer drew strength from the fact that he had been one of those Halifax magistrates to cooperate with Joseph Howe when court action ensued as a result of the latter's attempt in 1835 to bring certain local officials to account for alleged corruption and incompetence': D.A. Sutherland, 'Starr, John Leander,' *DCB* 11: 846 at 847.

39 What the *Novascotian* had been to the 1834 grand jury, the *Halifax Journal* was to the Court of Session: 'Shortly after the publication of the letter recited in this indictment,' observed Howe, 'a notice appeared in the *Halifax Journal* requesting the public to suspend their opinions until the magistrates could come forward and prove the falsity of the charges in a court of justice': Chisholm, *Speeches*, 1: at 32. 'Another of the People,' which was published in the Halifax *Journal* on 12 Jan. 1835, had clearly been written by someone who supposed – wrongly – that Howe was going to be privately prosecuted or sued for libel.

40 During the 1935 centenary celebration, Chief Justice Sir Joseph Andrew Chisholm made the following jejune observation on the action of the grand jury: 'No other course was reasonably open to them': J.A. Chisholm, 'The King v. Joseph Howe: Prosecution for Libel,' *CBR*, vol. 13 (1935), 584 at 587. Chisholm's point was that, while proof of publication by the accused was by no means sufficient grounds (as it had been previous to the passage of the Libel Act of 1792) to find the accused guilty, it remained sufficient grounds for the 'court of preliminary inquiry' to commit the accused for trial. On the implications for sedition law of the Libel Act of 1792, see Wright, 'Sedition in Upper Canada,' at 15.

41 The treasurer was presumably the provincial official, not the county official, whose accounting practices and management of fiscal affairs were to receive close, hostile scrutiny by Howe in his defence speech.

42 For Tremain's leading role in the affair, see D.A. Sutherland, 'Tremain, Richard,' *DCB* 8: 891 at 892, which argues persuasively that 'it was in character for Tremain to initiate the magisterial demand that Howe be tried for criminal libel.'

43 *Acadian Recorder* (Halifax), 28 Feb. 1835, at 3. The chief justice may have been implying that the magistrates should have considered changing the nature of the proceeding from prosecution to action, which would have answered the purpose of their resolution. If so, the proposal was belated. Once the grand jury had returned a true bill on the indictment, it was no longer possible even for the attorney general to stay the prosecution.

44 'Sessions/1834.'

45 None of the current active magistrates was a lawyer, and so perhaps – despite their collectively broad experience of criminal and civil adjudication – they did not know any better.

46 Chisholm, *Speeches*, 1: at 33. The six-week period would have been *c.* 1 Jan.–10 Feb. 1835: from the publication of the alleged libel to the delayed commencement of Hilary Term.

47 Ibid. Howe was mistaken in his view that witnesses for the defence could not be called at the trial of an indictment for high misdemeanour. That applied only to the preliminary inquiry before the grand jury – in camera – at which the indictee could neither be present nor represented by counsel.

48 Chisholm, *Speeches*, 1: at 82.

49 Beck, *Howe*, 1: at 136.

50 One of the government officials who may have been involved was the long-time (since 1814) secretary of the province, Sir Rupert Denis George. Though an ultramontane Tory hypochondriac at the nerve centre of the Government House clique, George was not a member of Council; nevertheless, he was ex officio clerk of that body.

51 Chisholm, *Speeches*, 1: at 52.

52 An omnibus Juries Act, consolidating and repealing four earlier acts, 1796 through 1833, was passed in Nova Scotia in 1838: 1 Vic., c. 6.

53 Spencer, 'Criminal Libel.'

54 J.R. Spencer, 'The Press and the Reform of Criminal Libel,' in *Reshaping the Criminal Law: Essays in Honour of Glanville Williams*, ed. P.R. Glazebrook (London: Stevens and Sons 1978), 266 at 271n.33. Archibald 'was the Sir James Scarlett of Nova Scotia, the greatest verdict-getter we have ever known and, like Sir James too, he proved to be a better advocate than judge': George

Patterson, *Studies in Nova Scotian History* (Halifax: Imperial 1940), at 49; see also J.M. Beck, 'Archibald, Samuel George William,' *DCB* 7: 21 at 22: 'In 1835 he [Archibald] participated in the prosecution of Joseph Howe for criminal libel but gave only a moderate speech to the jury, knowing full well that although Howe was guilty in law [*sic!*] he could not get a jury to convict him.'

55 J.M. Beck, 'Rise and Fall of Nova Scotia's Attorney General: 1749–1983,' in *Law in a Colonial Society: The Nova Scotia Experience*, ed. J.A. Yogis (Toronto: Carswell 1984), 125 at 129. Beck's characterization of Archibald as 'the last non-party attorney general of Nova Scotia' (ibid., at 130) speaks volumes about his discomfiture during the Howe trial, though of course non-party did not mean non-political.

56 Wright, 'Sedition in Upper Canada,' at 18.

57 So inimical were the new grand jurors to the reformist initiatives of their immediate predecessors that they ordered the last 'Memorandum' (which may have had something to do with the continuing controversy as to the prerogative of selecting the foreman) 'expunged' from the official record of proceedings: RG 34–312, series P, vol. 13, PANS.

58 Beck, *Howe*, 1: at 31.

59 Spencer, 'Criminal Libel,' at 387.

60 Spencer points out that 'political libel prosecutions ... continued in large numbers for the next 40 years [after the passage of Fox's act], and in many of the cases the government was seeking to silence discussion of what would now indisputably be regarded as legitimate topics of public interest': ibid., at 385. The analogy with *Howe* is unmistakable.

61 The summoning of a special jury was one of a number of distinguishing features that marked political-libel prosecutions: Spencer, 'Criminal Libel,' at 384. On special juries in criminal cases, which ('according to the course of the common law') were obtainable only in trials for misdemeanour, see Murdoch, *Epitome*, 3: at 175–8. The provision was based on a section of the English statute (1730) 3 Geo. II, c. 25, which 'has been held to apply to criminal indictments or informations in cases of misdemeanor.' Murdoch also pointed out, however, that the corresponding provincial act of 1796 was 'more general and extensive in its expressions than the English statute, though possibly the same interpretation would be given to both acts.'

62 J.M. Beck, 'Nugent, Richard,' *DCB* 8: 656 at 657. (The reference is to actions for defamation, but it applies equally to prosecutions for public libel.)

63 Beck, *Howe*, 1: at 136, gives a very helpful prosopography of the jury; see also Sutherland, 'Merchants of Halifax,' at 264n.77. Sutherland's occupational analysis shows one butcher [?], six merchants, one ship chandler, one 'gentleman,' and three tradesmen.

64 *Times* (Halifax), 3 March 1835, at 7. Here again was a contemporary Tory perspective on the blurring of what in England 'was always the clearest of distinctions between government prosecutions of dangerous critics of the established order on the one hand, and prosecutions by or on behalf of private persons who had been defamed on the other': Spencer, 'Criminal Libel,' at 384. So completely misunderstood, or perhaps deliberately misrepresented, by a rival organ was *Howe* that it is misconstrued as a civil proceeding by the crown for defamation.

65 Chisholm, *Speeches*, 1: at 82.

66 Ibid., 1: at 70. 'Your verdict will protect me to-day against the persecution of the sessions': ibid., 1: at 69. The jurisdiction of the Quarter Sessions over libel was such a well-settled part of the common law that a statute was required to abolish it: (1842) 5 and 6 Vic., c. 38, s. 1.

67 Chisholm, 'More Letters,' at 482.

68 Beck, *Howe*, 1: at 140. 'The law was completely against him': Beck, *Politics*, at 109. Simply to regurgitate the weak arguments supporting the crown's unsuccessful case does not make for a balanced historical analysis of the legal character of the trial. In one sense the law was for rather than against Howe, the Libel Act of 1792 having made certain that a person accused of libel could plead innocence of intention and false innuendo directly to the jury.

69 Beck (*Howe*, 1: at 135), again following Archibald, seems to regard this as a defence argument requiring rebuttal by the crown. Common law, in the sense of judge-made case law, was no less substantive for not being 'positive' in the sense of a statutory enactment.

70 Attorney General Archibald did not exploit 'the strategic advantage of the last word to the jury (which was not enjoyed by other prosecutors)': Wright, 'Sedition in Upper Canada,' at 18. Whether or not the defence called any witnesses was immaterial to the law officers' prerogative right of reply.

71 Chisholm, 'King v. Joseph Howe,' at 592. Beck (*Howe*, 1: at 141) approvingly quotes this passage from Chief Justice Chisholm, with whom he is in broad agreement on the legal meaning of the trial. To state, as does Chisholm, that 'no new rule of law was established,' however, is not only to depreciate Howe's defence but also to fail to grasp the jury's reason for acquitting him. The 'new rule of law' propounded by Howe was established by the jury through their verdict, which would have operated as a *de facto* judicial reception of the Libel Act of 1792 had it not already formed part of the corpus of formally received English criminal law.

72 M.G. Crawford, *The Journalist's Legal Guide*, 2nd ed. (Toronto: Carswell 1990), at 2.

73 Wright ('Sedition in Upper Canada,' at 17) explains why Upper Canada's

retrospective statutory reception of English criminal law may coincidently have barred reception of the Libel Act of 1792. The leading Canadian case on the reception of Fox's act is *R. v. Dougall et al.*, (1874) 18 LC Jurist 85 (Que. QB), for criminal defamation.

74 *Uniacke v. Dickson*, (1848) 2 NSR 287 at 291 (NS Ch), *per* Chief Justice Halliburton. Halliburton was articulating – in the very words of his predecessor, Blowers, who served as chief justice from 1797 to 1833 – the *sole* criterion for common-law reception of English statute law in Nova Scotia. The stenographic report of *Howe* is perhaps the strongest empirical evidence that the Libel Act of 1792 was good law. On this subject, see this book's introduction.

75 Chisholm, *Speeches*, 1: at 32.

76 As late as 1923 counsel for the appellant in *McLachlan v. R.* argued, 'The law in regard to seditious libel is as it was before the passage of Cox's [*sic*: Fox's] Libel Act': (1924) 56 NSR 413 at 417 (NSSC in Banco), *per* Harrington KC.

77 Chisholm, *Speeches*, 1: at 74.

78 See Murdoch's 'Rules of construing Statutes,' *Epitome*, 1: 23 at 24.

79 Beck, *Howe*, 1: at 38.

80 Ibid., 1: at 141.

81 'Criminal Libel,' at 470–1. Spencer is referring, of course, to private persons. It is arguable that in the nineteenth century, as earlier, minor public officials (for example, magistrates) who were libelled in a newspaper did not have the option of suing for damages or bringing a private prosecution.

82 Ibid., at 390.

83 'Sessions/1834,' 5 March 1835. Mover of the resolution was J.L. Starr (see n.38), seconder John Howe Jr (see n.16). (I owe this reference to the unpublished research of D.C. Harvey: MG 1, vol. 441, file 108 [Daniel Cobb Harvey fonds], PANS.)

84 Beck, *Howe*, 1: at 37.

85 Chisholm, *Speeches*, 1: at 33.

86 Three of the four reform bills died on the order paper, however, and were not reintroduced at the next (1836) session – Howe's first as Reform MHA for Halifax County: JHANS, February 1835, passim.

87 Sutherland, 'Merchants of Halifax,' at 263n.74; see also Beck's intriguing speculation, which imputes this motive to Howe himself: *Howe*, at 31n.22.

88 Beck, 'Nugent, Richard,' at 657, and 'Rise and Fall,' at 130. The two *Nugent* cases of 1843 illustrate the trend away from private-libel prosecutions and towards private-libel actions. The reason why civil actions of a pseudo-criminal character proliferated in the wake of *Howe* was that crown prosecutions for public or political libel were no longer viable. However, the effects of the attitudinal change, which was shortly to manifest itself in the failure of the

Libel Act of 1843 (Lord Campbell's Act) to address public or political libel, were only beginning to be felt in Nova Scotia.

89 'Zenger, John Peter,' *Encyclopaedia Britannica* (1965 ed.), vol. 23, at 944.

90 See n.29. 'John Peter Zenger in the British colony of New York in 1735 and Joseph Howe in Nova Scotia in 1835 won their cases despite the fact that they were prosecuted rather than sued': W.H. Kesterton, *The Law and the Press in Canada* (Toronto: McClelland and Stewart 1976), at 3.

91 Zenger, moreover, again like Howe, published a full account of the trial in his newspaper; this passed through several editions as a pamphlet and even found its way into Howell's State Trials, which Howe is known to have perused: (1735) 17 St. Tr. 675 (NYSC). *Zenger* nevertheless was not adduced by Howe in his defence, which drew exclusively upon English precedents. Howe's knowledge of American jurisprudence was confined to his reading of Chancellor Kent, who discussed liberty of the press under the heading 'law of libels' but nowhere cited *Zenger*: James Kent, *Commentaries on American Law*, rev. ed. (Philadelphia: Blackstone 1889), 2: at 19; Chisholm, *Speeches*, 1: at 71.

92 Chisholm, *Speeches*, 1: at 66.

93 See David Frank, 'The Trial of J.B. McLachlan,' in Canadian Historical Association, *Historical Papers/Communications Historiques* (Vancouver: 1983), 208 at 221 (comparison with *Howe*). See also Barry Cahill, '*Howe* (1835), *Dixon* (1920) and *McLachlan* (1923): Comparative Perspectives on the Legal History of Sedition,' *University of New Brunswick Law Journal*, vol. 45 (1996); and idem, 'A Forerunner of J.B. McLachlan?: Sedition, Libel and Manipulating the Myth of Howe,' in Royal Nova Scotia Historical Society *Collections*, vol. 44 (1996).

94 Chisholm, *Speeches*, 1: at 74 ('The Attorney General's Reply').

95 This paraphrases Frank, 'Trial of J.B. McLachlan,' at 208–9.

96 See this volume's introduction. The problem of definition justly complained of by Frank ('Trial of J.B. McLachlan,' at 219) is an old one: 'I can't separate from the idea of a seditious libel the tendency to excite sedition': *R. v. Woodfall*, (1774) 98 ER 914 (KB), *per* Harding, counsel for the accused. This reflects the common lawyer's conundrum – originating in case law and subsisting until Lord Brougham's dismissal of it as a legal fiction – of the inseparability of the idea of defamatory libel upon public officials and the tendency to create a breach of the peace. The distance between defamation and sedition might be short indeed.

97 Howe nevertheless read into the record extracts from the indictment, a copy of which had been given him by the attorney general – as if he were the accused in a treason trial – which make clear that he stood charged with sedition, not defamation: Chisholm, *Speeches*, 1: at 36–7, 52.

98 On this subject, see the popular biography by John Mellor, *The Company Store:*

James Bryson McLachlan and the Cape Breton Coal Miners 1900–1925 (Toronto: Doubleday 1983), at 203, 224, 230, 234–7. A scholarly biography of McLachlan is in preparation by David Frank.

99 Wright, 'Sedition in Upper Canada,' at 56. Wright's conclusions regarding sedition in pre-rebellion Upper Canada are generally applicable to Nova Scotia and to *Howe* in particular. Howe, more so perhaps than the Upper Canadian Reformers, including Robert Gourlay, typifies those subject to the sedition proceedings examined in Wright's article, for whom 'the fact that there was resort to criminal law as the means of repression yielded opportunities for contesting it' (ibid., at 50). If the study of sedition in Upper Canada 'centres on the Gourlay affair' (ibid., at 8), moreover, then the study of sedition in Nova Scotia must centre on the trial of Joseph Howe for seditious libel.

Appendix 1

Approaching an Iceberg: Some Guidelines for Understanding Archival Sources Relating to State Trials

PATRICIA KENNEDY

The investigation of treason, sedition, and related offences perceived to threaten the political order or state security requires both comprehensive, accurate source materials and certain skills for their interpretation. Is it reasonable to presume that the reports from colonial governors to the imperial authorities offer consistent and thorough, if not exhaustive, recounting of such matters? Or did these reports mention only selective cases, using carefully chosen types of documentation? How will an understanding of administrative structures and bureaucratic processes – possibly even more than any knowledge of the law and judicial structures – facilitate the interpretation of documents generated within them?

Where and how one approaches the mass of administrative records determines the quantity and quality of data one may find and how effectively a document and its context may be assessed. Is an action typical or anomalous? A research strategy is essential. The strategic questions for locating documents are: Who would have had reason to record the information one desires? What form might that record take? Where and by whom might the record be preserved?

The nature and fashion of recording information reflect the interests and concerns of the document creator, whether those concerns were chosen by or dictated to him.[1] Detailed, comprehensive lists of persons brought for trial might be compiled by any of a number of officials, but only two types were likely to identify the category of offences. The calendars compiled by clerks of the courts were a means of reporting judicial activities to the governor, through his civil secretary, and should have been filed by the latter. Court clerks, as well as the attorney general and solicitor general, incorporated lists of cases (often specifying charges for drafting and filing documents) in their accounts submitted for audit, as justification for expenses. Such documents should have been preserved by the clerk of the Executive Council in his capacity as secretary to the Board of Audit (a committee of the Executive Council).[2] Archivists preserve the surviving documents in *fonds* and series which reflect the work of the officials who accumulated incoming letters, petitions, and other documents or maintained letterbooks and registers to record texts of outgoing communications and used daybooks, registers, and other control systems to record their activities.[3]

Interpreting the records requires a similar set of questions. What concerns of the author and recipient might affect the content? How many and which details are recorded? How did an official's responsibilities affect what he recorded? The governor might be satisfied with reporting his actions to London – the fact that he had issued a commission, pardon, or warrant. By contrast, the provincial secretary and registrar was responsible for recording in his registers the full texts of all documents issued over the Great Seal, to provide a copy for future reference. Recognizing that is the key to locating the commission issued 24 May 1797 to authorize the treason trial of David McLane.[4]

To determine the incidence of crimes against the state and to obtain the fullest range of information on any one case – be it designated treason, sedition, or otherwise – one must understand the hierarchy of administrative structures and bureaucratic processes within which the official records[5] were created, transmitted, and accumulated for preservation purposes. For the colonies of British North America, that hierarchy is illustrated in the accompanying diagram. Within the hierarchy, documents served to communicate information both horizontally between administrative structures and vertically from one level of authority to another. The records created at each level reflect the authority exercised by and the concerns of specific officials.

The characteristics of the information recorded in the documents created at specific levels and transmitted to others vary significantly. The nature, quality, and quantity of details at each level epitomize the focus of the record keepers. Delegation of authority downward may be specific or general, as circumstances warranted. Reports of compliance, or justifying non-compliance, sent upward would include or exclude details likely to satisfy or displease the recipient. A wise governor chose carefully those individual cases or specific incidents mentioned in his dispatches. They fell into three broad categories: matters of pride, of protection, and of precedent. The supporting documents he enclosed were carefully selected to illustrate how well he merited promotion, to counteract the reports of his detractors and thus prevent demotion, or to refer to London exceptional matters beyond the governor's delegated powers and the expertise of his immediate advisers. Thus, it is not surprising that in 1765, expecting to be recalled and ques-

Apex	Colonial Office Governor dispatches &c	*Imperial Superstructure*
Centre	Executive Council Civil Secretary Provincial Secretary Attorney General, &c Court of King's Bench, &c internal correspondence &c	*Central Structures of Colonial Administration*
Base	Sheriffs Court of Quarter Sessions Clerks of the Peace/of Assize	Infrastructure

The Pyramid of Power

tioned on his conduct as governor of Quebec, James Murray chose not to inform his superiors of the attorney general's bungling attempt to try Jean-Marie Ducharme and François Cazeau for offences against the state.[6]

The principle cannot be overemphasized. Consistent with the nature of bureaucratic structures, justificatory or supporting documentation submitted to higher authorities was tailored to satisfy its intended audience, whether that audience's interests had been stated or were presumed. Due recognition must be given to one other factor: some matters may not have been recorded on paper. The size of the colonial administration was often so small that written reports may have seemed redundant. Much was done on verbal instructions.[7]

The authority structures at the apex of the pyramid focused on policy and strategy. Documents generated at this level emphasize grand concepts, the 'political reality.' The documents brought up from lower levels to support or justify the governor's reports share that focus. The structures operating at the central level exercised authority throughout the colony and had jurisdiction co-terminous with the colony's boundaries. Documents they generated emphasize the implementation of policy, the inception of operations. Again, documents from lower levels might be used to illustrate or justify contentions. At the base of the pyramid, institutions with limited jurisdiction (functionally, geographically, or temporally) focused on the actual implementation of operations. Documents they generated emphasize the specific details, the 'human reality.' Reports of state prisoners from the sheriff of various districts in Upper Canada tell of leg-irons and manacles, rations, specific medical attendance, shrouds and coffins, and the logistics of transporting men under guard by wagon or steamship.[8]

Examination of records accumulated at the central and infrastructure levels enable us to assess the gloss put on events in the governor's reports to London: how his reportage shaped the events to suit his and imperial purposes by selective reporting of both the incidents and their details. The imperial authorities indulged in the same tactics. Scrutiny shows that the lists of state prisoners printed in the British *Parliamentary Papers* are neither complete nor accurate. They omit names and details found elsewhere. Imprecise phrasing may cause misinterpretation of dates, circumstances of discharge, and other factors. The lists, trial proceedings, and certain accompanying dispatches were selected and printed in 1839–40 to satisfy parliament. There is every reason to believe that confidential dispatches were excluded to avoid compromising colonial and imperial security. When governors were instructed not to reveal confidential dispatches even to the Executive Council, who would authorize their publication?

Close examination also shows the lists in the Executive Council minute books[9] to be fallible. The jail registers and returns of prisoners compiled by sheriffs, and a return for the Toronto General Hospital, are the most comprehensive and probably the most reliable source for names of individuals and dates of their incarceration. However, these lists do not specify the charges preferred against the prisoners nor the terms under which they were released. Such legal niceties are better documented at higher levels. Indeed, the principal enclosures with the dispatches were copies of trial proceedings, affidavits, opinions of the law officers of the crown, petitions for clemency, and various letters. Rarely do the dispatches offer evidence of the physical reality: how prisoners were treated, use of manacles and leg-irons, meat or tea supplied to supplement the basic jail ration of bread and soup, soap and laundry services, and medical care accorded to sick or wounded men[10] – women are conspicuous by their absence from these lists.

Consideration of the strengths and weaknesses of records at each level demonstrates that the only way to locate the details necessary for painting a comprehensive picture of state trials and the definition of offences against the state is to examine the records produced and preserved at all administrative levels. It may prove impossible to determine the optimum strata to investigate first, the level most likely to provide names or dates and other details essential to locating information recorded elsewhere. Almost invariably, discoveries made during an investigation necessitate a review of sources to locate additional material or examine data previously ignored and a reinterpretation of preliminary conclusions. Taking a strategic approach to the mass of records in several archives should minimize the likelihood of heading down dead-end trails or otherwise attacking the records to little purpose. Determining that certain officials did not record particular categories of information can be an effective strategy for eliminating unrewarding lines of research.

Exploring below the tip of the iceberg reveals not only a wide range of little known cases but also unfamilar aspects of the well-known treason trials. A few examples are worth mentioning to illustrate what remains to be investigated regarding crimes against the state.

The term book for the Court of King's Bench[11] solves a long-standing puzzle regarding Gideon Tiffany, sometime government printer of Upper Canada. Tried on a charge of blasphemy during the Easter Term, 1797, Tiffany entered a plea of guilty. Sentence was recorded 19 July: that he pay a fine of £20, be confined one calendar month in the jail at Newark, and find securities for three years of £100 himself and two others of £50 each. Should this charge be considered the equivalent of extreme seditious libel, a crime against the state? Given that his conviction disqualified him from public office – effecting his dismissal as government printer – was this prosecution analagous to those of Francis Collins and William Lyon Mackenzie? Suspect for his republican sentiments and American origins, Tiffany was no less a thorn in the government's flesh than were later newspaper editors. Was subverting the authority of the state church the first charge the government could pin on a man of suspect political affiliations?[12]

Clemency was often effected by means other than legislative or judicial processes. Throughout the British regime, there are cases of the release without trial of persons whom the attorney general and associated officials determined to be not worth prosecuting, either because they were unsuitable objects for show trials or for lack of evidence. The number of such cases is relatively easy to determine by using jail registers and court calendars. Those who made the decision not to prosecute rarely committed their rationale to paper, but their oblique references abound – notably when the costs of prosecution, or a prisoner's state of health, were discussed.

The state might be merciful with respect to property as well as to persons. To what extent was confiscation of estates actually effected after the rebellions of 1837–8? The amnesty statutes specify that the state had not carried attainder of estates to its logical conclusion in Upper or Lower Canada. The two Province of Canada acts 10 Victoria c. 106 (reversing attainder generally) and 12 Victoria c. 12 (granting free and general pardon to those previously considered to have participated in the rebellions) offer no comprehensive lists of individuals – and indeed name only John Montgomery and Peter Matthews, for whom specific legislative provision had been made by the acts 8 Victoria c. 106 and 9 Victoria c. 105. While the confiscation of property during the War of 1812 is documented in court records, the audited public accounts, and a range of administrative reports in Upper Canada, the same is not true during and after the rebellions of 1837–8. The sheriffs submitted exhaustive accounts for their expenditures in apprehending and guarding state prisoners in Upper Canada, but they were conspicuously silent on the question of confiscation. If the seizures of *Patriote* property that took place in Lower Canada were effected not pursuant to judicial processes but rather in the heat of military operations, then the claims of the amnesty acts are valid.[13]

The two specific statutes reversing attainder merit investigation. The first was sought by Montgomery's creditors, the second was achieved through the persistent petitioning of Hannah Matthews. Refraining from comment on the execution of her husband, Peter, she used a plea of distraint of dower rights.[14] The attainder question serves to remind us that the authority for an action should not be construed as evidence of its being carried into effect. A well-designed search to locate documents must be balanced with careful interpretation of what is found – or not found – in the records.

The image of an iceberg is an appropriate analogy for the mass of archival records in that researchers are most familiar with its tip and many have distorted perceptions of the size and shape of what lies below. Recognition of the parallels between hierarchical administrative structures and the stratification of records they produced may come through equally potent images of pyramids or funnels. Regardless of the metaphor, researchers must recognize that choosing to investigate any one level of records will determine the range, quality, and quantity of information to be found and one's ability to interpret it in context. Choice of starting point may also determine the effectiveness of investigation at other levels by revealing or concealing names, dates, and evidence of procedures that form essential links between records in the various strata. The available indexes are few and fallible.

Documents accumulated at the apex of the administrative hierarchy record the government's rationale for the major state trials. To determine the names of all who might have been prosecuted and why and how action was taken or suspended requires an investigation of records accumulated at lower levels. The details necessary to draw a comprehensive picture of where, how, and when offences against the state were defined and punishment effected were never consistently recorded by any one official at any one level. An appropriate research strategy should uncover the desired details from the best sources.

NOTES

1 The use of *he* and *him* for record-creators during the British regime is appropriate because government officials were exclusively male. (Queen Victoria was not a mere official.) Furthermore, the women who wrote to the government consciously used a rhetoric acknowledging (and taking significant advantage of) male concerns.

2 Indeed, large numbers of such records are scattered through the audited public accounts of Quebec and Lower Canada (RG 1, E 15 A, NA) and of Upper Canada (RG 1, E 15 B, NA), as well as the civil secretary's correspondence files (RG 4, A 1 and RG 5, A 1, NA).

3 The dispersal of records in imperial, federal, and provincial archives may seem random but is in fact a reflection of record-*keeping* practices and principles. Pre-1867 records of the former Province of Canada were apportioned to Ottawa, Toronto, and Quebec in accordance with Article 143 of the BNA Act: where the responsibility went, there also would go the personnel and the records. Crown lands became a provincial responsibility, and so the surveyor general's records went to the provinces. While most entrybooks of land grants and leases maintained by the provincial secretary and registrar went to the provinces, Ottawa retained those for Indian lands (see RG 68, NA). Clemency being a viceregal prerogative, the entrybooks of pardons were also retained in Ottawa (again, see RG 68, NA).

4 In his dispatch to the Duke of Portland on 27 May 1797, Governor Robert Prescott reported issuing the commission but did not enclose a copy (see CO 42/109). The text was recorded in the first Register of Commissions and Special Court Pardons for Lower Canada (RG 68, vol. 130: 76–8, NA).

5 The private or personal papers of individuals and such public documents as newspapers do offer information on specific incidents. The prosecution of

cases (and the state's decision not to prosecute), however, are most comprehensively documented in official, administrative records – particularly when one considers the rarity of private prosecutions in the colonial context.

6 The editors address George Suckling's mishandling of the case in the introduction to this volume. Ducharme and Cazeau repeated their roles as incompetent gun-runners when the Americans invaded Quebec in 1775, evading prosecution through flight.

7 The frequency of verbal instructions can be assessed only when there is more than random evidence. As justification for the accounts he submitted to the Board of Audit (see RG 1, E 15 B, NA), the attorney general of Upper Canada obtained letters from the civil secretary confirming the number and nature of verbal instructions. A preliminary review of these records showed that this practice continued through the 1830s.

8 Numerous statements and vouchers for expenditures in the period 1837–40 have survived among the Board of Audit records for Upper Canada (RG 1, E 15 B, NA). These include monthly nominal returns of state prisoners detailing the dates of receipt and discharge, deaths, and transfers between hospitals and jails. They offer the most comprehensive listing of known or suspected rebels.

9 The minute books for Lower Canada, Upper Canada, and the united Province of Canada are all found in RG 1, E 1 (NA). The submissions on which the minutes were based are scattered in several NA series, notably RG 4, A 1; RG 1, E 3; and RG 1, E 7.

10 Detailed statements and vouchers of expenditures by officials of the civil establishment in each colony of British North America were sent to London for presentation to the Audit Office. The dispatches do not record their transmittal in a fashion likely to alert anyone to their existence, nor the wealth of detail in them. Investigation of Audit Office 3 at the Public Record Office reveals that disappointingly few of those documents were preserved in London. Duplicates retained with submissions to the Board of Audit in Quebec, Lower Canada, and Upper Canada have survived in significant quantities (see RG 1, series E 15 A and E 15 B, NA). These accounts both complement and supplement jail registers, court calendars, and the attorney general's correspondence. The surviving jail registers and court calendars (scattered in several NA series, notably RG 4, B 20 and B 21 for Lower Canada and RG 5, B 27 for Upper Canada) emphasize legal matters, such as crimes and dates of conviction, while the accounts focus more on number of days for which food was supplied than on the specific dates.

11 I am indebted to Alix McEwen for examining the term book for 1794–6 (RG 22, series 125, vol. 1: 51–2, 55–6, AO) in 1990, when my interest in Tiffany focused on his career as a printer. Searching the accounts of various officials for refer-

ences to printing accidentally brought to light the solicitor general's charges for prosecuting Tiffany.

12 Barry Wright is pursuing these and other questions about Tiffany's career.

13 This question awaits investigation; the delights of resolving such questions as this should not be mine alone.

14 With one major exception, the petitions submitted by Hannah Matthews in 1843–5 and related correspondence have survived with the numbered files and letterbooks of the Provincial Secretary (RG 5, series C 1 and C 2, NA).

Appendix 2

Note on Sources

PATRICIA KENNEDY

ABBREVIATIONS AND ACRONYMS

The abbreviations and acronyms listed below reflect practice common to archival and historical works. Abbreviations for jurisdictions in the colonial era have been expanded beyond the representation in the *Canadian guide to uniform legal citation/ manuel canadien de la référence juridique* (Toronto: Carswell 1992), which we have adopted as our base guideline for legal citation to supplement the University of Toronto Press/Osgoode Society style guide.[1]

AHR	*American Historical Review*
ANQ	Archives nationales du Québec (Quebec City, Que.)
AO	Archives of Ontario (Toronto, Ont.)
APC	*Acts of the Privy Council of England. Colonial Series. 1613–1783*
BCARS	British Columbia Archives and Records Service (Victoria, B.C.)
CHR	*Canadian Historical Review*
CIHM	Canadian Institute for Historical Microreproductions
BL	British Library (formerly, British Museum; London, England)
CON DOCS	*Documents Relating to the Constitutional History of Canada, 1791–1828* (ed. Adam Shortt and Arthur Doughty)
CSPC	*Calendar of State Papers, Colonial* (America and West Indies). 1513–1737
CSPD	*Calendar of State Papers, Domestic, 1547–1718*
CSPF	*Calendar of State Papers, Foreign*

DAB	*Dictionary of American Biography*
DCB	*Dictionary of Canadian Biography*
DNB	*Dictionary of National Biography* (Great Britain)
EHR	*English Historical Review*
JCTP	*Journal of the Commissioners for Trade and Plantations*. 1704–82 (verbatim publication of the minutes now designated CO 391/17–89)
JHA	*Journal* of the House of Assembly (followed by the intials of the province in question)
JLC	*Journal* of the Legislative Council (followed by the initials of the province in question)
MA	Massachusetts Archives (Boston, Mass.)
MSRC	*Mémoires et comptes rendus de la Société royale du Canada* (also, MCSRC)
MTRL	Metropolitan Toronto Reference Library
NA	National Archives (Ottawa, Ont.)
NBM	New Brunswick Museum (Saint John, N.B.)
NYCD	*Documents Relative to the Colonial History of the State of New York*
OH	*Ontario History*
PACR	*Public Archives of Canada Report*
PANB	Provincial Archives of New Brunswick (Fredericton, N.B.)
PANL	Provincial Archives of Newfoundland and Labrador (St John's, Nfld.)
PANS	Public Archives of Nova Scotia (Halifax, N.S.)
PARO	Provincial Archives and Records Office of Prince Edward Island (Charlottetown, P.E.I.)
PRO	Public Record Office (London, England)
PRSC	*Proceedings and Transactions of the Royal Society of Canada* [also, PTRSC]
RAQ	*Rapport des archives du Québec*
RHAF	*Revue d'histoire de l'Amérique française*
SOQ	Statutes of the Old Province of Quebec, 1764–91

NON-LEGAL ABBREVIATIONS

Archival Sources

Documents consulted in published collections, such as the *Acts of the Privy Council of England, Colonial Series*, the *Calendar of State Papers, Colonial*, or *Constitutional Documents*, and the works of T.B. Akins and Ernest Cruikshank *et al.*, are identified by citations to those works. While many of the principal sources have been consulted in microforms, citations identify the original records according to the style of their custodial institutions (such as CO 217/38 from the PRO or RG 5, A 1, vol. 16 from the NA). For major collections of private papers, citations use a short form of the title proper (as in Prescott Papers, vol. 24: 6; or Neilson Collection, vol. 14: 72) rather than the formal archival call number where such practice is deemed to combine brevity with benefit to the reader.

The National Archives holds microfilm of the major imperial records relevant to all areas of Canada (and provides a loan service), while each provincial archives holds microfilm of selected imperial records relevant to its region. Microforms of certain provincial holdings are available in the National Archives, and vice versa.

Citation styles reflect the preferred practice of the custodial institutions. Wherever this is unique or distinct in style (notably the BL and PRO), citations may omit the institutional acronym. Widespread use of Record Group and Manuscript Group in Canadian archives requires the inclusion of the archives' acronyms with each citation of an RG or MG. *The list below identifies the formal (archival) titles of the series of records and collections/fonds of private papers for which abbreviated forms of citation have been used.*

British Library

Add. MSS 19069–19071	Rev. Andrew Brown collection
Add. MSS 21661–21892	Sir Frederick Haldimand papers
Add. MSS 58855–59478	William Wyndham Grenville papers

Public Record Office

The PRO uses the terms *class* and *piece* where North Americans would use series and volume. The style for PRO citations used in this volume separates letters and numbers in class codes, which are then separated from the piece/volume by a stroke (unspaced), followed by folio/page numbers or subdivisions within a volume, as CO 226/39/232–44. Volume sequences are indicated as *CO 42/75–9.*

The texts of early legislation, particularly ordinances and acts not printed at the time of passage, may be found in the relevant PRO classes for the jurisdiction. Thus, CO 44 holds the Ordinances of Quebec, 1764–91, while CO 219 holds the Ordinances of Cape Breton, 1784–1820, as well as those of Nova Scotia before 1758. Texts of proclamations may be found with dispatches or the acts, or in the gazettes (for example, CO 230). Minutes of the Executive Council and journals of the legislatures were segregated in the class Sessional Papers.

Admiralty:	ADM
Audit Office:	AO (for example, AO 12 Claims, American Loyalists. Series I)
Colonial Office:	
CO 1	Colonial Papers. General Series
CO 5	America and West Indies. Original Correspondence (received)
CO 42	Canada. Original Correspondence (including Quebec, Lower Canada, Upper Canada, and Province of Canada, 1764–1867)
CO 43	Canada. Entrybooks
CO 44	Canada. Acts
CO 188	New Brunswick. Original Correspondence
CO 189	New Brunswick. Entrybooks
CO 190	New Brunswick. Acts
CO 194	Newfoundland. Original Correspondence
CO 195	Newfoundland. Entrybooks
CO 217	Nova Scotia. Original Correspondence (including Cape Breton, 1784–1820)
CO 218	Nova Scotia. Entrybooks
CO 219	Nova Scotia. Acts
CO 220	Nova Scotia. Sessional Papers
CO 226	Prince Edward Island. Original Correspondence
CO 227	Prince Edward Island. Entrybooks
CO 228	Prince Edward Island. Acts
CO 229	Prince Edward Island. Sessional Papers
CO 230	Prince Edward Island. Government Gazettes
CO 323	Colonies, general. Original Correspondence
CO 391	Board of Trade. Registers (Entrybooks of minutes, the text of which was printed verbatim in the *Journals of the Commissioners of Trade and Plantations*)
CO 537	Original Correspondence, Supplementary
PRO 30/8	Chatham Papers
PRO 30/55	British Headquarters Papers (or Carleton Papers) (This collection was first titled the American Manuscripts in the Royal Institution. After being held some years in the United States, it was returned to Britain and placed in the PRO. Transcript copies made for the NA and PANS were termed the Carleton Papers and the Dorchester Papers, respectively. These transcripts reflect the original order, while the microfilm (available at the NA in MG 23, B 1) was made after a massive reorganization. The microfilm is prefaced by a four-volume calendar, annotated to correlate modern document numbers with the original volume and page numbers.)

National Archives

The preferred style for NA citations separates letters and numbers.
Government Documents in Record Groups:

RG 1   Executive Council. Quebec, Lower Canada, Upper Canada, and the Province of Canada

RG 1, E 1   Quebec, Lower Canada, Upper Canada, Province of Canada. Executive Council. Minute Books on State Matters (commonly known as the State Books, when identified by letter designations in the style Quebec State Book B or Canada State Book M)

RG 1, E 3   Upper Canada. Executive Council. Submissions on State Matters (commonly termed the State Submissions – *erroneously* called State Papers. Files were numbered in alpha-numeric sequences, which were repeated periodically)

RG 4   Civil and Provincial Secretaries. Quebec, Lower Canada, and Canada East

RG 4, A 1   S Series (formally titled: Quebec and Lower Canada. Civil Secretary, correspondence received)

RG 4, B 16   Quebec, Lower Canada, and Canada East: Court Records

RG 4, B 20   Quebec, Lower Canada, and Canada East: Provincial Secretary and Registrar. Applications for pardons or clemency

RG 4, B 21   Quebec, Lower Canada, and Canada East: (Civil Secretary). Gaol calendars and prison returns

RG 4, C 1   Canada East. Provincial Secretary. Numbered Correspondence files

RG 4, C 2   Canada East. Provincial Secretary. Letterbooks

RG 4, D 1   *Quebec Gazette/gazette de Québec*

RG 5   Civil and Provincial Secretaries. Upper Canada and Canada West

RG 5, A 1   Upper Canada Sundries (formally titled: Upper Canada. Civil Secretary. Correspondence received)

RG 5, B 3   Upper Canada: Petitions and Addresses

RG 5, C 1   Canada West. Provincial Secretary. Numbered Correspondence files

RG 5, C 2   Canada West. Provincial Secretary. Letterbooks

RG 5, D 1   *Upper Canada Gazette*

RG 7   Governor General (including pre-confederation records from lieutenant governors' offices, except Newfoundland)

RG 7, G 1   Quebec, Lower Canada, Upper Canada, Province of Canada, Canada. Despatches received from the Colonial Office

RG 7, G 2   Quebec, Lower Canada, Upper Canada, Province of Canada.

Supplementary despatches received from the Colonial Office

RG 7, G 6	Despatches from the British Minister at Washington
RG 8	British Military and Naval Records
RG 8, series I	British Military and Naval Records. 'C Series' (The C series contain the principal adminstrative records generated or accumulated by the commander of the forces and his staff in British North America. Records of the Ordnance Department and the Admiralty form series II and III.)

Private Papers in Manuscript Groups
at the National Archives

A short or common title is usually formed from the surname (or peerage title) plus Papers, Fonds, or Collection. Several of the collections/fonds listed below include microfilm or transcript copies of originals held elsewhere, in Canada, Britain, or the United States.

MG 8, C 5	Nouvelle-France: Greffes des jurisdictions royale et seigneuriale du district de Montréal
MG 17, B 1	Society for the Propagation of the Gospel in Foreign Parts (SPGFP)
MG 18, M	Northcliffe Collection
MG 23, A 1	William Legge, second Earl of Dartmouth Papers
MG 23, A 2	William Pitt, first Earl of Chatham Papers
MG 23, A 4	William Petty Fitzmaurice, second Earl of Shelburne Papers
MG 23, A 6	George Sackville Germain Papers
MG 23, G II 10	Jonathan Sewell and Family Papers
MG 23, G II 17	Robert Prescott Papers
MG 23, G II 19	Monk Family Papers
MG 23, H I 1	John Graves Simcoe Papers
MG 24, A 45	Sir John Thomas Duckworth Papers
MG 24, B 1	John Neilson Collection
MG 24, B 2	Louis-Joseph Papineau et famille
MG 24, B 3	Herman Witsius Ryland Papers

Foreign Government Records in Manuscript Groups
at the National Archives

While scholars have long relied on the transcripts of colonial records made between the 1870s and the 1940s, these copies must be recognized as greatly inferior to the microfilm copies made since 1950. When transcription began, the British authorities prohibited the transcription of marginal notes and minutes – the commentary of the recipients recording their initial impressions and intentions for responding. The prohibition was not lifted until all of the Q Series had been transcribed.

Public Archives of Nova Scotia

MG 2, v. 732	Sir William Young Papers
RG 1, vol. 17	Transcripts of Correspondence to the Board of Trade
RG 1, vols. 29–34	Despatches from the Board of Trade and Secretary of State, 1748–99
RG 1, vols. 134–137	Inland letterbooks of the Governor and Provincial Secretary, 1753–6, 1760–91
RG 1, vols. 163–165	Commission Books, 1749–1872 and 167–176½ (entrybooks recording documents issued over the seals and so on)
RG 1, vols. 186–203	Executive Council. Minutes, 1749–1870
RG 1, vols. 215–218DDD	Legislative Council. Journals, 1758–1835
RG 1, vols. 219–249	Manuscript Documents of Nova Scotia, 1751–91 (an artificial series, organized by Thomas B. Akins; volumes 221–3 relate to the settlement of townships, 1751 ff.)
RG 1, vols. 342–343	Crown Prosecutions, 1749–1832
RG 1, vol. 347	Royal Warrants, Writs of Mandamus, Commissions, 1753–1840
RG 1, vol. 364	Transcripts (from Massachusetts public records) Relating to the American Invasion of Nova Scotia, 1775–1805
RG 1, vol. 377	List of Causes in the Court of Escheats and Forfeitures, 1770–1839
RG 1, vol. 470	Catalogue of Special Subjects
RG 36	Court of Chancery Records
RG 39, series C	Supreme Court, Halifax County Bench Books
RG 39, series J	Supreme Court, Entry and Judgment Books
RG 48	Probate Court Records

Primary Sources in Printed Format

An important distinction is that between documents printed contemporaneously and the publication of historical documents at later date. Broadsides and pamphlets, proclamations, statutes, and the *Journals* of legislatures most directly reflect the intentions of their creators. Collections of historical documents published in the nineteenth and early twentieth centuries suffer from highly subjective selection criteria and editorial emendations, the accretion of errors in transcription and typography, and formats that may obscure the identity and relationships of documents. Few compilations achieved the meticulous standards of the Public Record Office, yet even the *Acts of the Privy Council of England, Colonial Series*, and the *Journal of the Commissioners for Trade and Plantations* exhibit inconsistencies. The nature of the publication process and the quality of the transcriptions upon which Thomas B. Akins, E.A. Cruikshank, Beamish Murdoch, Adam Shortt and Arthur Doughty, or J.R. Brodhead and E.B. O'Callaghan relied renders their publications highly susceptible to errors and ommissions. Shortt and Doughty took their texts for *Constitutional Documents* from the Q Series and other transcripts notorious for their omission of marginalia. The translation of texts from French to English, or vice versa, for publication in the annual reports of the Public Archives of Canada created even greater opportunities for distortion, error, and omission. Nobody need rely on these printed collections, nor antique transcripts. It is an easy matter to trace the trail from transcript citations to original documents. Microforms offer a window on the original documents – which distance and budgetary constraints may render inaccessible.[2] The National Archives and the provincial archives of Quebec, New Brunswick, and Ontario provide microform loan services. Using microform, one can see and assess interlinear annotations, whether marginalia are in several hands, and myriad other details. Reduction ratios of the film do not distort the content. The only significant limitation is the absence of color, in particular for maps.

Caution must be exercised in the consultation of contemporary printed works. The series of *Confidential Prints* were compiled for the Colonial Office and the Foreign Office to serve specific purposes. These printed texts were selected for the information of the Privy Council, to illustrate and support cases brought forward by the secretaries of state responsible for colonial and for foreign affairs. Compilers were concerned with accuracy and so respected the legal importance of treaties and like documents, but supporting documents were chosen for political reasons.

Selection criteria were even more rigorously applied to the documents printed in the *Parliamentary Papers* and the *Imperial Blue Books*. Secret and confidential dispatches are conspicuous by their absence. The layout of the printed text may obscure details leading the unwary researcher to misinterpret details or draw false conclusions from incomplete data. A comparison of the documents relating to the rebellions of 1837–8 are an excellent example of this and shall be addressed in volume 2.

Certain printed documents merit a reader's trust. The texts of proclamations, statutes, government regulations, and notices were published in the colony's official gazette, as broadsides or in compilations (as appropriate), to inform both those who were to enforce them and the general populace. Every effort was made to ensure accuracy in these government documents.[3] In each colony, the provincial secretary and registrar was responsible for maintaining copies of record, from which he could make an *exemplification* should need arise, as well as for preparing texts for printing and the duplicates to be sent to the imperial authorities in London. Owing to these bureaucratic practices, we may choose among manuscript originals/duplicates and printed texts in imperial, federal, and provincial archives. While the originals and contemporary imprints may be rare and difficult of access, microfilm copies are readily accessible.[4] Most important, librarians and archivists make no objection to photocopying from the microforms.

Pamphlets and broadsides produced by individuals, at their own cost, may be presumed to be accurate reflections of their thoughts. Contemporary newspapers, however, reflect the interests and biases of their editors/publishers, which may affect their reporting of trials and other proceedings. The skills of the shorthand reporter should also be considered. Because of the work of the Canadian Institute for Historical Micro-reproduction (CIHM), tens of thousands of pre-1900 pamphlets, broadsides, and other printed ephemera are readily available for examination. The close cooperation between bibliographers and CIHM has ensured that virtually any text mentioned in the classic bibliographies by Olga Bishop, Patricia Fleming, and Marie Tremaine[5] can be found in the CIHM collection of microfiche.

To use published collections of historical documents is to limit a search to the sources their compilers were able to locate and considered significant. Going back to the original sources widens the range of documentation available and strengthens the conclusions drawn from the investigation.

NOTES

1 We have encouraged authors to coin short titles for those statutes enacted before short titling became common drafting practice. Statutes or other events in England or the empire before 1752 that fell between 1 January and 24 March are cited as in the *Dictionary of Canadian Biography* (vol. 1:3), with both old style and new style years given. Two relevant examples are: Statute of Treasons, 1351/2 and the Treason Act, 1695/6. We have chosen to use British North

America Act, 1867 as the short title in texts for the Constitution Act, 1867, 30 and 31 Vict., c. 3.

2 Conservation policies in many archives dictate the substitution of microforms for originals as a protective measure. Thus, a visit to Halifax, Ottawa, or Toronto no longer guarantees access to the original documents.

3 A recent investigation of two broadsides issued by Thomas Dunn, administrator of Lower Canada, in August 1811 revealed that a significant typographical error had been hand-corrected on each copy, in a print run of 200. The bilingual text also appeared in the Quebec *Gazette*.

4 Government-document specialists at the National Library (Ottawa, Ont.), having compiled a comprehensive listing of microforms for the *Journals*, statutes, gazettes, and associated printed records, can advise on locations or loans.

5 *Publications of the Government of the Province of Canada, 1841–1867; Publications of the Province of Upper Canada and of Great Britain Relating to Upper Canada, 1791–1840; Publications of the Governments of Nova Scotia, Prince Edward Island, and New Brunswick, 1758–1952; Atlantic Canadian Imprints, 1801–1820; Upper Canada Imprints, 1801–1841; A bibliography of Canadian Imprints, 1751–1800.* Also, see *Les imprimés dans le Bas-Canada, 1801–1810* by John Hare and J.P. Wallot. The location codes given in these works follow the Canadian Library Association standard.

Appendix 3

Supporting Documents Summary

A: Peter N. Moogk, The Crime of *Lèse-Majesté* in New France: Defence of the Secular and Religious Order
Document 1: The definition of offences against the crown
Document 2: The arrest, interrogation, and trial of Louis Cotin, Laurent Dubeau, and Charles Routhier, farmers, for incitement to rebellion among the countryfolk of the north shore in the Quebec district, 1714–15

B: Barry Cahill, The 'Hoffman Rebellion' (1753) and Hoffman's Trial (1754): Constructive High Treason and Seditious Conspiracy in Nova Scotia under the Stratocracy
Document 1: Bill of indictment for high treason
Document 2: Bill of indictment for seditious conspiracy

C: Thomas Garden Barnes, 'Twelve Apostles' or a Dozen Traitors? Acadian Collaborators during King George's War, 1744–7
Document 1: 'Representation of the State of His Majesties Province of Nova Scotia,' November, 1745
Document 2: Mascarene to Newcastle, December 1745
Document 3: Representation on the state of the province since the outbreak of war

D: Douglas Hay, Civilians Tried in Military Courts: Quebec, 1759–64
Document 1: Extracts from the correspondence of Deputy Judge Advocate General Charles Gould, 1763–4

E: Jean-Marie Fecteau and Douglas Hay, 'Government by Will and Pleasure Instead of Law': Military Justice and the Legal System in Quebec, 1775–83
Document 1: Haldimand to Germain, June 1779
Document 2: Haldimand to Germain, October 1780
Document 3: Chief Justice Livius to secretary of state, March 1782
Document 4: Petition of Mary Hay, May 1781
Document 5: Valentin Jautard to Matthew, September 1782

F: Ernest A. Clarke and Jim Phillips, Rebellion and Repression in Nova Scotia in the Era of the American Revolution
Document 1: An act to suspend habeas corpus, 1777

G: D.G. Bell, Sedition among the Loyalists: The Case of Saint John, 1784–6
Document 1: New Brunswick's statute against political petitioning, 1786

H: F. Murray Greenwood, Judges and Treason Law in Lower Canada, England, and the United States during the French Revolution, 1794–1800
Document 1: Extract from 'Cursory Strictures on the Charge Delivered by Lord Chief Justice Eyre to the Grand Jury,' October 1794
Document 2: Extract from Justice James Iredell's address to the grand jury, Circuit Court, District of Pennsylvania, April 1796
Document 3: Extract from Chief Justice James Monk's address to the grand jury, District of Montreal, March 1797
Document 4: Extract from a retrospective letter by Attorney General Jonathan Sewell to Civil Secretary Samuel Gale, July 1799
Document 5: Extract from a letter from Civil Secretary Herman Ryland to George Francklin, May 1797
Document 6: Extract from Chief Justice William Osgoode's charge to the trial jury in McLane
Document 7: The sentencing and execution of McLane (July 1797)
Document 8: Extract from Montreal lawyer Stephen Sewell's letter to brother Jonathan Sewell after the McLane trial
Document 9: Extract from Osgoode's letter to Under-Secretary John King, July 1797

I: Christopher English, The Official Mind and Popular Protest in a Revolutionary Era: The Case of Newfoundland, 1789–1819
Document 1: '[Affidavits] concerning riots in Bay Roberts'

J: Jean-Marie Fecteau, F. Murray Greenwood, and Jean-Pierre Wallot, Sir James Craig's 'Reign of Terror' and Its Impact on Emergency Powers in Lower Canada, 1810–13
Document 1: Extract from an 'Act ... to Secure and Detain Such Persons As His Majesty Shall Suspect Are Conspiring Against His Person and Government,' 1794
Document 2: Extracts from letters by John Richardson to Jonathan Sewell, 1797
Document 3: An Act for the Better Preservation of His Majesty's Government, 1797
Document 4: Extracts from debates in United States House of Representatives on a Senate bill to suspend habeas corpus, January 1807
Document 5: Extract from Chief Justice Sewell's judgment in *Bedard* (1810)
Document 6: Resolutions of the House of Assembly on martial law, 1813

K   Paul Romney and Barry Wright, State Trials and Security Proceedings in Upper Canada during the War of 1812
Document 1: The Sedition Act, 1804
Document 2: Proclamation, February 1812
Document 3: Proclamation, November 1812
Document 4: Act to detain persons suspected of treasonable adherence, 1814
Document 5: The Alien Act, 1814
Document 6: An Act for More Effectual Trial and Punishment of Treason, 1814
Document 7: Robinson to Loring, April 1814
Document 8: Robinson to Loring, June 1814
Document 9: Commission of Sequestration, January 1818

L: F. Murray Greenwood and Barry Wright, Parliamentary Privilege and the Repression of Dissent in the Canadas
Document 1: Bowen to Sewell, August 1814
Document 2: Law officers' opinion on the privileges of the House of Assembly of Lower Canada, December 1815

M: Evelyn Kolish and James Lambert, The Attempted Impeachment of the Lower Canadian Chief Justices, 1814–15
Document 1: Heads of impeachment

N: Barry Wright, The Gourlay Affair: Seditious Libel and the Sedition Act in Upper Canada, 1818–19
Document 1: Address to the jury, notes, August 1818
Document 2: Extrajudicial opinion, November 1818

O: Paul Romney, Upper Canada in the 1820s: Criminal Prosecution and the Case of Francis Collins

Document 1: Indictment of Francis Collins for libel, April 1828
Document 2: *Canadian Freeman*, 16 October 1828
Document 3: Indictment of Francis Collins for libel, October 1828
Document 4: Judge Sherwood's charge to the jury
Document 5: Sherwood to Mudge, December 1828
Document 6: Committee on the petition of Francis Collins
Document 7: Resolutions of the committee on the petition of Collins
Document 8: Sherwood to Colborne, March 1829
Document 9: Robinson to Colborne, April 1829

P: J.M. Bumsted, Liberty of the Press in Early Prince Edward Island, 1823–9
Document 1: Letter of Charles Binns to the *Prince Edward Island Register*, October 1823

Q   Barry Cahill, *R. v. Howe* (1835) for Seditious Libel: A Tale of Twelve Magistrates
Document 1: Howe to Austen, March 1835

A
The Crime of *Lèse-Majesté* in New France:
Defence of the Secular and Religious Order
Peter N. Moogk

1. THE DEFINITION OF OFFENCES AGAINST THE CROWN

The best, short summary of offences against the crown is provided by Guy Du Rousseaud de la Combe. The following consists of extracts from his Traité des Matieres criminelles, suivant l'Ordonnance du mois d'Août 1670, & les Edits, Declarations du Roi (Paris: Theodore Le Gras 1753), at 61–3.

Concerning the Crime of Earthly Lèse-Majesté

... The crime of earthly lèse-Majesté is an offence committed against kings and princely sovereigns, who are the living images of God on earth, and who represent, in their states' government, the authority that God exercises in the regulation of the universe ...

These are the crimes of lèse-Majesté under the first heading and which require loss of life [*confiscation de corps*] and confiscation of [the offender's] goods to the King, and for which the posterity of those found guilty of this crime, will be declared ignoble, commoners [*routurière*], and unworthy of any dignity, grace or privilege, and who may even be tried after their death:

1. Those who commit an attempt against or conspire against the person, life or authority of the King,

2. Those who have assisted in or have known of such conspiracies, yet have not straightaway revealed or declared them,

3. Those who rise up in arms against the King's authority, and who occupy or hold by force his towns, castles, and other fortified places,

4. Those who arouse the people to sedition, rebellion, in defiance of the King's authority, whether in writing or by their actions, or have maliciously sown [dissent] by words or speeches made in public,[1]

5. Those who undertake or enter into any conspiracies, associations, offensive or defensive leagues within the realm, with the King's subjects, or externally, with foreigners, directly or indirectly, by themselves or through intermediaries, [communicating] by word or by writing,

6. Those who deliver to foreigners or to the King's enemies defended places, armed forces, or subjects of the realm, by allowing them [enemies] to enter into such locations by whatever means, without the authority and permission of the

King, or who attempt by any way to give them up to the said enemies of the King and Kingdom, by aiding them, favouring them and maliciously fortifying places to His [Majesty's] prejudice,

7. Those, who being officers or councillors of the King, communicate with foreign princes or states, receive wages or pensions from them, disclose the secrets of the King and Kingdom, or otherwise aid and favour the said foreigners to the detriment of the King's service.

By the Edict of Francis I, given at St-Germain-en-Laye, in July 1534, those who receive letters or messages from a foreign prince, the King's enemy with whom he is at war, are criminals [guilty] of lèse-Majesté, if they do not inform the King or his officers of them. ...

Monsieur le Bret ... says that whenever an astrologer uses his science, false though it might be, to know the duration of the prince's lifetime, he is is reputed guilty of lèse-Majesté ...

The crimes of lèse-Majesté under the second heading are those that would impair or usurp the King's majesty and authority, and which are nonetheless punishable by loss of life and confiscation of goods to the King alone, without punishment of the offender's posterity, such as:

1. Those who, without the responsibility, power, permission, or order of the King, gather together and take counsel in private on matters of state, whether under the pretext of the public good or other cause whatsoever,

2. Those who levy or enlist men-at-arms without the authorization and permission of the King in letters-patent, as well as those so enrolled,

3. Those who create a common treasury, solicit contributions, or tax the King's subjects for money, munitions, magazines, or other support whatsoever, for any cause, without his authorization and permission in letters-patent,

4. Those who draw on his funds and taxes or undertake to command the same without his expressed power and authority,

5. Those entrusted with the government of any province, town or castle, or command over armies or companies of men-at-arms, who retain and hold on to their government or command after it has been revoked by the King,

6. Those who maliciously hinder the King's service, or encroach on the authority belonging to Him alone, outrage, threaten, and intimidate His magistrates and officers [who are] carrying out or exercising their office, or otherwise prevent them from freely exercising them,

7. Those who counterfeit the signatures or seals of the King,

8. Those who have money struck on their authority [alone], or who forge [lawful] money, clip, alter, or knowingly circulate the same.

It is also a secondary crime of lèse-Majesté to spread defamatory libels against the King's honour, especially if they would ignite the fire of sedition in people's minds.

Article 13 of Charles IX's ordinance of December 1567 and that of Henri III in January 1580 declare that this crime is punishable by death, with confiscation of property for the King, and [they state] that those who print such [defamatory] works are punishable by bodily penalties, even by capital punishment, according to the circumstances.

There are still other crimes associated with the crime of lèse-Majesté, and whose punishments for the guilty are not comparable to the preceding ones. They are:

1. Those who gather armed men for some private dispute, call upon them to fight, provide a location for the same, are sponsors of or aid those who are fighting, will be punished by loss of life and property as appropriate,

2. Those who cast artillery pieces, to wit: cannons, demi or medium culverins [coulevrines batardes and moyennes], without the King's order contained in letters-patent, are to be punished by confiscation of said pieces, by levelling the castle and places where they were made, and by a fine of four thousand écus.

3. Those who enclose towns [bourgs] and villages [with walls], fortify them, build new fortresses in towns, build bulwarks [boulevards], bastions, and other regal fortifications for castles, [or who] demolish the said fortifications and town walls, raze towns and castles without the King's permission will be sentenced to heavy, arbitrary fines ... and the demolished works will be restored at their expense.

2. The arrest, interrogation, and trial of Louis Cotin, Laurent Dubeau, and Charles Routhier, farmers, for incitement to rebellion among the countryfolk of the north shore in the Quebec district, 1714–15.

In August 1714, soon after the grain harvest, the rural population of the north shore near Quebec City gathered to protest the shortage of food and the high cost of retail goods. The three men suspected of having incited and led the protesters were Louis Cotin dit Dugal (1679–1726), Laurent Dubeau (1672–1731), and Charles Routhier (1677–?). All three were farmers born in New France, aged thirty-five to forty-two, and with large families.[2]

The criminal investigation followed the conventional pattern under the 1670 criminal ordinance: a report of an offence was received and a 'plainte' was presented to the tribunal by a crown attorney for action. If a trial seemed warranted, the accused were arrested, and interrogated in prison, and witnesses were summoned and interviewed in camera. In this case, the attorney general asked the questions while another member of the Superior Council acted as the witnessing magistrate, as required by law. This investigative stage was called 'information.' The accused, who had no legal counsel and often did not know the *charge against them until the trial's conclusion, were present when the witnesses were called upon to affirm their recorded testimony. After this procedure, known as 'récolement des témoins,' the accused had the opportunity to challenge the witnesses or their statements at the confrontation. Taking into account the evidence, testimony, and jurisprudence, the crown attorney would then present his recommendations to the presiding magistrates, who had the discretionary power to set the penalty for non-capital offences.*

In the following case, we do not have the witnesses' statements or the interrogation records. It appears that the testimony received was contradictory or insufficient to permit a conviction for the capital offence of incitement to armed rebellion. French magistrates always preferred to have a watertight case. Upon reflection, the members of the Superior Council at Quebec may have decided that the voluntary dispersal of the protesters mitigated their offence and that strong action was not warranted because there had been no danger of an insurrection. The protesters wanted officials to hear their complaints; they did not threaten to usurp the government's regulatory powers. Two of the accused had spent the cold winter months in prison and this uncomfortable sojourn might have been adjudged punishment enough. These translated extracts come from the Jugements et Déliberations du Conseil Souverain, 6 vols. (Quebec: J. Dussault 1891), 6: at 834–5, 838–9, 842–3, 926, 988–9, 997–1000.

The 24th September 1714 – The [Superior] Council [at Quebec] was specially convened, at which session were M. [Michel Bégon] the Intendant, Mr. [Claude de Bermen] de la Martinière, [François-Mathieu Martin] de Lino, [Abbé Joseph] de la Colombière, [François] Aubert, [Charles] Macart, [Dr Michel] Sarrazin, [Martin] Cheron, [Guillaume] Gaillard, [Eustache] Chartier de Lotbinière, [Jean-François] Hazeur, [Paul Denis] de St-Simon, all councillors and [Mathieu-Benoit Collet] the King's Attorney-General.

Considering the indictment [*requisitoire*] presented in council by the King's Attorney-General [asking] that he might be authorized to gather information against several residents of the surrounding settlements [*costes*], who gathered together on the eve of [the Feast of] St. Bartholomew [23 Aug.], set out armed with muskets, and made threats to enter this town as a group if no one listened to their remonstrances, and who only withdrew when they learned that the [regular garrison] troops and this town's militia had been ordered to march against them. And [this indictment is] against one Dugal [Louis Cotin called Dugal] for having given a seditious speech in Côte St-Augustin, and for having made threats against the [militia] captain of the settlement who opposed his designs.

[The attorney general listed the following documents]: An order having been issued on the second of this month authorizing him to gather information before Maître François-Mathieu Martin de Lino, designated [investigating] councillor for this case. Request of the Attorney-General on the twelfth of this month, asking that he be given an hour and a day to summon the witnesses before Sieur de Lino; an order of the thirteenth of the same month stating that the witnesses be summoned for next Tuesday, at two o'clock sitting in this council's chamber; copies of the summonses given to the witnesses by Dubreuil and Meschin, court bailiffs [*huissiers*], on the fifteenth of this said month. Testimony heard before Sieur de Lino in the council chamber on the eighteenth of the same month; his subsequent order that the [findings] be communicated ...[and the] indictment of the King's Attorney-General dated the twentieth of this same month.

[Having] heard the report of Sieur de Lino, appointed councillor for [reporting on the investigation of] this case, the council having considered the indictment of the King's Attorney-General, has ordered and does order that, at this time, Laurent Dubault [Dubeau] be summoned before Sieur de Lino to be heard on the facts gathered during the information and, in answer to the Attorney-General's conclusions, [orders] that one Routtier will be arrested and taken to the royal prison of this town to be heard and interrogated before Sieur de Lino about the facts resulting from the said charges and investigation that, among others, the Attorney-General would like to know. If [it is] not [possible to find him to deliver the written summons], after a search for his person, he will be summoned to appear on the fifteenth by a single public outcry in the following week, his goods seized, and annotated for which an agent will be established. With regard to the said Louis Dugal, he will be led to the [governor's] residence where he is to be detained in the said prison and locked up, at the Attorney-General's request, to be interrogated there before the said Sieur de Lino, commissioner, upon the facts gathered by the investigation, and then to proceed to the judgment of his case, as [the law] will require.

[signed:] Begon

Monday, the first of October, 1714 – Considering the judgment [*l'arrest*] reached in this council on September 24th last, requiring among other things that one Louis Dugal, settler of Côte De Maure, be taken to the Chateau St-Louis [the governor's residence], where he was detained in the royal prison of this town, and where he would be locked up at the request of the King's Attorney-General, there to be heard and interrogated before Maître François-Mathieu Martin de Lino ...; report of the delivery made of the said Dugal's person to this town's jail on the 28th of the same month; extract of the act of confinement on that date of the said Dugal from the prison register, [a copy of which was] delivered to the said Dugal on the same day; the King's Attorney-General's charge on the same day; the order of Sieur de Lino on the 29th of that month, notifying that he would [had] come to the gaol [ante-]room of the said prison on the preceding day at 2 p.m. to proceed with the interrogation; [and] the investigation of that date, the 28th of September last; Considering also the interrogation undergone by the said Dugal yesterday before the said Sieur de Lino, his order for which has been communicated to the said Attorney-General and is attached; [along with the] Conclusions of the said King's Attorney-General dated yesterday, and having heard the report of Sieur de Lino, as councillor assigned to this case, and having considered all, the Council has ordered and orders that the matter will be more amply investigated, concerning the facts noted in the case against the said Louis Dugal and, nonetheless, [orders] that he will be released and freed from this town's prison, upon his verbal bond, on condition that the said Dugal will appear whenever summoned, under penalty of [summary] conviction, and to this end he will be required to elect domicile in this town [to which address all writs may be delivered].

[signed:]   C de Bermen   de Lino

On Wednesday, the third of October, one thousand, seven hundred and fourteen, at eight in the morning, the preceding decree was read in the presence of My Lord de Lino, reporting councillor, to Louis Dugal in the jail room by me, appointed Clerk of the Council, undersigned, and immediately, after having sworn the oath to appear whenever and wherever he is required by justice, and [stating] that he has elected domicile with François Badeau on Rue Champlain [in Quebec], he was unshackled and put outside the prison and discharged from confinement by the appointed councillor aforementioned, [done] at Quebec on the day and year given above.

[signed:]   de Lino   Rivet [clerk]

Friday, the fifth of October, 1714 – The Council [was] specially assembled In view of the indictment of the King's Attorney-General on this day, containing [the statement] that he had been informed that several inhabitants of the neighbouring settlements [costes] had gathered together on the eve of St. Bartholomew's [day] last, some armed with muskets, and had made threats to enter the town as a body if no one listened to their remonstrances, of which he laid a complaint, upon which he had been authorized to gather information before Maitre François-Mathieu Martin de Lino, councillor ..., a decree was registered on the 24th of September, to summon for interrogation Laurent Dubault [sic] and for the arrest of one Routtier, but since then the said King's Attorney-General has learned that the said Dubault and Routtier, who were the authors of this gathering, and who, among other things, went into the farmers' [habitants] dwellings to solicit [their support] and to urge them to gather together, as they did, on the eve of St. Bartholomew last. He requires that, if it please the council, to permit him to continue the said enquiry before My Lord de Lino, upon the aforesaid facts, circumstances, and consequences, and principally into the fact that it was the said Dubault and Routtier who went from house to house, enjoining the residents to gather together [s'attrouper]. Having obtained that additional information, [that he might] submit whatever conclusions as will be warranted. The Council, considering the indictment, has permitted and permits the said King's Attorney-General to continue the said enquiry ... into the facts contained in the said indictment, their circumstances and consquences, and principally about the fact that it was Dubault and Routtier who went from house to house, encouraging the colonists to come together, so that, with the said additional information delivered to the King's Attorney-General, the council may, [guided by] his conclusions, order whatever will be appropriate.

[signed:] C de Bermen

Monday, the eleventh of March, 1715 – Considering the decree given in council on the 29th of October last, in which a charge is laid against Laurent Dubault (sic), tenant of De Maure seigneury, and that he be summoned to appear in person within a week [huitaine] before Maitre François-Mathieu Martin de Lino, designated councillor for this case, to be heard and interrogated on the facts obtained in the investigation of September 18th last and on any other details that the King's Attorney-General would like to investigate; The writ of subpoena issued at the request of the King's Attorney-General, delivered to Dubaut [sic] by Meschin the bailiff on February 19th last; Interrogation undergone on the first day of this month by the said Dubault before Sieur de Lino, whose report of the same is attached; [and the] Indictment of the said King's Attorney-General on the second of this said month.

Having considered all, The Council has ordered and does order that the witnesses heard in the interrogations undertaken at the request of the said King's Attorney-General, and the others who will have been interviewed again, will be asked to confirm their depositions and, if need be, confronted with the accused, Dubault. This is communicated to the said King's Attorney-General to be carried out so that he may present his recommendations for action, as required.

[signed:] de Lino

Monday, the fifth of August, 1715 – The Council assembled with M. the Intendant, Messrs. de la Martinière, de Lino, de la Colombière, Aubert, Macart, Sarrazin, Cheron, Gaillard, Chartier de Lotbinière, councillors, and the King's Attorney-General in attendance.

In view of the decree in this council on September 24th last; ... the order of Maitre François-Mathieu Martin de Lino, councillor designated to deal with this case, the said decree dated yesterday, directing that he go this day to the gaol [ante] room in this town's prison, to proceed with the interrogation of Charles Routtier, resident [habitant] of Ancienne Lorette; the interrogation before Sieur de Lino, his attached ruling, [and] the charge of the King's Attorney-General also dated this day. Having considered all, the Council has ordered and does order that the witnesses heard in the enquiry undertaken at the request of the King's Attorney-General, and the other persons who might be interviewed again, be summoned to confirm their depositions and be confronted with the accused Routtier. This decision has been communicated to the said Attorney-General, so that the council may rule as the case may require.

[signed:] Begon

Monday, the twelfth of August, 1715 – The Council having assembled with M. the Intendant, Messrs. de la Martinière, de Lino, Aubert, Macart, Sarrazin, Cheron, Gaillard, Chartier de Lotbinière, and the King's Attorney-General in attendance:

Between the King's Attorney General, plaintiff and accuser, on one hand, and on the other, Laurent Dubault, resident of St-Augustin, and Charles Routtier, resident of Lorette settlement, defendants and the accused. Considering the complaint laid by the said Attorney-General, stating that he had been informed that one the eve of St. Bartholomew last year several residents of the surrounding settlements had gathered together under the pretext of the dearness of goods and to make known their misery; that among them there were even some bold enough as to arm themselves with muskets – and they were observed by different persons; that they pushed their insolence to the point of uttering threats to enter the town, thus assembled, if no one listened to their remonstrance; and that they only retreated when they learned that the [garrison] troops and the town militia [companies] were commanded to march against them.

... The report [l'Information] was drawn up at the request of the said Attorney-General on the 18th of the said month [September 1714] containing the testimony of ten witnesses; [a résumé of all previous actions follows] ... The order of the said Sieur de Lino on the seventh of this said month [March 1715], asking that Sieurs d'Artigny, Haimard, Pinguet de Vaucours, and Sedillot, witnesses,[3] be summoned to appear on the tenth of the same month in the prison of this council to be asked to confirm their depositions, and be confronted with Routtier at nine in the morning, and at two o'clock on the same day to be confronted by the said Dubault. The summonses to appear were delivered to the said witnesses by Meschin the bailiff on the eighth and ninth of that month. ... The reports of the confrontations were later conveyed [to the council]. The King's Attorney-General presented his conclusions yesterday, and the said Sieur de Lino was heard as reporter. Having considered all, the Council has ordered and orders that more information be gathered on the matters mentioned in the case against the said Dubault and Routtier. Nonetheless, the said Routtier will be released and let out of prison upon the surety of his oath, to answer all summonses, when he is ordered by justice to appear, under penalty of a [summary] conviction. Likewise, the said Dubault will be held to answer all summonses and under the same threat, and to this end, the said Routtier and Dubault will be obliged to elect domicile in this Town.

[signed:]   Begon   de Lino

The present order has been read and pronounced to the said Dubault at the adjournment of the council this 12th of August, 1715, by me the Chief Clerk of the said council. The said Dubault agrees to [obey] the terms of the said order and, in conformity with it, has promised to present himself when ordered to do so, and he has elected domicile in the home of Sieur d'Artigny, Lieutenant General of this town's Prévoté Court. He declared that he did not know how to sign when required to [sign his release agreement].

[signed:]   de Monseignat

[Charles Routhier was also released from prison on the same terms and elected domicile in the home of the notary Etienne Dubreuil. Routhier and Laurent Dubeau were then free to return to their families and farms. No further action was taken on this case.]

NOTES

1 In seventeenth- and eighteenth-century England, conspiracy to riot against enforcement of the law, concealment of treasonable plotting, and seditious libel were misdemeanours punishable by fines, pillory, and imprisonment (usually one to two years except in the case of concealment – misprision of treason where it was life).

2 Biographical information on the accused is from René Jetté, *Dictionnaire généalogique des familles du Québec* (Montreal: Les presses de l'Université de Montréal 1983), and Cyprien Tanguay, *Dictionnaire généalogique des familles canadiennes depuis la fondation de la colonie jusqu'à nos jours,* 7 vols. (Montreal: Eusèbe Senecal 1871–80).

3 Louis Rouer d'Artigny was a seigneur and a legal official, while Jacques
  Pinguet de Vaucour was a royal notary. 'Haimard' might be Pierre Haimard, a
  merchant and seigneur. 'Sedillot' cannot be identified with certainty, but, like
  the others, he may have been a social superior of the protesting farmers.

B

The 'Hoffman Rebellion' (1753) and Hoffman's Trial (1754): Constructive High Treason and Seditious Conspiracy in Nova Scotia under the Stratocracy
Barry Cahill

1. Bill of indictment for high treason (RG1, vol. 342 [Depositions and Other Papers Connected with Crown Prosecutions between 1749 and 1780], doc. 32, PANS).

Province of } Halifax: 1 s———
Nova Scotia }

At a General Court, Court of Assize and General Gaol delivery held in and for the County of Halifax and Province of Nova Scotia at the Court House in the Town of Halifax in the same County On the last Tuesday in April In the Twenty seventh year of the Reign of our Sovereign Lord George the second of Great Brittain ffrance and Ireland King Defender of the ffaith &c. Before His Honour Charles Lawrence Esq$^{r.}$ President of His Majesties Council for the Province aforesaid, Benjamin Green, William Steele John Collier, William Cotterell, Robert Monckton Esq$^{rs.}$ Members of His Majesties said Councill By His Majesties Commission and Royall Instructions Assigned to See the Peace of our Sovereign Lord the King kept in the County, Town, & Province aforesaid And the Gaol of our said Sovereign Lord the King of Halifax of the Prisoners therein being By their proper hands to deliver here in Court of Record in form of Law to be Determined And also all Treasons, Misprision of Treason, Riotts, Routs unlawfull Assemblies, Murders, Manslaughters, Rapes, Ravishments, Burglaries, ffelonies, Trespasses, Assaults & misdemeanors In the Town and County aforesaid To hear and Determine By the Oath of Joshua Mauger John Webb Malachy Salter Benjamin Gerrish Charles Procter Charles Hay George Saul Henry ffurguson Joseph Rundle Jacob Hurd Thomas Greenoak Jonathan Hoar Joseph ffairbanks Henry Wilkinson Joseph Pierpoint John Anderson James ffillis James Hall George Gerrish Thomas Amies John Wheeler Jonathan Prescott Jonathan Binney. ———Good and lawful men of the County & province aforesaid Here and there duly returned Sworn & Charged to Inquire for our Sovereign Lord the King and for the Body of the said County It is presented in manner and form as followeth That is to say Province of Nova Scotia, Halifax: ss. The Jurors ffor our Lord the King upon their Oath Do Present That John William Hoffman of the Town of Lunenburg in the Province & County aforesaid Gentleman or Esq$^{r.}$ being a Person of a Seditious & Rebellious Disposition and not having the fear of God before his Eyes, nor weighing the Duty of his

Allegiance But conspiring and wickedly Intending to create groundless Jealousies & Discontents amongst His said Majesties Subjects in this province And the Peace & Welfare of the said Province to Disturb And the Government of our said Lord the King in the same Province to Destroy On the ffifteenth—— day of November In the Twenty seventh year of the Reign of our said Sovereign Lord George the second now King of Great Brittain &c. And at diverse other days & times as well before as after at Halifax and Lunenburg aforesaid In that Province aforesaid with force & Arms Did wickedly, maliciously & traitorously and as a false Traitor Conspire, compass and imagine The Death of our said Lord the King Then and now his supream dread Sovereign Lord and King And to raise Sedition and Rebellion in this his said Majesties Province of Nova Scotia And that for the Accomplishment of his said Treasons and Traitorous Imaginations and Purposes He the said John William Hoffman on the said ffifteenth—— day of November——In the s$^{d.}$ Twenty seventh year of his Majesties said Reign And at diverse other days & times as well before as after at Halifax and Lunenburg aforesaid Did use diverse Indirect practices to create and raise Sedition and Rebellion amongst His Majesties Subjects in this Province And for that purpose at the time and times aforesaid at Lunenburg aforesaid Did contrive and frame and then and there did maliciously & seditiously read and publish to one John Peterquin and to diverse other Persons a false, scandalous & seditious Letter or Libel in writing highly reflecting on the Administration of His said Majesties Government in this Province which he the said John William Hoffman pretended to have received from England from one George Surleau for the said John Peterquin And That amongst other things reflecting on the Administration of the Government in this province The said John William Hoffman by the said Letter or Libel falsely & seditiously Insinuated That His said Majesties foreign Subjects at Lunenburg aforesaid had been oppressed by the Persons Intrusted with the Administration of the said Government And That the said Government had contrary to his Majesties orders & desires[?] wrongfully deprived and kept back from His Majesties said Subjects at Lunenburg aforesaid great part of the different species of Provisions and great Quantities of Boards, Bricks, nails, Timber, Touls; Materials for ffishing and cultivating Land And also three shillings per day which had been granted to them by His said Majesty And thereby further seditiously, falsely & scandalously Insinuated & pretended That the said Government had contrary to his said Majesties Intentions wrongfully & oppressively Imposed upon and obliged His Majesties said foreign Subjects at [?] and persuade the said John Peterquin to Aid & Assist him to publish and make known the Contents of the said Seditious, false & scandalous—— Letter or Libel to His Majesties said Subjects at Lunenburg aforesaid And to encourage him therein promised to Support him with all his Power and Offered to pay him for the Time he might loose thereby By Occasion and means of which said Seditions & Scandals contained in the said Letter or Libel and reading & publishing thereof to the said John Peterquin and others The Peace & Tranquility of His Majesties said Government of Nova Scotia hath been greatly Disturbed & destroyed And the said John William Hoffman hath thereby Incited and caused to be Incited great Numbers of his said Majesties said Subjects at Lunenburg aforesaid to the Jurors unknown To Disown the present Authority and Government in this Province and to cast off their Obedience to his Majesties said Government by means aforesaid And diverse Traitors (to the Jurors unknown) then at Lunenburg aforesaid appeared in Arms and open Rebellion against His said Majesty And that the said John William Hoffman at the time aforesaid and at diverse other times afterwards at Lunenburg aforesaid was Privy to the said last mentioned Treason and Rebellion And then & there did knowingly Traitorously Conceal & Consent to the same And then & there did Traitorously Councill Aid & Abett the said Unknown Traitors in the Treason & Rebellion aforesaid Against the Duty of his Allegiance Against the Peace of our said Lord the King that now is his Crown and Dignity And Against the fform of the Statute in That Case made and Provided.———

Exa^{tur} p Geo: Suckling [sgd.] Cl[ericus] Coron[ae]

April General Court
1754 No. 8
Our Lord The King
ag^t
John William Hoffman

Bill of Indictm^t for
High Treason.
Ignoramus
Josh^a Mauger [sgd.] [?...]

2. Bill of indictment for seditious conspiracy (RG1, vol. 342 [Depositions and Other Papers Connected with Crown Prosecutions between 1749 and 1780] doc. 31, PANS).

At a Gener.^{l} Court held for the Town & County Halifax April 30th 1754 ———
County Halifax ——— }
Province Nova Scotia }
    The jurors of our Lord the King upon their oaths do present that John William

Hofman late of Lunenburg in the province afors.[d] Esq.[r] being a pernicious and Seditious man and a person depraved and of disquiet mind and Seditious disposition & Conversation and Contriving practising & Falsely Maliciously turbulently and Seditiously Intending the peace and Common tranquillity of our Lord the King and his Majestys Subjects of this province of Nova Scotia afors.[d] to Molest and disturb and the Government of Said province to bring into Hatred and Contempt with all his Majestys Liege & Faithfull Subjects of Said province, and he the s[d] John William Hofman his wicked Contrivances practices & Intentions afors[d] to Compleat perfect and render Effectuall did on the 15th 16th 17th or 18th of Novemb.[r] one Thousand Seven hundred & fifty three or on Some one day of said month of November at Lunenburg in the province afors.[d] having then Conversation with one or more of his Majestys Subjects at Lunenburg afors.[d] did publish and utter in the hearing of one or more of his Majestys Subjects a Certain false and Scandalous Libel by way of [a] Letter which he the s.[d] John William Hofman pretended & declared was directed to one John Peterquin of Lunenburg afors.[d] from his friend in England In which s.[d] Scandalous Libel He the s[d] John William Hofman woud Insinuate and did Say that his Majestys foreign Subjects meaning the Germans Dutch and French Settled at Lunenburg in the province afors.[d] were greatly oppressed and Injured and woud Insinuate they had not the Allowance of provisions and other necessaries the King allowed them, and that they his Said Majestys foreign Subjects were Imposed on if they paid for their passage to the province for that his Majesty had allowed they Should be transported at his Cost, and amongst many other Scandalous false and Seditious words which he the s[d] John William Hofman did then publish and utter he the s[d] John William Hoffman did in the hearing of one or more of his Majestys Subjects at Lunenburg afors[d] declare and Say there was no good to be done in this province, that he (meaning himself) the s[d] John William Hofman woud in the Spring of the Year [1754] get a number of the Inhabitants of this province to quit this province and that he and they woud go to the French (meaning the Settlements belonging to the king of France) and did also further Say and declare in the hearing of one or more of his Majestys Subjects that the Governor of Halifax [Colonel Lawrence] and the Governor of Lunenburg [Captain Sutherland] were both rogues & both drank out of one cup, and many Such other false & Scandalous & Seditious words, all tending to alienate the minds of his Majestys Subjects within this province from their Allegiance to his Majesty and to disturb the Tranquillity of the Government of this province and bring s.[d] Government into Contempt and Hatred, did he the s.[d] John William Hofman then and there publish utter and declare, by reason & Means of which Scandalous Libel & Seditious and false words So published uttered and declared by the s.[d] John William Hofman as afors.[d] Great Numbers of his Majestys Subjects at Lunenburg afors.[d] on or about the 15th day of December last [1753] with force & Arms and Contrary to his Majestys peace In a most riotous and tumultuous Manner did assemble to the great fear and dread of his Majestys peacefull Subjects, and they this s.ᵈ Rioters So assembled in such riotous Manner one of his Majestys S.ᵈ Subjects [Jean Petrequin], being then in the peace of our Lord the King did Seize he and Confine & Even put to torture, and this the s.ᵈ Rioters did & Confined S.ᵈ person & most Cruelly used him in the Guard house where he the s.ᵈ John William Hofman as Captain of Militia that Night Had the Guard. And that he the S.ᵈ John William Hofman did aid Comfort and abett the s.ᵈ Rioters So unlawfully Assembled and useing Such Crueltye to his Majestys Subjects, by distributing Tobaco to them that very Night they Committed those disorders, and afterwards translated Seditious papers for those very rioters & told them what to Insert in those papers, & those Rioters Continuing to Augment their Numbers Rose in arms, fired on his Majestys guardhouses and Committing divers others Insolencies were Still aided abetted Comforted and Councelled by him the s.ᵈ John William Hofman, who was Secretly in councell with Severall of the ringleaders of S.ᵈ rioters who would not act without the Concurrence of him the S.ᵈ John William Hofman and that he the s.ᵈ John William Hofman behaved in a Very Insolent Manner on his Examination before the Honb.ˡᵉ Robert Monckton Esq.ʳ one of his Majestys Councill for this province, and did in the presence and the hearing of many of his Majestys Subjects, call out to the Dutch and German deputys (So called) to Stand by him in order to rescue him the Sᵈ John William Hofman out of the Hands of the Guards who had him in Custody and after the aforsᵈ facts he the sᵈ John William Hofman did by Letters in his hand writing most Artfully Endeavour to move and Stir up the people to Disturb the peace of this province and the good government thereof by Insinuating that he was Oppressed and Cruely treated. all which actings and doings of him the sᵈ John William Hofman are Calculated & Intended to disturb the Common Tranquillity of this province and are Contrary to his Majestys Peace Crown and Dignity &.c —

E.ˣᵈ by Wᵐ Nesbitt Attorney for the King.

Nᵒ 9
Easter 1754
Bill of Indictment the King
agˢᵗ John William Hofman
for High Crimes Misdemeanors
and Breach of the Peace
A True Bill
Josh.ᵃ Mauger [sgd.]

11th May Guilty of ——
Misdemeanors for advising to
add to Peterquins Declaration
and for Misbehaviour To the
Honble Col.º Monckton

C

'Twelves Apostles' or a Dozen Traitors? Acadian Collaborators during King George's War, 1744–7

Thomas Garden Barnes

1. 'Representation of the State of His Majesties Province of Nova Scotia and Fort and Garrison of Annapolis Royal, Drawn up by a Committee of Council and Approv'd in Council, Annapolis Royal 8th Novr. 1745' (CO 217/39/218, reproduced in *Minutes of His Majesty's Council at Annapolis Royal, 1736–1749*, ed. C.B. Ferguson [Halifax: Public Archives of Nova Scotia 1967], at 80–4).

The Province of Nova Scotia with its Inhabitants after the Reduction of the Fort of Annapolis Royal in the Year 1710 was ceded or yielded up by the French to Her Brittanick Majesty and Her Successors at the Treaty of Utrecht.

That the Year following the said French Inhabitants not having taken the Oaths of Allegiance took Arms and Joind the Enemy Indians and held the Fort in some measure block's up for a considerable Time –

That after the Treaty of Utrecht altho' they were kindly treated by the English Government pursuant to Her late Majesty's Queen Annes Letter conformable to an Artickle of Said Treaty insisting upon the promise made to them in the said Letter which not being granted in manner as they requir'd they continued obstinate in refusing to Swear Allegiance to the Crown of Great Britain publickly Declaring that they look'd upon the French King to be their Sovereign 'till the year 1720 when Governour Philipps arriv'd and demanded it of them in Form but which to a man they still absolutely refus'd.

That afterwards the said Inhabitants suffer'd several small Bodys of Indians to seize and plunder the English Trading Vessels in the midst of their principal Settlements and the Crews &ca to be carried away Prisoners and in the year 1724 the Fort of Annapolis was insulted by about 60 or 70 Indians who were several days up the River amongst the Inhabitants before they made their attempt without their giving the least Intelligence thereof to the Governour.

That in the year 1726 Lieut Governour Armstrong again summon'd the Inhabitants to take the Oaths of Allegiance which they absolutely refus'd to a man throughout all their Settlements and in particular those of Chignecto Declared that they were resolv'd to continue True and Faithful to their Good King, the King of France, but those of the River of Annapolis Royal being Summond into the Fort after an obstinate refusal at lst consented to take the oath prescribed but first insisted that the Lieut. Governour should give them an assurance under his Hand that they should not be oblig'd to take Arms upon any account whatsoever which the Lieutenant Governour accordingly granted them and the other Settlements afterwards follow'd their Example on the like conditions.

That the year 1730 when General Philipps returned to his government he again in the mildest Forms requir'd them to repair their past misbehaviour by voluntarily Swearing Allegiance (without Stipulation) to their Lawfull Sovereign His Majesty King George the Second, and those of Annapolis Royal at first comply'd but on the governours making the same demand on the more numerous Settlements, they at first absolutely refus'd; but on expostulation they at last Swore Allegiance after having extorted the same Assurance from under the Generals Hand that they should not be oblig'd to bear arms, and the Inhabitants of Annapolis have since looked upon themselves to be included in the Same Conditions –

That since the year 1730 they have look'd on and suffer'd at sundry times about a dozen vagabond Indians to Seize and plunder the English Traders who ventur'd amongst them to supply them with necessarys and this in the midst of their most populous Villages, buying and Shareing with them these unlawfull Spoils even in the time of profound Peace between Britain and France.

That in the month of June 1744 after the War with France was proclaim'd the Fort of Annalpolis was attack'd by Surprise by a Party of about 3 or 4 hundred Indians headed by a French Officer & a Priest, and altho' the Enemy had march'd thro' the heart of the Province amongst the thickest of our Inhabitants we had not Intelligence of them 'till two Days before they murder'd two of our Men in the Gardens within a few yards of the Fort Gate and during their Stay were furnish'd plentifully with provisions messengers and other necessarys even Fire arrows while we were entirely Deserted by them. So soon as the Enemy left us, the Inhabitants sparingly brought in fresh Provisions at higher prices than usual, furnish'd us with Timber and Stones for the Repairs of the Fort with several Labourers for the same purpose.

That in the month of August following the fort was again attack'd by a more powerful Body of the Enemy, consisting of 6 or 700 regular Troops and Indians, not without some of our French Inhabitants amongst them ...

During the Enemies Stay here they were plentifully Supply'd with Provisions, Several hundred Scaling Ladders boats, Canoes and in short every other necessary the Countrey could afford but as to the English we could not get the least knowledge of the strength of our Enemy ...

During all which Transactions His Majesties Government could not procure the least account of the Enemy tho' we frequently sent out Partys in the night for that purpose, but the Inhabitants who were most liable to be met with left their houses and would never suffer themselves to be surpris'd, nevertheless both men, women and children frequented the Enemies Quarters at their Mass, prayers, dancing and all other ordinary occasions; After the Enemy was retir'd we were

again supply'd with Building materials and fresh provisions with more chearful-
ness than formerly but as some of themselves acknowledg'd the Enemy advis'd
them to it telling them tht whatever we might be able to do towards putting the
Fort in Repair we should certainly fall into their hands the following Spring
which seems agreeable to the Instructions given by the Bishop of Quebec to the
Missionarys here to keep themselves and the people from giving any occasion of
being expell'd the Province, that as the French were giving any occasion of being
expell'd the Province, that as the French were in hopes to reduce it they might
find it inhabited and the Inhabitants even concealed the Ammunition and Arms
left them by the Enemy –

Accordingly a fresh Body of French Canadians and chosen Indians enter'd the
Province in February following at Chignicto, carried on a Correspondence with
the Inhabitants of Mines immediately on their arrival and afterwards with the
Inhabitants of this River and were within twelve hours march of the Fort without
our having any certain Intelligence 'till the 1st of May, when by chance we Discover'd that some of our people who liv'd within a mile of the Fort held a Correspondence with them who suffer'd themselves to be severly treted by us before
they could be made to own they had the least knowledge of the Enemy, who ont
he 4th day of May was with us, and by the good accounts received from the
Inhabitants were enabled to surprise seven of our Rangers who were out on Party,
which Design was the only reason that encourag'd the Enemy to come to Annapolis and we have since been well inform'd ...

That his Majesties said French Subjects are esteem'd to be no less that 5000
Fighting men all Roman Catholicks and from the Circumstances before mention'd
may be said to be entirely devoted to the Interest of France; The Province is full of
Corn and Cattle which is of little use to the English, but rather a support to the
Enemy and themselves should they again attempt to revolt which we may reasonably expect they may do should they be encourag'd by an Expedition of any Consequence from France or Canada.

That the said Inhabitants pay no Taxes towards the Support of His Majesties
Government, only a Small Quit Rent for their Lands in Fowles and Wheat
amounting in the whole to about 15 Sterling excepting what they voluntarily
allow to their Priests, who, as they are subjects of France and receive a Yearly Sal-
lary from that King must be accounted as Spies on the English.

Upon consideration of the above Several indusputable Facts, if they are not
absolutely to be regarded as utter Enemies to His Majesties Government they cannot be accounted less than unprofitable Inhabitants for their conditional Oath of
Allegiance will not entitle them to the Confidence and Privileges of Natural British Subjects nor can it even be expected in Several Generations especially whilst
they have French Priests among them ...

The Garison is very inconsiderable, not having as yet had any reinforcement from Europe, that which we had from New England eighteen months ago being greatly diminish'd, and the men discontented, uneasy and desirous to be dismiss'd; neither have we any Vessels for the Defence of the Harbour or the least Bark for the Conveyance of packetts upon any extraordinary occasion, by which the Kings Provisions and other Necessaries for the Support of the Garrison is greatly expos'd even in the Harbour and the Garrison itself liable to be block'd up by a very insignificant force by Sea, several vessels having been taken in the Bason among which two Board of Ordnance Vessels with Stores for the Fort and two others with necessaries for the Officers and Troops.

'Tis true the Reduction of the City of Lewisburgh lying about 100 Leagues from us is of some advantage towards the safety of Annapolis provided a Squadron of Ships of War is constantly kept Cruising in those Seas when the Season permitts, but 'tis well known how much we are expos'd in the naked Condition we now are in to a Surprise by Sea should be French be so lucky as to make use of this favourable opportunity.

Upon the whole it is most humbly submitted whether the said French Inhabitants may not be transported out of the Province of NOVA SCOTIA and be replac'd by good Protestant Subjects.

P. Mascarene

2. Mascarene to Newcastle, 9 Dec. 1745 (CO 217/39/215 [new f. 314]).

I humbly refer to the papers inclos'd which contain a representation of the state of this Province with regard particularly to the temper and behaviour its inhabitants with an other annex'd to it from these inhabitants setting forth their case and a copy of my leter to Governour Shirley [f.324v] shewing my views and the motives of my conduct towards them. My principal aim in the management of this people has been to keep them from joyning in arms with the enemy and in making them as serviceable as I could in furnishing materials and other assistance to put this ruinous fort in a tolerable condition of deffence, which I have hitherto effect[ed]. But I can not answer that if the French should send a fleet and forces from Europe to attack this Province these inhabitants will not yield to the inclination they still retain for their old masters, tho' they seem to be sensible of the success they enjoy under His Majesty's government.

3. Representation on the state of the province since the outbreak of war (CO 217/39/216 [f.316]).

As these inhabitants have always been represented to be inclin'd to the French interest from their tyes of relation and religion; the suggestions on their behaviour seem to flow naturally with respect to that inclination and it is less to be wonder'd at that the enemy has had so much influence on this people lately as that he has not had much more. What weight the annexed representation these inhabitants make of their case will have must be left to consideration ... [since being brought to take oaths of fidelity] I have look't upon them as grafted in the body of the British Nation, as an unsound limb indeed, and therefore to be nurtur'd, and by time and good care to be brought to answer the purposes expected from them; first to become subjects and after that good subjects; which I have represented might be effected in some generations by good usage and by removing some impediments, to wit, the influence of the French at Cape Bretton and that the missionaries which have been suffer'd to remain amongst this people and which hitherto it has been reckon'd dangerous to attempt to drive away, as it has been a question how farr the Treaty of Utrecht was binding in this case which certainly can not be resolv'd here ...

[If the idea is to remove the Acadians and have British settlers take their place, Mascarene advances the following considerations: 1) how far Utrecht 'bind the Crown towards this People'; 2) if they are removed and acquired by the French, the latter will be much strengthened; 3) there are 'great difficulties' in removing, he estimates, 20,000 Acadians; 4) to suggest removal when the enemy is in the province would throw the Acadians into despair, and the nature of the country makes it hard to do anything with the inhabitants.]

This last consideration has occasion'd my using these French inhabitant in a very tender manner particularly of late, and to check those, who by too much zeal or forwardness loaded the behaviour of these inhabitants so as to make them all equally guilty and involv'd in the same threatened ruin

I have endeavour'd after the recess of the ennemy to raise an emulation amongst these inhabitants by telling them I knew there were some amongst them who had acted with a determinate ill will towards us and that I wanted to distinguish them from others, in which I have made some steps, but not with that success I might have expected, but reason of some impediments which would take to much room to explain.

D
Civilians Tried in Military Courts: Quebec, 1759–64
Douglas Hay

Extracts from the correspondence of Deputy Judge Advocate General Charles Gould, 1763–4, WO 72, PRO [reproduced in F.B. Wiener, *Civilians under Military Justice: The British Practice since 1689 Especially in North America* (Chicago: University of Chicago Press 1967), at 251–5].

Gould to Governor Murray of Quebec, 11 Aug. 1763
... I beg leave to acquaint you, that a Pardon is passing the Great Seal of Great Britain (and will be forwarded to you by the very first opportunity) for Joseph Corriveaux, as Accessary to the Murder of Louis Helene Dodier at St. Vallier.

I thought it proper to make this the Subject of a Separate Letter, not choosing that any thing should appear officially concerning his Case, as the King's Pardon Signified by the Judge Advocate would not be effectual, and as the Court Martial appear to have exceeded their jurisdiction in his trial as well as in those of Marie Josephe Corriveaux [see WO 71/137] for the same Murder, and of Isabella Silvain for Perjury; neither of them being military Persons, nor Subject to the Mutiny Act or Articles of War. I was in hopes, it might have been expedited, so as to be transmitted herewith; but the Lord Privy Seal, Lord Chancellor, and others, thro' whom Pardons of this nature necessarily pass, being out of Town, the delay occasioned by sending it to their respective Seats has made it impracticable. I took the liberty of mentioning my thoughts to [Secretary of State] Lord Egremont, who saw the Matter in the same light; and his Lordship, to whose Province it belonged to move His Majesty for the Pardon, preferred it's passing in a private manner through me, rather than Signifying the King's Commands from his Office. Although there has been no Substantial injustice done in this case, – on the contrary the Guilt of the Person, who has suffered, was evident, and the necessity of Example great, – Nevertheless you are so well apprised, how many there are in this Kingdom, who view the Military Arm with a jealous Eye and are ever ready to take advantage of the least mistaken excess of Power, though proceeding from the best intention, that I persuade myself, you will not think the delicacy used upon this occasion unnecessary, and that I have thought it my duty to Suggest will meet with your candid Acceptance.

Murray to Gould, 12 Nov. 1763 (also Murray Letterbook, MG 23, G11, 1, NA).
Sir,
I cannot delay, a moment, to return Thanks for your Favor of the 11th August. I

must forever think myself greatly obliged to you for the tenderness, and delicacy you have shewn in the Business of Josephe Corrivaux &c. &c:: You must be persuaded that tho' we have erred, our Intentions were most Upright, and I declare to You, I think it was lucky we did not know, how limited our Jurisdiction has been here for four years past. His Majesty's new Subjects, already prejudiced against us by every popish Art, must have conceived a Strange Opinion of their new Masters, who had no Law to punish the most notorious Murder, that perhaps has ever been committed.

I understand a civil Jurisdiction will soon be established here, when that happens, we can no longer be at a loss, in the mean Time, I have communicated to the Governors of Trois Rivieres, and Montreal, the Knowledge I have learnt from your Letter; I am confident the Information was as necessary for them, as it was for me, and I am astonished I was not apprised of the irregularity of our proceedings in time to have prevented them, as I am certain it is near three years ago, since two Canadians (*not Soldiers, nor in any respect subject to a military jurisdiction, according to your Explanation of the Articles of War,*) were hanged at Montreal, agreeable to the Sentence of a General Court Martial, approven of by Major General Gage, the Governor of that place, to which I add, the Paragraph, of the Secretary of States Letter quoted to you by Mr Cramahé; I certainly must do you the Justice to believe that the Proceedings of that Court Marshal were never sent to Your Office, but I can with difficulty reconcile Lord Egremonts Letter, to His Lordships seeing the Affair of Corrivaux in the same light that you do ...

General Thomas Gage, commander-in-chief, North America, New York, to Gould, 10 April 1764
Sir,

I am obliged to you for your Favor of the 11th Febry, in which you are pleased to make some observations on the Proceedings of the Genl Courts Martial, which have been held at Montreal; and till the Receipt of your Letter, I must own to you, I had not the smallest Doubt of their being consistent with Law. The utility of such Proceedings you are sensible of, where no Civil Judicature was in Force; you must therefore be sensible of the Necessity of passing Laws for the Direction of Officers in such Circumstances, to prevent Anarchy & Confusion, Murder, Robbery, & every heinous Crime being committed, without Restraint or Controul.

These Matters have been debated here; we have been told in Genl, That it is a Maxim held by all Civilians That no Government can subsist without Law, That in Conquered Countrys, The Laws of Such Countrys Subsist, till it shall please the Conqueror to give Them new Laws. In Canada, all Justice ceased upon the Conquest, for every Court of Civil or Criminal Judicature left the Country. The Genl therefore constituted new Courts of Judicature, and Criminal Cases were ordered to be tried by Genl courts Martial only. This Method was approved of by the King, and was accordingly followed.

If this Method was not strictly Warranted in Law, I should think it worth asking the opinion & advice of the Heads of the Law, how Canada in such Circumstances, ought to be governed ...

E
'Government by Will and Pleasure Instead of Law':
Military Justice and the Legal System in Quebec, 1775–83
Jean-Marie Fecteau and Douglas Hay

1 Haldimand to Germain, 7 June 1779 (CO 42/39/93–4).

This turbulent and seditious behaviour of a Cabal at Montreal has also laid me under the necessity of confining two French Men whose names are Mesplet and Jautard, the former a Printer sent here by Congress in 1774 to publish and disperse their Letters, the latter has been an Attorney, and is an unprincipled Adventurer, so soon as their Papers have been examined, Your Lordship shall have a circumstantial account of their Affairs, and if this does not in some measure check the licentious spirit that was beginning to rise, I shall not hesitate to make more examples. I heartily lament that those who misbehaved in 1775 and 1776 were not severely punished, it was easy then but now is difficult; nevertheless, my endeavours shall not be wanting to promote the King's Interests, serve the Public, and secure the Province – Objects which engross all my Attention, and which always have been, and ever shall be the sole Aim of all my Actions.

2 Haldimand to Germain, 25 October 1780 (CO 42/40/183–6).

It was with great regret that I found myself obliged not to Communicate the Instruction relative to the Security of Personal Liberty. The Citizens in No Country ought to be liable to Long imprisonments. Persons accused of Crimes ought Certainly to be brought in a limited Time to Trial, but in time of war and Rebellion, it would be impolitic, and in the present Circumstances of the Province, highly dangerous to attempt an innovation of the Kind. I have been under the disagreeable necessity of imprisoning several Persons for corresponding with Rebels or assisting them to Escape, and I have great Reasons to suspect many more of being guilty of the same Practices, but have Made it a Rule to pretend Ignorance as often as I can, and am Satisfied with guarding against the bad Consequences of their Treachery except where their Crime is publickly known, and then I think it my Duty to take Notice of them, as a contrary conduct would betray weakness, and encourage others to follow their Example, this was the case with Mr. Charles Hay of Quebec and Mr. Cazeau of Montreal. The Clerk of the Former was detected and apprehended last March as he was Setting off for Albany. He had a Certificate from Charles Hay whose Brother is a Quarter Master General in the

Rebel army, desiring credit to be put in him. The Clerk has confessed before a Magistrate that his Master sent him, and that Mr. Cazeau procured him a Guide. The first applied by Petition to the Court of King's Bench in the sessions last May for the District of Quebec praying a writ of Habeas Corpus. The Petition was rejected by the unanimous opinion of the Commissioners for executing the office of Chief Justice, who by that means and a Public Declaration which they made in 1779 at the trial of Mr. Stiles of the Viper on an indictment for Murder, of the King's having a Legal Right to impress mariners for the Navy in Time of War, have very much strengthened the hands of Government. The Province is surrounded by Enemies from without, and as happens in all Civil Wars, is infected with Spies and Secret Enemies from within – Your Lordship must be sensible how necessary it is that Government should be supported. I confide in Your Lordship's zeal for the King's Service to give me every Assistance in your Power, and in your Candor and Regard for myself, to assure His Majesty that my views on the Civil and Military affairs of the Province, shall and can have no end but the advantage of His Service and the Good of his People. I cannot finish this long letter without requesting Your Lordship to be Convinced that whatever System I may adopt, and whatever Opinion I may have formed of Men and things, is and will be the Result of my own Reflection and of my Attention to my Duty, and not the Suggestion of Persons influenced by attachment to former systems or plans of their own, at the same time that I cannot alter or Reject former measures, which I think for the Good of the King's Service agreeable to the Wishes and Suitable to the Wants of the People over whom I preside, because they may be agreeable to Men who perhaps have had private views and resentments.

3 Chief Justice Livius to secretary of state, 13 March 1782 (CO 42/42/109).

Mr. Livius Chief Justice of the province of Quebec previous to his return in the next convoy, thinks it his duty to state the following matter.

When the last ships left Quebec there were then in the Military prison in the province several persons of merely civil capacities who had been apprehended in virtue of the orders of General Haldimand (it must be presumed on strong grounds of suspicion) but without the warrant of any Magistrate, they have been continued in prison many months, some of them very near two years, without any knowledge being given them of the cause of their imprisonment, and without any examination.

The Agents these persons have sent over hither have applied to Mr. Livius, from them he understands that as soon as he arrives in the province, formal applications will be made to him as Chief Justice for legal redress. By the Act of parliament 14 Geo III, c.83 the Criminal Law of England is established in Canada in the fullest and most express terms, and the Chief Justice is under every obligation of honour, office and oath to grant that relief which the Law of England affords in cases of illegal imprisonment, he cannot possibly act otherwise, and tho' he will endeavour to preserve all the temperament and moderation that can possibly consist with his Office, yet unless the General recedes the consequence must be a contention between his Majesty's Military and civil servants attended with such public scandal as ought to be avoided at all times, but in the present Crisis would be very detrimental.

The Chief Justice therefore begs leave to suggest the necessity of some preventive measures, before his embarkation.

4 Petition of Mary Hay, Court of King's Bench, Province of Quebec, 1 May 1781 (Quebec T–0006–14, ANQ).

To the Honourable Adam Mabane, Thomas Dunn and Jenkin Williams Esquires his Majesty's Comissioners for executing the office of Chief Justice for the said Province

The Petition of Mary Hay, wife of Charles Hay of the City of Quebec, Master Cooper

Humbly sheweth, That your Petitioner's Husband was on the fifteenth day of April which was in the year of our Lord One Thousand seven hundred and eighty, apprehended and committed to Prison by Miles Prenties of this city, in whose custody he is still detained without his or your Petitioner's knowing the cause.

That your petitioner at the Session of this Court in the month of May last, did humbly petition your Honours to award a writ of Habeas Corpus ad subjiciendum to bring up the Body of her said Husband, to be dealt with according to law, annexing to the said petition, as by the Statute is directed and required, an Affidavit of the said Miles Prenties's refusal of a copy of the warrant of Commitment and Detainer.

That your petitioner did also at [the] same time humbly pray your Honours to assign Council to her said Husband to advise him and your Petitioner in matters of Law respecting his case, when your Honours were accordingly pleased to assign Robert Russel[l] Esquire to be of Council for her Husband.

That the said Robert Russell Esquire, did, for some time afterwards correspond with her said husband by the hands of the said Miles Prenties but on application made to the said Robert Russell Esq. by your Petitioner to prepare a petition to the Governour in Council for a writ of Habeas Corpus, as aforesaid, Mr. Russel not only refused preparing the same but declined sitting any further as Council for your Petitioner's husband, as appears by his letter to your Petitioner, a copy of which is hereunto annexed.

That your Honours were pleased to dismiss the Petition presented to your Honours aforesaid for a writ of Habeas Corpus, grounding your judgement, as far as your Petitioner can recollect, on the five following reasons; on which your Petitioner humbly begs leave to make a few remarks, which she hopes, your Honours will regard in a favourable light, and impute any improprieties that may be in them, to the true cause, that is, ignorance of the subject, and being deserted by her Council.

First reason alledged by your Honours:

That the Petition was grounded on the Statute 31 Chas. 2 chap.2 and demanded a writ of Habeas Corpus under that Statute as a matter of right, whereas my Lord Chief Justice Vaughan and Sir William Blackstone say that it is not a matter of Right; that it had been sometimes denied in England; that Sir Edward Coke denied one to a Pirate.

– Answer: the petition was general for a writ under the Statute of Chas 2 or at Common law, which ever your Honours should think to be the legal mode: but if your Honours considered the Petition to be for a writ under the Statute, it was certainly inaccurate to offer as a reason for refusing the writ, the opinion of Sir John Vaughan and Sir Edward Coke, who were both in their graves some years before the Statute of Chas. 2 was past and who therefore must be supposed to speak of the law as it stood in their time, subject to many abuses, to remedy which that Statute was enacted. To itself alone therefore recourse ought to be had for its meaning.

Second reason alledged:

Application ought to have been made the first day of the assize or the first week of the Term, and it was not made till the last day.

– Answer: Your Honours did not seem to lay much stress on this objection, and neither shall your Petitioner, only to observe that the assertion is not true in fact, for the application was made to the Court some days before the end of the Term and the delay in filing the Affidavit till the last day was owing to Thomas Scott Esquire One of his Majesty's Commissioners of the Peace having refused to take the affidavit of John Hay and Robert Connor in order to be annexed to the petition to this Court.

Third reason alledged:

That the Petition did not state that the Prisoner is not confined for any offences for which Bail is denied by the Statute, which it ought to have done.

– Answer: Had your Petitioner obtained a Copy of the warrant of Commitment upon her application, it would have appeared upon what offences the Prisoner was detained and whether or not they were within the exceptions of the Statute, but as such Copy was denied her, your Petitioner could state to the Court no more that she knew, viz that her husband was detained in the custody of Mr. Prenties without knowing the Cause and that a Copy of the warrant of Detainer was denied her.

Fourth reason alledged:

That the writ of Habeas Corpus is not introduced into the Province by the Quebec Act.

– Answer: That Statute enacts that the Criminal Law of England shall be observed as law in this Province, as well in the description and quality of the offences, as in the method of Prosecution and Trial. Now your Petitioner is informed that in England the most attrocious offender cannot be denied a writ of Habeas Corpus upon due application to the Judges, and annexing thereto an affidavit that a copy of the warrant of Commitment and Detainer has been denied. Such then being the method of Prosecution in England your Petitioner apprehends that the same is by the above recited clause of the Quebec Act, the legal method of Prosecution in this Province.

Fifth reason alledged:

The Statute of 17 Geo 3 cap.9

– Answer: Your Petitioner apprehends that how proper soever it might be to alledge this Statute as a reason for not granting her Husband his liberty, had the offences therein been certified on the return to the writ of Habeas Corpus prayed for, it can never be alledged as a reason for refusing to award the writ of Habeas Corpus itself. The writ of Habeas Corpus does not necessarily imply that the Prisoner shall thereon obtain his liberty, it is only a mode prescribed by the law to come at the knowledge of the cause of the Detention of the Prisoner; and there have been numberless instances in England and some even in this Province, wherein the Judges have remanded the Prisoners brought before them by a writ of Habeas Corpus, it having appeared on the return that their Detention was legal. Your Honours therefore in mentioning this Statute must have considered the information given by Mr. Prenties in Court equivalent to a return on a writ of Habeas Corpus.

Your Petitioner will observe upon this,

1st. That by the law, after affidavit produced of a Denial of a Copy of the warrant of Commitment and Detainer, the Court ought not to receive any information concerning the cause of the Capture and Detainer of the Prisoner, otherwise than certified on the return to the writ, by which means the return being filed in Court, the Prisoner would be able to procure a copy thereof.

2ndly. Mr. Prenties's answers to the Questions put to him are not sufficient to ground any Judgement upon; he was not sworn to declare the Truth, and when asked by the Court whether mention was not made in the warrant, that your Petitioner's Husband was charged with Treason, or suspicion of Treason, or Treasonable Practices, Mr. Prenties answered, 'I think there is something like that mentioned in it.' Your petitioner also thinks that this answer requires very little comment.

3rdly. Had your Honours been pleased to award a writ of Habeas Corpus, and Mr. Prenties had returned the same with the cause of the Caption and Detainer certified thereon, the body of the Prisoner not being brought up, this Court could not legally enquire into the sufficiency of the return; for the Law is express (and indeed the name of the writ implies it) that the Body of the Prisoner must be brought up, to do, submit to and receive whatsoever the Court shall consider in his behalf.

But supposing the writ of Habeas Corpus actually issued, and a return made thereof, according to the Judgement of the Court, "that your Petitioner's Husband was arrested by Mr. Prenties upon the warrant of the Lieutenant Governor by his Excellency's command on suspicion of Treasonable Practices" – your Petitioner is of opinion that nothing contained in that Statute would, on such a return, prevent the Prisoner from having his liberty, for the following reasons.

This is a penal Statute a temporary Statute of necessity and being totally repugnant to the Spirit of the British constitution, it ought to be construed with the greatest strictness, or whatever latitude as allowed in the interpretation thereof, ought to be beneficial for the Subject.

1st Your Petitioner submits it, whether, from the Preamble and the enacting part of the aforesaid statute, it extends, or was ever meant to extend to the Inhabitants of any province in America in the King's Peace or to have any other Persons in view than the Inhabitants of the Provinces in America declared by the Statute 16 Geo 3 chap 5th to be in Rebellion.

2ndly The Act requires that the Persons committed under it should be committed by a Magistrate having competent authority in that behalf, and your Petitioner is of the opinion that his Excellency the Governor, by whose authority alone it appears the commitment has been made, is not such a Magistrate.

3rdly Commitment under the Statute can be only to the Common Gaol, for that Statute empowers the King to erect new Gaols in the Realm of England only but in no other part of his Dominions.

4thly The only offences mentioned in the Statute are High Treason and Piracy, & by the Hypothesis, the Prisoner is detained on Suspicion of Treasonable Practices, which are less Criminal than High Treason, not subjecting the offender to a Capital punishment, and being less Offences than High Treason, are surely not the same as High Treason, for which reason as they do not come within the words of the Act, they ought not to be construed to come within the meaning of it. And therefore as persons committed for suspicion of Treasonable Practices are bailable by the law of England, your Petitioner's Husband ought to be admitted to bail, even allowing the Crime of which he is accused should be the same as is alleged in the Judgement of the Court.

That your Petitioner hereby declares that her Petition of the fifteenth of May last to your Honours was not for the writ of Habeas Corpus under the Statute of Cha 2d only but an application for the writ of Habeas Corpus either under the Statute of Cha 2d or at Common Law, as your Honours might think most expedient and Legal. And that this Petition also is for either of those writs.

Your Petitioner therefore humbly prays your Honours to consider how ill qualified she is for discussing points of Law, and, on that account, to pardon anything your Honours may find improper in this Petition; to grant your Petitioner's Husband once more the assistance of his Council aforesaid, by giving that Council an assurance that whatever he may legally do in behalf of her said Husband, shall be so far from giving offence, that he will receive therein the Countenance and protection of this Court; and also that your Honours will be pleased to reconsider your former Judgement, with your Petitioner's remarks thereon, and award a writ of Habeas Corpus, under the Seal of this Court, returnable immediate, to bring up the Body of her Husband, and when brought up, to admit him to bail, your Petitioner having very unexceptionable Bail ready for that purpose. But if your Honours will persist in refusing to award the Writ of Habeas Corpus, above prayed for, then your Petitioner prays that her Husband may now have a Trial by his Country, and if found guilty, he is willing to undergo the Sentence of the Law.

5 Valentin Jautard to Matthew, 19 Sept. 1782 (MG 21, Copies of Documents in the the British Library, Haldimand Collection, MS 21661–892, vol. 185–1: 108–9. Also printed in Jean-Paul De Lagrave and Jacques G. Ruelland, *Premier journaliste de langue française au Canada, Valentin Jautard, 1736–1787* (Quebec: Griffon D'Argent 1989, at 314–15).

Monsieur,

Comme il n'est pas injuste de penser que la qualité d'affaires dont vous êtes chargé ne vous ait distrait de la pétition et de la lettre que j'eus l'honneur de vous servir, je pense que vous ne trouverez pas mauvais que je les rappelle à votre mémoire.

Si je m'en rapporte à la réponse verbale que le sieur Prenties m'a faite de votre part, Monsieur, je ne trouve que le langage des années précédentes. Chaque automne, il a passé pour constant qu'après le départ des bâtiments les prisonniers devaient être élargis. Ce terme que l'on mettait à leurs peines leur a toujours été fatal. Le quatrième hiver approche, les bâtiments sont partis et revenus. [Ce sont] toujours le même propos sans effet. J'aurais donc tort de me flatter.

Je ne suis cependant pas sans quelque lueur d'espérance car je ne serais penser que dans le temps que le roi, le parlement et le peuple d'Angleterre s'empressent *by every consideration of humanity* de delivrer leurs prisonniers le plus promptement possible quand ils prennent toutes les mesures convenables a cet effet, qu'ils declarent que: *in which [measures] not only the comfort but the rights of individuals are concerned,* je n'ose penser, dis-je, que dans cette seule partie, dans ce seul petit point de l'Empire Britannique, les droits des individus sont regardés indifféremment et qu'une disposition aussi sage des sentiments, aussi conforme à l'humanité et aux constitutions nationales, ne soit pas suivie. Je me tais, car je pourrais me rendre coupable. Je sais qu'il m'est permis de penser, mais j'ignore si je dois dire ce que je pense.

Je ne désespère donc point de ma liberté, mais je ne m'en flatte pas. C'est pourquoi je demande une satisfaction qui ne peut m'être refusée en loi ni en équité. C'est que la cause pour laquelle j'ai été et suis detenu me soit notifiée afin que je sache s'il y a compensation de la faute à la peine. Si c'est ainsi, je me tairai et prendrai patience.

J'espère, Monsieur, qu'il vous plaira de communiquer a presence a Son Excellence et que vous daignerez me faire une réponse ecrite; car toute autre prendrait trop [de temps] avant qu'elle me fut parvenue ...

Rebellion and Repression in Nova Scotia in the Era of the American Revolution
Ernest A. Clarke and Jim Phillips

'An Act to Impower His Majesty to Secure and Detain Persons Charged with, or Suspected of, the Crime of High Treason, Committed in Any of His Majesty's Colonies or Plantations in America, or on the High Seas, or the Crime of Piracy' [(1777) 27 Geo III, c. 9].

WHEREAS a rebellion and war have been openly and traiterously levied and carried on in certain of his Majesty's colonies and plantations in America, and acts of treason and piracy have been committed on the high seas, and upon the ships and goods of his Majesty's subjects, and many persons have been seised and taken, who are expressly charged or strongly suspected of such treasons and felonies, and many more such persons may be hereafter so seised and taken: and whereas such persons have been, or may be brought into this kingdom, and into other parts of his Majesty's dominions, and it may be inconvenient in many such cases to proceed forthwith to the trial of such criminals, and at the same time of evil example to suffer them to go at large; be it therefore enacted by the King's most excellent majesty, and by and with the advice and consent of the lords spiritual and temporal, and commons, in this present parliament assembled, and by the authority of the same, That all and every person or persons who have been, or shall hereafter be seised or taken in the act of high treason committed in any of his Majesty's colonies or plantations in America, or on the high seas, or in the act of piracy, or who are or shall be charged with or suspected of the crime of high treason, committed in any of the said colonies, or on the high seas, or of piracy, and who have been, or shall be committed, in any part of his Majesty's dominions, for such crimes, or any of them, or for suspicion of such crimes, or any of them, by any magistrate having competent authority in that behalf, to the common gaol, or other place of confinement as is herein-after provided for that purpose, shall and may be thereupon secured and detained in safe custody, without bail or mainprize, until the first day of January, one thousand seven hundred and seventy-eight; and that no judge or justice of peace shall bail or try any such person or persons without order from his Majesty's most honourable privy council, signed by six of the said privy council, until the said first day of January, one thousand seven hundred and seventy-eight, any law, statute, or usage to the contrary in any-wise notwithstanding.

II. And whereas it may be necessary to provide for such prisoners within this realm some other places of confinement besides the common gaols; be it enacted by the authority aforesaid, That it shall and may be lawful for his Majesty, by warrant under his sign manual, to appoint one or more place or places of confinement within the realm, for the custody of such prisoners; and all and every magistrate and magistrates, having competent authority in that behalf, are hereby authorised to commit such persons as aforesaid to such place or places of confinement, so to be appointed, instead of the common gaol.

III. Provided always, and be it enacted, That no offences shall be construed to be piracy within the meaning of this act, except acts of felony committed on the ships and goods of his Majesty's subjects by persons on the high seas.

IV. Provided also, and it is hereby declared, That nothing herein contained is intended, or shall be construed to extend to the case of any other prisoner or prisoners than such as shall have been out of the realm at the time or times of the offence or offences wherewith he or they shall be charged, or of which he or they shall be suspected.

V. And be it further enacted by the authority aforesaid, That this act shall continue and be in force until the said first day of January, one thousand seven hundred and seventy-eight, and no longer.

G
Sedition among the Loyalists: The Case of Saint John, 1784–6
D.G. Bell

New Brunswick's statute against political petitioning, 1786 (SNB 1786, c. 58).

Resurrected from the reign of King Charles II, this remarkable measure was rushed through the General Assembly in March 1786 to counteract a wave of anti-government petitioning in all the counties from Saint John to Fredericton. Although no one is ever known to have been prosecuted under it, its requirements were still being observed into the 1830s. It disappeared quietly from the statute book in 1854.

An Act against Tumults and Disorders, upon pretence of preparing or presenting Public Petitions, or other Addresses, to the Governor, or General Assembly.

To prevent tumultuous and other disorderly soliciting, and procuring of Hands, by private persons, to Petitions, Complaints, Remonstrances, and Declarations, and other Addresses, to the Governor, Council and Assembly, or any or either of them for alteration of matters established by Law, redress of pretended grievances in Church or State, or other public concernments, being made use of to serve the ends of factious and seditious persons, to the violation of the Public peace.

I. Be it enacted by the Governor, Council and Assembly, That no person or persons whatsoever, shall solicit, labour, or procure the getting of Hands, or other consent, of any persons above the number of Twenty or more, to any Petition, Complaint, Remonstrance, Declaration or other Address, to the Governor, Council and Assembly, or any or either of them, for alteration of matters established by Law in Church or State, unless the matter thereof have been first consented unto, and ordered, by three or more Justices of that County, or by the major part of the Grand Jury of the County or division of the County, where the same matter shall arise, at their Public Assizes or General Quarter Sessions; and that no person or persons whatsoever, shall repair to the Governor, Council or Assembly, upon pretence of presenting, or delivering any Petition, Complaint, Remonstrance or Declaration, or other Addresses, accompanied, with excessive number of people, or at any one time with more than the number of Ten persons; upon pain of incurring a penalty, not exceeding the sum of One Hundred Pounds in money, and Three Months Imprisonment without bail or mainprize for every offence; which offence [is] to be prosecuted in the Supreme Court, or at the General Quarter Sessions, within Six Months after the offence committed; and proved by two or more credible witnesses.

II. Provided always, That this Act, or anything therein contained, shall not be construed, to extend to debar, or hinder any person, or persons, not exceeding the number of Twenty aforesaid, to present any public or private grievance, or complaint, to any Member or Members of the Council or Assembly, during the sitting of the General Assembly, or to the Governor, for any remedy to be thereupon had; nor to extend to any Address whatsoever, to the Governor, by all or any of the Members of the Council and Assembly, or either of them during the sitting of the General Assembly, but that they may enjoy their freedom of access to His Excellency, as heretofore hath been used.

H

Judges and Treason Law in Lower Canada, England, and the United States during the French Revolution, 1794–1800
F. Murray Greenwood

1. Extract from 'Cursory Strictures on the Charge Delivered by Lord Chief Justice Eyre to the Grand Jury, October 2, 1794,' as printed in 24 St. Tr. 199 at 225–8.

... The chief justice then, having hitherto talked of every thing that is not to the purpose, comes at last to speak of the matter in hand. Here he employs all his ingenuity, exerts all his arts, and displays his utmost intrepidity of countenance. This part of the case is opened as follows:

'Whether the project of a convention, having for its object the collecting together a power which should overawe the legislative body but not suspend it, or entirely determine its functions, if acted upon, will also amount to high treason, and to the specific treason of compassing and imagining the king's death, is a more doubtful question. Thus far is clear: a force upon the parliament, must be immediately directed against the king. It must reach the king, or it can have no effect at all. The laws are enacted in parliament by the king's majesty, by and with the advice and consent of the Lords and Commons in parliament assembled. A force meditated against the parliament, therefore, is a force meditated against the king, and seems to fall within the cases described.'

Nothing can be more gross to the view of any one who will attentively read this paragraph, than its total want of all definite and intelligible meaning. The chief justice talks of 'collecting together a power,' and of 'a force' exercised upon the parliament. What is here intended by the words power and force? Under the kindly ambiguity of these words, the chief justice seems very willing to slip upon us the idea of an armed power and a military force. But this can scarcely by any construction be reconciled to the idea of a convention. An army of delegates was an idea reserved for chief justice Eyre to introduce into the world. Well then: let us suppose that arms and violence are not intended; yet the chief justice says, that the project of a convention has for its object 'the collecting together a power, which should overawe the legislative body.' This word is still more ambiguous than any of the rest. What are we to understand by the phrase 'to overawe?' Awe in its true acceptation has always been understood to mean deference or respect. It cannot mean any thing else here, since, as we have already seen, armed power and military force are out of the question. But in this sense what is the object of every species of convention or political association whatever? It is always intended to produce deference and respect. Thus the chief justice very properly observes, that 'a convention, having for its sole object a dutiful and peaceable application to parliament,' does not fail to find that application attended with 'respect and credit, in proportion to its universality.' Indeed there can be no doubt, that there are but two ways of operating upon men's conduct, the one, by exhibiting arguments calculated to prevail upon their own inclinations and conviction, the other a perceiving how much the thing required accords with the sense of numerous bodies of men, and bodies of men entitled to eminent credit.

Such being the substance of the most material paragraph in the charge to the grand jury, let us see in what manner this paragraph is concluded, and what are the inferences drawn from it. What is the treatment due to this force which is no force; this collecting together a power, unarmed, and entitled to credit only for its universality? What shall be done to the men who thus overawe the legislative body, by exciting its deference and respect; or, failing this, do not overawe it at all, inasmuch as they have no power to inforce their demands? 'Whether or not,' as chief justice Eyre sagaciously observes, 'the project of such a convention will amount to high treason, is a more doubtful question.' He adds, 'in this case it does not appear to me, that I am warranted by the authorities, to state to you as clear law, that the mere conspiracy to raise such a force' [recollect what has been said about the nature of this force], and the entering into consultations respecting it, will alone, and without actually raising the force, constitute the crime of high treason. What the law is in that case, and what will be the effect of the circumstance of the force being thus meditated, will be fit to be solemnly considered and determined when the case shall arise.'

Here the chief justice speaks with a proper degree of modesty and precaution, so far as relates to the supposed guilt of the persons under confinement; but when he has occasion to resume the subject, he, in his usual manner introduces a variation into the statement. 'It may perhaps be fitting,' says he, 'if you find these persons involved in such a design, and if the charges of high treason are offered to be maintained against them upon that ground, that, in respect of the extraordinary nature, the dangerous extent, and at the best, the very criminal complexion of such a conspiracy, this case, which I state to you is a new and doubtful case, should be put into a judicial course of inquiry, that it may receive a solemn adjudication, whether it will or will not amount to high treason.'

It is difficult to conceive of any thing more abhorrent to the genuine principles of humanity, than the doctrine here delivered. The chief justice, after having enumerated various types of treason, respecting which he speaks ardently at first, and peremptorily at last, which are all the mere creatures of his own imagination, comes to a case upon which even he hesitates to decide. He dares not aver the proceeding described in it to be treason. Well, then; what is the remedy he proposes? Surely a new act of parliament; the remedy prescribed by the act of

Edward 3rd, 'in cases of treason, which may happen in time to come, but which could not then be thought of or declared.' No such thing. Upon this case, which he does not venture to pronounce to be treason, he directs the grand jury to find the bills to be true bills! He tells them, 'that it is fitting that this case,' which he 'states as new and doubtful, should be put into a judicial course of inquiry, that it may receive a solemn adjudication, whether it will or will not amount to high treason!'

The chief justice, in this instance, quits the character of a criminal judge and a civil magistrate, and assumes that of a natural philosopher or experimental anatomist. He is willing to dissect the persons that shall be brought before him, the better to ascertain the truth or falsehood of his preconceived conjectures. The plain English of his recommendation is this: 'Let these men be put upon trial for their lives; let them and their friends, through the remotest strainers of connexion, be exposed to all the anxieties incident to so uncertain and fearful a condition; let them be exposed to ignominy, to obloquy, to the partialities, as it may happen, of a prejudiced judge, and the perverseness of an ignorant jury: we shall then know how we ought to conceive of similar cases. By trampling upon their peace, throwing away their lives, or sporting with their innocence, we shall obtain a basis upon which to proceed, and a precedent to guide our judgment in future instances.'

This is a sort of language which it is impossible to recollect without horror, and which seems worthy of the judicial ministers of Tiberius or Nero. It argues, if the speaker understood his own meaning, or if the paper before me has faithfully reported it, the most frigid indifference to human happiness and human life. According to this methods of estimate, laws, precedents, cases, and reports are of high value, and the hanging of a few individuals is a very cheap, economical and proper way of purchasing the decision of a doubtful speculation ...

2. Extract from Justice James Iredell's address to the grand jury, Circuit Court, District of Pennsylvania, 12 April 1796, as printed in *Life and Correspondence of James Iredell, One of the Associate Justices of the Supreme Court of the United States* [c. 1857], 2 vols., ed. Griffith J. McRee (New York: Peter Smith 1949), 2: 467–74 at 468–9.

As it is not only natural, but the duty of every government to take care of its own preservation, this crime in all countries is considered of the highest rank; the object of it being the total destruction of the government itself, and of course of all the order, peace, security, and happiness connected with it, thus involving (where the government is a good one) the greatest accumulation of public and private misery which any crime can possibly occasion. But where so much is at stake an extraordinary degree of jealousy is usually proportioned to it, which jealousy will be entertained by a bad government as well as a good one, and always in a greater degree from a consciousness of deserving ill. Accordingly it has in fact happened, that in most countries, in all ages, and under all forms of government, the abuses which have been committed in prosecutions for this offence have been among the most atrocious ever perpetrated to the injury of mankind. Suspicion has supplied the place of evidence, the most distant approaches of danger have armed the hand of power against the greatest of men, and not unfrequently the highest instances of public virtue have been doomed to the punishment of the highest public offences. Happily for the United States, such scenes have been known to them only by the history of other nations. The mildness of their own governments has long been one of the most distinguished, as well as one of the most honorable characteristics of their country. But the framers of the present Constitution of the United States were too wise to depend for permanent security on occasional temper, or even the strong and tried basis of a national character. Knowing well the mischiefs which prosecutions for this offence had occasioned, glowing with proper indignation at the tyrannies of other countries, and thinking no precaution too great to exclude them from their own, they took especial care to guard against the danger of such, by provisions in the constitution anxiously adapted to that end. Every person conversant in such subjects knows, that the great engines of this species of judicial tyranny have been these: 1. So loose a definition of the crime that it was easy, by means of plausible subterfuges, to charge that as an act of treason which was never intended to be deemed such. 2. The admission of such slender proof that an unprincipled government in tempestuous times, taking advantage of favorable conjunctures, could often find means to obtain the conviction of an obnoxious though innocent man. 3. (And which is scarcely credible, if the proofs if [of] it were not too numerous and too plain to be questioned) A spirit of rapacity, which dictated accusations of treason upon insufficient grounds, in order to obtain the benefit of the forfeiture of property, annexed to the crime. Thus infamously taking away a man's life to rob himself and his family of his estate! Such have been the methods by which man has preyed on his fellow-man, and inhuman tyrants, without one spark of feeling, have sported with the happiness, the peace, the security, of the human race! The provisions in our constitution meet each of these causes of so many evils, and I trust will for ever prove a sufficient barrier against them, should it be the fate of this country, at any future unhappy period, to have to dread a tyrannical disposition it has never yet experienced.

3. Extract from Chief Justice James Monk's address to the grand jury, District of Montreal, March 1797, as printed in the Montreal *Gazette*, 20 March 1797.

... You will observe, Gentlemen, that every person, being a Subject, or living under the protection of our Laws, who may associate with the Enemies of the Crown, for the purpose of aiding those Enemies, in their hostile designs against the government of Great Britain, whether in Canada or elsewhere, is guilty of High Treason.

And you will distinguish, Gentlemen, that every person, living under the protection of our Laws, who may know of any treasonable conduct committed by others against the Government of Society, and does not make that knowledge known to the Magistrates, is guilty of a high Misdemeanor – termed a misprision of Treason.

That every degree of aid or assistance to such Enemies, whether by joining in their motives and designs, or by correspondence of advice, plans, projects or open attempts to attack, and subvert the Government of the Country, are acts of High Treason – And in which all are considered as principals, there being no accessories in this crime.

There is another species of Treason, that deserves consideration, and peculiarly so, by the advisers of public meetings and assemblies.

Our Laws declare, that every insurrection or rising of the Kings Subjects with intention to oblige the King to change the measures of His Government or alter the Laws, amounts to the crime of High Treason.

And all those who join in such treasonable practices, fall under the like criminality and are considered as Traitors.

The same degree of crime and its consequent punishment, attaches upon all those who rise in tumultuous assemblies, and openly, by force, oppose the execution of the Laws.

Such are the crimes affixed to the conduct of men, when levelled against the existence or the due execution of our Government.

Our Laws provide also for the repose of Society, by declaring as criminal those persons who spread false news, intending to produce alarm and discontent in the minds of the King's Subjects. They are guilty of a Misdemeanor, and punishable by fine and imprisonment, proportioned to their evil intentions.

Of the same description of crime is a Tumultuous assembly, a meeting of numbers to the disturbance of the peace and good order in Society.

The advisers of such meetings & assemblies are considered as criminal, and also punishable for a Misdemeanor.

Yet, let it not be understood, that the people have not the power of assembling for lawful purpose as of representing, to the Government, or the Legislature, any hardship they may conceive they labor under, though [through] the operation of particular laws. But it must ever be carefully guarded, that those assemblies are *made* with a peaceable and lawful intention, and that they are *conducted* to those purposes *alone*.

It is the causes, and the manner of forming such an assembly, and the deportment of that assembly, when collected, that will justify or render criminal, the persons who compose it. It is the intention of the characters who excite such public meetings, that will determine their guilt or innocence. Nor can any be executed by a plea of ignorance of the laws that sustain the first principles of our Government, namely – That every assembly of numbers, with intention to resist the laws, and of taking means to bring about a change, by the impetuous voice and the force of an intimidating public, is highly criminal, and, as such, punishable, either as Misdemeanor, or extended to the crime of Felony or High Treason, according as the circumstances of resistance against, or attack upon the laws and Government, may have involved the adventurous offenders. No man can be brought to punishment for a reasonable exertion of his civil rights. Nor will our Law, with impunity, *permit* that the Government of Society should be undermined, or overturned, by any plausible artifice practised upon a deluded multitude.

It is a leading principle, in the administration of Justice, that wherever an offence has been committed, the cause and instrument of the crime, should be brought to answer, on a public Trial, for the wrong done, through his inadvertent or criminal conduct.

Nor it is less a principle of Justice, that those whose criminal intentions have been manifest, though unsuccessfully executed, should be brought to alike public trial and Judgment.

On the one hand, Gentlemen, the individual, has a claim to your protection against groundless charges; but on the other hand, the society of which he, you, and all, form the aggregate has a right to the duty enjoined of you, by the sacred oath of your office, which is – to present to this Court, without fear or favor, every crime and offence, that has been committed in this District against the Laws which guard the peace and security of civil Society; and particularly so, against those, that form the first principles of Government under which we live, and that, at this moment, are, for their due execution, committed to the vigilance, the probity, and care of you, Gentlemen of the Grand Jury.

4. Extract from a retrospective letter by Attorney General Jonathan Sewell to Civil Secretary Samuel Gale, 9 July 1799, concerning events in 1797 (S series, RG 4, A 1, vol. 68: 21,772–6, NA).

... Upon the arrival of Mr. Cushing at Quebec, he persisted in the declaration made to my Brother, and he at once informed me that he expected some recompense from Government for the discovery [revelation] he should make not in money, but in land – I communicated to him the letter Marked No. 2, but he remarked that it was not specific, he did not ask a pecuniary recompense, but he expected a Grant of one Township to himself and Associates ... and of another on the same terms to a Friend of his, who, he informed me, could give material testimony on the subject matter of his information. He also observed that his discovery might endanger his life, and he trusted that in such case his family would be provided for. He added that he would not say anything, unless his terms were complied with. This conversation took place on the morning of the 19th [November] for on the 18th he was very unwell & kept his bed.

As I could not of myself make any answer to these proposals, I told him I should submit them to the Governors consideration & let him know his determination. This I accordingly did and the annexed paper No. 3 is a copy of the letter which I received early the next morning from Mr. Secy. Ryland, expressly declaring that his Excellency would *as early as possible* grant to Mr. Cushing a Patent as Leader of a Township ... and that in case of his death, provision should be made for his family.

I immediately sent for Mr. Cushing, read this answer to him, & said it closed with the terms which he himself had proposed the day before, so far as they respected himself, I conceived that every difficulty would be obviated. Mr. Cushing however informed me that he expected a specific Township should be promised, and that he should be permitted to take immediate possession, and observed that no mention was made of the second Township. He then produced to me a list of twelve to fourteen Townships ...

As he positively refused to give any information before these promises were made, I was compelled again to have recourse to Mr. Ryland for further Instructions. I went to the Chateau, and Mr. Ryland after speaking to the Governor, informed me that his Excellency desired that I should inform the Chief Justice of the situation in which matters then stood, & take his opinion. Mr. Ryland accordingly accompanied me and we had a long conference with the Chief Justice. The result of it was, that we were all of opinion, that the expected information appeared of sufficient importance to justify an absolute promise of the Township of Shipton to Mr. Cushing as he asked it, with permission to occupy it immediately ... But, with respect to the Township of Brompton, it was thought best to say, that it should be reserved for future disposition on the terms proposed until a knowledge of Mr. Cushings information should enable the Government to decide upon its importance.

With this opinion I returned to the Chateau, and had the honor of an interview with the Governor in the presence of Mr. Ryland, and as his Excellency was then pleased to concur in this opinion, I wrote to Mr. Cushing the letter of which a copy is annexed (marked No. 4) as you require. To the terms proposed in this letter Mr. Cushing acceded, & gave full information of the designs of David McLane against his Majestys Government and in consequence of this information David McLane was afterwards convicted & executed for High Treason.

5. Extract from a letter from Civil Secretary Herman Ryland to George Francklin, Elmer Cushing's lawyer, who would soon become one of David McLane's defence counsel, 18 May 1797 (Prescott Papers, MG 23, G II 17, vol. 9: 109, NA).

Sir,

The approaching Trial of Mr. McLane will probably afford Mr. Cushing an opportunity to clear up his own Conduct with regard to the Circumstance referred to in the inclosed letters[1] and evince how far he is deserving of the attention and favor of Government.

6. Extract from Chief Justice William Osgoode's charge to the trial jury in *McLane* (*R. v. Maclane* [sic] (1797), 26 St. Tr. 721 at 794–7).

... Perhaps, gentlemen, at this distance from the place of the king's personal residence, you may think it unreasonable to impute to the prisoner the crime which constitutes the first charge brought against him, namely that of compassing the king's death; but, if the facts laid, are found to be true in contemplation of law, they have a tendency to that fatal end; and such compassing always forms a charge in indictments for this sort of treason. True it is, that the overt acts seems to range themselves most naturally under the second count, for adhering to the king's enemies, which is a distinct and positive head of treason. If then you find any difficulty in referring the acts charged to the first count, you may, if you think proper, direct your attention to the evidence given as tending to prove the second count in the indictment, which contains the charge of a declared treason and is therefore sufficient, if found, to support a conviction.

Gentlemen, it ought to be a matter of satisfaction, both to the court and the jury, that from a repeated course of determinations on this subject, the law is perfectly clear, and that we are travelling upon a well trodden path. The words of the statute are in themselves plain and intelligible. – If a man do adhere to the king's enemies, giving them aid and assistance in the realm, or elsewhere it is declared to be treason. Such is the text, but the cases that have been determined under this clause, go a considerable degree farther; for it is not necessary, in order to complete the crime, that the aid and assistance should be actually given, nay, it is not necessary to be proved, as I shall explain to you by and by; but it is necessary that you should see that the aid and assistance was intended and that you should find it so. On the subject of intention, the distinction that was made by the attorney general, respecting the nature of crimes, by the English law, is certainly true, that crimes in general are not consummate by the intention, and that they must, in order to complete the guilt, be carried into execution; but that treason is an exception to this rule: there is no doubt, that the observation, generally speaking, is just; for, an attempt to commit larceny, robbery, or murder, does not constitute the capital crime, yet there is a capital crime which is not unfrequently brought before a court of justice, and of course the nature of it must have been often explained in your hearing, gentlemen, which offers the strongest analogy to high treason, and may therefore give you a better insight into it, I mean the crime of burglary. Burglary is defined to be the breaking and entering into a dwelling house by night, with intent to commit a felony; it is not necessary that any thing should be carried away, not even of the value of this pen; but the intent is left for the finding of the jury, from the nature of the overt acts proved; if evidence be given of the breaking and entering, these are overt acts sufficient to call upon the jury to determine with what intent this was done; and if they believe it was with a felonious intent, the crime is complete, though, as I said before, no property is carried away. So in the case of treason, if a traitorous intention is disclosed by words or writings, and they are followed up by any acts tending to execute such design, although it be not complete, it is sufficient to ground a charge of treason, and it is left to the oaths and conscience of a jury to say with what view such a step was taken, although the party is stopped short before the final purpose was carried into effect; for, common sense tells us, we ought not to wait till the mischief is completed.

... The point of law which ought to govern the present case ... is this: every attempt to subject this province, or any part thereof, to the king's enemies, is high treason, and every step taken in furtherance of such attempt is an overt act of high treason ...

7. The sentencing and execution of McLane, July 1797 (*McLane* at 826–8).

It remains that I should discharge the painful duty of pronouncing the sentence of the law, which is, 'That you David Mac Lane [*sic*], be taken to the place from whence you came, and from thence you are to be drawn to the place of execution, where you must be hanged by the neck, but not till you are dead; for, you must be cut down alive and your bowels taken out and burnt before your face; then your head must be severed from your body, which must be divided into four parts, and your head and quarters be at the king's disposal; and the Lord have mercy on your soul.'

... On Friday, the 21st of July, the prisoner, David Mac Lane [*sic*], pursuant to his sentence, was taken from the common gaol and placed upon a hurdle, which moved in slow solemnity towards the place of execution, attended by the sheriff and peace officers of the district, a miliary guard of fifty men and a great multitude of spectators. About a quarter after ten the hurdle drew up close to the gallows erected upon the *Glacis* without the garrison wall. As soon as it stopt, Maclane rose up, he was dressed in white linen grave cloaths, and wore a white cap on his head. The reverend Mr. Mountain and the reverend Mr. Sparks attended him, and with them he continued in fervent prayer for some minutes. He then informed the executioner that he was ready, and was by him directed to ascend the ladder which he immediately did. But the executioner observing that he was too high, he descended a step or two, and then addressed the spectators in the following words, 'this place gives me pleasure; I am now going where I have long wished to be, and you, who now see me, must all follow me in a short time, some of you perhaps in a few days; let this be a warning to you to prepare for your own deaths.' Then addressing himself to the military who were drawn up in a hollow square about the gallows, he added, 'you with arms in your hands, you are not secure here, even with your arms, I am going where I shall be secure without them.'

He immediately drew the cap over his face exclaiming 'Oh God receive my soul! I long to be with my Jesus' and dropped his handkerchief as a signal for the executioner, who instantly turned him off. – He appeared to struggle with death but a short time.

The body hung for five and twenty minutes and was then cut down. A platform, with a raised block upon it, was brought near the gallows, and a fire was kindled for executing the remainder of the sentence. The head was cut off, and the executioner holding it up to public view proclaimed it 'the head of a traitor.' – An incision was made below the breast and a part of the bowels taken out and burnt; the four quarters were marked with a knife, but were not divided from the body.

The whole of the execution took up about two hours, and the conduct of the unhappy sufferer was in every respect composed and becoming his situation.

8. Extract from Montreal lawyer Stephen Sewell's letter to brother Jonathan Sewell after the McLane trial, 17 July 1797 (Sewell Papers, MG 23 G II 10, vol. 3: 1104, NA).

Agreeable to your request Mr. Buchanan communicated to me your letter containing the account of McLane's trial, the conduct of which as well in what depended on yourself as on the Court and jury, and the issue of the same so perfectly consonant to justice and the laws, are subjects which draw from me most sincerely congratulations, for where the public mind is fully satisfied you in your official capacity cannot fail of feeling at the same time a far superior degree of satisfaction – The officers of the Canadian Volunteers [a locally raised army of English residents and Canadiens] have said that rather than McL. should want a hangman they would go down themselves and execute him.[2] It must be evident to every one that the Energy of the government at this day has saved the province. It is astonishing what an alteration there is in the Canadians in this district (I will not say in their principles for those I am sure are not changed) but in their behavior, they are more observant of the laws than can be expected of the best subjects, they work when and whenever they are commanded, (tho not without Grumbling) and the roads are universally good in consequence.

9. Extract from Osgoode's letter to Under-Secretary John King, 22 July 1797 (CO 42, MG 11, vol. 22, NA).

David McLane was Yesterday executed in pursuance of his Sentence for High Treason. He was well qualified for the undertaking had he had suitable materials to work withal, but his want of Confederates (at least in this City) was manifest from his indiscreet avowal of his Designs to a perfect stranger those [whose] Conduct on this Occasion has been highly meretorious the man had been imprisoned by Mr. Monk [then attorney general] in his wholesale Rage in the Year 1794 but never was brought to a Trial. McLane thought of necessity He must be disaffected sent for him into a wood near to Quebec and imparted the whole of his Project – Black[3] the Depositary of his Secret gave into all his Proposals invited him to come into Town at Night and made an instant disclosure of all he knew.

McLane's Mission being well known We had spies upon him in the States but he eluded all their Vigilance, avoided the Posts and came into the Province through the Woods. The first Intimation we had of his arrival was when he was in Bed at Black's House in the Lower Town ...

Inclosed I send a Quebec Gazette giving an Account of the Trial which lasted 14 Hours the Thermometer varying from 80 to 90. It is hoped that his Majestys Courts of Justice in his Province of Quebec will not be found obnoxious to the Censure cast on them in other quarters.[4]

NOTES

1 This 'Circumstance' has not been discovered.

2 There was initially a problem finding an executioner. In the end a mystery man with a gift for extortion (he received $900) performed the deed.

3 John Black, master shipwright and a key witness, with Barnard and Cushing, at McLane's trial. Black had been interned as a suspected subversive during the suspension of habeas corpus, 1794–5. His business had been ruined and he later recalled that 'I had passed for a disturber of publick peace & villen an Enemy to my King and Country the scoff & reproach of the time': Black to John Neilson, n.d., Neilson Collection, MG 24, B 1, vol. 1: 113–14, NA. Black's performance in the McLane affair resulted in his social rehabilitation but little concrete reward.

4 A reference to criticism by Edmund Burke and others of the 1794 acquittals.

I

The Official Mind and Popular Protest in a Revolutionary Era: The Case of Newfoundland, 1789–1819
Christopher English

'[Affidavits] concerning riots in [the district of] Bay Roberts in the past winter [1819–21]' (Colonial Secretary's Correspondence, GN 2/1/A, vol. 31 [1819–21], Harbour Grace Sessions Court, sitting at Bareneed, at 122, 125–6. 130).

a) William Snow sworn, Bareneed, 19 June 1817:

Saith in the month of March Seven men with Guns and fourteen with sticks came over the Ice towards my house. I went out to meet them, and asked them if they were going sealing. They answered No – that they were coming to search my house to see what was in it, and that they would have part of it. I told them that they should not, but that if they came like Men instead of Robbers that I would give them every satisfaction in my power. When John McGrath forced his Musquet against my breast which pushed me some paces back, I called him a damned Rascal and wanted to know what he done that for. He then cracked his Gun and swore that he would blow my soul to Hell if I said another word. I then said fine and be damned as I am not to be frightened by an Irish Rascal. Another of the gang upon this lifted up the stock of his Gun over my head and swore that he would knock my brains out ...

Now the elder Keefe intervened and took a Gun out of the hands of a Boy who was holding it carefully, and laid it across his own arm, upon which I observed to him that he had no occasion to come and rob me and it was but two days ago that I had distressed my own family by letting him have a barrel of potatoes for which he then paid me, he answered I am not come to do you any harm but to prevent Mischief. The Younger Keefe now said he would have no compassion for potatoes. I asked him if a Newfoundlandsman had nothing else to do but to support damned Irish Horses. Upon this the gang rushed into my Potatoe Cellar and those who could not get in for want of room seized upon the others as they came out and scuffled with them for their share of the plunder. Mr Matthew Stevenson of Harbour Grace happening to pass by just at this moment ordered them to put the potatoes back again which they did excepting one barrel and returned across the Ice.

[signed] William Snow

b) Affidavit of William Elenes of Bay Roberts [his mark], 17 June 1817:

Late in March John McGrath with a gun and two men came to his house asking for potatoes. Twenty–one or 22 men armed with guns and sticks stood a short distance off.

'I answered McGrath that I had no potatoes on my own room but what my own family required and asked him if he had any authority for acting as he was doing and why a Constable had not come with him? He said they were authority enough of themselves and had no need of a Constable.'

McGrath went to break open the lock and door. Elenes asked time to get the key 'as I am a poor Man, and cannot buy another.'

The men then found three and a half barrels and decided to take two. Elenes resisted and they took one. When he further resisted 'one of the gang seized me by the throat and would have strangled me but for the assistance of my wife. I recognized [and goes on to list nine men].'

c) Harbour Grace Sessions Court, *Foley v. Fogerty*, 16 June 1817, before Carrington, JP.:

Plaintiff testified that on 13 or 14 March the defendant 'came into Plaintiff's house ... and told plaintiff what the Law was at Carbonear, that to break locks and doors and take out whatsoever they wanted – that the Hair of a hungry Man was not to suffer and repeated the same three days.'

He then asked for the loan of bread, and the plaintiff refused 'saying he had none to spare upon which defendant replyed that he would soon see locks and doors broken open and Bread taken out.'

Upon the defendent being required to post security or go to jail, Matthew Kearney stood bail.

J
Sir James Craig's 'Reign of Terror' and Its Impact on Emergency Powers in Lower Canada, 1810–13
Jean-Marie Fecteau, F. Murray Greenwood, and Jean-Pierre Wallot

1. Extract from 'An Act to Impower His Majesty to Secure and Detain Such Persons As His Majesty Shall Suspect Are Conspiring Against His Person and Government' (34 Geo. III (1794), c. 54).

Whereas *a traitorous and detestable conspiracy has been formed for subverting the existing laws and constitution, and for introducing the system of anarchy and confusion which has so fatally prevailed* in France: *therefore, for the better preservation of his Majesty's sacred person, and for securing the peace and the laws and liberties of this kingdom;* be it enacted by the King's most excellent majesty, by and with the advice and consent of the lords spiritual and temporal, and commons, in this present parliament assembled, and by the authority of the same, That every person or persons that are or shall be in prison within the kingdom of *Great Britian* [*sic*] at or upon the day on which this act shall receive his Majesty's royal assent, or after, by warrant of his said Majesty's most honourable privy council, signed by six of the said privy council, for high treason, suspicion of high treason, or treasonable practices, or by warrant, signed by any of his Majesty's secretaries of state, for such causes as aforesaid, may be detained in safe custody, without bail or mainprize, until the first day of *February* one thousand seven hundred and ninety-five; any law or statute to the contrary notwithstanding ...

III. Provided always, and be it enacted, That nothing in this act shall be construed to extend to invalidate the ancient rights and privileges of parliament, or to the imprisonment or detaining of any member of either house of parliament during the sitting of such parliament, until the matter of which he stands suspected be first communicated to the house of which he is a member, and the consent of the said house obtained for his commitment or detaining.

2. Extracts from letters written by merchant-magistrate John Richardson, head of provincial counter-intelligence, to Attorney General Jonathan Sewell, 19 Jan. [1], 13 Feb. [II], 23, 30 March [III and IV] 1797 (MG 23, Sewell Papers, G II 10, vol. 3, NA).

I. I think Provencale should be apprehended without further delay.[1] It appears to me of importance that this should happen before the Legislature is prorogued, because so pointed a proof of intended invasion and insurrection would do away every argument the evil disposed in the Assembly might urge, against a renewal of the Alien Bill, and particularly if accompanied, as it ought to be, with the Clauses suspensive of the Habeas Corpus, as it stood the first year – The Democratic Members might affect to treat a general communication on the subject, (if such His Excellency should think fit to make) as unfounded, but the circumstances that must necessarily come to light on P's Arrest, would confound them – If still refractory, I should not hesitate (were I a Member) to treat them in Debate as Traitors abbetting the Invasion ...

II. We have at last succeeded in tracing the Treasonable Addresses to at least ten hands ... They pretend they are all burnt, and that they never show'd them to any person, but I am persuaded that there is hardly a Common Canadian in Town or a Democrat of the higher order, who did not know of them ... Such secrecy for such a length of time, without one having loyalty enough to discover [reveal], marks in my mind, either the extent of the conspiracy or at least a general disposition to do nothing against the French, or in favor of our Govt. – A Power to proclaim Martial Law when the Lt. Govr. in Council may judge it necessary, I more and more think is indispensable to our society ...

... Permit me to say, that I dread the consequences of the measure of submitting the whole of the Papers collected relative to the Emissaries [of Adet] etc., to the two houses – There certainly are names [of informers] that ought to remain inviolably secret ... If the Papers are sent down, they must go to a Committee – It is true you may call it a secret one, but as some who wish success to the Plot may get upon it, every thing will soon get abroad – It is not like a British House of Commons, and in this case they cannot safely be treated as such – There the Minister had influence Enough to get trusty members alone on the Secret Com:, but what security have you against their being here of another stamp – I therefore shall feel unhappy till I hear you drop that measure – With a view to render such a step unnecessary, We have been labouring to procure a body of information, which is consequential only (it offering hardly anything new) inasmuch as, that it can be submitted freely to the House, no promise of secrecy being made, and no necessity to conceal the Deponents ...

Pray how does Papineault look since these discoveries[2] – The Democrates here since the Arrests, wear faces almost a yeard long – Guilty consciences perhaps tell them their turn may not be far off ...

I hope you may be able to carry through the Alien Bill etc: before you leave Quebec [for the Monteal assizes], as it is of moment to make the most of first impressions – If it is delayed, the late discoveries will lose part of their effects, and the disaffected have time to muster up new excuses for avoiding the salutary measures contemplated ...

III. Mr. Reid sent you by last Post Copies of the Indictments, and by that of today you will receive from him Copies of the Convictions and Judgments and of the Presentment.[3]

With all this Artillery I should hope you would be able to beat down all opposition to the Alien Bill – If the Objects hoped for can be attained, it is immaterial whether they are in the Shape of one or two Bills, but I have generally seen in the last Legislature, and I should conceive the same principale would hold good in the present, that there was a great saving of time in concentrating matters as much as possible, to avoid unnecessary & ridiculous debate – There is no occasion for an entire Suspension of the Habeas Corpus Act – It is enough to do so in cases of Treason or suspicion of Treason – The Alien Bill as it originally stood, went no further –

If more palatable in the way you mention, I conceive it will answer the purpose, equally well, as one of the Chief Justices will always be accessible without much loss of time[4] –

But what think you of lodging also a Power with the Govr. in Council to proclaim Martial Law? – I conceive that would make a more forcible public impression than any other Measures ...

IV. I thank you for the humorous description of the caricature regarding Citizen P. [apineau] & suite – I should hope that Gentleman does not now stand quite so high at Head Quarters, as he did before the recent discoveries.[5]

I really did not think he had impudence enough, after what has happened, to venture openly to oppose the Alien Act – If the [separate] Habeas Corpus Bill contemplated by you should fall through, it will evince not only the extent of our danger, but that the imperious Majority in the Assembly, are determined under cover of their Legislative liberty of action, to deliver us over (as far as in them lies) bound hand & foot to the Sans Culottes – If you unhappily fail in that Bill, a necessity may arise of His Excellency taking upon himself the measure of proclaiming Martial Law, and trusting to Parliament for an indemnity[6] ...

3. An Act for the Better Preservation of His Majesty's Government As by Law Happily Established in this Province (SLC 1797, c. 6).

WHEREAS it is necessary to defend and secure His Majesty's good and loyal subjects against every traiterous attempt that may be formed for subverting the existing Laws and constitution of this Province of Lower-Canada, and for introducing the horrible system of Anarchy and confusion, which has so fatally prevailed in France; therefore and for the better preservation of His Majesty's Government, and for securing the Peace, the Constitution, Laws and Liberties of the said Province; Be it enacted by the King's most Excellent Majesty, by and with the advice and consent of the Legislative Council and Assembly of the said Province of Lower-Canada ... And it is hereby enacted by the authority of the same, that every person or persons who are or shall be in prison within this Province of Lower-Canada, at or upon the day on which this Act shall receive High Majesty's Royal Assent or after, by warrant of His said Majesty's Executive Council of and for the said Province, signed by three of the said Executive Council, for High Treason, misprision of High Treason, suspicion of High Treason or Treasonable practices; may be detained in safe Custody without Bail or mainprize until the first day of May, which will be in the Year of Our Lord one thousand seven hundred and ninety-eight; And that for and during the continuance of this Act, no Court or Courts, Judge or Judges, Justice or Justices of the Peace, shall bail or try any such person or persons so committed, without a Warrant for that purpose from His Majesty's Executive Council, signed by three of the said Executive council, any Law, Statute, Act or Ordinance to the contrary notwithstanding.

II. And be it further enacted by the authority aforesaid, that for and during the continuance of this Act, it shall not be lawful to or for any Justice or Justices of the Peace within this Province, or in any District or part thereof, to bail or admit to bail any person or persons charged with the crime of high Treason, or misprision of High Treason or suspicion of High Treason or Treasonable practices, any Law, Statute or Ordinance to the contrary notwithstanding.[7]

III. And be it further enacted by the authority aforesaid, that for and during the continuance of this Act, in all and every case, in which application shall be made for His Majesty's writ of *Habeas Corpus* to any Court or Courts, Judge or Judges within this Province, or in any district or part thereof, by an person or persons who are or shall be in prison within this Province, at or upon the day on which this Act shall receive His Majesty's Royal Assent or after, charged with High Treason, Misprision of High Treason, suspicion of High Treason or Treasonable Practices, such writ of *Habeas Corpus* (if allowed by such Court or Courts, Judge or Judges) shall not be made returnable in less than fourteen days from the day on which such writ of *Habeas Corpus* shall be allowed, and in all and every such case, it shall be the duty of such Court or Courts, Judge or Judges and of each and every of them, and they are hereby required when and so soon as such applicaiton for such writ of *Habeas Corpus* shall to them be respectively made, to give notice and information thereof in writing, together with Copies of such application and of the affidavit or affidavits or other paper writings, on which such application shall be founded, to the Governor, Lieutenant Governor or Person administering the Government of this Province for the time being.

IV. Provided always, and be it enacted, that such writ of *Habeas Corpus*, or the benefit thereof, shall not be allowed by such Court or Courts, Judge or Judges to any person or persons detained in prison at the time of his, her or their application of such writ of *Habeas Corpus* by such warrant of His said Majesty's Executive Council as aforesaid, for such causes as aforesaid or any or either of them, and that in all and every case, where such writ of *Habeas Corpus* shall be allowed, if upon the return made to such writ of *Habeas Corpus* at the expiration of fourteen days, from the day on which such writ of *Habeas Corpus* shall be so allowed, it shall appear that such person or persons shall be then detained in prison by such warrant of His said Majesty's Executive Council, as aforesaid, for such causes as aforesaid or any or either of them, any Law, Statute, Act or Ordinance to the contrary notwithstanding.

V. And be it further enacted by the authority aforesaid, that this Act shall continue and be in force, from the day on which it shall receive the Royal Assent, until the first day of May in the Year of Our Lord one thousand seven hundred and ninety-eight; and that after the said first day of May one thousand seven hundred and ninety-eight, all and every person or persons so committed shall have the benefit and advantage of the Laws relating to, or providing for, the liberty of the subjects in this Province.

VI. Provided always and be it enacted by the authority aforesaid, that nothing in this Act shall extend or be construed to invalidate or restrain the lawful rights and privileges of either Branch of the Provincial Parliament in this Province.

4. Extracts from the debates in the United States House of Representatives, 26 Jan. 1807, on a Senate bill to suspend habeas corpus: taken from the *Annals of Congress*, vol. 16, cols. 402–25.

MR. ELLIOT – Have we a right to suspend it in any and every case of invasion and rebellion? So far from it, that we are under a Constitutional interdiction to act, unless the existing invasion or rebellion, in our sober judgment, threatens the first principles of the national compact, and the Constitution itself. In other words, we can only act, in this case, with a view to national self-preservation. We can suspend the writ of habeas corpus only in a case of extreme emergency; that alone is *salus populi* which will justify this *lex suprema* ...

Mr. EPPES – When I feel a decided hostility to a principle, it is not material to me in what form I meet it. Decidedly opposed to the principle of this bill, I shall vote against it in all its stages, and cannot but hope that the motion of my colleague to reject it will prevail. By this bill, we are called upon to exercise one of the most important powers vested in Congress by the constitution of the United States. A power which suspends the personal rights of your citizens, which places their liberty wholly under the will, not of the Executive Magistrate only, but of his inferior officers. Of the importance of this power, of the caution which ought to be employed in its exercise, the words of the Constitution afford irresistible evidence ... It is not in every case of invasion, nor in every case of rebellion, that the exercise of this power by Congress can be justified under the words of the Constitution. The words of the Constitution confine the exercise of this power exclusively to cases of rebellion or invasion, where the public safety requires it. In carrying into effect most of the important powers of Congress, something is left for the exercise of its discretion. We raise armies when, in our opinion, armies are necessary ... But we can only suspend the privilege of the habeas corpus, 'when, in cases of rebellion or invasion, the public safety requires it.' Well, indeed, may this caution have been used as to the exercise of this important power. It is in a free country the most tremendous power which can be placed in the hands of legislative body. It suspends, at once, the chartered rights of the community, and places even those who pass the act under military despotism. The Constitution, however, having vested this power in Congress, and a branch of the Legislature having thought its exercise necessary, it remains for us to inquire whether the present situation of our country authorizes, on our part, a resort to this extraordinary measure ...

MR. J. RANDOLPH – I put it to any man, whether, now that we have received information of the extent of this conspiracy, and when we find that Catiline, Cethegus, and Lentulus, have not as many brother conspirators as themselves, this conspiracy is equal to that in Pennsylvania in 1794 or 1795? In physical force it is not comparable to it, however in intellectual talent it may be. I conceive then that according to the Constitution of the United States, there is but one case in which the writ of habeas corpus can be suspended, and I should not go into this view of the subject, if it had not been misstated by all those who have preceded me in debate. My view of the subject is this – that this privilege can only be suspended in cases, in which, not merely the public safety requires it, but that the case of the public safety requiring it, must be united with actual invasion or actual rebellion.

MR. SMILIE – I shall not detain the House long by the remarks which I propose to make on this subject. I shall waive all observations on the mode of proceeding on this occasion – whether we shall reject the bill on its first, or suffer it to go to a second reading. The question is now put, and I am called upon to give my vote, either in the affirmative or negative. I, therefore, feel under a necessity to put my negative upon it. I consider this one of the most important subjects upon which we have been called to act. It is a question which is neither more nor less than, whether we shall exercise the only power with which we are clothed, to repeal an important part of the Constitution? It is in this case only, that we have power to repeal that instrument. A suspension of the privilege of the writ of habeas corpus is, in all respects, equivalent to repealing that essential part of the Constitution which secures that principle which has been called, in the country where it originated, the 'palladium of personal liberty.' If we recur to England, we shall find that the writ of habeas corpus in that country has been frequently suspended. But, under what circumstances? We find it was suspended in the year 1715, but what was the situation of the country at that time? It was invaded by the son of James II. There was a rebellion within the kingdom, and an army was organized. The same thing happened in the year 1745. On this occasion it was found necessary to suspend it. In latter times, when the Government had grown more corrupt, we have seen it suspended for an infinitely less cause. We have taken from the statute book of this country, this most valuable part of our Constitution. The convention who framed that instrument, believing that there might be cases when it would be necessary to vest a discretionary power in the Executive, have constituted the Legislature the judges of this necessity, and the only question now to be determined is, Does this necessity exist? There must either be in the country a rebellion or an invasion, before such an act can be passed. I really doubt whether either of these exist. I really doubt whether a single law of the United States has been, as yet, violated. I will not say this is the fact; but I do not know anything to prove the contrary. But, supposing that a rebellion does exist, we are then left at liberty to decide whether it is such an one as to endanger the peace of society to such a degree that no ordinary remedy will answer ...

5. Extract from Chief Justice Jonathan Sewell's judgment, *In the Case of Pierre Bedard*, 1810 (*Stuart's Reports* 1 at 13–19).

We are fully satisfied that the motion cannot be granted. The facts which constitute the case before us are few in number. The late Provincial Parliament was dissolved by Proclamation on the first of March last, and, by the same Proclamation a new Parliament was summoned to meet on the 21st of April. On the 19th of March Mr. *Bedard* was arrested, and committed to the common goal of this District, by a Warrant under the hands and seals of three Members of the Executive Council, for 'treasonable practices,' and the object of the motion before us, is to release him from confinement upon the grounds that he served in the last Parliament as a representative of the City of Quebec. That on the 27th of this present month, he was elected to serve in the same capacity for the County of Surrey in the new Parliament, and therefore that he is entitled to his discharge, by reason of his privilege as a Member of the House of Assembly. The commitment of Mr. Bedard is made under the authority of the *Provincial Statute* 43rd Geo. III. c. 1. which authorizes the detention of every person committed by Warrant, signed by three of the Executive Council, for High Treason, Misprision of High Treason, or 'treasonable practices,' without bail or mainprize, during the continuance of the Act. It is however, provided by the sixth Clause of this Statue, 'That nothing in the Act contained shall extend or be construed to extend, to invalidate or restrain the lawful rights and privileges of either branch of the Provincial Parliament;' and it is contended that Mr. *Bedard* is within the letter of this exemption. But to bring this case within this proviso, it is obvious, that in the first instance he must be proved to be a Member of the Legislative Council, or of the House of Assembly; and in point of fact, there is no evidence of either. We have nothing, indeed, before us but two papers, which we are told are Indentures, executed between Mr. Bedard and the Electors of the City of Quebec, and of the County of Surrey. I say 'told,' because of this assertion no proof whatever has been offered, nor is any thing adduced, from which the authenticity of these papers can in any way be inferred ... I should be sorry, however, to have it supposed that this Court concedes what has been argued, viz., 'That there is privilege of Parliament against arrest for treasonable practices,' or to have it believed that we should hold ourselves bound by law, in any future instance, to admit a claim of privilege against arrest under circumstances similar to the present. The circumstances to which I allude, (assuming all facts to be as they have been stated,) are the arrest of Mr. *Bedard* eighteen days after the dissolution of the last Parliament and his Election to the new Parliament during his confinement ... the last Provincial Parliament met in Quebec, in the very place for which Mr. *Bedard* was returned a Member, and in which he resides; and as, therefore, it is impossible to say that he had not a convenient time for his return home, for transporting himself from one, to another, part of Quebec, between the first and the nineteenth day of March, it is clear that the day on which he was arrested was not within the period to which the privilege of the last Parliament extended.

Let us now examine whether this claim can be supported under the privilege of the new Parliament. There is certainly a material difference between the election of an individual who is at large, and the election of one already in confinement, which is the present case. In the former instance, the electors, having chosen a free man, are without blame, and ought not to be deprived of his services by any act of his, to which the privilege of Parliament extends; in the latter they make choice of one who visibly is not in a situation to perform the services which they require of him, and they have, therefore, only themselves to blame if they are deprived of them. In England, again, upon these principles, it has been decided that the privilege of a Member of the House of Commons from arrest, commences at his election [4. Bacon, fol. ed. 233] unless he has been arrested, or be in execution before his election, in which case it has also been decided, that he is not entitled to privilege [2. Siderfin 42. R. in Parl. 12th March, 1592]. Freedom from arrest, in all cases to which privilege legally extends, may be considered to be as indispensably necessary to the existence of a Provincial House of Assembly, as to an English House of Commons. But there is no principle upon which it should be admitted in this Province, under circumstances which are held in England to be such as must exclude it. It is argued that 'there is privilege of Parliament from arrest for treasonable practices,' and to support this assertion it is contended that this privilege extends to all offences except treason, felony and breach of the peace, (which may be admitted) and that treasonable practices do not amount either to treason, to felony, or to breach of the peace. The Court is of opinion that *'treasonable practices'* are within the meaning of the words *'breach of the peace,'* and that the privilege from arrest does not extend to cases of this description. All indictable crimes (and all treasonable practices must be indictable) are held in law to be *contra pacem domini regis*; and upon this ground, in England, it is now understood that the claim of privilege does not comprehend the case of any indictable crime. Such being the opinion of the court, we are not called upon to make any enquiry as to the distinction between treason and treasonable practices. It may be well, however, to observe, after what has been argued, that the precise import of the phrase 'treasonable practices' has never been settled by any legal decision; and if by the word *'practices'* we are to understand *'Acts,'* it certainly will be difficult to mark the line of distinction. In the course of the argument, to shew that 'treasonable practices' are entitled to privilege, the case of *John Wilkes* has been entirely relied on. It has been said, that by this decision it was settled that a Member of Parliament charged with having written and published a seditious libel was entitled to privilege; and from thence it has been inferred that a Member, charged with 'treasonable practices,' must also be entitled to his privilege. Now, admitting this case for the present, to be law, it by no means follows because a seditious libel is entitled to privilege, that treasonable practices must also be entitled to it. If indeed, the latter was the minor offence of the two, it might be inferred; but this is not the case, for in point of fact, it is the major and not the minor offence. To constitute treason, there must be an actual design against the King or his Government in contemplation; and it is in this that it is distinguishable from sedition, which comprehends such offences (not being capital) as are of like tendency, but without any actual design against the King or his Government. A charge therefore, of doing a thing *seditiously* cannot amount to a charge of *high treason*; since that which is seditious, and no more, can only partake of the nature of sedition. But, for the same reason, that which is treasonable must partake of the nature of treason, and consequently be a crime of greater magnitude than any act which is merely seditious. The case of *Wilkes* then, if admitted to be law, proves that the privilege of Parliament extends thus far, that is, to *seditious acts*, but affords no proof whatever that it extends beyond them to *'treasonable practices.'* But the decision in the case of *John*

Wilkes the Court cannot receive as law, because it has been solemnly disclaimed by both Houses of the British Parliament. The Judgment, in this well known case, (pronounced May 3rd, 1763) at the first meeting of Parliament afterwards, was taken into the consideration of both Houses, and the discussion ended on the 29th Nov. 1763 in a joint vote, by which it was resolved, 'That the privilege of Parliament doth not extend to the case of writing and publishing seditious libels, nor ought to be allowed to obstruct the ordinary course of the laws in the speedy and effectual prosecution of so heinous and dangerous an offence' [Comm. Journ. 24th Nov. 1763. Lords' Journ. 29th Nov. 1763. Almon's Deb. comm. for 1763]. Let the order therefore be, 'that he take nothing by his motion.'

6. Resolutions of the House of Assembly of Lower Canada on Martial Law, 1813 (JHALC, 1812–13 [26 Jan. 1813, 178]).

RESOLVED,

That it is the opinion of this Committee, that Martial Law, and the power of declaring and executing it, are known in the Laws of this Province, only in so far as they are recognized in the constitutional or public Law of England, which has been introduced into this Province.

RESOLVED,

That it is the opinion of this Committee, that according to the constitutional or public Law of England, making part of the Laws of this Province, Martial Law in the cases in which it may be lawfully declared and executed in respect of his Majesty's Subjects, hath been, and is limited in its operation to military persons.

RESOLVED,

That it is the opinion of this Committee, that all occasion or pretence for recurring in this Province, to Martial Law, in the sense, in which it is understood, in the constitutional or public Law of England, hath been taken away by the Act of the Parliament of the United Kingdom of *Great Britain* and *Ireland*, intituled, 'an Act for punishing Mutiny and desertion, and for the better payment of the Army, in their quarters' by the 'Rules and articles for the better Government of His Majesty's Forces,' and by the Militia Laws of this Province; whereby the Executive Government hath become, and is vested with all the powers necessary to enable it to provide for the safety of this Province, in the present conjuncture.

RESOLVED,

That it is the opinion of this Committee, that the limits and operation of Martial Law, as above stated, could not, nor can, be legally enlarged in this Province, without the authority of the Provincial Parliament.

NOTES

1 In September 1796 Provencale had attended a Montreal meeting where support for a French invasion had been discussed. He and two others were acquitted in a treason trial held a year later.

2 MPP Joseph Papineau, a leader of the *parti canadien* and father of Louis-Joseph, the 1837 rebel leader. Most of the English elite suspected, erroneously, that Papineau and house speaker Jean-Antoine Panet were working for Citizen Adet.

3 In early March three Canadien Montrealers, along with an absent agent of Adet's (also a Montrealer) who had organized the circulation of French propaganda, were indicted for high treason by the grand jury. J. Reid was clerk of the peace for the judicial district of Montreal.

4 Richardson was here referring to Sewell's decision to proceed with a separate bill based on British legislation. This became the Better Preservation Act. In the assembly, Sewell likely made the suspension more palatable by citing the British model (the Alien Act's suspending provisions had been *sui generis*) and stressing that responsibility would be vested in the Executive Council (which always included the two chief justices and other judges) and not a single magistrate as in 1794–5.

5 Prior to the session Governor Prescott offered Papineau a magistrate's commission (which he declined) and lionized him socially at the Chateau.

6 In fact, Papineau later reversed course to become a supporter of the Better Preservation Bill. The Richardson-Sewell strategy of providing the assembly with official evidence of the 'plot' appears to have worked: John Fleming as 'A British Settler,' *Political Annals of Lower Canada* (Montreal: Montreal Herald 1828), at 29–31.

K

State Trials and Security Proceedings in Upper Canada during the War of 1812
Paul Romney and Barry Wright

1. The Sedition Act, 1804 (U.C. Stat. 44 Geo. III, c.1)

'An Act for the Better Securing this Province Against All Seditious Attempts or Designs to Disturb the Tranquility Thereof.'

Whereas it is necessary to protect His Majesty's Subjects of this Province from the insidious attempts or designs of evil-minded and seditious persons; and, whereas much danger may arise to the Public Tranquillity thereof, from the unrestrained resort and residence of such persons therein; Be it therefore enacted ... That, from and after the passing of this Act, it shall and may be lawful, for the Governor, Lieutenant Governor or person administering the Government of this Province, for the Members of the Legislative and Executive Councils, the Judges of His Majesty's Court of King's Bench, for the time being, respectively, or for any person or persons authorized in that behalf, by an instrument under the hand and Seal of the Governor, Lieutenant Governor, or person administering the Government for the time being, or any one or more of them, jointly or separately, by Warrant or Warrants, under his or their hand and seal, or hands and Seals to arrest any person or persons not having been an inhabitant or inhabitants of this Province for the Space of six months, next preceding the date of such Warrant or Warrants, or not having taken the Oath of Allegiance to our Sovereign Lord the King, who by words, actions or other behaviour or conduct hath or have endeavoured, or hath or have given just cause to suspect that he, she or they, is or are about to endeavour to alienate the minds of His Majesty's Subjects of this Province from his person or Government, or in any wise with a seditious intent to disturb the tranquility thereof, to the end that such person or persons shall forthwith be brought before the said person or persons so granting such Warrant or Warrants against him, her or them, or any other person or persons duly authorized to grant such Warrant or Warrants by virtue of this Act; and if such person or persons not being such inhabitant or inhabitants aforesaid, or not having taken the Oath of Allegiance, shall not give to the person or persons so granting such Warrant or Warrants so authorized as aforesaid, before whom he, she or they shall be brought, full and complete Satisfaction, that his, her or their words, actions, conduct or behaviour had no such tendency, or were not intended to promote or encourage disaffection to his Majesty's person or Government, it shall and may be lawful for each or any of the said persons so granting such Warrant or Warrants, or so authorized as aforesaid, and he and they is and are hereby required to deliver an Order or Orders, in writing to such person or persons, not being such inhabitant or inhabitants as aforesaid, or not having taken such Oath of Allegiance, requiring of him, her, or them to depart this Province within a time to be limited by such order or orders, or if it shall be deemed expedient, that he, she or they should be permitted to remain in this province, to require from him, her, or them, good and sufficient security, to the satisfaction of the person or persons acting under the Authority hereby given, for his, her, or their good behaviour, during his, her, or their continuance therein.

II. And be it further enacted, by the Authority aforesaid, That if any person or persons not being such inhabitant or inhabitants as aforesaid, or not having taken such Oath of allegiance, who by any order or orders so delivered to him, her, or them is or are required to depart this Province, within a time limited by that order, should by sickness, or other impediment, be prevented from paying due obedience to the same, it shall and may be lawful for the person or persons who hath or have issued such order or orders as aforesaid, or for any other person or persons as aforesaid authorized by this Act so to do, (the person or persons acting under the authority hereby given, being first satisfied that such impediment by sickness, or otherwise, ought to be admitted as a reason for such order as aforesaid not having been obeyed) by an endorsement in writing upon the said order or orders, or otherwise in writing to enlarge the time specified in the said order or orders, from time to time, as occasion may require; and if any person or persons so having been required or ordered to quit this Province, as aforesaid, and not having obtained an enlargement of such time, in manner herein before Specified, should be found at large therein, or return thereinto, after the time limited by any or either of such orders, without licence from the Governor, Lieutenant Governor, or person administering the Government for the time being in that behalf; or in case any person or persons who shall have been served with any or either of such order or orders as aforesaid; or who shall have been permitted to remain in this Province, upon such security as aforesaid, shall by words, actions, or otherwise endeavour, or give just cause to suspect, that he, she, or they, is or are about to endeavour to alienate the minds of His Majesty's Subjects of this Province from his person or Government, or in any wise with a seditious intent to disturb the tranquility thereof, it shall and may be lawful for any one or more of the said person or persons so authorized by this Act as aforesaid, and he and they is and are hereby required by Warrant or Warrants under his or their hand and seal, or hands and Seals, to commit such person or persons so remaining at large, or returning into this Province without such licence as aforesaid, or so endeavouring or giving cause to suspect that he, she, or they is or are about to endeavour so to alienate the minds of His Majesty's Subjects of this Province, or in any wise with a seditious intent to disturb the tranquility thereof to the common Gaol, or to the Custody of the Sheriff of the District, in such districts in which there shall be no gaol at that time, there to remain, without bail or mainprize, unless delivered therefrom by special order from the Governor, Lieutenant Governor, or person administering the Government for the time being, until he, she, or they can be prosecuted for such Offence in His Majesty's Court of King's Bench, or of Oyer and Terminer and general gaol delivery in this Province, or under any Special Commission of Oyer and Terminer to be issued by the Governor, Lieutenant Governor, or person administering the Government of this Province for the time being; and if such person or persons, not being such inhabitant or inhabitants as aforesaid, or not having taken such oath of allegiance, shall be duly convicted of any of the Offences herein before described, in either of the said Courts respectively, he, she, or they shall be adjudged by such Court forthwith to depart this Province; or to be imprisoned in the Common gaol, or be delivered over to the Custody of the Sheriff in such districts in which there shall be no gaol at that time for a time to be limited by such Judgment, and at the expiration of that time, to depart this Province; and if such person or persons so convicted as aforesaid, shall remain in this province, or return thereunto, after the expiration of the time to be limited by the said Judgment, without licence from the Governor, Lieutenant Governor, or person administering the Government for the time being, in that behalf first had and obtained, such person or persons, on being duly convicted of so remaining or returning, before either of the said Courts, shall be deemed guilty of felony, and shall suffer death as a felon, without benefit of clergy – Provided always, that if, in the Execution of the powers hereby given any question shall arise touching or concerning the space of time during which any person or persons shall have been an inhabitant or inhabitants of this province, previous to any warrant or warrants having been issued against him, her, or them, or touching or concerning the fact of any person or persons having taken such oath of allegiance, the proof shall, in all such cases, lay on the party or parties against whom any such Warrant or Warrants shall in virtue of the Powers hereby given, have been granted or issued.

III. And be it further enacted by the Authority aforesaid, That if any person or persons, at any time shall be sued or prosecuted for any thing by him or them done in pursuance, or by Colour of this Act, or of any matter or thing therein contained, such Action or prosecution, shall be commenced within three Calendar months next after the Offence shall have been committed, and such person or persons may plead the general issue, and give the special matter in evidence for his, her, or their defence, and if, upon trial, a verdict shall pass for the defendant or defendants, or the plaintiff or plaintiffs shall become non-suited, or shall discontinue his, her, or their suit, or prosecution, or if Judgment shall be given for the defendant or defendants, upon demurrer or otherwise, such defendant or defendants, shall have treble costs to him or them awarded against the plaintiff or plaintiffs.

2. Proclamation, 24 Feb. 1812 (York *Gazette*, 11 March 1812)

Province of Upper Canada
ISAAC BROCK, Esquire, President administering the Government of the Province of Upper Canada, and Major General commanding His Majesty's Forces within the same.

Whereas information has been received, that divers persons have recently come into this Province with a seditious intent to disturb the tranquility thereof, and to endeavour to alienate the minds of His Majesty's Subjects from His Person and Government; I hereby require and enjoin the several persons authorized, to carry into effect a certain Statute, passed in the forty-fourth year of His Majesty's Reign, intituled, 'An Act for the Better securing this Province against all seditious attempts or designs to disturb the tranquility thereof,' to be vigilant in the execution of their duty, and strictly to enquire into the behaviour and conduct of all such persons as may be subject to the provisions of the said Act; and I do also charge and require all His Majesty's good and loyal Subjects within this Province, to be aiding and assisting the said persons in the execution of the powers vested in them by the said Act.

Isaac Brock, Esq., President &c

3. Proclamation, 9 Nov. 1812 (York *Gazette*, 14 Nov. 1812)

WHEREAS divers persons residing within the limits of this Province, claim to be exempt from Military Service, on pretence of being Citizens of the United States of America; I have thought proper, by and with the advice of His Majesty's Executive Council for the affairs of this Province, to direct and require, and I do hereby direct and require that all such persons residing in the Western, London and Niagara Districts, do forthwith report themselves to the Board appointed at Niagara to examine into such claims; And that all such persons residing in the Midland, Johnstown and Eastern Districts, do report themselves to the Board appointed at Kingston; And that all such persons residing in the Home and Newcastle Districts, do in like manner report themselves to the Board appointed at York for the same purpose, in order that if recognised to be Citizens of the United States of America, they may be furnished with proper Passports to leave the Province. – And it is hereby made known, that every Citizen of the United States of America in this Province, who shall not before the first of January 1813, have reported himself to one of the said boards, shall be liable to be treated as a Prisoner of War, or as a Spy, as circumstances may dictate.

R.H. Sheaffe, President, &c.

4. 'An Act to Empower HIS MAJESTY, for a Limited Time, to Secure and Detain Such Persons as HIS MAJESTY Shall Suspect of a Treasonable Adherence to the Enemy' (U.C. Stat. 54 Geo. III [1814], c.6)

Whereas it is necessary for the Public Safety that His Majesty be empowered to secure and detain such Persons as he shall suspect of Treasonable practices in aid of the Enemy; Be it therefore enacted by the King's Most Excellent Majesty, by and with the advice and consent of the Legislative Council and Assembly of the Province of Upper Canada ... that every person or persons who are, or shall be in prison within this Province of Upper Canada, at or upon the day in which this Act shall receive His Majesty's Royal Assent, either by the verbal or written Order of the Commander of the Forces within the said Province, for the time being, or of any General, or Field Officer Commanding any District of the same, for high Treason, Misprision of High Treason, suspicion of High Treason, or Treasonable Practices, and also every person or persons who shall, after the passing of this Act, be arrested within this Province, by Warrant of His Majesty's Executive Council, signed by one or more of the said Executive Council, or by Warrant of one or more Commissioners as may be specially authorized in each and every District for that purpose by virtue of a Commission, under the Hand and Seal of the Governor, Lieutenant Governor, or person administering the Government, for High Treason, Misprision of High Treason, suspicion of High Treason or Treasonable Practices, shall immediately be carried before three or more of His Majesty's Executive Council, or three or more of the aforesaid Commissioners, residing within the District in which such person or persons, so arrested, may be found, or in case a sufficient number of Commissioners or Executive Councillors cannot be had in such District, then before three or more of the nearest Commissioners, who, after such examination as may appear to them necessary, either private or public, not disclosing the name or names of the person or persons so accusing, shall have full power and authority, by Warrant under their Hands and Seals, to commit the person or persons, so arrested and brought before them, to any Gaol in the province, or to discharge the said person or persons, so arrested and brought before them, as to them shall appear just and expedient, and if committed, such person or persons may be detained in safe custody, without Bail or Mainprise during the continuance of this Act, and that for and during the continuance of this Act, no Court or Courts, Judge or Judges, Justice or Justices of the Peace, shall bail or try any such person or persons, so committed, without a Warrant for that purpose signed by one or more of the said Executive Council, any Law to the contrary notwithstanding.

II. *And be it further enacted* ... That for and during the continuance of this Act, it shall not be lawfull to or for any Justice or Justices of the Peace, within this Province, or in any District or Part thereof, to bail or admit to bail any person or persons charged with the crime of High Treason, or Misprision of Treason, or suspicion of High Treason, or Treasonable Practices, any Law or Statute to the contrary thereof notwithstanding.

III. *And be it further enacted* ... That for and during the continuance of this Act, in all and every case in which application shall be made for His Majesty's Writ of Habeas Corpus, to any Court or Courts, Judge or Judges, within this Province or in any District, or part thereof, by any persons who are or shall be in prison within this Province, at or upon the day on which this Act shall receive His Majesty's Royal Assent, or after charged with High Treason, Misprision of High Treason, suspicion of High Treason or Treasonable Practices, such Writ of Habeas Corpus (if allowed by such Court or Courts, Judge or Judges) shall not be made returnable in less than thirty days from the day on which such Writ of Habeas Corpus may be allowed, and in all and every such case and cases, it shall be the duty of such Court or Courts, Judge or Judges, and of each and every of them, and they are hereby required, when and so soon as such application for such Writ of Habeas Corpus shall to them be respectively made, to give notice and information thereof in writing, together with copies of such application, and of the affidavit or affidavits, or other paper writings on which such application shall be founded, to the Governor, Lieutenant Governor, or person administering the Government of this Province for the time being.

IV. Provided Always, *And be it further enacted* ... That such Writ of Habeas Corpus or the benefit thereof shall not be allowed by such Court or Courts, Judge or Judges, to any person or persons detained in Prison at the time of his, her, or their application for such Writ of Habeas Corpus by such Warrant of his said Majesty's Executive Council or Commissioners as aforesaid for such causes as aforesaid, or any, or either of them, and that in all and every case where such Writ of Habeas Corpus shall be allowed, no Court or Courts, Judge or Judges, shall bail or admit to bail the person or persons to whom such Writ of Habeas Corpus shall be allowed, if upon the return made to such Writ of Habeas Corpus at the expiration of thirty days as aforesaid from the day on which such Writ of Habeas Corpus shall be so allowed, it shall appear that such person or persons shall then be detained in prison by such Warrant of his said Majesty's Executive Council or Commissioners as aforesaid, for such causes as aforesaid, or any or either of them, any Law, Statute, Act or ordinance to the contrary, notwithstanding.

V. Provided nevertheless, *and be it further enacted* ... That any person, or persons, in prison at the time of passing this Act, against whom any Bill or Bills of indictment for High Treason, Misprision of High Treason, suspicion of High Treason, or Treasonable practices have been already found, shall and may be tried on such Indictment as if this Act had never passed.

VI. Provided always, *and be it further enacted* ... That nothing in this Act contained shall extend or be construed to extend to authorize the imprisonment or detaining of any member of the Legislative Council, or House of Assembly during the setting of the Legislature until the matter of which he stands suspected shall first be communicated to the House of which he is a member, and the consent of the said Council or Assembly respectively obtained for his commitment or detainer.

VII. *And be it further enacted* ... That this Act shall continue and be in force until the end of the next ensuing session of Parliament, or to the end of the present War with the United States of America, should it sooner terminate, and that from and after the expiration of this Act all and every person, or persons committed under the authority of the said Act, shall have the benefit, and advantages of the Laws relating to or providing for the Liberty of the Subjects of this Province.

5. The Alien Act, 1814 (U.C. Stat. 54 Geo. III [1814], c.9)

Whereas many persons, inhabitants of the United States of America, claiming to be subjects of his Majesty, and renewing their allegiance as such by oath, did solicit and receive grants of lands from his Majesty, or became seized of lands by inheritance or otherwise, within this province, which persons, since the declaration of war by the said United States of America, against his Majesty and his subjects of the United Kingdom of Great Britain and Ireland, have voluntarily withdrawn themselves from their said allegiance, and the defence of the said province; be it enacted ... That all such persons as aforesaid, who, having received grants of land, or may have become seized of lands, within this province, by inheritance or otherwise, as shall voluntarily have withdrawn themselves from this province into the United States of America, since the first day of July, one thousand eight hundred and twelve, or who may hereafter during the present war, voluntarily withdraw themselves from this province into the United States, without license, granted under the authority of the governor, lieutenant governor, or person administering the government of this province, shall be taken and considered to be aliens born, and incapable of holding lands within this province.

II. And be it further enacted ... That it shall and may be lawful for the governor, lieutenant governor, or person administering the government, by commission under the great seal of this province, to authorize any sheriff, coroner, or other person or persons in the several districts of this province, to inquire by the oath of twelve good and lawful men of their respective districts, and by inquisition indented under the hands and seals of the said jurors, and of the said commissioner or commissioners, to return to his Majesty's court of king's bench all such persons as aforesaid, who, seized of lands in the respective districts, shall have voluntarily withdrawn from the province into the United States of America since the said first day of July, and before the conclusion of the existing war with those states, without license granted under the authority of the governor, lieutenant governor, or person administering the government, and from and after the said finding by such inquisition, his Majesty shall become seized of the lands so found to have been in the seisin of such person on the said first day of July: Provided always, That nothing in this act contained, shall be construed to prevent any persons interested in the said lands from traversing any inquisition or office respecting the same, at any time within one year after the peace shall be established between his Majesty and the United States of America, or within one year after the finding of such inquisition.

III. Provided always, That nothing in this act shall extend or be construed to extend to affect the claim of any bona fide creditor, or to defeat any just lien or security of or upon any lands, tenements, or hereditaments whatsoever.

6. 'An Act for the More Impartial and Effectual Trial and Punishment of High Treason, and Misprision of High Treason, and Treasonable Practices in This Province' (U.C. Stat. 54 Geo. III [1814], c.11)

For the more impartial and effectual: Trial and Punishment of all offences of High Treason and Misprision of High Treason and Treasonable practices committed in this Province, and for taking away hopes of impunity from persons guilty of Crimes so dangerous to His Majesty's Government, Be it therefore enacted... That from and after the passing of this Act all offences of High Treason, and Misprision of High Treason, and of Treasonable Practices already committed, or to be committed within this Province, may be enquired of, heard, tried and determined in the court of King's Bench within the same, in the District where that court shall sit, or before such Justices of Oyer and Terminer and Gaol Delivery within such District of the Province as shall be assigned by the Governor, Lieutenant Governor or person administering the Government of this Province by Commission under the great Seal thereof in like manner and form and to all intents and purposes as if such offences had been done or committed in the same District when they shall be so enquired of, heard and determined as aforesaid.

II. That all inquiries and trials for High Treason or Misprision of High Treason or Treasonable practices, committed, or to be committed in the said Province, may be had by good and lawful men of the District where the said Court of King's Bench shall sit, or of the District when the said Justices of Oyer and Terminer and Goal Delivery shall execute their said Commissions by virtue of the Provisions of this Act, and that no challenge to Jurors for not being of the District where the offence was committed shall be allowed.

III. That his Majesty's Chief Justice of the said Province, and the Justices of the Court of King's Bench therein shall be named and assigned Justices in every such commission, whereof one to be of the Quorum.

IV. That all persons convicted or attainted of High Treason or Misprision of High Treason or Treasonable practices pursuant to this Act, shall be subject and liable to the same corruption of Blood, pains, penalties, and forfeitures as persons convicted and attainted at High Treason or Misprision of High Treason or Treasonable practices in the same District where such offences have been committed.

V. That this Act shall remain in force for and during the term of two years unless the present War with the United States of America shall sooner terminate, and from thence to the end of the then next ensuing session of the Provincial Parliament and no longer.

7. J.B. Robinson to Capt. Loring, secretary to Gen. Drummond, 4 April 1814 (RG 5, A 1, vol. 16: 6761-71, NA)

I have delayed all communication on the very important subject of the trial of the traitors confined here until I had made an abstract of the evidence I have against them, and learned exactly the extent of every man's crime. I have now done so, and beg permission to report to you that out of sixty men against whom I have informations, chiefly for treasonable practices it will be necessary to prefer Indictments for High treason against 30 and sufficient evidence may be had to entitle the Crown to convictions.

Far the greater part of these however, and some of them the most notorious offenders are with the enemy, and consequently out of the reach of punishment except by the confiscation of their estates.

Eight or nine remain, against whom I have witnesses bound in recognizance to appear whose evidence I am sure is amply sufficient to convict them of High treason, unless the Jury are at all events determined to acquit them.

Of these *three* ought, (I mean by the rules of the common law) to be tried in the District of Niagara where their offences were committed – besides whom about 20 remain to be indicted and six or more to be tried for treasons committed in the District of *London*.

When I had last the honor of conversing with Genl. Drummond upon the most adviseable means of bringing these men to justice I found the idea of difficulties that were likely to occur had suggested the expediency of trying them at York. Several obvious objections, however, dissuaded him from that opinion, and it was finally decided that the Court should be holden at Burlington in the District of Niagara. I acquiesced at the time, for this even was a nearer approach to what I thought desirable than had been contemplated. I have thought much upon the subject since, and beg leave with the most respectful deference to His Honor, the President to submit these considerations to his attention.

It becomes me first to apologise to His Honor for what would in almost any other case than mine have been unwarranted, namely not promptly complying with the positive orders delivered me before your departure to send immediately for His signature a special Commission for the trial of the Civil Prisoners at Burlington at as early a day as possible.

My present situation, and the consciousness of the responsibility attached to it, induce me rather to incur the censure of a little necessary delay than hazard any measure which may involve the Government and produce difficulties which after-consideration cannot repair.

The Act passed by the Legislature in their last session certainly does authorise the Government to bring these Offenders to trial in whatever District they please, but upon the best consideration I can give to this matter, the exercise of this new power would be improper in this instance upon several grounds. These prosecutions are very rightly conceived by the Government, and especially by His Honor as measures of great public importance. It is wished, and very rightly, to overawe the spirit of disaffection in the Province by examples of condign punishment by the law of the Land. Executions of Traitors by military power would have comparatively little influence: the people consider them as arbitrary Acts of punishment, but would not acknowledge them as the natural effects of justice. Now to give the condemnation of traitors by the law of the land, and by a Jury of the Country the full effect, the common course of Justice should be as much as possible observed. If these offenders are tried out of the proper District by virtue of this Statute, it will be said, and perhaps with some appearance of reason, that the law was passed entirely with a view to try them out of the ordinary course, and is so far in its intention, and operation[,] ex post facto. The reason of the law in requiring trials to be had only in the District where the offence was committed is just and obvious, and whether the Jury's local knowledge of the characters and their witnesses be to the advantage of the Prisoner or against him it is in favor of public justice that they should have it.

But it appears to me, and this I take the liberty of urging as a very powerful reason for wishing these trials to be had if possible in their proper Districts, that the local acquaintance of the Jurors, if taken from the District of London will be much in favor of the success of the prosecutions. Here, as in the District of Niagara, and in most other Districts of this Province, more especially in those inhabited by emigrants from the United States, the Jurors[,] I fear, are in general very indifferent to the honor, or interests of Government; indeed if they are not wholly indifferent, their bias is the other way. The Inhabitants of the District of London, however, know perfectly well the designs, and intentions of this rebellious party – they felt that their persons and property were in danger from their violence, so much so, that they voluntarily resorted to arms to subdue them – and it is fair to suppose that men who risqued their lives in the apprehension of these traitors will be well satisfied to have them punished as they deserve. Add to this that our witnesses, not a few, live in that District, and may not be easily obtained out of it – besides that being in the District gives the Prosecutor opportunity of making continual inquiry, and discovering testimony that might not otherwise be had.

I am well aware that some difficulties present themselves which may render these trials in the District of London very inconvenient, particularly those relating to the personal accommodation or safety of the court of which I must not expect to experience the least – but all considerations of this kind must give way to the necessities of public justice, and unless it is deemed impracticable to hold the Court there, every inconvenience should be suffered, to effect it.

His Honor best knows whether the District of London is liable to be so disturbed, within the next two months, by the enemy that Courts can not be held, nor Juries obtained there. If this is expected to be the case, or in other words if it is considered impossible to try the prisoners in that District, nothing need be said, we are bound by the necessity, and must do what under these circumstances will be certainly most adviseable – open the Court at Burlington.

I hesitate not to say that I make this representation to His Honor that the trial of these offenders out of the proper District, if it is ordered, may appear to stand upon the footing of necessity alone that I may not be said to have advised it, or be in that event so much responsible for the success of the prosecutions.

His Honor must be sufficiently sensible how necessary it is in my peculiar situation to have every step in this proceeding thoroughly understood. I am only acting in the office of Attorney General, and have no colleague whose Judgment I can consult, and who is to share with myself the responsibility of the prosecutions. It is therefore natural that I should feel more than commonly anxious to have every measure explained in which I can be supposed to be concerned, and these reflections will, I hope, justify me to His Honor for delaying after the matter was conceived to be determined to represent more fully my wishes and opinions as Prosecutor for the Crown, and to wait for positive instructions after those representations are made.

I must expect that every step in these important prosecutions will be long, and thoroughly canvassed, and I certainly desire that, whatever may be their success, it may not be doubtful, what part I have taken in every question of justice or expediency they may involve.

The Special Commission now out for the District of London is in force until the 20th June next, which would allow time for the trials. But in order that there may be no time lost, I send now a Special Commission under the Act, for the trial of the prisoners at Burlington, as His Honor when here was pleased to order. If therefore His Honor adheres to that intention this Commission and the Dedimus potestatem may be returned immediately with his signature.

You will perceive that the Commission also empowers the Commissioners to try treasons committed in the Home District. I found it necessary to prefer two Indictments for High treason at this last Court, they were found by the Grand Jury, and if it is determined that the other traitors should be tried at Burlington, the same reason exists for including these two.

Whatever may be His Honor's decision with respect to the District wherein these men are to be tried, I beg that you will in your written order to me for my fiat express his commands on that head explicitly, and if they are to be taken out of the proper District assign the reasons which render it difficult or impossible to proceed in the ordinary course.

I think it proper to inform His Honor while submitting this representation for his decision that the Judges appear to wish the trials to be had at Burlington. It was my duty to lay before His Honor what presented itself to my mind upon the subject, and whatever may be his determination I will anxiously endeavor to discharge my duty in bringing these men speedily to Justice.

8. J.B. Robinson to Capt. Robert Loring, Ancaster, 18 June 1814 (RG 5, A 1, vol. 16: 6845–52, NA)

... Respecting the Special Commission – It was the business of the Chief Justice, or the Commissioners generally (and I presume it has before this been done) to report to his Honor the cases that have occurred with sentiments on the several convictions, to assist His Honor in the exercise of that discretion which now devolves upon him.

If this has not yet been done I lament the delay that will necessarily follow the sentence of the law and which will in some measure destroy the effects of the example. Executions should be done while the facts are recent in the memory of the public.

Allow me to report briefly for His Honor's information by his order contained in your letter – that about 70 persons stand indicted for High treason of these about 50 have left the Country, and of course will be pursued by the ordinary process to Outlawry.

During the Commission 17 persons have been tried for High treason – of these 13 are convicted, and 4 acquitted. The Convicts are –

1. Jacob Overholser
2. Aaron Stevens
3. Garrett Neill
4. John Johnson
5. Samuel Hartwell
6. Stephen Hartwell
7. Daton Lindsay
8. George Peacock Junr.
9. Benjamin Simmonds
10. Adam Chrysler
11. Isaiah Brink
12. Isaac Pettit
13. Cornelius Howey

Four are yet to be tried. *Two* will be tried to morrow viz. – Noah P. Hopkins and John Dunham. If they are convicted, I know of no claim either of them have to mercy. The latter has most certainly none. He was one of the ringleaders in a band of rebels in the London District who carried several Militia Officers, and Inhabitants prisoners to Buffaloe. His house was their headquarters. I have no doubt I shall convict him.

The former is from Queenston charged with having acted as a Commissary in the American service and with having given them information in many instances. I know nothing of the man – his acts are not of a nature so atrocious as Dunham's, tho' I believe his principles are certainly dangerous. I am not equally confident of his conviction.

As to the others –

1. *Jacob Overholser*. An ignorant man from Fort Erie of considerable property – a good farmer convicted of having accompanied in arms parties of American Soldiers to the houses of four of his neighbours, who were by them made prisoners, and by them sent to Buffaloe about 1 Decr. last. He followed them himself next day voluntarily, and went before Col. Chapin, & Genl. Porter, and gave evidence against them charging them with having broken their parol by volunteering in our service after they had been parolled by the enemy. He is not a man of influence or

enterprise, and it is thought acted as he did from motives of personal enmity to the persons thus taken away who are not of themselves men of good characters. I state these facts fairly, and submit them to His Honor's consideration.

2. *Aaron Stevens.* A man formerly in the confidence of Government of respectable family, and property, convicted of having acted as a spy for the enemy – going for that purpose to Burlington when Genl. Vincent commanded there, surveying the works, and garrison, and communicating the result of his observations to Genl. Boyd for a large pecuniary reward. He was besides constantly with the enemy when they possessed Fort George, and often seen there in arms.

3. & 4. *Garrett Neill & John Johnson.* Two ignorant, inconsiderable men from the London District convicted of being two of the party of rebels acting under Chapin's orders in that District in Novr. last in open rebellion, making prisoners, and marching to attack Dover.

5. & 6. *Saml. Hartwell & Steph[e]n Hartwell.* Two young men formerly living near the Beaver-dam in the Niagara District. They were from the U. States, and had been about 10 years resident in this Country before the present War. Immediately on the Declaration of War they fled to the United States, leaving their wives, and families here. They were taken by Genl. Brock in arms at Detroit, and not being known to be subjects were parolled. They afterwards appeared in this Country as soon as the enemy had gotten possession of the Niagara frontier and returned to their former place of residence. On the 10th June they endeavoured to make prisoner in the name of the enemy of one of our militia men who was called out with his arms, for which they are convicted of High treason.

7. 8. 9. *Daton Lindsay, George Peacock Junr., Benjamin Simmonds.* Three of the rebels in the service of the enemy in the District of London in Novr. last making prisoners of our Militia officers and Inhabitants, and taking them to Buffaloe – and advancing to destroy Dover, and take the public stores there – these men were taken in open rebellion by Col. Bostwick's Party of Volunteer Militia and surrendered their arms to him.

10. 11. 12. *Adam Chrysler, Isaiah Brink, Isaac Pettit.* Three more of the same party of rebels, the two first very active and concerned in almost every act. They were not of the number taken in Arms by Col. Bostwick.

13. *Cornelius Howey.* Another of these rebels – he was taken in arms by Col. Bostwick's party, and received a shot through the body in the skirmish, under which wound he is yet languishing, it is thought without much probability of recovering.

Besides these as I have before observed Hopkins & Dunham will be tried on Monday. Two more, William Stevens and John Phelps are also in custody for Treason. The charges against them were made so late in the Commission that they cannot be tried without detaining the Court and Jury to the end of the week.

Upon a consideration of circumstances – Every public object proposed by assembling the Special Commission having been already achieved, it being now in the power of His Honor to make certainly a sufficient number of examples of [sic] punish the guilt of past offences, and to over-awe for the future the spirit of disaffection, the Militia of this District being ordered to the frontier, and a proportion of the best men with many of the most useful officers being attendant on the Court, I conceive it inexpedient on public grounds to pursue the prosecutions at present any further, and to keep the Juries who have patiently borne, and most creditably discharged a laborious duty for many days at a great private inconvenience, a week longer together for the trial of two men in whose cases there is nothing of extraordinary interest or importance. I have made this representation to the Court, and I imagine the Commission will be adjourned on Tuesday to the usual time of the Circuit Courts – about two months hence, when the remaining trials can be had. In doing this I exercised a discretion which appeared to me to belong to my situation under the present circumstances, and I trust His Honor will admit the propriety of my representation, and the consequent adjournment.

The Court before adjournment will pass sentence on the Convicts and, I imagine, will respite the execution of it until His Honor's pleasure may be known. Tho' it is a duty extremely unpleasant to the feelings, it is perhaps, proper that I should give some opinion on the different convictions. I hope His Honor will be guided in his discretion by more satisfactory advice but that no more delay may be produced by want of necessary information, I beg to make a few remarks, by no means wishing that any thing may be taken from me if a representation is made from a more proper source.

Of the persons convicted, I fear (2) Aaron Stevens, (5) Daton Lindsay, (6) Benjamin Simmonds, (7) George Peacock the Younger, (4) Adam Chrysler, (3) Isaiah Brink, and (1) John Dunham (if convicted) must be considered the most proper objects of punishment, placing them in the order as numbered.

John Johnson is an ignorant man, appeared to enter reluctantly into the plans of the rebels, and to have been at first deceived by them in a false account of the objects they proposed. He behaved with humanity to prisoners taken by the party, and expressed his regret at some of their outrages while they were together.

Saml. and Stephn. Hartwell are certainly by law traitors – they owed by residence, and the protection afforded by this Government to their families a local allegiance which they forfeited – but when war commenced they returned to their native Country at once, & avowed their hostility, they were acknowledged (tho' ignorantly) by us as Prisoners of war and were paroled as such. From the former relations between the two countries many cases of such nice discrimination may arise that perhaps from political motives even, it is better not to strain the law to its utmost rigor. By substituting as an Act of royal clemency banishment for execution in the case of these young men the principle of allegiance will be equally well maintained, and perhaps in natural justice it is fairer. Their act was a single one, they did not perfect their intention, nor indeed did they obstinately persevere in the attempt.

Of the rest I say nothing. I hope their cases are correctly stated, and His Honor's discretion will determine. I only take the liberty of suggesting that to prevent delay His Honor may write as soon as he has satisfied himself upon the subject directing the Judges to order the immediate execution of one or two of the Offenders of whose cases no doubt is entertained, that the objects of the prosecutions may not by any unforeseen accident be entirely defeated. Also, that an unconditional, and free pardon should in *no* case be granted. No person now convicted should be suffered to remain in the Country. The security of those who have disclosed their treasons, and been active in their apprehension makes this precaution necessary & just. I trust too, that His Honor will see the necessity from every consideration of some immediate example, and that in the meantime the same vigilance and care in guarding the prisoners will be directed to be continued.

9. Commission of Sequestration, 16 Jan. 1818 (RG 22, series 143 [High Treason (1814) Records, 1814–24], box 2, env. 5)

To our Trusty and well beloved Abraham Nellis and William Crooks of the District of Niagara, Esquires, Greeting.

Whereas at a Special Session of Oyer and Terminer, and General Gaol Delivery, held at the Township of Ancaster, in the District of Niagara, (now the District of Gore) and Province of Upper Canada, on Monday the twenty second day of May, in the fifty fourth year of our Reign, before the Honorable Thomas Scott, late Chief Justice of our Court of our Bench, in our said Province of Upper Canada, the Honorable William Dummer Powell, and the Honorable William Campbell, Justices of our Court of our Bench, for the Province aforesaid, assigned to hold Pleas before us, by our letters patent to the same Justices before named, and others their Associates, or any two or more of them, of whom we willed, that any one of them, the said Thomas Scott, William Dummer Powell, and William Campbell, made to enquire by the Oath of Good and Lawful men, of the District aforesaid, and by other ways, methods, and means, whereby they should or might better know, as well within liberties as without, more full the truth of all treasons, Misprisions of treason, and treasonable practices, against us committed, as well within the District of London, or within the Home District, as within the District of Niagara, of the Province aforesaid, by whomsoever or howsoever, had done, perpetrated and committed, and when, how, and in what manner, and of all articles, or circumstances whatsoever the Premises every or any of them concerning, and the same treasons, and other the Premises, for that time to hear and determine, according to the Law and Custom of England, and the Laws of our said Province, by the oath of James Crooks, Henry Haigh, James Durand, Abraham Nelles, Thomas Butler, George Adams, John Ball, Robert Grant, John Servos, Robert Hammilton, Thomas Cummings, Samuel Street the younger, Amos Chapman, Daniel Secord, Levi Lewis, and William Crooks, good and Lawful men of the District of Niagara, aforesaid, being sworn and charged to enquire for us, for the body of the District of Niagara, District of London and Home District aforesaid, it was presented, that long before and at the several times therein after mentioned, open and public War was and is yet carried on by the Government of the United States of America, against us, and that the people of the said United States of America, under persons exercising the said Government, were open and public Enemies of us, to wit at the Town of Niagara, in the District of Niagara aforesaid, And that during the said War, to wit on the Twenty seventh day of May, in the fifty third year of our Reign, the aforesaid Enemies of us, did hostilely invade, the District of Niagara aforesaid, and with their Fleets and Armies, forcibly did occupy and seize, and remain in possession of a part thereof against us for a long space of time, to wit, from the said twenty seventh day of May, in the said Fifty third year of our Reign aforesaid to the tenth day of December in the Fifty fourth year of our Reign. And that Aaron Stevens late of the Township of Niagara aforesaid, yeoman, being a subject of us and well knowing the Premises, but not having the fear of God in his Heart, nor weighing the duty of his allegiance, and being moved and seduced by the instigation of the Devil, as a false Traitor, against us, and wholly withdrawing the Love, obedience, fidelity and allegiance, which every true and faithful subject of us, should and of right ought to bear towards us, on the Eighteenth day of November in the fifty fourth year of our Reign, and on divers other days and times as well before as after during the continuance of the said War, and during the Invasion of the said District of Niagara by the Armies of the aforesaid Enemies of us, with force and arms at the Town of Niagara, in the District of Niagara aforesaid, unlawfully and traitorously was adherent to aiding and comforting the Enemies of us. And in pursuance, performance, and execution of the said Treason and Treasonable adhering aforesaid, he the said Aaron Stevens as such false Traitor as aforesaid, with force and arms on the Eighteenth day of November aforesaid, in the said fifty fourth year of the reign aforesaid, falsely, wickedly, maliciously and traitorously did enter as a Soldier into the service of the aforesaid Enemies of us with the intent of aiding and assisting, and thereby aiding and assisting the aforesaid Enemies of us to prosecute and wage War against us within this Province of Upper-Canada. And that in further pursuance, performance and execution of His Treason and Treasonable adhering aforesaid, he the said Aaron Stevens as such false Traitor as aforesaid, with force and arms, afterwards and during the continuance of the said War, and while the aforesaid Enemies of us were hostilely remaining in the said District of Niagara, to wit, on the Eighteenth day of November in the said fifty fourth year of our reign aforesaid, at the Town of Niagara, in the District of Niagara aforesaid, falsely, wicke[d]lly, maliciously, and traitorously, did enlist himself in a Corps commanded by one Joseph Willcox, then and there being in the service and employment of the said Enemies of us, and then and there armed and arrayed in a hostile manner, with Swords, Guns, Pistols, and divers other Weapons as well offensive and defensive, therein did serve against us as a Soldier under the command of the aforesaid Enemies of us in prosecuting and waging War against us within this Province of Upper Canada. And in further pursuance, performance and execution of the said treason, and treasonable adhering as aforesaid, the said Aaron Stevens as such false Traitor as aforesaid, with force and arms on the Seventeenth day of November in the fifty fourth year of our reign, and on divers other days and times, as well before as after, during the continuance of the said War, at a place called Fort Niagara, at that time in the possession of [and] garrisoned by the aforesaid Enemies of us, and being in the said United States of America, falsely, wickedly, maliciously and traitorously did enter as a Soldier in the service of the aforesaid Enemies of us with the intent of aiding and assisting and thereby aiding and assisting the aforesaid Enemies of us, to prosecute and wage a cruel War against us and our subjects of this Province of Upper Canada. And that in further pursuance, performance and execution of the said Treason and Treasonable adhering aforesaid, he the said Aaron Stevens as such false Traitor as aforesaid with force and arms on the Twenty fifth day of October in the fifty fourth year of our Reign and on divers other days and times as well before as after, during the continuance of the said War, and during the said Invasion of the said Province of Upper Canada by the aforesaid Enemies of us, at the Town of Niagara in the District of Niagara aforesaid, did falsely and traitorously engage with the said Enemies of us, to act as a Spy for them the aforesaid Enemies of us, and did then and there undertake with and promise the said Enemies of us to seek, obtain and procure intelligence of the situation, disposition and strength of the forces of us, then opposed to the Enemies of us and of other matters and things required to be known by the aforesaid Enemies of us, and to convey and carry such intelligence to the aforesaid Enemies of us with intent to aid and assist by such intelligence, as aforesaid, the said Enemies of us in their attempt to conquer and subdue the said District of Niagara. And that the said Aaron Stevens, as such Spy as aforesaid, and in order to obtain and procure Intelligence for the aforesaid Enemies of us, afterwards, to wit on the twenty fifth day of October in the fifty fourth year of the reign aforesaid, did go and enter into the Garrison of Burlington in the said District of Niagara then in possession of and defended by the Troops and other leige Subjects of us, and did then and there secretly, knowingly, unlawfully and traitorously enquire for, seek, obtain, procure, and get information and intelligence of the number of the troops, and other leige Subjects of us, and of the state of the aforesaid garrison and of divers other matters and things relative to the defence of the said District of Niagara and of the said Province of Upper Canada, and the situation of the troops of us therein with the intent to convey the same to the aforesaid Enemies of us, thereby intending to aid and assist the aforesaid Enemies of us to prosecute and wage War against us in this Province of Upper Canada and to conquer and subdue the same. And that in further pursuance, performance, and execution of the said Treason and Treasonable adhering of the said Aaron Stevens to the aforesaid Enemies of us, he the said Aaron Stevens, as such false Traitor, and spy as aforesaid, with force and Arms on the Twenty fifth day of October in the said fifty fourth year of our Reign and on divers other days and times as well before as after during the continuance of the said War, at the Town of Niagara in the District of Niagara aforesaid, and while the aforesaid enemies of us were in possession of the said Town of Niagara in the said District of Niagara aforesaid, falsely, wickedly, maliciously and traitorously, did disclose and make known to the aforesaid Enemies of us the number, situation and disposition of the Troops and Armies of us in the said District of Niagara, and the number of troops at that time stationed in the Garrison of Burlington and other important intelligence respecting the said District of Niagara and the said Garrison of Burlington, thereby aiding and assisting the aforesaid Enemies of us to prosecute and wage War against us within this Province of Upper Canada, in Contempt of us and our Laws and to the Evil example of all others in the like case offending, contrary to the duty of the Allegiance of him the said Aaron Stevens, against the form of the Statute in such case made and provided and against our Peace, our Crown and Dignity. And it was further presented that the said Aaron Stevens being a Subject of us as aforesaid, as a false traitor against us, to wit on the Eighteenth day of November in the fifty fourth year of our Reign aforesaid, and on divers other days and times, as well before as after the said last mentioned day, with force and arms within the said Province of Upper Canada, to wit at the Town of Niagara in the District of Niagara aforesaid, wickedly, maliciously and traitorously with divers other false Traitors, whose names were to the said Jurors unknown, being armed and arrayed in a warlike manner, with swords, guns, Pistols, and divers other Weapons as well offensive as defensive, did falsely and traitorously join himself with the said other false traitors, whose names were to the said Jurors unknown against us, and then and there with force and arms, with the aforesaid Traitors and Rebels, whose Names were to the said Jurors then unknown, as aforesaid did falsely and traitorously and in a warlike and hostile manner array and dispose himself against us, And then and there, he the said Aaron Stevens, with Force and arms, in pursuance and execution, of such his wicked traitorous intentions and purposes aforesaid, did falsely and traitorously prepare, order, wage and levy a public and cruel War, against us, in contempt of us and our Laws, against the duty of the allegiance of him the said Aaron Stevens, to the evil example of all others in the like case offending, against the form of the Statute in such case made and provided, and against our Peace our Crown and Dignity.

And whereas afterwards to wit at our same Session of Oyer and Terminer, and General Gaol Delivery, of our District of Niagara, District of London and Home District aforesaid, on the said Twenty second day of May, in the Fifty fourth year of our Reign, before our said Justices above named and others their fellows aforesaid there came the said Aaron Stevens, under the Custody of Thomas Merrit[t] Esquire, Sheriff of the District of Niagara, aforesaid, in whose custody, in the District of Niagara aforesaid, for the cause aforesaid, he had been before committed, being brought to the Bar, there, in his proper person, by the said Sheriff, to whom he was then also committed: And forthwith being Demanded concerning the premises in the said Indictment above specified, and charged upon him how he would acquit himself thereof; he said he was not Guilty thereof, and thereof for good and Evil he put himself upon the Country, And whereas it was thereupon awarded, that a Jury should thereupon immediately come, there, before our said Justices above mentioned, and others their fellows aforesaid, of free and Lawful men of the said District of Niagara, aforesaid, by whom the truth of the matter might be better known, and who were not of kin, of the said Aaron Stevens; to recognize upon Oath whether the said Aaron Stevens, was Guilty of the High Treason in the Indictment aforesaid specified, or not Guilty, because the said Aaron Stevens had put himself upon the said Jury. And whereas the Jurors of the said Jury, by the said Sheriff, for that purpose impannell'd, and returned, being called, came, Who being elected, tried and sworn to speak the truth of and concerning the premises, upon their oath, said that the said Aaron Stevens, was Guilty of the High Treason above charged in the form aforesaid, as by the Indictment aforesaid was supposed against him. And whereas upon that, it was forthwith demanded of the said Aaron Stevens, if he had or knew, any thing to say, wherefore the said Justices, there, ought not, upon the Premises and Verdict aforesaid to proceed to Judgement and execution against him, Who nothing further said, unless as before he had said[.] And Whereas thereupon all and Singular the Premises being seen; and by the said Justices fully understood, it was considered by the Court there, that the said Aaron Stevens, be taken to the place from whence he came, and then to be put on a hurdle, and from thence, to the place of Execution drawn, and then by the neck to be hung, and cut down alive to the

Ground, and that his privy Members be cut off, and that his entrails be taken out of his belly and be put into the fire and be burned and that his head be cut off, and that his body be divided into four parts, and that his head and those Quarters, should be put where we should appoint them. By reason whereof all the Goods and Chattels, Lands, Tenements, and Hereditaments, whatsoever, of which the said Aaron Stevens was possessed, or seized in use of possession, by any right, title or means, within this Province of Upper Canada, became, and are forfeited to us. Know, therefore, that we in your fidelity, industry and prudent circumspection, in the management of our affairs greatly confiding, have assigned you to be our Commissioners in this behalf, and by the Tenor of these Presents, give to you or either of you, full power and authority to enquire, as well by the Oath of Good and Lawful men of our District of Niagara, aforesaid, in our said Province of Upper Canada, by whom the truth of the matter may be the better known, as by the examinations and depositions of Credible Witnesses before your [sic] or either of you to be called and examined by their oaths, and by all other ways methods and Means, whereby you or either of you shall or may better know, what Lands, Tenements and Hereditaments and of what yearly value the said Aaron Stevens or any other person to his use, had on the said Eighteenth day of November in the said fifty fourth year of our Reign aforesaid, on which day he committed, the High Treason aforesaid, or ever after, And also what, and what manner of Leases, or Grants of any Lands Tenements and Hereditaments, and of what and what man[n]er of Goods and Chattles, and of what price; and of what Debts, Specialties and Sums of money the said Aaron Stevens, or any other person to his use has in your District, and of all other articles and Circumstances, concerning more fully the Truth, and those Lands Tenements, Goods and Chattles, and other the Premises aforesaid, with the appurtenances so as aforesaid to be found, to enter, take, and seize into our hands. And therefore we command you that a certain day and Place or days and places, which you or either of you for this purpose shall appoint, you diligently of the Premises make an Inquisition or Inquisitions, and that or those distinctly and openly made, you or either of you return to our Court of our Bench without delay under your or either of your seals together with these our Letters Patent. We Command also by the Tenor of these Presents, Our Sheriff of the District of Niagara aforesaid that at a certain day and place or days and places, which you or either of you shall appoint, and to him in our behalf shall give notice, he cause to come before you or either of you, so many and such of good and Lawful men of his Bailiwick as well within liberties as without, by whom the truth of the matter might be better known and inquired into. We also give you or either of you full power and authority to Summon and Cause to appear before you or either of you what persons soever proper to be examined in the Premises, and them of and in the premises, before you or either of you on their

Oaths corporally to be taken diligently to Examine, and their examinations to receive, and in writing to reduce, lest that our Present Command should remain further to be executed. We give moreover to all and Singular Sheriffs, Bailiffs Constables, and all others our Officers Ministers and Subjects whomsoever, by the Tenor of these Presents strictly in Command that you or either of you, in the execution of the Premises they observe, obey and attend as it behoveth.

L

Parliamentary Privilege and the Repression of
Dissent in the Canadas
F. Murray Greenwood and Barry Wright

1. Edward Bowen, judge, Court of King's Bench, to Jonathan Sewell, chief justice of Lower Canada (MG 23 GII 10, vol.5 [Sewell Papers] NA).

Quebec, 2 August 1814

My Dear Sir,
... I shall now beg leave to call your Attention to a Subject, I may with truth say is of Vital Interest to the Government of this Province, and to all who prefer the Security which naturally flows from a well organised and well administered System of Law and Politicks in the Colony, to the truly dangerous and alarming course which we see daily pursued here, by the false Patriots of Canada styling themselves 'Les Anti-Jacobins,' who at the same time they profess to admire and uphold the happy Constitution of the Mother Country and the Government in this Colony, do every thing in their power as well as in the House of Assembly as out of it, and particularly by sundry slanderous and libellous Publications in their Newspaper 'Le Spectateur,' published at Montreal, to sap both, and to create amongst the Inhabitants a general mistrust of the constituted Authorities, a want of confidence in and contempt of the Executive and Legislative Councils of the Province, and of the Judges and the Administration of Justice in general, with what motives or with what views, I shall not now stop to enquire, suffice it to say the fact is so. Looking forward however to the consequences and having before me 'Le Spectateur' of the 12th April last containing a most scandalous Libel upon the Legislative Council which I am strongly led to believe the Members of it will not be disposed to pass over in silence at their next Session. It will follow, should they resolve that the Publication alluded to contains libellous matter and is a breach of their Priviledges and a Contempt of that House, that the Authors, Editors, Printers and Publishers thereof will in all probability be ordered to be arrested and committed to the custody of the Genetleman Usher of the Black Rod.

The Persons so imprisoned will severally seek relief from the Judges of K.B. Quebec by Writs of Hab.Corp. in which case We shall necessarily be driven to a decision of the questions important as they are to this Colony.

What are the Priviledges, if any, to which the Legislative Council and the Assembly of the Province constituted by the Sta.31 Geo.III c.31 are entitled?

Have they of right any priviledges whatever which are not set forth in the said Statute, which might be aptly called their Charter of Constitution?

Ought they to profess any other priviledges than such as are essentially necessary to their political Existence, as 1st Freedom of Speech. 2nd Freedom from arrest in civil causes during the Sessions only, with a reasonable time for coming thither & returning home. 3rd The right of punishing their own Members or any others for Contempts committed within the Body of their own house whilst in Session?

Independent of the Publications to which I have alluded, there have been several others issued from different Presses in the Province, since the dissolution of the Provincial Legislature, and amongst them a well written Pamphlet under the signature 'Aristides.' It contains some home truths and censures in pretty strong language the proceedings of the last House of Assembly.

This I am also given to understand, the present house of Assembly composed as it is of all the violent and factious Characters which the last Session exhibited, and of many others of the same Stamp added to them by the late general Election will also take [it] up, as they consider it, by reflecting on the proceedings of the last house to be a contempt and a breach of the Priviledges of the present one.

Whether even conceding to them the right of punishing, and that the publication in question 'Aristides' contains a Libel upon the former house, the present one can legally take Notice of it, would not I conceive be a question very difficult to decide, but with the spirit of Party that has hitherto prevailed and must still prevail in the house, without some very decisive measures are adopted with respect to it, by the Government at home, I am thoroughly convinced that whatever Judgement we may feel ourselves compelled to give upon the Subject of their Priviledges, if that Judgement should prove unfavorable to their pretensions, they will exclaim against us, move to commit us for a breach of their Priviledges, or will refuse to continue their proceedings and petition for our removal from office as Judges.

The right of the Legislative Council, the Members of which hold their Seats for life, to punish for Libels, if that power be vested in them, may perhaps differ from the Members of the Assembly, tho' the Libel may have been published after the dissolution of the Provincial Parliament, for the Legislative Council is still the same body.

Knowing the interest you feel for the welfare of the Province, and as I view these questions to embrace Matters rather of State Policy than of Law, I feel in common with my Brethern upon the Bench anxious that you will lose no time in collecting such Information upon this Subject as may be within your reach, and particularly whether the Government at home is thought disposed to concede to this provincial legislature in a dependant Colony, all the Rights Priviledges and

Immunities of the Imperial Parliament or not, and favor us with your Opinion as to the correct line of Demarcation applied to both Houses in repect of their privileges, and particularly to punish for Libels which do not arise within the body of their respective houses.

Libellers certainly ought not to escape Punishment, but it appears to me that the Attorney General has a course to pursue in the Courts of Common Law, amply sufficient to check this growing Evil.

I need scarcely urge to you the necessity of giving early attention to this Subject and that I may if possible hear from you in Answer prior to the next Session of the Provincial Parliament which will probably be in January.

I am my Dear Sir with every Sentiment of Esteem, and anxiously awaiting your return to the province,

Very Truly and sincerely yours, Edw. Bowen

2. Opinion of the British law officers on the privileges of the House of Assembly of Lower Canada (CO 42/134(1)/127, NA, reproduced in *Con Docs* 2: at 480–3).

2 Lincoln's Inn
30th December 1815

My Lord,

We have had the honor to receive your Lordship's letter of the 20th Instant, transmitting to us two papers containing questions which have arisen on the construction of the Act of 31st Geo: 3rd Chap. 31. respecting the Government of Canada; and desiring us to take the same into our consideration, and to report to you our opinion thereupon in point of Law; we have accordingly considered the same, and as to the questions stated in the paper No. 1 which we have returned with our report, first 'Whether by the several Clauses referred to the Assembly of Lower Canada is entitled to any privileges under that Statute,' we beg to report to your Lordship that we consider the Members of the Assembly of Canada entitled to such Privileges as are incidental to, and necessary to enable them to perform, their functions in deliberating and advising upon, and consenting to laws for the peace, welfare & good Government of the Province.

In answer to the second question, 'Whether the Assembly is entitled to all the 'Privileges to which the House of Commons of the imperial Parliament are entitled under their own peculiar Law, the Lex Parliamentaria.'

We beg to report, that we think they are not so entitled. The Privileges of the High Court of Parliament composed of the King, The Lords spiritual, and temporal, and Commons of the Realm, are founded on the antient law and Custom of Parliament and we conceive arise from the supremacy, or as it is sometimes called, the omnipotence of this High Court, when the Parliament or great Council of the Nation thus composed sat together in one Assembly; Tho' the period when the two houses separated in their sittings, is not ascertained, yet whenever that event took place, each house retained certain privileges and powers; The Lords the judical power; the Commons the power of accusation and impeachment, and to both remained the right to pass bills of Attainder, and of pains and penalties to be assented to or rejected by the King, and each retained the original right of asserting, deciding upon, and vindicating the mighty privileges of their separate houses, but still we apprehend as constituent parts of our great Council or High Court of Parliament by virtue of their united Supremacy. To measure by this standard the privileges of Legislative Assemblies created either by the King's Charter, or by Act of Parliament, for the purpose of enacting Laws for the peace, welfare & good Government of any particular Colony, or district, part of the Dominions of the Crown of the United Empire, would be to give to subordinate bodies the mighty power of supremacy. The King, by his charter, could not, we apprehend, grant such powers, and tho' Parliament might, if it should deem it expedient, bestow them, yet unless it has so specifically done, such powers cannot belong to them as incident to their Creation and Constitution. If these powers and privileges belong to colonial Legislatures as arising from or by analogy to the Law & custom of Parliament, they must belong as well to the Legislative Council as to the House of Assembly, and then the judicial power in the last resort upon matters arising in the Colony, would be in the Legislative Council; the right to impeach would be in the House of Assembly; and the right to try & adjudge such impeachment would belong to the legislative Council; they would each have a power with the assent of his Majesty to enact Bills of Attainder, and of pains and penalties; it is however clear that by the Statute the Legislative Council have no judicial powers, belonging to them, neither have the House of Assembly any power of Impeachment in the legitimate sense of the word, however they may use the term in any accusation or complaint they may make, either to his Majesty in Council or in any petition they may present to the Parliament of the United Empire.

This claim to possess the same privileges as belong to the House of Commons has sometimes been asserted by certain colonial assemblies, as was done in the year 1764 by the House of Assembly of Jamaica, but we apprehend it has never been admitted or recognized, tho' in that particular instance it appears to have been thought expedient, so far to comply with their complaint, as to direct the succeeding Chancellor of the Island to vacate and annul the proceeding which had given offence to the House of Assembly. That the House of Assembly of a Colony is not entitled to the same privileges, nor has the same power in vindicating them as belong to the House of Commons of the imperial Parliament has been the opinion of very great and eminent Lawyers in former times. – Such was the opinion of the late Lord Camden, when Attorney General, as expressed in these words, 'Our house of Commons stands upon its own laws, the lex Parliamenti, whereas Assemblies in the Colonies are regulated by their respective Charters, Usages, and the Common Law of England, and will never be allowed to assume those privileges which the house of Commons is entitled to justly here upon principles that neither can nor must be applied to the Assemblies of the Colonies. Such appears also to have been the opinion of Lord Mansfield & Sir Richard Lloyd, and the same is to be collected from an opinion given by Sir Simon Harcourt and Sir Edward Northey in the year 1704, and from the opinions of other persons of Eminence, on Cases on which this question has individually arisen. Thirdly, it is enquired, if the House of Assembly are not entitled to the privileges founded upon the lex Parliamentaria to what extent they are entitled? We beg leave to observe that as no particular privilege is stated, as that, to which claim is now made, it is difficult to give a precise answer to this question, or to point out the privileges to which they are by Law entitled, otherwise than by giving a general outline. –

The House of Assembly of Upper Canada [sic] has not existed long enough to have established privileges by usage; the Act of Parliament has not delineated any, and we therefore conceive the outline to comprize and to be confined to such only as are directly & indispensably necessary to enable them to perform the functions with which they are invested, and therefore may be fairly said to be incidental to their constitution. We mention some of these as examples; personal liberty, eundo, redeundo et morando, or freedom from arrest, in civil Cases; a power to commit for such Acts of contempt in the face of the House of Assembly as produce disturbance and interruption of their proceedings, the freedom of debate upon the subjects of the Laws to be enacted or considered, they think also they would have the power of expelling a Member convicted by any competent Tribunal of a crime of an infamous nature, and as to this latter instance, we are warranted by an opinion of Lord Mansfield and Sir Richard Lloyd in the year 1755. The right of regulating and ordering their own proceedings in their Assembly consistently with the Statute must necessarily be incident to them, and as to the privilege of deciding upon the right of sitting either in legislative Council, or the house of Assembly, this can no longer be a question of privilege, because such right is in certain cases given by the 31st of Geo: 3d Ch. 31 to the Legislative Council as to their Members and is enacted by the Provincial Statute of the 48th Geo. 3d Chap. 21 as to the houses of Assembly ...

We have the honor to be My Lord, Your Lordship's most obedient Servants

W. Garrow [Attorney General],
S. Shepherd [Solicitor General]

M
The Attempted Impeachment of the Lower Canadian Chief Justices, 1814–15
Evelyn Kolish and James Lambert

1. *Proceedings in the Assembly of Lower Canada on the Rules of Practice of the Courts of Justices and the* **Impeachments** *of Jonathan Sewell and James Monk Esquires* (Printed by order of the House, 1814).

HOUSE OF ASSEMBLY,
Saturday, 26th February, 1814.

Mr. Stuart from the Committee appointed to prepare Heads of Impeachment against *Jonathan Sewell*, Esquire, Chief Justice of the Province, and *James Monk*, Esquire, Chief Justice of the Court of King's Bench for the District of *Montreal*, acquainted the House, that the Committee had prepared Heads of Impeachment accordingly, and also an Humble Representation to His Royal Highness the PRINCE REGENT, which they had directed him to report to the House: And he read the Report in his place, and afterwards delivered it in at the Table, where the same was read, and the said Heads of Impeachment and humble Representation so reported are as follows:

Heads of Impeachment of *Jonathan Sewell*, Esquire, Chief Justice of the Province of *Lower-Canada*, by the Commons of *Lower-Canada*, in this present Provincial Parliament assembled, in their own name, and in the name of all the Commons of the said Province.

FIRST. – That the said *Jonathan Sewell*, Chief Justice of the Province of *Lower-Canada*, hath traitorously and wickedly endeavoured to subvert the Constitution and established Government of the said Province, and instead thereof, to introduce an arbitrary tyrannical Government against Law, which he hath declared by traitorous and wicked opinions, counsel, conduct, judgments, practices and actions.

SECONDLY. – That, in pursuance of those traitorous and wicked purposes, the said *Jonathan Sewell*, hath disregarded the authority of the Legislature of this Province, and in the Courts of Justice wherein he hath presided and sat, hath usurped powers and authority which belong to the Legislature alone, and made regulations subversive of the Constitution and Laws of this Province.

THIRDLY. – That the said *Jonathan Sewell*, being Chief Justice of this Province, and President of the Provincial Court of Appeal, in pursuance of the traitorous and wicked purposes aforesaid, did, on the nineteenth day of January, in the year of our Lord one thousand eight hundred and nine, make and publish, and cause to be made and published, by the Court of Appeals, various regulations, under the name of 'Rules and Orders of Practice,' repugnant and contrary to the Laws of this Province, whereby the said *Jonathan Sewell*, wickedly and traitorously, in so far as in him lay, endeavoured and laboured to change, alter and modify, and to cause to be changed, altered and modified, by the said Court of Appeals, the Laws of this Province, which he was sworn to administer, and assumed legislative authority, and by the said regulations imposed illegal burthens and restraints upon His Majesty's subjects in the exercise of their legal rights, and attributed to the said Court unconstitutional and illegal powers and authority, altogether inconsistent with the duties of the said Court, and subversive of the liberty and just and legal rights of His Majesty's subjects in this Province.

FOURTHLY. – That the said *Jonathan Sewell*, being Chief Justice of this Province, and as such presiding in His Majesty's Court of King's Bench for the District of Quebec, in pursuance of the traitorous and wicked purposes aforesaid, did, in the Term of October, in the year of our Lord one thousand eight hundred and nine, make and publish, and cause to be made and published, by the said last mentioned Court, various regulations, under the name of '*Rules and Orders of Practice*,' repugnant and contrary to Law, by which regulations the said *Jonathan Sewell*, in so far as in him lay, endeavoured and laboured to change, alter and modify, and cause to be changed, altered and modified, by the said last mentioned Court, the Laws of this Province, which he was sworn to administer, and assumed legislative authority, and by the said regulations imposed illegal burthens and restraints upon His Majesty's subjects in the exercise of their legal rights, and thereby attributed to the said last mentioned Court unconstitutional and illegal powers and authority, altogether inconsistent with the duties of the said Court, and subversive of the liberty and just and legal rights of His Majesty's subjects in this Province.

FIFTHLY. – That the said *Jonathan Sewell*, being such Chief Justice and President of the Provincial Court of Appeals, as aforesaid, and as well by the duties as the oaths of his Offices, bound to maintain, support and administer the Laws of this Province, and award justice to His Majesty's subjects, according to the said Laws, hath nevertheless, in contempt of the said Laws, and in violation of his said duty and oaths, set aside the said Laws, and substituted his will and pleasure instead thereof, by divers unconstitutional, illegal, unjust and oppressive rules, orders and judgments, which he hath made and rendered, to the manifest injury and oppression of His Majesty's subjects in this Province, and in subversion of their most important political and civil rights.

SIXTHLY. – That the said *Jonathan Sewell*, being Chief Justice, as aforesaid, and also Speaker of the Legislative Council of this Province, and Chairman of His Majesty's Executive Council therein, did, by false and malicious slanders against His Majesty's Canadian Subjects, and the Assembly of this Province, poison and incense the mind of Sir *James Craig*, being Governor in Chief of this Province, against them, and mislead and deceive him in the discharge of his duties as such Governor, and did, on the fifteenth day of May, in the year of our Lord one thousand eight hundred and nine, advise, counsel, and induce the said Sir *James Craig*, being Governor in Chief as aforesaid, and being under the influence of the false and pernicious suggestions of the said *Jonathan Sewell*, as aforesaid, to dissolve the Provincial Parliament, without any cause whatever, to palliate or excuse that measure, and did also counsel, advise, and induce the said Sir *James Craig*, to make and deliver on that occasion a Speech, wherein the Constitutional rights and privileges of the Assembly of Lower Canada were grossly violated, the Members of that body insulted, and their conduct misrepresented.

SEVENTHLY. – That the said *Jonathan Sewell*, being such Chief Justice, Speaker of the Legislative Council and Chairman of the Executive Council as aforesaid, in pursuance of his traitorous and wicked purposes aforesaid, and intending to oppress His Majesty's Subjects and prevent all opposition to his tyrannical views, did counsel and advise the said Sir *James Craig*, being Governor in Chief as aforesaid, to remove and dismiss divers loyal and deserving Subjects of His Majesty from Offices of profit and honour, who were accordingly removed and dismissed, without the semblance of reason to justify it, but merely because they were inimical, or supposed to be inimical, to the measures and policy promoted by the said *Jonathan Sewell*, and in order, in one instance, to procure the advancement of his brother.

EIGHTHLY. – That the said *Jonathan Sewell*, in order in the strongest manner to mark his contempt for the liberties and rights of His Majesty's Subjects in this Province, and the disrespect for their Representatives, and for the Constitution of this Province, did in the Summer of the year one thousand eight hundred and eight, among other removals and dismissals from office as aforesaid, counsel, advise, and induce the said Sir *James Craig*, being Governor in Chief, as aforesaid, to dismiss *Jean Antoine Panet*, Esquire, who then was and during fifteen years preceding, had been, and still is Speaker of the Assembly of Lower Canada, and in the full enjoyment of the esteem and confidence of his Country, from His Majesty's Service as Lieutenant Colonel of a Battalion of Militia, in the City of Quebec, without any reason to palliate or execute such an Act of injustice.

NINTHLY. – That the said *Jonathan Sewell*, being such Chief Justice, Speaker of the Legislative Council, and Chairman of the Executive Council as aforesaid, regardless of the dignity and duties of his high offices, and in pursuance of his traitorous and wicked purposes aforesaid did, by an undue exercise of his official influence, in the month of March in the year of our Lord one thousand eight hundred and ten, persuade and induce *Pierre Edouard Desbarats*, Printer of the laws of this Province, to establish a News Paper, under the name of the 'Vrai Canadien,' to promote his factious views, and for the purpose of calumniating and vilifying part of his Majesty's Subjects, and certain Members of the Assembly of this Province, who were obnoxious to the said *Jonathan Sewell*, into which paper the said *Jonathan Sewell* caused to be introduced various articles containing gross libels on part of His Majesty's Subjects, and on the Assembly of Lower Canada: and that the said *Jonathan Sewell* did compromise the honour and dignity of His Majesty's Government, by pledging its support to the said Paper, and holding out assurances of its favour to those by whom the said Paper might be conducted and supported.

TENTHLY. – That the said *Jonathan Sewell*, being such Chief Justice, Speaker of the Legislative Council and Chairman of the Executive Council as aforesaid, in pursuance of his traitorous and wicked purposes aforesaid, and intending to extinguish all reasonable freedom of the Press, destroy the rights, liberties and security of His Majesty's Subjects in this Province, and suppress all complaint of tyranny and oppression, did in the month of March in the year of our Lord one thousand eight hundred and ten, counsel, advise, promote and approve the sending of an armed Military force to break open the dwelling House and Printing Office of one *Charles Le François*, being one of His Majesty's peaceable Subjects in the City of Quebec, and there arrest and imprison the said *Charles Le François*, and seize and bring away forcibly a Printing Press, with various private papers; which measure of lawless violence was accordingly executed, and the said Press and papers have since remained deposited in the Court House in the City of Quebec, with the knowledge and approbation, and under the eye of the said *Jonathan Sewell*.

ELEVENTHLY. – That the said *Jonathan Sewell*, being such Chief Justice, Speaker of the Legislative Council and Chairman of the Executive Council of the said Province, in pursuance of his traitorous and wicked purposes aforesaid, with the intention of oppressing individuals supposed to be suspicious of his character and views, and inimical to his policy, and for the purpose of ruining them in the public estimation, and preventing their re-election as Members of the Assembly of Lower Canada, did counsel, advise, promote and approve the arrest of *Pierre Bedard, François Blanchet*, and *Jean Thomas Taschereau*, Esquires, upon the false and unfounded pretext of their having been guilty of Treasonable Practices, whereby they might be delivered of the benefit of Bail, and by means of the influence derived from his high offices, under the Government, caused them to be imprisoned on the said charge, in the common Gaol of the District of Quebec, for a long space of time, and at length to be discharged without having been brought to a trial.

TWELFTHLY. – That the said *Jonathan Sewell*, availing himself of the influence of his said Offices, in pursuance of his traitorous and wicked purposes aforesaid, and in order to mislead the Public, deceive His Majesty's Government, and obtain pretexts for illegal and oppressive measures, instigated and promoted various acts of tyranny and oppression similar to those last mentioned, in other parts of the province, whereby divers individuals upon the false pretext of having been guilty of treasonable practices were exposed to unjust prosecutions, imprisoned and oppressed and one of them *François Corbeil*, being old and infirm, was by the rigour of his imprisonment deprived of life, and whereby general alarm and apprehension were excited in His Majesty's Subjects.

THIRTEENTHLY. – That the said *Jonathan Sewell*, being Chief Justice, Speaker of the Legislative Council, and Chairman of the Executive Council as aforesaid, in pursuance of his traitorous and wicked purposes aforesaid, on the twenty first day of March, in the year of our Lord one thousand eight hundred and ten, being a time when profound tranquillity prevailed in the province, and when no murmurs were heard, or discontents felt, other than those produced by the tyrannic and oppressive measures previously adopted by the advice of the said *Jonathan Sewell*, and when the loyalty of His Majesty's subjects and their attachment to his Government were, nevertheless, unimpaired, did maliciously, traitorously, and wickedly infuse into the mind of the said Sir *James Craig*, being Governor in Chief, as aforesaid, the most false and unfounded suspicions and alarms, respecting the disposition and intentions of His Majesty's Canadian subjects; and did counsel, advise, and induce the said Sir *James Craig*, to issue a Proclamation, extraordinary and unprecedented as well in style as in matter, wherein the arbitrary, unjust, and oppressive imprisonment of the said *Pierre Bedard*, *François Blanchet*, and *Jean Thomas Taschereau*, was referred to in such manner, as might induce a belief of their Guilt, and excite the greatest venom against them, and wherein such statements were made as implied that the Province was in a state approaching open insurrection and rebellion, whereby the character of His Majesty's Canadian subjects was most falsely calumniated, great injustice done to private individuals, and foreign states may have been drawn, and there is the greatest reason to believe from subsequent events were drawn, in to a belief of such disloyalty in His Majesty's Canadian subjects as would render the Province an easy conquest.

FOURTEENTHLY. – That the said *Jonathan Sewell*, being such Chief Justice as aforesaid, in pursuance of his traitorous and wicked purposes aforesaid, did labour and endeavour, by means of his official influence, to extend and confirm the unfounded imputations made, and alarm excited by the said Proclamation, and in the Term of the Court of Criminal Jurisdiction held in the said month of March, one thousand eight hundred and ten, read the said Proclamation in open

Court, for the purpose of influencing the minds of the Grand and Petit Juries, in the exercise of their respective duties.

FIFTEENTHLY. – That the said *Jonathan Sewell*, being such Chief Justice, Speaker of the Legislative Council, and Chairman of the Executive Council as aforesaid, in pursuance of his traitorous and wicked purposes aforesaid, hath laboured and endeavoured to produce in His Majesty's Government an ill opinion of His Majesty's Canadian Subjects, with a view to oppress them, and favour the progress of American influence in this Province, and hath traitorously and wickedly abused the power and authority of his high offices, to promote the advantageous establishment of Americans, being Subjects of the Government of the United-States of America, in this Province, and to pave the way for American predominance therein, to the great prejudice and injury of His Majesty's Canadian Subjects, and with a view to the subversion of His Majesty's Government.

SIXTEENTHLY. – That the said *Jonathan Sewell*, influenced by a desire to accelerate a political connexion of this Province, with part of the United-States of America, and to deprive His Majesty's Canadian Subjects of their present Constitution and Laws, did in or about the month of January, in the year of our Lord one thousand eight hundred and nine, enter into a base and wicked confederacy with one *John Henry*, an adventurer of suspicious character, for the purpose of sowing and exasperating dissention among the Subjects of the Government of the said United-States, and producing among them insurrection and rebellion, and a consequent dismemberment of the union, and in furtherance of the objects of the said confederacy, did, by artful and false representations, counsel, advise and induce Sir *James Craig*, being Governor in Chief of this Province, to send the said *John Henry* on a mission to the said United States, whereby the attainment of the views of the said *Jonathan Sewell* was to be promoted, and the said *Jonathan Sewell* became and was a channel for the correspondence of the said *John Henry*, respecting his mission aforesaid: by which conduct the said *Jonathan Sewell* hath exposed His Majesty's Government to imputations reflecting on its honour, and hath rendered himself unworthy of any place of trust under his Majesty's Government.

SEVENTEENTHLY. – That the said *Jonathan Sewell* being such Chief Justice, Speaker of the Legislative Council, and Chairman of the Executive Council as aforesaid, hath laboured and still doth labour to promote disunion and animosity between the Legislative Council and Assembly of this Province, and hath exerted his influence as Speaker as aforesaid to prevent the passing, in the said Council, of Salutary Laws, which had been passed in the said Assembly, and hath during the present war with the United States of America fomented dissension among His Majesty's Subjects in this Province, and endeavoured, by various arts and practices, to prevent a reliance on the Loyalty and Bravery of His Majesty's Canadian

Subjects, and produce a want of confidence in the administration of His Majesty's Government, and thereby weaken its exertions.

All which crimes and misdemeanors, above mentioned, were done and committed by the said *Jonathan Sewell*, Chief Justice of the Province of Lower Canada, whereby he the said *Jonathan Sewell*, hath traitorously and wickedly and maliciously laboured to alienate the Hearts of His Majesty's subjects in this province from His Majesty, and to cause a division between them, and to subvert the constitution and laws of this Province, and to introduce an arbitrary and tyrannical Government, contrary to his own knowledge, and the known Laws of this province: and thereby he the said *Jonathan Sewell*, hath not only broken his own oath but also as far as in him lay, broken the King's oath to his people, whereof the said *Jonathan Sewell*, representing His Majesty in so high an Office of Justice, had in this province the custody: For all which the said commons do impeach the said *Jonathan Sewell*, hereby reserving to themselves the liberty of exhibiting at any time hereafter any other accusation or impeachment against the said *Jonathan Sewell*, and adopting such conclusion and prayer upon the premises, as law and Justice may require.

Heads of Impeachment of *James Monk*, Esquire, Chief Justice of His Majesty's Court of King's Bench for the District of *Montreal*, in the Province of *Lower-Canada*, by the Commons of *Lower-Canada*, in this present Provincial Parliament assembled, in their own name, and in the name of all the Commons of the said Province.

FIRST. – That the said *James Monk*, Chief Justice of His Majesty's Court of King's Bench for the District of Montreal, in the Province of Lower Canada, hath traitorously and wickedly endeavoured to subvert the Constitution and established Government of the said Province, and instead thereof to introduce an arbitrary tyrannical Government, against Law, which he hath declared by traitorous and wicked opinion, counsels, conduct, judgments, practices and actions.

SECONDLY. – That in pursuance of those traitorous and wicked purposes, the said *James Monk* hath disregarded the authority of the Legislature of this Province, and in the Courts of Justice wherein he hath presided and sat, hath usurped powers and authority which belong to the Legislature alone, and made regulations subversive of the Constitution and Laws of this Province.

THIRDLY. – That the said *James Monk*, being Chief Justice of the said Court of King's Bench for the District of Montreal, and President of the Provincial Court of Appeals, in causes appealed from the Court of King's Bench for the District of Quebec, in pursuance of the traitorous and wicked purposes aforesaid, did, on the nineteenth day of January in the year of our Lord one thousand eight hundred and nine, make, consent to, concur in, approve and publish, and caused to be made and published, by the said Court of Appeals, various regulations, under the name of *'Rules and Orders of Practice,'* in the Provincial Court of Appeals, repugnant and contrary to the Laws of this Province, whereby the said *James Monk* wickedly and traitorously, in so far as in him lay, endeavoured and laboured to change, alter and modify, and cause to be changed, altered and modified, by the said Court of Appeals, the Laws of this Province, which he was sworn to administer, and assumed legislative authority, and by the said Regulations imposed illegal burthens and restraints upon His Majesty's subjects in the exercise of their legal rights, and attributed to the said Court unconstitutional and illegal powers and authority, altogether inconsistent with the duties of the said Court, and subversive of the liberty and just and legal rights of His Majesty's subjects in this Province.

FOURTHLY. – That the said *James Monk*, being Chief Justice of the said Court of King's Bench for the District of Montreal, as aforesaid, in pursuance of the traitorous and wicked purposes aforesaid, did, in the term of February, in the year of our Lord one thousand eight hundred and eleven, make and publish, and cause to be made and published by the said last mentioned Court, various Regulations, under the name of 'Rules and Orders of Practice,' repugnant and contrary to the laws of this Province, by which Regulations the said *James Monk*, in so far as in him lay, endeavoured and laboured to change, alter and modify, and to cause to be changed, altered and modified, by the said last mentioned Court, the Laws of this Province, which he was sworn to administer and assumed Legislative authority, and by the said Regulations, imposed illegal burthens and restraints upon His Majesty's Subjects, in the exercise of their legal rights, and thereby attributed to the said last mentioned Court unconstitutional and illegal powers and authority, altogether inconsistent with the duties of the said Court, and subversive of the liberty, and just and legal rights of His Majesty's Subjects in this Province.

FIFTHLY. – That the said *James Monk*, being such Chief Justice and President of the Court of Appeals as aforesaid, and as well by the duties as the oaths of his offices bound to maintain, support and administer the laws of this Province, and award Justice to His Majesty's Subjects, according to the said laws, hath, nevertheless, in contempt of the said laws, and in violation of his said duties and oaths, set aside the said laws, and substituted his will and pleasure instead thereof, by divers unconstitutional, illegal, unjust and oppressive Rules, Orders and Judgments, which he hath made and rendered, to the manifest injury and oppression of His Majesty's Subjects in this Province, and in subversion of their most important political and civil rights.

SIXTHLY.- That the said *James Monk*, being such Chief Justice as aforesaid, in pursuance of his traitorous and wicked purposes aforesaid, hath, in the exercise of his Judicial powers, openly and publicly ascribed to the said Court of King's

Bench, the power of altering, changing and modifying the laws of this Province, and hath alleged and declared, that such power had been recognized by all the Judges of the land in the Provincial Court of Appeals, and on such his false, traitorous and wicked opinions and declarations, hath founded judgments of the said Court.

SEVENTHLY. – That the said *James Monk*, being such Chief Justice as aforesaid, and bound by the laws of this Province to protect and maintain the personal liberty of His Majesty's Subjects, and relieve them from illegal and unjust imprisonment, hath, nevertheless, contrary to his duty, and in contempt of the said laws, denied Writs of *Habeas Corpus* to persons legally entitled to them, and thereby deprived His Majesty's Subjects of their dearest and most important rights, and hath wilfully oppressed them.

EIGHTHLY. – That the said *James Monk*, being such Chief Justice as aforesaid, hath, in certain cases, promoted, counselled and advised Criminal Prosecutions, and hath afterwards exercised his judicial powers, as such Chief Justice, and hath sat in Judgment upon such Prosecutions.

All which crimes and misdemeanors abovementioned, were done and committed by the said *James Monk*, Chief Justice of the Court of King's Bench for the District of Montreal, whereby he the said *James Monk* hath traitorously, wickedly and maliciously laboured to alienate the hearts of His Majesty's subjects in this province from His Majesty, and to cause a division between them, and to subvert the constitution and laws of this province, and to introduce an arbitrary and tyrannical Government, contrary to his own knowledge, and the known laws of this province: And thereby he the said *James Monk* hath not only broken his own oath, but also, as far as in him lay, hath broken the King's Oath to his people, whereof the said *James Monk*, Esquire, representing His Majesty in so high an office of Justice, had in the said District of Montreal, the custody.

For all which the said commons do impeach the said *James Monk*, hereby reserving to themselves the liberty of exhibiting at any time hereafter any other accusation or impeachment against the said *James Monk*, and adopting such conclusions and prayer upon the premises as law and Justice may require.

N
The Gourlay Affair: Seditious Libel and the Sedition Act in Upper Canada, 1818–19
Barry Wright

1. Address to the jury, Kingston, 15 August, and notes, 20 August 1818 (RG 1, Pamphlet Collection 1-1051, file: Address to the the Jury, 1–4, 6, 21–2, NA).

PRELIMINARY NOTE, &c.

The subject of the following Address, and the manner in which it has been brought forward to notice, will, I am convinced, induce serious reflections, and make a lasting impression on the public mind. The right of free petitioning, has, for years, engaged my own special attention: – it is a subject which I have again and again agitated, at home, by my writings, and, the more it is considered, the more important will it appear. From the moment of my arrest, I looked forward to the trial, now over, as an occasion, almost enviable, for displaying, to full effect, this invaluable privilege, and, for having a clear and strong sense, of the liberty of exercising it, stamped on the minds of the people of Upper Canada. I had resolved to do my best in preparing for the trial, so that every particular, and every view of the subject, should be exhibited. For this purpose, I had resolved on going to New York, to have access to law books, &c. not, here, to be found; and, from thence, meant to have brought a short-hand writer, that every word spoken on the trial, might have been handed down to posterity. The unexpected appointment of the assizes nearly a month earlier than usual, balked these purposes: – it left me only time to cross the lake from Niagara; and, still more luckless, a bilious disorder held me feeble and feverish, almost to the hour of my appearance in court. Considering the greatness of the subject, I am truly sorry that I have not been able to do it justice. My Address is far from being equal to my wishes; it is much inferior to what it might have been made, under other circumstances; but, I trust, these explanations will find for it some excuse.

A copy of the warrant of my arrest is subjoined, in lieu of the indictment, refused; and I trust, recording the names of the worthy men who were empanelled as Jurors, will make others zealous for maintaining, unimpaired, the blessings of our glorious constitution, should any attempt, be ever again made, to deprive us of them.

WARRANT:
The King v. Robert Gourlay

MIDLAND DISTRICT – To Robert Young, high constable, or to any other constable in the town of Kingston – Greeting. – Whereas, information and complaint hath been made before me, (Thomas Markland, Esquire one of His Majesty's Justices of the peace, in and for, the said District) on oath, that Robert Gourlay late of Kingston, in the said District, Gentlemen at Kingston, in the said District, on or about the first day of June instant, unlawfully, maliciously, and wickedly, did publish and utter a false, wicked and seditious libel styled 'Principles and Proceedings of the Inhabitants of the District of Niagara, for addressing His Royal Highness the Prince Regent respecting claims of sufferers in war, lands to militia men, and the general benefit of Upper Canada, printed at the Niagara Spectator office, 1818; price one shilling, Halifax,' intending, thereby the peace and common tranquility of our lord the King, and this his Province of Upper Canada, to disquiet, molest, and disturb, and to bring the Government of our aid lord the King, in this his Province, into great hatred, contempt, and scandal, with all his faithful and liege subjects of the said Province.

These are: therefore: to charge and command you to apprehend and arrest the said Robert Gourlay, if he shall be found within your Bailiwick, and bring him before me, or some other of His Majesty's Justices of the Peace, to be dealt with as the law directs.

ADDRESS
MY LORD: GENTLEMEN OF THE JURY,

I stand before you, accused of 'unlawfully, maliciously, and wickedly, publishing, a *false, wicked,* and *seditious* libel, styled *Principles and Proceedings of Inhabitants of the District of Niagara, &c.* – intending thereby, the peace and common tranquility of our Lord the King and this his Province of Upper Canada, to disquiet, molest, and disturb, and to bring the Government of our Lord the King, in this his Province, into great hatred, contempt, and scandal, with all his faithful and liege subjects of the said Province.' These words I take from the warrant for my arrest, as a copy of the indictment has been refused ... and it is impossible for me to know, accurately, the charges preferred, from a mere hearing of the indictment read before the court.

You have just heard, Gentlemen, this accusation supported and enforced by the trained arts and eloquence of a lawyer ... Gentlemen, you feel that I address you from a written paper, and in this, had I given the Solicitor General credit for eloquence. I must retract my compliment. Never till this day did I witness, before a court of justice, such weakness – such vulgarism – such illiberality. Gentlemen, the speech of this Solicitor General of Upper Canada needs no reply: it has not set forth a single argument: indeed scarcely two of its sentences hang together; but I shall recall to your memory a few of the Solicitor's pretty assertions and insinuations ... He told you, in proof of the bad effects of my writings, that two persons were indicted for sedition at the present Assizes. Gentlemen, it is *infamous*, even to hint at such occurrences. Their bearing on my case is nothing: – towards the parties indicated, it is base and malignant. Every man stands innocent in the eye of the law until he is proved guilty; and no man, especially in the situation of a Solicitor General, has a right to prejudge and prejudice the cause of another.

This Solicitor General, after eulogizing the liberty of the press, has the assurance to tell you that I labour to obstruct it!– He has told you that all the seditious people of this Province come from home! He has compared my conduct to that of Wilcox; and expressed his expectation that my fate will be the same!– He has asked if you will join my banners in a time of peace to overturn the constitution! – He says that I have not courage to come before a Court of Justice; but that I take refuge behind a printer's desk, from whence I abuse the Government! Gentlemen, I have no patience for the whole of his stuff – it is *all infamous*. It is a disgrace to the British Government to have such a thing as this acting as Solicitor General: – it is lamentable and ruinous for the Province; – but let us proceed ...

... – Gentlemen, when I am accused of wicked intentions, and not a single proof can be given of such intention, – nay, when there is not a single motive to be discovered which could tempt me to evil; and, when a most glaring irregularity of procedure presents itself on the part of my accuser who should not only be regular, but impartial and above all influences, I am entitled to bring forward a surmise which may throw light on motions and motives otherwise so unaccountable; – but, Gentlemen, let us quit this theme, so sickening, and proceed to examine witnesses as to the fact already advanced, that I am only an accessary, not a principal, in publishing the pamphlet complained of, – a pamphlet, with which I have no more to do, as to its publication, than hundreds besides, nor any thing like so much as some others ... The rules of courts of law, Gentlemen, are seldom founded on parliamentary statutes. They are often the capricious and selfish decrees of men greedy of power; and however unreasonable – however baseless they may be, it is often difficult to get them changed for better. I could mention many instances where such rules now exist, completely subversive of justice. I shall particularize one which was happily overturned, because it will be in point to direct you in your present duty. It had been long insisted on that jurors should give their verdict, in cases of libel *only* as to the fact of publishing; and as to the law, they were governed by the judge. The present Lord Erskine gained immortal honor by overturning this rule, by the bold and persevering expression of his opinion; and as it was of infinite consequence to the liberty of the Press. – Mr. Fox, and he, introduced a bill into Parliament, and had it enacted, that in cases of libel, jurors should be free to decide for themselves upon the whole matter in issue – both fact and law.

[In the NA the following paragraph appears at the end of the preliminary note (697), cross-referenced to this spot]:

This act was passed the year after the Constitution was given to this Province. The right of Juries, therefore, is here, still, only an arbitrary right. It might be well, therefore, to have it made absolute by provincial statute.

It now only remains to be wondered at, how a free people could be so long subjected to the contrary of this, now confirmed, right. – Whoever will reflect on the nature of libel, will perceive that it is infinitely varied by circumstances, that no positive rule could possibly determine the limits of judgment; and to leave this to the dictum of the bench, would be a dangerous sacrifice of liberty. It is now therefore the established and undeniable right of jurors, impannelled for the trial of libel, to give the verdict at their own discretion on the whole matter before them. The judge may advise, but he cannot dictate as to the law. My fate, then, Gentlemen, and that of this great question, which concerns the invaluable right of free petitioning, rests entirely with yourselves; and as you decide, God and your consciences will decide for your future peace. Think not, for a moment that this is a common case, whoever may tell you so, to throw you from your guard, – think not that it only concerns me. A verdict of acquital will not only clear me of unwarrantable scandal and reproach: – it will establish for yourselves and fellow subjects, your most valuable constitutional privilege, now most, wantonly and audaciously assailed. A verdict of condemnation on the contrary, must call a strain on thousands; and as I said before, should you commit me to durance, your country's reputation and your country's freedom must also be imprisoned.

Extracted from the Kingston *Gazette*, 18 August 1818

MR. GOURLAY'S TRIAL

On Saturday, the 15th instant the case of the *King* v. *Robert Gourlay* for publishing a seditious Libel, was tried before the court of Assizes; now sitting in this Town. The publication charged as libellous was the Niagara Petition to the Prince Regent. It being a cause of great expectation, the Court House was thronged beyond what was ever known on any former occasion. The solicitor general opened the prosecution, and produced Stephen Miles, Printer, as a witness, to prove the publication of the pamphlet, which not being precisely proved, was admitted by the defendant. –Mr. Gourlay entered into a very full defence, which, we understand, will probably be published. He called John Clark, Esq. of Niagara, to prove his character and conduct in that District, & that the Petition charged to be libel, although written by the defendant, was examined, approved and published by a Committee of the Representatives of that District, with their names annexed to the publication. The defendant also called James Wilkie, Esq. Ordnance store-keeper, of Kingston, who testified that, from his earlier years, he had been well acquainted with Mr. Gourlay, having been brought up in the same neighbourhood and served under his command as a commandant of volunteers in Fifeshire; also that Mr. Gourlay's character in his native country was fair and irreproachable, and his family and connections, of the first respectability. The solicitor General replied at great length. Judge Campbell, who had exercised much patience and candour during the arguments, delivered a learned and able charge to the Jury, who withdrew, and in about half an hour returned into Court, with a verdict of *NOT GUILTY*. As soon as the verdict was delivered, an instantaneous and general burst of applause, which continued for some minutes, marked the state of the public feeling on this interesting subject.

Thus the verdict of a Jury, after a full and fair discussion in Court, has established the right of uniting in a Petition to the Prince Regent, and using the requisite means of forming such union; and has refuted the most extraordinary charge, that a large proportion of the loyal inhabitants of this Province have been guilty of a seditious Libel, by the circulating and adopting the Petition in question.

2. Extrajudicial Opinion, November 1818 (RG1, E3, Upper Canada, Executive Council Submissions, reproduced in E.A. Cruikshank, 'The Government of Upper Canada and Robert Gourlay,' *OH*, vol. 33 (1936), 65 at 164.

REPORT OF THE JUDGES TO SIR PEREGRINE MAITLAND

Having had under our consideration the statute passed in the fourty-fourth year of his Majesty's reign entitled 'an act for the better securing of this province against all seditious attempts or designs to disturb the tranquillity thereof,' we are of the opinion that in the sound Construction of that Act, the word Inhabitant is used in its popular sense, as in divers other statutes of this province, and especially in that of the fifty-sixth of the King imposing statute labour on all inhabitants, comprehending persons who have no settled abode; and that it denotes any person living in this province for the continued term of six months, although not an inhabitant householder in the strict sense of the word to entitle to any franchise the inhabitant of a town or vill.

Although otherwise for the purposes of this act we might admit proof of having taken the oath of allegiance in any of his Majesty's dominions as satisfactory, yet we are of the opinion, in conformity to the spirit of the act, that the oath of allegiance, to exempt the person from its operation, must have been taken within this province as the law was obviously enacted to guard against the seditious practices of natuaral born subjects as well as aliens, and against such as it might be presumed, had taken the oath of allegiance in the United Kingdom or some of its plantations.

We are further of the opinion that such an Inhabitant having resided six months and not taken the oath of allegiance, by an absence of some weeks in a foreign country, within the six months immediately preceding the warrant of arrest, leaving no fixed residence behind him, becomes subject, on his return, to the full operation of the statute.

YORK, 10th November 1818　　　　　　　　　　Wm. Dummer Powell, C.J.
[handwriting of Powell]　　　　　　　　　　　　Wm. Campbell, J.
　　　　　　　　　　　　　　　　　　　　　　　　D'Arcy Boulton, J.

O
Upper Canada in the 1820s:
Criminal Prosecution and the Case of Francis Collins
Paul Romney

1. Indictment of Francis Collins for libel, 10 April 1828 (JHAUC, 1829, Appendix, Report on Collins' Case; also CO 42/388/114–15).

UPPER CANADA, Home District, to Wit. The jurors for our Lord the King, upon their oath present, that Francis Collins, late of the town of York, in the Home District aforesaid, printer, being an evil disposed person and maliciously intending to scandalize and vilify the government of this province, and to excite the people of this province, to hatred of His Excellency Sir Peregrine Maitland Lieutenant Governor of the said province, on the 3rd of April in the ninth year of the reign of our Sovereign Lord George the Fourth by the Grace of God of the United Kingdom of Great Britain and Ireland, King Defender of the Faith, with force and arms, at the town of York aforesaid in the said [H]ome [D]istrict, did wickedly and maliciously print and publish, and cause and procure to be printed and published in a Newspaper entitled, 'Canadian Freeman,' a certain false, scandalous and malicious libel of and concerning the said Lieutenant Governor, in which said libel are contained amongst other things, divers scandalous and malicious matters and things of and concerning the said Lieutenant Governor, to the tenor and effect following, that is to say. 'On Thursday morning last His Excellency the Lieutenant Governor, (meaning the said Lieutenant Governor) returned to his farm at Stamford, to look after the Buck wheat and Indian corn. His Excellency (meaning the said Lieutenant Governor) looked sickly, and we hear he took his coffin with him.' Again, 'He [meaning the said Lieutenant Governor] has left town without paying our £113 10 voted to us now three times by the commons of the country. His Excellency [meaning the said Lieutenant Governor] has sworn to administer justice impartially in this Colony; How has he complied with this obligation? He has paid Mr. Fairbanks [as the Attorney General stated in the House] for work and labor done, and materials furnished by order of Duncan Cameron Esq. [meaning Esquire] without a vote of the Assembly, and he has refused to pay the Editor of the Freeman [meaning the said Francis Collins] as was properly observed by Captain Matthews, for work and labor done, and materials furnished by order of the commons of the country, after the amount having been three times voted by the Representatives of the people! Is this the impartial administration of justice? or is it partiality, injustice, and fraud?' meaning thereby falsely and wickedly to insinuate and to cause it to be believed, that the said Lieutenant Governor of this province had disregarded an oath by him taken to administer justice, and had been guilty of partiality, injustice, and fraud, to the great scandal of the said Lieutenant Governor, in contempt of our said Lord the King and his laws; to the evil example of all others in the like case offending; and against the peace of our said Lord the King, his crown and dignity.

2. *Canadian Freeman*, 16 October 1828

York Assizes. – Our Assizes commenced here on Monday last, and the Attorney and little Boulton[1] have put their heads together again on Tuesday, to see if they can do anything in the way of *libel*. On that morning the Attorney General called upon the Editor of the *Freeman* to take his trial upon one of the cases of libel held over since last assizes. The Editor, who pressed the Attorney to trial last court, when his counsel had been brought to town at a very heavy expense, by express, rose and said that he was not ready for trial neither of his counsel being in court, and that from the undetermined manner in which the Attorney General spoke last assizes, he did not expect that the proceedings would be followed up. As he had not been arraigned, however, he said he would traverse the indictment. The Attorney General, with a view of bringing us to trial unprepared, first rose, and stated an open palpable falsehood in Court – namely, that we had been arraigned last Assizes. When we contended to the contrary, to the satisfaction of the Court, the Attorney, in his native malignancy, took till next day [yesterday] to hunt up authorities to see if he could force us to trial without the privilege of traverse, contrary to the universal practice of the Court. This he attempted to show yesterday, and our old *customer* Judge Hagerman[2] was in favour of the measure. Mr. Robert Baldwin, in our behalf, stated that he was taken by surprise – that he thought from the observations of the Attorney General last Assizes, these cases were quashed – such was the opinion of Mr. [John] Rolph, leading counsel, and the defendant himself, and that as he did not think the Attorney General would refuse the right to traverse, he was not prepared to reply to his argument against it. The question is to be decided today; in the mean time, we expect Mr. Rolph here daily, and when he arrives, we shall show the Attorney and little Boulton that we are not afraid to meet them.

———

Mr. Strowbridge[']s case against the Burlington Canal Commissioners came on yesterday. The Attorney General, who brought the bill into Parliament for the relief of Mr. Strowbridge against the tyranny of the Commissioners, acted as leading Council for the Commissioners to prevent his own law from taking effect. This we view as a monstrous piece of injustice. The Attorney General argued for a nonsuit upon the principle that the Commissioners as public officers could not be sued for a Public debt of this kind. The argument was held good by the bench. The case in the end went to the Jury who acted uprightly and brought a verdict for the Contractor, £3234 14s. 8d. damages. This no doubt, from the opinion of the Judge and Attorney, will be set aside, and poor Strowbridge will be worried to beggary by the Commissioners, without the colour of justice. We have taken down the proceeding which shall soon appear.

3. Indictment of Francis Collins for libel, 21 Oct. 1828 (same as doc. 1; also CO 42/388/117–23).

UPPER CANADA

Home District, to Wit. The Jurors for Our Lord the King upon their oath present that on [M]onday the 13th day of October, in the ninth year of our Sovereign Lord George the Fourth by the Grace of God of the United Kingdom of Great Britain and Ireland King, Defender of the Faith, at York in the Home District aforesaid, a session of Oyer and Terminer and general gaol delivery, in and for the said Home District, was begun and holden at the town of York in and for the said district, before the Honorable Levius Peters Sherwood one of the Judges of His Majesty's Court of King's Bench in this province, the Honorable Wm. Allan and others their fellows, Justices of Oyer and Terminer and general gaol delivery assigned for the said district, and that the said session was duly continued by adjournment and was duly holden by the said Justices and others their fellows as aforesaid on Tuesday, the 14th of October in the year aforesaid and also on the 15th day of October ... on which said last mentioned day the said court was duly holden before the Honorable Christopher Alexander Hagerman another of the Judges of His Majesty's Court of King's Bench in this province, and also one other of the justices of Oyer and Terminer and general gaol delivery assigned for the said district as aforesaid, the Honorable William Allan, and others their fellows; and that a session of assize and Nisi Prius for the said Home District was also begun and holden on Monday the said thirteenth day of October in the year aforesaid at the Town of York in the said Home District, before the said Honorable Levius Peters Sherwood ... and was duly continued by adjournment from day to day, until and on the said fifteenth day of October ... when the same was duly holden before the said Christopher Alexander Hagerman ... And that at the said session of Oyer and

Terminer and general gaol delivery ... John Beverly Robinson, then and still being Attorney General for our said Lord the King for his province of Upper Canada, and Henry John Boulton, Esquire, then and still being Solicitor General of our said Lord the King for the said province attended and were present to prosecute for our said Lord the King in the due discharge of the duty of their aforesaid offices, and that one Francis Collins late of the town of York aforesaid, printer, stood bound by recognizance of himself and certain sureties to appear at the said court of Oyer and Terminer and general gaol delivery to be tried on a certain indictment for libel depending against him, & that at the said court of assize and Nisi Pruis holden as aforesaid on the 15th day of October ... a certain issue came on to be tried in due form of law in a cause wherein one James Gordon Strowbridge was plaintiff, and William Chisholm, Alexander Chewett, Robert Nelles and William Munson Jarvis, commissioners appointed under the authority of an Act of the Provincial Parliament of Upper Canada ... entitled 'An Act to provide for the constructing a navigable Canal between Burlington Bay and Lake Ontario,' were defendants, in a certain plea of debt, and was then and there tried before the Honorable Christopher Alexander Hagerman by a jury of the country in that behalf duly sworn and taken between the said parties. And that the said John Beverly Robinson ... was one of the counsel for the said Defendants upon the trial of the said cause. And that the said Francis Collins being an ill disposed person, and contriving and maliciously intending to bring into scandal and contempt the Administration of justice in this Province, and to defame, vilify and abuse the said Hon. Christopher Alexander Hagerman ... and the said John Beverly Robinson and Henry John Boulton so acting in the discharge of the duties of their respective offices as aforesaid on the sixteenth day of October ... with force and arms, at the town of York aforesaid ... did wickedly and maliciously print, and publish and cause and procure to be printed and published in a newspaper entitled, 'Canadian Freeman,' a certain false scandalous, and malicious libel, entitled as follows. 'York assizes,' of and concerning the proceedings of the said session of Oyer and Terminer and general gaol delivery ... against him the said Francis Collins, and of and concerning the said Christopher Alexander Hagerman ... and of and concerning the said John Beverly Robinson and Henry John Boulton, in the execution of the duties of their respective offices as aforesaid, and also of and concerning the trial of the said issue before the said Honorable Christopher Alexander Hagerman ... Which said false, scandalous and malicious libel is according to the tenor and effect following, that is to say ... [the two paragraphs printed as doc. 3 are recited] ... [and is] to the great scandal and reproach of the administration of justice in this province, in contempt of our said Lord the King and his laws, to the evil example of all others in the like case offending and against the peace of our said Lord the King his crown and dignity.

4. Judge Sherwood's charge to the jury, as taken down by Francis Collins and printed in the *Journal* of the House of Assembly[3] (Source: same as doc. 1)

The defendant Francis Collins, stands indicted for a libel, and has pleaded Not Guilty. It now becomes your duty to enquire whether he is guilty or not. The learned counsel told you very properly that you are judges of both the law and the fact. This I admit; you are so not only in this particular case, but in all criminal cases; you have the same power in all. The court will express an opinion to you; but you will exercise your own opinion and give your verdict as you may think proper.

The first witness is Allan Wilmot, a clerk in Mr. Stegman's store. It appears by this witness, that Mr. Stegman was a subscriber to this paper, and that it was the duty of the defendant in conformity with engagement to send the papers to him, which he did by a boy, who usually carries the papers through town. If you think this sufficient proof, well and good; if not, you will acquit the defendant upon this ground. With respect to the libel, you are to take the whole of his language into consideration, in order to form an opinion whether any particular parts of it be libellous, – for whoever reads this article must admit that many parts of it are not libellous. I will, therefore, read it to you, Gentlemen, and point out what I consider libellous.

It is here said that the Attorney General stated 'an open palpable falsehood' in court. You probably know whether the Attorney General did so or not; but even if he did, the defendant is not justifiable in law in publishing it in this manner. The very nature of a libel, is that which has a tendency to cause a breach of the peace; and any thing of that kind, whether true or false, is punishable by law, because, to keep the public peace, is paramount to every thing else, and whether true or false, it has the same tendency to excite public feeling, and drive persons to a breach of the peace. Therefore in my opinion, Gentlemen, to tell the Attorney General or any other respectable counsel at the bar – that he asserted 'an open palpable falsehood,' is an indictable offence, and is what the law terms libel. The learned counsel for the defendant told you that the term 'falsehood,' was very different from 'a lie,' – that the former was simply an untruth, while the latter was an untruth known to be such: – But my opinion is, that the terms 'open palpable falsehood,' and 'a lie,' are synonimous.

Then the Attorney General assumed a question in court, whether or not the defendant had a right to traverse, and said he would take the pains to examine law authorities on the point to shew that he had not that right, and the defendant accuses him of doing this in his 'native malignancy.' Now, Gentlemen, this I consider a most improper assertion. In Johnson's Dictionary, you will find that 'malignancy,' means *an inclination to hurt others!* and if this sense be adopted, the assertion is tantamount to this, *that the Attorney General* possesses a *natural inclination to injure others*. It is then for you gentlemen to consider the character of the Attorney General, and the high office which he fills, and say whether he be a man of this kind. If you cannot answer this question in the affirmative, if you cannot say that the Attorney General possesses a natural inclination to hurt others, must you not determine that such an assertion is calculated to injure his feelings and lead to a breach of the peace. Would not any of you be disposed to break the peace, and disturb society, under similar circumstances? And if you met a man in the streets who thus libelled you, would you not knock him down? If so, then it amounts to *a libel*, as having a tendency to lead to a breach of the peace.

In another part of this paper, the case of Mr. Stro[w]bridge is alluded to. The Attorney General is accused of becoming leading counsel for the Burlington Bay Canal Commissioners, to prevent his own law (the bill which he brought into parliament for the relief of Mr. Stro[w]bridge,) from taking effect. This is an assertion, Gentlemen, that I consider very injurious to the Attorney General as a member of parliament and a barrister of the country. The Editor says this law was his own, because he introduced the bill into the house. Now this is not correct, because a member cannot introduce a bill without leave of a majority of the house, and when brought in, it must go through a first, second and third reading: any member may object to it; and if the majority go with him it cannot pass. But this is not all, gentlemen: It has to pass another branch of the legislature also, and further, to receive the assent of the representative of his majesty, before it can become a law. All these formalities are to be gone through, gentlemen, and can you believe that the editor, who is a man of information, believed his own assertion, when he stated that this was the Attorney General's *own law?* I would be sorry gentlemen, that it should be an objection to any person as a member of Parliament, that he belonged to the Bar. It would be a great loss to the country, if no Lawyers were to be elected. They are men of information, and ought to be mixed with other honest men in Legislative Assemblies. In England, at one time when lawyers were not elected, it was called 'the lack learning Parliament;' but now gentlemen of the Bar are returned as frequently as others.

The editor goes on to say, that this we view as monstrous injustice. The counsel said that what the editor meant by the words 'this we view,' was merely to give his own opinion, and not to speak positively: but I consider this gentlemen *as a positive assertion*, and if so, it is libellous. You heard the objections of the Attorney General himself to this part; and he took a view of it which I must confess, the language will not, in my opinion, bear, unless very much strained. An editor has a right to comment on the courts of justice, and it has an excellent effect, when his remarks are temperately brought out with a view to give information; but when an editor descends to scurrility and intemperance, it is most improper and dangerous to the administration of justice. Here the liberty of the press is abused by licentiou[s]ness in going beyond the proper bounds. It is easy for you, gentlemen, to see when the line is passed between that which is proper and decorous, and that which is indecent and scurrilous, which ought to be punished; and the improper liberty of the press restrained.

In the next place the editor speaks of his *'old customer,'* Judge Hagerman. Now, I view the expression *'customer,'* [as] a figurative allusion to the business of merchants or mechanics, and it clearly implies that the editor of this paper, has made remarks upon this gentleman before, *as a retailer of calumny; but, in my opinion gentlemen, this editor is no petty retailer, but a wholesale retailer of calumny.* This is my opinion gentlemen, and, as a Judge of this court, I have a right to express it. It is contended by some, that a judge has not the power to express his opinion in this way; but I contend that he has the power; a constitutional power to express his opinion on all matters that come before him – a power too that ought always to be exercised by a judge in the discharge of his duty; and I shall always give my opinion freely, where I think my duty calls me to do so. I think, gentlemen, that this is a libel; a gross and scandalous libel; but you can determine as you think proper; and whether you determine that it is a libel, or is not, I shall still have the same good opinion of you; as I know you will determine as you think right, and I have done my duty.

5. Levius P. Sherwood to Z. Mudge, 5 Dec. 1828 (Source: same as doc. 1; also CO 42/388/70–2, 129–30).

The following are the principal grounds of my judgment, in the case of the King vs. Francis Collins, lately convicted of a libel on the Att'y. General. I think all publications of this kind have the effect to create ill blood in society, and therefore manifestly tend to a breach of the public peace, which is always regarded of the greatest importance by all civilized governments. Such publications also have a direct and undoubted tendency to impede the due administration of public justice, by generating a bad feeling and injurious prejudice in the public mind, & more particularly in the minds of the jurors who are summoned for the trial of causes. This libel, in my opinion, was intended to obstruct the administration of justice, because it was printed and published during the sitting of the court, and just before the defendant was tried for printing and publishing an alleged libel on Sir Peregrine Maitland, then the Lieutenant Governor of the province. Any person who writes and publishes fair and candid opinions on the system of government and constitution of the country, or points out what he honestly conceives to be grievances, and in a proper and decent manner, proposes legal means for the redress of such grievances; or if any person in his publications enters into a just and useful criticism of the productions of others, and shews the public their errors and absurdities; or if any one in a decent and proper manner exposes the errors & wrong opinions of public men; or if he exhibits the evil tendency & unconstitutional bearing of public measures, such person, in my opinion, deserves encouragement. If such publisher, however, steps aside from the high road of decency and peaceable deportment, and adopts a course of public calumny and open abuse against the officers of government generally, or particularly against the principal law officer of the crown in the legal execution of his duty in the King's courts, as the defendant did, then I think he should be published to the extent, which, in human probability, would prevent a recurrence of the offence; any thing short of this would be nugatory, and have an effect contrary to the ends proposed by all punishments.

Taking all the circumstances of the case into consideration, Mr. Justice Hagerman and myself deemed the sentence which we passed on the defendant, both proper and necessary, for the public good, and what the case itself required.

6. Excerpts from the evidence taken by the select committee on the petition of Francis Collins (Source: same as doc. 1.)

John Beverley Robinson, Attorney General: [Q: On what authority is it, that persons are held to bail for good behavior, before they have been convicted of the offences?] I have not had occasion to argue this question but I have always considered that the power exercised by Judges and Justices of the Peace of binding to their good behaviour persons indicted for libels scandalizing the government as well as persons indicted for some other offences, rests upon the Statute 34 Edward 3rd ch. 1 – but I am not prepared to say, that it rests exclusively on that Statute. The power is recognized by the best authorities known to our law, and has been exercised both in antient and modern times. It has been applied without question being made, (so far as I have found) of its propriety, even in a case of words not indictable, but which tended to bring a court of Justice into contempt.

This authority, confided by the law of England to those who are appointed to administer the laws, does not seem to have been regarded as unconstitu[t]ional in other countries. In Lower Canada it has been exercised by the court, after the legality had been questioned and solemnly argued, and in the United States, where the freedom of the press is generally understood even to be more unrestricted than in England, it will be found to have been used, as it appears, without hesitation or question as to the right, in a case of libel, even before any Indictment had been found.

Mr. McKean, a lawyer of eminence formerly Chief Justice, and afterwards Governor of Pennsylvania, in a charge delivered to the grand Jury of the city and county of Philadelphia, on the 27 November 1797, after an exposition of the law relative to libels, informs them, 'that a certain printer in that city, (meaning Cobbet[t] the publisher of Porcupine's Gazette)[4] was, and long had been in the habit of offending against the law by the publication of scandalous, and malicious libels[,] that he had interfered and endeavoured to arrest the progress of this offender *by binding him over to be of good behaviour,* but that the printer in contempt of this recognizance, and in defiance of the authority of the law, persisted in his mischievous course, and that the duty of arresting him now devolved on the grand jury, by whom alone the strong correctives appearing to be necessary could be applied.'

I cite this instance not because it is of so much weight as the English authorities upon the same point, but because it may be satisfactory to shew that our system of jurisprudence does not sanction a more rigorous control over the evils of a licentious press than has been exercised in another country where the freedom of the press is often erroneously supposed to exist almost without control.

It is to be borne in mind, that ... neither the principal nor his sureties can suffer any penalty, until the former has been found guilty by a jury of an offence subsequent to the taking of the recognizance.

John Beverley Robinson (second appearance): [Q: Were you present when Judge Sherwood said in court, that the law allowing jurors to find a special verdict in case of libel, was not in force in this province; – but as it was the practice of the court to receive special verdicts, although it was not the law, he would, had he been in court when the jurors brought in the verdict, have received it.] I took no part in the argument upon the objection raised by the Prisoner's Counsel after verdict ... I was present, and I think the whole time. It is not my impression that Mr. Justice Sherwood made any remark of the kind mentioned in the conclusion of the question, or say what he would, or would not have done, had he been present when the verdict was given.

I recollect that some discussion arose in the course of the argument as to whether the British Act 32 Geo. 3rd respecting libels was in force in this Province and that both at the Bar and on the Bench different opinions were expressed. What Mr. Justtice Sherwood's impression was at first I do not now recollect, but I remember perfectly, that having it distinctly impressed upon my mind, from former investigation, that that Statute was in force here, I did, in the manner of an Amicus Curioe, state, that it was in force, & that I produced from the library of the Law Society in the adjoining room the volume of the Statutes at large, containing that particular act, and shewed from the month in which it was passed, that it must have been an existing Statute in England, at the period up to which we adopted the criminal law, viz. September, 1792.

Donald Bethune, MPP: [Q: Do you consider it legal to incarcerate a person charged with Libel, before conviction.] By the Statute 34 Edward 3d cap. 1 Justices are empowered 'to take of all them *that be* not of good fame, where they shall be found, sufficient surety and mainprize of their *good behaviour*, towards the King and his people, &c.' It is holden that under this Statute, a man may be bound to his *good behaviour*, for speaking words of contempt of an inferior magistrate, as a Justice of the Peace, or Mayor of a Town; or for words that either directly tend to a breach of the peace, or to *scandalize the government*, by abusing those who are entrusted by it with the administration of Justice; and this *without* any trial pending, in the same manner as sureties for keeping the peace are required. There are many other words that would justify a justice in binding a man over to his good behaviour under this Statute, which it would be useless to particularize. After Indictment found for libel, there is an absolute necessity for requiring Bail; and in that case there is a greater necessity than *before* indictment, for requiring also that the party against whom the Indictment is found, shall be bound to his good behaviour, if the libel be such as would justify such a course in the first instance. In case of refusal to give sureties for his good behaviour, the justices, where no trial is pending, and the court, where a Bill of Indictment is found, are of course bound to imprison the person complained of, otherwise the provisions of the law would be nugatory.

[Do you consider any such Law consistent with the rational liberty of the Press.] I do; and in giving this opinion, I trust, I shall not be considered an enemy to 'the rational liberty of the Press[.]' I consider a press conducted upon sound principles, inestimable – but, when all principle is set at nought, it then becomes an engine of great moral evil, and should undoubtedly be restrained and kept within proper bounds. The Statute 34 Edward 3d cap. 1, I do not think at all opposed to a press conducted upon proper principles, but it is most decidedly opposed to its licentiousness. It will be observed, that this law is calculated to *prevent* the commission of crime; and it has always been considered by wise legislators, that those laws which tend to the *prevention* of crime, are much more salutary and desirable than those which only provide a punishment for offences actually committed. It is plain that the law which *prevents* a man from doing mischief is much more humane and perfect, and less arbitrary and oppressive, than those which merely provide a punishment for that mischief. To prevent an improper exercise of the discretion which the law gives to the Magistrate in cases where no trial is pending, he is bound, when he commits a man for want of sureties, to express with 'convenient certainty,' the cause thereof; and it is at his peril, if he commit without good cause.

James A. Sampson, MPP: [Q: Do you consider that the existence of any law authorising incarceration of a person charged with Libel, before conviction, (is) consistent with the rational liberty of the Press?] The terms of the question are too vague for a direct answer, but by reference to the first question of Mr. Bethune's examination and to the object for which this Committee was appointed, I understand 'incarceration' intended to mean imprisonment on refusal of Sureties of the peace.

From the *manner* of the question, I assume that the committee are perfectly acquainted with the law on the subject as it now stands, and as it has stood for centuries. It is therefore unnecessary to quote precedents or refer to experi[e]nce to prove its' utilily [sic]. Leaving the law therefore entirely out of view, I will reply: That nothing in my opinion contributes so much to the support of a good Government, as the freedom of the Press. It is emphatically a terror to evil doers, and a praise to them that do well. This freedom, I consider as firmly established as Magna Charta. It's own licentiousness MAY, but no other cause, or power, or combination ever can destroy or abridge the rational liberty of the Press.'

It is therefore the duty of every man, but particularly and imperatively of our Judicature to withstand every attempt to check its usefulness or to extend its abuse. Happily for British Subjects the Spirit of the English Law is to prevent the commission of an offence, rather than to retaliate by the punishment of an offender. If therefore those whom the State has appointed to administer this preventive justice, have just and reasonable grounds shown to them that an offence, either by libel or otherwise, is about to be committed, it is their duty to require from the person so accused, such surety as will in probability deter him from his purpose, and ensure his good behaviour. The principle is much strengthened, if an accusation for a similar offence is pending against the same offender. This is not to punish a man for his *intentions*, but to secure the public from an anticipated injury. In cases of libel, and particularly libel on the administration of justice, without such restriction, an offender might ensure impunity by a repetition of his offence. Such a restriction can never injure a good man. It may and does afford some security to the public, against the malice and wickedness of the bad.

For these and many other reasons, I consider the law as it at present exists, authorising imprisonment in case of refusal of sureties for good behaviour, not only consistent with, but absolutely necessary to maintain the rational liberty of the press.

7. Resolutions reported by the committee on the petition of Francis Collins and adopted by the House of Assembly (Source: same as doc. 2; also CO 42/388/97–100).

1st. RESOLVED, that while prosecutions have been instituted and encouraged against Francis Collins, Hugh C. Thomson, M. P. and William Lyon McKenzie,

M. P. editors of papers opposing the injurious policy pursued by the late provincial administration, other papers under the patronage and pay of the provincial government, have been allowed to disseminate with impunity far grosser and more dangerous libels against the house of assembly, as well as against many public and private men.

...

5. Resolved, that the select committee of the Imperial House of Commons upon Canada affairs, urged in the most especial manner upon His Majesty's government, that a strict and instant enquiry should take place into all the circumstances attending the prosecutions for libel instituted in Lower Canada, with a view to giving such instructions upon them as should be consistent with justice and policy – which recommendation was properly respected and observed in Lower Canada, and ought not to have been slighted and disregarded in this province.

6. Resolved, that the document marked D ... contains a true report of material parts of the charge delivered by Mr. Justice Sherwood to the jury; which charge was an unwarrantable deviation from the matter of record, and a forced construction of language, contrary to the ends of fair and dispassionate justice.

7. Resolved, that Mr. Justice Hagerman who was one of the persons alleged on the record to be libelled, refused to receive the verdict as first tendered by the jury, viz: 'guilty of libel against the Attorney General only,' – and directed them to find a general verdict of Guilty, – with which direction the jury complied, whereby the defendant was made to appear on record guilty of charges of which the jury had acquitted him, and whereby false grounds were afforded upon the record for an oppressive and unwarrantable sentence.

8. Resolved, that it appears from the appended copy of the letter of Judge Sherwood to His Excellency [doc. 5 above] that Mr. Justice Hagerman alleged on the record to be libelled, did concern himself with Mr. Justice Sherwood, in measuring the punishment of the defendant, thereby, without necessity for it, further violating the rule, that a man shall not be judge in his own case.

9. Resolved, that from the language of Judge Sherwood in his said letter, viz: 'if such publisher, however, steps aside from the high road of decency and peaceable deportment, and adopts a course of public calumny and open abuse against the officers of the Government generally, or particularly against the principal law officer of the crown, in the legal execution of his duty in the King's Courts, as the defendant did, then I think he should be punished to that extent, which in human probability, would prevent a recurrence of the offence: any thing short of this would be nugatory, and have an effect contrary to the ends proposed by all punishments,' it too plainly appears that the punishment inflicted upon the said

Francis Collins, was not confined to the verdict as originally tendered by the jury.

10. Resolved, that the punishment inflicted upon Francis Collins ... is, considering the state of the province and circumstances of the defendant, shamefully disproportioned to his offence, – subversive of the freedom of the press, under pretence of correcting its excesses; and destructive of the liberty of the subject, under pretence of punishing an offender.

...

14. Resolved, that the doctrine laid down in the letter of Judge Sherwood, viz: that the extent of punishment should be such as will in all human probability, prevent the recurrence of the offence – and that any thing short of it would be nugatory, and have an effect contrary to the ends proposed by all punishment – is an unjust and imperfect view of such a question, dangerous in a Judge entrusted with the administration of criminal justice of this country, and calculated to render the criminal law so administered a scourge to the community.

15. Resolved, that it is inconsistent with the liberty of the press, that a person should, before conviction, be called to find bail for good behaviour, upon so indefinite an offence as libel; and that the law under which such proceeding is justified in this province, is well objected to by Lord Ashburton in the following terms: 'I never heard till very lately, that Attornies General, upon the caption of a man supposed a libeller, could insist on his giving securities for his good behaviour. It is a doctrine injurious to the freedom of every subject, derogatory from the old constitution, and a violent attack if not an absolute breach of the liberty of the press. It is not law, and I will not submit to it.'

16. Resolved, that an earnest appeal be made to His Majesty, to relax, in this case, the rigor of that law, which was made for the happiness and welfare of the people, who pray for its relaxation – and that His Majesty be requested to lay these resolutions and documents before the Imperial Legislature.

8. Judge Sherwood to Sir John Colborne, 26 March 1829 (Source: CO 42/388/134–41).

... Every person conversant with judicial proceedings must be well aware that in prosecutions for libels made up of a variety of matter containing abstract allusions and ambiguous insinuations it is necessary for the Judge who looks to the ends of Justice to be explicit in his charge. The Jury always expect this since the passing of the Statute 32 Geo. 3 Cap. 60 relative to the trial for libel. That act expressly requires the Judge to give his opinion according to his discretion on the matter in issue between the Crown and the Defendant. It must always be well known to those who are in the constant habit of attending Courts of Justice that charges to Juries on the trial of causes during the hurry and press of public business at the Assizes are not expected to be so free from error as opinions of the Court delivered on solemn argument in Term time. When however the charge of a judge appears to be right in the main and generally applicable to the circumstances of the case under consideration, such charge, I conceive, ought not to be arraigned on account of occasional or casual expressions which upon more mature reflection might possibly be found incorrect. Juries are too well informed at this day to be mislead [sic] by any such accidental remarks, because they regard the strong features of a case much more than its fainter lineaments and very rarely form their opinion on extraneous or irrelevant matter.

The Jury who tried Collins were, as I am told, respectable and well informed men and the circumstance of their confining their verdict to the particular part of the indictment which relates to the Attorney General, clearly proves their capacity to discriminate and their inclination to exclude every thing doubtful. The House of Assembly even could find no fault with the Jury. It seems to me when a Jury arrives at a just and legal conclusion that the great object of a public trial is attained and that it is not reconcileable [sic] to natural Justice or to legal usage to examine with eagle eyes the whole proceedings for no other purpose but to discover some unintentional and trifling mistake. I have always considered it the bounden duty of a Judge to cause Justice to be done to the utmost of his ability in every case. His oath requires it and his conscience cannot be satisfied without it. In all capital cases the Judge is certainly the constitutional Counsel for the prisoner but the maxim can signify nothing more than that the Judge shall take care the prisoner is not unlawfully convicted, but if the prisoner in truth appears to be guilty the Judge should not be designedly instrumental in an unlawful acquittal. On trials for misdemeanours the Defendant may always have Counsel and Collins at his trial had two, who very properly used their best endeavours to ensure a favourable result to the cause of their client, although I have never heard that they themselves doubted the propriety and Justice of his conviction. Indeed the case of Collins is one whose bearing and object could not readily be mistaken. The Defendant offered no evidence in his defence and the case rested solely on the Testimony for the Crown. Under these circumstances it appeared to me the natural and only true inference which could be drawn by the Jury from the publication itself must be that it was malicious and the general tenor of all my remarks to the Jury went to support that opinion. If the Defendant had proved any circumstances to justify the publication in Law the presumption of malice would have been taken away but this was not done and the evil tendency of the matter appeared by the record in such a way as not to be misunderstood. Malice according my opinion was therefore proved by the publication without the aid of extrinsic evidence and the only remaining essential necessary to prove an indictable misdemeanour and to complete the offence was the tendency of the Defendant's publication to a breach of the peace. Upon reading the indictment when the cause came on for trial it struck me that there was a difference in the law respecting libels against a public Magistrate acting as a Judge and the law respecting libels against the Attorney General acting as such. I supposed however that the general law of libel against private individuals was also applicable to this case so far as it concerned the Attorney General and I shaped my remarks to the Jury principally but not altogether on this impression for I was fully convinced the libel against the Attorney General had a tendency likewise to obstruct the administration of Justice. With respect to the incidental remarks I made on the circumstance of the Attorney General being a member of the Legislature they were suggested by a part of the matter charged in the indictment as libellous and were only alluded to as indicative of the Defendant's intention which was to be determined by the Jury.

When the Jury retired for deliberation they carried with them the paper containing the alleged libel and therefore had the opportunity and the means of forming their own opinion of the Defendant's intention as well as the tendency of his act. The latter essential the law always implies from a libel like the one of which the Defendant was convicted but I thought it necessary to explain to the Jury the reason of this legal implication although I think the Jury should admit the principle and ought not to reject it in any case where malice is implied. I am quite sensible of the imperfections of my charge and few Judges perhaps upon mature consideration would find all their charges exactly as they intended but at the same time I am not aware of its having produced any illegal result. The House of Assembly themselves do not deny the guilt of the Defendant. To what useful purpose then can these resolutions tend? After the verdict was recorded the Counsel for the Defendant raised several objections in Law which were afterwards argued and determined, but no objection whatever was made to the verdict on the ground of misdirection or mistake of the Court, and the Committee that framed the resolutions formed their opinion altogether from a statement made out by the Defendant himself ...

[He next refers to his letter of 5 Dec. 1828 (doc. 5 above).]

... I did not mean to intimate in that letter, and no unprejudiced person can think I did that a punishment not allowed by the laws of nature and society and not commensurate to the offence should ever be inflicted upon any one. The time, place and manner of committing an offence, the age, character and circumstances of the offender should always be considered before his sentence is passed, and they were fully considered in the case of Collins and in that of every other person convicted before me. That the chief end of human punishment is the prevention of crime and that the measure of such punishment should be adapted to that end and in such manner as the Law allows in each case has always been my opinion and my conduct as a Judge has uniformly accorded with it. No other men or body of men but the House of Assembly have ever presumed to intimate that I am inclined to severity either as a man or a Judge and the uncourteous style in which some of the resolutions are drawn up afford abundant reason to suspect that prejudice has been allowed indulgence and party spirit has been called in active exercise. The short letter I wrote in compliance with Your Excellency's directions, and which is so frequently alluded to in the resolutions of the House of Assembly Your Excellency must be well aware could not be intended as a grave treatise on crimes and punishment because its only object was to assist Your Excellency in Council to determine how far it would be proper to release Collins from the penalties of the whole sentence according to the prayer of his petition. I gave my honest sentiments to the best of my Judgment without the most distant idea of advancing any new doctrine respecting crimes and punishments or any opinion not approved of by the best writers on criminal jurisprudence. In what particulars the House of Assembly have discovered that the doctrine expressed in my letter differs from the doctrine advanced by such writers I have yet to learn, for they have not found it convenient to be so explicit as to lead to the discovery. Your Excellency, I have no doubt, obtained every information respecting the circumstances of Collins' case and of his character in society before you finally determined not to release him from the imprisonment to which the Court sentenced him and I have every reason to believe the matter was previously submitted to the opinion of His Majesty's Council for their report on the case and that they are most probably as capable of determining on the correctness of legal doctrine as the House of Assembly are. If any regret for the past or inclination to better habits for the future could have been discovered on the part of Collins I have no doubt they would not have escaped Your Excellency's notice or have failed to produce the usual and proper effects.

The ninth resolution of the House of Assembly appears to be wholly formed from an isolated part of my letter and contains a positive assertion that the punishment of Collins was not confined to the verdict as originally tendered by the Jury, and a direct insinuation when connected with the seventh resolution, that the sentence was grounded on other parts of the indictment as well as that to which the verdict applied. The assertion and insinuation are both incorrect. It should always be presumed that public Magistrates are actuated by justifiable motives unless the contrary can clearly be made to appear but this resolution contravenes the legal presumption in favour of magistrates and unjustly imputes illegal conduct to the Judges upon the pretended evidence arising from an unfair and perverted interpretation of the meaning of my letter. I there particularly confined my remarks so far as they regarded Collins to the offence of a public calumny and open abuse of the principal Law officer of the Crown, meaning the Attorney General, in the discharge of his legal duty in the King's Courts and of which offence Collins had been convicted, but I never intimated that he had been convicted or even accused of the offence of public calumny and open abuse of the officers of Government generally. The sentence in my letter to which I allude consists of two distinct parts connected together by the disjunctive conjunction *or* and each part so connected contains a distinct subject. In the former part the officers of Government generally are mentioned, in the latter part one particular officer the principal Law officer of the Crown is alluded to and I expressed an opinion that if a publisher libelled the persons referred to in either part of the sentence he should be punished to the extent I mentioned and I further alleged that Collins had done what was expressed by the latter part of the sentence, that is to say adopted a course of calumny and open abuse against the principal Law officer of the Crown in the legal execution of his duty in the King's Courts. The affirmation of the act of Collins was intended to refer to the latter part of the sentence only according to the real truth of the case. The very first sentence in my letter alleges that Collins had been convicted of a libel on the Attorney General and can any candid person suppose that after I had expressly confined his conviction by my first statement to a libel against one particular person I could possibly wish to intimate that he should be punished for a libel on the Officers of Government generally? That the ninth resolution does in fact allege so gross an absurdity I will not positively assert, but that it unjustly conveys an opinion that the Court of Oyer and Terminer sentenced a man to punishment for some offence of which he was never convicted no one I think can doubt. They impute no sinister motives to the Judges and give no reason for their opinion but the one which I have examined and shewn to be visionary and groundless. They do not deny the legality and justice of the verdict but arraign the conduct of the Judges for not confining their sentence to that verdict when the real truth is that it was so confined. The Committee who reported this resolution after sitting some months and calling before them a number of witnesses among whom were several of the Jury themselves at last came to a conclusion expressly stated to be drawn from premises which every candid man must see are wholly insufficient to warrant it ...

I will now take the liberty of making a few observations on the seventh and eighth resolutions of the House of Assembly which go to impeach the conduct of Mr. Justice Hagerman. It was not intended that Gentleman should take any part in the judicial proceedings against Collins but I was during the whole Court afflicted with indisposition and great dibility occasioned by a severe attack of the prevailing fever of the Country. The trial continued from an early part of the day to a late hour in the evening and during the whole of that time I was almost incapable of attending to any public business but after the Jury retired I became so ill as to be obliged to request the favour of his attending in Court the verdict, which was returned late in the night. The presence of one of the Judges of the Court of King's Bench is indispensably necessary to constitute a Court of Oyer and Terminer. After the verdict was rendered it appeared the Defendant had not been found guilty of any part of the charge which related to Mr. Justice Hagerman and it was then supposed that no legal objection could possibly be taken against the discharge of his duty as a Judge and he therefore remained on the Bench during the subsequent proceedings in this case precisely as he did in all others. Although the Judges have never interfered in the least with politics, although their enemies do not accuse them of it and the libel in question has no allusion to politics, yet all attacks on the Court of King's Bench seem to have originated with a political party. No sinister or corrupt motives are imputed to the Judges, all disapprobation appears confined to casual errors of the natural Judgment at most, no partiality or prejudice is found in the Jury, no comparison is attempted to be made between the sentence of Collins and that of other persons convicted of libel in England and in this Province, yet the majority of the House of Assembly condemn the Judges for their proceedings in the most unqualified terms. Without descending to further particulars I must leave it to Your Excellency to determine from your own observation and experience what motives have produced so much public heat and sensibility in the cause of a printer who in my opinion has been justly convicted of an offence destructive in its consequences to the best interests of the community.

As a British subject and a British Judge I have uniformly endeavoured to do my duty in an upright manner to the best of my judgment and abilities and according to the dictates of my conscience without prejudice or favour and without the least regard to the views or feelings of any party in the Community and the House of Assembly have been able to discover but one solitary case against which they find the least pretext for objection. It is my opinion that the animadversions and censures which the resolutions contain must weaken the administration of Justice by lessening the authority and respectability of the Bench in the opinion of those who do not understand or who wish to oppose the laws of this country. All the well disposed and enlightened men of the Province are convinced of the absolute necessity of endeavouring to prevent the bad effects arising from frequent publications tending to the obstruction of Justice, the deterioration of a fair and unbiassed trial by Jury, and the consequent taking away from all Courts a proportion of their power to do justice, and it may not be considered unworthy of observation that the first resolution of the House expressly declares two of the Members of the House of Assembly to be editors of newspapers and actually indicted for libel. I have the utmost confidence in the honor, Justice and liberality of His Majesty's Government and their well known anxiety to countenance morality and good order in society and promote the peace and happiness of his Majesty's loyal and faithful subjects in this Colony and I have equal confidence in the acknowledged Justice and ability of your Excellency to discover the motives and appreciate the worth of public men and public measures...

9. John Beverley Robinson to Sir John Colborne, 4 April 1829 (Source: CO 42/388/150–61).

... In obedience to Your Excellency's commands, I beg to remark –

Upon the first resolution – that in a period of sixteen years during which I have been a Crown Officer, I believe, I have brought to trial but three Cases of Indictment for libel against the Editors of Newspapers.

One of these was in 1819 in consequence of an address of the House of Assembly to the Lt. Governor requesting that the Defendant might be prosecuted – And the other two were against Francis Collins, upon one of which he was acquitted, and on the other convicted. Several other indictments have within this twelve-month been found against the same defendant, but I have foreborne to proceed upon them, for reasons which I have had occasion to state in former communications that have been transmitted to His Majesty's Government–

These were not all cases of proceedings instituted by me ex officio; some of them originated in presentments of the Grand Jury – and others upon the complaint of persons libelled –

The Mr McKenzie mentioned in this resolution, with the addition of M.P., was not a Member of the Assembly, and never had been, at the time when the Grand Jury made the presentment against him for libel upon which he was afterwards indicted – I mention this because any stranger might naturally imagine that it was intended to insinuate in the resolution that he was selected as an object for punishment, because he had taken a particular part in the Assembly – Though the paper on which he was indicted was sufficiently scurrilous, it is not of that class of libels that I think should be selected for prosecution in preference to others of a more criminal nature, and with Your Excellency's concurrence, I have signified to the Defendant's Counsel my intention not to proceed upon it.

Mr. Thomson another Member of the Assembly concurring in these resolutions was indicted at the last Assizes in the Midland District for a libel upon the then

Lieutenant Governor of an aggravated description. It consisted not of that mere unmeaning ribaldry, and vulgar abuse, which so much disfigure political discussions in this Province, but it was a grave statement of certain supposed facts in which the Lieutenant Governor was charged with having from motives of favoritism corruptly licensed a person to smuggle goods – I not only knew the statement to be false, but I had also the best reason to know that the printer, from particular inquiry made by him some months before, was perfectly well aware, when he admitted so injurious a statement into his paper, that it was utterly without truth – Mr. Thomson traversed at the last Assizes, and these cases of libel against him and Mr. McKenzie were therefore both pending, when in their places in the Assembly they concurred in passing these resolutions —

With respect to the latter part of this resolution it contains an assertion, of which I do not admit the truth, and of which I could scarcely admit that it could possibly be true, to the extent of the statement – That other papers besides those prosecuted have of late years contained articles against the House of Assembly as clearly libellous as any that for a series of years before had been teeming from the presses of Mr. Collins and Mr. McKenzie is, I dare say, true – Why I have hitherto not selected for punishment any printer or publisher of articles of this description (confined I mean to the Assembly and to the conduct of its Members) I am perfectly ready to explain, if required, as I have indeed done both in the Courts of Justice and in the Assembly – I am convinced that such an explanation can not be necessary here – and if it be desired in any other quarter, then certain facts which are perfectly notorious must be stated, however extraordinary they may appear – In the mean time it is to be observed that it is not for any libel of that description that Mr. Collins has been convicted, or indicted.

With respect to libels upon 'private men,' I have only to remark that I have never prosecuted for a libel upon any private individual unless at his desire, and that I have never refused to prosecute upon the application of any individual making a complaint, and furnishing proof – I can not admit that a comparison can with any degree of justice be instituted between the papers published by Mr. Collins and Mr. McKenzie, and any other newspapers published in this Country, or, (I am not sure that I might not add), in any other. If the numbers of Mr. Collins [sic] paper published since his conviction have any parallel in libels as atrocious directed against the Judges of a superior Court in any part of the British dominions, I am ignorant of that fact. In this province I consider that they are without parallel – Under any imputation of undue rigor against these printers I am perfectly easy, but I will confess that I can not so readily acquit myself for suffering them to continue unpunished for years in a licentious abuse of the press which has been pernicious as an example, and which I fear has had an unfavorable effect upon public morals, and been injurious to the character and interests of the Province. Why I did forbear so long I have fully explained on a former occasion – I was actuated by reasons which have had many able advocates in most Countries, and if I have been disappointed in the result I anticipated, it has been an error in judgment which I much regret, but of which most certainly the persons alluded to have no reason to complain ...

I need only say of [the fifth] Resolution, that no recommendation of a Committee of the English House of Commons with respect to prosecutions depending in Lower Canada, was ever made the matter of instruction to me, and that I must think it would have been rather extraordinary, if it had been – In the absence of any order from the Government I must exercise my own discretion, and for the manner in which I have exercised that discretion I am of course responsible – I had no idea, however, that a Committee of the English House of Commons ever meant to recommend that libels on Courts of Justice should ever be protected from punishment in the ordinary Course of law, and I am at a loss to know in what manner the Assembly intended to apply the Report they allude to the case of Francis Collins –

Resolution 15th. If, in any case, a person indicted for libel but not yet tried may be required to find surety for good behaviour, it would be in a case of a person of libel published by a person so indicted during the sitting of a Court, traducing the Judge, the Crown officers, and the parties in a Cause, and evidently designed to procure his own acquittal in the case depending before the same Court. The exacting such security in this case was purely the act of the Court – I did not move it, or press it, but I have never found reason to doubt that the legality of such a proceeding is supported by unquestionable authority, and I must remark that, without inquiring on what occasion it was, or in what capacity Lord Ashburton maintained the doctrine he is supposed to have advanced in the passage on which the Assembly so implicitly relies, a judicial decision would have derived little weight from its being clinched with the declaration 'It is not law, and I will not submit to it.' If it was in the course of a Parliamentary discussion that Lord Ashburton undoubtedly a most eminent lawyer made this bold assertion, it would be easy to shew that in more modern times, and on a similar occasion, the power which His Lordship exclaims against, has been more dispassionately asserted, and vindicated as incontrovertible by even higher authority –

I have not presumed to offer any remark upon those resolutions which are intended to cast reproach upon the Judges and I shall only add that there is no Country in the world in which the Press enjoys by law more freedom than in Upper Canada, that I sincerely believe there is none in which that freedom has been more shamefully abused, and that, whether lenity in dealing with such abuse be praiseworthy, or censurable, greater lenity has never been shewn than has been observed towards the Press in this Province.

NOTES

1 Henry John Boulton, the solicitor general.
2 Christopher Hagerman, collector of customs at Kingston, who had been temporarily appointed to the King's Bench pending the replacement of Judge Willis.
   See Robert L. Fraser's biography of Hagerman in *DCB* 7: 365.
3 Despite its provenance, this stenographic account is printed in preference to
   Sherwood's subsequent reconstruction of his charge, submitted to the lieutenant governor several months after the trial. Of his version, Sherwood wrote:
   'The precise words, I cannot undertake to state but I believe they were in no
   part of this charge materially different from those I have used in the report; the
   juxtaposition of the sentences and their dependence on each other, I think, are
   retained.' CO 42/388: 134–41 at 134 (Levius P. Sherwood to Sir John Colborne,
   26 March 1829). In the author's opinion, the differences between the two texts
   are sufficient to justify the selection of the stenographic account as being probably the more accurate.
4 On this see Norman L. Rosenberg, *Protecting the Best Men: An Interpretive History of the Law of Libel* (Chapel Hill, N.C.: 1986), at 95–6.

P
Liberty of the Press in Early Prince Edward Island, 1823–9
J.M. Bumsted

1. Letter of Charles Binns to the *Prince Edward Island Register*

SIR,

– There is perhaps nothing more dear to the hearts of British subjects, than the legitimate freedom of the press, and as you have been pleased to suggest a wish, that I would give you my best advice for your future government in regard to the insertion of public proceedings in general in your paper, I feel it my bounden duty as a small return for your many acts of kindness, at once to commence my compliance with your wish. I shall probably take the liberty to trouble you with a contination of my correspondence on subjects which I may consider particularly to affect the welfare of this Colony, and to require immediate attention, and in doing so, I shall always endeavour to list to the pure voice of reason, and that wise instructor of a Briton, the genuine spirit of freedom. I will follow guides that cannot deceive me, disregarding the envenomed tongue of calumny, the lampooning pen, the frown of the literary, pretended legal pride, imperious rank or authority, and the dogmatical dictates of hateful despotism from whatever quarter, and as a friend and well wisher of the press and of this Island, like yourself, will freely and fearlessly commit my sentiments to you. In my present communication I will state some cases which clearly point out your duty as it respects the publishing of the proceedings in Courts, in the House of Assembly, and of public meetings under the Bill of Rights, but heaven forfend the necessity of any of those meetings, in this, or any other part of the realm, for I wish my fellow subjects no grievances.

One of our best living writers on Law in England (Holt on Libel) says 'the Constitution of this country acknowledges in every man a right to set forth a *general* or individual hardship and to suggest error even in the highest branch of the magistracy, it is too wise not to consider that its best interest is truth. It opens therefore a ready ear to honest and useful truth of all kinds, and as it receives this truth from human beings and therefore can only expect it as mingled up and adulterated with human passions, it will often pardon and overlook a natural untruth for the sake of the fruit which it produces. This is the character of the Constitution in good times. The people have reserved to themselves the right to petition and remonstrate with the King and two houses of Parliament, every resolution of one or both of the two Houses upon constitutional points not merely recognizes, but expressly and ostentatiously repeats in the people – the right of petitioning and all the liberty of speech and writing which are built upon it are founded in and deduced from general analogies of the the Consitution. It is necessary to the safety of every government that the power and the will of the Governors should not be overawed and overwhelmed. No Government could support itself if every demagogue could come forward every year and call a meeting to petition government to dissolve itself. No person must endanger the fundamentals of the Constitution; he must not shake what is rooted, nor bring again into discussion, with a view of disturbing, what is settled, he must not provoke the passions of the populace to overawe the Laws, and recast the system of the State – as far as is necessary to make truth known, the Law allows him and only interposes to controul where he trespasses beyond the necessity. The right claimed by the Press, to examine and censure the conduct of public men is partly made up of the natural right of thinking and speaking, and is a peculiar right expressly recognized by the British Constitution under the form of petitioning.' The same writer says[:] 'To publish the proceedings of Parliament partially and injuriously is both an injury in itself, and a breach of that implied contract which the parties permitted by the House to take them, have entered into with the House.' King vs. Wright; 8 T[erm] R[eport], 293 rule having been obtained calling on the defendant (a bookseller) to shew cause why a criminal information should not be granted against him for publishing a libel on J. Horne Tooke, the defendant made an affidavit in which he stated that the charge on Mr. Horne Tooke was a paragraph contained in the report of the Committee of secrecy of the House of Commons, a literal copy of which he had published, and that he did not publish the report with a view to calumniate Mr. Horne Tooke.

The paragraph complained of and which was contained under the title 'attempts to assemble a convention of the people of England' was as follows, some of the persons so arrested were prosecuted for high treason. 'A Grand Jury for the County of Middlesex found a bill against Thomas Hardy, the Secretary of the London corresponding Society and eleven others, three of the persons so indicted, viz. Thomas Hardy, John Horne Tooke, and John Thelwall were tried, and on their trials were acquitted of the charge in the indictment, but the evidence given on those trials established in the clearest manner the grounds on which the Committee of the two Houses of Parliament had formed their report in 1794, and shewed beyond a possibility of doubt that the views of those persons and their confederates were in their nature completely hostile to the existing government and constitution of this kingdom, and went directly to the subversion of every established and legitimate authority.'

After a learned argument by counsel on both sides, the Judges delivered their opinions *seratim*, and discharged the rule *nisi*.

Lawrence J. observed, 'this case has been chiefly argued on two grounds. First it is said that the report of the House of Commons is itself unjustifiable inasmuch as it imputed a crime to the prosecutor and deprives him of his privileges. It is said that this report charges him with being guilty of high treason notwithstanding a verdict of the Jury had ascertained his innocence, but that is not the fair import of the paragraph. It is possible that a man may have views hostile to the government and constitution of the kingdom, without being guilty of high treason, especially of the particular treason imputed to the persons therein mentioned. It does not therefore follow that this report charges those persons with the same crime of which they had been before acquitted. But the chief ground taken by the prosecutor's counsel is, that though the report of the House of Commons cannot itself be considered a libel, the defendant not acting under the authority of the House may be indicted for publishing it with a view to general circulation. It has been said that the publication of the proceedings of Courts of Justice when reflecting on the character of an individual is a libel, to support which position, the case of *Waterfield v the Bishop of Chichester*, has been cited, but on examining the charge there was, that the plaintiff had not published a true account. There the plaintiff suggested for a prohibition that the Bishop had excommunicated him for refusing to take the oath *ex officio*, on his being chosen church-warden of Arundel; it afterwards appeared that he was excommunicated for having refused to take the oath of a church-warden according to Law, and the ground of the prohibition being false, a consultation was awarded, then the plaintiff published a supposed account of the prohibition entitled, 'a true copy of a writ of prohibition granted, &c. against the Bishop of Chichester, who had proceeded against and excommunicated T. Waterfield, a church-warden for refusing to take the oath usually tendered to persons in such office, by which writ the illegality of all such oaths is declared, &c.' Now that publication was not a true statement of the proceedings of the Court, he at first obtained a prohibition on a false representation of the fact, and after the consultation was awarded, he published a false account of the proceedings in prohibition, and the Court declared that such false account was a seditious libel. Therefore I do not think that the case established the proposition to support which it was cited. I am not aware of any authority that does support it. The proceedings of Courts of Justice are daily published, some of which highly reflect on individuals, but I do not know that an information was ever granted against the publishers of them. Many of these proceedings contain no point of law, and are not published under the authority or sanction of the Courts, but they are printed for the information of the public. Not many years ago, an action was brought in the Court of Common Pleas by Mr. Currie against Walter, proprietor of 'The Times' for publishing a libel in the paper of 'The Times' which supposed libel consisted in merely stating a speech made by a counsel in this Court on a motion for leave to file a criminal information against Mr. Currie. – Lord Chief Justice Eyre, who tried the cause, ruled that this was not a libel nor the subject of an action, it being a true account of what had passed in this Court, and in the opinion, the Court of Common Pleas afterwards, on a motion for a new trial, all concurred, though some of the Judges doubted whether or not the defendant could avail himself of that defence on the general issue. Though the publication of such proceedings may be to the disadvantage of the particular individual concerned, yet it is of vast importance to the public that the proceedings of Courts of Justice, should be universally known. The general advantage to the country in having these proceedings made public, more than counterbalances the inconveniences to the persons whose conduct may be the subject of such proceedings; the same reasons also apply to the proceedings in Parliament; it is of advantage to the public, and even to the Legislative bodies, that true accounts of their proceedings should be generally circulated; and they would be deprived of that advantage if no person could publish their proceedings without being punished as a libeller. Though therefore the defendant was not authorised by the House of Commons to publish the report in question, yet as he only published a true copy of it, I am of opinion that the rule ought to be discharged.

2 Campb. N.P. 571,–Rex vs Fisher and another.

Lord Ellenborough said, 'Trials at law fairly reported; although they may occasionally prove injurious to individuals have been holden to be privileged: let them continue so privileged. The benefit they produce is great and permanent, and the evil that arises from them is rare and incidental.'[1]

Rex vs. Lord Abingdon, 1 Esp. N.P.C. 226.

Prosecution for a libel against one Sermon, an attorney, by the defendant as a member of the House of Lords. The report says his Lordship read his speech in the House of Lords from a written paper, which paper he had at his own expence sent and caused to be printed in several of the public papers, and Lord Kenyon, Ch. J. observed, 'that, in the present case, the offence was the publication under the defendant's authority and at his expence.' The Jury found his Lordship guilty.

Rex vs. Creevey, a member of the House of Commons.

This was nearly a similar case to the last, and the defendant was found guilty; it is evident from the facts stated that the gist of the offences in the two last cases consisted in the malice which induced these defendants thus to act and which justly ousted them of the benefit of privilege under the bill of rights. – The law infers no such thing against printers of public newspapers who truly report speeches and trials for general information in the usual and regular course of public news.[2]

The above cases are the most modern in point with which I am acquainted. Lord Kenyon was succeeded by Lord Ellenborough, and he by the present Lord Abbott[;] I stated this as the cases mentioned when compared with those of

ancient date, shew, that liberty has expanded in England as the times became
more modern, and I believe these cases to be genuine law at this day – from them
and many others which might be quoted, it appears that you may safely publish
true reports of Parliamentary and Law proceedings, unless you are absolutely
notified of an order to the House or Court to the contrary. Holt observes on that
point[:] 'it is a contempt to publish against order. Every Court or Council has necessarily its own proceedings within itself: it has the discretion to open or shut its
doors. All Courts and all Councils are virtually open to the Country. In the Courts
of Law the country is present by the Jury, and the Parliament by its Representatives. Either House therefore has an undoubted right to withhold its proceedings
and speeches from publication.' This injunction has often been laid *pro. tem* both
by Parliament and the Courts and the breach of it punished.

As to the proceedings of public meetings to petition the King, the common Law
right of the people, has been declared and recognized by the Bill of Rights, 1 W. &
M. St. 2, cap. 2, sec. 1, where it is declared 'That it is the right of the subjects to
petition the King, and all commitments and prosecutions for such petitioning are
illegal.' I never could bring myself to see that there was not a perfect and complete
analogy in all respects between the freedom of speech in Parliament as declared in
the Bill of Rights, and the right of the subjects to petition the King, for as I have
stated, Holt observes, the right of petitioning and all the liberty of speech and
writing, which are built upon it are founded in and deduced from the general
analogies of the Constitution, so it is from these analogies I must deduce my opinion. Now the only ground for freedom of speech in Parliament, is thus declared in
the Bill of Rights 'that the freedom of speech and debates or proceedings in Parliament ought not to be impeached or questioned in any Court or place out of Parliament.' This is only placing Parliament exactly on the same footing with the
people, for if Parliament are not to be questioned and the people are not to be
prosecuted or committed, it must be the same thing, then it appears to me that the
privileges of Parliament and the people in this respect are co-equal and co-exten-
sive, and if so, it manifestly follows that if the speeches and proceedings in Parliament may be published legally at any time, so may the speeches and proceedings
of the people with a view to their proper object petitioning the King; but if the
people, or any of them should act as Lord Abingdon and Mr. Creevy did in the
House of Parliament by evidently using the pretence of petitioning (as they did
their speeches in Parliament,) only for a cloak of maliciousness and not with any
real or bona fide view to petition, and that should be proved against them, then
such people could not be justified under the Bill of Rights, any more than Lord
Abingdon or Mr. Creevy were, nor you either under the acknowledged liberty of
the press. If you knew of their mal intention before you published their speeches
and proceedings, and if this be proved against you, but not otherwise. I believe it

has been the invariable practice of the United Kingdom to publish all the debates and proceedings of such public meetings, and I never have understood that it was even supposed to be illegal so to do, any more than to publish the debates and proceedings of Parliament or reports of the proceedings of Courts of Justice.

I am Sir, your's faithfully, C. Binns
Charlotte Town, Oct. 25, 1823

NOTES

1 Ellenborough adds in this case that preliminary examinations are not so privileged.
2 Holt goes on to add that, because a member may speak as he pleases in parliament, 'he may therefore publish his speech in the shape of an appeal to the people; that he may convert a parliamentary speech into a popular harangue, and carry his privilege of parliament as a shield against legal responsibility, where the reason of such privilege totally ceases. The privilege is not absolute, but relative; it is not personal, but local; and where the reason ceases, and the condition of place does not exist, the promulgation or publication of slanderous and libellous matter (the privilege being divested with the reason and consideration of it), necessarily stands forth in its own nature, subject to the controul and punishment of law' (at 195).

R. v. Howe (1835) for Seditious Libel:
A Tale of Twelve Magistrates
Barry Cahill

Excerpt from Joseph Howe's letter to his sister, probably Jane Austen, 17 March 1835 (holograph transcript in George Johnson fonds, MG 30, D9, file 6: 40–1, NA. Neither the original of this letter nor the indictment is known to be extant.)

The trial here has been, even taking the soberest view of it, a tremendous triumph & might have turned my head a few years ago. I had to plead before the Chief Justice [Brenton Halliburton] whose Conduct & emoluments on several occasions I had roughly handled, against [Attorney General S.G.W.] Archibald who though friendly enough outwardly, had been sorely galled at times by attacks on his policy & the general doings of the Assembly – surrounded by the Bar – many of whom had had their professional & political taints exposed. The Body who filed the Bill [of indictment] were formidable enough – but with the exception of themselves & their immediate friends all ranks and classes from the highest to the lowest were in my favour.

Still as the charges were so glaring & gross & as evidence was shut out by the form of action [prosecution] all parties feared & all the lawyers believed that I must be convicted. The Community were prepared therefore to console me during a three months' imprisonment and to pay from £100 to £300 of fine which would have been done in two hours by subscription. Having studied the law deeply & gathered the facts, I felt more sanguine & though I did not mention the hope to others, told Mrs Howe a week before that if I had the nerve & power to put the whole case before a Jury as it rested in my own mind & they were fair and rational men they must acquit me. This was my strong belief but as the situation was to me a novel one, of course I was not such a fool as to have no distrust of my own powers. The speech you can form your own opinion of from the report which is pretty accurate, but the scene in the Court [now Legislative Library, Province House] beggars all description. It was crammed to overflowing & as hot as a furnace. For six hours & a quarter I defended myself & scourged my prosecutors in a style that of course I was too busy to judge of but which startled & astonished the multitude who devoured every word like manna & what was better awed the Bench, scattered & confounded the prosecutors & what was best of all convinced the Jury. Though I was afraid the adjournment might spoil the verdict by giving the other side an advantage, still I was certain on that night [2–3 March 1835] that they could not get a verdict against me for one old man in the box cried like a child. However the triumph was greater from them having the whole night to reflect & clear heads to listen to the other side. The verdict is most important to all the Colonies as it fixes principles of the highest value, & had it gone the other way it would have taken twenty years to reverse it ... My father [Joseph Howe, Sr] laughed till his sides shook when it was all over & as he shook me by the hand said 'I knew you'd thrash them. I thought they would better let you alone'. He is delighted & feels satisfied that the exposure was needed. Their worships have been in a precious mess ever since; resignations, investigations & new appointments are the order of the day. I mean to dive, for a month, into the old English poet [Shakespeare?] to sweeten my imagination & let them fight as they will. Some of them are blustering about private actions, but they won't meddle with me in a hurry.

Index